D Volume 5

The World Book Encyclopedia

World Book, Inc.
a Scott Fetzer company

Chicago London Sydney Toronto

The World Book Encyclopedia

Dd

D is the fourth letter of our alphabet. It was also the fourth letter in the alphabet used by the Semites, who once lived in Syria and Palestine. They named it *daleth,* a word that meant *door.* It is believed that this word came from one of the *hieroglyphs* (picture writings) the ancient Egyptians used. They drew a picture of a door with panels. See **Alphabet.**

Uses. *D* or *d* ranks as about the tenth most frequently used letter in books, newspapers, and other printed material in English. When used on a report card, *D* usually means poor work or near failure in a school subject. In music, it names one note of the scale. As an abbreviation, *D* stands for the isotope *deuterium* in chemistry, for *electric displacement* in electronics, and for *500* in the Roman numeral system. The symbol *d* denotes *drag* in aeronautics, and the fourth known quantity in algebra. The symbol *D* or *d* stands for *diameter* in mathematics and physics, or a wider-than-average shoe.

Pronunciation. In English, a person pronounces *d* with the tongue touching the roof of the mouth just back of the teeth. In French, Dutch, and Italian, the tongue touches the upper front teeth. In German, a *d* at the beginning of a word, followed by a vowel, resembles the English *d* sound. Otherwise, it usually has a *t* sound. The Spanish *d* is expressed more softly than in English when it is at the beginning of a word. Elsewhere, it has a *th* sound, similar to *the* in English, not the *th* of *thin.* See **Pronunciation.** Marianne Cooley

Development of the letter D

The ancient Egyptians drew this symbol of a door with panels about 3000 B.C. The Semites adapted the symbol and named it *daleth,* their word for *door.*

The Phoenicians used a triangle in their alphabet about 1000 B.C.

The Greeks, about 600 B.C., shaped the letter as an equilateral triangle. They called their letter *delta.*

The Romans rounded the letter and gave it its capital form about A.D. 114.

The small letter **d** developed about A.D. 500 from Roman writing. Monks who copied manuscripts reshaped the letter during the 800's. By about 1500, the letter had developed its present shape.

A.D. 500   1500   Today

Special ways of expressing the letter D

International Morse Code

Braille

International Flag Code

Semaphore Code

Sign Language Alphabet

Common forms of the letter D

Handwritten letters vary from person to person. *Manuscript* (printed) letters, *left,* have simple curves and straight lines. Cursive letters, *right,* have flowing lines.

Roman letters have small finishing strokes called *serifs* that extend from the main strokes. The type face shown above is Baskerville. The italic form appears at the right.

Dd *Dd*

Sans-serif letters are also called *gothic letters.* They have no serifs. The type face shown above is called Futura. The italic form of Futura appears at the right.

Computer letters have special shapes. Computers can "read" these letters either optically or by means of the magnetic ink with which the letters may be printed.

D-day is the term for a secret date on which a military operation is to begin. Peacetime planning of military operations is also based on hypothetical D-days. Terms such as *D-plus-3* (three days after initial attack) and H-hour (the hour of an attack) are used to plan the sequence of operations. The expression *D-day* became current in World War II when it defined the dates set for Allied landings on enemy-held coasts. The most famous D-Day is June 6, 1944, when the Allies invaded Normandy. John W. Gordon

See also **World War II** (D-Day).

Da Nang, *dahn ahng* (pop. 492,194), is one of the largest cities in Vietnam. Da Nang is also called Tourane (*too RAHN*). The city's location on the South China Sea has made it an important trading center since the 1600's. For the location of Da Nang, see **Vietnam** (map). The city produces soap and textiles.

Da Nang became a city of South Vietnam in 1954, when that country was created. Da Nang was a key city during the Vietnam War (1957-1975) because of its location near North Vietnam. United States military forces established bases there, and the city became a favorite target of the North Vietnamese forces. The North Vietnamese Communists took control of South Vietnam in 1975. They unified North and South Vietnam into the single nation of Vietnam in 1976. David P. Chandler

Dacca. See Dhaka.

Dachau, *DAH kow,* was the first permanent concentration camp set up in Germany by the Nazis. It stood near the town of Dachau, 10 miles (16 kilometers) from Munich. Dachau was built in 1933 as an extermination camp for Jews and political prisoners. After 1943, many prisoners worked in arms factories that were built there. The Nazis performed brutal medical experiments on over 3,500 people. Almost all of these prisoners died. Thousands more were executed or died of starvation and epidemics. United States forces liberated about 32,000 prisoners on April 29, 1945. William A. Jenks

Dachshund, *DAHKS hund,* is a dog known for its long, low-slung body and short legs. The breed originated in Germany, where it was trained to hunt badgers. The word *dachshund* is German for *badger hound.* The dachshund has a cone-shaped head, a slim, tapering

WORLD BOOK photo
A dachshund has a long body and short legs.

muzzle, and long, drooping ears. Its front legs are slightly curved. Its glossy coat usually is black or tan, but it may be red, yellow, gray, spotted, or striped. Many dachshunds have short, smooth hair. Two other varieties are the long-haired, with long, silky hair; and the wire-haired, with a rough coat. The dachshund makes a good watchdog and a wonderful pet. See also **Dog** (picture: Hounds). Critically reviewed by the Dachshund Club of America

Dacia. See **Romania** (Early days).

Dadaism, *DAH duh ihz uhm,* a protest movement in the arts, was formed in 1916 by a group of artists and poets in Zurich, Switzerland. The Dadaists reacted to what they believed were outworn traditions in art, and the evils they saw in society. They tried to shock and provoke the public with outrageous pieces of writing,

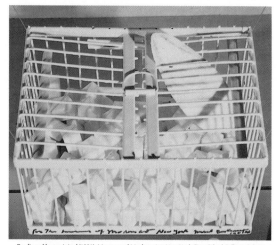

Replica of lost original (1921); Museum of Modern Art, New York City, Gift of Galleria Schwarz
A Dada sculpture by Marcel Duchamp called *Why Not Sneeze Rose Sélavy?* is a painted metal bird cage containing 151 marble blocks, a thermometer, and a piece of cuttlebone.

cabaret skits, poetry recitals, and art exhibitions. Much Dada art was playful and highly experimental. The name *Dada,* a French word meaning *hobbyhorse,* was deliberately chosen because it was nonsensical.

The founders of the movement included the French poet Tristan Tzara, the French artist Jean Arp, and the German poet Hugo Ball. Later members included the French artist Francis Picabia, the French poets Louis Aragon and André Breton, and the German artist Max Ernst. Perhaps the best-known Dadaist was the French artist Marcel Duchamp. He was not a member of the Zurich group, but was working in the Dada spirit as early as 1913. About that year, he completed his first *ready-made.* Ready-mades were common objects, such as bicycle wheels, exhibited as though they were works of art. In this way, Duchamp ridiculed the idea that art was something profound. Marcel Franciscono

See also **Arp, Jean; Breton, André; Duchamp, Marcel; Ernst, Max; Painting** (Dadaism).

Additional resources

Bigsby, C. W. E. *Dada & Surrealism.* Methuen, 1972.
Erickson, John D. *Dada: Performance, Poetry, and Art.* Twayne, 1984.

Rubin, William S. *Dada and Surrealist Art.* Abrams, 1968.
Short, Robert. *Dada & Surrealism.* Octopus Books, 1980.

Daddy longlegs is a popular name in North America for a harmless, long-legged creature related to the spider. Its legs are bent and its body hangs close to the ground. It is not an insect, but an *arachnid* (see **Arachnid**). Another name for it is *harvestman.*

WORLD BOOK illustration by John F. Eggert
Daddy longlegs

Daddy longlegs prey on small insects. They also eat dead insects and fallen fruit. When disturbed, many species of daddy longlegs can give off a bad odor, but they do not bite. In the tropics, some species gather in great enough numbers to cover a small bush. If disturbed, all the daddy longlegs will shake violently, causing the entire bush to move.

In England, the *crane fly* is called *daddy longlegs.* The crane fly is an insect that has wings and looks much like a large mosquito, but it does not bite.

Scientific classification. The harvestman belongs to the class Arachnida. It makes up the order Opiliones. The crane fly belongs to the class Insecta, order Diptera, and family Tipulidae.

Edwin W. Minch

Daedalus, *DEHD uh luhs,* in Greek mythology, was a skilled Athenian craftsman and inventor. Daedalus took his nephew Perdix, or Talos, as an apprentice. Perdix proved to be such a brilliant craftsman that Daedalus killed him in a jealous rage. After his crime, Daedalus fled to Crete. Minos, the king of Crete, hired Daedalus, who created many ingenious inventions while in the ruler's service. His work included the *labyrinth,* a maze-like building, which imprisoned a monster called the Minotaur (see **Minotaur**).

Daedalus helped Minos' daughter Ariadne elope with Theseus, the slayer of the Minotaur. As punishment for the crime, Minos imprisoned Daedalus and his young son, Icarus, in the labyrinth. In order to escape, Daedalus made two pairs of wings from feathers, wax, and thread. Daedalus and Icarus used the wings to fly from Crete. However, Icarus flew too close to the sun. The wax in his wings melted and he plunged to his death in the sea. Minos pursued Daedalus to Sicily. According to one story, Daedalus killed the king by scalding him in a specially constructed bathtub. Justin M. Glenn

See also **Airplane** (picture: An ancient Greek story).

Daffodil is a yellow flower that blooms in the early spring. It is a type of *narcissus,* and comes from Europe, where it grows wild in the woods. The daffodil is also widely grown in gardens in North America and other regions.

There are many kinds of daffodils. The best-known daffodil is also called the *trumpet narcissus.* It has one blossom at the end of each stalk. The daffodil has a large flower and five or six bluish-green leaves about 15 inches (38 centimeters) long. Daffodil bulbs should be planted in autumn. They should be planted about 8 inches (20 centimeters) deep, and about 5 inches (13 centimeters) apart. Daffodil bulbs are poisonous if eaten.

WORLD BOOK illustration by Robert Hynes
The daffodil is a yellow narcissus that blooms in the early spring. The best-known daffodil is the trumpet narcissus, *above.*

Scientific classification. Daffodils belong to the amaryllis family, Amaryllidaceae. They are *Narcissus pseudo-narcissus.*

August A. De Hertogh

See also **Bulb; Narcissus.**

Da Gama, *duh GAM uh,* **Vasco,** *VAS koh* (1469?-1524), was a Portuguese sea captain and explorer. He commanded the first fleet to reach India from Europe. Da Gama sailed around the Cape of Good Hope to India in the late 1490's. His voyage opened the first all-water trade route between Europe and Asia.

Early life. Da Gama was born in Sines, Portugal. He probably attended school in the town of Évora. As a young man, Vasco learned astronomy and navigation. Da Gama became a naval officer in 1492 and commanded ships along the coast of Portugal.

Another Portuguese sea captain, Bartolomeu Dias, had discovered a route around the southern tip of Africa in 1488. He had sailed around the Cape of Good Hope. In 1497, King Manuel I of Portugal asked da Gama to find a sea route to India by sailing around Africa. The king wanted da Gama to establish trade with India. Da Gama's father had been chosen to lead the expedition, but he died before the plans were completed.

Voyage to India. Da Gama commanded four ships, including the *Berrio,* the *Saint Gabriel,* and the *Saint Raphael.* He had a total crew of about 170 men. His navigational equipment included compasses, an instrument called an *astrolabe,* and astronomical charts.

Da Gama sailed from Lisbon, Portugal, on July 8, 1497. He rounded the Cape of Good Hope on November 22, headed north, and stopped at trading centers that are now Moçambique, Mozambique; and Mombasa and Malindi, Kenya. Arab traders in Moçam-

Detail of an engraving by Broegg, Lisbon Geographical Society
Vasco da Gama

Vasco da Gama sailed from Portugal to India in 1497 and 1498. His historic voyage, which is shown on this map, opened a new trade route between Europe and Asia.

bique and Mombasa hated the Portuguese and tried to seize their ships. The people at Malindi were friendlier and arranged for a guide to lead the fleet to India.

On May 20, 1498, da Gama reached Calicut, India. But the Indian ruler felt insulted because he thought the gifts da Gama had brought him were of little value. In addition, Muslim merchants controlled trade in Calicut and resented European interference in their business. They continually threatened the Portuguese and would not trade with them. In August 1498, da Gama sailed for home with only samples of Indian goods. Many of the sailors died of disease during the voyage, and only 55 survived. Da Gama arrived in Lisbon in September 1499. King Manuel rewarded him and gave him the title of Admiral of the Sea of India.

Later life. The king sent another fleet to India in 1500 to break the Muslims' control of trade in that country. The Portuguese succeeded this time, and da Gama made a second voyage to India in 1502 to establish and expand trade there. He sailed from Lisbon with a fleet of 15 ships. Da Gama killed many innocent Indians and Muslims in revenge for violence against Portuguese sailors. Portugal soon became one of the most important trading and naval powers in the Indian Ocean.

After returning to Portugal in 1503, da Gama retired from the sea. In 1519, he was made Count of Vidigueira, which entitled him to collect taxes and rents in two Portuguese villages. In 1524, King John III named him viceroy of India. Da Gama sailed to India, where he died that same year.   John Parker

See also **Exploration** (The voyage around Africa).

Additional resources

Jones, Vincent. *Sail the Indian Sea.* Gordon & Cremonesi, 1978. Da Gama's life and voyages.
Knight, David. *Vasco de Gama.* Troll, 1979. For younger readers.
Sanderlin, George. *Eastward to India: Vasco da Gama's Voyage.* Harper, 1965. Suitable for younger readers.

Dagger is a small, handheld weapon with a short, pointed blade. Daggers are chiefly used for self-defense and sudden attack, but some have served purely ceremonial or decorative purposes. Daggers typically measure from 6 to 20 inches (15 to 51 centimeters) in length. Both edges of the blade are sharpened.

Daggers have been used since prehistoric times. Most daggers have had metal blades, but some have been made of stone, bone, wood, and plastic. The earliest form of bayonet was a dagger with a tapered handle that would fit into the muzzle of a musket.

Walter J. Karcheski, Jr.

See also **Bayonet; Bowie knife.**

A dagger is a short-bladed weapon. The dagger shown above was used by British commandos during World War II.

Daguerre, *dah GAIR,* **Louis Jacques Mandé,** *lwee zhahk mahn DAY* (1787-1851), a French stage designer and painter, introduced the first popular form of photography. His pictures were called *daguerreotypes.*

Daguerre was born in Cormeilles-en-Parisis, near Paris. He became a talented theater artist and operated a scenery theater called the Diorama in Paris. There he displayed huge painted scenes from nature, using lighting to create the illusion of changing views. A desire to improve these scenes led him to work with J. N. Niépce, a French scientist who had invented the first photographic technique. Experimenting with this technique, Daguerre discovered the daguerreotype process in 1837. The permanent mirrorlike images produced through the process brought him worldwide fame.

Reese V. Jenkins

See also **Photography** (History).

Daguerreotype, *duh GEHR uh typ,* was the first popular method of photography. It was named for Louis J. M. Daguerre, a French stage designer and painter who perfected the process in 1837. The word *daguerreotype* also refers to photographs produced by this process.

Daguerre's process involved treating a thin sheet of silver-plated copper with fumes from heated crystals of iodine to make the silver plating sensitive to light. The sheet was then placed inside a camera and exposed through the camera lens for 5 to 40 minutes. After the sheet was removed from the camera, it was developed by vapors from heated mercury. The mercury combined with the silver at the points where it had been affected by light, and formed a highly detailed image. The image was then *fixed* (made permanent) by treating the sheet with sodium thiosulfate.

Daguerre first published a description of his process in 1839. The process was soon improved by several other inventors. By 1841, for example, the exposure time for the pictures had been reduced to less than a minute.

Daguerreotype portraits were tremendously popular during the 1840's and 1850's, especially in the United States. But the daguerreotype was eventually replaced

International Museum of Photography at George Eastman House

A daguerreotype was an image on a copper plate.

by other processes, chiefly because it produced no negatives from which copies could be made.

Richard Rudisill

See also **Daguerre, Louis J. M.; Photography** (History); **Talbotype.**

Dahlia, *DAL yuh,* is the name of a popular group of flowers cultivated from the original dahlia of Mexico. Some dahlias are ball-shaped; others have long, flat petals. *Cactus dahlias* have double blossoms with long, twisted petals. Dahlias are now grown throughout the United States, in southern Canada, and in Europe. They are named for the Swedish botanist Anders Dahl.

Dahlias grow from *tuberous,* or thick, fleshy roots that look somewhat like bulbs. They should be planted in rich, well-drained soil, and in full sun after all danger of

WORLD BOOK illustration by Robert Hynes

The dahlia is a popular garden flower.

frost has passed. After the first frost, the roots should be dug up and stored for the winter in a cool, dry place. Storing the root clump with soil attached will stop shriveling. At planting time, the roots should be separated and planted about 6 inches (15 centimeters) deep. Dahlias flower in the late summer.

Scientific classification. Dahlias belong to the composite family, Compositae. Garden dahlias are *Dahlia pinnata.*

W. Dennis Clark

See also **Flower** (picture: Garden perennials [Bulbs]).

Dahomey. See Benin (country).

Dáil Éireann. See Ireland (The Easter Rebellion).

Daimler, *DYM luhr,* **Gottlieb,** *GAHT leeb* (1834-1900), a German engineer, developed an internal-combustion engine light enough to power an automobile. He and Wilhelm Maybach worked with motors for years, and produced a motor-bicycle in 1885. They made a four-wheeled car in 1886. The Daimler Company was founded in 1890, and produced the Mercedes car. The Daimler and Benz companies merged to make the Mercedes-Benz car in 1926.   Smith Hempstone Oliver

See also **Automobile** (The gasoline car); **Benz, Karl; Manufacturing** (table: 25 leading manufacturers); **Motorcycle** (picture); **Maybach, Wilhelm.**

Daimyo. See Samurai; Japan (Rise of the shoguns).

Dairy Belt. See Milk (The milk industry).

Dairying is the branch of agriculture concerned with the production of milk, butter, evaporated milk, ice cream, cheese, and dried milk products. It includes the care and feeding of the cattle that give the milk. Dairy farming is one of the leading agricultural activities in the United States. Milk sales total about $18 billion a year, or 12 per cent of all money made from agriculture. Dairying accounts for most of the income of about 170,000 U.S. farms.

There are about 11 million milk cows on farms in the United States today. They produce about 17 billion gallons (64 billion liters) of milk each year. The average yearly milk production per cow is 1,600 gallons (6,100 liters). The largest amount of this milk—40 per cent—is used for fluid milk and cream. Thirty-two per cent is used for cheese, 16 per cent for butter, 10 per cent for ice cream, and 2 per cent for dry, condensed, or evaporated milk.

Dairy farms

There is dairy farming in every state, but the industry is concentrated in a group of states in the East and Midwest, from New York to Minnesota. Dairy farming is also important on the Pacific Coast, particularly in California. The average size of U.S. dairy herds is 39 cows. Large commercial dairy farms may have more than 1,000 cows. Wisconsin leads the states in milk production, producing about 3 billion gallons (11 billion liters) per year. The other leading milk-producing states are California, New York, Minnesota, and Pennsylvania, in that order. Quebec ranks as the leading milk-producing province. Its cows produce about 750 million gallons (2.8 billion liters) of milk a year.

Dairy cattle. The six most important breeds of dairy cattle in the United States are the Holstein-Friesian, Jersey, Guernsey, Ayrshire, Brown Swiss, and Milking Shorthorn. They vary in size and color. Holsteins are black and white. Jerseys are fawn to brown, with or

Robert Barclay, Grant Heilman

In a loose-housing system, *above,* individual freestalls allow the cows to enter and leave at any time to eat, drink, and exercise. Large dairy farms may have more than 1,000 cows.

without white markings. Guernseys are pale fawn or fawn and white. Ayrshires are deep red, brown, or a combination of these colors with white. Brown Swiss are solid brown, and Milking Shorthorns are red, white, or *roan* (a mixture of red and white). The Brown Swiss is generally the largest breed, weighing about 1,500 pounds (680 kilograms). The Jersey, at 1,000 pounds (450 kilograms), is the smallest. The breeds are also distinguished by the composition of their milk and the amount they produce.

The breed of cattle kept on a dairy farm depends upon the farmer's preference and the market for milk. Eighty-five per cent of all dairy cattle in the United States are Holstein. They are the most popular breed because they produce a high volume of milk. Holsteins can produce an average of 1,700 gallons (6,400 liters) per year. Jerseys are the next most popular because their milk is the richest. It has 5 per cent *butterfat* (the natural fat in milk), and is the highest in protein. Jerseys are easier to handle and tolerate heat better than other breeds.

Dairy cattle whose ancestry can be traced to the original animals of a breed are called *purebred*. A *registered* animal is one whose ancestry has been recorded with a breed association. Most dairy cattle are not registered with a breed association. Such cattle are called *grade cows*. Most grade cows are the offspring of unregistered parents of the same breed. But many are born of unregistered cows and registered purebred bulls.

Milking. Dairy farmers usually milk their cows at regular times, once each morning and once each evening at 12-hour intervals. Most dairy farmers milk their cows by machine. These machines attach to the cows' teats and pump the milk directly from the cow through a glass pipeline into a separate milk house. This system keeps the milk clean. The milk also tastes better if it is not exposed to the air in the barn. The milk house has vats for washing equipment and a tank where the milk is cooled and stored until the farmer can ship it.

Most of the milk marketed as *Grade A* fluid milk comes from dairy farms that meet strict quality codes and standards. On some farms, workers step into a pan of disinfectant before entering the milking parlor. They carefully wash the cows' udders to remove impurities before milking. During the milking, the workers rinse the utensils periodically. After they are finished milking, they wash and sanitize all equipment. They also wash the milk house and milking parlor floors.

Housing. There are two main types of housing systems for dairy cattle: *confinement housing* and *loose housing*. In confinement housing, farmers keep their cows in individual stalls at all times, except for milking and brief exercise periods. Some confinement stalls have *stanchions,* metal pipes that go around the cow's neck to keep her in place in the stall. Dairy workers can open or close each stanchion separately. Other cows live in *tie stalls.* In a tie stall, cows are tied on two or three feet of chain and have more room to move.

In the confinement system, the cows have separate *feed bunks* (troughs) and drinking cups. A *gutter* runs behind the stalls to collect the cattle's manure and urine. Many gutters are equipped with mechanical devices called *barn cleaners*. A barn cleaner is a chain with paddles that pull the manure into a manure spreader or holding area. The spreader is used to scatter manure onto the land to make the soil more fertile.

In the loose-housing system, cows are free to move around as they please. When it is warm, they may go out to the pasture between milkings. In cold weather, they may rest in a *loafing barn,* a large shed that is open on one side. Farms that do not have a loafing barn usually have individual *freestalls* that allow the cows to enter and leave at any time to eat, drink, or exercise.

Modern dairy farmers keep their barns very clean. On many farms, workers wash the barns with a disinfectant to kill germs and prevent diseases from spreading through the herd. Barns should also have adequate ventilation to protect the cows' health and the flavor of the milk.

Feeding. A good dairy cow may weigh up to 1,700 pounds (770 kilograms) and produce 2,300 gallons (8,700 liters) or more of milk during a year. To do this, the cows eat large amounts of *concentrates* and *forages.* Concentrates are grains and by-product feeds. By-product feeds include corn gluten feed and meal, dried beet pulp, molasses, and wheat millfeeds. Forages consist of *pasture* (grasses, legumes, and other plants), hay, and *silage* (chopped-up stalks of corn and other crops). Farmers usually store hay in the barn loft or in a hay shed. Silage is stored in a silo, where it ferments. Most high-producing herds are fed in *dry lots,* rather than put out to pasture. Workers bring the feed to the lots, and the cows eat together from long feed bunks.

Cows that produce a large amount of milk need feed that provides energy, protein, and essential vitamins and minerals. Dairy farmers try to balance a cow's ration and provide all food nutrients in the proper amounts and proportions. For example, if farmers feed their cows a low-protein forage, such as corn silage, they increase the amount of protein in the concentrate mixture. Typical energy feeds include barley, corn, grain sorghums, oats, and wheat. Cottonseed and soybean meal are typical protein supplements. Some forages that supply both protein and energy are alfalfa, clover, corn silage, mixed hays, sorghum silage, and many varieties of pasture.

The economics of dairying. Dairy farming requires large financial investments. Dairy farmers in the Northern States invest an average of $804,000 for a farm with 52 cows. This amount includes the price of land, cattle, buildings, and equipment. Each cow must produce about 1,600 gallons (6,100 liters) of milk per year to cover all costs of production. Profits for dairy farmers are usually small. However, dairy farmers can make a good profit with high milk-yield per cow, efficient operation, and the use of labor-saving technology.

Improvements in dairy farming. Today's farmers have greatly increased milk production efficiency through improved methods of breeding, feeding, and managing dairy cattle. Although the average yearly production of milk per cow in the United States has risen to 1,600 gallons (6,100 liters), many good dairy herds average 2,400 gallons (9,100 liters) of milk per cow. In 1975, one Holstein cow named Beecher Arlinda Ellen produced 6,472 gallons (24,499 liters)—a world record.

Various organizations have contributed to the increased efficiency of dairy farming. Among these organizations are dairy herd improvement (DHI) associations, the United States Department of Agriculture, colleges of agriculture, and the Purebred Dairy Cattle Association. DHI associations are cooperative organizations of dairy farmers. Each association employs trained supervisors to keep monthly milk, protein, and butterfat production records on association herds. Supervisors advise members on how to feed and care for the cattle. They also help farmers decide which cows are not good producers and should be removed from the herd. Cows in DHI association herds produce an average of about 1,800 gallons (6,800 liters) of milk annually.

More than half of all dairy cows in the United States are now bred by *artificial insemination.* Dairy farmers artificially inseminate cows by placing *semen* (sperm-containing fluid) from a donor bull in the reproductive organs of their fertile cows. The average bull used by an artificial insemination organization can be mated to over 3,000 cows a year. This method enables farmers to increase their use of outstanding purebred bulls.

Dairy farming regulations

Many states and local governments have laws regulating the conditions under which dairy farmers can produce and sell milk. These laws are essential because of the many ways in which milk can become contaminated. All the containers that the milk passes through as it travels from the cow to the consumer must be clean, sterile, and dry. Some cattle diseases can infect human beings through impure milk. Tuberculosis spread in this way until farmers removed tubercular cows from their dairy herds. Brucellosis is a disease that strikes some herds. Farmers control brucellosis by testing their cattle, vaccinating the calves, and eliminating animals.

Most laws regulating dairies require that the operator have a license. Dairy inspectors make sure that the farms meet sanitary regulations. Workers in dairies and milk plants undergo periodic physical examinations to make sure they are healthy. The milk is tested to be certain that its composition meets the legal standard and that it contains no impurities or disease-causing bacteria.

Grant Heilman

The milking parlor of a dairy farm is a special room where the cows are milked by machines. The milk is then piped to a refrigerated tank.

Most communities have regulations dealing with Grade A milk. These laws cover the health of cows and the sanitary conditions under which milk is produced and handled. About 85 per cent of all milk sold is Grade A. With today's processing equipment and refrigerated tank trucks, dairy managers can ship milk long distances easily and safely.

Dairying around the world

Dairying is carried on in most countries of the world. Denmark, New Zealand, and Switzerland are famous for their dairy products. The Soviet Union led the world in annual milk production in the late 1980's with 27 billion gallons (102 billion liters). With 17 billion gallons (64 billion liters), the United States ranked second, followed by France.

People in other countries use the milk of various animals. Goats are an important dairy animal in many countries. In the United States, however, goats provide only a small share of the milk supply. In France and Greece, sheep's milk is used in making certain cheeses. People in Arab lands drink camel's milk, and in the Soviet Union some people drink mare's milk. Laplanders drink reindeer milk, and the people of Egypt and India use the milk of the water buffalo.

History of dairying

Norwegian Vikings may have brought the first cattle to the Americas in the early 1000's. Historians are certain that Christopher Columbus carried cattle on his second voyage to America in 1493. English colonists brought cows to the Jamestown settlement in the early 1600's. Later, they took cows with them to Plymouth and other New England settlements. Cattle raising spread quickly.

An important advance in dairying developed in colonial Massachusetts in the late 1600's. Before that time, cows gave milk only during the spring, summer, and fall, when they could feed in open pastures. Farm families used up what little milk the cows gave, and had very little to sell. Then, the colonists began feeding grain and hay to cattle during the winter. The cows gave milk all winter. This method of feeding cattle, called *stall-feeding,* made it possible to produce milk year-round.

When the pioneer families moved westward, much of their food consisted of butter, cheese, and milk. They found that cattle manure fertilized the soil. They kept more cattle, and sold the surplus milk.

The biggest development in the growth of dairying in the United States came after 1840, when the large cities began to expand. Before that time it had not been difficult to supply the cities with dairy products because farm and city were close together. After the cities grew, shipping milk to the consumer became a problem. However, after 1830, the number of railroads in the Eastern United States multiplied rapidly, and the first trainloads of milk arrived in New York City in 1841. In a few years, city dwellers all over the United States were drinking milk from farms as far as 50 miles (80 kilometers) away.

For many years, farmers manufactured dairy products on the farm. In 1850, farmers in the United States churned almost 315 million pounds (143 million kilograms) of butter. But as city markets increased, it became necessary to process milk on a larger scale. The first *creamery* (butter factory) was set up in New York about 1856. Soon, there were many creameries scattered throughout the Eastern and Midwestern states. The manufacture of milk products has become highly industrialized. Today, there are creameries throughout the country.   Michael F. Hutjens

Related articles in *World Book* include:

Agriculture	Cheese	Milking machine
Barn	Cooperative	Pasteurization
Butter	Hay	Pasture
Cattle	Milk	Silo

Daisy is a name given to many flowers. The name comes from the Old English words for *day's eye.* It refers to the fact that daisy blossoms, like an eye, close at night and open at dawn. Daisy blossoms actually consist of many small flowers of two types—tiny *disk flowers* in the center and petallike *ray flowers* around the edge.

Several species known as daisies are included in the *genus,* or scientific grouping, *Chrysanthemum.* These species usually have yellow disk flowers and white or yellow rays. One member of this group—the oxeye, or white, daisy—is the most common wild daisy in North America. It originally came from Europe and western Asia. The oxeye daisy grows in fields and on roadsides. It grows up to 3 feet (1 meter) tall, with blossoms up to 2 inches (5 centimeters) across.

The Shasta daisy is a popular cultivated member of the chrysanthemum group. It was developed by the famous American horticulturist Luther Burbank. It is a large, sturdy plant that grows over 3 feet (1 meter) tall, with blossoms that measure as much as 4 inches (10 centimeters) across.

English daisies belong to the genus *Bellis* and are called true daisies. The leaves are bunched at the bottom of the stem, leaving the stalk naked. The blossom consists of yellow disk flowers and white, pink, red, or purplish rays. English daisies rarely grow over 6 inches

WORLD BOOK illustration by Robert Hynes

The oxeye daisy is a common plant that has a center of tiny yellow disk flowers surrounded by white petallike ray flowers.

(15 centimeters) tall. The blossoms measure nearly 2 inches (5 centimeters) across.

Scientific classification. Daisies belong to the composite family, Compositae. The oxeye daisy is *Chrysanthemum leucanthemum.* The Shasta daisy is *C. X superbum.* The English daisy is *Bellis perennis.*   Margaret R. Bolick

See also **Black-eyed Susan; Composite family.**

Dakar, *dah KAHR* (pop. 978,523), is the capital and largest city of Senegal and the westernmost city on the mainland of Africa. Dakar is Senegal's major seaport and an important industrial and transportation center. For location, see **Senegal** (map).

Dakar's port is a center of trade. The city's economic activities include food processing, printing, tourism, and the manufacture of cement, cigarettes, shoes, soap, and textiles. An international airport and the University of Dakar are in the city. Dakar has modern buildings and buildings of French colonial architecture. It also has *shantytowns* (areas of shacks and huts).

Dakar began to grow in 1857, when a French fort was built on the site of a settlement there. It later became the capital of French West Africa. Senegal became an independent nation in 1960. Many people have since moved to Dakar from rural areas, and the city faces housing and unemployment problems.   Lucy E. Creevey

Dakota. See **North Dakota; South Dakota.**

Dakota Indians. See **Sioux Indians.**

Daladier, *DAH lah DYAY,* **Édouard,** *ay DWAHR* (1884-1970), served as French premier in 1933, 1934, and from 1938 to 1940. He agreed at Munich in 1938 to let Hitler partition Czechoslovakia (see **Munich Agreement**). After France fell to Germany, he was imprisoned from 1941 until 1945. He testified against Marshal Henri Philippe Pétain in 1945, accusing him of collaborating with Germany. Daladier was born in Carpentras, in Vaucluse, France.   Ernest John Knapton

Dalai Lama. See **Tibet** (Religion and culture; History and government).

Daley, Richard Joseph (1902-1976), a Democrat, was mayor of Chicago from 1955 until his death in 1976. During that time, he was one of the most powerful political leaders in the United States. He was elected to his first term as mayor in 1955, and was reelected in 1959, 1963, 1967, 1971, and 1975.

Daley headed the Cook County Democratic organization, perhaps the strongest political machine in the United States. He became an adviser to President John F. Kennedy and to President Lyndon B. Johnson. Under Daley's leadership, Chicago reorganized its police department, encouraged the construction of many major downtown buildings, and pushed an urban renewal and rebuilding program that removed many slums.

In the early 1970's, Daley's administration was rocked by several scandals and trials involving corruption. None involved Daley. But many high officials were found guilty. Over 50 police officers were convicted of taking bribes from tavern owners.

Daley suffered a political setback in 1972 when the city's regular Democratic delegates were barred from the party's national convention in a fight over delegate selection procedures. But he won renewed national prestige with a decisive reelection victory in 1975.

Daley was born in Chicago. He received undergraduate and law degrees from DePaul University. He was elected to the Illinois House of Representatives in 1936 and later served in the Illinois Senate and as state revenue director. His son Richard M. Daley was elected mayor of Chicago in 1989.   Charles E. Nicodemus, Jr.

See also **Chicago** (Government).

Dali, *DAH lee,* **Salvador** (1904-1989), was a famous surrealist painter. His unusual pictures made him one of the most publicized figures in modern art.

Dali called his surrealist paintings "hand-painted

Salvador Dali

dream photographs." The pictures show strange, often nightmarish combinations of precisely detailed figures and objects. Many of his paintings have strong sexual associations. The barren landscapes and fantastic rock formations of the Spanish region of Catalonia, where Dali was born, appear in a number of his works. Dali's *Gala and the Angelus of Millet Immediately Preceding the Arrival of the Conic Anamorphoses* illustrates his realistic technique and his use of complicated, puzzling symbols. This painting is reproduced in color in the **Painting** article. Dali also created many etchings and lithographs. He designed many of these prints to illustrate books.

Salvador Felipe Jacinto Dali was born in Figueras, Spain. He was also a sculptor and jewelry designer. Dali worked with the Spanish film director Luis Buñuel on two surrealist motion pictures—*An Andalusian Dog* (1929) and *The Golden Age* (1930).   Willard E. Misfeldt

See also **Surrealism.**

Additional resources

Ades, Dawn. *Dali and Surrealism.* Harper, 1982.
Descharnes, Robert. *Salvador Dali.* Abrams, 1985. Abridgment of original 1976 edition.
Secrest, Meryle. *Salvador Dali.* Dutton, 1986.

Collection of Julien Levy, Bridgewater, Conn., WORLD BOOK photo by Robert Crandall

Dali's *Accommodations of Desire* was completed about 1929. This oil and collage painting shows the mysterious combination of realistic figures and objects typical of the artist's style.

Dallapiccola, *DAH lah PEE koh luh,* **Luigi,** *loo EE jee* (1904-1975), was an Italian composer. He became best known as a pioneer of *dodecaphony* in Italy. Dodecaphonic music is a 12-tone technique. Dallapiccola's musical style is characterized by delicate *counterpoint* (multiple melodies), lyrical lines and textures, and subtle tone colors. His work was influenced by the modern Austrian composers Alban Berg and Anton Webern as well as by Italian Renaissance vocal music.

Dallapiccola's two-act opera *Ulisse* (1968) first brought the composer international fame. His compositions for solo voice and instrumental ensemble of the 1950's and 1960's rank among his finest works. Dallapiccola also composed two one-act operas, a ballet, the oratorio *Job,* numerous choral and solo vocal works, and a few works for piano and for chamber ensemble. He was born in Pazin (now in Yugoslavia), near Trieste.

Vincent McDermott

Dallas, *DAL uhs,* is the second largest city in Texas and one of the largest in the United States. Among Texas cities, only Houston has more people. Dallas is a center of banking, fashion, manufacturing, trade, and transportation. Dallasites often call their city "Big D."

Dallas lies on the rolling prairies of north-central Texas, about 30 miles (48 kilometers) east of Fort Worth. It is the county seat of Dallas County. Historians believe the city may have been named for George M. Dallas, who served as Vice President of the United States from 1845 to 1849 during the Administration of President James K. Polk.

John Neely Bryan, a lawyer and trader, founded Dallas in 1841, when he built a trading post on the Trinity River. Trade and transportation accounted for much of Dallas' early development. Rapid industrial expansion from 1940 to 1970 resulted in a tripling of the city's population.

President John F. Kennedy was assassinated in Dallas on Nov. 22, 1963 (see **Kennedy, John F.** [pictures]). Vice President Lyndon B. Johnson took the oath of office as President aboard the presidential plane at Love Field in the city (see **Johnson, Lyndon B.** [picture]).

The city. Dallas covers about 378 square miles (979 square kilometers), or about two-fifths of Dallas County. The city's metropolitan area covers 4,659 square miles (12,067 square kilometers) and includes 6 counties—Collin, Dallas, Denton, Ellis, Kaufman, and Rockwall. About 15 per cent of Texas' people live in this area.

Three separate towns, each with its own government, are completely surrounded by Dallas. They are Cockrell Hill, Highland Park, and University Park. Suburbs that have populations of more than 60,000 include Garland, Grand Prairie, Irving, Mesquite, and Richardson.

A network of freeways links Dallas with its suburbs and forms a loop around the city. The Trinity River di-

Facts in brief

Population: *City*—904,078. *Metropolitan area*—1,957,378. *Consolidated metropolitan area*—2,930,516.
Area: *City*—378 sq. mi. (979 km²). *Metropolitan area*—4,659 sq. mi. (12,067 km²). *Consolidated metropolitan area*—7,198 sq. mi. (18,643 km²).
Altitude: 512 ft. (156 m) above sea level.
Climate: *Average temperature*—January, 46° F. (8° C); July, 85° F. (29° C). *Average annual precipitation* (rainfall, melted snow, and other forms of moisture)—34 ½ in. (88 cm). For the monthly weather in Dallas, see **Texas** (Climate).
Government: Council-manager. *Terms*—2 years for the council members; manager appointed.
Founded: 1841. Incorporated as a town, 1856; as a city, 1871.

Squire Haskins Photography, Dallas

Downtown Dallas includes such landmarks as the 72-story NCNB Plaza building, the city's tallest skyscraper, and the domed Reunion Tower. Dallas is one of the largest U.S. cities.

City of Dallas

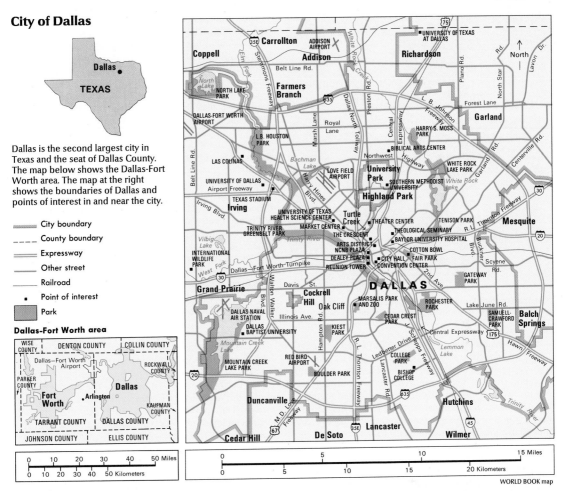

Dallas is the second largest city in Texas and the seat of Dallas County. The map below shows the Dallas-Fort Worth area. The map at the right shows the boundaries of Dallas and points of interest in and near the city.

City boundary
County boundary
Expressway
Other street
Railroad
• Point of interest
Park

Dallas-Fort Worth area

WORLD BOOK map

vides Dallas into two sections. The main business district of Dallas lies north and east of the river. Oak Cliff, a residential area, is south and west of the river.

The 72-story NCNB Plaza building in downtown Dallas is the tallest structure in the city. The famous Neiman-Marcus department store on Main and Ervay streets attracts crowds of shoppers. At the south end of downtown Dallas, the Dallas Convention Center provides a meeting place for business people and organizations from throughout the country. An observation deck in the nearby 50-story Reunion Tower offers visitors a spectacular view of Dallas.

The county government center at the west end of the downtown area includes a restored version of the log cabin built by John Neely Bryan, who founded Dallas. City Hall stands at the south end of downtown Dallas. The building was designed by American architect I. M. Pei. A sculpture by the English sculptor Henry Moore decorates the plaza.

Warehouses, light industries, and office buildings occupy the Trinity Industrial District, which adjoins downtown Dallas. The Dallas Market Center, off Stemmons Freeway northwest of the downtown area, provides facilities for trade shows.

The people. About 94 per cent of the people of Dallas were born in the United States. Although many of

Dallas' first residents were Southerners, people from all parts of the country have settled there. The city's population includes people of Asian, English, French, German, Irish, and Mexican ancestry. American Indians of many tribes live in the city. Blacks make up about a third of the population.

Dallas has had relatively few racial disturbances, though there have been some sit-ins, picketings, and other incidents. A citizens' group, called the Interracial Council for Business Opportunity, has aided in the peaceful integration of public facilities.

Symbols of Dallas. The red, white, and blue in the flag of Dallas, *left,* represent the United States and Texas, which use these colors in their flags. The star is the chief symbol of Texas, the Lone Star State. The flag, which was adopted in 1967, also bears the city seal, *right.*

LTV Aerospace and Defense

Airplane manufacturing is one of Dallas' chief industries. Most of the planes go to the United States armed forces.

Economy. Dallas is one of the nation's major centers for the manufacture of electronics and electrical equipment, aircraft and missile parts, oil field equipment, and women's clothing. Other important manufacturing activities in Dallas include the production of printed materials, nonelectrical machinery, and food products. More than a fourth of the people who work in the city are employed in some type of manufacturing. The city has about 4,000 factories.

Texas ranks as the nation's top cotton-producing state, and Dallas is one of the world's leading cotton markets. Dallas serves as the headquarters of more oil firms than any other U.S. city. More than three-fourths of the known oil reserves in the United States, excluding Alaska, are located within 500 miles (805 kilometers) of Dallas.

The Eleventh District Federal Reserve Bank in Dallas makes the city an important financial center for the Southwestern United States. Over 100 banks are located in the Dallas metropolitan area. Dallas is the headquarters of more insurance companies than any other Southern city.

Dallas is the Southwest's most important transportation center. Seven interstate highways serve the city. The Dallas-Fort Worth Airport, which lies about midway between the two cities, is the nation's largest in area. It is also one of the nation's busiest airports.

Education. Southern Methodist University, in University Park, is the oldest and best-known university in the Dallas area. Baylor College of Dentistry, Dallas Baptist University, Dallas Theological Seminary Graduate School, and the University of Texas Southwestern Medical Center are in Dallas. Other schools of higher education in the Dallas area include the University of Dallas, in Irving, and the University of Texas at Dallas, in Richardson. In addition, the Dallas County District Community College System consists of seven two-year community colleges in the Dallas area.

The Dallas public school system includes 185 elementary and high schools, with a total enrollment of about 130,000. Dallas has 37 church-supported schools, with a total enrollment of more than 12,000 students. Greenhill, Hockaday, and St. Mark's are well-known private schools.

Cultural life. Dallas is a cultural center of the Southwest. The Dallas Opera performs in the Music Hall of State Fair Park. The Dallas Symphony Orchestra performs in the Morton H. Meyerson Symphony Center. The city also has a Civic Ballet Society, a Metropolitan Ballet, a Civic Chorus, and a Chamber Music Society. The Dallas Theater Center stages classic and modern plays in two buildings, one of which was designed by the American architect Frank Lloyd Wright. Touring Broadway productions appear regularly at the restored Majestic Theatre in downtown Dallas. Summer musicals at Fair Park attract many people.

The Dallas Health and Science Museum features such displays as transparent models of the human body. The Southwestern Historical Wax Museum has over 100 figures from Texas history. The Dallas Museum of Natural History exhibits wildlife and fossils from the Texas area. The Dallas Historical Society runs the Texas Hall of State, a museum built for the 1936 Texas Centennial Exposition.

The Dallas Museum of Art exhibits American and European paintings and sculptures. It is part of the Dallas Arts District, a development project covering 17 blocks on the northeast edge of downtown. The district also includes the Arts District Theater and a two-story pavilion for visual and performing arts. Other features of the Arts District include the Meyerson symphony center, which opened in 1989.

The Dallas Public Library System includes a downtown unit and 15 branches throughout the city. Dallas has about 35 radio stations and 9 television stations. The city's two daily newspapers are the *Morning News* and the *Times Herald.*

Recreation. The Dallas park system covers about 14,000 acres (5,670 hectares). The Marsalis Park Zoo has more than 2,000 animals. The Dallas Cowboys of the National Football League play in Texas Stadium, in Irving. The Texas Rangers of the American League play baseball in Arlington Stadium in the nearby city of Arlington. The Dallas Mavericks of the National Basketball Association play at Reunion Arena. Dallas is the home of the Cotton Bowl, a stadium. Every New Year's Day, the Cotton Bowl football game features two of the nation's outstanding college teams.

Other interesting places to visit include:

Fair Park, about 2 miles (3 kilometers) east of downtown Dallas. It includes picnic grounds, concession stands, rides, the Cotton Bowl, and most of Dallas' museums. The State Fair of Texas attracts about 3 million people to the park during its 16 days every October.

Observation deck, atop Reunion Tower in downtown Dallas. On clear days, viewers can see Fort Worth.

Dealey Plaza, in downtown Dallas. A memorial plaque stands near the site where President John F. Kennedy was assassinated.

International Wildlife Park, in Grand Prairie. Visitors can drive through a wild game preserve and see wild animals roaming in a natural setting.

Summer Rodeo, in Mesquite. Rodeo events are held on weekends, from April through September.

Six Flags over Texas, in Arlington. This amusement park offers a variety of exhibits and rides.

Biblical Arts Center, about 6 miles (10 kilometers) north of downtown. It has an international collection of religious art.

Government. Dallas has a council-manager form of government. The voters elect a mayor and 10 other city council members to two-year terms. The mayor and council members set up general policies for governing the city. The council hires a city manager who is administrative head of the government. This official carries out the policies set up by the council, prepares the budget, and appoints and dismisses department heads. The city's chief sources of revenue are fees, fines, and property and sales taxes. Revenue bonds and federal grants have also provided funds.

The Dallas city government faces a number of problems, including air and water pollution and a rising crime rate. Dallas leaders are also working to prevent a large shift of population and retail trade from the city to the suburbs.

History. In 1841, John Neely Bryan built a home and trading post along the Trinity River, near what is now the county government center. Bryan traded with westward-bound wagon trains, Indians, and buffalo hunters. Soon he began selling lots in a town a half-mile (0.8 kilometer) square. The town became the county seat in 1846, when Dallas County was created.

In 1855, a group of French scientists, writers, artists, and musicians settled near Dallas to form a cooperative community. The community failed and many of its residents moved to Dallas.

Dallas was incorporated as a town in 1856. It became a stop for stagecoaches and for cowboys driving longhorn cattle to markets in Missouri and Kansas. During the Civil War (1861-1865), Dallas served as an administrative center of the Confederate Army. Two railroad lines—the Houston and Texas Central, and the Texas and Pacific—reached Dallas in the early 1870's. Farm tool manufacturers then began opening branches in Dallas. Hunters brought buffalo hides to the city. Small factories started to produce leather goods. Wholesalers began to supply retail stores around Dallas.

Dallas was incorporated as a city in 1871. The growth of transportation and trade caused the population of Dallas to increase by more than 12 times between 1870 and 1890, when it reached 38,067. In 1890, Dallas replaced Galveston as the largest city in Texas. By 1930, Dallas' population had grown to 260,475, but Houston had replaced it as the state's largest city. Discovery of the great East Texas oil field southeast of Dallas in 1930 helped boost Dallas' economy and growth.

World War II (1939-1945) brought aircraft plants and other defense industries to Dallas. After the war, Dallas became a leading U.S. center for the manufacture of electrical and electronics equipment, and aircraft and missile parts. Many large companies, including Chance Vought Aircraft, moved to Dallas. In 1961, Chance Vought became part of the Ling-Temco-Vought corporation (now LTV Corporation), then the largest business firm in Dallas. Other companies that had been founded in Dallas, such as Texas Instruments, also expanded rapidly. This industrial growth helped the population of Dallas increase by more than half a million people from 1940 to 1970—from 294,734 to 844,401.

During the 1960's and 1970's, population and retail trade grew in both Dallas and its suburbs. But suburban growth was faster than the growth in the city. To reverse this trend, Mayor Erik Jonsson helped form a "Goals for Dallas" program. In 1967, Dallas voters passed a $175-million bond issue—the largest in the city's history—to fulfill some of the goals. The plans led to construction of the Dallas-Fort Worth Airport, which opened in 1974, and other improvements.

Large companies continued to move their headquarters to Dallas during the 1970's. Much construction took place in the city during this period, and the building boom continued in the 1980's. By 1980, the city's population had reached 904,078.   Henry K. Tatum

Dallas, George Mifflin (1792-1864), served as Vice President of the United States from 1845 to 1849 under President James K. Polk. He was a loyal supporter of Polk's policies. His tie-breaking vote in favor of a low tariff bill Polk favored in 1846 destroyed him politically in Pennsylvania, his home state.

Dallas served as a Democratic U.S. senator from Pennsylvania from 1831 to 1833, as minister to Russia from 1837 to 1839, and as minister to England from 1856 to 1861. While in England, Dallas helped settle disputes over the Clayton-Bulwer Treaty (see **Clayton-Bulwer Treaty**). Dallas also held office as mayor of Philadelphia, United States district attorney, and attorney general of Pennsylvania. In addition, he served as secretary to Albert Gallatin, the diplomat who helped negotiate an end to the War of 1812. Dallas was born in Philadelphia.
Irving G. Williams

See also **Vice President of the United States** (picture).

Dalles, *dalz,* are deep gorges where rivers flow rapidly over, or have cut through, hard rock or slabs. The name comes from a French word meaning *slab* or *tile.* The singular form of dalles in English is *dell,* and in many parts

Artstreet

Dalles, also called *dells,* are deep gorges. The scenic Wisconsin Dells, *above,* are located on the Wisconsin River.

of the country these gorges are called *dells* instead of *dalles*. French explorers gave the name *dalles* to scenic gorges of North American rivers, especially those in the northern part of the United States. Notable dalles in the United States include the Wisconsin Dells on the Wisconsin River, near Wisconsin Dells, Wis.; the Saint Louis River Dalles near Duluth, Minn.; the Saint Croix River Dalles between Wisconsin and Minnesota; and The Dalles on the Columbia River between Oregon and Washington. See also **Wisconsin** (Places to visit; picture); **Wisconsin River.**   Richard G. Reider

Dallin, *DAL ihn,* **Cyrus Edwin** (1861-1944), an American sculptor, used American Indian life as the theme for many of his greatest works. *The Appeal to the Great Spirit* (1908) shows his realistic and dramatic style. Other works include *Signal of Peace* (1890), *Medicine Man* (1899), *Brigham Young and the Pioneers* (1900), and *Paul Revere* (1940). His *Sir Isaac Newton* (1895) is in the Library of Congress in Washington, D.C. Dallin was born in Springville, Utah. He studied at the École des Beaux-

Stuart Cohen, Stock, Boston
Dallin's *The Appeal to the Great Spirit* is a bronze statue that stands outside the Museum of Fine Arts in Boston.

Arts and the Académie Julian in Paris. He taught in Boston. See also **Massasoit** (picture).   Bess L. Hormats

Dalmatia, *dal MAY shuh,* a district of Yugoslavia, is a long, narrow strip of land extending over 200 miles (320 kilometers) along the eastern shore of the Adriatic Sea. Dalmatia is part of Croatia, one of six republics of Yugoslavia. The Dalmatian coast is deeply indented and fringed with hundreds of islands. Dalmatia lies in the Dinaric Alps. The chief rivers are the Neretva and the Krka. They flow into the Adriatic Sea. The most important cities are Split, Dubrovnik, Šibenik, and Zadar.

Most of the people are Croatians. Tourism is Dalmatia's main industry. Each year, millions of people flock to the warm, sunny coast for boating, swimming, and sunbathing. Cherries, grapes, olives, and other fruits are grown in valleys near the coast.

Dalmatia was once part of the ancient kingdom of Illyria. The Romans conquered Dalmatia in the 200's B.C. Later, between the A.D. 600's and 1400's, the Slavs invaded Dalmatia. After the defeat of Napoleon in 1815, the Great Powers gave Dalmatia to Austria. In 1918, after World War I ended, Dalmatia became part of what is now Yugoslavia.   Alvin Z. Rubinstein

Dalmatian, *dal MAY shuhn,* is a medium-sized dog. It is white, covered with many black or liver-colored spots. Dalmatian puppies are pure white when born. The spots appear after about three or four weeks. Dalmatians make good watchdogs. They are alert, curious, clean, and useful. They also can be taught to hunt. Another name for the Dalmatian is the *coach dog.* These dogs used to run along between the wheels of coaches or carriages, and were companions to the horses. The breed was named for Dalmatia, an area on the Adriatic Sea, but experts are not sure where the dogs were first raised. See also **Dog** (picture: Nonsporting dogs).
                    Critically reviewed by the Dalmatian Club of America

Dalton, John (1766-1844), an English chemist, proposed an atomic theory of matter that became a basic theory of modern chemistry. His theory, first presented in 1803, states that each chemical element is composed of its own kind of atoms, all with the same relative weight. It explained why a fixed weight of one substance always combines with a fixed weight of another substance in forming a compound.

Dalton was born in Eaglesfield, near Carlisle. In 1794, Dalton published the first major study of color blindness, an affliction he had. In 1802, he published a law now known as *Dalton's law of partial pressures.* The law states that the total pressure exerted by a mixture of gases is the sum of the pressures of all individual gases in the mixture.   Melvyn C. Usselman

See also **Atom** (The birth of the modern atomic theory); **Chemistry** (Dalton's atomic theory; picture: John Dalton).

Daltonism. See **Color blindness.**

Daly, Marcus (1841-1900), helped establish Montana's copper-mining industry. Daly developed mines in Butte and built a copper smelting plant in Anaconda. He founded the Anaconda Copper Mining Company in 1895. Daly, Henry Rogers, and William Rockefeller founded the Amalgamated Copper Company in 1899. Daly was a leader of the Democratic Party in Montana. Born in Ireland, he came to the United States in 1857, when he was a boy. See also **Montana** (Statehood).

Dam is a barrier placed across a river to stop the flow of water. Dams vary in size from small earth or rock barriers to concrete structures that rise as high as a skyscraper. People have always had to gather water during wet seasons to have enough for themselves, their animals, and their crops in dry spells.

Throughout history, wherever people settled, an important first concern was to locate an adequate water supply. In many regions, streams full of water during certain seasons of the year become dry at other times, perhaps when water is most needed. At first, people built small dams of brush, earth, and rock that would store enough water for immediate needs. But floods frequently washed these small dams away. As communities grew and populations increased, people learned to construct larger dams that would provide a more permanent and abundant water supply. These dams could store enough water to meet people's needs during seasonal drops in the water supply and during drought periods covering several years. Later, people learned how to harness the energy of falling waters and use it to produce electric power for homes and industries.

What does a dam do?

As a barrier across a river or stream, a dam stops the flow of water. A dam stores the water, creating a lake or reservoir above it. The stored water is then made available for irrigation, town and city water supplies, and many other uses. The dam also raises the water surface from the level of the original riverbed to a higher level. This permits water to be diverted by the natural flow of gravity to adjacent lands. The stored water also flows through hydraulic turbines, producing electric power that is used in homes and industries. Water released from the dam in uniform quantities assures water for fish and other wildlife in the stream below the dam. Otherwise, the stream would go dry there. Water released in larger quantities permits river navigation throughout the year. Where dams create large reservoirs, floodwaters can be held back and released gradually over longer periods of time without overflowing riverbanks.

Reservoirs or lakes created by dams provide recreational areas for boating and swimming. They give refuge to fish and wildlife. They help preserve farmlands by reducing soil erosion. Much soil erosion occurs when rivers flood their valleys, and swift floodwaters carry off the rich topsoils.

Types of dams

Dams are classified by the material used to construct them. Dams built of concrete, stone, or other masonry are called *masonry dams.* Dams built of earth or rocks are called *embankment dams.* Engineers generally choose to build embankment dams in areas where large amounts of earth or rocks are available.

Masonry dams. Today, nearly all masonry dams are built of large blocks of concrete. There are three main kinds of masonry dams: *gravity, arch,* and *buttress.*

Gravity dams depend entirely on their own weight to resist the tremendous force of the oncoming water. They are the strongest and most massive dams built today. A gravity dam is built on a solid rock foundation. The dam transfers the force of the water downward to the foundation below. Gravity dams can hold back enormous amounts of water. However, they are costly to build because they require so much concrete.

Arch dams curve outward toward the flow of water. They are usually built in narrow canyons. As the water pushes against the dam, the arch transfers the water's force outward to the canyon wall. An arch dam requires much less concrete than a gravity dam of the same length.

Buttress dams depend for support on a series of vertical supports called *buttresses.* The buttresses run along the dam's *upstream face*—that is, the side facing away from the water's flow. The upstream face of a buttress dam usually slopes outward at about a 45-degree angle. The sloping face and the buttresses serve to transfer the force of the water downward to the dam's foundation. Buttress dams, like gravity dams, are usually built in

---

Larry W. Mays, the contributor of this article, is Professor of Civil Engineering and Director of the Center for Research in Water Resources at the University of Texas at Austin.

Shasta Dam in California creates a huge reservoir on the Sacramento River. It is one of the highest gravity dams in the United States.

Fort Peck Dam is one of the largest earth-fill dams in the world. It extends about 4 miles (6 kilometers) across the Missouri River in northeastern Montana. The dam controls flooding, provides irrigation water, and generates electricity for the surrounding area.

U.S. Army Corps of Engineers Fort Peck Project

wide valleys where long dams are needed.

Embankment dams are constructed of materials dug out of the ground, including rocks, gravel, sand, silt, and clay. They are also known as *fill dams.* An *earth-fill dam* is an embankment dam in which compacted earth materials make up more than half the dam. Earth-fill dams are constructed by hauling the earth materials into place and compacting them layer upon layer with heavy rollers. The materials are graded by density, and the finest, such as clay, are placed in the center to form a waterproof core. In some cases, concrete cores are used. The coarser materials are placed outside the core and covered with a layer of rock called *riprap.* The riprap serves as an outer protection against water action, wind, rain, and ice. In addition, thinned-out cement, called *grout,* is pumped into the foundation to fill cracks. This process makes the foundation watertight.

Where rocks are available, it may prove most economical to build a *rock-fill dam.* Most dams of this type are constructed of coarse, heavy rock and boulders. Many of them have a covering of concrete, steel, clay, or asphalt on the upstream side. This covering makes the dam watertight. Combinations of rock and earth result in a type of dam called an *earth-and-rock fill dam.*

Other types of dams. *Timber dams* are built where lumber is available and the dam is relatively small. The

World's highest and largest dams

Highest dams

Dam	Location	Type	Height In feet	In meters	Year completed
Rogun	Soviet Union	Earth-fill/ Rock-fill	1,099	335	1989
Nurek	Soviet Union	Earth-fill	984	300	1980
Grand Dixence	Switzerland	Gravity	935	285	1961
Inguri	Soviet Union	Arch	892	272	1980
Chicoasén	Mexico	Rock-fill	856	261	1980
Tehri	India	Earth-fill/ Rock-fill	856	261	†
Kishau	India	Earth-fill/ Rock-fill	830	253	†
Sayano-Shushensk	Soviet Union	Arch	804	245	†
Guavio	Colombia	Rock-fill	797	243	†

Largest dams*

Dam	Location	Type	Volume In cubic yards	In cubic meters	Year completed
Chapeton	Argentina	Earth-fill/ Gravity	387,400,000	296,200,000	†
Pati	Argentina	Earth-fill/ Gravity	311,400,000	238,100,000	†
Tarbela	Pakistan	Earth-fill/ Rock-fill	194,200,000	148,500,000	1976
Fort Peck	United States	Earth-fill	125,600,000	96,050,000	1937
Lower Usuma	Nigeria	Earth-fill	121,600,000	93,000,000	†
Cipasang	Indonesia	Earth-fill/ Rock-fill	117,800,000	90,100,000	†
Atatürk	Turkey	Rock-fill	111,200,000	85,000,000	†
Rogun	Soviet Union	Earth-fill/ Rock-fill	93,300,000	71,300,000	1989
Guri	Venezuela	Rock-fill/ Gravity	92,720,000	70,889,000	†

*Based on volume of dam structure.   †Under construction.
Source: Arthur H. Walz, Jr., United States Committee on Large Dams.

Larry W. Mays

The Feitsui Dam in Taiwan is a large concrete arch dam. The arch transfers the water's force outward to the canyon walls.

timber is weighted down with rock. Planking or other watertight material forms the facing. *Metal dams* have watertight facings and supports of steel.

Dams with movable gates are built where it is necessary to let large quantities of water, ice, or driftwood pass by the dam. A *roller dam* has a large roller located horizontally between piers. It can be raised and lowered to allow ice and other materials to pass through the dam without much loss of reservoir water level.

How dams are built

Planning. In order to construct a dam, the builders must first gather and study much information. The site where the dam is to be erected must be examined for its formation, quality of foundation, and the availability of suitable construction materials. A careful analysis must be made of the stream-flow characteristics. The area to be covered by the reservoir that the dam creates must be outlined when determining the height of the dam at any given site. This requires detailed topographic mapping and geologic studies. Subsurface drillings are necessary to determine the condition, quality, and location of the rock formation under the damsite.

All property in the reservoir area must be bought or relocated. This occasionally requires the relocation of entire towns, highways, railroads, and utilities. Engineers must also determine the amount of mud, silt, and debris which the dam will stop. This will determine the useful life of the reservoir, because when the reservoir becomes filled with this material it can no longer store water. If the dam is to be used for generating power, outlets must be provided which will connect to generating equipment. If the water is to be used for irrigation or municipal supply, outlets to control its release to canals or aqueducts must be built.

Construction. When the damsite has been selected, means must be found to remove or bypass the flow of the stream from the riverbed so that the foundation can be excavated and the concrete, earth, or rock placed. To divert the flow of the river from the area, frequently half of the riverbed is excavated at one time. The other half of the riverbed is used for the flow of the river. In some cases, it is more economical to bore a tunnel through an adjacent canyon wall. The tunnel permits the entire flow of the river to pass around the damsite. To accomplish this diversion, *cofferdams* (small dams placed temporarily across a stream) are built upstream to divert the river into the tunnel. After the dam has been built high enough, the diversion tunnel is closed with gates, and permanently plugged.

Dam safety. In designing the dam, some provision must be made to bypass water when the reservoir is full, without overtopping the dam. For this purpose, a *spillway* is constructed. Spillways act as safety valves by releasing excess waters that the reservoir cannot contain. A spillway may be a channel apart from the dam or a section of the dam over which water can flow freely. The excess water flows from the reservoir through the spillway and back to the downstream river or drainage channel. A spillway must be large enough to handle the water from a major flood.

Dams can create serious safety hazards. If a dam collapses, it can cause enormous property damage, injury, and sometimes death. A dam can collapse because of faulty construction or an earthquake. Erosion can also lead to a dam's collapse. A dam can be eroded from the inside by water leaking into the embankment, the foundation, or structures attached to the dam. If the spillway is too small, water may flow over the top of the dam and cause erosion.

History

Dams have influenced civilization for thousands of years, especially cultures that depended on irrigation. The Egyptians built the earliest known dam on the Nile River about 2800 B.C. But dams probably were built much earlier. The ancient Romans built dams of cut stone throughout the Roman Empire. Some of these dams are still in use today.

The earliest dams in North America provided power for grist mills and sawmills. American colonists probably built their first dam in 1634 to operate a sawmill in South Berwick, Maine. In the 1800's, significant advances were made in the design and construction of masonry dams, especially in Europe. Dams built in the United States during the late 1800's and early 1900's supplied

© Steve Solum, Bruce Coleman, Inc.

U.S. Army Corps of Engineers Fort Peck Project

Water from Fort Peck Dam's reservoir is used by two powerhouses, *left,* to generate electricity. The dam's spillway, *right,* carries excess water to the Missouri River.

A World Book Science Project

Building a model dam

The purpose of this project is to show how a dam can turn a nearly useless river into a valuable asset. One part of the model represents a shallow, almost useless, stream. The other part shows how a dam can make the stream a source of power, irrigation, and recreation.

Illustrated by Art Lutz for WORLD BOOK

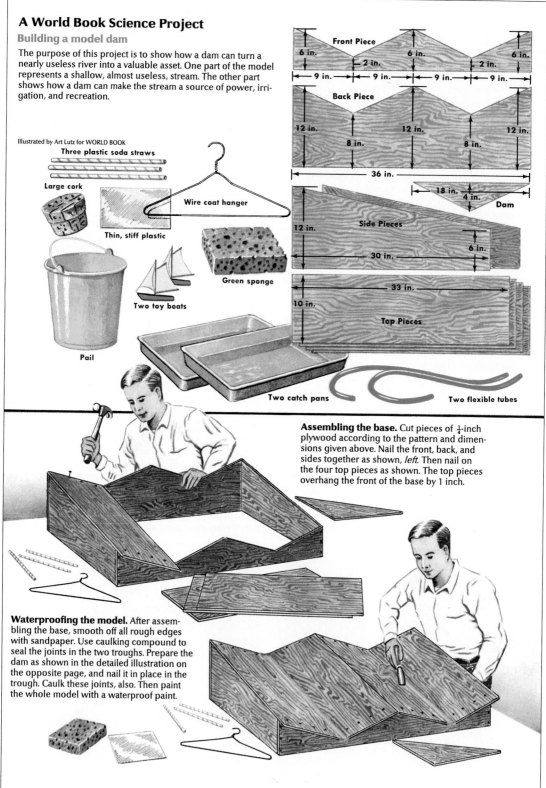

Front Piece

6 in.   6 in.   6 in.
2 in.   2 in.
9 in.   9 in.   9 in.   9 in.

Back Piece

12 in.   12 in.   12 in.
8 in.   8 in.

36 in.

18 in.   4 in.

Dam

12 in.   **Side Pieces**   6 in.
30 in.

33 in.
10 in.   **Top Pieces**

Three plastic soda straws

Large cork

Thin, stiff plastic

Wire coat hanger

Green sponge

Two toy boats

Pail

Two catch pans   Two flexible tubes

Assembling the base. Cut pieces of ¼-inch plywood according to the pattern and dimensions given above. Nail the front, back, and sides together as shown, *left.* Then nail on the four top pieces as shown. The top pieces overhang the front of the base by 1 inch.

Waterproofing the model. After assembling the base, smooth off all rough edges with sandpaper. Use caulking compound to seal the joints in the two troughs. Prepare the dam as shown in the detailed illustration on the opposite page, and nail it in place in the trough. Caulk these joints, also. Then paint the whole model with a waterproof paint.

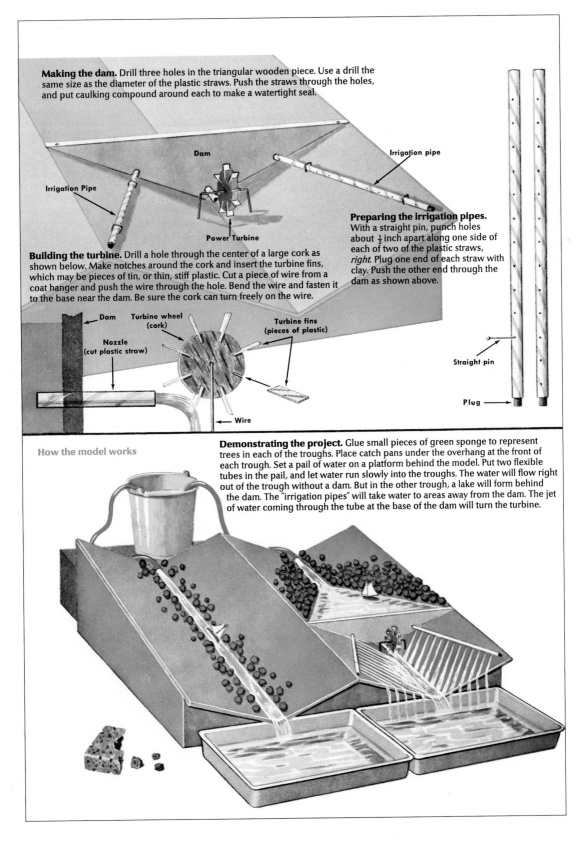

Making the dam. Drill three holes in the triangular wooden piece. Use a drill the same size as the diameter of the plastic straws. Push the straws through the holes, and put caulking compound around each to make a watertight seal.

Irrigation pipe

Dam

Irrigation Pipe

Power Turbine

Preparing the irrigation pipes. With a straight pin, punch holes about $\frac{1}{2}$ inch apart along one side of each of two of the plastic straws, *right.* Plug one end of each straw with clay. Push the other end through the dam as shown above.

Building the turbine. Drill a hole through the center of a large cork as shown below. Make notches around the cork and insert the turbine fins, which may be pieces of tin, or thin, stiff plastic. Cut a piece of wire from a coat hanger and push the wire through the hole. Bend the wire and fasten it to the base near the dam. Be sure the cork can turn freely on the wire.

Dam

Turbine wheel (cork)

Nozzle (cut plastic straw)

Turbine fins (pieces of plastic)

Straight pin

Plug

← Wire

How the model works

Demonstrating the project. Glue small pieces of green sponge to represent trees in each of the troughs. Place catch pans under the overhang at the front of each trough. Set a pail of water on a platform behind the model. Put two flexible tubes in the pail, and let water run slowly into the troughs. The water will flow right out of the trough without a dam. But in the other trough, a lake will form behind the dam. The "irrigation pipes" will take water to areas away from the dam. The jet of water coming through the tube at the base of the dam will turn the turbine.

water to dry lands in the West and opened the area to settlement. During the 1900's, improvements in engineering techniques and building materials have led to the construction of higher and longer dams than ever before. These dams have brought electricity to remote areas and water to arid regions.   Larry W. Mays

Related articles in *World Book.* See the *Electric power* section of various state, province, and country articles, such as **Alabama** (Electric power). See also:

Dams

Aswan High Dam	Glen Canyon Dam	Owyhee Dam
Bonneville Dam	Grand Coulee Dam	Parker Dam
Detroit Dam	Hoover Dam	Pensacola Dam
Fort Peck Dam	Mud Mountain Dam	Roosevelt Dam
Fort Randall Dam	Oahe Dam	Ross Dam
Garrison Dam	Oroville Dam	Shasta Dam

Other related articles

Arizona (picture)	Reservoir
Brazil (picture: The Itaipú Dam)	Rio Grande Project
Central Valley Project	Saint Lawrence Seaway (The
Electric power	hydroelectric power project)
Energy supply (Water power)	
Flood	Tennessee Valley Authority
Irrigation	Turbine (Water turbines)
Kentucky Lake	Water power
Lake (picture)	

Outline

I. What does a dam do?
II. Kinds of dams
  A. Masonry dams   C. Other types of dams
  B. Embankment dams
III. How dams are built
  A. Planning   C. Dam safety
  B. Construction
IV. History

Questions

Why do we need dams?
What is the world's highest dam? The world's largest dam?
How do dams help farmers?
What materials are commonly used in building a dam?
How do builders decide where to construct a dam?
What is a *cofferdam*?
Under what circumstances are *roller dams* necessary?
What is the purpose of a *spillway*?

Additional resources

Level I
Farb, Peter. *The Story of Dams: An Introduction to Hydrology.* Harvey, 1961.
Kelly, James E., and Park, W. R. *The Dam Builders.* Addison-Wesley, 1977.

Level II
Goldsmith, Edward, and Hildyard, Nicholas. *The Social and Environmental Effects of Large Dams.* Sierra Club, 1984.
Smith, Norman A. *A History of Dams.* Lyle Stuart, 1972. First published in 1971.

Damages, in law, means money that a court orders one person to pay to another person for violating that person's rights or for breaking a contract. To collect damages, a victim ordinarily must show that loss or injury has been suffered because of the other person's fault or carelessness or breach of contract.

The main types of damages include *compensatory, general, nominal,* and *punitive* damages. Compensatory damages are recovered only for actual damage, such as the cost of repairing an automobile damaged in an accident. Most damages are compensatory. General damages are based on indications of harm, including pain

and suffering. They are awarded most often in *libel* and *slander* cases where it may be hard to show how one's reputation was harmed by a person making false statements. Nominal damages are small token awards given in cases where a person's rights have been violated, but where no harm has occurred. Suits fought on principle are often settled in this way. Punitive damages are in effect a fine levied against the wrongdoer. They are given in addition to other damages, when the wrongdoer has purposely harmed the other person.

There are few rules of law on how to measure damages. Damages may vary with each case, because the circumstances may be different. Also, many damage suits are tried before juries, and each jury may award different damages. Damages may include elements that are hard to measure in money, such as pain and suffering. Some damages may have to be measured for harm that will occur only in the future.   Sherman L. Cohn

See also **Negligence; Tort.**

Damascus, *duh MAS kuhs* (pop. 1,200,000), is the capital and largest city of Syria. It may have been founded about 5,000 years ago and is one of the world's oldest cities. Damascus is Syria's cultural, economic, and political center. It lies in southwest Syria, between the Anti-Lebanon Mountains on the west and the Syrian Desert on the east (see **Syria** [map]).

The city is on an oasis in a semiarid plain. The Barada River flows through Damascus and has provided the area with water for thousands of years.

The southern section of Damascus includes an area that is hundreds of years old. There, on narrow, winding streets, merchants sell a wide variety of goods in bazaars called *suqs,* just as their ancestors did. This area contrasts with the main business district in the northwest, which has many tall buildings erected during the 1900's. Many parts of Damascus and its suburbs have residential areas. Most of the people live in apartments, but some have beautiful houses.

Cultural attractions in Damascus include the University of Damascus, the National Library, museums, and

Shostal

Damascus is the capital and largest city of Syria. Some sections of the city are hundreds of years old, but the main business district, *above,* has many buildings erected in the 1900's.

theaters. The city has many fine works of Islamic architecture. Among them are the Umayyad, or Great Mosque; the Mosque of Sultan Suleiman; and the tomb of Saladin, a Muslim leader of the 1100's.

Economy. Damascus is the chief Syrian center of manufacturing, trade, tourism, and banking and other financial activities. Textile production and food processing are two of the city's largest industries. Fruit grown in nearby orchards is processed and canned in Damascus. In the old section of the city, craftworkers sell fabrics, metalware, and many other products. Most of the people of Damascus use buses and taxis for local transportation. An international airport lies just outside the city.

History. Historians believe Damascus may have been founded about 3000 B.C. The city was important during the rule of several early empires, including those of the Assyrians, Greeks, Romans, and Byzantines. The Muslim Arabs captured Damascus from the Byzantines in A.D. 635. Under the leadership of the Umayyad dynasty, the Muslim Arabs made Damascus the capital of their vast empire in 661. But the Umayyads lost control of Damascus during the 700's, and the city went through a long period of anarchy and decline.

In 1154, the Syrian leader Nur al-Din made Damascus the capital. Saladin, the Muslim ruler of Egypt, took control of Damascus in the late 1100's. The city became a center of trade. Most of its main historical monuments date from the late 1100's and the 1200's.

In 1516, the Ottoman Turks conquered Damascus. The city prospered as trade increased with neighboring countries and with European nations. The Ottomans controlled the region until World War I (1914-1918). Combined Allied and Arab forces captured Damascus during the war. France took control of Syria in 1920.

Syria became independent in 1946, with Damascus as its capital. By the early 1980's, the city had almost four times as many people as it had in 1946, and a housing shortage resulted. New towns were established near Damascus to solve the problem.   Malcolm C. Peck

See also **Syria** (picture).

Damask, *DAM uhsk,* is a firm, lustrous fabric that may be woven from any fiber. Its flat, woven design appears on both sides of the fabric. Damask was originally a silk fabric produced in China. Traders introduced it to Europe by way of Damascus, Syria.

In table damask, the design may be sateen weave with *floats* (longer, raised threads) in the *filling* (crosswise) threads. The background may be a satin weave with floats in the *warp* (lengthwise) threads. Single table damask has a four-float construction, and double damask has a seven-float construction. Damask's luster depends on length of floats, length of fibers, closeness of weave, and uniformity of yarns.   Christine W. Jarvis

D'Amboise, *dahm BWAZ,* **Jacques,** *zhahk* (1934-   ), an American dancer, won fame as a featured performer with the New York City Ballet. He earned particular recognition as the male lead in George Balanchine's ballet *Apollo.* Athletic jumps and a sparkling stage presence marked his style.

Jacques Joseph d'Amboise was born in Dedham, Mass. He trained under Balanchine at the School of American Ballet. D'Amboise is remembered for roles in the ballets *Western Symphony* (1954), *Movements for Piano and Orchestra* (1963), *Meditation* (1963), and *Union*

Martha Swope

Jacques d'Amboise danced with Suzanne Farrell in the ballet *Diamonds* at the New York City Ballet in 1967.

Jack (1976). As a *choreographer* (creator of dances), he created *Irish Fantasy* (1964) and other ballets.

D'Amboise appeared on TV and in motion pictures and directed or choreographed several Broadway musicals. In 1976, he established the National Dance Institute to introduce children to the arts through dance.

Dianne L. Woodruff

Dame school. See **Colonial life in America** (The school).

Damien de Veuster, *DA MYAN duh vus TAIR,* **Joseph** (1840-1889), was a Roman Catholic priest who gave his life to the care of lepers in a colony at Molokai, Hawaii. Father Damien was born in Belgium and became a member of the Fathers of the Sacred Hearts of Jesus and Mary. He asked to be sent to Molokai as resident priest (see **Hawaii** [Molokai]). But because of the difficulty in getting doctors, he was obliged to serve as a doctor as well. He was stricken with leprosy in 1885. Hawaii has placed a statue of Father Damien in the United States Capitol in Washington, D.C.   Marvin R. O'Connell

Damocles, *DAM uh kleez,* was a member of the court of Dionysius II, who ruled Syracuse, Sicily, from 367 to 344 B.C. Damocles was an excessive flatterer. The Roman orator Cicero said that Damocles once talked too much about the happiness and good fortune of Dionysius. To teach Damocles a lesson, Dionysius invited him to a big feast. When he was seated, Damocles found a sword, suspended by a single hair, dangling over his head. This sword represented the constant danger that went with the wealth and material happiness of Dionysius. The *sword of Damocles* has become a byword for the threat of danger.   Peter Krentz

Damon and Pythias, *DAY muhn, PIHTH ee uhs,* were two noble youths in Greek legend. Their friendship and loyalty to each other made them famous. Pythias had been condemned to death by Dionysius, ruler of the city of Syracuse. Pythias was allowed to leave Syracuse to put his affairs in order after Damon agreed to die in his place if Pythias failed to return. Although Pythias was delayed, he arrived just in time to save Damon from death. Dionysius so admired this display of friendship that he pardoned Pythias and asked the two to become his friends. The name of Pythias was originally spelled *Phintias.* During the Middle Ages, scribes accidentally spelled it *Pythias.* That form of the name has been common since the 1500's.   William F. Hansen

Damp is a dangerous gas found in mines. It is most often found in coal mines, where it is a hazard to miners. *Firedamp* is the most common kind of damp. It is chiefly *methane,* a tasteless, odorless gas. Firedamp forms when decaying plant matter produces coal. It is trapped in seams or cracks in rock. When miners cut into the seams or cracks, the gas is released. The gas burns readily and can explode when mixed with air in certain proportions. Exploded firedamp leaves *afterdamp,* a deadly gas that contains poisonous carbon monoxide and nonpoisonous nitrogen and carbon dioxide.

Chokedamp and *blackdamp* are common names for carbon dioxide, CO_2, a gas that is denser than air. This gas gathers at the bottom of pits and low places in mines, reducing the amount of oxygen in the air. If too much CO_2 is present, miners will suffocate. Miners once carried canaries to test for gases. They knew gas was present if the birds collapsed. Today, various mechanical, chemical, and electrical devices are used to test for the presence of gases.   George B. Clark

See also **Methane; Coal** (Mine safety).

Dampier, *DAM pee uhr* or *DAMP yuhr,* **William** (1651-1715), was an English seaman and explorer. He explored Australia and the far South Pacific, and wrote one of the first English accounts of the region. His journal, *A New Voyage Around the World* (1697), helped increase English interest in the Pacific. Dampier also strengthened racial prejudices when he wrote that the people then living in Australia were "the miserablest People" in the world.

Dampier was born in East Coker, England. He went to sea as a boy, and joined the navy in 1672. In 1688, he sailed to Australia (then called New Holland). In 1699, he reached Australia again in a voyage financed by the British Admiralty. Dampier also reached New Britain and New Ireland, islands that are near New Guinea.

Robin W. Winks

Damping-off is a plant disease caused by certain fungi that live near the surface of the soil (see **Fungi**). The disease affects many kinds of plants. Damping-off kills *seedlings* (young plants) before they grow above the ground, or it destroys the stems of seedlings just above the surface of the soil. Damping-off cannot be cured. But growers can prevent the disease by planting seeds in soil free from fungi, or by treating the seeds or the soil with fungicides.   Jerry T. Walker

Damrosch, *DAM rahsh,* was the family name of a father and son who spent their lives educating Americans to serious music. They came from a family of German musicians.

Leopold Damrosch (1832-1885), violinist and conductor, founded the New York Symphony Society in 1878, and conducted its orchestra until his death. Damrosch was born in Posen, Prussia (now Poznan, Poland). After receiving his degree in medicine from the University of Berlin in 1854, he joined the Weimar court orchestra as violinist under Franz Liszt. Damrosch came to the United States in 1871 to become conductor of the German Male Choral Society. He introduced German opera at the Metropolitan Opera House.

Walter Johannes Damrosch (1862-1950), son of Leopold, conducted the New York Symphony Orchestra in 1925 in the first symphonic program ever broadcast on radio. From 1928 to 1947, Damrosch served as musical counsel for the National Broadcasting Company. Children throughout the nation learned about great music by listening to the Music Appreciation Hour he directed. The music of such composers as Wagner, Stravinsky, Gershwin, Ravel, and Elgar became popular, in part, through Damrosch's efforts.

Damrosch was born in Breslau, Silesia, and came to America with his father in 1871. He succeeded his father as director of the Oratorio and Symphony societies of New York City in 1885. Later he founded the Damrosch Opera Company to present Wagnerian operas. Damrosch reorganized the New York Symphony Society in 1903, and then served as its conductor until 1927.

In addition to his conducting and educational work, Damrosch composed such operas as *The Scarlet Letter, Cyrano de Bergerac, The Man Without a Country,* and *Manila Te Deum,* celebrating Admiral George Dewey's victory. He wrote several songs, including "Danny Deever" and "Mandalay."   Irving Kolodin

Damsel fly. See Dragonfly.

Dana, *DAY nuh,* **Charles Anderson** (1819-1897), editor and part owner of the New York *Sun,* built it into one of the most important newspapers of its time. Dana and his associates paid $175,000 for the *Sun* in 1868. Under his management its value rose to an estimated $5 million. He made the *Sun* a witty, terse, and outspoken newspaper.

Dana was born on Aug. 8, 1819, in Hinsdale, N.H. He studied at Harvard University. In 1842, he became a member of the Brook Farm Association, an experimental social community at West Roxbury, Mass., and wrote for its publications, *The Harbinger* and *The Dial* (see **Brook Farm**). He joined the staff of the New York *Tribune* in 1847, and later became its managing editor. He resigned in 1862 because he disagreed with *Tribune* owner Horace Greeley about the newspaper's stand on the Civil War. Dana served as an assistant secretary of war from 1863 to 1865.   John Eldridge Drewry

Dana, *DAY nuh,* **Richard Henry, Jr.** (1815-1882), was an American author known for his sea adventure story *Two Years Before the Mast* (1840). The book became one of the most popular and influential sea stories ever written. Herman Melville said the excitement he felt while reading Dana's book helped inspire him to write his famous sea novel, *Moby Dick.*

Dana was born in Cambridge, Mass. He was forced to leave his studies at Harvard University because of poor eyesight caused by an attack of measles. In 1834, Dana sailed as a seaman from Boston around Cape Horn, arriving in California in January 1835. After spending about 17 months in California, he returned by sea to Boston. Dana kept a journal of his two voyages and his visit to California that became the basis of *Two Years Before the Mast.* He wrote the book in the form of a diary, realistically describing life at sea and providing a vivid account of Spanish California in the 1830's.

Dana was active in the antislavery movement before the Civil War (1861-1865) and helped form the antislavery Free Soil Party in 1848. He was also a noted lawyer and wrote *The Seaman's Friend* (1841), a manual of customs, terms, and laws relating to the sea. *To Cuba and Back: A Vacation Voyage* (1859) describes one of Dana's later sea voyages.   Edward W. Clark

Danaë. See Perseus.

Alwin Nikolais Dance Theatre

A performance of the modern dance *Imago*

Patson Travel, Chicago (WORLD BOOK photo)

Religious dance of India

© Ebet Roberts

Dancing to rock music

Marc & Evelyne Bernheim, Woodfin Camp, Inc.

An African dance

Dancing

Dancing is an act of moving the body in rhythm, usually in time to music. People seem to have a natural urge to express their feelings through rhythmic movement. For example, most children jump up and down when they are excited and sway gently when content or at rest. In dancing, people organize the expressive movements of their bodies into rhythmic and visual patterns.

Dancing is both an art and a form of recreation. As an art, a dance may tell a story, set a mood, or express an emotion. A ballet dancer's movements, for example, can effectively describe the fluttering of a wounded swan.

Some Oriental dances consist of symbolic gestures that tell a story completely through movement.

As a form of recreation, dancing has long provided fun, relaxation, and companionship. On the American frontier, for example, square dances gave pioneer families a welcome chance to socialize. Today, dancing at a party or other gathering remains a popular way for people to enjoy themselves and to make new friends.

Prehistoric paintings found in Africa and southern Europe show people dancing. Social scientists believe that

Selma Landen Odom, the contributor of this article, is Associate Professor of Dance History at York University.

dancing may have played an important part in hunting and many other activities of prehistoric life. Scientists study the dances of various cultures because the kinds of dances a people do—and how and why they do them—can reveal much about their way of life.

Why people dance

Most people dance simply to have fun or to entertain others. But dancing also serves many other purposes.

For many people, dancing provides one of the most personal and effective means of communication. A dancer can express such feelings as joy, anger, or helplessness without saying a word. Many elementary and high schools, colleges, and private studios offer classes in *modern dance*. These classes encourage students to express themselves through rhythmic movement. The field of dance therapy uses modern dance to treat physically handicapped and emotionally disturbed people.

In many societies, dancing plays a role in courtship. It serves as a way for men and women to become acquainted before they marry. Among some African peoples, girls announce their readiness for marriage by taking part in special dances. In the United States, high school and college students get to know one another at school dances.

Throughout human history, dancing has been used in worship. Prehistoric people probably made up religious dances to gain the favor of their gods. Many North American Indian tribes danced in appealing for rain and good crops. During the 1800's, a Christian religious group called the *Shakers* tried to "shake out the Devil" by doing lively, whirling dances. Many traditional religious dances are still done today. In Australia, for example, a few tribes of Aborigines follow their age-old custom of imitating the gestures of hunting during a religious dance before an actual hunt. In some English villages, children dance around a ribboned Maypole on May 1 in a springtime celebration. This custom goes back to the ancient religious dances of the Romans, who ruled Britain from A.D. 43 until the early 400's. On May 1, the Romans worshiped Flora, the goddess of spring, by dancing around a Maypole decorated with flowers.

Dancing often serves to create a feeling of unity among the participants. In New Guinea, tribal war dances before a battle draw the community together and inspire the warriors to fight bravely. Some secret societies in Africa do a special initiation dance known only to their members. When new members learn the dance, it represents their acceptance into the group. In a similar way, American teen-agers often gain the admiration and acceptance of their classmates by mastering the latest popular dances.

Kinds of dancing

There are two major kinds of dancing—theatrical and social. *Theatrical dancing* is performed for the entertainment of spectators. Theatrical dance forms include ballet, modern dance, musical comedy dances, and tap-dancing. Theatrical dancers may take great personal satisfaction in creating something beautiful. However, their own enjoyment and need for self-expression are less important than their ability to interpret the dance effectively for the audience.

In *social dancing,* the participants dance for their own pleasure rather than for the entertainment of an audience. There are many types of social dances. Most of them have specific steps and rhythms, but many newer ones allow the dancers to compose their own movements as they dance.

All types of theatrical and social dancing involve movement, energy, rhythm, and design. *Movement* is the action of dancers as they use their bodies to create organized patterns. *Energy* provides the force needed to perform movement. *Rhythm* is the pattern of timing around which the dance movement is organized. Most dance movement is related to the rhythm of accompanying music. *Design* refers to the visual pattern made by the movements of a dancer's body.

The rest of this section deals with four of the most important kinds of dance in the Western world. They are the theatrical forms of ballet and modern dance and the two types of social dancing, folk dancing and popular dancing. The next two sections discuss dancing in Asia and in Africa.

Ballet began in the royal courts of Italy in the 1400's. The special movements of ballet still include bows and other elegant manners that reflect its courtly origin.

Ballet dancers learn how to hold their bodies to achieve the ideal upright posture of ballet. Their bearing is open and direct as they perform their movements. Classical ballet technique is based on positions and movements in which the legs rotate outward from the hip joint. This rotation is known as the *turnout*. It enables the dancer to move freely in any direction.

In ballet, the trunk of the body remains relatively calm, while the arms and legs extend outward to form meaningful designs. The *line* of a dancer's body is very important in both performing and appreciating ballet. Line refers to the way a dancer displays clarity of design and to how closely a dancer's body proportions express the ideal for ballet. Today, ideal proportions include long arms and legs and a thin, well-shaped trunk.

© Jack Vartoogian

Ballet dancers combine technical precision with the ability to express emotion through movement. Rebecca Wright and Kirk Peterson of the American Ballet Theatre are shown above in a performance of *Harlequinade* (1965) by George Balanchine.

Ballet themes and styles have changed greatly over the years. The first works called ballets were based on stories that had a moral or political meaning. These works resembled plays, but they featured dance sections known as *entrées*. The movements of early ballet dancers differed from those of dancers today because the early dancers were court nobles, who performed special versions of social dances of their times. In addition, heavy, elaborate costumes limited their movements.

Many ballets of the 1800's told stories of delicate, imaginary creatures. These ballets emphasized the quick, light movements of graceful women dancers performing on their toes. Male dancers served mainly to lift the women to show how light they were. In the early 1900's, a famous Russian company, the Ballets Russes, introduced new strength and energy to male technique.

Since about 1900, the length of ballets has varied from short works lasting about half an hour to full-length ballets several hours long. Some modern ballets tell a story. Others describe a mood or express the feelings and movements aroused by the music or by some other factor, such as a painting or nature. Current dance styles reflect the speed, pressures, and complexity of modern life. For an extensive discussion of ballet, see the article **Ballet**.

Modern dance developed in the early 1900's. The leaders of the modern dance movement believed that the techniques of ballet were artificial and meaningless. They searched for fresher, more personal ways to express ideas through dancing. Pioneers of the movement included Isadora Duncan, Loie Fuller, and Ruth St. Denis of the United States; Emile Jaques-Dalcroze of Switzerland, and Rudolf von Laban of Hungary.

Isadora Duncan was one of the most free-spirited of the modern dance pioneers. She danced in her bare feet and wore loose-fitting garments that allowed her freedom of movement. She permitted no scenery onstage, which might draw attention from her dancing. Duncan ignored the formal, set movements of ballet. Her own flowing movements were inspired by nature, classical music, and Greek drama and sculpture. Duncan's ideas greatly influenced the development not only of modern dance but also of ballet.

Oriental religions inspired the dances of Ruth St. Denis. She won fame during a tour of Europe from 1906 to 1909. In 1915, St. Denis and her husband, Ted Shawn, opened the famous Denishawn School of Dancing in Los Angeles. The school moved to New York City in 1922. After leaving Denishawn, many former students developed more personal styles than the ones they had been taught. Several of these students, including Martha Graham and Doris Humphrey with her partner, Charles Weidman, formed their own dance companies.

Mary Wigman became Europe's first great modern dancer. She founded an influential dance school in her native Germany in 1920. Dancers from her school performed throughout Europe and the United States.

Since the 1940's, creativity in modern dance has centered on U.S. dancers and dance companies. The most experimental dancers have included Merce Cunningham, Alwin Nikolais, Paul Taylor and Twyla Tharp. Modern dance works today place less importance on emotion and personal expression. Instead, they explore

Martha Swope

American musical comedy has inspired some of the most imaginative dances ever created. The dance above is from the brilliant Broadway musical *A Chorus Line* (1975)—a show that pays tribute to the chorus dancers in musical comedies.

movement for its own sake. For example, dancers may make patterns with their bodies merely to form interesting pictures. Dancers may also use movements, such as walking, that are more natural than the movements used by earlier performers. Today's dances even include tumbling, rolling, and other acrobatics. Ballet companies have adopted some modern dance techniques and have begun to invite modern dance *choreographers* (dance composers) to work with them. As a result, the gulf between ballet and modern dance has narrowed greatly.

Folk dancing is a form of social dancing that has become part of the customs and traditions of a people. Well-known folk dances include the square dance, the Irish jig, and the polka. Most folk dances developed among people in villages and were passed on from gen-

David Hurn, Magnum

Folk dancing is the traditional form of social dancing of a particular nation or ethnic group. The couples shown above are performing a folk dance that originated in Scotland. This type of dance is passed down from generation to generation.

eration to generation in a particular region. In many of these dances, groups of dancers form such basic patterns as a circle, a line, or a curved, moving line called a *chain*. In some folk dances, women and men dance together in couples. But in many other dances, such as Greek village dances, only men or women perform.

Although folk dances are preserved by repetition, they gradually change over the years. For example, the polka danced in the United States today looks different from the polka danced in Europe during the 1800's. The music and basic steps resemble the original style. But many things, such as modern clothing styles and the surface on which the dance is done, may affect the dancers' movements and make the polka look different.

During the 1800's and 1900's, immigrants to the United States and Canada continued to enjoy the folk dances of their homelands. However, most of their children and grandchildren abandoned the dances and other family traditions. Today, folk dance classes and clubs in the United States and Canada are rediscovering traditional dances from all over the world. These groups perform in costume for entertainment and so help preserve the heritage of the folk dance.

For additional information on folk dancing, see the article **Folk dancing.**

Popular dancing is the kind of dancing people do for fun. They may dance to the music of live bands in ballrooms or to recorded music in nightclubs called *discothèques,* or *discos*. People also dance at parties and other social gatherings. Popular, or social, dances include such old favorites as the waltz and the cha-cha, as well as the latest rock dances. Early social dances known as *court dances* developed among the European nobility in the 1100's from the folk dances of the peasants. However, these social dances were more dignified than the high-spirited folk dances from which they originated.

Social dancing differs from folk dancing in several ways. For example, the steps of many social dances have been carefully recorded on paper. In addition, social dancing has been formally taught by dancing masters since as early as the 1400's. Folk dances, on the other hand, have been largely unrecorded, and most people learn to do them simply by watching folk dancers and then imitating their steps. Social dances often spread quickly throughout much of the world, but folk dances usually remain closely identified with the regions where they developed.

Most social dances are fads that become associated with the period in which they were popular. The most fashionable dances of one period are generally out of date in the next. Some popular dances were considered shocking when they first appeared. Many people in the early 1800's thought the waltz was disgraceful because it required close contact between partners. In the 1920's, "cheek-to-cheek" dancing to jazz music was condemned as sinful. The suggestive movements of some rock dances of the 1950's and 1960's were criticized as vulgar.

Oriental dancing

In parts of Asia, dance traditions are thousands of years old. Most theatrical dance forms of Asia were performed originally as part of religious worship or for entertainment. Many folk dances also developed in Asia,

but modern social dances reflect Western influences. Asians have deep respect for tradition, which has encouraged dancers to make existing theatrical dance forms perfect rather than to create new styles.

In most of Asia, dance, drama, and opera did not develop as separate art forms, as they did in the West. Traditional forms of Asian theater combine dance, music, pantomime, speech, and sometimes puppetry. The performers often wear elaborate costumes and fantastic masks or makeup. In some Asian theatrical dances, slight movements of the upper body—especially facial expressions and hand gestures—communicate the message of the dance. Every movement, even a raised eyebrow, may have significance. Many dances describe, through gesture, a historical event, a legend, or a myth.

Some theatrical dance performances in Asia take place outdoors and last all night. People in the audience leave and return as they please. A famous performance of this type held in Burma is called *pwe* (pronounced *pweh*). At a pwe, spectators may shout out comments, tease the performers, and go backstage to watch them put on costumes and makeup.

Religion and magic are major themes of much Oriental dancing. *Bharata Natyam,* a dance originally performed in the temples of India, combines rhythmically complicated dancing with Hindu legends told in song and pantomime. Like other Indian dance forms, this temple dance uses *mudras*—hand gestures that have recognized meanings.

In Southeast Asia, *trance dances* blend superstitions with Buddhist, Hindu, and Islamic beliefs. During the *Barong,* a theatrical dance form performed on the Indonesian island of Bali, dancers in a trance act out a legendary battle between a dragon and a witch. The dancers turn knives on themselves. But in most cases, the trance prevents them from feeling pain and helps protect them from injury. Members of the audience rescue performers who become too violent, unless they themselves go into a trance.

© Jack Vartoogian

Oriental dancing is based on thousands of years of tradition. These two dancers from the Indonesian island of Bali perform a dance with stylized movements and expressive gestures.

Hand-colored woodcut (about 1685) by Sugimura Jihei; Mary Andrews Ladd Collection, Portland Art Museum, Portland, Ore.

The lion dance, which originated in China, is a Japanese folk dance. It is performed in the streets during harvest festivals and other celebrations and in theatrical dance productions.

Some of the most important theatrical dances of Asia began as entertainment for royalty. Two famous Japanese dance dramas, *no* and *kabuki,* developed from a majestic court procession called the *bugaku,* which started in the 800's. The Peking Opera began in the court of the Chinese emperor in the late 1700's. The opera's dances and other traditional features, such as skillful acrobatics and pantomime, colorful costumes, and symbolic makeup, still delight audiences today. During the 1950's, China began to develop a dance form called *revolutionary ballet.* This form uses the strength and speed of Western ballet style to express Communist themes.

African dancing

Dancing developed in Africa as an essential part of village life. It emphasizes the unity among the members of a village. As a result, African dancing is nearly always a group activity. On important occasions, ceremonial dances with special symbolic movements may be performed by professional dancers. But in most village dances, all the men, women, and children join in the dancing, or they clap their hands or form a circle around the dancers and call out to them.

Every important event in African life is observed by dancing. Such events include birth, death, the planting of crops, and even the dedication of a public building. Dancing is a major feature of festivals held to thank the gods for a rich harvest. Ceremonial hunting dances are performed throughout Africa. Other dances celebrate the passage of young people from childhood to adulthood. In addition, Africans dance for entertainment at weddings and on other occasions.

African dances vary widely from region to region, but most dances share certain characteristics. Participants

usually dance in a single line, in two parallel lines, or in a circle. They seldom dance alone or with a partner. African dances feature as many as six rhythms at once. Each part of the dancer's body—the head, the trunk, the arms, and the legs—may follow the rhythm of a different instrument at the same time. Precise control of the parts of the body and of the designs they make is less important than the continuous, natural flow of movement. African dancers sometimes wear masks. They may also decorate their bodies with paint to make their movements even more expressive.

The development of Western dance

Prehistoric times. Dancing was one of the earliest forms of artistic and personal expression. Prehistoric paintings of dancers have been found on cave walls in Africa and southern Europe. These paintings may be more than 20,000 years old. Religious ceremonies that combined dancing, music, and drama probably played an important part in the lives of prehistoric people. These ceremonies may have been held to worship the gods and to ask them for success in hunting and in battle. Ceremonial dances may also have been performed for such reasons as to celebrate a birth, heal the sick, and mourn the dead.

Ancient times. Both sacred and nonreligious dancing existed during ancient times, especially in the regions along the Mediterranean Sea and in the Middle East. The paintings, sculptures, and writings of ancient Egypt provide information about early Egyptian dancing. For example, decorative carvings found in Egyptian tombs show that dances were performed during funerals, parades, and religious ceremonies. The Egyptians were an agricultural people, and their major religious festivals centered on dances honoring Osiris, the god of vegetation. Dancing also provided private entertainment. For example, slaves danced to entertain wealthy families and their guests.

The ancient Greeks regarded dancing as essential to education, worship, and drama. The Greek philosopher Plato urged that all Greek citizens be taught to dance to develop self-control and skill at warfare. Weapon

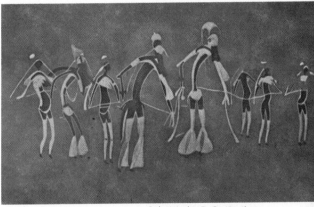

Rock painting from Tassili-n-Ajjer, Algeria (Henri Lhote's expedition document)

Prehistoric dancers are pictured in paintings up to 20,000 years old. Such paintings, found on rock surfaces, prove that dancing is one of the oldest forms of human expression.

Mural (about 1350) by an unknown Danish artist; Ørslev Church, near Sorø, Denmark (National Museum, Copenhagen)

The chain dance became one of the most popular kinds of folk dances in the Middle Ages. Like other folk dances, it began among the peasants and was adopted by the nobility, *above*. Folk dancing played a major part in the celebration of weddings, holidays, and other festive occasions.

dances had already become part of the military education of boys in the city-states of Athens and Sparta. Colorful social dances were performed at weddings, harvesttime, and many other occasions.

Religious dances played a major part in the birth of Greek drama. During the 500's B.C., serious dramas called *tragedies* developed from a ceremony of hymns and dances in honor of Dionysus, the god of wine. The *emmeleia,* a dignified dance performed in tragedies, included a set of recognized gestures. A trained dancer could tell the entire story of a play through these gestures. Greek comedies and short, humorous plays called *satyrs* included lively dances.

By the time the Romans conquered Greece in 197 B.C., they had already adopted much of the Greek culture, including Greek dancing. Like the Greeks, the Romans developed dances for religious festivals. Roman entertainers danced as they juggled and performed acrobatics. In spite of the popularity of dancing, some important Romans disapproved of it. The famous orator Cicero claimed, "No man dances unless he is drunk or insane." In time, professional dancers came to be considered immoral.

The Middle Ages. During the Middle Ages, which lasted from about the A.D. 400's to the 1500's, the Christian church became the most influential force in Europe. Church officials in many areas prohibited theatrical dancing because some dances had become vulgar and included sexually suggestive movements. However, wandering dancers kept theatrical dancing alive by performing at fairs and in villages. By the 1300's, associations of craftworkers put on elaborate religious plays in which dancing was a popular feature (see **Drama** [Medieval drama]).

During the 1300's, a plague known as the *Black Death* swept across Europe, wiping out a fourth of the population. The constant threat of disease and death tormented some people to near madness. People sang and danced frantically in graveyards. They believed such acts would drive away demons and keep the dead from escaping from their coffins to infect the living. Disease, superstition, and fear of the plague drove some people to dance wildly in procession from place to place until they fainted or fell dead.

Throughout the Middle Ages, Europeans continued to celebrate weddings, holidays, and other festive occasions with folk dances. The peasants, adults as well as children, performed sword dances and danced around Maypoles. Other folk dances included chain dances and

such dance games as ring-around-the-rosy, which still delights children today. The nobility developed more elegant versions of the peasants' folk dances. Lords and ladies danced a circle dance called the *carol* in a slower, more dignified manner than the peasants' original lively style. During the late Middle Ages, dancing became part of the spectacle associated with the splendid banquets, tournaments, and parades of the nobility.

The Renaissance was a period of great economic and cultural growth. The Renaissance began in Italy about 1300, during the late Middle Ages, and spread throughout most of Europe by 1600. In Italy, the nobility of nearly every prosperous city tried to outdo the nobles of other cities in staging elaborate entertainment at the royal courts. They hired professional dancing masters to create original court spectacles that included dances called *balli* or *balletti.*

Spectacles were presented to celebrate such events as birthdays, weddings, and visits by foreign officials. Members of the court took turns performing for one another in various groupings and arrangements. The productions combined poetry, dancing, music, and scenic effects. Some spectacles included fireworks, water shows, mock battles, and parades. Leading composers wrote the music, and the most talented artists, including the great Leonardo da Vinci, designed costumes and special effects.

Catherine de Médicis, a member of the ruling family of Florence, Italy, became queen of France in 1547. She introduced Italian dance and spectacle into the French court. For a royal wedding in 1581, Catherine commissioned a group of Italian artists to come to Paris to create the magnificent *Ballet Comique de la Reine,* one of the first ballets ever produced. This kind of ballet became widely imitated throughout Europe.

In addition to producing spectacles, dancing masters taught social dances to the nobility. Lords and ladies danced such dances as the bouncy galliard, the dignified pavan, and the lively volta. Dancing also had special philosophical meaning during the Renaissance. Many people believed harmony of skilled dance movement reflected harmony in government, nature, and the universe.

The 1600's and 1700's. King Louis XIV of France, who lived from 1638 to 1715, greatly encouraged the development of ballet. His support of dancing and the other arts helped make France the cultural center of Europe. Louis himself enthusiastically danced in court ballets for 20 years. One of his favorite roles, that of the

Greek sun god Apollo, helped earn him his famous nickname, "the Sun King."

During Louis' reign, ballet came to have its own professional performers and a formal system of movements. Performances were gradually moved from the royal ballroom to a theater. The theater had a *proscenium arch,* which framed the stage and set it apart from the audience. The arch symbolized the separation developing between the performers and the spectators.

Ballet technique for women became freer during the 1700's. Before that time, women wore long, heavy skirts, tight corsets, and heeled slippers—all of which severely limited their ability to jump and perform other energetic movements done by male dancers. But during the 1700's, women shortened their skirts to about mid-calf and eventually began to wear shoes without heels. Marie Sallé, a French dancer, wore loosely draped cloth to allow greater freedom of movement. Jean Georges Noverre, a French choreographer, helped develop a form of dance drama called *ballet d'action.* It stressed the use of movement to communicate a story or idea rather than merely to show off a dancer's skills.

The dances of the court ballets had been based on the social dances of the period. The most popular dances of the 1700's included the gavotte, the allemande, and the minuet. These graceful dances consisted of a complicated pattern of steps, glides, rises and dips, and bows and curtsies. Lively English folk dances called *country dances* also became favorites of the middle and upper classes throughout Europe. The invention of written systems of *dance notation* enabled people to learn dances by following diagrams printed in books. Some European dancing masters sailed to America, especially to the Southern Colonies, to teach dancing and other social graces to the families of wealthy merchants and plantation owners.

The rise of romanticism revolutionized the subject matter and technique of ballet during the 1800's. Romanticism was a movement in the arts that glorified individuality and freedom of personal expression. Previously, most ballets were about gods and goddesses, but they now focused on common people. Many ballet stories of the 1800's also included delicate, imaginary beings, such as fairies and *sylphs* (spirits of the air). Women portrayed these creatures by dancing on their toes. They wore fluffy knee-length or calf-length skirts called *tutus* and glided across a stage that was specially lighted to produce a magical atmosphere. The best-known romantic ballets include two works by French composers, *La Sylphide* (1832) by Jean-Madeleine Schneitzhoeffer and *Giselle* (1841) by Adolphe Adam.

Marius Petipa, a French choreographer who worked in Russia, and Lev Ivanov, his Russian assistant, transformed classic fairy tales into spectacular ballets during the late 1800's. They set their works to the beautiful music of the Russian composer Peter Ilich Tchaikovsky. Their best-known ballets—*Sleeping Beauty* (1890), *The Nutcracker* (1892), and *Swan Lake* (1895)—combine graceful movement with technical precision.

Throughout the 1800's, most of the new social dances that became popular in Europe and the United States began among the common people. Instead of largely setting the fashion, the European nobility again imitated the peasants, who danced the waltz and the polka. Social dancing in ballrooms became popular among the middle and upper classes.

In the United States, new forms of theatrical dancing developed or first became popular among the working class and the poor. Blacks developed tap-dancing by combining traditional African dances with the Irish jig and a lively English folk dance called the *clog.* Black performers tap-danced in such places as taverns and on street corners. By the 1870's, they also performed in traveling variety shows. Chorus girls danced the high-kicking cancan, which originated in France, to entertain cowboys in dance halls along the American frontier.

Engraving (1682) by Antoine Trouvain;
Bibliothèque Nationale, Paris

Magnificent court balls were often staged in France under the reign of King Louis XIV, who ruled during the late 1600's and early 1700's. Louis' enthusiastic support of social dancing and ballet made France the dance center of Europe.

Detail of *Der Hofball* (about 1900), a gouache
painting on canvas by Wilhelm Gause;
Vienna State Museum, Vienna, Austria

The romantic waltz became the most fashionable social dance of the 1800's. It originated in Germany and Austria and soon spread to other countries. Waltz music also added beauty and elegance to some of the period's best-loved ballets.

Watercolor (about 1890) by Albert Meyers; Museum of
Modern Art, New York City. 22 by 22 in. (56 by 56 cm)

The cakewalk started among American slaves as a high-stepping promenade that poked fun at the haughty ways of plantation masters. Dancers improvised steps to syncopated music. Whites began to dance the cakewalk about 1890.

Dancing since 1900 has shown a wide range of styles and much experimentation, beginning with the introduction of modern dance. The development of modern dance, which was based on freedom of movement and expression, is discussed in the subsection *Modern dance* earlier in this article.

The revolutionary ideas of modern dance led to major changes in ballet. The Ballets Russes, the great Russian company formed by Sergei Diaghilev, produced powerful and even shocking ballets during the early 1900's. One of Diaghilev's most famous new works was *The Rite of Spring* (1913). Its primitive-style dances by the Russian choreographer and dancer Vaslav Nijinsky and radical music by the Russian composer Igor Stravinsky set off a riot in the audience at the ballet's opening in Paris. Diaghilev and his great choreographers, such as Michel Fokine, influenced the development of ballet for many years. By the 1960's, the leading ballet choreographers included George Balanchine, who had worked for Diaghilev and moved to the United States in 1933; Jerome Robbins; Antony Tudor; and Sir Frederick Ashton. Today's ballet styles and techniques include elements of jazz, modern dance, and rock.

Theatrical dancing won its greatest commercial success in motion pictures and musical comedies. During the 1930's, many movie musicals featured the elegant ballroom dancing of Fred Astaire and Ginger Rogers and the spectacular production numbers of choreographer Busby Berkeley. Some of the best later movie musicals were *An American in Paris* (1951), *Singin' in the Rain* (1952), and *Seven Brides for Seven Brothers* (1954)—all of which included highly imaginative dance numbers. Many outstanding American ballet choreographers created brilliant dances for musical comedies, such as the work of Agnes de Mille in *Oklahoma!* (1943) and Jerome Robbins in *West Side Story* (1957).

Hundreds of new social dances have come and gone during the 1900's. About 1900, the strutting, high-stepping cakewalk was at the height of its popularity. A few years later, the ballroom dancers Vernon and Irene Castle introduced the tango, the first in a long series of popular Latin-American dances. During the 1920's, people danced the Charleston and the black bottom. In the 1930's and 1940's, they did the big apple and the jitterbug to the *swing* music of big dance bands.

With the birth of rock 'n' roll in the mid-1950's, social dance styles became freer. Partners did not touch each other, and they made up their own dance movements on the spot. During the 1960's and 1970's, blacks created many dances that white people enthusiastically adopted. A popular style of dancing in the 1970's called "disco" rejected the "do-it-yourself" choreography of earlier rock dances. Instead, dancing partners held each other and followed a set pattern of steps. During the 1980's, young black males popularized *break dancing*, which consisted largely of acrobatic movements performed to rock music.   Selma Landen Odom

Related articles in *World Book* include:

Biographies

For biographies of ballet dancers and choreographers, see the *Related articles* in the **Ballet** article. See also:

Ailey, Alvin	Cunningham,	Dunham, Katherine
Astaire, Fred	Merce	
	Duncan, Isadora	Graham, Martha

Greco, José	Saint Denis, Ruth
Kelly, Gene	Shawn, Ted
Nikolais, Alwin	Tharp, Twyla
Robinson, Bill	

Kinds of dances

Ballet	Folk dancing	Square dancing
Bolero	Fox trot	Tango
Cotillion	Minuet	Tarantella
Flamenco	Rumba	Waltz

Pictures of dancers

The following articles have pictures of dancers:

Africa	Indonesia	South Dakota
Asia	Kenya	Spain
Clothing	Latin America	Thailand
Folklore	Motion picture	Union of Soviet
France	Pacific Islands	Socialist Repub-
Greece	Pygmies	lics
Gypsies	Roaring Twenties	United States
Indian, American	Romania	Yugoslavia

Other related articles

Buffalo ceremonials	Musical comedy
Castanets	Pantomime
Gymnastics (Rhythmic	Rain dance
gymnastics)	Rhythm
Mask	

Outline

I. Why people dance
II. Kinds of dancing

A. Ballet	C. Folk dancing
B. Modern dance	D. Popular dancing

III. Oriental dancing
IV. African dancing
V. The development of Western dance

Questions

What is the difference between theatrical dancing and social dancing?
What are folk dances?
How did Isadora Duncan rebel against the ballet techniques of her time?
What are some of the reasons that folk dances change gradually over the years?
What were the *balli* ?
How did the birth of rock 'n' roll influence popular dance styles of the mid-1950's?
What are some reasons why people dance?
How did women's ballet costumes change in the 1700's?
What are *mudras*?
How do scholars know that prehistoric people danced?

Reading and Study Guide

See *Dancing* in the Research Guide/Index, Volume 22, for a *Reading and Study Guide.*

Additional resources

Level I
Berger, Melvin. *The World of Dance.* Phillips, 1978.
McDonagh, Don. *The Complete Guide to Modern Dance.* Doubleday, 1976.
Price, Christine. *Dance on the Dusty Earth.* Scribner, 1979. Folk dances around the world.

Level II
Emery, Lynne F. *Black Dance.* 2nd ed. Princeton Book Co., 1987.
Jacob, Ellen. *Dancing: A Guide for the Dancer You Can Be.* American Alliance for Health, 1981.
Quirey, Belinda. *May I Have the Pleasure?* London Dance Books, 1987. First published in 1985. A history of popular dance.
Sachs, Curt. *World History of the Dance.* Norton, 1937. A classic study.
Wallace, Carol M., and others. *Dance: A Very Social History.* Rizzoli, 1987.

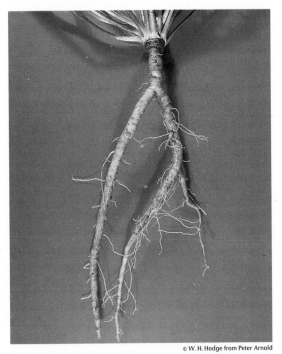

© W. H. Hodge from Peter Arnold

The dandelion root is long, thick, and pointed.

Dandelion is a bright-yellow wild flower that grows in lawns and meadows. Throughout the temperate regions of the world, gardeners usually consider the dandelion a troublesome weed that is difficult to control.

The early colonists brought the dandelion to America from Europe. Its name comes from the French words *dent de lion,* meaning *lion's tooth.* It has smooth leaves with coarse notches, which look like teeth. The golden-yellow head is really a cluster of flowers. The dandelion has a smooth, straight, and hollow stem, and the entire plant contains a white, milky juice. The root is long, thick, and pointed, and it has hairlike root branches growing from it.

WORLD BOOK illustration by Lorraine Epstein

The dandelion is a yellow wild flower.

The dandelion differs from most other plants in the manner in which it reproduces. The ovaries of the dandelion form fertile seeds without having to be pollinated (see **Pollen**).

Young dandelion leaves can be used in salads or they can be cooked. They taste best when they are young, before the plant has blossomed. Wine sometimes is made from the dandelion flowers.

In order to keep dandelion plants from growing on lawns, gardeners must cut deep into their roots. The roots grow to about 3 feet (91 centimeters) long in soft, rich earth. Slicing close under the surface only encourages the plants to grow. Gardeners sometimes spray dandelions with chemicals that destroy the dandelions but do not harm grass.

Scientific classification. The dandelion is a member of the composite family, Compositae. The common dandelion is *Taraxacum officinale.*   Anton A. Reznicek

Dandie Dinmont terrier is a dog that got its name from a book. In Sir Walter Scott's novel *Guy Mannering,* a farmer named Dandie Dinmont raised an unusual pack of short-legged terriers that were all the color of either pepper or mustard. In the book, the dogs were famous as hunters of foxes, badgers, and otters. A new breed was later called Dandie Dinmont for the farmer in the book.

The Dandie Dinmont terrier has a big head and large, soft brown eyes. Its forehead is covered by a silky *topknot* (tuft of hair). Its coat is crisp to the touch on the back and soft and downy underneath. Dandies weigh from 18 to 24 pounds (8 to 11 kilograms) and stand 8 to

Roy and Betty-Anne Stenmark
(Fox & Cook Photography)

The Dandie Dinmont terrier has short front legs.

11 inches (20 to 28 centimeters) high at the shoulder. See also **Dog** (picture: Terriers).

Critically reviewed by the Dandie Dinmont Terrier Club of America

Dandruff is a condition in which flakes of dead skin are shed from the scalp. The flakes may be yellow and oily, or white and dry. The scalp normally sheds some dead skin cells. Dandruff results when it sheds thick layers of them. Physicians do not fully understand what causes the condition, and most people have it at some time. In most cases, mild dandruff can be controlled by washing the hair frequently. Dandruff does not cause baldness.

A condition called *seborrhea* may produce severe dandruff and a red, itchy scalp. Dandruff shampoos help treat the problem. If the condition continues, a physician should be consulted.   Orville J. Stone

Danes. See Denmark; England (The Anglo-Saxon period).

Daniel, Book of, is a book of the Bible. It is named for a Jewish hero who lived in Babylon from the end of the 600's B.C. to the late 500's B.C. In Jewish forms of the Bible, the book is part of a collection called the *Writings.* Christian editions include it in a group called the *Prophets.*

The Book of Daniel is divided into two parts. Chapters 1-6 contain six stories that deal with historical events over a period of almost 50 years in Babylon and emphasize Daniel's loyalty to his faith. Chapters 7-12 include stories of four visions. In these visions, Daniel describes four empires that will rule the world until the triumph of God's kingdom.

In one famous story in the book (6: 1-28), Daniel is thrown into a den of lions for refusing to worship Darius the Mede as a god. The animals refuse to harm Daniel. Another story tells how Daniel interpreted mysterious handwriting that appeared during a feast held by the Babylonian ruler Belshazzar (5: 1-31). In chapter 3: 1-30, Daniel's companions Shadrach, Meshach, and Abednego are cast into a fiery furnace because they refuse to worship a golden idol. The flames do not hurt them.

Biblical scholars do not agree on the date of the book. Some once believed that Daniel was the author. Today, scholars believe the book was written much later. Many think it was written during the 100's B.C. These scholars say the author wanted to use Daniel as a heroic model to encourage Jews in a revolt against the Seleucid king Antiochus IV. The revolt was led by Judah Maccabee in the 160's B.C.   Eric M. Meyers

See also **Bible** (The Old Testament); **Handwriting on the wall.**

Daniel-Rops, *da NYEHL ruhps,* **Henri,** *ahn REE* (1901-1965), was the pen name of Henri-Jules Periot, a French author and religious historian. He gained his greatest recognition for *Jesus in His Times* (1945), a brief and readable history of the life of Jesus Christ. His 10-volume *History of the Church of Christ* (1948-1965) traces the history of the Christian church.

Daniel-Rops was born in Épinal, France. In the 1920's and 1930's, he wrote novels and essays that radiated religious devotion and concern for humanity's loss of genuine religion. During World War II, the Nazis tried to destroy his *Sacred History* (1943), a history of the Jews. But a few copies survived, and the book was reissued after the war. In 1955, Daniel-Rops was elected to the French Academy.   Roland N. Stromberg

Dannay, Frederic. See Queen, Ellery.

D'Annunzio, *duh NUN see oh,* **Gabriele,** *GAH bree EH lee* (1863-1938), was an Italian author and political figure. His poetry deals with nature, the sea, and his own desire for passionate experiences. The poems show an unusual sensitivity for colors, moods, and feelings. His style is imaginative and melodious, but often flowery. His best poetry is contained in the collection *Alcyone* (1904). D'Annunzio wrote many novels, several based on his scandalous personal life. *The Flame of Life* (1900) is based on his love affair with actress Eleonora Duse (see **Duse, Eleonora**). His plays include *La Gioconda* (1898) and *The Daughter of Jorio* (1904).

D'Annunzio was born in Pescara. In 1910, his extravagant living forced him to declare bankruptcy, and he moved to Paris. He returned to Italy to campaign for his country's entry into World War I. In 1919 and 1920, he served as the self-appointed ruler of the city of Fiume (now Rijeka) after seizing the city with a military force.   Richard H. Lansing

Dante Alighieri, *DAHN tay ah lee GYA ree* (1265-1321), an Italian author, was one of the greatest poets of the Middle Ages. His epic poem *The Divine Comedy* ranks among the finest works of world literature. Critics have praised it not only as magnificent poetry, but also for its wisdom and scholarly learning.

Dante was a great thinker and one of the most learned writers of all time. Many scholars consider *The Divine Comedy* a summary of medieval thought. Dante

Oil painting on canvas; National Gallery of Art, Washington, D.C., Ailsa Mellon Bruce Fund

Daniel in the Lions' Den was painted by the Flemish artist Peter Paul Rubens. The picture shows Daniel praying at dawn after safely spending the night in the lions' den. Completed about 1615, it is one of the few large works Rubens painted without assistants.

had a tremendous influence on later writers. Geoffrey Chaucer and John Milton imitated his works. Dante influenced such writers of the 1800's as Henry Wadsworth Longfellow, Percy Bysshe Shelley, Lord Byron, Lord Tennyson, Victor Hugo, and Friedrich Schlegel, along with T. S. Eliot in the 1900's.

His life. Dante was born in Florence. He received a rich education in classical and religious subjects. He may have studied at Bologna, Padua, and possibly Paris.

Dante's idealized love for a beautiful girl, Beatrice Portinari (1266-1290), provided much inspiration for his literary works. He saw her only twice, once when he was almost 9 and again nine years later. Her death at a young age left him grief-stricken. Sometime before 1294, Dante married Gemma Donati. They had at least three children.

Dante was active in the political and military life of Florence. He entered the army as a youth and held several important positions in the Florentine government during the 1290's. Dante became involved in a political dispute between two groups, the Guelphs and the Ghibellines, who were fighting for control of Tuscany. A political group within the Guelphs gained control of Florence in 1301. This political group was hostile to the poet and banished him in 1302, condemning him to death if he returned to Florence. Dante spent the rest of his life in exile and died in Ravenna, where he was buried.

His works. Among Dante's early writings, the best known is *La Vita Nuova* (*The New Life*), written about 1293. It is a collection of 31 poems with prose commentary describing his love for Beatrice. *The New Life* shows the influence of troubadour poetry, a style that flourished in southern France in the 1100's and 1200's.

Dante began *The Divine Comedy* about 1308. The poem relates his spiritual development and focuses on the theme of life after death. For more information about this work, see **Divine Comedy.**

Dante also wrote several nonfiction works. About 1303 and 1304 he wrote *De Vulgari Eloquentia* (*On Eloquence in the Vernacular*). This work in Latin prose stresses the importance of writing in a common Italian language, rather than in Latin or a minor dialect. Dante hoped that the Italians would develop a national literary language to help unite the country.

Il Convivio (*The Banquet,* 1304-1307) is an unfinished work written in Italian, consisting of three odes, each followed by long, detailed commentaries on their meaning. The work is filled with Dante's wide knowledge of philosophy and science. *The Monarchia* (*On World-Government,* 1313?) is a long essay in Latin prose. Dante called for the state, in the form of the Holy Roman Empire, to join with the church in guiding people to a better life on earth and joy in heaven. Other works include a group of poems and several letters. Richard H. Lansing

See also **Allegory; Virgil** (His influence).

Additional resources

Bergin, Thomas G. *Dante.* Greenwood, 1976. First published in 1965.
Holmes, George. *Dante.* Oxford, 1983. First published in 1980.
Quinones, Ricardo J. *Dante Alighieri.* Twayne, 1979. Concentrates on Dante's works, especially *The Divine Comedy.*

Danton, *DAN tuhn,* **Georges Jacques,** *zhawrzh zhahk* (1759-1794), was a great leader of the French Revolution. His policy was "boldness, and more boldness, and ever more boldness, and France is saved!" He per-

haps did more to create and defend the French Republic than any other person. Danton was partly responsible for the massacres of the Reign of Terror, which he considered necessary for the safety of his country. When he believed that safety was assured, he advocated more humane policies. He wished to restore, rather than to destroy, the normal life of France.

Danton was born in Arcis-sur-Aube, of middle-class parents. At the beginning of the revolution he was a successful lawyer in Paris, and a leader of the Cordeliers Club, one of the militant factions of the extreme Republicans. This group favored ridding France of the monarchy. They achieved their purpose on Aug. 10, 1792, when they forced the legislative assembly to imprison Louis XVI. Danton, who is called "the Man of August 10th" because of his leadership in the movement to imprison Louis XVI, became minister of justice.

Danton and his associates, Camille Desmoulins, Maximilien Robespierre, and Jean Paul Marat, established a national convention of revolutionary leaders and a revolutionary tribunal. These two bodies ruled France for the next three years. Almost anyone could be brought before the jury of the tribunal. Their victims were not only traitors, but also persons suspected of being too mild in their political views. Danton and Desmoulins soon recognized the need for stamping out this violence. They felt that the convention should relax its policy and prepare a workable republican constitution for an orderly government. Danton suggested halting the violence.

Robespierre was jealous of Danton's success. He ordered Danton arrested for disloyalty and brought before the tribunal. Danton's fiery and eloquent denunciation alarmed the tribunal members, who feared loss of power. Danton was condemned and executed. His execution climaxed the Reign of Terror. André Maurois

See also **French Revolution; Marat, Jean Paul; Robespierre.**

Danube River, *DAN yoob,* is the second longest river in Europe. Only the Volga River is longer. The Danube flows 1,777 miles (2,860 kilometers) from its source in southern Germany to its mouth at the Black Sea in Eastern Europe. The river drains about 315,000 square miles (815,800 square kilometers) of land.

The Danube begins at the merger of two small rivers in the Black Forest in Germany. The river winds eastward through Germany and Austria, and along part of the border between Czechoslovakia and Hungary. The Danube curves southward near Budapest, Hungary. The river then flows through Hungary and enters northeastern Yugoslavia. Farther on, it forms part of the border between Yugoslavia and Romania and most of the border between Romania and Bulgaria. Then it flows northeast through Romania and splits into three branches before emptying into the Black Sea. The northernmost branch forms part of the border between Romania and the Soviet Union.

Commercial ships and barges transport large amounts of freight on the Danube. They carry agricultural goods, chemicals, mineral ores, steel, and other products. About 35 major ports lie along the Danube.

Several countries have dams and electric power plants on the Danube. The largest dam is the Iron Gate Dam. It stands at the Iron Gate, a gorge at the border between Yugoslavia and Romania. The power plant of the

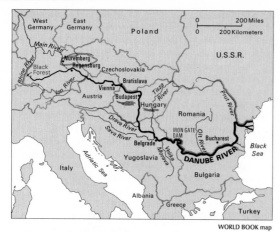

Location of the Danube River

dam produces electricity for Romania and Yugoslavia.

Many canals connect the Danube to other waterways. The Main-Danube Canal, scheduled for completion in the early 1990's, will connect the Danube to the Main River, which is a branch of the Rhine. This canal will make it possible for ships to travel between the Black and North seas.   Warren E. Yasso

Danzig. See Gdańsk.

Daoism. See Taoism.

Daphne, *DAF nee,* was a nymph in Greek mythology. She was the daughter of a river god, either Ladon or Peneus. The best-known myth about Daphne recounts her flight from the god Apollo. The god Eros shot both Daphne and Apollo with arrows in revenge against Apollo for insulting his skill as an archer. Eros shot Apollo with a gold-tipped arrow, causing him to fall madly in love with Daphne. He shot the nymph with a leaden one, making her hate all suitors. Apollo pursued Daphne relentlessly. One day, when he was finally about to catch her, Daphne prayed for escape, and was transformed into a laurel tree. Although Apollo could not possess her, he made the laurel his sacred tree and wore a crown of laurel leaves on his head. See **Apollo; Cupid.**   Nancy Felson-Rubin

Dapsang. See K2.

DAR. See Daughters of the American Revolution.

Dar es Salaam, *DAHR ehs suh LAHM* (pop. 870,020), is the capital and largest city of Tanzania, and a chief seaport in eastern Africa. The city lies on the east coast of Tanzania. For location, see **Tanzania** (map).

Dar es Salaam is a major transportation center. It has an international airport and a port, and railroads and highways link it with the rest of Tanzania. The city also has many churches, libraries, and research centers. The University of Dar es Salaam, the National Art Gallery, and the National Museum of Tanzania are in the city.

Foreign trade plays a key role in the economy of Dar es Salaam. Large quantities of imported and exported goods pass through the city's port. Products manufactured in Dar es Salaam include cigarettes, footwear, furniture, soft drinks, and textiles.

The sultan of Zanzibar, the ruler of a nearby island, founded Dar es Salaam in 1862 as a trading post. Germany took control of the city in 1887 and made it a major trading center for eastern Africa. British forces captured the city in 1916, during World War I. It became the capital of Britain's Tanganyika Territory in 1919. Tanganyika gained independence from Britain in 1961 and became part of Tanzania in 1964.

Since 1964, the population of Dar es Salaam has increased from about 150,000 to about 870,000. In 1973, Tanzanians voted to move the capital from Dar es Salaam to the inland city of Dodoma. The move was expected to be completed in the 1990's.   L. H. Gann

See also **Tanzania** (picture).

Dardanelles, *DAHR duh NEHLZ,* is a strait that joins the Aegean Sea with the Sea of Marmara. The strait is part of a waterway that leads from the landlocked Black Sea to the Mediterranean. Also part of this waterway is the Bosporus, a strait joining the Black Sea and the Sea of Marmara. The word *Dardanelles* comes from the ancient Greek city of Dardanus, on Asia's side of the strait. The ancient Greeks called this strait the *Hellespont.*

At its narrowest point, the Dardanelles is about 1 mile (1.6 kilometers) wide from the European shore to the Asiatic. The average width of the strait is 3 to 4 miles (5 to 6 kilometers). It is about 37 miles (60 kilometers) long, and the average depth is 200 feet (61 meters). It usually has a strong surface current in the direction of the Aegean Sea, but a powerful undercurrent flows east and carries salty water through the Sea of Marmara and the Bosporus into the Black Sea. This undercurrent keeps the Black Sea from becoming a freshwater body.

In 480 B.C., Xerxes I of Persia built a bridge of boats across the Dardanelles near Abydos and led an army over it to invade Europe. In 334 B.C., the Macedonian general Alexander the Great led his army over a similar bridge across the Dardanelles into Asia. Hundreds of years later, the strait was important to the defense of the Byzantine Empire. After that empire fell, the Ottoman Turks ruled the Dardanelles. See **Byzantine Empire.**

In 1841, the great powers of Europe—Great Britain, France, Prussia, and Austria—agreed to give Turkey control of the passage of ships through the Dardanelles. This agreement was renewed in 1856, 1871, and 1878. The Treaty of Lausanne in 1923 opened the Dardanelles to all nations. In 1936, the Montreux convention gave Turkey permission to remilitarize the strait.

Early in World War II, the strait was closed to all ships except those with special permission from Turkey. Al-

WORLD BOOK map

The Dardanelles lies between Europe and Asia.

though the possession of the Dardanelles was threatened during the war, Turkey kept control of this important waterway. After World War II, the Soviet Union unsuccessfully attempted to gain control of the Dardanelles. The Western Powers supported Turkey's rights to the strategic strait.   Robert O. Reid

Related articles in *World Book* include:

Aegean Sea	Hellespont	World War I (The
Black Sea	Marmara, Sea of	Dardanelles)
Bosporus	Turkey	

Dare, Virginia (1587-   ?   ), was the first English child born in America. Her parents were Ananias Dare and Eleanor White, two members of a band of 117 colonists who settled on Roanoke Island in 1587. She was born on August 18 and named Virginia in what may have been the first English christening ceremony in America. See also **Lost Colony.**   Joseph Carlyle Sitterson

Darío, *dah REE oh,* **Rubén,** *roo BAYN* (1867-1916), was the pen name of Félix Rubén García Sarmiento, one of the most important poets to write in Spanish. Darío was the outstanding figure among a group of Spanish-language authors whose work is associated with a literary movement called *modernism.*

A collection of verse and prose called *Azul . . .* (1888) established Darío's reputation. The verse brought a new rhythmic beauty to literary Spanish. Considered even more innovative are the short prose selections, which stress description over narration and sensory appeal over statement. In *Profane Prose* (1896), Darío perfected his poetic technique. The poems feature unusual rhythmic patterns and sound effects, scholarly references, and luxurious settings.

In *Songs of Life and Hope* (1905), Darío retreated from the ornamental, artful poetry of his earlier works and sought a plainer and more down-to-earth form of expression. This collection includes poems about human doubt and sadness and verse of social commentary. In *Wandering Song* (1907), Darío continued to move toward poetry that responded more directly to common human problems.

Darío was born in Metapa (now Ciudad Darío), Nicaragua. He held several diplomatic posts, including Nicaraguan consul in Paris and minister to Brazil and Spain.

Naomi Lindstrom

See also **Latin-American literature** (Modernism).

Darius I, *duh RY uhs* (550?-486 B.C.), ruled the Persian Empire from 522 B.C. until his death. He is often called Darius the Great. Darius extended the Persian Empire, which was based in southwest Asia, eastward into what is now southern Pakistan and westward into southeastern Europe. He tried to conquer Greece, but failed.

Darius seized the Persian throne after King Bardiya of Persia was murdered in 522 B.C. Armies led by Darius put down a rebellion in Egypt in 519 B.C. and conquered Thrace in southeastern Europe about 513 B.C. Later, Persian forces conquered what is now southern Pakistan. Darius efficiently ruled his empire by dividing it into 20 *satrapies* (provinces). The officials he chose to govern the satrapies raised taxes locally for the royal treasuries and provided Darius with soldiers.

During the 490's B.C., Greeks in Asia Minor (now Turkey) rebelled unsuccessfully against Persian rule. In 492 B.C., a Persian attempt to invade Greece failed. In 490 B.C., Darius sent another expedition to conquer Greece.

The army landed northeast of Athens on the plain of Marathon. The Greeks, though outnumbered, defeated the Persians (see **Marathon**). Darius died before he could organize another invasion of Greece. His son Xerxes I succeeded him.   Jack Martin Balcer

Darius III, *duh RY uhs* (380?-330 B.C.), was the last of the Achaemenid kings of Persia. This family had developed one of the world's greatest empires in western Asia during the 500's B.C. Darius tried to prevent Alexander the Great, the king of Macedonia, from conquering the Persian Empire, but failed.

Ineffective kings and rebellions by provincial governors had weakened the Persian Empire for almost a hundred years when Darius became king in 336 B.C. He tried to reorganize the central government and build a strong army. In 333 B.C., Alexander the Great defeated Darius' forces at Issus in what is now southern Turkey. In 331 B.C., Alexander again defeated Darius in the Battle of Arbela, also called the Battle of Gaugamela, in what is now northern Iraq. Darius was murdered by his own nobles in 330 B.C.   Jack Martin Balcer

See also **Alexander the Great.**

Darjeeling, *dahr JEE lihng* (pop. 57,603), is the summer capital of the state of West Bengal in eastern India. It lies on the lower slopes of the Himalaya, north of Calcutta, about 7,100 feet (2,160 meters) above sea level. The high altitude makes the city cool and pleasant the year round. People who live in the Indian lowlands seek relief from the heat by going up to Darjeeling in September and October. Mount Everest is visible from just outside the city. The well-known Darjeeling tea grows on hillsides near the city. A small railway climbs to the city over steep slopes and through tea plantations and teakwood forests. A wide square serves as an open-air bazaar for trading.   Robert LaPorte, Jr.

Dark Ages is a term once used to describe the Middle Ages, especially the early Middle Ages, which lasted from the A.D. 400's to the 900's. The word *dark* referred to a supposed lack of learning during the period. Actually, the Middle Ages were not completely "dark." The period only seemed dark to scholars of the more advanced Renaissance and to historians later influenced by them.

In the early Middle Ages, civilization sank low in Western Europe. Knowledge from the ancient Romans survived only in a few monastery, cathedral, and palace schools. Knowledge from ancient Greece almost disappeared. Few people received schooling. Many artistic and technical skills were lost. In their ignorance, writers accepted popular stories and rumors as true. Population decreased, and economic life became more primitive.

While such darkness existed in Western Europe, life was brighter elsewhere. The Byzantine Empire preserved many features of Greek and Roman life (see **Byzantine Empire**). The Arabs spread a splendid civilization from Spain to the borders of China (see **Muslims**).

In the early 1000's, economic and political life began to revive in Western Europe. This revival led to a remarkable improvement of culture during the 1100's.

Joel T. Rosenthal

For a description of the life and culture of the Dark Ages, see **Middle Ages; Feudalism; Renaissance.**

Dark horse. See **Political convention** (Planning strategies).

Dark matter is the invisible substance that makes up most of the mass of galaxies and clusters of galaxies. Dark matter is unlike other forms of matter because it does not give off, reflect, or absorb light. Scientists believe that unless the current theory of gravity is wrong, the mass of the universe consists of at least 10 times more dark matter than visible matter.

Scientists are not sure of the composition of dark matter. One theory suggests it is ordinary matter in the form of isolated planet-sized gas balls too small to shine as stars. But many astronomers argue it is unlikely that so many of these gas balls could have formed without some of them becoming visible stars. Another possibility is that dark matter consists of *neutrinos* of low mass. Neutrinos are subatomic particles that have no electrical charge. According to a third theory, dark matter could be "cold." *Cold dark matter* includes such hypothetical particles as *weakly interacting massive particles,* called *WIMPs,* and *axions.*

Scientists first suggested in the 1930's that clusters of galaxies contained much more mass than could be seen. The theory was not taken very seriously until the 1970's, when astronomers began measuring the rotational speeds of spiral galaxies. In these measurements, astronomers first determined the orbital speeds of stars and gas clouds in a galaxy. Then, they used these speeds to calculate the amount of matter in the galaxy. Astronomers made these calculations for many galaxies and found that the calculated mass was always greater than the visible mass. Similarly, astronomers have concluded from the velocities of galaxies in clusters that most of the matter in clusters is dark.   Joel R. Primack

Darling, Ding (1876-1962), was an American editorial cartoonist. During the Great Depression of the 1930's, his work often ridiculed the relief programs of President Franklin D. Roosevelt. Darling also took a strong interest in the conservation of natural resources. Many of his cartoons criticize those who threaten wildlife. Darling won the Pulitzer Prize for cartooning in 1924 and 1943.

Jay Norwood Darling was born in Norwood, Mich., and was nicknamed Ding while a student at Beloit College. He became a cartoonist for the *Sioux City* (Iowa) *Journal* in 1901 and joined the *Des Moines Register* in 1906. From 1917 until his retirement from the *Register* in 1949, the *New York Tribune* (later called the *Herald Tribune*) distributed his cartoons to newspapers across the United States. In 1934 and 1935, he served as chief of the U.S. Bureau of Biological Survey.   Michael Emery

Darling, Grace Horsley (1815-1842), became a famous English heroine by helping save nine survivors of a shipwreck. She lived at Longstone Lighthouse on one of the Farne Islands, off the English coast. Her father was keeper of the lighthouse. The steamer *Forfarshire* was wrecked on Sept. 7, 1838. Through a telescope, she saw several people clinging to a rock. During a storm, she rowed to the rescue with her father. The Humane Society awarded both of them gold medals. She was born in Bamborough, Northumberland.

Darling River is the longest river in Australia. It flows 1,702 miles (2,739 kilometers) and drains more than 251,000 square miles (650,000 square kilometers) of land.

The Darling rises in the Great Dividing Range in the state of Queensland, in eastern Australia, and flows southwest across the state of New South Wales. Near the town of Wentworth, it flows into the Murray River, which empties into the Indian Ocean. This part of the Indian Ocean is called the Southern Ocean in Australia. In winter, the Darling is dry along most of its course. But in summer, it is an important source of water for the Murray (see **Australia** [terrain map; Rivers]; **Murray River**). During the 1800's, the Darling served as an important waterway for barges and steamboats. Today, the river is important chiefly as a source of water for livestock and crops.   Garry R. LeDuff

Darrow, Clarence Seward (1857-1938), was the most famous American lawyer of the early 1900's. He was clever and eloquent, and earned a worldwide reputation as a brilliant criminal defense attorney.

Darrow was born in Kinsman, Ohio, near Youngstown. He studied law for a year at the University of Michigan and began practicing law in Ohio in the early 1880's. Darrow moved to Chicago in 1887 and later worked as an attorney for the city of Chicago and the Chicago & North Western Railway. Darrow represented Eugene V. Debs and other officials of the American Railway Union who were arrested for supporting the Pullman strike of 1894, which disrupted mail delivery. This case made him famous as a defender of labor interests.

Darrow became active as a defense attorney for labor unions and served in the Illinois House of Representatives from 1903 to 1905. In 1911, Darrow went to Los Angeles to defend John J. and James B. McNamara. The brothers, both labor leaders, were charged with dynamiting the Los Angeles Times Building. Darrow had the McNamaras plead guilty and saved them from a probable death sentence. But he lost union support forever.

N.Y. Herald Tribune and *Des Moines Register*

"Why Call Them Sportsmen?" Through his cartoons, Ding Darling fought for the conservation of wildlife in America.

Clarence Darrow, *left,* opposed William Jennings Bryan, *right,* during the famous John Scopes trial at Dayton, Tenn., in 1925.

WORLD BOOK illustration by Colin Newman, Linden Artists Ltd.

The Johnny darter, like other darters, is a small freshwater fish of the perch family. The fish gets its name from the way it swims, darting quickly from one resting place to another.

Darrow returned to Chicago and started to specialize in criminal cases. He was nearly 70 years old when he tried his two most spectacular cases. In 1924, Darrow defended Nathan F. Leopold, Jr., and Richard A. Loeb, who admitted kidnapping and murdering 14-year-old Bobby Franks in an attempt to commit a perfect crime. Darrow used psychiatric evidence and argued that the 19-year-old Leopold and 18-year-old Loeb were mentally ill. Darrow's goal was to keep the youths from receiving the death sentence, which he strongly opposed. Leopold and Loeb each received a sentence of life imprisonment plus 99 years.

In 1925, Darrow helped attract widespread attention to the Scopes trial in Dayton, Tenn. In this case, he defended the right of John T. Scopes to teach the theory of evolution in public school.   Kevin Tierney

See also **Idaho** (Early statehood); **Scopes trial.**

Additional resources

Gurko, Miriam. *Clarence Darrow.* T. Y. Crowell, 1965. Suitable for younger readers.
Tierney, Kevin. *Darrow: A Biography.* T. Y. Crowell, 1979.
Weinberg, Arthur and Lila. *Clarence Darrow: A Sentimental Rebel.* Atheneum, 1987. First published in 1980.

Dart. See **Blowgun; Darts.**

Darter, a bird. See **Anhinga.**

Darter is any of about 140 species of small freshwater fish belonging to the perch family. Darters are found in North American waters east of the Rocky Mountains, from central Canada to northern Mexico. The fish gets its name from the way it swims, darting quickly from one resting place to another.

Most darters live in clear, fast-moving streams that have gravelly bottoms. Others thrive in lakes and rivers. During the breeding season, male darters of many species develop brilliant colors. Male *rainbow darters,* which become blue, red, and yellow, are especially striking. Female darters lay eggs in spring or early summer. Darters eat a variety of water insects and other fish. The young feed on microscopic organisms called *zooplankton.* Darters range in size from the *least darter,*

which measures less than 2 inches (5 centimeters) long, to the *freckled darter* and the *logperch,* which grow nearly 8 inches (20 centimeters) long. Most species measure from 2 to 4 inches (5 to 10 centimeters).

Several species of darters have become endangered because the fish are particularly sensitive to changes in their environment. Concern over the *snail darter* delayed completion of the Tellico Dam on the Little Tennessee River during the late 1970's. The dam, which was completed in 1980, destroyed what was then the only known habitat of the snail darter. However, the species was later discovered in a few other Tennessee streams and is no longer considered endangered.

Scientific classification. Darters belong to the freshwater perch family, Percidae. The snail darter is *Percina tanasi.*

Henry W. Robison

See also **Fish** (picture: Fish of temperate fresh waters).

Dartmouth, N.S. (pop. 65,243), is the second largest city in Nova Scotia. It lies on the eastern shore of Halifax Harbor, opposite Halifax, the province's capital and largest city. For location, see **Nova Scotia** (political map).

Dartmouth is one of Canada's chief distribution centers for many products, including imported automobiles. The Dartmouth-Halifax area is also the manufacturing center of Nova Scotia. Industries in Dartmouth include boat building and repairing; petroleum refining; and the manufacture of tires and naval supplies. Part of the Halifax naval base is on Dartmouth's shore, and the Shearwater naval air station is nearby.

Dartmouth is the home of the Bedford Institute of Oceanography and several other research centers. Cultural attractions in the area include a museum and a symphony orchestra.

Micmac Indians once lived in what is now the Dartmouth area. Dartmouth was founded in 1750 by British settlers who named their village after Dartmouth, England. From 1941 to 1961, the growth of defense establishments in and near Dartmouth helped increase its population by about 50 per cent. Dartmouth was incorporated as a city in 1961. Micmac Mall, the largest shopping mall in the Atlantic Provinces, opened in Dartmouth in 1973. The city has a mayor-council form of government.   Basil W. Deakin

Dartmouth College is a private coeducational liberal arts school in Hanover, N.H. Associated with it are three graduate schools: Dartmouth Medical School, Thayer School of Engineering, and the Amos Tuck School of Business Administration. Courses lead to bachelor's, master's, and doctor's degrees. Baker Library is one of the largest college libraries in the United States. It is noted for its Stefansson Arctic and Robert Frost collections.

Dartmouth was founded at Hanover in 1769 under a charter granted to Eleazar Wheelock, a Congregational minister, by King George III of England. It developed from Moor's Indian Charity School, founded by Wheelock about 1750 in Lebanon, Conn. For enrollment, see **Universities and colleges** (table).

Critically reviewed by Dartmouth College

Dartmouth College case, also called *Dartmouth College v. Woodward,* upheld the constitutional freedom from unreasonable government interference with contracts. The Supreme Court of the United States decided this case in 1819. The decision helped protect the rights of private property and encouraged the development of the free enterprise system.

In 1769, King George III of Great Britain granted Dartmouth College a charter as a private school. This charter was to last "forever." The various states succeeded to the rights and obligations of such charters when they became independent. But in 1816, New Hampshire tried to make Dartmouth College the state university by canceling the charter. Former trustees of the college claimed that the royal charter was still valid. They sued to recover the school seal and records from William H. Woodward, the college secretary. Daniel Webster, a graduate of Dartmouth, presented the trustees' case before the Supreme Court in one of his greatest arguments. The court held for the trustees. It ruled that the state had "impaired the obligation" of the charter in violation of Article I, Section 10 of the Constitution. Because of this case, legislatures today put time limitations in charters or include provisions allowing cancellation by the government under proper circumstances.

Jerre S. Williams

Darts is a game in which the players throw darts at a target called a *dartboard.* A regulation dartboard meas-

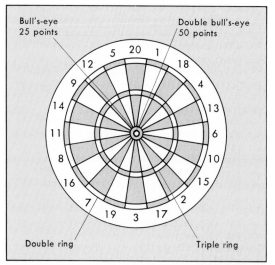

Bull's-eye
25 points

Double bull's-eye
50 points

Double ring

Triple ring

WORLD BOOK diagram

Darts is a game in which the players try to score points by throwing darts at a target. The target is divided into wedge-shaped areas. The wedges are worth from 1 to 20 points. A dart that lands in a ring scores double or triple the wedge's value.

ures about 18 inches (46 centimeters) in diameter. It is divided into 20 equal-sized areas shaped like wedges of a pie. A player scores from 1 to 20 points by hitting different wedges. The board is further divided by a narrow outer ring called the *double ring* and a narrow inner ring called the *triple ring.* A dart that hits one of the rings scores either double or triple the value of the wedge. The *bull's-eye* is worth 25 points. A *double bull's-eye* inside the bull's-eye is worth 50 points.

The dartboard is mounted so the bull's-eye is 5 feet 8 inches (1.73 meters) from the floor. In tournaments, players stand at one of two authorized distances from the board, 7 feet $9\frac{1}{4}$ inches (2.37 meters) or 8 feet (2.44 meters). They take turns throwing three darts that measure up to $8\frac{1}{4}$ inches (21 centimeters) long. To win, a player must score a certain number of points — in most cases 301, 1001, or 3001. The winner must start and end the game by hitting the double ring or the double bull's-eye.

Robert T. McLeod

Darwin (pop. 72,937) is the administrative center and largest city of the Northern Territory of Australia. It is an air gateway to Australia and the chief port in the Northern Territory. For location, see **Australia** (political map). The discovery of uranium south of Darwin in 1949 stimulated its growth.

Darwin was planned in 1869 as the first station in Australia on a telegraph line connecting Australia with Europe. It was named for Charles Darwin. On Christmas Day, 1974, a cyclone struck Darwin and destroyed most of the city in Australia's worst natural disaster. The Australian government appointed a commission to manage the reconstruction of Darwin. The commission completed its work in 1978.   Ken White

Darwin, Charles Robert (1809-1882), was a British naturalist who became famous for his theories on evolution. Like several other scientists before him, Darwin believed that, through millions of years, all species of plants and animals had *evolved* (developed gradually) from a few common ancestors.

Darwin set forth his theories in his book *On the Origin of Species by Means of Natural Selection, or the Preservation of Favoured Races in the Struggle for Life* (1859). He gathered facts that supported the idea of evolution, and he proposed that evolution occurred through a process called *natural selection.*

Darwin's theories shocked most people of his day, who believed that each species had been created by a separate divine act. His book, which is usually called simply *The Origin of Species,* presented facts that disputed this belief. It caused a revolution in biological science and greatly affected religious thought.

Darwin's life. Darwin was born in Shrewsbury, England. He was the grandson of the noted physician and naturalist Erasmus Darwin, who had proposed a theory of evolution in the 1790's. As a boy, Charles often heard his grandfather's theories discussed.

Darwin studied medicine at the University of Edinburgh and theology at Cambridge University. He received a bachelor's degree from Cambridge in 1831. From 1831 to 1836, Darwin served as a naturalist with a British scientific expedition aboard the H.M.S. *Beagle.* The expedition visited places throughout the world, and he studied plants and animals everywhere it went.

In South America, Darwin found fossils of extinct animals that closely resembled modern species. On the Galapagos Islands in the Pacific Ocean, he noticed many variations among plants and animals of the same general type as those in South America. Darwin collected the fossils and other specimens of organisms for future study.

Brown Bros.

Charles R. Darwin

Darwin returned to England in 1836 and settled in London. He spent the rest of his life studying specimens, doing experiments, and writing about his findings. His early books included *The Structure and Distribution of Coral Reefs* (1842) and a journal of his research aboard the *Beagle.*

In 1839, Darwin married his cousin Emma Wedgwood. The family moved to Downe, near Croydon, in 1842, and Darwin lived there until his death. He was buried in Westminster Abbey in London.

Darwin's theories. The study of the specimens from the voyage of the *Beagle* convinced Darwin that modern species had evolved from a few earlier ones. He documented the evidence and first presented his theories on evolution to a meeting of scientists in 1858.

In most cases, according to Darwin, no two members of any species are exactly alike. Each organism has an individual combination of traits, and most of these traits are inherited. Darwin pointed out that gardeners and farmers commonly developed special kinds of plants and animals by selecting and breeding organisms that had desired traits. He believed that a similar kind of selective process took place in nature. Darwin called this process *natural selection,* or *the survival of the fittest.*

Darwin showed that living things commonly produce many more offspring than are necessary to replace themselves. The earth cannot possibly support all these organisms, and so they must compete for such necessities as food and shelter. Their lives also are threatened by animals that prey on them, by unfavorable weather, and by other environmental conditions.

Darwin suggested that some members of a species have traits that aid them in this struggle for life. Other members of the species have less favorable traits and therefore are less likely to survive. On the average, the members with favorable traits live for a longer period of time and produce more offspring than do the others. They also pass on the favorable traits to their young. The unfavorable traits eventually die out. In different places and at different times, some traits will be favored and others will be eliminated. In this way, varieties of organisms appear and gradually become separate species.

Darwin wrote several books that further discussed his theories of evolution. These included *The Descent of Man and Selection in Relation to Sex* (1871) and *The Expression of the Emotions in Man and Animals* (1872).

The influence of Darwin's ideas. Darwin's theories of evolution through natural selection set off a bitter controversy among biologists, religious leaders, and the general public. Many people thought Darwin had implied that human beings were descended from mon-

keys, and they angrily criticized his revolutionary ideas. But such noted British scientists as Thomas Henry Huxley and Alfred Russel Wallace supported Darwin's work, and many groups eventually accepted his theories. These theories, and the facts that supported them, gave biologists new insight into the origin of living things and the relationship among various species.

Darwin's theory of evolution by natural selection stimulated studies in biology, particularly in paleontology and comparative anatomy. During the first half of the 1900's, discoveries in genetics and developmental biology were used as evidence for theories of evolution that regarded natural selection as unimportant. However, after World War II ended in 1945, Darwin's theories again became the dominant influence in evolutionary biology in a form often called *Neo-Darwinism.* Neo-Darwinism gave a fuller explanation for the genetic origin of variation within individual species and for how species are formed. Beginning in the late 1960's, discoveries in molecular biology and paleontology have been used to support non-Darwinian theories of evolution. But few biologists reject the basic propositions of Neo-Darwinism, and Darwin's theories continue to be the basis for most contemporary biological studies.

Darwin's work has had a tremendous impact on religious thought. Many people strongly oppose the idea of evolution—and the teaching of it—because it conflicts with their religious beliefs. For example, they claim that the theory of evolution disagrees with the Biblical account of the Creation. Some people argue against the theory of natural selection because they believe it diminishes the role of divine guidance in the universe. Darwin suggested that human beings are similar to other animals in many ways. This idea contradicts the belief that God created human beings and gave them special emotional and intellectual gifts. In spite of these arguments, many religious people have no difficulty in accepting evolution. They maintain that God's wisdom and guidance underlie the process of evolution.

Darwin avoided discussing the sociological aspects of his work, but other writers used his ideas in developing their own theories about society. The German philosopher Karl Marx compared the struggle for survival among organisms to the struggle for power among social classes. Certain other writers referred to natural selection to justify the concept of the development of superior races of human beings. Scholars called social Darwinists used Darwin's ideas to promote the belief that people in a society—and societies themselves— must compete for survival.   Caroline M. Pond

See also **Evolution; Natural selection; Social Darwinism.** For a *Reading and Study Guide,* see *Darwin, Charles,* in the Research Guide/Index, Volume 22.

Additional resources

Brent, Peter. *Charles Darwin: "A Man of Enlarged Curiosity."* Harper, 1981. Title also appears as *Darwin.*
Clark, Ronald W. *The Survival of Charles Darwin: A Biography of a Man and an Idea.* Random House, 1985.

Dasheen. See Taro.
Dasyure. See Native cat.
Data processing. See Computer.
Database. See **Computer** (Storing and retrieving information).

Date Line, International. See International Date Line.

Date palm is the tree that produces dates. Date palms thrive in hot, dry climates. They grow throughout northern Africa and the Middle East, and they flourish in desert oases where few plants can grow. The date palm is one of the oldest crop plants. Early civilizations began to cultivate date palms at least 5,000 years ago. Today, dates still form an important part of the diet in many desert countries.

Uses. Date palms have many uses. They provide nourishment, shade, building materials, and fuel. They are especially important to Muslim peoples of the Middle East. According to Muslim legend, the date palm represents the tree of life.

Dates have a high sugar content, making them rich in carbohydrates. People eat dates fresh or dried. Dried dates can be used in cooking and can be easily stored and preserved. Sugar obtained from the sap of the tree and juice pressed from dates serve as sweeteners. Date mash ferments into an alcoholic drink called *arak,* also spelled *arrack.*

People use the trunk and leaves as building materials. They weave the leaves into baskets, mats, and other articles. Fiber from the bark makes strong rope. Even the pits are burned as fuel or are used as animal feed when ground up.

The tree. Date palms grow as tall as 100 feet (30 meters). They have a straight, rough trunk of about the same thickness from base to top. Featherlike leaves from 10 to 20 feet (3 to 6 meters) long fan out from the top of the trunk. Growths called *suckers* sprout near the base of the trunk and may develop into new plants. For this reason, date palms tend to grow in clumps.

Flowers bloom on the trees between February and June, and the fruit ripens from June to December. Male and female flowers grow on separate trees. Male flowers produce pollen, and female flowers develop into fruit.

The date is an oblong fruit that measures 1 to 2 inches (2.5 to 5 centimeters) in length. Thick, sweet flesh, covered by tough skin, surrounds a single large seed. Dates range in color from yellow to orange, red, or green, depending on the variety.

Dates grow in clusters at the end of stalks. A single cluster on some mature varieties of date palm can hold between 600 and 1,700 dates at time of picking. Date palms bear much fruit. They commonly produce at least 100 pounds (45 kilograms) of fruit annually for about 60 years.

Cultivation and production. Dates require warm temperatures and low humidity to ripen properly. The roots of the date palm need a regular supply of water, such as that provided by irrigation or an underground spring. Date palms may be raised from seeds. But growers more commonly raise them from suckers cut from a parent plant. They plant the suckers in rows about 30 feet (9 meters) apart. Trees begin to flower and bear fruit about four years after planting.

Pollen influences the size, shape, and ripening time of the fruit. Pollination can occur naturally by means of wind. But growers usually pollinate trees by tying a male flower cluster to a female cluster. Paper bags placed above the ripening fruit help prevent damage from rain. Netting or porous cloth placed over the clusters protect the fruit from insects and birds.

Workers harvest the clusters of dates by hand. They treat the dates with carbon bisulfide fumes to kill insects. They then put the dates in a warm place to ripen further and dry. This additional ripening increases the sugar content and reduces acidity.

Growers produce nearly 3 million short tons (2.7 million metric tons) of fresh dates annually. Egypt and Saudi Arabia are the largest producers of dates. Other impor-

© Dan Porges, Peter Arnold

Date palms thrive in hot, dry climates, such as the Middle East, northern Africa, and the deserts of California and Arizona. The date orchard shown above grows in Israel.

© Derek Fell

Clusters of dates that may include as many as 1,700 dates each and weigh up to 25 pounds (11 kilograms) grow on palm trees. The dates have a rich red or golden color while on the tree.

tant producers include Algeria, Iran, Iraq, and Pakistan. In the United States, cultivation occurs primarily in the desert valleys of Arizona and California.

Scientific classification. The date palm belongs to the palm family, Palmae. It is *Phoenix dactylifera.*   Michael G. Barbour

See also **Palm.**

Dating. See Sex (Boy-girl relationships); **Adolescent; Marriage; Etiquette.**

Datura, *duh TYUR uh,* is a group of poisonous shrubs and trees, including jimsonweed and angel's trumpet. These large bushy plants, also called *thorn apple,* have toothed, ill-smelling leaves, prickly fruit, and white to lavender trumpet-shaped flowers. Native to the tropics, datura now grow in eastern North America as well.

Scientific classification. Daturas make up a genus in the nightshade family, Solanaceae. The jimsonweed is *Datura stramonium.*   J. J. Levison

See also **Jimsonweed; Nightshade.**

Daudet, *doh DAY,* **Alphonse,** *al FAWNS* (1840-1897), is sometimes called the French Dickens. Like the English author Charles Dickens, Daudet wrote about poor and suffering persons and the outcasts of society. Both writers often softened their pictures of the cruelty of reality with a sympathy that occasionally became too sentimental. Daudet had a clear, graceful style. His simple observations of society and his humor and fantasy have made him a favorite with young readers.

Daudet is best known for his humorous short stories in *Letters from My Mill* (1866) and the patriotic stories in *Monday's Tales* (1873). The comic adventures of his boastful character Tartarin appear in two novels, *Tartarin of Tarascon* (1872) and *Tartarin over the Alps* (1895). Daudet also wrote serious realistic novels that contain excellent pictures of his time. These books include *The Nabob* (1877) and *Sapho* (1884).

Daudet was born in Nîmes. His parents were poor and he was bullied in school by his classmates and teachers. He described his unhappy youth in *Little What's Your Name* (1868), his first novel.

Thomas H. Goetz

Daugherty, *DAW hur tih,* **James Henry** (1889-1974), was an American artist and author of children's books. He won the 1940 Newbery Medal for *Daniel Boone,* which he wrote and illustrated. Daugherty also wrote and illustrated *Andy and the Lion* (1938), *Poor Richard* (1941), *Abraham Lincoln* (1943), *Of Courage Undaunted* (1951), and *Magna Charta* (1956). Daugherty was born in Asheville, N.C.   Virginia L. Wolf

Daughters of the American Revolution (DAR) is an organization of women directly descended from people who aided in establishing American independence. Women over 18 years of age who can prove such descent are eligible for membership. The chief goal of the DAR is to teach and promote good citizenship among youths, adults, and immigrants. Its programs promote appreciation of the past, patriotic service in the present, and educational training for the future. The DAR helps preserve shrines that keep alive the memory of people who won American independence. It encourages the study of American history and maintains relics and records of early America.

The organization owns a boarding school and a day school in remote mountain areas of Alabama and South Carolina. It also aids four other schools and colleges. It

Larry Walker, DAR

Memorial Continental Hall in Washington, D.C., is the original headquarters building of the Daughters of the American Revolution. Its cornerstone was laid in 1904.

publishes a *Manual for Citizenship* to help foreign-born residents of the United States in becoming citizens. The DAR sponsors Junior American Citizens Clubs for schoolchildren, provides scholarships for American Indians, and runs an annual Good Citizens contest in U.S. high schools. The organization's official publication is *The Daughters of the American Revolution Magazine.*

The DAR's official name is the National Society of the Daughters of the American Revolution. The DAR was founded in Washington, D.C., in 1890. It was chartered by Congress in 1896 and must report to Congress each year. The DAR has more than 212,000 members in over 3,100 chapters in the United States and other countries.

Headquarters of the DAR consist of three adjoining buildings at 1776 D St. NW, Washington, DC 20006. Memorial Continental Hall houses one of the largest genealogical libraries in the United States. The building also contains 30 State Rooms that are furnished in historic American styles. The Administration Building houses the society's business offices and a museum. Constitution Hall is an auditorium where the society holds its annual Continental Congress, and where many of Washington's cultural events are held.   Critically reviewed by the National Society of the Daughters of the American Revolution

Daughters of the Confederacy, United, is an organization of women directly descended from members of the army and navy of the Confederacy. The organization was founded in 1894 at Nashville, Tenn., by the widows, wives, mothers, and sisters of Confederate fighting men. The original purposes of the group were to honor the memory of the Confederacy and to help needy Confederate soldiers and sailors and their families. The organization has about 27,000 members. There are about 800 chapters in the United States, and one chapter in Paris, France. The group engages in educational, patriotic, and philanthropic activities, and preserves records and data of the Confederacy. The national office of the United Daughters of the Confederacy is in the Memorial Building to the Women of the South, 328 North Boulevard, Richmond, VA 23220.

Critically reviewed by the United Daughters of the Confederacy

Daughters of the Nile. See Masonry (Organization).

D'Aulaire, *doh LAIR,* is the family name of a husband and wife who wrote and illustrated children's books.

Edgar Parin d'Aulaire (1898-   ) and his wife, Ingri Mortenson d'Aulaire (1904-1980), won the Caldecott Medal in 1940 for their picture-book biography, *Abra-*

ham Lincoln. The couple also won the Regina Medal in 1970. They drew directly on lithographic stone in making their illustrations. Their career as book collaborators began in 1931 with *The Magic Rug.*

Their books include *Ola, Ola and Blakken, Children of the North Lights, Conquest of the Atlantic, George Washington, Benjamin Franklin,* and *Pocahontas.* They also illustrated *The Lord's Prayer, East of the Sun and West of the Moon,* and *Johnny Blossom.*

Edgar was born in Campoblenio, Switzerland, and Ingri in Kongsberg, Norway. They met in Munich, Germany, and were married in 1925. They moved to the United States in 1929. Jill P. May

Daumier, *doh MYAY,* **Honoré,** *aw naw RAY* (1808-1879), was a French artist and one of the most influential social critics of the 1800's. Daumier worked mainly in *lithography* (a type of printmaking), but he also gained recognition for his painting and sculpture. During his life, Daumier was best known for his satirical cartoons and *caricatures* (satirical portraits).

Daumier's works range from light satire to grim realism. Many of his caricatures ridicule middle-class tastes and values. He especially enjoyed attacking doctors and lawyers because he believed they used confusing language and special costumes to conceal their fraudulent practices. An example of his satirical lithographs appears in the article on **Cartoon.**

Daumier often made small clay sculptures to use as models for his lithographs. One of the best examples of these sculptures is *Ratapoil,* a caricature of Emperor Napoleon III. This figure appears in several of Daumier's lithographs as a political troublemaker. Many of Daumier's paintings portray the working-class people of Paris. These works include *The Third Class Carriage* (about 1862) and *The Washerwoman* (1863).

Daumier was born in Marseille and grew up in Paris, where he worked as a lawyer's errand boy. His experiences in the courts and on the streets of Paris gave him insight into the social struggles of the period. While in his 20's, he studied drawing. He later worked as a cartoonist for French political magazines and newspapers. In 1832, he served six months in prison because of a caricature he drew of King Louis Philippe. Albert Boime

For other examples of Daumier's works, see **Painting**

Crispin and Scapin (after 1860), an oil painting on canvas; Louvre, Paris (SCALA/Art Resource)
A Daumier painting shows characters in a comedy by French playwright Molière. The theater inspired many Daumier works.

(What do painters paint?); **Realism; Bronze** (picture: Modern French sculpture).

Dauphin, *DAW fuhn,* was the official title of the oldest son of the king of France from 1349 to 1830. The title was similar to that of "Prince of Wales" in England. The lords of Viennois and Auvergne, whose lands were known as Dauphiné, first used the title. The last lord of Viennois had no heir. He gave his lands to Philip VI, on condition that either the king or the heir to the throne should be lord of Dauphiné and have the title "Dauphin of France."

At first the dauphin had many privileges as ruler of his lands. But the title became merely honorary after Dauphiné was put under the same rule as the other provinces of France. J. Salwyn Schapiro

D.A.V. See Disabled American Veterans.

Davenant, *DAV uh nuhnt,* **Sir William** (1606-1668), was an English playwright. He became poet laureate of England in 1638. His name is also spelled D'Avenant.

Davenant was born in Oxford. During the 1630's, he wrote elaborate spectacles called *masques* and romantic plays such as *Love and Honour* (1634) and *The Platonic Lovers* (1635). During the civil war and Commonwealth periods in England (1642-1660), when plays were banned, Davenant attempted a new theatrical form, the opera. In 1656, he wrote and produced *The Siege of Rhodes,* generally considered the first English opera.

Davenant supported the crown during the civil war. After the restoration of Charles II to the English throne in 1660, Davenant became one of two men authorized to reopen the theaters in London. Davenant thus had tremendous influence over theater productions and the careers of playwrights and performers. He oversaw the appearance of the first actresses permitted on the English stage. Albert Wertheim

Davenport (pop. 103,264; met. area pop. 383,958) is the third largest city in Iowa. Only Des Moines and Cedar Rapids have more people. Davenport lies on the west bank of the Mississippi River (see **Iowa** [political map]). It is the largest city in a metropolitan area commonly called the Quad-Cities. The name Quad-Cities originally referred to what were then the four largest cities of the area—Davenport and the Illinois cities of Rock Island, Moline, and East Moline. As other area cities grew and the population of Bettendorf, Iowa, exceeded that of East Moline, the term came to be used for the entire area. The Quad-Cities is a manufacturing and transportation center surrounded by rich farmland.

The downtown business district of Davenport extends along the riverbank. Large Victorian houses add grace to Davenport's tree-lined streets. The area's main products include aluminum, cement, construction and farm equipment, and processed meats. Marycrest College, St. Ambrose College, and Palmer College of Chiropractic are in the city.

Until 1832, the site of Davenport was part of an area controlled by the Indian chief Black Hawk. U.S. Army troops defeated Black Hawk in the Black Hawk War that year. Whites then gained control of the Davenport area. Antoine LeClaire, a part-Indian and part-white interpreter, helped found the city. He named it for his friend George Davenport, an English trader. In 1856, the first bridge across the Mississippi River was built at Davenport by the Chicago and Rock Island Railroad.

Davenport has a mayor-council form of government. It is the seat of Scott County. Daniel K. Hayes

Davenport, Thomas. See **Electric railroad** (History).

David (1030?-965? B.C.) was the second king of Israel and one of the greatest figures in the history of the Jews. He succeeded Saul as king about 1000 B.C. and ruled for about 40 years, longer than any other king of ancient Israel.

More chapters of the Bible are devoted to David's reign than to that of any other monarch. The Old Testament also tells more about David as a person than about any other king. The prophets declared that a descendant of David would become the *Messiah,* an ideal king. This king would bring a golden age of peace, justice, and prosperity to Israel. The New Testament traces the ancestry of Jesus Christ back to David.

Marble statue (1504) by Michelangelo; Galleria dell' Accademia, Florence, Italy (Scala/EPA)

David

The Old Testament portrays David as a great warrior and as a strong, popular leader. It also tells of his talents as a musician and poet. When David was a youth, his lyre playing endeared him to King Saul. Later, David composed one of his most beautiful and sensitive poems as a tribute to Saul and his son Jonathan after they died in battle. According to tradition, David also wrote many of the Psalms in the Old Testament (see **Psalms, Book of**).

Early life. David was born in Bethlehem. His father was a shepherd named Jesse. David was the youngest of eight brothers and spent his early years tending his fa-

Detail of a fresco (1509); Scala/Editorial Photocolor Archives

David and Goliath is one of many Biblical scenes painted by Michelangelo on the ceiling of the Sistine Chapel in the Vatican.

ther's sheep. He later became a member of King Saul's court, where he formed a close friendship with Saul's son Jonathan. At that time, the Philistines were Israel's main enemy. The most famous story of David's youth tells of his battle with a Philistine warrior named Goliath. Armed only with a sling and five stones, David killed the giant Goliath.

David's courage and skill in battle quickly made him a hero among the people of Israel. As his popularity grew, however, Saul became extremely jealous of David and tried to kill him. David fled to the area of Israel where the tribe of Judah lived. There he gathered an army of followers. After Saul was killed in battle against the Philistines, David became king of Judah. David ruled Judah for 7½ years and then was named king of all Israel.

King of Israel. During his reign, David established Israel as a major power in western Asia. His troops defeated the Philistines, ending their threat to Israel's security. David also greatly expanded Israel's territory through a series of wars against the Ammonites, Moabites, and other neighboring peoples. He formed an alliance with the Phoenicians, who sent badly needed craftworkers and supplies to Israel.

David was an able ruler and administrator. He united his people and overcame the disunity that had interfered with Saul's reign. He established his capital in Jerusalem, which was centrally located and acceptable to all Israel's tribes. He also made Jerusalem the spiritual center of Israel by having the Ark of the Covenant moved to the city. The Ark was the sacred chest that contained the tablets inscribed with the Ten Commandments.

During the last years of David's reign, his sons plotted and struggled among themselves to determine who would succeed him. David's son Absalom rebelled against him and forced him to flee Jerusalem. David's troops eventually killed Absalom and regained control of the kingdom. However, David mourned bitterly for his son. According to the Bible, these troubles were punishment for a sin. Years earlier, David had committed adultery with a beautiful woman named Bathsheba. David also had Bathsheba's husband killed in battle so he could marry her.

David died about 965 B.C. His son Solomon then became king. Eric M. Meyers

Related articles in *World Book* include:

Goliath
Hittites
Philistines
Saul

Sculpture (picture: *David* by Donatello)
Solomon

Additional resources

Bright, John. *A History of Israel.* 3rd ed. Westminster, 1981.
Encyclopaedia Judaica, Vol. 5. Macmillan, 1972. Article on David appears on pp. 1318-1338.
Gaubert, Henri. *David and the Foundation of Jerusalem.* Hastings, 1969. Vol. IV of *The Bible in History.*
Orlinsky, Harry M. *Ancient Israel.* 2nd ed. Cornell Univ. Press, 1960.

David was the name of two kings of Scotland.

David I (1084-1153), the youngest son of Malcolm III Canmore, became king of Scotland in 1124. He invaded England twice, once to support his niece Matilda's claim to the English throne, and again to gain the earldom of Northumbria for his son, Henry. During his reign, David won the support of the many Anglo-Norman barons in Scotland.

David II (1324-1371), the son of Robert Bruce, was married to Joanna, daughter of King Edward II of England, at the age of 4. He became king in 1329. David fled to France when England invaded Scotland. He later fought with France against England in 1346. The English captured him. They released him 11 years later, and he returned to Scotland.   Robert S. Hoyt

David, *dah VEED,* **Jacques Louis,** *zhahk lwee* (1748-1825), was the leading French painter during the French Revolution and the Napoleonic era. He painted primarily in the neoclassical style, which emphasizes solidly modeled forms, realistic details, and balanced composition. Neoclassicists often used subjects from ancient history to make observations about contemporary events. David's famous painting *The Oath of the Horatii* (1784) reflects neoclassical style and subject matter. This painting appears in **Painting** (The 1800's).

David was an active participant in the French Revolution and voted for the death of King Louis XVI. He started to depict the events of the revolution in the unfinished *The Oath of the Tennis Court,* begun in 1791. In 1793, he painted *The Death of Marat,* a moving portrait of the assassinated revolutionary leader. An ardent supporter of Napoleon, David also glorified some of the

Unfinished oil painting on canvas (1800); the Louvre, Paris (Giraudon)

Jacques Louis David's *Portrait of Madame Récamier* emphasizes solidly modeled forms, realistic details, and balanced composition. These qualities are typical of his neoclassical style.

main events of the emperor's life in his paintings.

David was born in Paris. His work influenced many of the major artists of the 1800's, including many members of the impressionist movement.   Ann Friedman

See also **Clothing** (picture: Women's clothing); **French Revolution** (picture: The death of Marat); **Napoleon I** (pictures: Napoleon I; *The Coronation of Napoleon*); **Socrates** (picture).

David, Saint (520?-589?), is the patron saint of Wales. Almost no authentic information exists on David's life. He is said to have founded a number of Welsh monasteries, including St. David's at Mynyw (Menevia) in southwestern Wales. Mynyw is now called St. David's. After David's death, a widespread belief grew that he had served as the leader of the Welsh church. Perhaps as a result, Mynyw became a center of religious authority for much of Wales.

According to legend, David was born into a prominent Welsh family and studied under the monk Saint Paulinus. In works of art, David is shown standing on a mound with a dove perched on one shoulder. His feast day is celebrated on March 1.   William J. Courtenay

David Copperfield. See Dickens, Charles (Dickens' life; The second phase).

Davidson, Jo (1883-1952), an American portrait sculptor, created heads of many famous people. His work is direct and lifelike. He has been called a "biographer in bronze." Davidson worked chiefly in terra cotta and bronze. His best-known works include portraits of General Pershing and Franklin D. Roosevelt.

Davidson was born in New York City. He studied for three years at the Art Students' League there, but then decided on a medical career. While at Yale Medical School, he saw work done by art students in a modeling class and chose to become a sculptor. He went to Paris in 1907 to work and study. Davidson served as a war correspondent during World War I (1914-1918).
    William L. MacDonald

Davies, Arthur Bowen (1862-1928), was an American painter and illustrator. His idealized figures, often taken from literature or legend and represented in a lyrical style, reflect a highly intellectual and poetic personal vision. However, he was keenly aware of the changing artistic ideas of his time. Davies saw value in the more down-to-earth style of painter Robert Henri and his group. He joined Henri's group, known as *The Eight,* or the *Ashcan School* (see **Henri, Robert**). Davies was instrumental in organizing the Armory show of 1913. Held in New York City, this exhibition is generally considered the artistic event that did most to awaken Americans to developments in modern art abroad. Davies was born in Utica, N.Y.   Charles C. Eldredge

Davies, Robertson (1913-   ), is a Canadian novelist, playwright, and journalist. He sets most of his novels in small Ontario towns. Davies' early novels satirize members of various professions, including ministers, journalists, and college teachers and students. In *A Mixture of Frailties* (1958), Davies described the artistic development of a gifted young Canadian singer. He explored the relationship between magic, religion, and psychology in three related novels. These novels are *Fifth Business* (1970), *The Manticore* (1972), and *World of Wonders* (1975). Davies also wrote the novels *Tempest-Tost* (1951), *Leaven of Malice* (1954), *The Rebel Angels* (1982), and *What's Bred in the Bone* (1985).

William Robertson Davies was born in Thamesville, Ont., and was educated in Canada and England. He worked in England as an actor, stage manager, director, and drama teacher. He later wrote critical studies in drama history and several plays.

In 1942, Davies became editor of the *Peterborough* (Ont.) *Examiner.* He wrote a syndicated column of witty observations on small-town American and Canadian life. Selections from this column were collected in *The Papers of Samuel Marchbanks* (1985). A collection of Davies' speeches and lectures was published as *One Half of Robertson Davies* (1978). From 1963 to 1981, Davies served as master of Massey College for graduate students at the University of Toronto.   Claude T. Bissell

See also **Canadian literature** (Modern English-Canadian fiction; picture).

Leonardo da Vinci's works include the *Mona Lisa, left,* probably the most famous portrait ever painted. *The Virgin and Child with Saint Anne, right,* illustrates how Leonardo organized his paintings in a pyramid design. Both pictures represent the artist's style in their blurred outlines, graceful figures, overall feeling of calm, and dramatic contrasts of dark and light.

Da Vinci, *duh VIHN chee,* **Leonardo** (1452-1519), was one of the greatest painters of the Italian Renaissance. His portrait *Mona Lisa* and his religious scene *The Last Supper* rank among the most famous pictures ever painted.

Leonardo, as he is almost always called, was trained to be a painter. But he became one of the most versatile geniuses in history. His interests and achievements spread into an astonishing variety of fields that are usually considered scientific specialties. Leonardo studied anatomy, astronomy, botany, and geology, and he designed machines and drew plans for hundreds of inventions.

Leonardo recorded his scientific observations and his ideas for inventions in notebooks. Many of the ideas and designs Leonardo preserved in his notebooks were far ahead of their time. For example, he drew plans for a flying machine and a parachute. Leonardo also stated that the sun does not move, though scientists of his day believed that the sun revolved around the earth. By the time Leonardo's scientific and technical investigations became widely known, other people had come up with many of the same ideas.

Although Leonardo explored an amazing number of areas of human knowledge, he was not a universal genius. For example, he had no interest in history, literature, or religion. He never developed his ideas systematically, and he did not formulate scientific laws or principles. But Leonardo was an excellent observer. He concerned himself with what the eye could see, rather than with abstract thoughts.

Early career. Leonardo was probably born outside the village of Vinci, near Florence in central Italy. At that time, Florence was an independent republic and a commercial center. Leonardo was the illegitimate son of Ser Piero da Vinci, a legal specialist, and a peasant girl. Ser Piero raised the boy.

During the late 1460's, Leonardo became an apprentice to Andrea del Verrocchio, a leading painter and sculptor in Florence. He remained with Verrocchio as an assistant after completing his apprenticeship.

Verrocchio and Leonardo collaborated on the painting *The Baptism of Christ,* which is reproduced in the *World Book* article on **John the Baptist.** Leonardo painted the head of the left angel, the distant landscape, and probably the skin of Christ. His parts of the painting have soft shadings, with shadows concealing the edges. The figures are shown in the act of moving from one position to another. Verrocchio's figures and objects in this work are sharply defined. They reflect the style called

Red chalk drawing on paper;
Reale Library, Turin, Italy (SCALA)

A self-portrait is the only authentic likeness of Leonardo that has been preserved. The artist drew it about 1512.

Early Renaissance. Leonardo's more graceful approach marked the beginning of the High Renaissance style. However, this style did not become popular in Italy for another 25 years.

From about 1478 to 1482, Leonardo had his own studio in Florence. During this period he received an important commission to paint a church altarpiece now known as the *Adoration of the Three Kings*. It exists today in an unfinished form, with the figures and the light and dark areas visible only as outlines.

The *Adoration of the Three Kings* shows three kings worshiping the Christ child. Leonardo abandoned the traditional treatment of this subject. Earlier versions had shown the figures in profile, with the Virgin Mary and Jesus on one side of the painting and the kings on the other. To give the Holy Family more emphasis, Leonardo placed them in the center, facing the viewer. The kings and other figures form a semicircle around Mary and Jesus. This arrangement resulted in a livelier scene and greater unity among the figures.

Years in Milan. Leonardo never finished the *Adoration of the Three Kings* because he left Florence about 1482 to become court artist for Lodovico Sforza, the duke of Milan. Leonardo lived in Milan for 17 years.

Leonardo had a variety of duties in the duke's court. As a military engineer, he designed artillery and planned the diversion of rivers. As a civil engineer, he designed revolving stages for pageants. As a sculptor, he planned a huge monument of the duke's father mounted on a leaping horse.

In Milan, Leonardo painted the *Madonna of the Rocks* (about 1485), his earliest major painting that survives in complete form. It is reproduced in the **Painting** article.

Leonardo finished painting *The Last Supper* about 1497. He created the famous scene on a wall of the dining hall in the monastery of Santa Maria delle Grazie. The painting appears in the article on **Jesus Christ**. It shows Christ and His 12 apostles just after Jesus has announced that one of them will betray Him. Leonardo changed the traditional arrangement of the figures from a line of 13 figures to several small groups. Each apostle responds in a different way to Christ's announcement. Jesus sits in the center of the scene, apart from the other figures. Leonardo's composition creates a more active and centralized design than earlier artists had achieved.

When painting *The Last Supper,* Leonardo rejected the *fresco* technique normally used for wall paintings (see **Fresco**). An artist who uses this fresco method must work quickly. But Leonardo wanted to paint slowly, revise his work, and use shadows—all of which would have been impossible in fresco painting. He developed a new technique that involved coating the wall with a compound he had created. But the compound, which was supposed to hold the paint in place and protect it from moisture, did not work. Soon after Leonardo completed the picture, the paint began to flake away. *The Last Supper* still exists, but in poor condition.

During his years in Milan, Leonardo began to produce scientific drawings, especially of the human body. He studied anatomy by dissecting human corpses and the bodies of animals. Leonardo's drawings clarify not only the appearance of bones, tendons, and other body parts, but also their function. The drawings are considered the first accurate portrayals of human anatomy.

Return to Florence. In 1499, the French overthrew Lodovico Sforza and forced him to flee Milan. Leonardo also left the city. He visited Mantua, where he made a famous drawing of Isabella d'Este, the wife of the duke of Mantua. He also visited Venice briefly before returning to Florence.

Leonardo's paintings during his stay in Milan had made him famous, and the people of Florence welcomed him as a returning hero. The early work that he did there had strongly influenced the young men who had become the leaders of the next generation of Florentine painters. These artists included Sandro Botticelli and Piero di Cosimo. The work Leonardo was to create in Florence also inspired a third generation of artists. This generation included Andrea del Sarto, Michelangelo, and Raphael.

When Leonardo returned, Florence was building a new hall for the city council. The Florentine government hired Leonardo and Michelangelo to decorate the walls of the hall with scenes of the city's military victories. Leonardo chose the Battle of Anghiari, in which Florence had defeated Milan in 1440. His painting showed a cavalry battle, with tense soldiers, leaping horses, and clouds of dust.

In painting the *Battle of Anghiari,* Leonardo again rejected fresco and tried an experimental technique called *encaustic.* As in the case of *The Last Supper,* the experiment did not work. Leonardo left the painting unfinished when he went on a trip. The paint began to run, and he never finished the project. The painting no longer exists. Its general appearance is known from Leonardo's sketches and from copies made by other artists.

While working on the *Battle of Anghiari,* Leonardo painted the *Mona Lisa,* which appears with this article.

Leonardo's notebooks Leonardo recorded his ideas about art, engineering, and science in several notebooks. About 4,200 pages still exist. Many pages include drawings that reveal Leonardo's powers of observation and skill as a draftsman. He wrote his notes backward, and so they can be read only with a mirror.

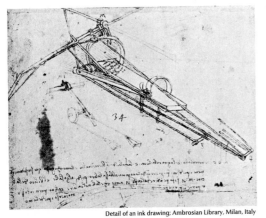

Detail of an ink drawing; Ambrosian Library, Milan, Italy

A sketch of an experimental flying machine

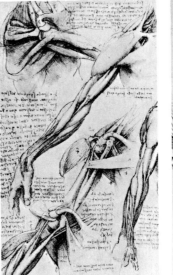

Detail of an ink drawing; Ambrosian Library, Milan, Italy

A design for a movable bridge

A drawing of a rock formation

Details of drawings; reproduced by Gracious Permission of Her Majesty Queen Elizabeth II (Royal Library, Windsor Castle, Windsor, England)

A study of the human shoulder

Ink drawing; Ambrosian Library, Milan, Italy

A construction crane

The *Mona Lisa* is a portrait of Lisa del Giocondo, the young wife of a Florentine merchant. It is often called *La Gioconda.*

The *Mona Lisa* became famous because of the mysterious smile of the subject. Actually, Leonardo showed the woman's face moving into or out of a smile. He arranged her folded hands so that the figure formed a pyramid design. Leonardo's technique solved a problem that had faced earlier portrait painters. These artists had shown only the head and upper part of the body, and the picture seemed to cut off the subject at the chest. Leonardo's placement of the hands of the *Mona Lisa* gave the woman a more complete, natural appearance.

Last years. Leonardo did little painting during his later years, but he produced many drawings of machines and of experimental inventions. These drawings rank among Leonardo's greatest masterpieces, especially in their delicate use of shadow and their sense of motion.

In 1517, Leonardo settled in France at the invitation of King Francis I. The king wanted to surround himself with

famous representatives of Renaissance culture. Leonardo spent his final two years near Tours in a large house provided by the king.   Creighton Gilbert

See also **Airplane** (History and development [picture]); **Parachute** (picture). For a *Reading and Study Guide,* see *Da Vinci, Leonardo,* in the Research Guide/Index, Volume 22.

Additional resources

Clark, Kenneth. *Leonardo da Vinci.* 3rd ed. Viking, 1988. Critical study of the artist's work.
Harris, Nathaniel. *Leonardo and the Renaissance.* Bookwright, 1986. For younger readers.
Wallace, Robert. *The World of Leonardo, 1452-1519.* Time-Life Books, 1966.

Davis, Benjamin Oliver, Jr. (1912-   ), was a United States Air Force officer. In 1959, he became the first black U.S. officer in history to be made a major general. He was promoted to lieutenant general in 1965.

Davis was born in Washington, D.C. His father, Benjamin O. Davis, a U.S. Army officer, had become the highest ranking black U.S. officer in 1940, when the Army made him a brigadier general.

In 1936, the younger Davis became the first black graduate of the United States Military Academy in nearly 50 years. In World War II (1939-1945), he earned the Distinguished Flying Cross. He became director of Manpower and Organization of the U.S. Air Force in 1961. Davis was made Air Force chief of staff in South

U.S. Air Force
Benjamin O. Davis, Jr.

Korea in 1965, and commander of the 13th Air Force at Clark Base in the Philippines in 1967. In 1968, he became deputy commander in chief of U.S. Strike Command at MacDill Air Force Base in Tampa, Fla. Davis retired from the Air Force in 1970. He served as an assistant secretary of the Department of Transportation from 1971 to 1975.

Richard Bardolph

Davis, Bette (1908-1989), was an American motion-picture actress known for her portrayals of strong-willed women. Davis won Academy Awards as best actress for her performances in *Dangerous* (1935) and *Jezebel* (1938). She received eight other Academy Award nominations.

Ruth Elizabeth Davis was born in Lowell, Mass. She studied acting in New York City and appeared in several plays before beginning her film career. Davis made her first film, *Bad Sister,* in 1931. She made

A.S.P. from Tom Stack & Assoc.
Bette Davis

85 movies, including *Of Human Bondage* (1934), *Dark Victory* (1939), *The Letter* (1940), *Now, Voyager* (1942), *The Corn Is Green* (1945), *All About Eve* (1950), and *Whatever Happened to Baby Jane?* (1962). Davis also wrote two autobiographies, *The Lonely Life* (1962) and *This 'n That* (1987).

Roger Ebert

Davis, David (1815-1886), an American judge and statesman, helped his close friend Abraham Lincoln obtain the nomination for President in 1860. Lincoln appointed Davis to the Supreme Court of the United States in 1862. Davis was nominated for President by the National Labor Reform Party in 1872, but he withdrew the nomination. He resigned from the Supreme Court in 1877, and was elected to the United States Senate from Illinois as an independent. His election prevented him from serving on the Electoral Commission in the disputed presidential election of 1876. Davis' vote might have elected Democrat Samuel J. Tilden (see **Electoral Commission**). Davis was born in Cecil County, Maryland.   Arthur A. Ekirch, Jr.

Davis, Henry Gassaway (1823-1916), was the Democratic candidate for Vice President of the United States in 1904. He and presidential candidate Alton B. Parker lost to President Theodore Roosevelt and Charles W.

Fairbanks. Davis, at the age of 80, was the oldest person ever chosen to run for Vice President. Davis served as a United States senator from West Virginia from 1871 to 1883. He was born in Woodstock, Md.   Irving G. Williams

Davis, Jefferson (1808-1889), served as president of the Confederate States of America during the Civil War. He has been called the man who "symbolized the solemn convictions and tragic fortunes of millions of men." He was not popular with the people of the South during the war, but he won their respect and affection after the war through his suffering in prison and also through his lifelong defense of the Southern cause.

Davis was a statesman with wide experience. He served in the United States House of Representatives and the Senate, and as a Cabinet member. He also won distinction as a soldier. He was a thoughtful student of the Constitution and of political philosophy.

Early life. Davis was born on June 3, 1808, in Christian (later Todd) County, Kentucky. His father, Sam Davis, was a veteran of the Revolutionary War. His older brother, Joseph, moved to Mississippi and became a successful planter. The Davis family moved there while Jefferson was still an infant, and he grew up in Wilkinson County. He attended the county academy, then entered Transylvania University in Kentucky. At the age of 16, he entered the U.S. Military Academy, and graduated with comparatively low grades in 1828.

Davis' Army career took him to Forts Howard and Crawford on the Wisconsin frontier. He fought in campaigns against the Indians, and took charge of Indian prisoner removal after the Black Hawk War. Davis resigned from the Army in 1835.

Davis' family. In 1835, Davis married Sarah Taylor, daughter of his commander, Colonel Zachary Taylor, who later became a general and President of the United States. Davis took his bride to Mississippi and settled down to live as a cotton planter. But within three months, both he and his wife became ill with fever, and Mrs. Davis died. Davis traveled for a year, while he regained his strength. For several years after his return to his plantation, Brierfield, on the Mississippi River, Davis studied history, economics, political philosophy, and the Constitution of the United States. He managed his plantation successfully, and became wealthy.

In 1845, Davis married Varina Howell, whose family lived on The Briars, an estate near Natchez, Miss. The couple had six children: Samuel, Margaret Howell Hayes, Jefferson, Joseph, William, and Varina Anne. Varina Anne, nicknamed Winnie, became known as the *Daughter of the Confederacy.* Mrs. Davis was a brillant and witty hostess. She did much to advance her husband's political career, and also ably helped him during the Civil War.

His political career. Davis became interested in politics in 1843, and won a seat as a Democrat in the U.S. House of Representatives in 1845. He resigned from Congress in June 1846 to become a colonel in a regiment of Mississippi volunteers in the Mexican War. He served under General Zachary Taylor in northern Mexico, and distinguished himself for bravery in the battles of Monterrey and Buena Vista. His deployment of his men in a V shape gave him credit for winning the battle of Buena Vista (see **Mexican War**). During the battle, Davis fought all day with a bullet in his foot.

The governor of Mississippi appointed Davis in 1847 to fill out the term of a United States senator who had died. The next year the state legislature elected him for the rest of the term, and in 1850 for a full term. Henry Clay's famous compromise measures came before the Senate in 1850, and Davis took an active part in opposing them in debate (see **Compromise of 1850**). He believed in a strict interpretation of the Constitution, and loyally supported Senator John C. Calhoun, a Southern states' rights leader (see **Calhoun, John C.**).

Davis believed that Mississippi should not accept the Compromise of 1850, and resigned from the Senate to become the candidate of the States' Rights Democrats for governor. He lost the election, and retired to his plantation in Wilkinson County.

Secretary of war. President Franklin Pierce appointed Davis secretary of war in 1853. Davis improved and enlarged the Army during his term. He introduced an improved system of infantry tactics, and brought in new and better weapons. He organized engineer companies to explore routes for railroads from the Mississippi River to the Pacific Coast. He even tried the experiment of importing camels for Army use in the western deserts. At the close of the Pierce Administration in 1857, Davis was reelected to the Senate from Mississippi. In the Senate, Davis no longer advocated secession, but he defended the rights of the South and slavery. He opposed Stephen A. Douglas' "Freeport Doctrine," which held that the people of a territory could exclude slavery by refusing to protect it. Davis also opposed Douglas' ambition to be the Democratic presidential candidate in 1860 (see **Douglas, Stephen A.**).

Photograph by Mathew Brady. National Archives, Washington, D.C.

Jefferson Davis became the provisional president of the Confederate States of America on Feb. 18, 1861.

Spokesman for the South. Davis became the champion of the constitutional right of a state to choose and maintain its own institutions. He demanded that Congress protect slavery in the territories. In the positions he took, Davis considered himself the heir of Calhoun.

After Abraham Lincoln was elected President of the United States, Mississippi passed an Ordinance of Secession, and Davis resigned from the Senate. Davis hoped to become head of the Army of the Confederate States. But shortly after his return to Mississippi, the convention at Montgomery, Ala., named him provisional president of the Confederacy. He took the oath of office on Feb. 18, 1861. He was inaugurated as regular president of the Confederacy on Feb. 22, 1862.

Leader of the Confederacy. Davis was probably not the wisest choice for president. His health was poor. Although he was a good administrator, he proved to be a poor planner. He had difficulties with his Congress, and bitter critics condemned his management of the war, charging that he was too watchful of his powers. Some modern historians view Davis as a rigid constitutionalist who was too inflexible in his ideas on command and strategy.

Soon after General Robert E. Lee surrendered, Davis was taken prisoner, and imprisoned at Fort Monroe. A grand jury indicted him for treason, and he was held in prison two years awaiting trial. Horace Greeley and other Northern men became his bondsmen in 1867, and he was released on bail. He was never tried.

His last years. Davis spent his last years writing and studying at "Beauvoir," his home at Biloxi, Miss., near the Gulf of Mexico. Davis published *The Rise and Fall of the Confederate Government* in 1881 as a defense against his critics. Davis appeared often at Confederate reunions, and eventually won the admiration of his fellow Southerners. He died on Dec. 6, 1889, and was buried in New Orleans. His body was moved to Richmond in 1893. The state of Mississippi presented a statue of Davis to Statuary Hall in the U.S. Capitol in 1931.

Davis' birthday, June 3, is a legal holiday in seven Southern states. Louisiana celebrates it as Confederate Memorial Day. Kentucky celebrates it as Confederate Memorial Day and as Davis' birthday.   Thomas L. Connelly

See also **Civil War; Confederate States of America; Richmond; Alabama** (picture: Home).

Additional resources

Davis, Burke. *The Long Surrender.* Random House, 1985. Describes Jefferson Davis' final years.

Eaton, Clement. *Jefferson Davis.* Free Press, 1977.

Warren, Robert Penn. *Jefferson Davis Gets His Citizenship Back.* Univ. Press of Kentucky, 1980.

Davis, John (1543-1605), also spelled *Davys,* an English mariner and explorer, was the first European to discover what is now Davis Strait, between Greenland and Canada. He led the way for such explorers of northeast Canada as Henry Hudson and William Baffin. Davis was one of the most skilled navigators of the late 1500's. He invented a type of *quadrant,* a device used in navigation, and developed what became the standard ship's log.

From 1585 to 1587, Davis headed three expeditions in search of the Northwest Passage, a route through Canada between Europe and Asia (see **Northwest Passage**). He discovered Davis Strait on his first trip. During his voyages, Davis explored the east coast of Baffin Island

and the west coast of Greenland but did not find a route west. From 1591 to 1593, he tried to find a passage to Asia via the Strait of Magellan in South America. He failed to do so but sighted the Falkland Islands, off the southeast coast of South America. Davis became a pilot for the East India Company's first fleet to East Asia. He was killed by Japanese pirates. Davis was born at Sand-ridge Barton in the county of Devon.   Barry M. Gough

Davis, John William (1873-1955), a famous American constitutional lawyer, was the unsuccessful Democratic candidate for the presidency of the United States in 1924, losing to Calvin Coolidge. Davis represented a wide range of clients as a constitutional lawyer. He ar-gued 140 cases before the Supreme Court of the United States, more than anyone had argued up to that time. Many considered him the most distinguished constitu-tional lawyer in the United States. But he lost his last and most famous case, his Supreme Court defense of South Carolina's public school segregation laws, in 1954.

Davis was born in Clarksburg, W. Va. He represented West Virginia in the U.S. House of Representatives from 1911 to 1913. He served as U.S. solicitor general from 1913 to 1918 and as ambassador to Great Britain from 1918 to 1921.   Eric F. Goldman

Davis, Miles (1926-   ), is an influential American jazz trumpeter and bandleader. He became famous for a trumpet style that is forceful but lyrical. His moody tone and original ideas made him one of the most imitated musicians of his generation.

Miles Dewey Davis III was born in Alton, Ill. In 1945, he went to New York City to study music at the Juilliard School. However, he spent most of his time performing with jazz bands, including a quintet led by alto saxo-phonist Charlie Parker. That group helped create the complex, modern form of jazz known as *bebop* or *bop*. In 1948, Davis formed a nine-piece recording unit that helped develop *cool jazz*, a style that emphasized rich ensemble colors and emotional restraint.

During the 1950's, Davis' bands performed in a more energetic style, though his playing continued to empha-size melody. His major recordings include *Miles Ahead* and *Porgy and Bess*, both arranged for trumpet and or-chestra by Gil Evans, and the sextet session *Kind of Blue*. Many musicians gained their first recognition in Davis' bands, including saxophonists John Coltrane and Wayne Shorter; pianists Red Garland, Bill Evans, and Herbie Hancock; bassists Paul Chambers and Ron Carter; and drummers Philly Joe Jones and Tony Williams. Since the late 1960's, Davis has pioneered in *fusion,* a movement that combined elements of rock music with jazz. His au-tobiography, *Miles,* was published in 1989.

Gary Giddins

See also **Jazz** (Cool jazz; New directions in jazz).

Davis, Paulina Wright (1813-1876), was an American social reformer. She worked for the right of women to own property and to vote.

In 1840, Davis joined a women's campaign against the property laws of the day. These laws made a man the owner of his wife's possessions. The campaign led to a New York law of 1848 that gave wives control of prop-erty they had owned before marriage.

From 1845 to 1849, Davis lectured to women's groups on the female anatomy. These talks encouraged some of Davis' listeners to join the small number of women who

became physicians.

Davis also helped organ-ize the first and second na-tional woman's rights con-ventions. She presided at these meetings, held in 1850 and 1851 in Worces-ter, Mass. From 1853 to 1855, she published a woman's rights magazine called *Una.* Davis was born in Bloomfield, N.Y.

Miriam Schneir

National Portrait Gallery, Smithsonian Institution

Paulina Davis

Davis, Richard Har-ding (1864-1916), was an American writer best known as a war correspondent. His exciting, colorful style of reporting earned him a reputation as one of the leading journalists of his time.

Between 1897 and 1916, Davis reported on six major conflicts for New York and London newspapers. He dra-matically described events in the Cuban revolution against Spanish rule, the Greco-Turkish War, the Span-ish-American War, the Boer War in South Africa, the Russo-Japanese War, and the early years of World War I. His vivid accounts of Lieutenant Colonel Theodore Roosevelt's Rough Riders during the Spanish-American War helped make Roosevelt famous.

Davis was born in Philadelphia. He began his journal-istic career in 1886 with the *Philadelphia Record,* and he served as managing editor of *Harper's Weekly* magazine in the early 1890's. Davis published seven volumes of his observations as a war correspondent. He also wrote novels, plays, and short stories.   Michael Emery

Davis, Samuel (1842-1863), a Confederate spy, was called the *Boy Hero of the Confederacy.* Union troops hanged him near Pulaski, Tenn., because he would not tell who gave him secret military information. Davis' last words were, "I would rather die a thousand deaths than betray a friend or be false to duty." Tennessee erected a statue to his memory on the Capitol grounds in Nash-ville. Davis' birthplace, near Smyrna, Tenn., is kept as a shrine.   Gabor S. Boritt

Davis, Stuart (1894-1964), was an American painter and illustrator. His bright, lively paintings deal with everyday life. Davis tried to combine a modern abstract style with distinctly American scenes and objects. Bold areas of intense, pure color and rugged written lines characterize his work. He often included words from street signs and billboards. Davis was inspired by such things as jazz, motion pictures, gas stations, storefronts, and mass-produced objects.

Davis was born in Philadelphia. At 19, he exhibited in the Armory Show of 1913. The works of Vincent van Gogh, Paul Gauguin, and Henri Matisse impressed him at this exhibition. His mature style also shows the influ-ence of such cubist painters as Fernand Léger and Pablo Picasso. He did murals for Radio City Music Hall and Rockefeller Center in New York City.   Sarah Burns

See also **Painting** (picture: *The Barber Shop*).

Davis Cup is a silver bowl trophy awarded each year to the nation that wins the world's men's tennis champi-onship. Dwight F. Davis, who was a leading American tennis player, donated the cup in 1900 and competition began that year. The competition consists of a single

Davis Cup tournament

Year	Winner	Runner-up	Score	Year	Winner	Runner-up	Score
1900	United States	Great Britain	3-0	1939	Australia	United States	3-2
1901	No competition			1940-1945	No competition		
1902	United States	Great Britain	3-2	1946	United States	Australia	5-0
1903	Great Britain	United States	4-1	1947	United States	Australia	4-1
1904	Great Britain	Belgium	5-0	1948	United States	Australia	5-0
1905	Great Britain	United States	5-0	1949	United States	Australia	4-1
1906	Great Britain	United States	5-0	1950	Australia	United States	4-1
1907	Australia and New Zealand	Great Britain	3-2	1951	Australia	United States	3-2
1908	Australia and New Zealand	United States	3-2	1952	Australia	United States	4-1
1909	Australia and New Zealand	United States	5-0	1953	Australia	United States	3-2
1910	No competition			1954	United States	Australia	3-2
1911	Australia and New Zealand	United States	5-0	1955	Australia	United States	5-0
1912	Great Britain	Australia and New Zealand	3-2	1956	Australia	United States	5-0
1913	United States	Great Britain	3-2	1957	Australia	United States	3-2
1914	Australia and New Zealand	United States	3-2	1958	United States	Australia	3-2
1915-1918	No competition			1959	Australia	United States	3-2
1919	Australia and New Zealand	Great Britain	4-1	1960	Australia	Italy	4-1
1920	United States	Australia and New Zealand	5-0	1961	Australia	Italy	5-0
1921	United States	Japan	5-0	1962	Australia	Mexico	5-0
1922	United States	Australia and New Zealand	4-1	1963	United States	Australia	3-2
1923	United States	Australia and New Zealand	4-1	1964	Australia	United States	3-2
1924	United States	Australia and New Zealand	5-0	1965	Australia	Spain	4-1
1925	United States	France	5-0	1966	Australia	India	4-1
1926	United States	France	4-1	1967	Australia	Spain	4-1
1927	France	United States	3-2	1968	United States	Australia	4-1
1928	France	United States	4-1	1969	United States	Romania	5-0
1929	France	United States	3-2	1970	United States	West Germany	5-0
1930	France	United States	4-1	1971	United States	Romania	3-2
1931	France	Great Britain	3-2	1972	United States	Romania	3-2
1932	France	United States	3-2	1973	Australia	United States	5-0
1933	Great Britain	France	3-2	1974	South Africa	India	*
1934	Great Britain	United States	4-1	1975	Sweden	Czechoslovakia	3-2
1935	Great Britain	United States	5-0	1976	Italy	Chile	4-1
1936	Great Britain	Australia	3-2	1977	Australia	Italy	3-1†
1937	United States	Great Britain	4-1	1978	United States	Great Britain	4-1
1938	United States	Australia	3-2	1979	United States	Italy	5-0
				1980	Czechoslovakia	Italy	4-1
				1981	United States	Argentina	3-1†
				1982	United States	France	4-1
				1983	Australia	Sweden	3-2
				1984	Sweden	United States	4-1
				1985	Sweden	West Germany	3-2
				1986	Australia	Sweden	3-2
				1987	Sweden	India	5-0
				1988	West Germany	Sweden	4-1
				1989	West Germany	Sweden	3-2

Source: United States Tennis Association.   *Won by default.   †Fifth match suspended by mutual consent.

elimination tournament among 16 qualifying nations. A separate tournament is held for nations that have not qualified. These nations are divided into four zones. The winner of each zone advances to the cup competition for the next year, replacing the nations with the poorest record. See also **Tennis** (Tennis today).   Arthur Ashe

Davis Strait. See **Northwest Passage.**

Davy, Sir Humphry (1778-1829), an English chemist, rose to fame as inventor of the miner's safety lamp. The Davy lamp, perfected in 1815, greatly reduced the risks of coal mine explosions. At the age of 20, Davy experimented with the use of nitrous oxide, or laughing gas, as an anesthetic. At 29, he became the first person to isolate sodium and potassium. He did this by passing an electric current through the fused hydroxides of these elements. He was also first to isolate barium, boron, calcium, magnesium, and strontium.

Davy was born in Penzance, England. In 1802, he became professor of chemistry at the Royal Institution in London. During his stay there, he took on the English chemist and physicist Michael Faraday as his assistant. Davy was knighted in 1812, and elected president of the Royal Society in 1820.   Seymour Harold Mauskopf

See also **Aluminum** (History); **Electric arc; Safety lamp; Faraday, Michael; Chlorine.**

Davy Jones, in sailors' folklore, is the wicked spirit who rules over the souls in the ocean deep. He is known chiefly through the proverbial term for the bottom of the sea, *Davy Jones's locker.* This is the final resting place of lost articles, sunken ships, and sailors who have drowned or been buried at sea. Thus, Davy Jones's locker has come to mean death. Some people have tried to trace Jones to Jonah, the Hebrew prophet who lived three days in the belly of a fish.   Octavia N. Cubbins

Davys, John. See **Davis, John.**

Dawes, Charles Gates (1865-1951), served as Vice President of the United States from 1925 to 1929 under President Calvin Coolidge. He shared the 1925 Nobel Peace Prize for arranging a plan for German reparations after World War I (1914-1918) (see **Dawes Plan**). Dawes entered national politics when he handled Republican Party finances in the 1896 campaign.

Dawes served on the Allied General Purchasing Board during World War I, and became the first director of the federal budget in 1921. He served as ambassador to Britain from 1929 to 1932. Dawes was chairman of the board of the City National Bank & Trust Company of Chicago from 1932 until his death. He was born in Marietta, Ohio.   Irving G. Williams

See also **Vice President of the U.S.** (picture).

Dawes Act. See Indian Territory; Indian, American (The fall of Indian America).

Dawes Plan was a program designed to help Germany pay its World War I *reparations* (payments for damages). The plan resulted from an international conference held in London in 1924. Charles G. Dawes, a banker who later became Vice President of the United States, led the committee that formed the plan.

In 1921, the Allies had set Germany's debt at $33 billion. The Dawes Plan did not reduce this total, but it did ease Germany's payment schedule. The plan also provided for an international loan to help Germany pay its debt. Germany accepted the plan in 1924. In 1929, the Dawes Plan was replaced by the Young Plan. But Germany defaulted on its payments during the Great Depression.   Robert H. Ferrell

See also **War debt; Ruhr** (History).

Dawson, George Mercer (1849-1901), was a Canadian geologist and the son of the geologist Sir John William Dawson. George Dawson joined the Geological Survey of Canada in 1875 and became its director in 1895. The Survey published much of his work, including the first detailed investigations of the geology and natural resources of British Columbia and the Yukon. Dawson also published geographical descriptions of Canada and was coauthor of a study of Indian languages. During the 1870's, he called attention to the rich beds of dinosaur fossils located in Alberta.

Dawson was born in Pictou, N.S. He attended McGill University in Montreal and the Royal School of Mines in London. Dawson, the capital of the Yukon Territory from 1898 to 1953, is named for him.   Dennis R. Dean

Dawson, Sir John William (1820-1899), was a Canadian geologist and educator. His major work was *Acadian Geology* (first published in 1855), a study of rock formations in Nova Scotia. The book vigorously opposed the theory of naturalist Louis Agassiz that a huge sheet of ice once covered large regions of the Northern Hemisphere. Dawson incorrectly believed that glaciers had covered only small areas of the earth.

Dawson also wrote about coal deposits and the fossils they contain. He discovered important early amphibians and reptiles. In addition, Dawson published on natural history, agriculture, evolution, fossils, and the relationship between science and religion.

Dawson was born in Pictou, N.S. He served as principal of McGill University in Montreal from 1855 to 1893. In 1882, Dawson became the first president of the Royal Society of Canada.   Dennis R. Dean

Day. While the earth travels through space around the sun, it also spins on its own axis. A *solar* day is the length of time that it takes the earth to turn around once with respect to the sun. We usually say *day* for the time when the sun is shining on our part of the earth, and *night* for the time when our part of the earth is dark, or turned away from the sun. But the night is really a part of the whole day. We also say *business day* sometimes to mean the hours of business in any one day.

Each day begins at midnight. In most countries, the day is divided into two parts of 12 hours each. The hours from midnight to noon are the a.m. (before noon) hours. Those from noon to midnight are the p.m. (afternoon) hours. The military services often designate the time of day on a 24-hour basis, such as 0100 for one o'clock in the morning, 1200 for noon, and 2400 for midnight.

The Babylonians began their day at sunrise. The ancient Jews began the day at sunset. The Egyptians and the Romans were the first to begin the day at midnight.

The length of daylight changes during the year in all parts of the world. It does so because the tilt of the earth's axis causes first one pole to slant toward the sun and then the other as the planet orbits the sun. The longest day in the Northern Hemisphere usually is June 21 and that in the Southern Hemisphere is December 21. Each of these days has 13 hours and 13 minutes of daylight at 20° latitude. The same days have 14 hours and 30 minutes of daylight at 40° latitude, and 18 hours 30 minutes at 60°. The shortest day in the Northern Hemisphere usually is December 21 and that in the Southern Hemisphere is June 21. Each has only 10 hours and 47 minutes of daylight at 20° latitude, 9 hours 9 minutes at 40°, and 5 hours and 30 minutes at 60°. The length of daylight changes very little during the year at the equator.

When the tilt of the earth's axis causes the North Pole to face the sun, the South Pole is continuously dark and the North Pole is always in daylight. As the North Pole is tilted away from the sun, it becomes dark there while the South Pole has constant daylight. These periods of darkness and daylight last about six months.

Astronomers use a day called a *sidereal day.* It is based on the period of the earth's rotation as measured by fixed stars. This day equals 23 hours, 56 minutes, and 4.09054 seconds of mean solar time.   James Jespersen

See also articles on the days of the week; **Daylight saving; Sidereal time; Time; Twilight.**

Day, Benjamin Henry (1810-1889), founded the first successful "penny paper," the *New York Sun,* in 1833. Day priced his little newspaper at one cent a copy, and sent newsboys onto the streets to sell it. This made the *Sun* a novelty in American journalism. Day also attracted readers by emphasizing the human and dramatic element in the news. By 1836, the *Sun* claimed a circulation of 30,000, the largest in the world at the time. Day sold the newspaper in 1837. Day was born in West Springfield, Mass.   John Eldridge Drewry

Day, Clarence (1874-1935), was an American writer. He became known chiefly for two books of humorous sketches about his family, *Life with Father* (1935) and *Life with Mother* (published in 1937, after his death). These books were made into the play *Life with Father* (1939), which became one of the most popular plays in American theater history.

In *Life with Father* and *Life with Mother,* Day describes the battle of wits between his stern but ineffective father and his slyly rebellious family. Day tells how his mother's illogical reasoning and cunning triumphed over his father in domestic matters. The works also provide an entertaining picture of upper-class life in New York City during the late 1800's. Day also wrote essays, stories, and reviews. Day's cartoonlike drawings added humor to his books.

Clarence Shepard Day, Jr., was born in New York City. He suffered from severe arthritis and was bedridden for much of his life.   Sarah Blacher Cohen

Day, Dorothy (1897-1980), was an American journalist and cofounder of the Catholic Workers, a Roman Catholic movement that supports social reform and opposes war. She founded the group with Peter Maurin, a

French-born philosopher and writer, in 1933. In that year, they began publishing a monthly newspaper, *The Catholic Worker,* to express the goals of the movement. The group works to defend the rights of working-class people and to promote peace, charity, and nonviolent social change.

Day was born in New York City. She joined the Socialist Party during her college years and later converted to Roman Catholicism. During the Great Depression of the 1930's, Day and Maurin established 33 houses of hospitality for poor and homeless people in cities throughout the nation. The houses provided food and shelter for about 5,000 people daily. Day also wrote for several publications, including the socialist newspaper *Call* and the Catholic journal *Commonweal.* Her autobiography, *The Long Loneliness,* was published in 1952.   Ed Marciniak

Marquette University Archives
Dorothy Day

Day-care center is a facility that cares for children outside the home. The parents can leave their children at such a center while they work. Most centers operate from 10 to 12 hours on weekdays and care for children who are less than 6 years old. They also care for school-age children before and after school and during school vacations.

Many programs for children in day-care centers offer social, emotional, educational, and nutritional benefits. For example, children may learn to play games cooperatively, work with clay, crayons, paints, paper, and paste, and go on field trips. Day-care centers try to increase the children's social abilities in a safe, stable, comfortable environment.

Many communities throughout the world have day-care centers. The centers include private homes in which an adult cares for 1 to 9 children. Larger centers look after as many as 150 youngsters. Day-care centers in the United States care for an estimated 6 million children daily, yet there is evidence of a demand for more facilities. Day-care has become essential to many families as more and more women join the work force. Some companies and universities maintain a center for the children of their employees.

The U.S. government operates many day-care centers for children of low-income families as part of the Head Start program. It also provides day-care service for some mothers who get welfare payments and are enrolled in a job-training program. Such programs teach them vocational skills so they eventually can support themselves and their children.   Edward Zigler

Day-Lewis, Cecil (1904-1972), was an Irish-born English poet and novelist. In 1968, Queen Elizabeth II appointed him poet laureate of England.

Day-Lewis was born in Ballintogher, near Sligo, and attended Oxford University in England. During the 1930's, along with W. H. Auden, Louis MacNeice, and Stephen Spender—all friends from Oxford—he gained fame by writing about modern political and social forces in a direct, informal, and often deliberately vulgar

manner. Much of Day-Lewis' later poetry deals with his Irish heritage and memories of his childhood in Ireland. Day-Lewis' *Collected Poems* were published in 1954. His novels include *The Friendly Tree* (1936) and *Starting Point* (1937). In 1952, he published a verse translation of Virgil's epic poem *Aeneid.* His autobiography, *The Buried Day,* was published in 1960. Day-Lewis wrote detective stories under the pen name of Nicolas Blake.

Michael Seidel

Day lily is a lily plant whose beautiful blossoms, usually yellow or orange, live only from sunrise to sunset. The flowers grow in loose clusters at the top of a leaf-

WORLD BOOK illustration by Lorraine Epstein

The lemon day lily, *above,* produces beautiful flowers in loose clusters at the top of a tall, leafless stalk.

less stalk 3 to 5 feet (91 to 150 centimeters) high. Six to twelve flowers make up a cluster, and two or three open each day. The plant's long smooth leaves, 1 to 2 feet (30 to 61 centimeters) long, spring from the fleshy, fibrous root. These hardy plants can be cultivated easily in rich soil and a moist, shady area. They bloom from June to September. The related *plantain lily* resembles the day lily, but it has white and blue flowers.

Scientific classification. Day lilies are in the lily family, Liliaceae. The tawny-orange day lily is *Hemerocallis fulva.* The fragrant, or lemon, day lily is *H. flava.*   Alfred C. Hottes

Day of Atonement. See Yom Kippur.

Dayaks. See Dyaks.

Dayan, *dy AHN,* **Moshe,** *MOY shuh* (1915-1981), was an Israeli military hero and political leader. He commanded the Israeli forces that won the Arab-Israeli war of 1956, and directed the Israeli victory in a six-day war against Egypt, Jordan, and Syria in June 1967. Dayan became Israel's foreign minister in 1977. He resigned in 1979 because he believed that the government was not doing

François Lochon, Gamma from Liaison
Moshe Dayan

enough to bring about peace with the Arabs. He was minister of defense from 1967 to 1974, minister of agriculture from 1959 to 1964, and chief of staff from 1953 to 1958.

In 1939, the British who ruled Palestine imprisoned Dayan for his work with the outlawed *Haganah,* a Jewish militia group. He was released in 1941 to fight with the British against the Vichy French. He was wounded during a battle in Lebanon, and lost his left eye. Dayan also fought in the first Arab-Israeli war of 1948. He was born in Deganiya, Palestine.   Ellis Rivkin

Daydream. See **Imagination.**

Daye, Stephen, also spelled *Day* (1594?-1668), with his son Matthew, set up and operated the first printing office in what is now the United States. The Dayes arrived in Cambridge, Mass., in 1638. Jose Glover, a British clergyman, financed their passage from England and supplied them with a press, type, and paper. The first book that came from the press was *The Bay Psalm Book* in 1640. Eleven copies of it survive. See **Bay Psalm Book.**

Stephen Daye was born in Cambridge, England, and first worked as a locksmith. He prospected for iron ore in New England. The first piece of print produced by the Daye press was *The Freeman's Oath.* It was issued in the late 1630's.   Ray Nash

Dayfly. See **Mayfly.**

Daylight saving is a plan in which clocks are set one hour ahead of standard time for a certain period. As a result, darkness comes one hour later than on standard time. The advantages of this plan include an additional daylight hour for recreation in the evening. Great Britain adopted daylight time as an economy measure during World War I. The United States adopted it in 1918. The U.S. Congress repealed the law in 1919, but many cities continued to use daylight time.

From 1942 to 1945, the United States observed daylight time year-round to reduce evening use of electricity. An act of Congress, which became effective in 1967, established daylight time from the last Sunday in April to the last Sunday in October. A state may remain on standard time if its legislature votes to do so. An amendment to the law in 1972 allows the states that lie in more than one time zone to use daylight time in one zone and not in the other zone. In an effort to conserve energy, the United States observed daylight time from January 6 to October 27 in 1974 and from February 23 to October 26 in 1975. In 1986, Congress passed a law that moved the beginning of daylight time from the last Sunday in April to the first Sunday of that month.

Donald B. Sullivan

See also **Standard time.**

Dayton (pop. 195,536; met. area pop. 942,083) is a leading manufacturing center in Ohio. It is called the *Birthplace of Aviation* because Orville and Wilbur Wright, who invented the first successful airplane, lived there. Dayton lies in the Miami River Valley in southwestern Ohio (see **Ohio** [political map]).

Settlers from Cincinnati founded Dayton in 1796. They chose the site because three major rivers—the Mad, the Great Miami, and the Stillwater—flow together there. This location makes Dayton a natural center of water transportation. The settlers named their town for Jonathan Dayton, the youngest signer of the Constitution of the United States.

Description. Dayton, the county seat of Montgomery County, covers 55 square miles (142 square kilometers). The Dayton metropolitan area occupies 1,692 square miles (4,382 square kilometers) and consists of Clark, Greene, Miami, and Montgomery counties.

Nearly a fourth of Dayton's workers are employed in its more than 1,000 manufacturing plants. Major products, in order of value, include nonelectrical machinery, rubber and plastic goods, transportation equipment, electrical equipment, and printed materials. Wright-Patterson Air Force Base, just outside Dayton, is its largest employer. NCR Corporation, the world's chief maker of cash registers, has headquarters in Dayton.

A major tourist attraction in the Dayton area is the U.S. Air Force Museum at the air base. The museum features more than 150 planes and missiles. Dayton also has an art institute and a museum of natural history. Educational institutions in the city include the University of Dayton and Wright State University. Dayton is also the home of the United Theological Seminary.

Government and history. Dayton has a council-manager form of government. The council is called the City Commission. Dayton's voters elect the five commission members to four-year terms. The commission hires a city manager to carry out its policies.

Miami and Shawnee Indians lived in the Dayton area before white settlers first arrived in 1796. During the 1800's, the city grew into a market and transportation center. Many factories were built in the 1800's, creating new jobs. The city's population rose from 38,678 in 1880 to 116,577 in 1910.

In March 1913, heavy rains caused the Mad, Great Miami, and Stillwater rivers to rise and flood the city. The flood killed more than 300 people and caused about $100 million damage. Later that year, the city adopted the council-manager form of government, with a professional city manager hired to handle the problems caused by the flood. The new system of government took effect in 1914, and Dayton became the first U.S. city with more than 100,000 people to adopt it.

The flood also led to the formation of the Miami Conservancy District in 1915. This agency constructed five dams upstream from Dayton between 1918 and 1922. Today, Dayton and the Miami River Valley have one of the world's most effective flood-control systems.

The Dayton Convention and Exhibition Center opened in the downtown Dave Hall Plaza in 1973. It includes an exhibition hall and a theater.   Steven L. Sidlo

Dayton, Jonathan (1760-1824), a New Jersey political leader, was the youngest signer of the Constitution of the United States. Dayton was 26 years old when he attended the Constitutional Convention in 1787. At the convention, Dayton spoke in favor of giving the states strong powers in the new nation.

Dayton was born in Elizabethtown, N.J. He graduated from the College of New Jersey at the age of 16. Dayton later became a captain in the Revolutionary War in America (1775-1783). After the war, Dayton pursued his interests in law, politics, and investment. He served as a U.S. representative from 1791 to 1799, and as Speaker of the House from 1795 to 1799. From 1799 to 1805, Dayton served as a U.S. senator.

Dayton was charged with high treason in 1807. He was believed to be involved in western political schemes with Aaron Burr, Vice President of the United States from 1801 to 1805. But Dayton was never tried, and he returned to state politics. Dayton took part in an unsuccessful attempt to buy land in the area of Dayton, Ohio, which is named for him.   Richard D. Brown

Dayton, William Lewis (1807-1864), was the Republican candidate for Vice President of the United States in 1856. He and presidential candidate John C. Frémont were defeated by Democratic candidates James Buchanan (President) and John C. Breckinridge. As a member of the Whig Party, Dayton served as a U.S. senator from New Jersey from 1842 to 1851. He was minister to France from 1861 to his death. Dayton was born in Basking Ridge, N.J.   Richard P. McCormick

Daytona Beach, Fla. (pop. 54,176; met. area pop. 258,762), a resort city, lies on the Atlantic Ocean and the Halifax River (see **Florida** [political map]). It has a hard-packed sand beach on which cars can be driven.

Harbors for yachts and other small boats lie in the Halifax River. Hotels, motels, and apartment buildings line its ocean front and riverbanks. The city offers many outdoor recreational facilities. Many championship automobile and motorcycle races are held at the Daytona International Speedway (see **Automobile racing** [picture]).

Daytona Beach's chief economic activities include tourism, fishing, and the manufacture of electronics components, cement, furniture, suntan products, and boats.

The city was founded in 1870, and incorporated as Daytona in 1876. In 1926, it consolidated with the peninsula towns of Daytona Beach and Seabreeze, and was chartered as Daytona Beach. The city is the home of Bethune-Cookman College and Embry-Riddle Aeronautical University. It has a council-manager form of government.   Tony Briggs

DC. See **Electric current** (Direct and alternating current).

DDT is an insecticide that has been widely used on crops for pest control. The three letters come from its chemical name, *d*ichloro-*d*iphenyl-*t*richloroethane. DDT is a grayish-white powder that, when used for pest control, is mixed with other substances.

DDT kills insects by affecting the nervous system. It differs from most other insecticides because it lasts a long time. DDT decays slowly and appears in plants and in animals that eat the plants. It also appears in human beings because it is absorbed into the body tissues from the animals and plants that people eat.

Large-scale application of DDT kills useful insects as well as harmful ones, and it may endanger other animal life, including birds and fish. It may also contaminate the food that people eat. In 1972, the United States Environmental Protection Agency banned almost all uses of DDT. But DDT is still used in other parts of the world.

DDT was first prepared as an insecticide by Paul Müller, a Swiss chemist, in 1939 (see **Müller, Paul H.**). It became well known during World War II (1939-1945), when the United States Army used it to fight an epidemic of typhus fever in Naples, Italy. The Army used DDT as a means of destroying body lice, which carry the disease.   Harold D. Coble

De facto segregation. See **Segregation** (De facto segregation).

De jure segregation. See **Segregation** (Jim Crow laws).

DEA. See **Drug Enforcement Administration.**

Deacon is one of the classes or ranks of Christian clergy. The term also refers to members of the laity assigned to help ministers and priests in such tasks as preaching and helping the sick and needy. The word *deacon* comes from *diakonos,* a Greek word that means *servant.* The office of deacon is called the *diaconate.*

In the Anglican, Eastern Orthodox, and Roman Catholic churches, the diaconate is mainly a stage of a year or less that precedes priesthood. These churches now also have deacons ordained to the diaconate as a lifetime vocation. These deacons assist in church work, especially if there is a shortage of priests. In many Protestant churches, deacons are lay members who help meet various needs of their congregation. The Anglican church and many Protestant churches have women members of the diaconate called *deaconesses.*   Robert S. Ellwood, Jr.

Dead-Mail Office. See **Post office** (Dead mail).

Dead reckoning. See **Navigation** (Dead reckoning); **Airplane** (Dead reckoning).

Dead Sea is a saltwater lake in southwestern Asia. Its shore, which lies about 1,310 feet (399 meters) below

Dead Sea

Area: 400 sq.mi. (1,040 km²)

Elevation: 1,310 ft. (399 m)
            below sea level

Deepest point: 1,312 ft. (400 m)

Area occupied by Israel since 1967

o   Historic site

——— Road   +—+—+ Railroad

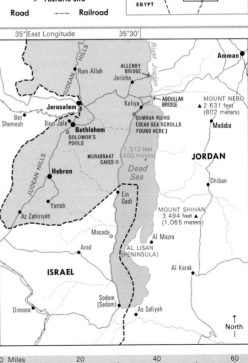

WORLD BOOK map

sea level, is the lowest place on the surface of the earth. The Dead Sea is the saltiest body of water in the world. It is about nine times as salty as the ocean. The lake lies at the mouth of the River Jordan and forms part of the border between Israel and Jordan.

The salty waters of the Dead Sea appear smooth and sparkling. Rocky and barren land surrounds the lake, and steep, brightly colored cliffs rise above its eastern and western banks. The lake is called the Dead Sea because few plants and no fish except brine shrimp live in its waters. In addition, little plant life grows in the salty soil around the Dead Sea.

The Dead Sea lies in the Ghor, a deep *fault* (break) in the earth's crust. The lake covers about 400 square miles (1,040 square kilometers). It is 11 miles (18 kilometers) wide at its widest point and about 50 miles (80 kilometers) long.

A peninsula called Al Lisan juts into the Dead Sea from its eastern shore. This peninsula divides the lake into a large northern basin and a smaller southern basin. The lake's deepest part is in the northern basin. In this area, the lake bottom lies 1,312 feet (400 meters) below the surface and about 2,622 feet (799 meters) below sea level.

Since the early 1900's, the water level of the Dead Sea has been slowly falling. The region receives less than 4 inches (100 millimeters) of rain annually. The River Jordan and several streams pour relatively fresh water into the lake. The fresh water mixes with salty water at the surface. However, extreme heat in the area causes this water to evaporate rapidly. As a result, the Dead Sea never grows less salty. The high salt content of the water provides great buoyancy, enabling swimmers to float with ease.

The Dead Sea contains large quantities of minerals, including common salt (sodium chloride), bromine, calcium chloride, and potassium chloride. An Israeli company called the Dead Sea Works extracts the minerals from the water for use in making such products as table salt, fertilizer, and drugs.

At the southern end of the Dead Sea, a network of dikes forms shallow pools that cover more than 40 square miles (100 square kilometers). These pools evaporate and leave behind mineral solids, which are then refined by the Dead Sea Works. Some people believe that bathing in the Dead Sea is healthful because of its high mineral content. Several health resorts in the area provide facilities for bathers.

The Dead Sea was probably formed millions of years ago when the Arabian Peninsula and the African continent shifted and formed the Great Rift Valley (see **Great Rift Valley**). The Dead Sea is mentioned in the Bible as the *Salt Sea* (Gen. 14:3). The ancient cities of Sodom and Gomorrah stood near the lake (see **Sodom and Gomorrah**).

Columns of salt rock on the shore of the Dead Sea may have been the basis for the Biblical story of Lot's wife (see **Lot**). Lot's wife was turned into a pillar of salt as punishment for disobedience to God (Gen. 19:26). Ancient manuscripts known as the *Dead Sea Scrolls* were found in caves near the Dead Sea. Most of these scrolls date from about 100 B.C. to about A.D. 70 (see **Dead Sea Scrolls**). John Kolars

See also **Israel** (Mining; picture); **Asia** (picture).

Dead Sea Scrolls are ancient manuscripts from Palestine. The scrolls were found in caves near the northwestern shore of the Dead Sea (see **Dead Sea** [map]). The first group of scrolls was discovered in 1947 in a cave in the *Wadi Qumran* (Qumran Valley). In the late 1940's and early 1950's, archaeologists and Bedouins found 10 more caves containing ancient writings.

The discoveries consist of scrolls and fragments of hundreds of documents. Most of the manuscripts are made of leather or papyrus, some written as early as 200 B.C. They were part of a library that many scholars believe belonged to a group of the Essenes, a Jewish sect (see **Essenes**). This group probably lived from about 150 B.C. to A.D. 68 in a settlement near the caves where the scrolls were found.

The Dead Sea Scrolls include all the books of the Old Testament except Esther. A few of the books are in nearly complete form. They are the oldest known manuscripts of any books of the Bible. The scrolls also include some fragments of the *Septuagint,* which is the first known Greek translation of the Old Testament, and parts of the Book of Job written in Aramaic. In addition, the scrolls include parts of some books of the Apocrypha written in Hebrew, Aramaic, and Greek.

The Dead Sea Scrolls also include writings of the Qumran community itself. The writings provide a rare picture of one group of Palestinian Jews about 2,000 years ago. Two manuscripts tell how the community organized its life. They indicate how one became a member and why. They also contain the rules that governed daily life in the community. Another manuscript gives directions for conducting the final battle that the community awaited, the War of the Sons of Light against the Sons of Darkness. Some texts record the prayers of the community. The Hymn scroll is a collection of hymns somewhat like the Book of Psalms. Other manuscripts are commentaries on the books of the Bible.

Caves near the western shore of the Dead Sea were excavated in the 1950's and 1960's. They also contained parts of Biblical and other documents. These texts date largely from a later historical period that preceded and included the second Jewish revolt against the Romans from A.D. 132 to 135. Terrance D. Callan

See also **Bible** (picture: The Dead Sea Scrolls).

Additional resources

Cross, Frank M., Jr. *The Ancient Library of Qumran and Modern Biblical Studies.* Rev. ed. Baker Book, 1980.
Vermès, Géza. *The Dead Sea Scrolls in English.* 3rd ed. Penguin, 1987.
Wilson, Edmund. *Israel and the Dead Sea Scrolls.* Farrar, 1978.

Deadbolt. See Lock (How door locks work; picture).
Deadly nightshade. See Belladonna.
Deafness is usually defined as the inability to hear and understand speech. There is no legal definition of deafness, however, and experts do not completely agree on when to use the term.

Hearing specialists generally distinguish between deafness and *hearing impairment.* People with impaired hearing can usually hear and understand at least some speech, especially when it is loud enough. However, they may be unable to hear some other sounds, such as doorbells or high musical notes. In addition, the quality of any sounds they do hear may be distorted.

Deaf children and children with severe hearing im-

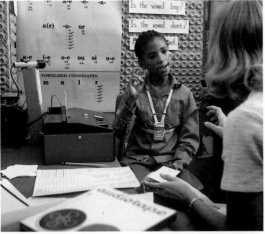

WORLD BOOK photo

Deaf students can be taught to communicate with the assistance of specially trained speech therapists. The therapist shown above is working with a youngster at a school for the deaf. The therapist is teaching the child how to make vowel sounds. The student is learning with the help of a powerful hearing aid.

pairments have tremendous difficulty learning to speak. Normally, children learn to speak by imitating the speech of others. But deaf children cannot hear speech. Many deaf people never learn to speak well enough to be understood. They use sign language and other special techniques to communicate.

Defective hearing is the most common physical disability in the United States. At least 15 million Americans have a noticeable hearing disorder, and about 2 million of these people are deaf.

Many deaf people earn college degrees, and most deaf men and women support themselves. Deafness need not hinder achievement in a wide variety of occupations. The famous German composer Ludwig van Beethoven wrote some of his finest music after he became deaf.

Types of hearing disorders

There are two major types of hearing disorders, *conductive disorders* and *sensorineural disorders.* Some people suffer a combination of these conditions called a *mixed hearing loss.*

Conductive disorders result from interference with the transmission of sound through the outer ear or the middle ear. Sound normally enters the outer ear and passes down the ear canal to the *tympanum* (eardrum). This thin membrane vibrates in response to sound and activates three tiny bones, called *ossicles,* in the middle ear. The ossicles transmit the vibrations to the inner ear. Most cases of conductive hearing loss are due to diseases that prevent the ossicles from functioning properly.

Sensorineural disorders involve some defect in the inner ear or the *auditory nerve,* which leads from the inner ear to the brain. The inner ear contains the actual organ of hearing, called the *organ of Corti.* This organ converts the vibrations transmitted to the inner ear into electrical impulses, which the auditory nerve carries to the brain. Damage to any of these delicate tissues can be caused by a wide variety of factors, and it cannot be repaired.

Causes of hearing disorders

Diseases cause most cases of conductive hearing loss. The leading cause of such disorders is *otitis media* (infection of the middle ear). In otitis media, a common cold or some other infection spreads to the middle ear and causes it to fill with fluid. The pressure of this fluid reduces the ability of the eardrum and ossicles to transmit vibrations. Otitis media occurs most commonly during early childhood and can lead to serious hearing loss if not treated promptly.

The other major cause of conductive hearing loss is *otosclerosis,* a disease of the ossicles. In this disorder, a bony growth forms around the base of the *stapes,* the bone next to the inner ear. The growth keeps the stapes from moving and so prevents it from passing on vibrations to the inner ear. Physicians believe otosclerosis is hereditary. It may begin to affect hearing at any age but is usually not detected until the teen-age years or later.

Some diseases can cause sensorineural disorders. *Meningitis* and other diseases accompanied by a high fever can severely damage the inner ear and the auditory nerve. A disorder of the inner ear called *Ménière's disease* also causes hearing loss, especially among people over 40. This disorder, which affects millions of people, often disturbs the sense of balance.

Birth defects account for many cases of sensorineural deafness or hearing impairment. Some people are born with inherited defects in their *auditory* (hearing) systems. Other inherited conditions may lead to hearing loss later in life.

A woman who has German measles during pregnancy may give birth to a child with a hearing defect. German measles, especially if it strikes during the first three months of pregnancy, may interfere with the development of the child's ears and nervous system.

A condition called *Rh disease* can cause a child to be born with a hearing disorder. The blood of some unborn children contains a substance called the *Rh factor,* which is not in the mother's blood. The mother's body may produce substances that attack the Rh factor and damage the baby's auditory system. See **Rh factor.**

Environmental factors, such as accidents and exposure to loud noise, can damage a person's hearing. A hard blow to the head can cause permanent hearing loss. Such injuries may affect the eardrum, the bones of the middle ear, or even parts of the inner ear. Exposure to loud noises can lead to serious hearing loss by damaging the organ of Corti. Extremely loud noises, such as explosions or gun blasts, can produce sudden deafness. In many of these cases, however, the victim eventually recovers much of the lost hearing.

Exposure to loud noise over a long period of time can gradually cause permanent loss of hearing. Many people who work in extremely noisy factories eventually suffer considerable hearing loss. Listening for long periods to the loud music played by many rock music bands can also damage hearing. In addition, many physicians believe that prolonged exposure to loud noises is a major cause of *tinnitus* (ringing in the ears). All loud sounds should be avoided if possible, or people should use ear plugs or other devices to muffle them.

Aging. Loss of hearing is one of the most common disorders among older people. In the United States, two-thirds of people over 65 years of age experience some loss of hearing. From 3 million to 6 million elderly Americans have hearing problems severe enough to seriously impair their ability to communicate. Hearing loss in old age, called *presbycusis,* may result from illness or exposure to noise earlier in life. Some hearing specialists believe aging may also cause changes in the auditory system or in the brain that reduce hearing ability.

Living with hearing disorders

Detection of hearing problems. Experts called *audiologists* are specially trained to detect and diagnose hearing problems. An audiologist uses an electric instrument called an audiometer to test a person's hearing in a soundproof room. There are two main types of audiometers: *pure-tone audiometers* and *speech audiometers.* Pure-tone audiometers use simple vibrations of various frequencies and intensities to measure hearing. Speech audiometers use spoken words or sentences.

Audiologists can also measure hearing ability without the conscious participation of the person being tested. They perform these tests by measuring alterations in brain waves and other bodily responses to sound. Such responses make it possible to test an infant's hearing. A child's hearing should be tested within a few days after birth if premature birth or some other condition suggests a possible hearing disorder. Many schools conduct hearing tests annually. Children found to have a hearing loss are referred to a clinic for complete testing.

Medical treatment. Physicians can restore hearing partially or completely in many cases of conductive hearing loss. Doctors use penicillin and other antibiotics to treat otitis media. In severe cases of this infection, a small incision is made in the eardrum to drain fluids that have collected in the middle ear.

Some conductive disorders are treated by surgery. For example, a ruptured eardrum can be repaired surgically. An operation called *stapes mobilization* can restore the ability of the middle ear to transmit sound in patients suffering from otosclerosis. This operation frees the stapes from the bony growth that has trapped it. In some cases, the surgeon completely removes the stapes and replaces it with an artificial device. Such an operation is called a *stapedectomy.*

Testing for hearing disorders is usually done by trained experts called *audiologists.* The audiologist shown above is using a device called an *audiometer* to test a child's hearing.

WORLD BOOK photo by Dan Miller

Most sensorineural disorders cannot be treated medically because damage to the inner ear or auditory nerve is permanent. However, a surgical operation called a *cochlear implant* can be helpful in some cases that involve damage to the cochlea, the part of the inner ear that contains the organ of Corti. In this operation, the surgeon implants a device that converts sounds into electric signals. These signals are picked up by the auditory nerve and transmitted to the brain. Such an operation may enable a profoundly deaf person to hear sounds and understand some speech. However, many physicians believe that the risks and cost of cochlear implants may outweigh their benefits.

Special aids and communication techniques. Many hearing-impaired people use electronic hearing aids to amplify sound. A hearing aid works much like a telephone. It converts sound to electrical energy, amplifies the energy, and then changes the energy back into sound. Hearing aids work for people with conductive disorders, but these devices may have only limited value in cases of sensorineural impairment. Amplification alone cannot make speech understandable to most victims of sensorineural disorders, but it may provide some improvement in hearing. An audiologist can recommend the proper hearing aid for a patient.

Many people who use a hearing aid also use *lip reading* and *manual communication* to help them communicate. Lip reading involves watching the movements of the speaker's lips. In manual communication, people communicate primarily with their hands. Some deaf people rely entirely on lip reading and manual communication because a hearing aid cannot help them.

Manual communication usually involves both *finger spelling,* in which each letter of the alphabet is represented by a different hand signal, and *sign languages,* in which hand signals stand for objects and ideas (see **Sign language** [picture]). The chief sign languages used in the United States are Signed English and American Sign Language (also called ASL or Ameslan). Deaf people use manual communication to converse with people who understand finger spelling and sign language. They also communicate by speaking and lip reading, or by writing. Some use a method called *cued speech,* in which hand signals and lip movements are combined to represent the sounds of spoken words. In addition, deaf people sometimes use professional interpreters who hear normally and know manual communication.

Some deaf people also use other aids in their daily lives. For example, the American Humane Association trains dogs to serve as "hearing ear dogs" for the deaf. These dogs alert their masters to various specific sounds, such as alarms, doorbells, and a baby's crying. Deaf individuals can make and receive telephone calls by using a special device called a *TDD* (Telecommunication Device for the Deaf) or *TTY.* This device is connected to a telephone by a special adapter. Both the caller and the person receiving the call must have a TDD. The message is typed in at the caller's TDD and typed out at the TDD on the receiving end.

Deaf people can enjoy TV and motion pictures if *captions* (printed dialogue) appear on the screen. The U.S. government sponsors Captioned Films for the Deaf, an agency that captions popular films and distributes them to deaf people. The Federal Communications Commis-

A special telecommunication device, called a *TDD* or *TTY,* enables a deaf person to make and receive telephone calls. The message appears on a screen or is printed on paper.

sion (FCC) has ordered television stations to caption weather warnings and all other emergency bulletins. The FCC also reserves part of the TV signal for the broadcasting of captions. In 1980, many television stations in the United States began *closed captioning* some of their programs over this part of the signal. The captions appear only on sets that have a special attachment.

Education and training. Many deaf children receive their elementary and high school education in special schools or in classes that have teachers specially trained to instruct them. Children with impaired hearing may attend special classes, or they may enroll in regular classes and obtain expert assistance when needed. Many deaf and hearing-impaired children have been placed in classrooms with children that have normal hearing. This practice is called *mainstreaming.*

Two main methods of training deaf children to communicate are the *oralist method* and *total communication.* In the oralist method, children are taught to speak and to lip-read. In total communication, they learn manual communication as well as speech and lip reading.

Deaf children can learn manual communication more easily than they can learn to speak. Supporters of the oralist method claim that children who learn manual communication will rely on it and never develop their potential for speech. However, supporters of total communication believe that deaf children should learn every means of communication—and use the methods that best meet their individual needs.

Teaching deaf children to speak requires special techniques. Normal speech development depends on hearing speech, but deaf children must use sight and touch to learn to speak. They watch their teacher make a vocal sound. They also touch the teacher's face and throat to feel the vibrations and the flow of breath involved in making the sound. Then they try to produce the same vibrations and breath effects themselves.

After deaf students graduate from high school, they may attend regular universities or go to special institutions of higher education. Gallaudet University, in Wash-

ington, D.C., is the world's only liberal arts college for deaf people. National Technical Institute for the Deaf, in Rochester, N.Y., also accepts only deaf students.

Treatment of hearing disorders and education of deaf students enable the deaf to lead fulfilling lives. Deaf people can do almost any kind of work. But some have difficulty finding jobs suited to their education and training. Such organizations as the Alexander Graham Bell Association for the Deaf, the Convention of American Instructors of the Deaf, and the National Association of the Deaf promote the education, training, and employment of deaf people.　　John B. Christiansen

Related articles in *World Book* include:

Audiology	Gallaudet
Bell, Alexander G.	Gallaudet University
Bridgman, Laura Dewey	Handicapped
Dog guide	Hearing aid
Ear	Keller, Helen A.
Education (picture: Special education programs)	Lip reading
	Sign language

Additional resources

Benderly, Beryl L. *Dancing Without Music: Deafness in America.* Doubleday, 1980.

Lane, Harlan L. *When the Mind Hears: A History of the Deaf.* Random House, 1984.

Levine, Edna S. *Lisa and Her Soundless World.* Human Sciences Press, 1984. For younger readers.

Ogden, Paul W., and Lipsett, Suzanne. *The Silent Garden: Understanding the Hearing-Impaired Child.* St. Martin's, 1982.

Dean, Dizzy (1911-1974), was one of baseball's greatest pitchers and most colorful personalities. He pitched for the St. Louis Cardinals and the Chicago Cubs from 1932 to 1941. He won 30 games in 1934. He and his brother Paul (Daffy) each pitched two victories for St. Louis over the Detroit Tigers in the 1934 World Series. St. Louis won this series, four games to three.

Dean loved to brag about his great pitching ability. One day in 1934, he walked into the Brooklyn Dodgers' clubhouse and told each Brooklyn player exactly how he would pitch to him. He beat Brooklyn that day, 13 to 0. Dean developed a sore arm in 1937 and was traded to the Chicago Cubs in 1938. His arm never returned to normal and early in the 1941 season he retired from baseball to become a sports announcer. Dean returned to baseball for one game in 1947, pitching four scoreless innings for the St. Louis Browns.

Dean was born in Lucas, Ark. His real name was Jay Hanna Dean, but he also used the name of Jerome Herman Dean. He quit school after the second grade. He picked cotton until he was 16 years old, and then served in the Army for three years. Dean became a professional baseball player in 1930.

As a radio and television sports announcer, Dean became famous for his quaint announcing style. He often used such expressions as "The runner *slud* into third," and "He *throwed* the ball." Dean was elected to the National Baseball Hall of Fame in 1953.　　Dave Nightingale

Dean, James (1931-1955), was an American motion-picture actor. He became famous for his intense, brooding portrayals of discontented, rebellious young men. Dean starred in only three films—*East of Eden* (1955), *Rebel Without a Cause* (1955), and *Giant* (1956). He died in an automobile accident at the age of 24. After his death, he became an idol to young people in many parts of the world. They considered Dean a symbol of their frustrations because of the characters he portrayed.

James Byron Dean was born in Marion, Ind. He studied acting at the University of California at Los Angeles and at the Actors Studio in New York City. Dean acted in TV dramas before beginning his film career. He also was in two Broadway plays, *See the Jaguar* (1952) and *The Immoralist* (1954).

Roger Ebert

Dennis Stock, Magnum

James Dean

Dean, John W., III. See **Watergate** (The break-in and cover-up).

Deane, Silas (1737-1789), was an early American diplomat. He helped gain vital French aid for the American Colonies during the Revolutionary War (1775-1783).

In 1776, the Continental Congress sent Deane to France to purchase military supplies, arrange trade agreements, and hire soldiers. Congress ordered him to return in 1777 to face charges of disloyalty and financial misconduct. Arthur Lee, one of Deane's fellow diplomats, had accused him of taking payment for supplies that the French intended as gifts. The charges were never proved. Deane became bitter over what he considered his country's ingratitude. He returned to France in 1780 and lived in Europe as an exile until his death.

Deane was born in Groton, Conn. He graduated from Yale College in 1758 and began practicing law in 1761. He represented Connecticut in the first and second Continental Congresses. William Morgan Fowler, Jr.

De Angeli, *dee AN juh lih,* **Marguerite Lofft** (1889-1987), was an American author and illustrator of children's books. She was best known for her stories about minority groups. *Thee Hannah!* (1940) is about a Quaker girl, and *Yonie Wondernose* (1944) tells the story of a Pennsylvania Dutch boy. *Bright April* (1946) describes a black girl's experience with racial prejudice. De Angeli won the 1950 Newbery Medal for *The Door in the Wall* (1949), a story of England in the 1300's. She collected and illustrated a *Book of Nursery and Mother Goose Rhymes* (1954). Her poems were published in *Friendship and Other Poems* (1981). De Angeli was born in Lapeer, Mich. Her first book, *Ted and Nina Go to the Grocery Store,* was published in 1935. Jill P. May

Dearborn, Mich. (pop. 90,660), is the home of the headquarters and main plants of the Ford Motor Company. In addition to automobiles made by Ford, the city's chief products include steel and heating and air-conditioning equipment. Dearborn lies along the Rouge River, on the southwestern outskirts of Detroit. For location, see **Michigan** (political map).

Dearborn's Greenfield Village, a group of historical buildings and landmarks, and the Henry Ford Museum attract large numbers of visitors to the city (see **Greenfield Village**). Fair Lane, Henry Ford's estate, is also in Dearborn. It was given to the University of Michigan in 1956. Dearborn is the home of a campus of the University of Michigan, Henry Ford Community College, and the Dearborn Historical Museum. The city maintains Camp Dearborn, a 626-acre (253-hectare) recreational fa-

cility 35 miles (56 kilometers) to the northeast.

Wyandot Indians were the first inhabitants of the area that is now Dearborn. White pioneers settled there in 1795. The village of Dearborn was formed in 1893. The village was incorporated as a city in 1927.

Between 1917 and 1919, Henry Ford built his main automobile plant in Fordson, adjacent to Dearborn. Dearborn annexed Fordson in 1929. Dearborn has a mayor-council form of government. William C. Tremblay

See also **Ford, Henry; Ford Motor Company.**

Dearborn, Henry (1751-1829), was an American soldier and political leader. Fort Dearborn in Chicago was named for him (see **Fort Dearborn**). He was born in North Hampton, N.H., and served as a captain in the Revolutionary War. He fought at Bunker Hill, went with Benedict Arnold to Quebec, and was serving as a major with General Horatio Gates when the British general John Burgoyne surrendered. Dearborn served twice in the U.S. Congress and was secretary of war in Thomas Jefferson's Cabinet from 1801 to 1809. He was a major general during the War of 1812 and served as minister to Portugal from 1822 to 1824. Richard N. Current

Death is the end of life. Every living thing eventually dies, but human beings are probably the only creatures that can imagine their own deaths. Most people fear death and try to avoid thinking about it. But the awareness of death has been one of the chief forces in the development of civilization. Throughout history, people have continually sought new medical knowledge with which to delay death. Philosophers and religious leaders have tried to understand the meaning of death. Some scholars believe that much human progress results from people's efforts to overcome death and gain immortality through lasting achievements.

Medical aspects of death. Scientists recognize three types of death that occur during the life of all organisms except those consisting of only one cell. These types are *necrobiosis, necrosis,* and *somatic death.*

Necrobiosis is the continual death and replacement of individual cells through life. Except for nerve cells, all the cells of an organism are constantly being replaced. For example, new skin cells form under the surface as the old ones die and flake off.

Necrosis is the death of tissues or even entire organs. During a heart attack, for example, a blood clot cuts off the circulation of the blood to part of the heart. The affected part dies, but the organism continues to live unless the damage has been severe.

Somatic death is the end of all life processes in an organism. A person whose heart and lungs stop working may be considered *clinically dead,* but somatic death may not yet have occurred. The individual cells of the body continue to live for several minutes. The person may be revived if the heart and lungs start working again and give the cells the oxygen they need. After about three minutes, the brain cells—which are most sensitive to a lack of oxygen—begin to die. The person is soon dead beyond any possibility of revival. Gradually, other cells of the body also die. The last ones to perish are the bone, hair, and skin cells, which may continue to grow for several hours.

Many changes take place after death. The temperature of the body slowly drops to that of its surroundings. The muscles develop a stiffening called *rigor mortis.*

The blood, which no longer circulates, settles and produces reddish-purple discolorations in the lowest areas of the body. Eventually, bacteria and other tiny organisms grow on the corpse and cause it to decay.

Defining death. Traditionally, a person whose breathing and heartbeat had stopped was considered dead. Today, however, physicians can prolong the functioning of the lungs and heart by artificial means. Various machines can produce breathing and a heartbeat even in a patient whose brain has been destroyed. These new medical procedures led many people to call for a new definition of death. The Uniform Determination of Death Act, which was drafted in 1980, has been adopted by most states of the United States. Under this act, a person is considered dead when breathing and the heartbeat irreversibly stop, or when brain function totally and irreversibly stops, a condition also called *brain death.* The act permits physicians to use reasonable medical standards in applying this legal definition.

The brain-death definition of death raises important medical, legal, and moral questions. People who support this definition argue that it benefits society by making vital organs available for transplants. In most cases, the organs of a person who is dead under the traditional definition cannot be transplanted. But many vital organs remain alive and functioning in an individual whose body processes are maintained by machine, even though brain activity has stopped. Physicians can remove these organs and use them in transplants—if brain death is accepted as a legal definition.

Critics of the brain-death definition point out that there are many unanswered questions regarding this concept. Such questions include: Who should decide which definition of death to use? When has brain death reached the point where it cannot be reversed?

The right to die. Many people believe that physicians should use every means to maintain a person's life as long as possible. But others argue that dying patients and their physicians have the right to choose whether life-maintaining treatments should be continued. Some people also feel that this decision should be left to the family and physician if the patient is no longer capable of expressing his or her wishes. People who hold these attitudes contend that physicians are not obligated to provide treatment that would only temporarily extend the life of a hopelessly ill or injured person. In 1990, the U.S. Supreme Court ruled that patients who have clearly made their wishes known have a constitutional right to discontinue life-sustaining medical treatment.

Some people draw up a document popularly called a *living will.* Such a document directs physicians to discontinue any treatment that serves no purpose except to delay the individual's inevitable death. Most states have laws that recognize the validity of living wills under certain circumstances.

Some people believe that hopelessly ill patients should not only have the right to refuse treatment, but also to be put painlessly to death if they desire. They contend that each person has the right to control his or her life and to determine the time of his or her death. Others maintain that this right should be extended to the family of dying patients who are no longer capable of expressing their own desires. In these cases, they argue, the family and physician should be permitted to pain-lessly end the patient's suffering. Putting hopelessly ill persons to death—with or without their requesting it—is called *euthanasia,* or *mercy killing.* Euthanasia is illegal in the United States, Canada, and most other nations.

Attitudes about death have changed during the 1900's. About 1900, the majority of deaths were those of children who died of diphtheria, pneumonia, or some other infectious disease. Most people died at home, surrounded by their families. People were familiar with dying and viewed death as a natural part of life.

Today, most people in industrial nations die from heart disease, cancer, stroke, or other diseases associated with aging. As a result, about 95 per cent of all children reach adulthood without experiencing a death in their family. In addition, most deaths now occur in hospitals. Therefore, many young people have never been present at someone's death. This lack of experience makes it difficult for many people to talk openly about death or to be with a dying person.

The increasing number of deaths among the elderly has also affected attitudes about death. Many people have come to view the elderly as having "lived out their lives," and as no longer deeply involved in the lives of their families and communities. Such people may experience the death of an elderly person as a minor social and emotional event. The death of a child or a young adult, on the other hand, is considered unexpected and unjust. Such a death generally has deep and longlasting emotional consequences.

Traditionally, people have confronted death within a set of religious beliefs that gave it meaning apart from the natural world. Mourning rites and funeral customs have helped them deal with the grief that accompanies the loss of a loved one. Many people still find comfort in these beliefs and customs. But a growing number of people now view death more in terms of a biological process. On the other hand, some people find death a threatening prospect and choose to deny it. Still others regard death as the greatest possible challenge. They seek to delay the aging process or to defeat death itself through medical science or by other means.

During the mid-1900's, many psychologists and other people became interested in the special emotional needs of dying people. For example, studies showed that friends, relatives, and even doctors and nurses avoided dying patients because of their own feelings about death. As a result, many critically ill patients suffered greatly from loneliness. To help solve this problem, a number of medical schools, hospitals, colleges, and churches began to give courses in death education. Such courses were designed to help people become more knowledgeable about death and more responsive to the needs of the dying.   Robert Fulton

See **Funeral customs** and its list of *Related articles.* See also **Euthanasia; Hospice; Immortality; Reincarnation; Resurrection.**

Additional resources

Death and Dying. Ed. by Janelle Rohr. Greenhaven, 1987. Suitable for younger readers. Presents controversial viewpoints.
DeSpelder, Lynne A., and Strickland, A. L. *The Last Dance: Encountering Death and Dying.* 2nd ed. Mayfield Pub. Co., 1987.

Death penalty. See Capital punishment.
Death rate. See Birth and death rates.

Death Valley lies chiefly in east-central California. A small part of it extends into Nevada. A group of pioneers named the valley for its desolate desert environment after they crossed it in 1849. It became part of the Death Valley National Monument, set up in 1933.

Death Valley is a deep trough, about 130 miles (209 kilometers) long and from 6 to 14 miles (10 to 23 kilometers) wide. The lowest elevation in the Western Hemisphere is near Badwater in Death Valley. It lies 282 feet (86 meters) below sea level. The Panamint Mountains stand west of the valley. Telescope Peak in the Panamint range is 11,049 feet (3,368 meters) high. The Amargosa Range, composed of the Grapevine, Funeral, and Black mountains, rises to the east.

The valley is a *graben*—a block in the earth's surface, dropped down by faults that form its east and west walls. *Faults* occur when the earth's crust breaks and slips into various positions. Erosion of the steep cliffs has formed beautiful canyons. In the northern part of the valley is Ubehebe Crater, a small volcano on the west side fault. Flows of lava issue from the faults in the southern part of Death Valley.

During glacial times, the climate was moister, and a large lake occupied Death Valley. Today, rainfall averages about 2 inches (5 centimeters) a year there. The highest temperature ever recorded in the United States, 134° F. (57° C), was reported there on July 10, 1913. Summer temperatures of 125° F. (52° C) are common. The valley's geological attractions and warm winter sunshine have made it a popular winter-resort area. Plants include the creosote bush, desert holly, and mesquite. Wildlife includes bobcats, coyotes, foxes, rats, rabbits, reptiles, and squirrels.

Borax deposits were discovered in Death Valley in 1873. Actual mining began in the early 1880's, and famous 20-mule teams hauled the borax out of the valley. Prospectors also discovered copper, gold, lead, and silver in the nearby mountains. Mining towns sprang up around Death Valley, with such colorful names as Bullfrog, Greenwater, Rhyolite, and Skidoo. The towns died when the ores were exhausted. Today only cluttered debris remains.   John Edwin Coffman

See also **United States** (picture).

Death Valley National Monument is in California and Nevada. It is a desert of scenic, scientific, and historical interest. The valley contains the lowest point in the Western Hemisphere (282 feet, or 86 meters, below sea level) near Badwater in California. The monument was established in 1933. For the area of the monument, see **National Park System** (table: National monuments). See also **Death Valley** (map).

Critically reviewed by the National Park Service

Death's-head moth is a large moth with a thick, hairy body. Many superstitions arose because of the skull-like pattern on its body. The death's-head moth is a type of *hawk moth* (see **Hawk moth**). The moth lives in Africa and southern Europe, and adults often migrate to northern Europe. They enter beehives to eat honey and may squeak loudly when disturbed. The caterpillar is bright yellow with violet stripes and blue spots. It feeds on the leaves of potato plants.

Scientific classification. The death's-head moth belongs to the family Sphingidae. It is *Acherontia atropos*.

Bernd Heinrich

Deathwatch is a name given to several kinds of small brownish beetles that communicate by knocking their heads against wood. This odd action produces a peculiar ticking or rapping sound. Superstitious people believe that the rapping, heard in the quiet of the night, foretells death in the house. Deathwatch beetles burrow into furniture and woodwork and are often very destructive. The *drugstore beetle,* which feasts on drugs and spices stored in shops, is sometimes called the deathwatch. But it belongs to a different beetle family.

Scientific classification. Deathwatch beetles belong to the family Anobiidae.   David J. Shetlar

DeBakey, Michael Ellis (1908-   ), an American surgeon, won fame for his work with the heart and for his techniques to replace damaged blood vessels. He pioneered in giving a patient an *assisting heart.* This machine is inserted into the chest. It helps a weak heart pump blood until either the heart recovers or surgeons transplant another person's heart. DeBakey has also worked on the development of an artificial heart.

DeBakey became the first person to surgically repair an *aneurysm,* a condition in which the wall of a blood vessel weakens and balloons out. He replaced the weakened part of the vessel with another blood vessel (see **Aneurysm**). He later developed artificial blood vessels made of Dacron.

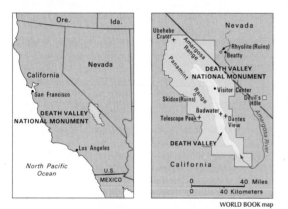

Location of Death Valley

WORLD BOOK map

Keith Gunnar, Bruce Coleman Inc.

Death Valley is in east-central California. The valley's Badwater area, *above,* lies at the foot of the Panamint Mountains.

DeBakey was born in Lake Charles, La., and earned an M.D. from Tulane University in 1932. He became head of the Department of Surgery at Baylor University in 1948 and president of the Baylor College of Medicine in 1969.

Isaac Asimov

Debate is a series of formal spoken arguments for and against a definite *proposition*. A proposition is a carefully worded statement that makes clear the positions of both the affirmative and negative sides.

Debate differs from discussion. *Discussion* is the process by which a problem is recognized, defined, and investigated, and then solutions are explored. *Debate* is the process that evaluates a probable truth, a judgment, a causal relationship, or a single solution.

Formal debate. In formal debating, the same number of people speak for each side. They have the opportunity to reply directly to opposing speakers. Affirmative and negative speakers usually alternate, and all the speeches are limited in time. In informal (as in conversation) and in legislative debating, though there is the same opportunity to reply to opposing speakers, the speeches are not necessarily limited in time. There may be no attempt to alternate opposing speakers, and the number of speakers on each side may be unequal.

Propositions. Subjects for debates are expressed in the form of propositions. Propositions should be:

(1) Appropriate to the knowledge, experience, and interests of both speakers and audience.

(2) Debatable—that is, not obviously true or false. The statements should involve an honest difference of opinion, with arguments and evidence on both sides.

(3) Phrased in the affirmative. Positive statements prevent confusion by making the issue clear-cut.

(4) Restricted to set forth only one idea. This policy keeps the debate within narrow limits.

(5) Worded clearly. The words should be ones that can be defined exactly, so the debate does not become a mere quibble over the meaning of words.

There are four kinds of propositions: (1) propositions of fact, (2) propositions of value, (3) propositions of explanation, and (4) propositions of policy.

A proposition of fact is a statement to be proven true or false as the evidence is gathered. For example, the proposition, "Resolved, that Main High School will defeat East High School in varsity football next week," is neither true nor false at the present time. It may be argued vigorously by comparing the players at each position, the coaches' skills, scores against common opponents, team records, and current injuries. After the game, the proposition is no longer debatable. It is a fact that Main High School either won, lost, or tied. Propositions of fact are usually resolved in debate by awarding the decision to the team that presents the best evidence and that establishes probable truth. A proposition of fact is not a fact. *Facts* are truths proved only through such means as experiment, testing, measurement, or scientific observation.

A proposition of value contains a relative term that makes a value judgment. For example, in the proposition, "Resolved, that John Jones did a good job as student council president," the word *good* cannot be precisely defined. The meaning of *good* depends on the value that is given to it. It may have several meanings: (1) John was kind to council members, (2) John was politi-

cally successful, (3) John accomplished his agenda, (4) John knew parliamentary procedure, or (5) John was moral. In order to debate a value proposition, debaters must define the value term, convince the audience that this definition is reasonable, and apply it to the subject of the proposition (in this example, John).

A proposition of explanation attempts to determine whether a cause and effect relationship exists between two actions or events. For example, the proposition, "Resolved, that oily rags left in the attic caused the fire," asks whether the rags were a necessary and sufficient factor to produce the fire.

A proposition of policy evaluates potential courses of action. It answers the question, "should we change?" A proposition of policy may argue for a new program: "Resolved, that the federal government should finance elementary and secondary public education in the United States." A proposition of policy may want to end a policy: "Resolved, that trial by jury should be eliminated in civil cases." It may also want to substitute one policy for another: "Resolved, that tackle football should be replaced by touch football."

Analysis. After a subject has been selected and the proposition carefully worded, the next step is analysis of the proposition by both debating teams. Analysis of the proposition begins with a broad understanding of it. As a team member, you should know as much about your opponents' case as you know about your own side. Good debaters study the origin and history of a proposition, define its terms, and survey carefully all the arguments and evidence for and against it. Policy analysis usually follows one of two outlines:

Does a new condition exist in the present system?
Is that condition harmful to people or nations?
Is the harm significant in scope and/or intensity?
Is the present policy the cause of the harm?
Can (or will) the present policy solve the harm?
Will the proposition solve the harm?
Will the proposition produce new harms?

or

Will the proposition create a new situation?
Is this new situation advantageous?
Are the advantages significant or widespread?
Are the advantages unique only to the proposition?
Will disadvantages result from adopting the proposition?

The case. Both affirmative and negative sides need to prepare a *case*. A case is a group of arguments. Two common affirmative cases are the *need case* and the *comparative-advantages case*. The need case attempts to show that a significant harm exists, that the present policy either has caused the harm or cannot solve it, and that the action proposed will solve the harm. The comparative-advantages case argues that there is an opportunity for improvement. The affirmative side argues that the action urged in the proposition will yield significant advantages that the present policy cannot produce. The negative approach to the affirmative case may defend the present policy as being good. The negative side may also offer a counterplan that rejects both the present policy and the proposition, and presents an alternative to both.

The plan. The affirmative side needs to present a workable procedure to put the proposition into effect. Such a procedure usually focuses on four steps: (1) the goal, (2) administration, (3) funding, and (4) enforcement. The negative side usually will raise one or more objections to the plan. Examples are: "The plan will not work." "The plan will not solve the harm." "The plan will create new harms."

The issues. The chief points of difference between the affirmative and the negative are the *main issues.* These may have divisions called *subordinate issues.* There must be a clash of opinion on both the main and the subordinate issues. A good way to help find the issues is to list the opposing arguments in parallel columns. In the subject, "Resolved, that the United States should abolish the Electoral College and adopt a system that would provide for the election of the President by direct popular vote," a listing of opposing arguments might lead to the following two main issues and six subordinate issues:

I. **Would electing the President by direct popular vote correct flaws in the present system?**
   A. Would it be more democratic and give each voter an equal voice in choosing the winner?
   B. Would it assure that the candidate with the most votes is elected?
   C. If no candidate receives a majority of the votes, would this system reduce the chances of political deals and an electoral crisis?

II. **Would electing the President by direct popular vote have disadvantages?**
   A. Would it weaken the power of the small states and threaten the federal system?
   B. Would it encourage the formation of small political parties and make it difficult for the winner to receive a majority of the votes?
   C. Would it reduce the power of minority groups to influence an election?

The evidence. After the issues have been determined, the next step for the debaters is to find the evidence that will prove the issue true or false. Evidence can be in the form of *factual evidence* or *testimonial evidence.* Factual evidence consists of current and historical examples (true incidents), statistics, physical evidence, and facts. Testimonial evidence consists of opinions of experts in the subject being debated. To evaluate testimonial evidence, the debater should ask: "Is this authority an expert and, thus, in a position to know the truth?" and "Is this authority biased, and, thus, in any position to tell the truth?"

Rebuttal. Next, the debaters must select the arguments and evidence of their opponents that they believe can be successfully attacked. Finally, they must prepare their own arguments and evidence that will be used in the attack.

Format. In the *traditional* form of debate, there are two speakers on each side, each of whom makes both a *constructive* speech and a *rebuttal* speech. The speaking order is:

  Constructive speeches (10 minutes each)
    1. First affirmative
    2. First negative
    3. Second affirmative
    4. Second negative
  Rebuttal speeches (5 minutes each)
    1. First negative
    2. First affirmative
    3. Second negative
    4. Second affirmative

Another type of debate is the *cross-examination* form,

which was developed at the University of Oregon. Each constructive speaker is cross-examined by an opposing speaker. The speaking order is:

  Constructive speeches (8 minutes) and
  Cross-examinations (3 minutes)
    1. First affirmative
    2. Cross-examination by second negative
    3. First negative
    4. Cross-examination by first affirmative
    5. Second affirmative
    6. Cross-examination by first negative
    7. Second negative
    8. Cross-examination by second affirmative
  Rebuttal speeches (4 minutes)
    1. First negative
    2. First affirmative
    3. Second negative
    4. Second affirmative

The decision. If a decision is to be given, one or more judges listen to all the speakers. Each judge decides which team made the most convincing argument and votes for that team. The team with the most votes wins.

Competitive debate. The National Forensic League sponsors debate competitions for high school students. The Cross-Examination Debate Association and the National Debate Tournament Committee of the American Forensic Association sponsor college debate tournaments.   James M. Copeland

See also **Lincoln, Abraham** (picture: The Lincoln-Douglas debates); **Logic; Oratory; Public speaking.**

Debenture bond. See Bond.

Deborah was a Biblical prophetess of Israel in the period of the Judges, the 1100's B.C. She was the wife of Lapidoth. She acted as an adviser to her people, and was a judge in their disputes. Deborah was admired for her wisdom, and she rose to a position of leadership among her people.

When she heard of the cruel treatment her people had received from the Canaanites, Deborah summoned Barak, the Israelite leader. Together they worked out a plan of action for the army of Israel. They hoped to defeat the Canaanite army under Sisera. They fought near Mount Tabor, on the plain of Esdraelon. A rainstorm aided Israel, turning the plain into mud and trapping the enemy chariots. Sisera fled on foot and was later murdered in his sleep. The victory was important in Israel's struggle with the Canaanites. One of the most notable victory odes of the Bible is the *Song of Deborah* in Judges 5.   Gary G. Porton

Debrecen, *DEH breh TSEHN* (pop. 211,823), is a commercial and industrial city in eastern Hungary. It serves as a market for nearby farming areas. For location, see **Hungary** (political map). Debrecen became a major center of Protestantism in the 1500's and was called the *Calvinist Rome.* Lajos Kossuth proclaimed Hungarian independence there in 1849. In 1944, during World War II, Hungary's provisional government met in Debrecen. Places of interest in the city include an art gallery, a museum, and a university.   Thomas Sakmyster

De Broglie, *duh braw GLEE,* **Louis Victor,** *lwee veek TAWR* (1892-1987), was a French physicist who won the 1929 Nobel Prize in physics for his theory of the wave nature of electrons. This theory became one of the foundations of *quantum mechanics,* a field of physics.

Since the early 1800's, physicists had believed that

light consisted of waves of energy. They also thought that all matter was composed of tiny particles that combined in various ways to make up the material world. In 1900, Max Planck, a German physicist, showed that light behaves as if it consists of particles. He called these particles *quanta.* In 1924, De Broglie proposed that, under certain conditions, electrons have characteristics of both particles and waves, as do quanta of light. His theory was later verified by experiments.

De Broglie was born in Dieppe, France, and studied at the Sorbonne. He joined the faculty of the University of Paris in 1926.　　Richard L. Hilt

See also **Quantum mechanics; Physics** (Quantum theory); **Planck, Max K. E. L.**

Debs, Eugene Victor (1855-1926), was a colorful and eloquent spokesman for the American labor movement and for socialism. He formed the American Railway Union (ARU) in 1893 as an industrial union for all railroad workers regardless of their craft. The ARU ordered its members not to move Pullman cars in 1894, in support of a strike by the workers making Pullman cars. President Grover Cleveland used federal troops to break the strike, charging that it interfered with the mails. Debs went to prison for six months when he refused to comply with a federal court injunction. He came out of jail a confirmed socialist.

Debs made a speech condemning war during World War I. He was convicted under the Espionage Law in 1918 and went to prison the next year, on a 10-year sentence. President Warren G. Harding commuted his sentence in 1921.

Debs ran for the presidency as a socialist candidate five times. He was the nominee of the Social Democratic Party in 1900, and of the Socialist Party in 1904, 1908, 1912, and 1920. Debs ran his 1920 campaign while still in prison, and received nearly 1 million votes. He wrote *Walls and Bars,* a book dealing with prison problems.

Debs was born in Terre Haute, Ind., and went to work in the railroad shops at the age of 15. Later he became a locomotive fireman, and joined the Brotherhood of Locomotive Firemen (later the Brotherhood of Locomotive Firemen and Enginemen). He was national secretary and treasurer of the group from 1880 to 1893. Debs served in the Indiana legislature in 1885.　　Jack Barbash

Additional resources

Ginger, Raymond. *The Bending Cross: A Biography of Eugene Victor Debs.* Russell & Russell, 1969. First published in 1949.
Salvatore, Nick. *Eugene V. Debs: Citizen and Socialist.* Univ. of Illinois Press, 1982.

Debt is anything owed, especially a sum of money that one person owes to another. A person who owes a debt is called a *debtor,* and the one to whom it is owed is the *creditor.* If the debtor is unwilling or unable to pay the debt, the creditor may bring suit to recover the money. If the court finds that the debt is owed, and if the debtor fails to pay, the creditor may appeal to the sheriff for an *execution* of judgment. This gives the creditor the right to seize enough property of the debtor to pay the debt and the costs of the process. But there are exceptions as to what may be seized. This law varies in different states, provinces, and territories.

In a special type of debt called *secured debt,* the debtor promises that, if the debt is not paid on time, the

creditor may seize specified property from the debtor before a suit is brought. If the value of the property is not enough to pay the entire debt, the creditor may then sue the debtor for the remaining amount. Most people purchase such expensive items as homes and automobiles through secured debt agreements.

Time limits on collection of debts. The courts ordinarily state that debtors should pay their debts, even though the creditor does not demand payment. But if the creditor makes no effort to collect the money within a certain number of years, the debt becomes *barred* by a *statute of limitations* and can no longer be collected.

Penalties for debts. In ancient times, a debtor was handed over to the mercy of his creditors to become a slave. This was true in Greece and Rome, among the Israelites, and among the Saxons in England. During feudal times, however, every man was first of all a soldier, and armies would have broken up if overlords jailed their men for the debts they owed.

As feudalism declined, and trade and industry rose, harsh treatment of debtors was revived. Prison terms were the usual punishment, and thus no money was recovered. Early American settlers included many fugitives from debtors' prisons.　　John Krahmer

Related articles in *World Book* include:

Attachment	Collection	Guaranty	National
Bankruptcy	agency	I.O.U.	debt
Bond	Garnishment	Moratorium	

Debt, National. See National debt.

Debussy, *dehb yoo SEE,* **Claude** (1862-1918), was an important French composer. His revolutionary treatment of musical form and harmony helped change the direction of music in the early 1900's.

Debussy felt closer to painters and poets than to other musicians, and he acknowledged the influence of literature and painting on his music. He sought a style of composition that was free from conventional musical forms, and he often used descriptive titles. He is regarded as the leader of impressionism in music.

Culver
Claude Debussy

Achille-Claude Debussy was born in St.-Germain-en-Laye. He entered the Paris Conservatory at the age of 10. Twelve years later, he won the 1884 Prix de Rome for his cantata *The Prodigal Son.* Other works of the late 1800's include the String Quartet in G minor (1893) and the three Nocturnes, the first two for orchestra (1900) and the third (1901) for female voices. The popular piano piece *Rêverie* (1890) is from this period, as is the *Suite bergamasque* (1890, revised 1905). Its third movement, "Clair de lune," is often played separately. The orchestral *Prelude to "The Afternoon of a Faun"* (1894), based on a poem by Stéphane Mallarmé, pointed to Debussy's later works.

The turning point in Debussy's career came in 1902 with his opera *Pelléas and Mélisande.* Written as a series of short scenes that end without climaxes, the opera emphasizes natural speech as opposed to brilliant singing. In spite of the controversy caused by its unconventional style, the opera was an immediate success and began an extremely productive period for Debussy. His following compositions greatly expanded previous limits of musical structure and *tonality,* the relationship among various tones. This period lasted about 15 years and included the orchestral masterpieces *La Mer* (1905) and *Images* (1913); the piano works *Estampes* (1903), *Masques* (1904), *L'isle joyeuse* (1904), two sets of *Images* (1905, 1907), and two books of Préludes (1910, 1913); and several sets of songs.

In 1909, Debussy suffered the first symptoms of cancer. He died of the disease nine years later. Probably because of his illness, he began working at a much slower pace. He started some operas and other large-scale projects but could not finish them.

From 1913 to 1917, Debussy abandoned impressionism for a more severe, abstract style. He returned to classicism with such works as the three chamber sonatas composed from 1915 to 1917. He also composed his most daring works. They include *Syrinx* for solo flute (1913), the 12 Études for piano (1915), and the ballet *Jeux* (1913). The ballet is sometimes considered Debussy's finest and most influential work.   Steven E. Gilbert

See also **Classical music** (The 1900's).

Debye, *deh BY,* **Peter Joseph William** (1884-1966), a Dutch physicist and chemist, won the 1936 Nobel Prize in chemistry for his studies of molecular structure. He was born in Maastricht, the Netherlands, and attended engineering school at Aachen, Germany. He served as chairman of the Cornell University chemistry department from 1940 to 1950.   Carl T. Chase

Decaffeinated coffee. See **Coffee** (Kinds of coffee).

Decal, *DEE kal* or *dih KAL,* is the process of transferring printed designs, letters, or pictures from specially prepared paper onto various surfaces. The word *decalcomania* (pronounced *dee KAL kuh MAY nee uh*) also describes this process. The print transferred is called a *decal* or *decal transfer.* Decals can be applied to such surfaces as glass, wood, plastic, and metal. They have many domestic and commercial uses. Manufacturers decorate dishes, furniture, and other products with decals. People use them to decorate toys, windows, and personal items. Decals are also used as automobile licensing stickers on windows because they are difficult to remove.

A decal is made of a thin film of oil paint and lacquer. It is coated on one side with a special adhesive and placed on a paper backing. Some decals can be lifted off the backing and applied directly to an object. Others must be soaked in water to soften the adhesive. The decal is then slid from the backing onto the desired surface. The adhesive dries in about a minute and makes the decal stick.

Decals were developed in Germany in the 1800's. They were first used on dinnerware as a cheaper decorative process than hand painting.   Dona Z. Meilach

Decalogue. See **Ten Commandments.**

Decameron. See **Boccaccio, Giovanni.**

Decathlon, *dih KATH lahn,* is a two-day contest in 10 events to determine an all-around track and field champion. Athletes compete in the 100-meter dash, long jump, shot-put, high jump, and 400-meter run, in that order, on the first day. They try the 110-meter hurdles, discus throw, pole vault, javelin throw, and 1,500-meter run on the second day. The athletes compete against time and distance standards, instead of against each other. Up to 1,200 points can be won for each event. The athlete scoring the most total points wins the decathlon.

The decathlon became a part of the Olympic Games in 1912. Nine U.S. athletes have won the Olympic decathlon title. Jim Thorpe won in 1912; Harold Osborn in 1924; James Bausch in 1932; Glenn Morris in 1936; Bob Mathias in 1948 and 1952; Milton Campbell in 1956; Rafer Johnson in 1960; Bill Toomey in 1968; and Bruce Jenner in 1976.   Bert Nelson

See also **Track and field** (The decathlon, heptathlon, and pentathlon; table: World track and field records).

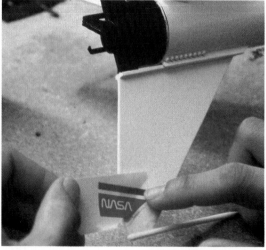

WORLD BOOK photos by Steinkamp/Ballogg

Decals can be applied to such surfaces as glass, wood, plastics, and metal. Some decals have a sticky coating and can be applied directly to a surface, *left.* Other decals must first be soaked in water. The decal is then slid from the backing and pressed into place, *right.*

Decatur (pop. 93,896; met. area pop. 131,375) is an industrial city located in a rich farming region of central Illinois. Decatur lies about 40 miles (64 kilometers) east of Springfield and about 170 miles (274 kilometers) southwest of Chicago. For the location of Decatur, see **Illinois** (political map).

Decatur's major industries process soybeans, make corn products and tires, and build tractors and motor graders. Decatur also has iron and brass foundries. Other factories make compressors, pharmaceuticals, pumps, store fixtures, and water and gas systems. Decatur was settled about 1830. The Grand Army of the Republic was founded there in 1866. The city is the home of Millikin University. Decatur has a council-manager government.   Richard D. Brautigam

Decatur, Stephen (1779-1820), was one of the most daring officers in the United States Navy during its early years. He is remembered for his toast: "Our country: In her intercourse with foreign nations may she always be right; but our country, right or wrong." Handsome, brave, and honorable, Decatur enjoyed great popularity with his men and with the public. He was one of a group of men who established the naval traditions of the United States. Others were John Barry, John Paul Jones, David Porter, Oliver Hazard Perry, Thomas Macdonough, and Isaac Hull.

Decatur was born in a log cabin in Sinepuxent, Md., on Jan. 5, 1779. He made his first long voyage at the age of 8, when he went to France on a ship commanded by his father, a merchant captain. He became a midshipman in 1798 during the naval war with France, and rose to lieutenant in 1799. Given command of the *Enterprise* during the war with Tripoli, he captured an enemy vessel that was renamed the *Intrepid.* In this ship he led a picked band into Tripoli Harbor on the night of Feb. 16, 1804, and set fire to the frigate *Philadelphia,* once commanded by his father, which the Tripoli pirates had captured. Not a man was killed and only one was wounded. The English Admiral Horatio Nelson called this exploit "the most bold and daring act of the age." Because of it, Decatur won a sword from Congress and a captaincy when he was only 25.

Commanding a squadron of three ships in the War of 1812, he captured the British frigate *Macedonian* after a desperate struggle. He became a commodore in 1813, and took command of a squadron in New York Harbor. He attempted to run the British blockade early in 1815, but his flagship, the *President,* struck the bar at Sandy Hook and was damaged. He was forced into a fight against heavy odds. Wounded, he had to surrender. The British sent him to Bermuda as a prisoner of war, but he was soon released.

He next sailed against Algiers, Tunis, and Tripoli, where he forced the rulers to release United States ships and prisoners and to stop molesting U.S. vessels. On his return he became a navy commissioner. Suspended Commodore James Barron, at whose court-martial Decatur had presided, challenged him to a duel in 1820. Decatur was killed by the commodore near Bladensburg, Md. Barron had accused certain officers, headed by Decatur, of persecuting him.   Bradford Smith

See also **Barron, James.**

Decay is the process by which dead animal or dead plant matter is broken down to simple compounds. These simpler products can then be used as food by living things, such as plants. Decay is an important process in the environment. The wastes that animals give off and the plants and animals that die are removed through this process. Decay is sometimes called *decomposition* or *putrefaction.*

The major part of the decay process is carried out by microbes, such as bacteria, molds, and yeasts. Such microbes feed on and completely digest dead animal or plant matter, or the waste products of live animals. During decay, enzymes in the microbes break down *macromolecules* (large molecules). For example, the enzymes convert proteins to amino acids and complex carbohydrates to simple sugars. The microbes use these products to build the materials they need. They also use some of the products to get energy for growth and reproduction. As the microbes grow and multiply, the decay process speeds up.

Warmth and moisture help microbes grow and thus assist the decay process. Refrigeration or cooking kills microbes and slows decay. Certain chemicals also can destroy microbes and prevent decay.   David Schlessinger

Related articles in *World Book* include:

Antiseptic	Fermentation	Ptomaine poisoning
Bacteria	Food preservation	
Biochemistry	Mold	Teeth
Decomposition	Pasteur, Louis	Yeast

Decay series. See **Isotope** (Radioactive isotopes).
Deccan. See **India** (The land; picture).
Deceleration. See **Motion** (Acceleration).

Oil painting on canvas (1863) by Alonzo Chappel; Chicago Historical Society

Stephen Decatur stands victoriously on the deck of a man-of-war after successfully forcing Algiers to sign a peace treaty.

December is the twelfth and last month of the year according to the Gregorian calendar, which is used in almost all the world today. It was the tenth month in the early Roman calendar and takes its name from the Latin word *decem,* which means *ten.* It became the twelfth month in a later Roman calendar. In 46 B.C., the Roman statesman Julius Caesar added two days to December, which before then had only 29 days.

Winter begins in December in the northern half of the world. Some people call it "the frosty month." But winter does not begin until December 21 or 22, and most of December is usually warmer than other winter months. On the first day of winter, the sun reaches the solstice, when it appears to have gone farthest south. In the Northern Hemisphere, it is the shortest day of the year. But it is the longest day in the southern half of the world. The latter part of December has long been a holiday season. The Romans honored Saturn, the god of agriculture, with a festival called *Saturnalia.* Today, Christmas is the chief holiday of the month in many countries. Christians celebrate it as the birthday of Jesus Christ. The Druids of northern Europe used mistletoe in a December festival. We still use mistletoe at Christmas.

Activities. In the Northern Hemisphere, most birds have gone to warmer climates. But many animals are active. Mink, ermine, beavers, and foxes grow beautiful coats of fur. Nature finishes preparing for the long winter ahead. Many people make feeding places for birds and squirrels.

Special days. People celebrate many holidays in December. They prepare for New Year's Eve parties on the last day of December. Some people in New England observe December 21 as Forefathers' Day in honor of the landing of the Pilgrims at Plymouth on Dec. 21, 1620. People in several European countries celebrate December 6 as the Feast of Saint Nicholas. Many of them exchange gifts on that day.

After Christmas Day on December 25, some Christian

Important December events

1   Iceland became a self-governing kingdom united with Denmark, 1918.
2   President James Monroe proclaimed the Monroe Doctrine in his message to Congress, 1823.
—   John Brown, American abolitionist, hanged at Charles Town, Va. (now W. Va.), 1859.
—   Scientists achieved the first controlled atomic chain reaction, in Chicago, 1942.
3   Illinois admitted to the Union, 1818.
—   Novelist Joseph Conrad born 1857.
—   Maria Callas, American-born opera singer, born 1923.
—   First human heart transplant performed by Christiaan Barnard, South African surgeon, 1967.
4   Thomas Carlyle, Scottish author, born 1795.
5   Phi Beta Kappa, honorary scholastic society, founded at the College of William and Mary, 1776.
—   Martin Van Buren, eighth President of the United States, born at Kinderhook, N.Y., 1782.
—   Motion-picture producer Walt Disney born 1901.
—   Amendment 21 to the United States Constitution, repealing prohibition, proclaimed, 1933.
6   Europeans celebrate the Feast of St. Nicholas.
—   Columbus discovered Hispaniola, 1492.
—   Dave Brubeck, American jazz pianist, born 1920.
7   Delaware ratified the Constitution, 1787.
—   Japanese forces attacked the U.S. naval base at Pearl Harbor in Hawaii in World War II, 1941.
8   Horace, Roman poet, born 65 B.C.
—   Eli Whitney, inventor of toothed cotton gin, born 1765.
—   Jan Sibelius, Finnish composer, born 1865.
—   The American Federation of Labor organized, 1886.
—   Chinese Nationalists flee the mainland, moving their capital to Formosa (today Taiwan), 1949.

8   John Lennon shot and killed in New York City, 1980.
9   John Milton, English poet, born 1608.
—   Joel Chandler Harris, American author of the "Uncle Remus" stories, born 1848.
10 William Lloyd Garrison, American journalist and abolitionist, born 1805.
—   Mississippi admitted to the Union, 1817.
—   Emily Dickinson, American poet, born 1830.
—   The Territory of Wyoming authorized women to vote and hold office, 1869.
—   Spain ceded Philippines to the United States, 1898.
11 Hector Berlioz, French composer, born 1803.
—   Indiana admitted to the Union, 1816.
—   Robert Koch, German bacteriologist, born 1843.
—   Edward VIII of Great Britain abdicated, 1936.
12 John Jay, American diplomat, born 1745.
—   Pennsylvania ratified the Constitution, 1787.
—   Gustave Flaubert, French novelist, born 1821.
—   Guglielmo Marconi received the first radio signal sent across the Atlantic Ocean, 1901.
13 The Council of Trent opened, 1545.
—   Sir Francis Drake left England to sail around the world, attacking Spanish possessions, 1577.
14 Tycho Brahe, Danish astronomer, born 1546.
—   George Washington died at Mt. Vernon, 1799.
—   Alabama admitted to the Union, 1819.
—   James Doolittle, American air pioneer and air force general, born 1896.
—   Roald Amundsen, Norwegian explorer, reached the South Pole, 1911.
15 The first 10 amendments to the Constitution, including the Bill of Rights, ratified, 1791.
—   Maxwell Anderson, American playwright, born 1888.

Dec. birthstone—
turquoise

Dec. flower—
poinsettia

Dec. 7—Japanese
attack on Pearl Harbor

Dec. 10—Emily
Dickinson born

churches observe the Feast of Saint Stephen on December 26, the Feast of Saint John the Evangelist on December 27, and Holy Innocents' Day on December 28.

Popular beliefs. A beautiful Bible story tells how the star of Bethlehem guided the wise men to the place where they found the Christ child. The star at the top of a Christmas tree symbolizes this star.

Symbols. Holly, narcissus, and poinsettia are special December flowers. The turquoise and the zircon are December birthstones.　　　　*Sharron G. Uhler*

Quotations

'Twas the night before Christmas, when all through the house
Not a creature was stirring, not even a mouse;
The stockings were hung by the chimney with care,
In hopes that St. Nicholas soon would be there;
The children were nestled all snug in their beds,
While visions of sugar-plums danced in their heads.
　　　　　Attributed to *Clement Clarke Moore*

Heap on more wood! The wind is chill;
But let it whistle as it will,
We'll keep our Christmas merry still.
　　　　　　　　Sir Walter Scott

The sun that brief December day
Rose cheerless over hills of gray,
And, darkly circled, gave at noon
A sadder sight than waning moon.
　　　　　John Greenleaf Whittier

I heard the bells on Christmas Day
Their old, familiar carols play,
And wild and sweet
The words repeat
Of peace on earth, good will to men.
　　　　Henry Wadsworth Longfellow

Related articles in *World Book* include:

Calendar	Nicholas, Saint	Solstice
Christmas	Santa Claus	Turquoise
Holly		

Important December events

16 English Parliament passed Bill of Rights, 1689.
　— Composer Ludwig van Beethoven born 1770.
　— Boston Tea Party, 1773.
　— Novelist Jane Austen born 1775.
　— Actor-playwright Sir Noel Coward born 1899.
　— Margaret Mead, American anthropologist, born 1901.
　— East Pakistan (today Bangladesh) achieved independence from West Pakistan (today Pakistan), 1971.
17 Sir Humphry Davy, English chemist, born 1778.
　— John Greenleaf Whittier, American poet, born 1807.
　— William Lyon Mackenzie King, three times prime minister of Canada, born 1874.
　— Orville Wright made first heavier-than-air flight at Kitty Hawk, N.C., 1903.
　— Willard Libby, American chemist, born 1908.
18 Charles Wesley, English clergyman and author of many hymns, born 1707.
　— New Jersey ratified the Constitution, 1787.
　— Amendment 13 to the U.S. Constitution, ending slavery, proclaimed, 1865.
　— Christopher Fry, British playwright, born 1907.
19 Continental Army camped for the winter at Valley Forge, Pa., in the Revolutionary War, 1777.
20 The United States took over Louisiana, 1803.
21 The Pilgrims landed at Plymouth, Mass., 1620.
　— Playwright Jean Baptiste Racine born 1639.
　— Benjamin Disraeli, twice prime minister of Great Britain, born 1804.
　— Joseph Stalin, Soviet dictator, born 1879.
22 James Oglethorpe, founder of Georgia, born 1696.
　— Opera composer Giacomo Puccini born 1858.
23 Richard Arkwright, British inventor, born 1732.
　— U.S. Federal Reserve System established, 1913.

24 "Kit" Carson, American frontier scout, born 1809.
　— United States and Great Britain signed the Treaty of Ghent to end the War of 1812, 1814.
25 Christmas, celebrated by Christians as the birthday of Jesus Christ.
　— Isaac Newton, English scientist who discovered the law of gravitation, born 1642.
　— George Washington and his men started across the Delaware River to Trenton, N.J., 1776.
　— Clara Barton, "Angel of the Battlefield" and founder of the American Red Cross, born 1821.
26 Battle of Trenton in the Revolutionary War, 1776.
　— George Dewey, American admiral, born 1837.
27 Johannes Kepler, German astronomer, born 1571.
　— Louis Pasteur, French chemist, born 1822.
　— Sir Mackenzie Bowell, prime minister of Canada from 1894 to 1896, born 1823.
　— Soviet troops invaded Afghanistan to crush a revolt against that country's Communist government, 1979.
28 Iowa admitted to the Union, 1846.
29 Woodrow Wilson, 28th President of the United States, born at Staunton, Va., 1856.
　— Andrew Johnson, 17th President of the United States, born at Raleigh, N.C., 1808.
　— William E. Gladstone, four-time prime minister of Great Britain, born 1809.
　— Texas admitted to the Union, 1845.
30 The United States acquired territory from Mexico in the Gadsden Purchase, 1853.
　— Rudyard Kipling, British writer, born 1865.
31 Andreas Vesalius, the first anatomist to describe the human body completely, born 1514.
　— Henri Matisse, French painter, born 1869.

WORLD BOOK illustrations by Mike Hagel

Dec. 14—Roald Amundsen reached South Pole

Dec. 17—first flight by Orville Wright

Dec. 21—Pilgrims arrival at Plymouth

Dec. 25—Clara Barton born

Decembrist Uprising. See Union of Soviet Socialist Republics (Alexander I).

Decemvirs. See Twelve Tables, Laws of the.

Decibel, *DEHS uh behl,* is a unit used in comparing sound pressure, voltage, power, and other related acoustical and electrical quantities. Its symbol is dB. A decibel equals one-tenth of a *bel,* a unit named for the Scottish-born inventor and scientist Alexander Graham Bell.

In acoustics, the decibel is frequently used to compare the intensity or pressure of sound with fixed reference levels. For measuring intensity, the most common reference level is 10^{-12} watts per square meter. This level equals 0 decibels. The common reference point for sound pressure level is 2×10^{-5} *pascals* (see **Pascal**). Thus, a sound pressure level of 60 decibels means that the sound pressure is 60 decibels above the reference level.

Sound at a level of 10 decibels is barely audible to the normal human ear. The level of sound pressure in a quiet room may be about 40 decibels, but a level of 70 decibels would be considered noisy. Sound at the 70-decibel level transmits 1,000 times as much energy as sound at 40 decibels.   Thomas D. Rossing

See also **Sound** (Measuring sound).

Deciduous tree, *dih SIHJ u uhs,* is the name for any tree that loses its leaves at a certain time each year and later grows new leaves. In northern temperate regions, most deciduous trees lose their leaves in the autumn. The twigs and branches stay bare all winter. The following spring the trees grow a new set of green leaves. Before the leaves die, some of the food material they contain is drawn back into the twigs and branches. There it is stored and used the following spring. Deciduous trees usually have broad leaves. Such trees include ash, beech, birch, maple, and oak. Larch is a common deciduous tree that has needlelike leaves.

Dried leaves continue to hang on the branches of some deciduous trees until the new leaves come out. In warmer climates, deciduous trees grow new leaves earlier in the spring and retain their leaves longer.

Scientists think that losing the leaves helps some trees to conserve water in the winter. Water normally passes into the air from tree leaves by a process called *transpiration.*   Richard C. Schlesinger

See also **Tree** (Broadleaf trees).

Decillion, *dih SIHL yuhn,* is a thousand nonillions, or a unit with 33 zeros, in the United States and France. One decillion is written 1,000,000,000,000,000,000,000,000,-000,000,000. A decillion is a unit with 60 zeros in Great Britain and Germany.

Decimal numeral system. See Decimal system.

Decimal system is a way of writing numbers. Any number, from huge quantities to tiny fractions, can be written in the decimal system using only the 10 basic symbols 1, 2, 3, 4, 5, 6, 7, 8, 9, and 0. The value of any of these symbols depends on the place it occupies in the number. The symbol 2, for example, has different values in the numbers 832 and 238, because the 2 is in different places in each of the numbers. Because the value of a symbol depends on where it is in a number, the decimal system is known as a *place-value system.*

The word *decimal* comes from *decem,* the Latin word for *ten.* The decimal system received its name because it is a *base-ten system.* The value of each place is 10 times greater than the value of the place just to its right. Thus, the symbols on the left of a number have larger values than symbols farther to the right. For example, the symbol 2 in 238 is worth much more than the symbol 2 in 832, because the 2 in 238 is farther to the left than is the 2 in 832.

The decimal system is also called the *Hindu-Arabic system.* It was developed by Hindu mathematicians in India more than 2,000 years ago. Arabs learned this system after conquering parts of India in the A.D. 700's. They spread knowledge of the system throughout their empire, including the Middle East, northern Africa, and Spain.

The decimal system and number words

In the English language, special number words are used to name the value of each place in the decimal system except the *ones place* (the place farthest to the right). The letters "ty" at the end of the words for numbers in the second place (just left of the ones place) indicate the number of tens. For example, *sixty* means *six tens.* The word *hundred* is used to show the size of the third place. There is another new word for the fourth place, *thousand,* but after that there are only new words for every third place to the left.

A comma is placed after each third place to make it easier to read a decimal system number. The words *ten* and *hundred* are used with *thousand* and the other special words to name all the places between the special places. Each group of three numbers is read as if it had only three places, and then the name of its group is added. For example, in the United States and Canada, the number 5,246,380,901,483 is read as "five trillion, two hundred forty-six billion, three hundred eighty million, nine hundred one thousand, four hundred eighty-three."

Large numbers in the decimal system can easily be expressed using *exponents.* An exponent is a symbol written to the right of and above a number. The exponent tells how many times a number is used as a *factor.* For example, the figure 10^6 is equivalent to the expression $10 \times 10 \times 10 \times 10 \times 10 \times 10$, in which 10 appears as a factor six times. Because multiplying by 10 moves a number written in the decimal system

Some large decimal system numbers

Number word	How many	Written in the decimal system	Written in exponents
Thousand	one thousand	1,000	10^3
Million	one thousand thousands	1,000,000	10^6
Billion	one thousand millions	1,000,000,000	10^9
Trillion	one thousand billions	1,000,000,000,000	10^{12}
Quadrillion	one thousand trillions	1,000,000,000,000,000	10^{15}

The names for the next thousands are quintillion, sextillion, septillion, octillion, nonillion, decillion, undecillion, duodecillion, tredecillion, quattuordecillion, quindecillion, sexdecillion, septendecillion, octodecillion, novemdecillion, and vigintillion. In Australia and Great Britain, the word *billion* refers to a million millions rather than to a thousand millions. *Trillion* refers to a million billions, and so on.

over one place to the left, the exponent for ten also tells how many zeros to write when that number is written in the decimal system. Thus, 10^6 is written as a 1 followed by six zeros—1,000,000.

Decimals less than one

In the decimal system, as the places go to the left of the ones place, each place gets ten times larger than the last. But the places can also go to the right of the ones place. As places go to the right, the values of those places get smaller. In the first place to the right, the one is divided into ten equal parts, called *tenths*. In the second place to the right, each tenth is itself divided into ten parts. As a result, in this place, the one has been divided into ten times ten—or one hundred—small parts. Each of these small parts, which are called *hundredths*, gets divided into ten smaller parts in the third place, and so on.

The names for the places to the right are like those for the places to the left, except that the letters "th" are added to the name for each place. The letters "th" show that the one is divided into that many small parts. The names for the places to the right sound as if the values are getting bigger, but the "th" at the end of the words shows that the values are really getting smaller. It takes only ten tenths to make one, but it takes a million millionths to equal one.

A period, called the *decimal point*, is written between the ones place and the first small decimal place to show when a decimal system number includes the small places to the right of the ones place. When a decimal system number does not include any places to the right of the ones place, a period does not have to be written. The period is usually read as "and" to show that the smaller places are starting. For example, 345.678 is read as "three hundred forty-five and six hundred seventy-eight thousandths." To name the places to the right, read the numbers as if they were to the left of the decimal point and then add the name of the place farthest to the right. The places in the decimal system are *symmetric* (balanced) around the ones place, not around the decimal point:

hundreds tens ones . tenths hundredths

Addition and subtraction

of decimals smaller than one are done in the same way as addition and subtraction of whole numbers. Only numbers in the same places can be added or subtracted. One number is written beneath the other number so that matching places line up—that is, tenths are beneath tenths, hundredths beneath hundredths, and so on.

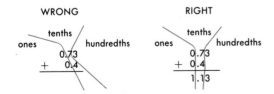

To add or subtract numbers with decimals less than one, write one number beneath the other number so that the decimal point of the bottom number is right beneath the decimal point of the top number. It does not

matter if one number has numerals sticking out to the right or left of the other number. You can put in zeros in any places that are missing numerals. Then add or subtract the numerals that are just above and below each other.

$$
\begin{array}{r} 7 - 2.61 \\ 7.00 \\ -2.61 \\ \hline 4.39 \end{array}
\qquad
\begin{array}{r} .356 + 27.9 \\ .356 \\ +27.9 \\ \hline 28.256 \end{array}
\qquad
\begin{array}{r} 548 - 6.08 \\ 548. \\ - \;\; 6.08 \\ \hline 541.92 \end{array}
$$

Multiplication of one whole number by another gives a number larger than the original number. But multiplication of a number by a decimal less than one gives a number *smaller* than the original number.

2×3 means two groups of three

$.1 \times 3$ means .1 group of three, or one-tenth of three, which is just part of three

The multiplication shift rule for multiplying a number by .1 (one-tenth) is that each digit in that number moves one place to the right—that is, it moves one place smaller.

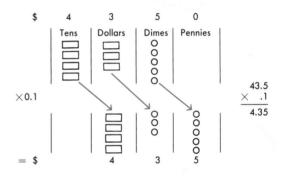

In this example, the amount $43.50 consists of four ten-dollar bills, three one-dollar bills, and five dimes. When multiplied by .1, each of the five dimes becomes a penny, because a penny is a tenth of a dime. Each of the three dollars becomes a dime, because a dime is one-tenth of a dollar. One-tenth of ten dollars is a dollar, so each of the 4 tens becomes a one. So the $43.50 becomes $4.35.

The multiplication shift rule for multiplying a number by .01 (one-hundredth) states that each digit in the number moves two places to the right. Each digit in a number multiplied by .001 (one-thousandth) moves three places to the right, and so on. In general, when a number is multiplied by any decimal smaller than one, the number moves as many places to the right as there are places smaller than one. Therefore, the rule for multiplying any number by a decimal number is: Multiply as usual. Then add the number of decimal places in the top number to the number of places in the bottom number and put that many decimal places in the answer.

$$
\begin{array}{r} 27.5 \\ \times \quad .03 \\ \hline .825 \end{array}
\qquad
\begin{array}{l} \text{one place} \\ \text{two places} \\ \text{three places} \end{array}
$$

In this example, there is one decimal place in the top number. Multiplying this number by .03 will move the number over two more places to the right. So there will be $1 + 2$ decimal places in the answer.

Division of a number by a decimal number smaller than one means finding out how many of those small decimal parts there are in that number. In problems involving the division of a whole number by a decimal smaller than one, the answer is always *larger* than the number being divided.

$6 \div 2$ means "How many twos in six?"

$6 \div .1$ means "How many tenths in six?"

Asking how many tenths there are in six is similar to asking "How many dimes in six dollars?" There are ten dimes in one dollar, so there are $6 \times$ ten (60) dimes in six dollars. Therefore, $6 \div .1 = 60$.

The division shift rule for tenths is just the opposite of the multiplication shift rule for tenths. Each place in the number being divided shifts one place to the *left* (gets one place larger). When a number is divided by .01 (one-hundredth), each place moves two places to the left, and so on.

To divide by a number with places smaller than one, write the problem in long division form.

$$1.08\overline{)75.6}$$

Move the decimal point in the divisor all the way to the right. Write a caret mark (^) for this new decimal place. Then in the number being divided, move the decimal point to the right *the same number of places*. Write zeros if more spaces are needed in the number being divided. Write a caret for the new decimal place. Then just divide as usual and put the decimal point in the answer above the caret in the number being divided.

Step 1	Step 2	Step 3
$1.08\overline{)75.6}$	$1.08\overline{)75.60}$	$\begin{array}{r} 70. \\ 1.08\overline{)75.\ 60} \\ \underline{75\ 6} \\ 00 \end{array}$

This rule works because you are just multiplying the problem by 1, which will not change the answer:

$$\frac{75.6}{1.08} = \frac{75.6}{1.08} \times 1 = \frac{75.6}{1.08} \times \frac{100}{100} = \frac{7560}{108} = 70$$

Decimals and fractions

In mathematics, any number that can be written in the form of a fraction—that is, as one number divided by another—is called a *rational number*. All rational numbers can be written in the decimal system. When rational numbers are changed to the decimal form, the result is either a *repeating decimal* or a *terminating decimal*. A repeating decimal is one that goes on repeating the same number or series of numbers, such as 0.333 . . . and 0.14851485. . . . The dots at the end show that the same pattern repeats over and over. This repetition may also be shown by writing a bar line above the repeating pattern: $0.\overline{3}$ and $0.\overline{1485}$. A terminating decimal is one in which the division at some point comes out even and so the decimal number stops.

Any repeating or terminating decimal can be written as a rational number—that is, in fraction form. But some decimal numbers, called *irrational numbers*, never repeat or end and cannot be written in rational form. Two examples of irrational numbers are $\sqrt{2}$ and pi (π). The symbol $\sqrt{2}$ represents the square root of two. This is the number which when multiplied times itself gives two. It is between 1.4142135 and 1.4142136. Pi is the number you get when you divide the *circumference* (the distance around) of any circle by its *diameter* (the distance across it through its center). The value of pi has been calculated to thousands of decimal places by computers. It is between 3.1415926 and 3.1415927. See **Circle; Pi.**

Changing fractions to decimals. To change a number from the fraction form to the decimal form, just carry out the division that is implied in the fraction. Divide the *numerator* (top number) by the *denominator* (bottom number). This division will always give either a terminating decimal or a repeating decimal, because the remainder will eventually be 0 or will repeat an earlier remainder. A repeating decimal can be rounded off to any place.

Terminating decimal		Repeating decimal
$\frac{3}{5} \rightarrow \begin{array}{r} 0.6 \\ 5\overline{)3.0} \\ \underline{3\ 0} \\ 0 \end{array}$ so $\frac{3}{5} = .6$		$\frac{2}{3} = \begin{array}{r} 0.666... \\ 3\overline{)2.000} \\ \underline{18} \\ 20 \\ \underline{18} \\ 20 \\ \underline{18} \\ 2 \end{array}$

Changing decimals to fractions. To change a decimal to a regular fraction, write the number without any decimal point as the top of the regular fraction. For the bottom of the regular fraction, write the numeral 1 followed by as many zeros as there are places to the right of the decimal point in the decimal. This bottom number is the value of the last place in the decimal.

$$0.28 = \frac{28}{100} \qquad\qquad 0.005 = \frac{5}{1000}$$

↑		↑	
hundredths place		thousandths place	
two	two	three	three
places $\rightarrow$	zeros	places $\rightarrow$	zeros

The exact procedure for changing a repeating decimal to a fraction varies with the form of the repeating decimal. If the repeating decimal starts in the tenths place and has no whole numbers in it, the fraction form of the repeating decimal has the repeating pattern as the top number and as many 9's as there are places in the repeating pattern for the bottom number.

$$0.\overline{581} = \frac{581}{999} \qquad 0.\overline{4628} = \frac{4628}{9999} \qquad 0.\overline{14} = \frac{14}{99}$$

In some repeating decimals, there are nonrepeating numbers before the pattern of the decimal starts repeating. If these nonrepeating numbers are whole numbers, the top number for the new fraction is made by writing the repeating decimal up to the first repeat of the pattern and subtracting from this the whole number. The bottom number is as many 9's as there are in the repeating pattern.

$$25.\overline{639} = \frac{25639 - 25}{999} = \frac{25614}{999}$$

In some repeating decimals, the nonrepeating numbers are to the right of the decimal point. In such cases, the top number is made by writing the nonrepeating part followed by one repeat of the pattern. The nonrepeating part is then subtracted from this number. The bottom number is made by writing as many 9's as there are places in the repeating pattern, followed by as many 0's as there are nonrepeating places to the right of the decimal point.

$$.74\overline{5} = \frac{745 - 74}{900} = \frac{671}{900}$$

$$5.1\overline{693} = \frac{51693 - 51}{9990} = \frac{51642}{9990}$$

History

Invention of the decimal system. The decimal system was invented in India, but no one knows exactly when or where. As early as 250 B.C., a base-ten number system was written in Brahmi, a script used for writing the Sanskrit language. The Hindu-Arabic numerals 1, 2, 3, 4, 5, 6, 7, 8, and 9 are based on the Brahmi symbols for the numbers one through nine. However, the Brahmi number system also used special symbols for ten, twenty, thirty, forty, fifty, sixty, seventy, eighty, ninety, one hundred, and one thousand.

By A.D. 595, all the extra symbols had been dropped from the system. All numbers were written by using just the symbols for one through nine. The place in which a symbol was written told its value. However, there was a problem with this place-value system. If a given place was empty, some new symbol was needed to hold that place empty so that all the other symbols would stay in their correct places. The first record of the use of such a new symbol in the Brahmi system is from A.D. 876. This symbol is what we now call zero. The Maya of Central America, who also invented a place-value system, used a zero before A.D. 300 (see **Zero**).

Spread of the decimal system. During the 700's, Arabs conquered parts of India. They learned the decimal system there, and during the next 300 years, spread it throughout their empire—through the Middle East to northern Africa, and into Spain.

The system was introduced into Europe by several people, including Pope Sylvester II about 1000 and Leonardo Fibonacci, an Italian mathematician, in 1202. At that time, however, new learning in books did not reach large numbers of people, chiefly because books were copied by hand and were therefore scarce. But soon after the printing press was invented in the mid-1400's, several arithmetic books that explained the use of the decimal system were published in England, France, Germany, the Netherlands, and other countries. Schools opened in many countries to teach decimal-system calculations, and the system was taught in universities.

The widespread interest in the decimal system was due largely to the number of advantages the system had over Roman numerals, which most people in Europe used at the time (see **Roman numerals**). Calculations are difficult with Roman numerals, so people used little round pieces of metal as counters. They performed their calculations with such devices as calculating boards or calculating cloths that had vertical columns drawn on them to make places for the counters. But because of the place-value nature of the decimal system, calcula-

tions could be performed with decimal numbers by using just a pen and paper. Counters and a counting board or cloth were no longer necessary. It also takes less space to write a number in the decimal system. Larger and larger numbers can be written in the decimal system without inventing any new symbols. Another advantage is that numbers smaller than one can be written in the decimal system, and calculations can be performed with these numbers.

Use of decimals smaller than one. The first books written in Europe about the decimal system did not say anything about decimals smaller than one. Such decimals were used in China many centuries before they were introduced into Europe and were used by Arab astronomers by at least the early 1400's. Some European mathematicians and astronomers had also known about decimals smaller than one, but the first evidence of their use by merchants and ordinary people appeared in a Flemish pamphlet called *De Thiende*, published in the Netherlands in 1585. John Napier, a Scottish baron who studied mathematics, published in 1619 an easier way to write decimals smaller than one, and we still use his method today. Such decimals gradually began to be used with the rest of the decimal system.

In the late 1700's, France adopted a metric system of weights and measures and a new money system. Both were based on the decimal system (see **Metric system**). They enabled many more people to use decimals less than one. By the late 1900's, nearly every country had converted, or planned to convert, to the metric system of measurement. Widespread use of the metric system placed greater importance on the use of decimals less than one, and decreased importance on fractions.

The importance of decimals smaller than one was further increased in the late 1970's and early 1980's by the development of inexpensive electronic calculators. Many problems that were previously solved with fractions could be done more easily with calculators that use the decimal system.   Karen Connors Fuson

Related articles in *World Book* include:

Abacus	Fraction	Percentage
Arabic numerals	Metric system	Rational number
Arithmetic	Numeration systems	

Decimeter. See Metric system (Using the metric system).

Decipher. See Codes and ciphers.

Declaration of Human Rights. See Human Rights, Universal Declaration of.

Declaration of Independence is the historic document in which the American Colonies declared their freedom from British rule. The Second Continental Congress, a meeting of delegates from the colonies, adopted the Declaration on July 4, 1776. This date has been celebrated ever since as the birthday of the United States.

The Declaration of Independence ranks as one of the greatest documents in human history. It eloquently expressed the colonies' reasons for proclaiming their freedom. The document blamed the British government for many abuses. But it also stated that all people have certain rights, including the right to change or overthrow any government that denies them their rights. The ideas expressed so majestically in the Declaration have long inspired freedom-loving people throughout the world.

Events leading to the Declaration. Friction between the American Colonies and Britain had been building for more than 10 years before the Declaration was adopted. During that period, the colonies had asked Britain for a larger role in making decisions that affected them, especially in the area of taxation. In 1765, the British Parliament passed the Stamp Act, which required the colonists to pay a tax on newspapers, legal and business documents, and various other items. The colonists protested so strongly against this "taxation without representation" that Parliament repealed the act in 1766.

Parliament then passed a law stating it had the right to legislate for the colonies in all matters. In 1767, it placed a tax on certain goods imported into the colonies. But colonial opposition led Parliament to remove these taxes in 1770—except for the tax on tea. In 1773, angry colonists boarded British ships in Boston Harbor and dumped their cargoes of tea overboard. Parliament then passed a series of laws to punish Massachusetts. These laws led the colonies to unite against what they called the Intolerable Acts.

The Continental Congress. In 1774, delegates from all the colonies except Georgia met in Philadelphia at the First Continental Congress. The delegates adopted an agreement that bound the colonies not to trade with Britain or to use British goods. They also proposed another meeting the next year if Britain did not change its policies before that time.

But Britain held to its policies, and the Second Continental Congress was called. The delegates met in Philadelphia's State House (now Independence Hall) on May 10, 1775. By that time, the Revolutionary War in America had already begun, with battles between Massachusetts colonists and British troops. Congress acted swiftly. It voted to organize an army and a navy and to issue money to pay for the war. Many delegates now believed that independence from Britain was the only solution. But others disagreed. Early in July, Congress therefore sent a final, useless appeal to Britain's King George III to remedy the colonies' grievances.

Richard B. Morris, the contributor of this article and of the explanatory notes with the Declaration, is the author of The American Revolution: A Brief History.

The independence movement grew rapidly early in 1776. The English writer Thomas Paine spurred the movement with his electrifying pamphlet *Common Sense.* This work presented brilliant arguments for the freedom of the American colonies. More and more Americans came to agree with the patriot Samuel Adams, who asked, "Is not America already independent? Why not then declare it?"

On June 7, 1776, Richard Henry Lee of Virginia introduced the resolution in Congress "That these United Colonies are, and of right ought to be, free and independent States. . . ." On June 10, Congress voted to name a committee to write a declaration of independence for the delegates to consider in case they adopted Lee's resolution. The committee, appointed the next day, consisted of John Adams, Benjamin Franklin, Thomas Jefferson, Robert R. Livingston, and Roger Sherman. Jefferson's associates on the committee asked him to draft the declaration. Jefferson completed the task in about two weeks. Franklin and Adams made a few minor literary changes in Jefferson's draft.

Adoption of the Declaration. On July 2, Congress approved the Lee resolution. The delegates then began to debate Jefferson's draft. A few passages, including one condemning King George for encouraging the slave trade, were removed. Most other changes dealt with style. On July 4, Congress adopted the final draft of the Declaration of Independence.

The Declaration, signed by John Hancock as president of Congress, was promptly printed. It was read to a large crowd in the State House yard on July 8. On July 19, Congress ordered the Declaration of Independence to be *engrossed* (written in beautiful script) on parchment. Congress also ordered that all its members sign the engrossed copy. Eventually, 56 members of Congress signed.

The importance of the Declaration was that it magnificently expressed the thoughts of all patriots. It thus did not contain new ideas. The Declaration actually reflected ideas on social and political justice held by various philosophers of the time, especially the English philosopher John Locke. Yet the eloquent language of the document stirred the hearts of the American people. It also aroused people in Europe to make their govern-

Signers of the Declaration of Independence

Fifty-six members of the Continental Congress signed the engrossed parchment copy of the Declaration. Most members signed on Aug. 2, 1776. The rest signed on later dates. *World Book* has a biography of each signer. The signers, in alphabetical order, were:

John Adams (Mass.)	John Hancock (Mass.)	Thomas Lynch, Jr. (S.C.)	Edward Rutledge (S.C.)
Samuel Adams (Mass.)	Benjamin Harrison (Va.)	Thomas McKean (Del.)	Roger Sherman (Conn.)
Josiah Bartlett (N.H.)	John Hart (N.J.)	Arthur Middleton (S.C.)	James Smith (Pa.)
Carter Braxton (Va.)	Joseph Hewes (N.C.)	Lewis Morris (N.Y.)	Richard Stockton (N.J.)
Charles Carroll (Md.)	Thomas Heyward, Jr. (S.C.)	Robert Morris (Pa.)	Thomas Stone (Md.)
Samuel Chase (Md.)	William Hooper (N.C.)	John Morton (Pa.)	George Taylor (Pa.)
Abraham Clark (N.J.)	Stephen Hopkins (R.I.)	Thomas Nelson, Jr. (Va.)	Matthew Thornton (N.H.)
George Clymer (Pa.)	Francis Hopkinson (N.J.)	William Paca (Md.)	George Walton (Ga.)
William Ellery (R.I.)	Samuel Huntington (Conn.)	Robert T. Paine (Mass.)	William Whipple (N.H.)
William Floyd (N.Y.)	Thomas Jefferson (Va.)	John Penn (N.C.)	William Williams (Conn.)
Benjamin Franklin (Pa.)	Francis Lightfoot Lee (Va.)	George Read (Del.)	James Wilson (Pa.)
Elbridge Gerry (Mass.)	Richard Henry Lee (Va.)	Caesar Rodney (Del.)	John Witherspoon (N.J.)
Button Gwinnett (Ga.)	Francis Lewis (N.Y.)	George Ross (Pa.)	Oliver Wolcott (Conn.)
Lyman Hall (Ga.)	Philip Livingston (N.Y.)	Benjamin Rush (Pa.)	George Wythe (Va.)

IN CONGRESS, JULY 4, 1776.

The unanimous Declaration of the thirteen united States of America.

WORLD BOOK photo

The original Declaration of Independence is displayed in an upright case in the National Archives Building in Washington, D.C. The Declaration stands above the United States Constitution and Bill of Rights. All these historic documents are sealed under glass.

ments more democratic. Over the years, many newly emerging nations have looked to the Declaration's expressive language in giving their reasons for seeking freedom from foreign control.

The original parchment copy of the Declaration is housed in the National Archives Building in Washington, D.C. It is displayed with two other historic American documents—the United States Constitution and the Bill of Rights.   Richard B. Morris

See also **Continental Congress; Independence Day; Locke, John; Revolutionary War in America; United States, History of the.** For a *Reading and Study Guide,* see *Declaration of Independence* in the Research Guide/Index, Volume 22.

Additional resources

Level I

Dalgliesh, Alice. *The Fourth of July Story.* Scribner, 1956.
Foster, Genevieve S. *Year of Independence, 1776.* Scribner, 1970.
Fradin, Dennis B. *The Declaration of Independence.* Childrens Pr., 1988.
Peterson, Helen S. *Give Us Liberty! The Story of the Declaration of Independence.* Garrard, 1973.

Level II

Becker, Carl L. *The Declaration of Independence: A Study in the History of Political Ideas.* Random Hse., 1958. First published in 1922.
Hawke, David F. *A Transaction of Free Men: The Birth and Course of the Declaration of Independence.* Da Capo, 1989. First published in 1964.

The Declaration of Independence

The Declaration of Independence can be divided into four parts: (1) The Preamble; (2) A Declaration of Rights; (3) A Bill of Indictment; and (4) A Statement of Independence. The text of the Declaration is printed in boldface. It follows the spelling and punctuation of the parchment copy. But unlike the parchment copy, each paragraph begins on a new line and is indented. The paragraphs printed in lightface are not part of the Declaration. They explain the meaning of various passages or give examples of injustices that a passage mentions.

In Congress, July 4, 1776. The unanimous Declaration of the thirteen united States of America,

[The Preamble]

When in the Course of human events, it becomes necessary for one people to dissolve the political bands which have connected them with another, and to assume among the powers of the earth, the separate and equal station to which the Laws of Nature and of Nature's God entitle them, a decent respect to the opinions of mankind requires that they should declare the causes which impel them to the separation.—

This paragraph tells why the Continental Congress drew up the Declaration. The members felt that when a people must break their ties with the mother country and become independent, they should explain their reasons to the world.

[A Declaration of Rights]

We hold these truths to be self-evident, that all men are created equal, that they are endowed by their Creator with certain unalienable Rights, that among these are Life, Liberty and the pursuit of Happiness.—

The signers of the Declaration believed it was obvious that "all men" are created equal and have rights that cannot be taken away from them. By "all men," the signers meant people of every race and both sexes. The rights to "Life" included the right to defend oneself against physical attack and against unjust government. The right to "Liberty" included the right to criticize the government, to worship freely, and to form a government that protects liberty. The "pursuit of Happiness" meant the right to own property and to have it safeguarded. It also meant the right to strive for the good of all people, not only for one's personal happiness.

That to secure these rights, Governments are instituted among Men, deriving their just powers from the consent of the governed,—

The Declaration states that governments exist to protect the rights of the people. Governments receive their power to rule only through agreement of the people.

That whenever any Form of Government becomes destructive of these ends, it is the Right of the People to alter or to abolish it, and to institute new Government, laying its founda-

tion on such principles and organizing its powers in such form, as to them shall seem most likely to effect their Safety and Happiness. Prudence, indeed, will dictate that Governments long established should not be changed for light and transient causes; and accordingly all experience hath shewn, that mankind are more disposed to suffer, while evils are sufferable, than to right themselves by abolishing the forms to which they are accustomed. But when a long train of abuses and usurpations, pursuing invariably the same Object evinces a design to reduce them under absolute Despotism, it is their right, it is their duty, to throw off such Government, and to provide new Guards for their future security.—**

People may alter their government if it fails in its purpose. Or they may set up a new government. People should not, however, make a revolutionary change in long-established governments for unimportant reasons. But they have the right to overthrow a government that has committed many abuses and seeks complete control over the people.

[A Bill of Indictment]

Such has been the patient sufferance of these Colonies; and such is now the necessity which constrains them to alter their former Systems of Government. The history of the present King of Great Britain is a history of repeated injuries and usurpations, all having in direct object the establishment of an absolute Tyranny over these States. To prove this, let Facts be submitted to a candid world.—

The Declaration states that the colonists could no longer endure the abuses of their government and so must change it. It accuses King George III of inflicting the abuses to gain total power over the colonies. The document then lists the charges against him.

He has refused his Assent to Laws, the most wholesome and necessary for the public good.—

All laws passed by the colonial legislatures had to be sent to Great Britain for approval. George rejected many of the laws as harmful to Britain or its empire.

He has forbidden his Governors to pass Laws of immediate and pressing importance, unless suspended in their operation till his Assent should be obtained; and when so suspended, he has utterly neglected to attend to them.—

The Continental Congress adopted the Declaration of Independence on July 4, 1776. In this famous painting by the American artist John Trumbull, the president of the Congress, John Hancock, sits at the right. Before him stand the five committee members named to draft the Declaration. They are, *left to right,* John Adams, Roger Sherman, Robert R. Livingston, Thomas Jefferson, and Benjamin Franklin.

Yale University Art Gallery

Royal governors could not approve any colonial law that did not have a clause suspending its operation until the king approved the law. Yet it took much time, sometimes years, for laws to be approved or rejected.

He has refused to pass other Laws for the accommodation of large districts of people, unless those people would relinquish the right of Representation in the Legislature, a right inestimable to them and formidable to tyrants only.—

The royal government failed to redraw the boundaries of legislative districts so that people in newly settled areas would be fairly represented in the legislatures.

He has called together legislative bodies at places unusual, uncomfortable, and distant from the depository of their public Records, for the sole purpose of fatiguing them into compliance with his measures.—

Royal governors sometimes had the members of colonial assemblies meet at inconvenient places.

He has dissolved Representative Houses repeatedly, for opposing with manly firmness his invasions on the rights of the people.—

Royal governors often dissolved colonial assemblies for disobeying their orders or for passing resolutions against the law.

He has refused for a long time, after such dissolutions, to cause others to be elected; whereby the Legislative powers, incapable of Annihilation, have returned to the People at large for their exercise; the State remaining in the mean time exposed to all the dangers of invasion from without, and convulsions within.—

After dissolving colonial legislatures, royal governors sometimes took a long time before allowing new assemblies to be elected.

He has endeavoured to prevent the population of these States; for that purpose obstructing the Laws for Naturalization of Foreigners; refusing to pass others to encourage their migrations hither, and raising the conditions of new Appropriations of Lands.—

The colonies wanted immigrants to settle in undeveloped lands in the west. For this reason, their laws made it easy for settlers to buy land and to become citizens. But in 1763, King George claimed the western lands and began to reject most new *naturalization* (citizenship) laws. In 1773, he prohibited the naturalization of foreigners. In 1774, he sharply raised the purchase prices for the western lands.

He has obstructed the Administration of Justice, by refusing his Assent to Laws for establishing Judiciary powers.—

The North Carolina legislature passed a law setting up a court system. But Britain objected to a clause in the law, which the legislature refused to remove. As a result, the colony had no courts for several years.

He has made Judges dependent on his Will alone, for the tenure of their offices, and the amount and payment of their salaries.—

The royal government insisted that judges should serve as long as the king was pleased with them and that they should be paid by him. The colonies felt that judges should serve only as long as they proved to be competent and honest. They also wanted to pay the judges' salaries.

He has erected a multitude of New Offices, and sent hither swarms of Officers to harrass our people, and eat out their substance.—

In 1767, Great Britain passed the Townshend Acts, which taxed various products imported into the colonies. Britain also set up new agencies to enforce the laws and appointed tax commissioners. The commissioners, in turn, hired a large number of agents to aid them in collecting the taxes.

He has kept among us, in times of peace, Standing Armies without the Consent of our legislatures.—

British armies arrived in North America to fight the French in the French and Indian War (1754-1763). The colonists resented the fact that Britain kept troops in the colonies after the war.

He has affected to render the Military independent of and superior to the Civil power.—

The British altered the civil government in Massachusetts and named as governor General Thomas Gage, commander of Britain's military forces in America.

He has combined with others to subject us to a jurisdiction foreign to our constitution, and unacknowledged by our laws; giving his Assent to their Acts of pretended Legislation:—

The Declaratory Act, passed by Britain in 1766, claimed that the king and Parliament had full authority to make laws for the colonies. But the Declaration of Independence maintained that the colonies' own laws did not give the British that authority.

For quartering large bodies of armed troops among us:—

The royal government passed various quartering acts, which required the colonies to provide lodging and certain supplies to British troops stationed in America.

For protecting them, by a mock Trial, from punishment for any Murders which they should commit on the Inhabitants of these States:—

In 1774, Britain passed the Impartial Administration of Justice Act. Under this act, British soldiers and officials accused of murder while performing their duties in Massachusetts could be tried in Britain.

For cutting off our Trade with all parts of the world:—

Britain passed many laws to control colonial trade. The Restraining Acts of 1775, for example, severely limited the foreign trade that several colonies could engage in. One of these acts provided that American ships which violated the law could be seized.

For imposing Taxes on us without our Consent:—

This charge referred to all taxes levied on the colonies by the British, beginning with the Sugar Act of 1764.

For depriving us in many cases, of the benefits of Trial by Jury:—

British naval courts, which had no juries, dealt with smuggling and other violations of the trade laws.

For transporting us beyond Seas to be tried for pretended offences:—

This charge referred to a 1769 resolution by Parliament that colonists accused of treason could be brought to Britain for trial.

For abolishing the free System of English Laws in a neighbouring Province, establishing therein an Arbitrary government, and enlarging its Boundaries so as to render it at once an example and fit instrument for introducing the same absolute rule into these Colonies:—

In 1774, the Quebec Act provided for French civil law and an appointed governor and council in the province of Quebec. The act also extended the province's borders south to the Ohio River.

For taking away our Charters, abolishing our most valuable laws, and altering fundamentally the Forms of our Governments:—

The Massachusetts Government Act of 1774 drastically changed the Massachusetts charter. It provided that councilors would no longer be elected but would be appointed by the king. The act also restricted the holding of town meetings and gave the governor control over all lower court judges.

For suspending our own Legislatures, and declaring themselves invested with power to legislate for us in all cases whatsoever.—

In 1767, Parliament passed an act suspending the New York Assembly for failing to fulfill all the requirements of the Quartering Act of 1765.

He has abdicated Government here, by declaring us out of his Protection and waging War against us.—

Early in 1775, Britain authorized General Gage to use force if necessary to make the colonists obey the laws of Parliament. The British fought the colonists at the battles of Lexington, Concord, and Bunker Hill. George declared the colonies to be in revolt and stated they would be crushed.

He has plundered our seas, ravaged our Coasts, burnt our towns, and destroyed the lives of our people.—

The British seized ships that violated the Restraining Act of December 1775. They also bombarded such seaport towns as

Falmouth (now Portland), Me.; Bristol, R.I.; and Norfolk, Va.

He is at this time transporting large Armies of foreign Mercenaries to compleat the works of death, desolation and tyranny, already begun with circumstances of Cruelty & perfidy scarcely paralleled in the most barbarous ages, and totally unworthy the Head of a civilized nation.—

The British used German *mercenaries* (hired soldiers) to help fight the colonists.

He has constrained our fellow Citizens taken Captive on the high Seas to bear Arms against their Country, to become the executioners of their friends and Brethren, or to fall themselves by their Hands.—

The British forced American seamen on ships seized under the Restraining Act to join the British navy.

He has excited domestic insurrections amongst us, and has endeavoured to bring on the inhabitants of our frontiers, the merciless Indian Savages, whose known rule of warfare, is an undistinguished destruction of all ages, sexes and conditions.

On Nov. 7, 1775, Virginia's royal governor proclaimed freedom for all black slaves who would join the British forces. British military plans included using Indians to fight colonists in frontier areas.

[A Statement of Independence]

In every stage of these Oppressions We have Petitioned for Redress in the most humble terms: Our repeated Petitions have been answered only by repeated injury. A Prince, whose character is thus marked by every act which may define a Tyrant, is unfit to be the ruler of a free people.

The Continental Congress had asked the king to correct many abuses stated in the Declaration. These appeals were ignored or followed by even worse abuses.

Nor have We been wanting in attentions to our Brittish brethren. We have warned them from time to time of attempts by their legislature to extend an unwarrantable jurisdiction over us. We have reminded them of the circumstances of our emigration and settlement here. We have appealed to their native justice and magnanimity, and we have conjured them by the ties of our common kindred to disavow these usurpations, which, would inevitably interrupt our connections and correspondence. They too have been deaf to the voice of justice and of consanguinity. We must, therefore, acquiesce in the necessity, which denounces our Separation, and hold them, as we hold the rest of mankind, Enemies in War, in Peace Friends.—

Congress had also appealed without success to the British people themselves.

We, therefore, the Representatives of the united States of America, in General Congress, Assembled, appealing to the Supreme Judge of the world for the rectitude of our intentions, do, in the Name, and by Authority of the good People of these Colonies, solemnly publish and declare, That these United Colonies are, and of Right ought to be Free and Independent States; that they are Absolved from all Allegiance to the British Crown, and that all political connection between them and the State of Great Britain, is and ought to be totally dissolved; and that as Free and Independent States, they have full Power to levy War, conclude Peace, contract Alliances, establish Commerce, and to do all other Acts and Things which Independent States may of right do.—

And for the support of this Declaration, with a firm reliance on the protection of divine Providence, we mutually pledge to each other our Lives, our Fortunes and our sacred Honor.

Because all appeals had failed, the signers of the Declaration, as representatives of the American people, felt only one course of action remained. They thus declared the colonies independent, with all ties to Britain ended.

Declaration of Rights. See Bill of rights; Continental Congress; Human Rights, Universal Declaration of; Rights of Man, Declaration of the.

Declaratory Act. See Revolutionary War in America (The quartering and stamp acts).

Declension is a listing of the different case forms of a noun or pronoun. Some languages, such as Latin, Greek, and Russian, have complicated case systems. They have many different forms for each noun or pronoun, varying with the way the words are used in sentences.

In English, the declension of nouns is extremely simple. English nouns have only two case forms: a *common* case, used for both subject and object, and a *possessive* case. For example, in "The scoutmaster instructed the young boy," *scoutmaster* is the subject and *boy* is the object, but the common case is used for both. The possessive form is marked by the inflection *-'s*, as in the sentence "The *scoutmaster's* instructions helped the *boy's* progress."

The pronouns *I, he, she, we, they,* and *who* show three case forms—subjective (sometimes called nominative), objective, and possessive. The following declension shows the differences among the forms. It also includes a variation in the possessive form in four of the pronouns:

Subjective	I	he	she	we	they	who
Objective	me	him	her	us	them	whom
Possessive	my	his	her	our	their	whose
Variation	mine		hers	ours	theirs	

The pronouns *it* and *you* show only two case forms, common and possessive. William F. Irmscher

See also **Case; Pronoun; Inflection.**

Declination. See Compass (Variation); Astronomy (table; picture).

Decoding. See Codes and ciphers.

Decomposition, in chemistry, is the breaking down of a substance into simpler products, or into the elements of which it is composed. Decomposition may be brought about in several ways. Heat decomposes red mercuric oxide into its elements of oxygen and bright metallic mercury. Heat breaks down limestone to form lime and carbon dioxide. Heat also decomposes many organic compounds. For example, table sugar breaks down mostly into carbon and water when heated. An electric current decomposes water into its elements hydrogen and oxygen. Many substances are decomposed by chemical action. Starch is broken down into a simple sugar, called *glucose,* by the action of a boiling, dilute acid. Decomposition may also be caused by the action of light, bacteria, or enzymes. The enzymes in yeast ferment sugar into simple products.

A distinction is sometimes made between decomposition caused by people, as in chemistry, and decomposition that occurs in nature. For example, animal and vegetable matter, when attacked by certain microorganisms, are said to *decompose,* or decay. Such natural decay is also called *putrefaction.* The decomposition of animals and plants is important in geology. For example, coal and petroleum are formed from plants that became buried in swamps and decayed. Albert G. Anderson

See also **Decay.**

Decompression sickness. See Bends.

Decoration, Interior. See Interior decoration.

Decoration Day. See Memorial Day.

Decorations, medals, and orders are honors that are awarded to people for bravery or merit. These honors are generally given by a monarch or head of state. People granted such honors receive a badge that may be worn or displayed. In most cases, the badges are suspended from a ribbon. The designs and colors of the ribbon usually symbolize the national colors of a country or such characteristics as virtue or bravery.

Decorations are usually in the shape of a cross or star, suspended from a ribbon. They are usually given in wartime for a single act of outstanding gallantry. In the military, decorations are generally more important than medals. The Victoria Cross of Great Britain is an example of a decoration.

Medals are usually round and bear the likeness of a head of state or other symbol surrounded by an inscription. Most medals are made of gold, silver, or bronze. Medals generally hang from a ribbon. Medals are usually presented for participation in a campaign, long service, or good conduct. An example of a medal is the United States Navy Civil War campaign medal.

Orders have a variety of shapes, but stars and crosses are used most frequently. The most common type of cross is the *Maltese cross.* Its four arms have V-shaped ends. Traditionally, orders have been exclusive societies with a limited membership determined by the head of state. In countries where orders exist, membership in an order is generally considered the highest degree of honor. The United States and Switzerland are among the few countries that do not have orders. The French Legion of Honor is an example of an order.

United States decorations and medals

Military awards. During the late 1700's and early 1800's, the idea of decorations and medals was unpopu-

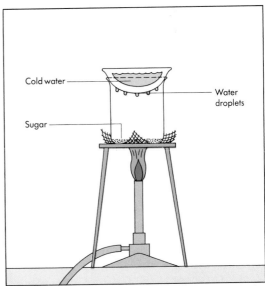

WORLD BOOK diagram by Arthur Grebetz

In decomposition, a substance is broken down into simpler products. Table sugar decomposes into carbon and water when heated. The carbon stays in the beaker. The water forms droplets at the bottom of an evaporating dish filled with cold water.

Medal of Honor
(Army)

Medal of Honor
(Air Force)

Medal of Honor
(Navy)

Decorations and medals of the United States

Distinguished
Service Cross
(Army)

Air Force
Cross

Navy
Cross

U.S. Army

(Defense)

Distinguished Service Medal
(Army)

(Air Force)

(Navy)

Purple Heart

Silver Star

Legion of Merit
(Chief Commander)

Distinguished
Flying Cross

NASA

NASA Congressional
Space Medal of Honor

Presidential Medal of Freedom

Young American
Medal for Bravery

lar in the United States because it was associated with customs of the European upper classes. As a result, no general system of military decorations or medals was organized until the Civil War. However, a few individual awards were granted during the Revolutionary War.

George Washington received the first American medal. In 1776, Congress gave him a gold medal for forcing the British to abandon Boston.

In 1782, Washington established the Purple Heart, formally called the Badge of Military Merit. This badge,

United States military decorations and medals

Name of medal	Year established	People eligible	Awarded for
Medal of Honor	1861 (Navy)	All ranks	Gallantry in action
	1862 (Army)	All ranks	Gallantry in action
	1963 (Air Force)	All ranks	Gallantry in action
Distinguished Service Cross (Army)	1918	All ranks	Exceptional heroism in combat
Navy Cross	1919	All ranks	Exceptional heroism in combat
Air Force Cross	1960	All ranks	Exceptional heroism in combat
Defense Distinguished Service Medal	1970	High-ranking officers assigned to Defense Department	Distinguished service
Distinguished Service Medal	1918 (Army)	High-ranking officers	Exceptional meritorious service
	1919 (Navy)	High-ranking officers	Exceptional meritorious service
	1949 (Coast Guard)	High-ranking officers	Exceptional meritorious service
	1960 (Air Force)	High-ranking officers	Exceptional meritorious service
Silver Star (citation)	1918	All ranks of the armed forces	Gallantry in action
(medal)	1932	All ranks of the armed forces	Gallantry in action
Legion of Merit	1942	Normally to officers or high foreign officials	Exceptionally meritorious service in peace or war
Distinguished Flying Cross	1926	All ranks of the armed forces	Heroism or extraordinary achievement in flight
Soldier's Medal	1926	All ranks of the Army	Heroism not involving conflict with the enemy
Navy and Marine Corps Medal	1942	All ranks of the Navy or Marine Corps	Heroism not involving conflict with the enemy
Airman's Medal	1960	All ranks of the Air Force	Heroism not involving conflict with the enemy
Coast Guard Medal	1951	Any person serving with the Coast Guard	Heroism not involving conflict with the enemy
Bronze Star	1944	All ranks of the armed forces	Heroic or meritorious achievement during military operations
Air Medal	1942	All ranks of the armed forces	Meritorious achievement in flight
Commendation Medal	1944 (Navy)	All ranks	Meritorious service in war or peace
	1945 (Army)	All ranks	Meritorious service in war or peace
	1947 (Coast Guard)	All ranks	Meritorious service in war or peace
	1958 (Air Force)	All ranks	Meritorious service in war or peace
Purple Heart (original)	1782	All ranks of the armed forces	Wounds or death in combat
(modern)	1932 (Army)	All ranks of the armed forces	Wounds or death in combat
	1942 (Navy)	All ranks of the armed forces	Wounds or death in combat

United States civilian decorations and medals

Presidential Medal of Freedom	1963	U.S. citizens	Nation's highest civilian honor for exceptional merit toward national security, world peace, culture, or other public service
Presidential Citizens Medal	1969	U.S. citizens	Exemplary deeds of service
Gold and Silver Lifesaving Medals	1874	Any person	Lifesaving in maritime waters at personal risk of life
National Security Medal	1953	Any person	Distinguished contribution to the U.S. national intelligence effort
President's Award for Distinguished Federal Civilian Service	1957	Federal employees	Outstanding service
Young American Medal for Bravery	1950	U.S. citizens under 19	Exceptional courage in lifesaving
Young American Medal for Service	1950	U.S. citizens under 19	Outstanding service
Congressional Space Medal of Honor	1969	Astronauts	Exceptional meritorious contribution to national welfare
National Aeronautics and Space Administration Distinguished Service Medal	1959	Federal employees	Contributions to aeronautical or space exploration

Grand Cordon of the Supreme
Order of the Chrysanthemum
(Japan)

Consulate General of Japan, New York

Order of Merit of
the Italian Republic
(Italy)

Royal Swedish Embassy, Washington, D.C.
Royal Order of the Seraphim
(Sweden)

Order of the
Aztec Eagle
(Mexico)

Victoria
Cross
(Great Britain)

Military Order
of William
(Netherlands)

Order of
Lenin
(Soviet Union)

Iron
Cross
(Germany)

Legion
of Honor
(France)

Decorations and medals of other countries

WORLD BOOK photos

which consisted of a heart made of purple cloth, was awarded to Revolutionary War soldiers for unusual bravery. The modern Purple Heart, established in 1932, is given to members of the armed forces who have been wounded or killed in action.

During the Civil War, Congress authorized the first permanent U.S. military decoration or medal—the Medal of Honor. Today this award, often called the Congressional Medal of Honor, is the highest military decoration that the United States grants to members of its armed forces. Congress approved the Navy Medal of Honor in 1861, and the Army Medal of Honor in 1862. Originally, the Army Medal of Honor was awarded only to noncommissioned officers and privates. In 1863, this honor was also given to officers. The Air Force Medal of Honor was approved by Congress in 1963. Before then, Air Force personnel received the Army Medal of Honor because the Air Force was originally a division of the Army.

Campaign medals, also known as war service medals, have been awarded to all ranks of the military for service in every war fought by the United States from the Civil War to the present. The first campaign medal approved by Congress was the Manila Bay Medal (Dewey Medal). It was awarded in 1898 to members of the Navy and Marine Corps who took part in the battle of Manila Bay during the Spanish-American War. The U.S. War De-

partment authorized the Army Civil War Campaign Medal in 1907—42 years after the conflict ended.

Civilian awards. Congress established the gold and silver Treasury Department Lifesaving Medals in 1874. They are awarded by the Coast Guard for extreme and heroic daring in rescue at sea.

In 1904, Andrew Carnegie established the Carnegie Hero Fund Commission. The commission provides awards in North America and Western Europe for saving or attempting to save lives. Carnegie Medals have been awarded in gold, silver, and bronze.

The Department of Justice awards the Young American Medal for Bravery and the Young American Medal for Service. Only two of each of these medals can be awarded each year to young people under the age of 19. The National Aeronautics and Space Administration (NASA) awards the Distinguished Service Medal to astronauts or any other federal employees who have made a great contribution to aeronautical or space exploration. Astronauts are also eligible for the Congressional Space Medal of Honor. The Presidential Citizens Medal is occasionally awarded to distinguished United States citizens. Recipients have included composer Irving Berlin and comedian Bob Hope. Congress awards the Medal for Merit to United States and foreign civilians who perform distinguished service in wartime. The

Presidential Medal of Freedom, the nation's highest civilian honor, is awarded by the President for outstanding service.

Other awards. Most of the states give members of their National Guard decorations and medals that resemble federal military awards. Some cities, schools, associations, and foundations also award decorations.

The Constitution forbids U.S. citizens who work for the federal government to accept foreign decorations without the consent of Congress. Congress has passed special laws authorizing specified people to accept decorations awarded by another country.

Foreign orders and decorations

Decorations and medals are awarded by nearly every country in the world. Most nations have national orders of merit. The highest awards for valor or service in some countries are the grand orders of knighthood. New systems of awards have developed as kingdoms have been replaced by other forms of government. Many former colonies that are now independent also have set up their own systems of awards.

The Americas. Mexico awards the Order of the Aztec Eagle to foreigners who have given distinguished service to Mexico. Bolivia's highest award is the National Order of the Condor of the Andes. It is given to foreigners and Bolivian citizens for exceptional civil or military merit. Peru awards the Order of the Sun of Peru to Peruvians and foreigners for distinguished service in civilian or military affairs. The Order of the Sun of Peru was established in 1821.

Europe. The Victoria Cross ranks as the highest honor in Great Britain. Queen Victoria instituted this award in 1856. It is usually given to members of the military for a single act of extreme heroism. Britain's Royal Humane Society is probably the world's best-known lifesaving society. Each year, this society grants more than 50 medals for lifesaving. France's highest award is the Legion of Honor. This award was instituted by Emperor Napoleon I in 1802. It is given to foreigners and French citizens for gallantry or civil achievement. The Legion of Honor was the first order based solely on merit and was open to all citizens. One of the oldest European awards is Denmark's Order of the Dannebrog. It was established

Decorations, medals, and orders of some other countries

Country	Name of award	Year established	People eligible	Awarded for
Belgium	**Order of Leopold**	1832	Belgians and citizens of other countries	General civilian and military merit
Brazil	**National Order of the Southern Cross**	1822	Citizens of other countries	Civil or military merit
British Commonwealth	**Victoria Cross**	1856	All ranks of the armed forces	Conspicuous bravery in action
	George Cross	1940	Civilians and military	Conspicuous bravery
Chad	**National Order of Chad**	1960	Chadians	Distinguished service to Chad
China	**Order of Socialist Labor**	1949	Chinese Communists	Distinguished service to China
Denmark	**Order of the Dannebrog**	1219; revived 1671	Danes and foreigners	General merit
France	**Legion of Honor**	1802	French citizens and citizens of other countries	General merit
Gabon	**Order of the Equatorial Star**	1959	All people over 29 years old	Contribution to the work of Gabon; acts of courage or devotion to duty
Great Britain	**Order of the Garter**	1348	Sovereign and 26 knights	Service to the British monarch
Greece	**Order of the Redeemer**	1829	Greeks and citizens of other countries	General merit
Israel	**Hero of Israel**	1949	Military personnel	Gallantry in combat
Italy	**Order of the Star of Italian Solidarity**	1947	All civilians	Contribution to the rebuilding of Italy after World War II
Japan	**Supreme Order of the Chrysanthemum**	1876 or 1877	Japanese male royalty and heads of state	Great service to the emperor
Nepal	**Order of Mahendra-Mala**	1961	Foreign monarchs	Service to Nepal
Pakistan	**Sign of Haider**	1958	Pakistani military	Acts of great heroism in action
Philippines	**Ancient Order of Sikatuna**	1951	Philippine and foreign diplomats and heads of state	Outstanding achievement
Somalia	**Order of the Somali Star**	1960	All people	Outstanding civil or military merit
Soviet Union	**Order of Lenin**	1930	Soviet and foreign individuals and organizations	Achievement in research, art, technology, or economics
Sweden	**Order of the Seraphim**	1748	Royalty and heads of state	Service to humanity
Syria	**Order of the Omayyad**	1924	All people	Outstanding civil or military merit
Turkey	**Independence Medal**	1924	Turkish citizens	Outstanding contribution to the formation of the Turkish Republic
The Vatican	**Order of Pius**	1847	Distinguished Roman Catholics	Personal service to the pope
West Germany	**Iron Cross**	1813	German and allied military	Exceptional bravery in combat and outstanding leadership of troops
Yugoslavia	**Order of Hero of Socialist Labor**	1948	Individuals and organizations	Exceptional contributions in industry and productivity

in 1219 and revived in 1671. It is given to Danes and foreigners for distinguished service in civilian and military affairs. The Soviet Union awards the Order of Lenin to outstanding Soviet and foreign individuals and organizations. This award was begun in 1930.

Middle East. Lebanon gives the National Order of the Cedar to foreigners and to Lebanese for exceptional service or for acts of extreme courage. Egypt's highest award is the Order of the Nile. This award is given to Egyptian citizens and foreigners for distinguished military or civilian service. Israel gives the Medal for Valour to members of the Israeli military who have performed acts of supreme heroism.

Africa. Kenya awards the Order of the Golden Heart of Kenya to citizens of Kenya and foreigners who have performed exceptional service to the country. Morocco's highest award is the Order of Muhammad. The Order of Muhammad award is given to members of the royal family, foreign heads of state, and civil and military leaders for exceptional service to Morocco. Malawi gives the Order of the Lion of Malawi to foreigners and citizens of Malawi who have performed distinguished and outstanding service to Malawi. The Order of the Pioneers of Liberia is Liberia's award for exceptional service to Liberia in the arts, science, or government, as well as for heroism.

Australia and Asia. Australia's highest award is the Order of Australia. It is given to Australians and foreigners for outstanding civil or military merit. India awards the Bharat Ratna (Jewel of India) to Indian citizens who have done exceptional work in art, literature, science, or public service. Thailand's greatest honor is the Most Illustrious Order of the Royal House of Chakri. Membership is limited to 43 people who have performed outstanding service to Thailand. The Supreme Order of the Chrysanthemum is Japan's highest award. This award is given to Japanese royalty, nobility, and foreign heads of state (male only). The Supreme Order of the Chrysanthemum was established in 1876 or 1877.

History

Since the beginning of history, monarchs and heads of state have rewarded individuals for bravery and merit. The ancient Greeks rewarded military and athletic heroes with wreaths made of laurel leaves. The tradition of the laurel wreath has had a lasting influence. Today, many medals have an image of a laurel wreath surrounding an inscription or the *bust* (sculpted head) of a head of state.

The ancient Romans crowned their heroes with gold laurel wreaths. Gold collars, chains, medallions, and arm rings were also awarded for outstanding bravery. The most significant award was the *phalera,* a gold or silver disk formed into the head of a god, man, or animal. These awards were given for bravery in battle and represented an early stage in the development of breast stars and chest decorations.

Knights of the Middle Ages formed orders. Each order created a distinctive badge that displayed the symbol of the order. A knight wore the badge on a chain around his neck. Knights also received medals of gold, silver, or bronze. These round medals were meant to be displayed on a table, not worn.

The first ribboned medals, similar to today's medals,

appeared in Austria and Russia during the 1600's. Most of these types of medals celebrated participation in famous battles, and they were generally awarded only to military officers.

By the mid-1800's, almost every country in Europe had at least one national order for merit. Orders were created to reward merit in many fields, including the arts, science, and agriculture, as well as for military and civil merit. During the last half of the 1800's, trade and the expansion of colonial empires led much of the rest of the world to adopt awards systems based on those of Western Europe.   J. Robert Elliott

See also **Knighthood, Orders of** (picture: Some leading orders of knighthood).

Additional resources

Borthick, David, and Britton, J. L. *Medals, Military and Civilian of the United States.* MCN Press, 1984.
Gaylor, John. *Military Badge Collecting.* 3rd ed. Secker & Warburg, 1983.
Rosignoli, Guido. *Ribbons of Orders, Decorations and Medals.* Arco, 1977. First published in 1976.
Werlich, Robert. *Orders and Decorations of All Nations: Ancient and Modern, Civil and Military.* 2nd ed. Quaker Press, 1974.

Decorative arts is a term used to designate a variety of categories including furniture, woodwork, and glass. The term decorative arts also refers to ceramics (porcelain and earthenware) and metalwork (gold, silver, bronze, and other metals).

The decorative arts are called the *applied arts* when referring to objects intended for actual use such as chairs, silver flatware, porcelain dishes, and glass vessels. *Minor arts* is another term occasionally used for decorative arts. This term does not mean that the decorative arts are inferior to other forms. It is intended to separate decorative arts from the *fine arts* of painting, sculpture, and architecture.

The decorative arts reflect the desire throughout human history to decorate the environment. For example, prehistoric peoples created small ivory sculptures. The Egyptians buried finely crafted furniture and jewelry with their dead. During medieval times, artisans deco-

Spring Flowers Egg, an enamel and gold shell enclosing a basket of wood anemones made of gold, diamonds, garnets, and chalcedony; the *Forbes* Magazine Collection, New York City

A masterpiece of the decorative arts, this Easter egg was crafted by the Russian jeweler Peter Carl Fabergé in 1890.

rated castles and churches with articles made from ivory, gold, and enamel. Artists of the Renaissance produced fine furniture, metalwork, and glass. People of the 1700's created beautiful porcelain pieces and carved woodwork. Today, the decorative arts continue to be an important division of art. Fine art and decorative art reflect important artistic trends in their form, color, and material.   John W. Keefe

Related articles in *World Book* include:

Beadwork	Interior decoration	Lace
Decoupage	Ironwork, Decora-	Mosaic
Enamel	tive	Pottery
Furniture	Ivory	Stained glass
Inlay	Jewelry	Tapestry

Decorator. See Interior decoration (Careers).

Decoupage, *DAY koo PAHZH,* is the art of using paper cutouts to decorate furniture and such accessories as boxes, lamps, plaques, and trays. The finished object looks and feels like fine enamel. Cutouts can be taken from such articles as calendars, greeting cards, magazine and newspaper illustrations, photographs, and wrapping paper. The word *decoupage* comes from the French word *decouper,* meaning *to cut out.*

Decoupage usually involves four steps. First, the sur-

WORLD BOOK photo

Decoupage is the art of decorating furniture and accessories with paper cutouts. The cutout is glued to a surface and covered with many coats of varnish. The final coat is waxed and polished.

face of the object to be decorated must be sanded and, if wood, painted or stained. A protective sealer is applied to the cutout, which is then glued to the object. Next, the decorated surface is covered with many coats of varnish until the edge of the cutout cannot be felt. Last, the final coat of varnish is smoothed, polished, and waxed.   Dona Z. Meilach

Deductive method is the process of reasoning by which we draw conclusions by logical inference from given premises. If we begin by accepting the propositions that "All Greeks have beards" and that "Zeno is a Greek," we may validly conclude that "Zeno has a beard." We refer to the conclusions of deductive reasoning as *valid,* rather than *true,* because we must distinguish clearly between *that which follows logically* from other

statements and *that which is the case.*

Starting premises may be articles of faith, assumptions, or conclusions based on earlier reasoning. In order to draw valid conclusions, the deductive method uses a special set of rules. These rules are based on the structures of premises and conclusions. Mathematics and logic make extensive use of the deductive method. The scientific method requires a combination of induction and deduction (see **Inductive method**).

Morton L. Schagrin

See also **Logic; Science** (Mathematics and logic).

Deed is a written document to transfer ownership of real estate. The deed must be signed by the *grantor,* the party transferring ownership. In many cases, it is also signed by the *grantee,* the party receiving ownership. The deed must describe the property transferred and show the intent to transfer ownership. The deed takes effect only when it is delivered to the grantee or to the grantee's agent.

There are two main types of deeds—*warranty deeds* and *quitclaim deeds.* A warranty deed guarantees the grantee that the grantor owns all the rights described in the deed. If it turns out that the grantor does not own the rights, the grantor must pay the grantee's resulting damages. A quitclaim deed contains no such guarantee and therefore is used less often.

Unlike the title to an automobile, a deed does not have to be submitted to the government to become valid. However, deeds may be recorded in the office of the recorder of deeds for the county or district in which the land is located. Recording the deed gives public notice of the rights the grantee is receiving. It thus helps protect the grantee against later claims by others to rights in the property.

Many land buyers obtain title insurance to protect themselves against later claims. Before the insurance company insures the buyer, it researches the title to the property and reports its findings to the buyer. Some land buyers hire a lawyer or other specialist to research the title and prepare a brief history of the land's ownership. The history is called an *abstract of title.* See **Abstract.**   James L. Winokur

Deep refers to any ocean area that has a depth of more than 18,000 feet (5,490 meters). More than 100 deeps have been discovered in ocean floors. Contrary to popular belief, they are not found in the center of the ocean. Most of them occur close to mountainous islands where steep shores plunge down to the bottom of the sea.

The deepest known ocean deep is located in the Mariana Trench 200 miles (320 kilometers) southwest of Guam. There, the ocean floor is 36,198 feet (11,033 meters) below the surface. The Milwaukee Deep, part of the Puerto Rico Trench north of Puerto Rico, has the greatest recorded depth in the Atlantic Ocean. This deep was found in 1939 and has a depth of 28,374 feet (8,648 meters).   Mark A. Cane

See also **Atlantic Ocean** (The ocean bed); **Ocean** (The world ocean; The land at the bottom of the sea); **Pacific Ocean** (Location and size).

Deep-sea animals. See Fish (pictures: Fish of the deep ocean); Ocean (pictures).

Deep-sea diving. See Diving, Underwater.

Deep Sea Drilling Project. See Atlantic Ocean (People and the Atlantic); Ocean Drilling Program.

Stephen Collins, N.A.S.

New antlers of a white-tailed deer, *above,* and moose, *below,* have a furry cover called *velvet* which the animals soon rub off.

D. Lichtenberg, N.A.S.

A mother white-tailed deer guards her fawns while they search for food. Fawns may stay with their mothers for more than a year.

Fritz Prenzel, Pix from Publix

Deer are the only animals with bones called *antlers* on their heads. Antlers differ from horns, which are strong, hard layers of skin with a bony core. Deer are among the most common large land mammals and are well-known for their running ability.

There are more than 60 species of deer, including caribou, elk, marsh deer, moose, mule deer, musk deer, and reindeer. Some deer live in the hot, dry deserts. Others live in cold regions above the Arctic Circle. However, most species of deer live in prairies, swamps, or woodlands that have a mild climate.

Deer vary widely in size. They are among the largest wild animals in North America and Europe. The North American moose is the largest deer in the world. Some males grow $7\frac{1}{2}$ feet (2.3 meters) tall at the shoulders and weigh over 1,800 pounds (816 kilograms). The smallest deer is the pudu of western South America. It is about 1

foot (30 centimeters) tall at the shoulders and weighs about 20 pounds (9 kilograms).

Among most species of deer, only the males have antlers. In caribou and reindeer, however, both males and females have antlers.

Most male deer are called *bucks*. But male caribou, elk, and moose are called *bulls,* and male red deer are *stags* or *harts*. Most female deer are called *does*. But female caribou, elk, and moose are *cows,* and female red deer are *hinds*. Most young deer are called *fawns,* but young caribou, elk, and moose are *calves*.

Since early times, people have used deer meat for food and deer skins for clothing. After white settlers came to North America, they killed so many deer that the animal was wiped out in large regions of the continent. In some areas, deer populations recovered after the animals were reintroduced from other regions and protected by hunting laws. However, hunting laws fail to protect many of the animals that prey on deer, such as coyotes and cougars. These predators are now scarce or absent in some areas where deer live, and some deer

Gregory K. Snyder, the contributor of this article, is Associate Professor of Biology at the University of Colorado.

populations have grown too large. As a result, today many deer are killed simply to reduce their numbers.

The body of a deer

Deer are *mammals*—that is, animals whose young feed on milk produced by the mother. Like other mammals, deer are *warm-blooded,* which means their body temperature remains fairly constant regardless of the surrounding temperature. Deer have a covering of hair on the body that helps keep them warm in cold weather. Caribou of the Far North have a thick coat of hair. Most other deer have shorter, shiny hair that lies flat so that the animals' coat looks smooth. Deer in tropical regions have a much thinner coat.

Legs and hoofs. All deer have long, thin legs and are good runners. They move their legs rapidly and take long strides. A deer's foot is really two center toes. Each of the two toes is protected by a hard covering called a *hoof.* A deer runs on tiptoe with a springing or bouncing motion. Two other toes, called *dewclaws,* grow higher on the leg and have no use when the animal runs. The dewclaws often leave dots at the back of a deer's track in snow.

Deer use their speed to avoid predators. A frightened white-tailed deer can run as fast as 40 miles (64 kilometers) per hour and can leap 15 to 20 feet (4.6 to 6.1 meters) forward. Even the moose, with its large, powerful body, can run about 20 miles (32 kilometers) per hour.

Head. Deer have narrower heads and somewhat smaller noses and mouths than do cattle. The deer's lips move easily, and the animal uses them to grasp food. Most kinds of deer have only bottom teeth in the front of the mouth. A thick pad of rough skin takes the place of upper front teeth. The lower teeth press against this pad of skin when the deer tears off leaves and twigs to eat. The upper and lower back teeth have many sharp-pointed tips. The deer uses these teeth to chew its food.

A deer has large eyes at the sides of its head. However, the animal depends on its ears and its nose to catch the first warnings of danger. A deer has keen hearing and smell. Its large ears are always erect, and they can be moved to catch sounds from any direction. A

The skeleton of a deer

WORLD BOOK illustration by John D. Dawson

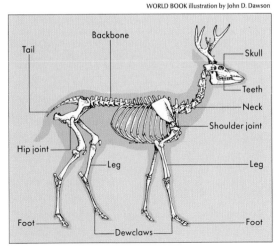

The tracks of a deer

WORLD BOOK illustration by Tom Dolan

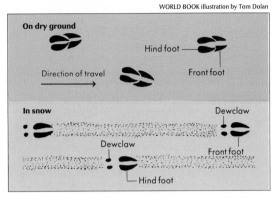

deer can identify the direction from which a sound is coming. A deer usually faces into the wind when it eats or rests. The wind carries sounds and smells of approaching predators.

Antlers are outgrowths of bone that are part of a deer's skull. Their hard, bony structure and sharp points make them extremely dangerous weapons. Male deer use antlers chiefly to fight for mates or for leadership of a herd. Deer that live in mild or cold climates shed their antlers each winter and begin to grow a new set in late spring. Deer that live in warm or hot climates may lose their antlers and grow new ones at other times of the year.

New antlers are soft and tender and grow rapidly. A thin layer of skin grows over the antlers and stimulates their development. This skin layer is called *velvet* because it is covered by short, fine hairs that give it a soft appearance. As the antlers reach full size, the velvet dries and the deer scrapes it off on the ground or against trees or bushes.

All antlers have branches that end in *tines* (points or prongs). But the shape of the antlers varies among species of deer. Moose and caribou are easy to distinguish from other deer by the antlers alone. Moose antlers have areas that are broad and flat. In caribou, a branch of one antler extends forward above the nose of the animal.

The size and shape of a deer's antlers depend on the animal's size, age, and health. A deer first grows antlers when it is 1 or 2 years old. In most deer, these first ant-

How a deer's antlers grow

Deer lose their antlers each winter and begin to grow new ones in late spring. The new antlers are soft and tender. Thin skin with short, fine hairs called *velvet* covers the growing antlers. Full-grown antlers are hard and strong, and have no velvet.

WORLD BOOK illustration by Tom Dolan

lers are short and somewhat straight. Each year, the antlers grow longer and larger, and form branches.

The life of a deer

Deer have no permanent homes, dens, or nesting sites. They spend their lives roaming an area called a *home range* in search of food. Deer also claim and defend areas within the home range to attract mates. Deer may live in groups or alone, depending on their age, sex, and species. Moose spend most of their time alone. But caribou may form herds with up to 100,000 animals.

Many deer move to more favorable locations when the seasons change. Deer that live in the mountains move to lower lands for the winter. These deer usually stay near the edges of forests. There, trees and grasses supply food, and bushes serve as a place to sleep, to hide from predators, or to give birth.

Some deer migrate long distances each year. Caribou may travel 1,000 miles (1,600 kilometers) between feeding grounds. They spend the summer in the flat, marshy land of the Arctic Circle. In late summer, they gather in large herds and travel to warmer areas for the winter. In early spring, the caribou return north.

Young. A female deer carries her young inside her body for about six to nine months, depending on the species. She chooses a hidden spot away from other deer to give birth. The young deer remain hidden until they can walk well enough to follow their mother.

Fawns of white-tailed deer weigh from $3\frac{1}{2}$ to 6 pounds (1.6 to 2.7 kilograms) at birth. They stay hidden for four to five weeks. Newborn moose calves weigh about 25 to 35 pounds (11 to 16 kilograms). They can follow their mother when they are about 10 days old. Caribou calves, most of which are born during the herd's spring migration, weigh about 10 pounds (4.5 kilograms) at birth. They can walk with the herd several hours later.

Most kinds of deer have one young at a time. Occasionally, twins are born. Chinese water deer, which live along the Yangtze River, give birth to the most young—four to seven fawns at a time.

Food. Deer eat a wide variety of plants and plant parts. In spring, when food is relatively plentiful, deer eat mostly grasses, flowers, buds, and young leaves. In summer, when grasses and leaves dry up, deer eat twigs, stems, and mature leaves. In winter, deer often gather in small herds and tramp the snow on their feeding grounds to reach twigs and small tree branches. When food becomes extremely scarce, deer will feed on bark and other hard parts of trees.

Deer do not chew their food well before swallowing it. A deer's stomach has four chambers. One chamber serves as a storage place, which enables deer to eat large amounts of food quickly. Thus, deer do not need to spend long periods at their feeding grounds, where predators might see them. Later, when a deer has found a safe place, the stored food is returned to the mouth in a ball-like glob. The deer then chews this food, called *cud.* After the chewed food has been swallowed, it goes to other parts of the stomach. Animals that digest their food in this way are called *ruminants* (see **Ruminant**).

Habits. Deer use their keen senses, their knowledge of their home range, and their speed to avoid enemies. A healthy deer can outrun most predators, including bears, cougars, wolves, and human beings. But a deer's primary means of escaping danger is to avoid detection. Unless startled, most deer will stand motionless and let a predator pass by. White-tailed deer and mule deer feed only at dawn and dusk at the edges of forests, where they blend in best with their surroundings.

Wild deer live 10 to 20 years. In captivity, some deer live longer. However, the roe deer of Europe lives 10 to 12 years in the wild but only 3 to 7 years in a zoo.

Kinds of deer

There are more than 60 species of deer. They live in North America, Central and South America, and Asia and Europe. Deer also have been introduced into places where they did not live naturally, including Australia, Hawaii, New Guinea, and New Zealand.

North American deer. The best known deer of North America include (1) white-tailed deer, (2) mule deer, (3) caribou, (4) elk, and (5) moose.

White-tailed deer, also called *Virginia deer,* are the most common large game animals of North America. A male white-tailed deer may stand $3\frac{1}{2}$ feet (1.1 meters) tall at the shoulders and weigh 200 pounds (91 kilograms).

Deer of North America These drawings show the differences in size, body shape, and antlers of the five major kinds of North American deer. The sizes given are the average shoulder height of the adult deer. Deer, especially the moose and elk, are among the largest wild animals of North America.

WORLD BOOK illustrations by John D. Dawson

Moose
6 feet (1.8 meters)

Elk (wapiti)
5 feet (1.5 meters)

Caribou
4 feet (1.2 meters)

Mule deer
$3\frac{1}{2}$ feet (1.1 meters)

White-tailed deer
$3\frac{1}{2}$ feet (1.1 meters)

Harry Engels, N.A.S.

An American elk stands alert for danger in the grassy high mountain meadow that is its summer feeding area.

Frederick Baldwin, Photo Researchers

A herd of reindeer scrambles over the rocky ground of the Arctic regions to find grass and moss to eat.

The deer's tail, for which it is named, grows about 1 foot (30 centimeters) long. The tail has brown hair on top and white hair underneath. When the deer is frightened and begins to run, its tail stands straight up, showing the white part. This deer has a reddish-brown coat in summer and a gray or bluish-gray coat in winter.

Mule deer, also called *black-tailed deer* in the Pacific Northwest, are much like white-tailed deer. Mule deer are named for their large, furry ears, which look somewhat like those of a mule. Buckskin was originally made from the hides of mule deer and white-tailed deer.

Caribou, which live in northern North America, are closely related to the reindeer. Unlike all other deer except reindeer, both males and females have antlers. Caribou grow about 4 feet (1.2 meters) high at the shoulders and vary in color from white to grey or brown. Arctic Eskimos and Indians eat caribou meat, carve the animal's bones into utensils, and make the caribou's hide into clothing and tents.

Elk, also called *wapiti,* are the second largest deer in the world. Only moose are larger. Male elk may stand about 5 feet (1.5 meters) at the shoulder and weigh up to 1,100 pounds (500 kilograms). Elk tend to form herds with up to 500 animals in summer and 1,000 animals in winter.

Moose are the largest of all deer. Some males stand $7\frac{1}{2}$ feet (2.3 meters) at the shoulders and weigh up to 1,800 pounds (816 kilograms). Their antlers may measure $4\frac{1}{2}$ feet (1.4 meters) wide and weigh up to 60 pounds (27 kilograms). In spite of its large size, a moose can move quickly and quietly through the forest. Moose are much darker in color than other deer, ranging from reddish-brown to black. Moose normally live alone.

Central and South American deer include (1) pudu, (2) marsh deer, (3) brocket deer, (4) pampas deer, and (5) huemul.

Pudu, also called *rabbit deer,* are the smallest of all deer. They live in the forests of western South America from sea level to altitudes of about 10,000 feet (3,000 me-

ters) in the Andes Mountains. Pudu grow only about 1 foot (30 centimeters) high and weigh about 20 pounds (9 kilograms). They have short, spikelike antlers. Their rough, brittle hair is brown or gray. Pudu are probably the shyest deer, and little is known about them.

Marsh deer are the largest South American deer. They grow about 4 feet (1.2 meters) high. These deer live in the swampy plains and forests of Brazil, Paraguay, and Uruguay. They can spread each hoof wide to help them walk on the soft ground. Indians hunt these animals for their skins, but the meat has a poor flavor.

Some members of the deer family

Common name	Scientific name	Where found
Brocket deer	*Mazama*	Central America
*Caribou and *reindeer	*Rangifer tarandus*	Asia, Europe and North America
Chinese water deer	*Hydropotes inermis*	Asia
Chital (Axis deer)	*Axis axis*	Asia
Fallow deer	*Dama dama*	Asia and Europe
Huemul (Andean deer)	*Hippocamelus*	South America
Marsh deer	*Blastocerus dichotomus*	South America
*Moose	*Alces*	Asia, Europe, and North America
*Mule deer (Black-tailed deer)	*Odocoileus hemionus*	North America
*Musk deer	*Moschus moschiferus*	Asia
Père David's deer	*Elaphurus davidianus*	Asia
Pudu	*Pudu*	South America
*Red deer and American elk (Wapiti)	*Cervus elaphus*	Europe, Asia, Africa, and North America
Roe deer	*Capreolus capreolus*	Asia and Europe
White-tailed deer (Virginia deer)	*Odocoileus virginianus*	North America

*Has a separate article in WORLD BOOK.

Where deer live

The yellow areas of the map show the parts of the world in which deer live. Deer live on every continent except Antarctica.

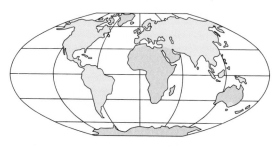

Brocket deer live from southern Mexico to Paraguay, in wooded areas from sea level to altitudes of 16,000 feet (4,880 meters). They grow about 20 inches (51 centimeters) high at the shoulders. Their antlers look somewhat like spikes.

Pampas deer are named for the tall pampas grasses of the South American plains in which they live. These deer grow about 3 feet (91 centimeters) high at the shoulders and have reddish-brown or yellowish-brown hair. The male has glands in its back hoofs that give off a strong odor.

Huemul, or **Andean deer,** are found in the Andes Mountains from Ecuador to southern Argentina. They live in thick forests and grassy plateaus at altitudes of about 16,000 feet (4,880 meters). Huemul grow about 3 feet (91 centimeters) high at the shoulders and have speckled coats of gray, yellow, and brown. The hair is rough and brittle, and grows longest on the forehead and tail.

Asian and European deer include (1) musk deer; (2) muntjac; (3) chital, or axis deer; (4) fallow deer; (5) red deer; (6) reindeer; and (7) Père David's deer.

Musk deer roam the forests of the mountains and high plateaus of central, eastern, and northeastern Asia. They grow to 24 inches (61 centimeters) tall at the shoulders and have no antlers. Two tusklike teeth grow downward from the top of the jaw. The deer are named for an oily substance called *musk,* which is produced by a gland in the skin of the male's abdomen. Musk is used in perfume.

Muntjac live in jungle areas in India, Nepal, Sri Lanka, southern China, and throughout most of Southeast Asia. They stand about 20 inches (51 centimeters) high at the shoulders. These deer make a barking noise when they are frightened and are sometimes called *barking deer.*

Chital, or *axis deer,* are found in the grasslands and open forests of India and Sri Lanka. Some people consider them the most beautiful and graceful of all deer. Chital grow about 3 feet (91 centimeters) high at the shoulders. Their sleek reddish-brown coats are spotted with white. Their antlers, which grow about 3 feet (91 centimeters) long, curve gracefully back from their heads. Like the male musk deer, male chital have two tusklike teeth that grow from the upper jaw. These deer are found in many zoos.

Fallow deer originally lived only in lands along the Mediterranean Sea. Today, they may be found in most parts of Europe. Many are kept in herds on estates or in parks. Fallow deer are about as large as chital. Unlike most European deer, they have broad, flat antlers shaped somewhat like those of the moose.

Red deer are found in Europe, Asia, and northern Africa. These animals also live in North America, where they are called *American elk.* Red deer have reddish-brown to grayish-brown hair and are famous for their beauty.

Reindeer, which live in the Arctic and in the northern regions of Europe and Asia, look like caribou. The male and female both have antlers. Reindeer are among the most important animals of the Far North. People eat reindeer meat, make clothing and tents from the hide, and carve utensils from the antlers and bones.

Père David's deer once roamed the plains and marshes of northern China. They are named for a French priest who first saw the deer in 1865. Today, only about 400 of these deer are still alive. They live in private parks and zoos in many parts of the world. All are related to deer that were brought to England about 1900 from a herd kept by the Chinese emperor in Beijing (also spelled Peking). The original herd in China died out in 1921, but the English herd did well. Père David's deer stand about $3\frac{1}{2}$ feet (1.1 meters) high at the shoulders and have a grayish-tan coat in winter and a reddish-tan coat in summer.

Endangered species. In the late 1980's, more than 20 species of deer were endangered with extinction. These species included Columbian white-tailed deer, key deer, marsh deer, and five kinds of Asian sikas. Many countries have banned deer hunting and have set up game preserves to protect the animals. Today, the destruction of natural habitats poses the greatest threat to deer populations. People have cleared away many areas where deer live for agricultural and housing developments.

Scientific classification. Deer are members of the class Mammalia and belong to the order of even-toed hoofed animals, Artiodactyla. They make up the deer family, Cervidae.

Gregory K. Snyder

Related articles in *World Book* include:

Outline

Questions

How many species of deer are there?
What are antlers? How do they grow?
What is a home range?
How far can a deer jump?
What do deer eat?
Which is the largest deer? The smallest?
How many toes does a deer have?
What are young caribou called?
Why does a deer face the wind when it eats or rests?
How do deer avoid enemies?

Deer fly is an insect related to the horse flies. Deer flies are found throughout North America. They have blotched or banded wings, and some of these wings are beautifully colored. Female deer flies bite large animals and people. Some deer flies carry germs that cause disease. The *snipe fly* is similar to the deer fly and is found in the Western United States. Snipe flies have two wings and six long legs. Some snipe flies have long beaks that are shaped like the bill of a bird called a *snipe*. A person may use mosquito repellents to avoid the bites of both deer flies and snipe flies.

WORLD BOOK illustration
by Shirley Hooper,
Oxford Illustrators Limited

Deer fly

Scientific classification. The deer fly belongs to the horse fly family, Tabanidae. It is in the genus *Chrysops.* Snipe flies belong to the snipe fly family, Rhagionidae.　　E.W. Cupp

Deer mouse. See Mouse (Deer mice).

Deere, John (1804-1886), was an American inventor and manufacturer. In 1837, he invented the first steel plow that efficiently turned the heavy American prairie sod. Deere became one of the world's greatest plowmakers.

Deere was born in Rutland, Vt. He became a blacksmith's apprentice at the age of 17. In 1836, he opened a blacksmith shop in Grand Detour, Ill. He soon learned that nearby farmers were dissatisfied with their plows. The heavy, gummy prairie sod stuck to the rough surface of the wood or iron moldboard that was used to turn the soil.

Deere built a smooth, hard moldboard out of an old circular steel saw in 1837. The new moldboard worked just as he had hoped. The soil fell away cleanly in furrows and polished the surface of the moldboard as it turned. Deere and a partner, Leonard Andruss, began making quantities of steel plows. Within 10 years, they were producing 1,000 plows annually. In 1847, Deere sold his interests to Andruss and started a new company in Moline, Ill. To improve the quality of his plows, Deere ordered a special type of hard steel from England. He then had a similar type of steel made in Pittsburgh. This project resulted in the first plow steel ever manufactured in the United States. By 1857, Deere was producing 10,000 plows a year. The business was incorporated as Deere and Company in 1868. Today the company ranks as one of the largest industrial corporations in the United States.　　Richard D. Humphrey

See also **Plow** (The sulky plow).

Deerhound is a Scottish breed of dog, close to the Irish wolfhound in ancestry. It was named for its skill at deer hunting, and it was bred to hunt game by sight. Today, it is seldom used for hunting. The deerhound is a member of the hound class of dogs. It measures from 28 to 32 inches (71 to 81 centimeters) tall at the shoulder and weighs from 75 to 110 pounds (34 to 50 kilograms). The coat of the deerhound is 3 to 4 inches (8 to 10 centimeters) long and is coarse and wiry. It may be gray or tan, with dark streaks or spots. The deerhound is a rugged but graceful dog. It makes an excellent pet.

Critically reviewed by the American Kennel Club

De Falla, Manuel. See Falla, Manuel de.

Defamation. See Libel.

Defenestration of Prague. See Thirty Years' War (The Bohemian period).

Defense, Civil. See Civil defense.

John Deere Co., Moline, Ill.

John Deere, *above,* became one of the world's leading manufacturers of plows. His Gilpin sulky, *right,* named for its designer, Gilpin Moore, was the first commercially successful riding plow. Deere introduced it in 1875.

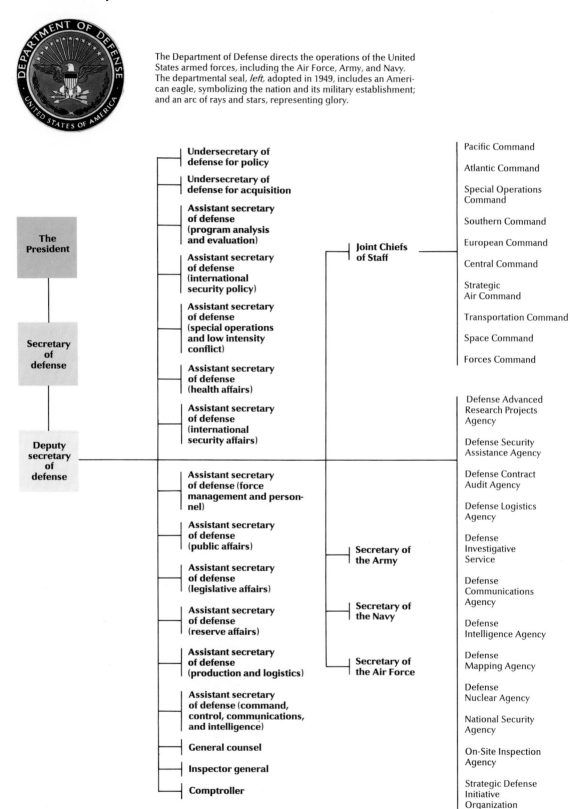

The Department of Defense directs the operations of the United States armed forces, including the Air Force, Army, and Navy. The departmental seal, *left,* adopted in 1949, includes an American eagle, symbolizing the nation and its military establishment; and an arc of rays and stars, representing glory.

The President

Secretary of defense

Deputy secretary of defense

Undersecretary of defense for policy

Undersecretary of defense for acquisition

Assistant secretary of defense (program analysis and evaluation)

Assistant secretary of defense (international security policy)

Assistant secretary of defense (special operations and low intensity conflict)

Assistant secretary of defense (health affairs)

Assistant secretary of defense (international security affairs)

Assistant secretary of defense (force management and personnel)

Assistant secretary of defense (public affairs)

Assistant secretary of defense (legislative affairs)

Assistant secretary of defense (reserve affairs)

Assistant secretary of defense (production and logistics)

Assistant secretary of defense (command, control, communications, and intelligence)

General counsel

Inspector general

Comptroller

Joint Chiefs of Staff

Secretary of the Army

Secretary of the Navy

Secretary of the Air Force

Pacific Command

Atlantic Command

Special Operations Command

Southern Command

European Command

Central Command

Strategic Air Command

Transportation Command

Space Command

Forces Command

Defense Advanced Research Projects Agency

Defense Security Assistance Agency

Defense Contract Audit Agency

Defense Logistics Agency

Defense Investigative Service

Defense Communications Agency

Defense Intelligence Agency

Defense Mapping Agency

Defense Nuclear Agency

National Security Agency

On-Site Inspection Agency

Strategic Defense Initiative Organization

Defense Legal Services Agency

Defense, Department of, is an executive department of the United States government. It directs the operations of the nation's armed forces, including the Army, Navy, and Air Force. The government maintains armed forces to ensure the security of the United States and to support the nation's policies and interests.

The secretary of defense, a member of the President's Cabinet, heads the Department of Defense. The secretary is a civilian and is appointed by the President with the approval of the Senate. All functions of the Department of Defense are carried out under the secretary's authority and control. The secretary is a member of the National Security Council and the North Atlantic Council. The secretary maintains close contact with governmental bodies, especially the Department of State.

Organization. The Department of Defense includes (1) the Office of the Secretary, (2) the Joint Chiefs of Staff, (3) the military departments, (4) the unified and specified commands, and (5) defense agencies.

The Office of the Secretary is made up of the secretary and a staff. The deputy secretary of defense is the secretary's chief assistant. The next senior officials are the undersecretary of defense for policy and the undersecretary of defense for acquisition. The undersecretary of defense for policy is the secretary's chief adviser on such subjects as arms limitation talks, intelligence gathering, and international affairs. The undersecretary of defense for acquisition is the secretary's main adviser and assistant for all matters relating to acquiring and constructing military weapons and materials.

Eleven assistant secretaries of defense have responsibilities in other areas. They deal with (1) command, control, communications, and intelligence; (2) legislative affairs; (3) health affairs; (4) international security affairs; (5) force management and personnel; (6) international security policy; (7) public affairs; (8) reserve affairs; (9) production and logistics; (10) program analysis and evaluation; and (11) special operations and low-intensity conflict. Other leading officials include the comptroller, the general counsel, and the inspector general.

The Joint Chiefs of Staff consists of a chairman, a vice chairman, the chiefs of staff of the Army and Air Force, the chief of naval operations, and the commandant of the Marine Corps. Members of the Joint Chiefs of Staff are the principal military advisers to the President, the National Security Council, and the secretary of defense. The members also transmit orders to the unified and specified commands.

The military departments are the departments of the Army, Navy, and Air Force. The Marine Corps is included in the Department of the Navy. Each military department is headed by a civilian secretary who administers the department under the direction, control, and authority of the secretary of defense. The military departments organize, train, equip, and maintain the readiness of their forces.

The unified and specified commands are the operating military units and perform continuing military missions. The President assigns combat forces to unified or specified commanders. Unified commands consist of large forces from more than one branch of service. Specified commands are made up of forces from only one branch of service. The unified commands are the Atlantic, Central, European, Pacific, Southern, and Special Operations commands. The Forces Command, the Space Command, the Strategic Air Command, and the Transportation Command are specified commands.

Defense agencies meet specific defense requirements. These agencies include the Defense Advanced Research Projects, Defense Communications, Defense Contract Audit, Defense Intelligence, Defense Mapping, Defense Nuclear, Defense Security Assistance, Defense Logistics, On-Site Inspection, and National Security agencies; and the Defense Investigative Service.

History. In 1789, Congress established the Department of War to administer and conduct military affairs. In 1798, Congress separated the naval forces from the land forces, creating the Department of the Navy. For the next 149 years, the Department of War and the Department of the Navy were the only two military departments. The secretaries of these departments were Cabinet members and reported directly to the President.

During World War II (1939-1945), President Franklin D. Roosevelt directed U.S. combat forces through a Joint Chiefs of Staff, which functioned without a formal charter. The armed services cooperated with one another through unified commands in overseas theaters of operation. At home, however, the Army and Navy competed for scarce personnel and materials. The Army Air Forces also pressed for equal status with the Army and Navy.

The National Security Act of 1947 created the National Military Establishment. It was headed by a secretary of defense and had three military departments. The Department of War became the Department of the Army. The Army Air Forces became a separate service under a new Department of the Air Force. The Navy and Marine Corps continued under the Department of the Navy. The secretary of defense became a member of the Cabinet. The secretary formulated general policies and programs for the National Military Establishment. Also in 1947, Congress formally chartered the Joint Chiefs of Staff and provided for a separate Joint Staff to help the Joint Chiefs.

In 1949, Congress set up the Department of Defense to replace the National Military Establishment. It withdrew executive status from the military departments and provided that they be administered separately under the

Secretaries of defense

Name	Took office	Under President
* James V. Forrestal	1947	Truman
Louis A. Johnson	1949	Truman
* George C. Marshall	1950	Truman
Robert A. Lovett	1951	Truman
Charles E. Wilson	1953	Eisenhower
Neil H. McElroy	1957	Eisenhower
Thomas S. Gates, Jr.	1959	Eisenhower
* Robert S. McNamara	1961	Kennedy, Johnson
* Clark M. Clifford	1968	Johnson
* Melvin R. Laird	1969	Nixon
* Elliot L. Richardson	1973	Nixon
James R. Schlesinger	1973	Nixon, Ford
Donald H. Rumsfeld	1975	Ford
* Harold Brown	1977	Carter
* Caspar W. Weinberger	1981	Reagan
Frank C. Carlucci	1987	Reagan
* Richard B. Cheney	1989	Bush

*Has a separate biography in *World Book*.

direction, authority, and control of the secretary of defense. At the same time, Congress also created the post of deputy secretary of defense.

In 1953, Congress passed a reorganization plan for the department, establishing a general counsel. In 1977, another reorganization created the posts of undersecretary of defense for policy and undersecretary of defense for research and engineering. In 1982, the department established the Space Command. This unit is responsible for space shuttle flights that carry military cargoes and for antisatellite warfare. In 1987, the position of undersecretary of defense for research and engineering was abolished, and a new position, undersecretary of defense for acquisition, was created.

Critically reviewed by the Department of Defense

Related articles in *World Book* include:

Air Force, United States	National Security
Army, United States	Agency/Central Security
Flag (picture: Flags of the United	Service
States government)	Navy, United States
Joint Chiefs of Staff	Pentagon Building
Marine Corps, U.S.	

Defense mechanism. See Neurosis (Neurosis as a psychological mechanism).

Deficiency disease. See Nutrition (Results of malnutrition); Disease (Nutritional diseases).

Defoe, Daniel (1660-1731), was an English novelist and journalist. He wrote *Robinson Crusoe,* one of the first English novels and one of the most popular adventure stories in Western literature. Some critics have called Defoe the father of the English novel. Others rate him as much less important. But he was one of the great masters of realistic narrative long before such writers as Theodore Dreiser and Ernest Hemingway.

His life. Defoe was born in London, the son of a butcher and candle merchant. He started a business career, but he went bankrupt and turned to writing. His earliest writings dealt with such controversial subjects as politics and religion. A political pamphlet led to his imprisonment in 1703 for about 4 months.

For about 25 years, Defoe earned his living writing for newspapers. He produced his own periodical, *The Review,* single-handedly from 1704 to 1713. Many politicians hired him to write for newspapers. At times he was secretly writing for the Whig Party in one paper and the Tories in another. Not much is known about his last years, but he continued to write much political journalism, as well as other kinds of work.

His writings. Defoe is unique in the quantity and variety of his works. It is difficult to tell how many works he produced, because most were published anonymously. The latest estimate is almost 550, including works of poetry, theology, economics, and geography.

For most readers today, Defoe is known primarily as a novelist. However, this was really a minor part of his writing, and not the part that gave him the most pride. Defoe's two most famous novels are *Robinson Crusoe* (1719) and *Moll Flanders* (1722).

Defoe's novels reflect the growing power and wealth the new English middle class developed through new business opportunities at home and abroad. Many of this new class were Puritans and they tended to believe in the glory of hard work and getting ahead through one's own efforts. The Puritans also stressed education, and therefore became a large part of the reading public. So for the first time, Defoe and other writers treated trade, capitalism, and individualism favorably.

Robinson Crusoe is the story of a man marooned on an island. It is a memorable adventure story and a study of what it is like to be truly alone. It is also a success story, because Crusoe's hard work, inventiveness, and ability to take advantage of others turns his island into a successful colony. See **Robinson Crusoe.**

Moll Flanders has been generally accepted as Defoe's best example of a genuine novel. Moll Flanders, the heroine, is a thief and a prostitute. Although her surroundings differ from those of Robinson Crusoe, there are basic similarities between the two characters. They both seem like real persons determined to get ahead and gain security. And eventually they both repent of their sins, and end very prosperously.

Defoe's novels marked an important break with the fiction of the past. He offered the ordinary lives of real people who were the normal products of their social and economic surroundings. Defoe makes us believe in the reality of what we are reading as we are hurried from scene to scene by his breathless prose. Only after we have finished do we realize that we have not really been given much psychological insight into the characters.   Ian Watt

De Forest, John William (1826-1906), was an American novelist. He was born in Seymour, Conn., but lived in Charleston, S.C., from 1856 until the outbreak of the Civil War in 1861. He then returned to Connecticut to serve as a captain in the Union army.

De Forest wrote about his war experiences and showed his knowledge of the South in his best novel, *Miss Ravenel's Conversion from Secession to Loyalty* (1867). This work and *Kate Beaumont* (1872) established him as one of the earliest realists in American fiction. De Forest's descriptions of war and of small-town Southern life before the war foreshadowed later antiromantic descriptions of the South. But they kept him from gaining a wide audience in his day. De Forest also wrote novels that exposed political corruption and satirized many customs of his time.   Dean Doner

De Forest, Lee (1873-1961), was an American inventor who pioneered in the technology of radio and television. In 1907, De Forest patented a three-electrode vacuum tube, which he called an *audion* (see **Vacuum tube**). The audion made it possible to amplify weak radio signals and transmit them over long distances. It was essential for later advances in broadcasting.

De Forest received a contract from the United States Navy to build radio stations for ship-to-shore communications. He also staged demonstrations of radio's potential to entertain the public. In 1910, he arranged to broadcast a performance by tenor Enrico Caruso from the Metropolitan Opera House in New York City.

During the 1920's, De Forest worked on a sound system for motion pictures. After 1930, he turned his attention to television's emerging technology. After the U.S. government authorized commercial telecasting in 1941, he encouraged the use of the new medium for public entertainment. De Forest was born in Council Bluffs, Iowa.   Joseph H. Udelson

See also **Electronics** (picture: Lee De Forest).

Deformity. See Birth defect.

Degas, *duh GAH,* **Edgar** (1834-1917), was a French impressionist painter. Like the other impressionists, he wanted to portray situations from modern life. However, he did not share his fellow impressionists' enthusiasm for light and color. Degas emphasized composition, drawing, and form more than did the other members of the movement. See **Impressionism.**

Degas is best known for his paintings of people in both public and unguarded private moments. He showed his figures in awkward or informal positions to free himself from what he felt were outmoded styles of portraying the human body. But he composed his pictures carefully to achieve formal balance.

Hilaire Germain Edgar Degas was born in Paris of wealthy parents. From 1854 to 1859, he spent much time in Italy studying the great Italian Renaissance painters to perfect his draftsmanship and style. Degas intended to become a painter of historical scenes, but he abandoned this career because he felt a need to paint modern subjects. Probably under the influence of the painters Gustave Courbet and Edouard Manet, Degas began to paint scenes from everyday life. He especially enjoyed painting pictures of race-track and theatrical life.

During the 1870's, Degas began to use daring compositional techniques, partly influenced by Japanese prints. He placed his figures at unusual angles and used odd visual viewpoints. For example, he tilted his perspective to emphasize a sudden or informal movement by a figure. He even cut off parts of the subjects at the edge of the picture. In the 1880's, Degas started to concentrate on intimate scenes, such as women bathing, shopping, or drying or combing their hair.

Degas painted many pictures in oil, but he also excelled in pastel. His pastel *At the Milliner's* is reproduced in the **Painting** article. Degas was a fine sculptor as well and produced many figurines of clay or wax.

Albert Boime

See also **Cassatt, Mary** (picture).

De Gaulle, *duh GOHL* or *duh GAWL,* **Charles André Joseph Marie** (1890-1970), became the outstanding French patriot, soldier, and statesman of the 1900's. He led French resistance against Germany in World War II, and restored order in France after the war. He guided the formation of France's Fifth Republic in 1958, and served as its president until his resignation in 1969.

As president of France, de Gaulle led his country through a difficult period in which Algeria and other

Bronze statue, 39 inches (1 meter) high; the Tate Gallery, London

Degas's *Young Dancer* was completed in 1881. The artist now ranks as an important sculptor, but he created statues only to study body movements, not for exhibition.

Oil painting on canvas (1874); the Louvre, Paris

The Dancing Class illustrates how Degas portrayed figures in informal poses. The picture's careful composition and unusual visual viewpoint are typical of Degas' style.

parts of France's overseas empire were granted independence. He fashioned a new role in Europe for France based on close association with a former enemy, Germany. His leadership restored political and economic stability, and again made France one of Europe's leading powers. De Gaulle provided France with a successful constitution, political system, and foreign policy.

Charles de Gaulle became a symbol of France to the French and to people in other parts of the world. Even his name suggested *Gaul,* the ancient Roman name for France. An imposing figure 6 feet 4 inches (193 centimeters) tall, de Gaulle was stern and aloof. Some thought him stubborn and arrogant. But de Gaulle had a deep love for France and great confidence in himself. He firmly believed that he was the one man who could make France a world power again.

Early life. Charles de Gaulle was born Nov. 22, 1890, in Lille. His father, Henri, was an officer in the Franco-Prussian War, then taught philosophy, literature, and mathematics. His mother, Jeanne Maillot de Gaulle, came from a literary and military family.

With his sister and three brothers, Charles grew up in an atmosphere that was both military and religious. As a boy, he enjoyed reading stories of famous French battles. When he played soldiers with his friends, Charles always had to be "France." After studying at the College Stanislas in Paris, de Gaulle served a year in the infantry. He was graduated with honors in 1911 from the famous French military school, St. Cyr.

During World War I, de Gaulle was wounded four times. He was captured at Verdun in 1916. After the war, he served with the French Army in Poland, then taught military history at St. Cyr for a year.

In 1921, he married Yvonne Vendroux, a devout Roman Catholic. They had a son and two daughters. Yvonne de Gaulle followed her husband wherever his duties took him, but essentially remained behind the scenes as a housewife and mother.

Between World Wars I and II, de Gaulle held various military commands and taught at the French War College. His book *The Edge of the Sword* (1932) stressed the importance of powerful leadership in war. In *The Army of the Future* (1934), he outlined the theory of a war of movement, in which tanks and other mechanized forces would be used. Most French military leaders ignored this theory. But the Germans studied it and used it in World War II.

Leader of the Free French. After the Germans invaded France in May 1940, de Gaulle was put in charge of one of France's four armored divisions. He became undersecretary for war in June. But just days later, on June 22, France surrendered to Germany.

De Gaulle, then a general, escaped to London. He refused to accept the surrender. Nor would he recognize the authority of Marshal Pétain, his former regimental commander and patron, who headed the Vichy government that

Wide World
Charles de Gaulle

cooperated with the Germans (see **Pétain, Henri Philippe**). For this, a French military court sentenced de Gaulle to death. De Gaulle declared that France had lost a battle but not the war. He broadcast such messages to France as: "Soldiers of France, wherever you may be, arise!" His broadcasts stirred French patriotism and kept French resistance alive.

De Gaulle organized the Free French forces in Great Britain and in some of the French colonies. In September 1941, he became president of the French National Committee in London. By 1943, the Allies accepted him as the unquestioned leader of the "Fighting French."

Peacetime leader. De Gaulle triumphantly entered Paris with the Allies in August 1944. In September, he became head of the provisional government.

De Gaulle got the machinery of government working again during the next 14 months. But France's left-wing parties did not support him, and he resigned in January 1946. He bitterly opposed the constitution of 1946 because it did not provide a strong executive power. In 1947, he organized a new party, the Rally of the French People (R.P.F.) to reform the constitution. But it lost strength after the elections of 1951 and 1956.

He lived at his country home during his retirement. He wrote his World War II memoirs and watched the political situation in France go from bad to worse. In 1957, though he was 67, de Gaulle still hoped that France would recall him. But early in 1958 he admitted, "Now I begin to fear that it is too late."

The Fifth Republic. Finally, in May 1958, the call came. France stood on the verge of civil war. Dissatisfied French officers, afraid they would lose the government's support against the Algerian rebels, seized power in Algiers. De Gaulle emerged as the only figure likely to prevent domestic chaos. In June, he accepted President René Coty's request to form a government on the condition that he have full powers for six months.

De Gaulle had a new constitution drawn up that established the Fifth Republic. It provided broad powers for the president, who was to be elected for seven years by an electoral college of 80,000 public officials. French voters approved the plan, and the electoral college chose de Gaulle as president in December 1958.

As president, de Gaulle acted with great firmness. After another revolt in Algeria in 1960, he arrested French officers there who had formerly supported him. He negotiated with Algerian nationalist leaders for a cease-fire agreement. The agreement they reached in March 1962, ended more than seven years of bloody war. At de Gaulle's urging, the French people voted almost 10 to 1 in April 1962 for Algerian independence.

The French Assembly ousted the de Gaulle-sponsored government in October 1962. But de Gaulle dissolved the Assembly and obtained the support of a majority coalition. In a separate referendum, the voters also approved de Gaulle's proposal to elect future French presidents by direct popular vote.

In January 1963, de Gaulle and Chancellor Konrad Adenauer of West Germany signed a treaty providing for political, scientific, cultural, and military cooperation. At the same time, de Gaulle blocked Great Britain's entry into the European Community (Common Market). In 1964, France became the first Western power to recognize Communist China. De Gaulle narrowly won a sec-

De Gaulle, leader of the Free French, led a triumphant parade down the Champs Élysées in August 1944, to mark the liberation of Paris after the German occupation of World War II.

ond seven-year term as president in 1965. In 1966, he announced his decision to withdraw French forces from the North Atlantic Treaty Organization (NATO) and remove the NATO headquarters from France. In 1967, de Gaulle again blocked Britain's entry into the Common Market. He also created an independent nuclear strike force and criticized U.S. involvement in the Vietnam War (1957-1975).

In 1968, French students and workers staged strikes and demonstrations. The economy suffered from inflation and currency problems, but de Gaulle maintained popular support. In April 1969, however, his proposals for constitutional changes were defeated in a referendum, and he resigned. De Gaulle died on Nov. 9, 1970, after suffering a heart attack.   Michael M. Harrison

Additional resources

Banfield, Susan. *De Gaulle.* Chelsea Hse., 1985. Suitable for younger readers.
Cook, Don. *Charles De Gaulle: A Biography.* Putnam, 1983.
Ledwidge, Bernard. *De Gaulle.* St. Martin's, 1982.

Degree is a name given to various small units of measure. In geometry and on maps, a degree is a unit of measurement of angles and of arcs of circles. An angle of 1 degree (1°) is $\frac{1}{90}$ of a right angle. An arc of 1° is $\frac{1}{360}$ of a whole circle. Because longitude and latitude lines are circles, they are also measured in degrees. Degrees in geometry are divided into 60 units called *minutes.* Some branches of higher mathematics measure angles in units called *radians.* See **Angle; Circle; Latitude; Longitude; Minute; Radian; Second.**

Degrees are also units of measurement of temperature. One degree of temperature on the Fahrenheit scale is $\frac{1}{180}$ of the difference between the temperatures of melting ice and boiling water. One degree on the Celsius scale of temperature is $\frac{1}{100}$ of the same difference. See **Thermometer.**   Colin C. Graham

Degree, College. A university or college awards a *degree* to a person who has completed a required course of study. The institution presents the degree in the form of a *diploma,* a document certifying the award.

The four basic kinds of degrees are called *associate, bachelor, master,* and *doctor.* An honorary degree may be awarded for an outstanding contribution in a field.

The associate degree is awarded by many colleges and universities in the United States and most community, or junior, colleges (see **Community college**). An associate degree usually indicates completion of two years of college work. The most commonly awarded associate degrees are the *Associate in Arts* and the *Associate in Science.*

The bachelor's degree. In the United States, a college student normally receives a bachelor's degree after four years of study in a university or college. Most students specialize in a field of study called a *major subject.* Many institutions require other types of study outside a major to ensure a liberal education. There are many kinds of bachelor's degrees, but the two most common are the *Bachelor of Arts* (B.A.) and the *Bachelor of Science* (B.S.). The B.A. usually includes majors in such subjects as history, literature, and fine arts, and, in certain cases, science and mathematics. The B.S. usually includes majors in the physical and natural sciences. Most engineering students receive B.S. degrees. Many colleges offer specialized degrees, such as the *Bachelor of Education* or *Bachelor of Architecture.* Law students obtain the *Doctor of Jurisprudence* (J.D.) after more training. Outstanding achievement in a bachelor's degree may be designated by the Latin phrases *cum laude* (with praise), *magna cum laude* (with great praise), or *summa cum laude* (with the highest praise).

British colleges and universities offer two types of bachelor's degrees, an ordinary, or *pass,* degree and an *honors* degree which requires more extensive and more advanced work. Canadian colleges and universities usually follow British or French tradition in their systems of degrees. See **Canada** (Education).

The master's degree. In the United States, students who desire a master's degree must complete one or two years of advanced study beyond the bachelor's degree. Many institutions require a *thesis,* a written report of a special investigation in the student's major field. The two most common master's degrees are the *Master of Arts* and the *Master of Science.*

In Great Britain, the master's degree is usually considered the highest requirement for an academic career, but a number of British universities also offer the doctorate. In Scotland, a student proceeds directly to the master's degree without taking a bachelor's degree.

The doctor's degree is the highest earned degree in the United States, France, Germany, and many other countries. There are two distinct types of doctor's degrees. One is a professional degree required to practice in certain professions, such as medicine. The other is a research degree that indicates the candidate has acquired mastery of a broad field of knowledge and the technique of scholarly research.

In the United States, the research doctorate requires at least two or three additional years of study beyond the master's degree. Most doctoral students are expected to have a reading knowledge in two foreign languages. The candidate must also complete examinations and present a written thesis or *dissertation.* The doctoral thesis represents an original contribution to knowledge, and is a more detailed study of a research problem than

Some common abbreviations for college degrees

A.A. Associate in Arts	**B.S. in Ed., B.S.Ed.** Bachelor of Science in Education	**D.O.** Doctor of Osteopathy	**M.M.Ed., M.Mus.Ed.** Master of Music Education
A.S. Associate in Science	**B.S. in E.E., B.S.E.E.** Bachelor of Science in Electrical Engineering	**D.V.M.** Doctor of Veterinary Medicine	**M.R.E.** Master of Religious Education
B.A., A.B. Bachelor of Arts	**B.S. in Elem.Ed.** Bachelor of Science in Elementary Education	**Ed.D., D.Ed.** Doctor of Education	**M.S.** Master of Science
B.A. in Ed. Bachelor of Arts in Education	**B.S. in L.S.** Bachelor of Science in Library Science	**J.D.** Juris Doctor	**M.S. in C.E., M.S.C.E.** Master of Science in Civil Engineering
B.Arch. Bachelor of Architecture	**B.S. in M.E., B.S.M.E.** Bachelor of Science in Mechanical Engineering	* **L.H.D.** Doctor of Humane Letters	**M.S. in Ch.E.** Master of Science in Chemical Engineering
B.B.A. Bachelor of Business Administration	**B.S. in Med.Tech.** Bachelor of Science in Medical Technology	* **Lit.D., D.Lit.** Doctor of Literature	**M.S. in Ed.** Master of Science in Education
B.D. Bachelor of Divinity	**B.S.J., J.B.S.** Bachelor of Science in Journalism	* **Litt.D.** Doctor of Letters	**M.S. in E.E., M.S.E.E.** Master of Science in Electrical Engineering
B.Ed. Bachelor of Education	**B.S.N.** Bachelor of Science in Nursing	**LL.B.** Bachelor of Laws	**M.S. in L.S.** Master of Science in Library Science
B.E.E. Bachelor of Electrical Engineering	**B.S.Pharm.** Bachelor of Science in Pharmacy	* **LL.D.** Doctor of Laws	**M.S. in M.E.** Master of Science in Mechanical Engineering
B.F.A. Bachelor of Fine Arts	**D.A.** Doctor of Arts	**LL.M.** Master of Laws	**M.S.J.** Master of Science in Journalism
B.L.S. Bachelor of Library Science	**D.B.A.** Doctor of Business Administration	**M.A., A.M.** Master of Arts	**M.S.W.** Master of Social Work
B.M., B.Mus. Bachelor of Music	**D.C.** Doctor of Chiropractic	**M.A. in Ed.** Master of Arts in Education	**Ph.B.** Bachelor of Philosophy
B.M.E., B.Mus.Ed. Bachelor of Music Education	* **D.D.** Doctor of Divinity	**M.A.T.** Master of Arts in Teaching	**Ph.D.** Doctor of Philosophy
B.S. Bachelor of Science	**D.D.S.** Doctor of Dental Surgery	**M.B.A.** Master of Business Administration	† **Sc.D., D.Sc., D.S.** Doctor of Science
B.S. in B.A., B.S.B.A. Bachelor of Science in Business Administration	**D.M.D.** Doctor of Dental Medicine	**M.D.** Doctor of Medicine	**S.T.M.** Master of Sacred Theology
B.S. in C.E., B.S.C.E. Bachelor of Science in Civil Engineering	* **D.Mus., Mus.D.** Doctor of Music	**M.Div.** Master of Divinity	**Th.M.** Master of Theology
B.S. in Ch.E., B.S.Ch.E Bachelor of Science in Chemical Engineering		**M.Ed.** Master of Education	
B.S. in Chemistry, B.S. Chem. Bachelor of Science in Chemistry		**M.F.A.** Master of Fine Arts	
		M.L.S. Master of Library Science	
		M.M., M.Mus. Master of Music	

*Honorary degree only.   †Usually honorary.

that required for the master's degree.

The *Doctor of Philosophy* degree is the most important research doctorate and may include specialization in almost any academic subject. The *Doctor of Education, Doctor of Medicine,* and *Doctor of Dental Surgery* degrees represent advanced professional training. Students in such professions as medicine and dentistry can obtain a doctor's degree without first receiving a bachelor's or master's degree. But most acquire a bachelor of science degree before entering medical training.

Honorary degrees. Many award honorary degrees to people for achievement in their chosen fields. Chief among these are the *Doctor of Letters* and the *Doctor of Laws.* These are given to prominent authors, scholars, and leaders in the professions, business, government, and industry.

History. College degrees date from the 1200's when schools in Europe won the right to examine and license their graduates. The system of degrees, which took form by the 1300's, was modeled on the guild system. A student spent a sort of apprenticeship as a candidate for a bachelor's degree. Receiving the bachelor's degree resembled becoming a journeyman in a craft. The master's degree represented the status of a master craftsman, and served as a license to teach. The student's thesis was his "masterpiece," just as a journeyman submitted an example of his work to become a master craftsman. If the student continued to study and teach in law, medicine, or theology, he might earn the title of doctor. The medieval system remained largely unchanged until the impact of science on education in the 1700's and 1800's. During the last hundred years, college degrees in the United States have been extended to include many new fields of knowledge.   Douglas Sloan

See also **Graduation.**

De Groot, Huig. See Grotius, Hugo.

De Hooch, *duh HOHK,* **Pieter,** *PEE tuhr* (1629-1684?), was a Dutch painter noted for his charming scenes of middle-class life. He painted housewives with maids or children, and ladies and gentlemen talking, drinking, or playing games. His style is distinguished by warm, often unmixed colors and the skillful portrayal of the effects of sunlight. Like other Dutch painters of his time, de Hooch experimented with showing depth and the illusion of space. Unlike earlier Dutch painters of everyday life, he often included glimpses through the open doors or windows into rooms, streets, or gardens. De Hooch and Jan Vermeer, another Dutch painter of the 1600's, probably influenced each other. De Hooch was born in Rotterdam.   Linda Stone-Ferrier

Dehumidifier, *DEE hyoo MIHD uh FY uhr,* is a device that removes moisture from the air. Dehumidifiers are commonly used to make homes more comfortable.

The amount of moisture the air can contain is related to the temperature of the air. The warmer the air is, the more moisture it can hold. On hot days, that moisture can make people uncomfortable. But when the moisture level of the air is reduced, moisture from the skin evaporates more readily. People then feel cooler even though the temperature of the air stays the same.

A dehumidifier consists of a set of cold coils, called the *evaporator,* and a set of hot coils, called the *condenser.* A fan in the dehumidifier draws moisture-filled air from a room and blows it across the coils. The air loses moisture as it passes over the evaporator and it is reheated to room temperature by the condenser. The air then reenters the room, absorbs moisture again, and recirculates through the dehumidifier. The moisture the air loses is carried by a hose to a drain or sink, or it is collected in a built-in container.   Evan Powell

See also **Air conditioning** (Controlling the moisture); **Humidifier; Humidity.**

Dehydrated food is food that has been preserved by drying. Adding water to such food makes it ready for eating or for cooking. Dried milk and milk products, soups, coffee, tea, spices, gelatin, dessert mixes, and macaroni are sold in most stores. Other common dehydrated foods include yeast, cheese, and egg products.

Important features of dehydrated foods are their lightness in weight and their compactness. More than 90 per cent of the water is removed during drying. When adequately packaged, most dehydrated foods can be kept for several months if stored below 75° F. (24° C).

Foods selected for drying must be fresh, clean, and at the proper stage of ripeness. Vegetables are usually *blanched* (briefly heated and cooled) to destroy enzymes before drying. Biological products such as serums and vaccines and such foods as chickens and mushrooms are freeze-dried. In the freeze-drying process, the product is frozen and held under conditions of low heat and a nearly perfect vacuum. As a result, the ice in the frozen food is vaporized without melting.   H. Jack Warner

See also **Food preservation** (Drying).

Dehydration is a condition characterized by the excessive loss of water from the body. In most cases of dehydration, the body also loses salt. Symptoms of mild dehydration include dryness of the mucous membranes of the nose, mouth, and throat; reduced ability to sweat and urinate; and doughy skin. In severe dehydration, rapid loss of salt and water leads to fast heartbeat, low blood pressure, shock, and even death.

Worldwide, the most common cause of dehydration is infectious diarrhea. Dehydration resulting from diarrhea is a major cause of death in children in developing countries. Other causes include vomiting, excessive sweating or urination, and extensive skin burns. Extended shortages of water may also produce dehydration. Some people in comas may become dehydrated because they are unable to respond to thirst.

People suffering from mild dehydration should drink plenty of fluids. Cases of severe dehydration usually require hospitalization. In treating diarrhea-related dehydration, doctors use a solution containing glucose to restore lost water and salt. This solution may be taken orally or by injection.   Laurence H. Beck

Deighton, *DAY tuhn,* **Len** (1929-   ), is an English author known for espionage and war novels. He belongs to the antiromantic school of spy novelists, presenting espionage as an unglamorous and ruthless activity. He carefully researches all his novels. He often uses footnotes and other scholarly devices to reflect his research and make his stories appear more realistic.

Deighton gained international recognition for his first spy thriller, *The Ipcress File* (1962). The novel introduces the anonymous British spy who narrates most of Deighton's novels. The story has the complicated plot and specific details typical of Deighton's work. Deighton has written two trilogies and a separate novel about British spy Bernard Samson. The first trilogy consists of *Berlin Game* (1983), *Mexico Set* (1985), and *London Match* (1985). Next came *Winter* (1987) and the second trilogy, *Spy Hook* (1988), *Spy Line* (1989), and *Spy Sinker* (1990). His other novels include *Funeral in Berlin* (1964), *SS-GB* (1978), and *XPD* (1981).

Deighton also has written popularized military history, including *Blitzkrieg* (1979) and *Battle of Britain* (1980). He was born in London.   Cynthia A. Davis

Deism, *DEE ihz uhm,* is a religious and philosophic belief. Deism rejects most conventional forms of religion, accepting reason as the only guide to truth. It embraces the concept of God, however, in the limited sense of a creator, or first cause, of the physical and moral laws of the universe. Deists compare God's act of creation to that of a watchmaker who builds a watch, sets it in motion, and then refuses to intervene in its actions.

Deism became popular during the 1700's. Deist ideas appear in the writings of such philosophers as Jean-Jacques Rousseau and Voltaire of France and Immanuel Kant of Germany. In America, deist ideas appear in the Declaration of Independence and the Preamble to the Constitution. Those ideas reflect the political influence of leading deists of the time: Benjamin Franklin, Thomas Jefferson, and Thomas Paine. The deist concept of God underlies such phrases as "In God We Trust" and "we are endowed by the Creator with certain inalienable rights."   Mark Juergensmeyer

See also **God; Theism; Atheism.**

De Kalb, Johann. See Kalb, Johann.

Dekker, Thomas (1572?-1632?), brought to Elizabethan popular literature a fresh emphasis on the life of his day. Dekker's best-known play is *The Shoemaker's Holiday* (1599). It is a zestful picture of Elizabethan life that combines patriotism and romance with a favorable portrayal of the rising merchant and artisan classes. Dekker's other plays include the romance *Old Fortunatus* (1599) and the comedy *The Honest Whore* (1604-1605).

Dekker wrote many dramas and pamphlets. Between 1598 and 1602 alone, he wrote all or part of over 40 plays, most of them now lost. Yet he usually had no money and apparently spent several years in prison for debt. From about 1604, Dekker turned increasingly to writing popular pamphlets, mainly satires of the London nderworld. *The Gull's Hornbook* (1609) is a lively record of London life of the time.   Stephen Orgel

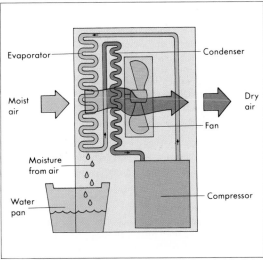

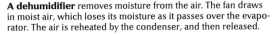

WORLD BOOK diagram by Arthur Grebetz

A dehumidifier removes moisture from the air. The fan draws in moist air, which loses its moisture as it passes over the evaporator. The air is reheated by the condenser, and then released.

De Klerk, *duh KLEHRK,* **Frederik Willem,** *FREH dehr ihk VIHL uhm* (1936-   ), became the head of South Africa's government in 1989. He succeeded Pieter W. Botha as state president after Botha resigned because of ill health. De Klerk was elected to the post later in 1989. De Klerk has worked to find a compromise between South Africans who favor the policy of racial segregation called *apartheid* and those who support increased rights for the country's black majority. In 1990, he released Nelson Mandela, deputy president of the African National Congress, from prison. This black group has helped lead the opposition to apartheid. De Klerk began meeting with Mandela to discuss political change in South Africa.

© Mark Peters, Sipa

Frederik W. de Klerk

Although de Klerk called for an end to apartheid, he sought to keep some privileges for the white minority.

De Klerk was born in Johannesburg. He attended Potchefstroom University in the Transvaal province and then practiced law. He served in the House of Assembly from 1972 to 1989. De Klerk was the head of the National Party in the Transvaal from 1982 to 1989. He became a member of Botha's cabinet in 1978.   Bruce Fetter

De Kooning, *duh KOO nihng,* **Willem** (1904-   ), is a leading abstract expressionist artist. He is best known for his hectic and violent paintings dominated by lunging brushstrokes, swirling paint patterns, and a strong emphasis on line. In later works, de Kooning simplified the surfaces of his paintings, sometimes working with purely linear patterns on clear, white canvas. But the mood of de Kooning's paintings and drawings is not always explosive. In his early tender portraits, his studies of women in the 1960's, and other works, he has shown skill with refined, delicate compositions and colors.

De Kooning was born in Rotterdam, the Netherlands, and moved to the United States in 1926. He gained his first critical acclaim for his abstract paintings of the late 1940's. Painted largely in black and white enamel, these pictures are composed of rhythmic curved lines mixed with oddly-shaped flat planes. In 1953, de Kooning exhibited a series of oils and pastels titled *Woman* in which he appeared to present a savage vision of woman as siren or dark goddess. *Woman, I,* a work from this series, is reproduced in the **Painting** article. The exhibition inspired many younger artists to seek new ways of representing the human figure. Many de Kooning paintings of the 1960's and 1970's contain landscape elements and suggest huge spaces and outdoor light.   Dore Ashton

Delacroix, *duh lah KRWAH,* **Eugène,** *oo ZHEHN* (1798-1863), was the chief representative of the romantic style of painting in France. Like many romantics, he painted exotic, faraway, emotional subjects. His painting was influenced by Flemish painter Peter Paul Rubens' bold, thick brushstroke and the deep, rich colors of the Venetian Renaissance painters.

Delacroix admired such English writers as William Shakespeare and Lord Byron, whose work provided subjects for his paintings. His sympathy for the Greeks' struggle for independence from Turkey inspired him to paint *Incidents from the Massacre at Chios* (1824). In 1830, he took part in the revolution in Paris, which freed France from an absolute monarchy. His painting *Liberty Leading the People* (1830) glorifies this event.

In 1832, Delacroix traveled to North Africa, where the effects of the intense sunlight led to his use of shimmering color highlights. The sketches of exotic people, animals, and events he made in Africa became subjects for many of his later paintings, starting with *The Women of Algiers* (1834). Ferdinand Victor Eugène Delacroix was born at Charenton, near Paris.   Ann Friedman

For examples of Delacroix's paintings see **Columbus, Christopher; Greece; Painting** (The 1800's; picture: *Jewish Wedding in Morocco*).

De la Madrid Hurtado, *day lah mah DREED ur TAH doh,* **Miguel,** *mih GEHL* (1934-   ), served as president of Mexico from 1982 to 1988. De la Madrid belongs to the Institutional Revolutionary Party. A financial expert, de la Madrid served as Mexico's secretary of planning and budget from 1979 until he became president of the country.

When de la Madrid became president, he faced severe economic problems

Oil painting and newspaper on canvas (1956); Metropolitan Museum of Art, Rogers Fund, 1956

A Willem de Kooning painting called *Easter Monday* is typical of the abstract style the artist developed in the mid-1950's. This style featured short, broken brushstrokes and bright colors.

United Press Int.

Miguel de la Madrid

The Bark of Dante was the first success achieved by Eugène Delacroix. The painting is based on an episode in Dante's poem *Inferno*. It shows Dante and the Roman poet Virgil crossing a lake in hell as the drowning damned clutch at their boat.

The Louvre, Paris, Art Reference Bureau

that resulted from government spending and reduced income from oil (see **Mexico** [Recent developments]). As president, he took steps to try to solve the problems, including inflation and a huge foreign debt. But the problems continued, and de la Madrid's critics charged him with a lack of leadership.

De la Madrid was born in Colima. He received a law degree from the National Autonomous University of Mexico in 1957. He taught there from 1958 to 1968. In 1964 and 1965, he took a leave of absence to earn a master's degree in public administration at Harvard University. He entered government service in 1960. Before becoming a Cabinet member, he served in government financial posts in the department of the Treasury and with Mexico's national oil company.   Roderic A. Camp

De La Mare, *duh luh MAIR,* **Walter** (1873-1956), was an English author noted for his romantic works for both adults and children. He wrote poems, short stories, novels, and plays distinguished by a unique mixture of dreams, reality, and the supernatural. De La Mare also edited books for children. His anthology of prose and verse called *Come Hither* (1923) is a children's classic. De La Mare's best collections of poetry include *Peacock Pie* (1913) and *Bells and Grass* (1942). His most popular short stories were published in *Collected Stories for Children* (1947). Perhaps his best-known work for adults is the novel *Memoirs of a Midget* (1921). It is a romantic fantasy about society as seen through the eyes of a midget. De La Mare was born in Charlton, near London. See also **Regina Medal.**   Jerome Bump

Delany, *duh LAY nih,* **Martin Robinson** (1812-1885), was a black American army officer, physician, journalist, and social reformer. He was trained as a physician at Harvard University. He practiced medicine occasionally in Pittsburgh, but spent most of his time fighting against slavery. He worked for the *Underground Railroad,* a system for helping slaves escape to the North before the Civil War. He also wrote for an abolitionist newspaper owned by the black crusader Frederick Douglass. In the 1850's, Delany joined a movement that urged free blacks to move to Africa. But Delany later lost his enthusiasm for this "back-to-Africa" movement.

Delany served as a Union Army surgeon during the Civil War. He became the first black to earn the rank of major. Delany was born in Charleston, W. Va. (then called Virginia).

Historical Picture Service, Inc., Chicago

Martin Delany

Richard Bardolph

De la Roche, *duh luh RAWSH,* **Mazo,** *MAY zoh* (1879-1961), became one of the most popular novelists in Canadian literature. She was best known for a series of 16 novels about the Whiteoak family. The first Whiteoak novel was *Jalna* (1927), and the last was *Morning at Jalna* (1960). These novels tell the story of several generations of the family from 1852 to 1954. The central character is Adeline Whiteoak, who emigrates with her husband from Great Britain to Canada. She builds a home called Jalna in the countryside west of Toronto and dominates the lives of the family members who live there. The books create a vivid picture of upper-class life on a country estate. The Jalna saga was made into a successful Canadian Broadcasting Corporation television series in 1972. De la Roche also wrote other novels, as well as plays, short stories, and an autobiography called *Ringing the Changes* (1957). De la Roche was born in Newmarket, Ont.   Laurie R. Ricou

De la Salle, Saint Jean Baptiste. See **Jean Baptiste de la Salle, Saint.**

A crop of Delaware barley grows on a farm west of Dover, in the central section of the state. Farmland covers about half of Delaware. Most of Delaware lies in the Atlantic Coastal Plain, a region of flat, fertile land.

Delaware   *The First State*

Delaware is the second smallest state of the United States. Only Rhode Island has a smaller area. And only three states—Alaska, Vermont, and Wyoming—have fewer people. Delaware lies close to many of the nation's largest industrial cities. The Delaware River, and networks of canals, highways, and railroads, carry products from Delaware to Baltimore, New York City, Philadelphia, and Washington, D.C.

Delaware lies along the Atlantic coastline. It shares the Delmarva Peninsula with parts of Maryland and Virginia. Most of Delaware lies in a low, flat, coastal plain. Rolling hills and valleys of the Piedmont region cover the northern tip of the state.

About 200,000 companies are incorporated in Delaware. They include many of the largest U.S. firms. Delaware's business laws favor corporations. It is easier and less expensive to incorporate in Delaware than in most other states—even for companies that do most of their

The contributors of this article are Barbara E. Benson, Director of the Library of the Historical Society of Delaware; and Peter W. Rees, Associate Professor of Geography at the University of Delaware.

business outside of Delaware. Several of the nation's biggest chemical companies have headquarters and research laboratories in or near Wilmington, the state's only large city. These firms include E. I. du Pont de Nemours & Company, one of the world's largest chemical manufacturers and marketers. Wilmington is also one of the nation's leading banking centers. Dover is the capital of Delaware.

Broilers (chickens from 5 to 12 weeks old) are the leading cash farm product in Delaware. Broiler raising has made Sussex County in the southern part of Delaware one of the nation's richest farm regions.

In 1609, Henry Hudson, an English explorer sailing for the Netherlands, reached what is now Delaware. In 1610, a ship from the Virginia colony sailed into what is now called Delaware Bay. The captain named the bay *De La Warr Bay* for Lord De La Warr, the governor of Virginia. Delaware is known as the *First State*, because on Dec. 7, 1787, it became the first state to approve the United States Constitution.

Delaware is the only state in which counties are divided into areas called *hundreds*. Delaware is also the only state in which the legislature can amend the state constitution without the approval of the voters.

Interesting facts about Delaware

WORLD BOOK illustrations by Kevin Chadwick

Christmas seals were first introduced to the United States in Wilmington. Emily P. Bissell, a Delaware artist, designed the seals, and organizers of a local tuberculosis fund drive put them on sale at the Wilmington Post Office in December 1907. The idea for Christmas seals came from a similar fund-raising campaign first used in Denmark.

Christmas seals

The first beauty contest in the United States was held at Rehoboth Beach in 1880. Contestants competed for the title of "Miss United States." The famous inventor Thomas Edison was one of the three judges. The contest became the forerunner of today's Miss America pageant.

Delaware's Coleman Du Pont Highway is the only privately financed major highway in the United States. A corporation called Coleman Du Pont Road, Inc., spent $4 million for its construction, which began in 1911 and was completed in 1924.

Delaware's northern boundary with Pennsylvania is formed by the arc of a perfect circle. Delaware is the only state to have such a boundary. The circle is centered at the dome of the Court House in the town of New Castle.

Log cabins were first introduced to North America in 1638 by Swedish immigrants who settled in southern Delaware. Log construction was already an established practice in Scandinavia and in other parts of Europe.

The first log cabins

Shostal

Rehoboth Beach, on Delaware's southeastern coast, attracts many summertime visitors. Vacationers enjoy the Atlantic Ocean breezes that sweep over the long stretches of beach.

Du Pont & Company

Delaware's chemical industry, centered in the Wilmington area, includes major chemical firms. This researcher works at Du Pont, one of the world's largest chemical manufacturers.

Floyd Dean, Inc.

Wilmington, in the far northeastern corner of Delaware, is the state's only large city. It is also the leading manufacturing center in Delaware. Wilmington's history dates back to the 1630's.

Delaware in brief

Symbols of Delaware

The state flag first appeared in its present form in 1913. It bears a shield with a sheaf of wheat, an ear of corn, and an ox, all of which symbolize agriculture. Above the shield is a sailing ship. A soldier and a farmer support the shield. "December 7, 1787" is the date Delaware became the first state. The state seal was adopted in 1777 and has the same design as the flag. The dates 1793, 1847, and 1911 are years when changes were made.

State flag

State seal

Delaware (brown) ranks 49th in size among all the states, and is the smallest of the Southern States (yellow).

The State Capitol is in Dover, the capital of Delaware since 1777. New Castle had been the capital since 1704.

General information

Statehood: Dec. 7, 1787, the first state.
State abbreviations: Del. (traditional); DE (postal).
State motto: *Liberty and Independence.*
State song: "Our Delaware." Words by George B. Hynson; music by William M. S. Brown.

Land and climate

Area: 2,044 sq. mi. (5,295 km²), including 112 sq. mi. (290 km²) of inland water but excluding 350 sq. mi. (906 km²) of Delaware Bay.
Coastline: 28 mi. (45 km).
Elevation: *Highest*—442 ft. (135 m) above sea level on Ebright Road in New Castle County. *Lowest*—sea level along the coast.
Record high temperature: 110° F. (43° C) at Millsboro on July 21, 1930.
Record low temperature: −17° F. (−27° C) at Millsboro on Jan. 17, 1893.
Average July temperature: 76° F. (24° C).
Average January temperature: 35° F. (2° C).
Average yearly precipitation: 45 in. (114 cm).

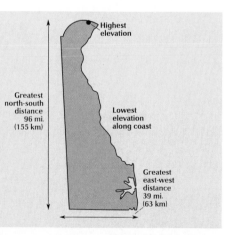

Greatest north-south distance 96 mi. (155 km)

Highest elevation

Lowest elevation along coast

Greatest east-west distance 39 mi. (63 km)

Important dates

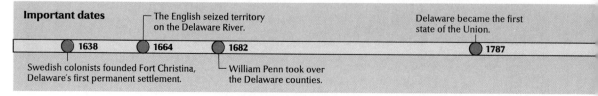

The English seized territory on the Delaware River.

Delaware became the first state of the Union.

| 1638 | 1664 | 1682 | 1787 |

Swedish colonists founded Fort Christina, Delaware's first permanent settlement.

William Penn took over the Delaware counties.

State bird
Blue hen chicken

State flower
Peach blossom

State tree
American holly

People

Population: 594,338 (1980 census)
Rank among the states: 47th
Density: 291 persons per sq. mi. (112 per km²), U.S. average 67 per sq. mi. (26 per km²)
Distribution: 71 per cent urban, 29 per cent rural

Largest cities in Delaware

Wilmington	70,195
Newark	25,247
Dover	23,507
Brookside*	15,255
Claymont*	10,022
Edgemoor*	7,397

*Unincorporated place.
Source: U.S. Bureau of the Census.

Population trend

Thousands

*All figures are census figures except 1985, which is an estimate.

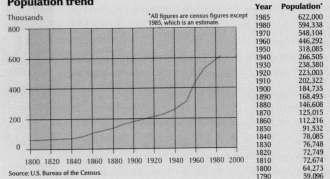

Source: U.S. Bureau of the Census.

Year	Population*
1985	622,000
1980	594,338
1970	548,104
1960	446,292
1950	318,085
1940	266,505
1930	238,380
1920	223,003
1910	202,322
1900	184,735
1890	168,493
1880	146,608
1870	125,015
1860	112,216
1850	91,532
1840	78,085
1830	76,748
1820	72,749
1810	72,674
1800	64,273
1790	59,096

Economy

Chief products

Agriculture: chickens.
Manufacturing: chemicals, food products, transportation equipment.

Gross state product

Value of goods and services produced in 1986, $11,706,000,000. *Services* include community, business, and personal services; finance; government; trade; and transportation, communication, and utilities. *Industry* includes construction, manufacturing, and mining. *Agriculture* includes agriculture, fishing, and forestry.

Sources: U.S. Bureau of Economic Analysis.

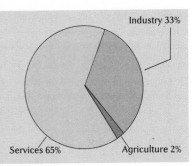

Industry 33%

Services 65%

Agriculture 2%

Government

State government

Governor: 4-year term
State senators: 21; 4-year terms
State representatives: 41; 2-year terms
Counties: 3

Federal government

United States senators: 2
United States representatives: 1
Electoral votes: 3

Sources of information

The Delaware Tourism Office handles requests for information about tourism in the state. The office also directs requests for information about the economy, government, and history of Delaware to the proper departments. Write to: Delaware Tourism Office, 99 Kings Highway, Box 1401, Dover, DE 19903.

Delaware established a state highway department.

The Delaware Coastal Zone Act prohibited construction of industrial plants in coastal areas.

1861-1865   **1917**   **1957**   **1971**

Delaware fought for the North during the Civil War.

The state began providing funds for needy students to attend the University of Delaware.

Population. The 1980 United States census reported that Delaware had 594,338 people. The state's population had increased $8\frac{1}{2}$ per cent over the 1970 census figure, 548,104. The United States Bureau of the Census estimated that by 1985 the state's population had reached about 622,000.

About three-fourths of the people in Delaware live in urban areas. That is, they live in or near cities and towns of 2,500 or more people. More than two-thirds of the people live in the Wilmington metropolitan area. This is the state's only Standard Metropolitan Statistical Area (see **Metropolitan area**). For its population, see the *Index* to the political map of Delaware with this article.

Wilmington is the only large city in the state. None of the other cities has a population of over 27,000. Dover is the state capital. See the separate articles on the cities of Delaware listed in the *Related articles* at the end of this article.

About 97 per cent of the people who live in Delaware were born in the United States. Of the few people born in other countries who live in the state, the largest groups came from Canada, Germany, Great Britain, Italy, and Poland.

Schools. The Dutch and Swedish colonists who settled the Delaware region in the 1600's made education an important part of their lives. Most of their early schools were run by churches. The English gained control of the region in the 1660's, and built schools of their own. But many wealthy English sent their children to schools outside the colony. Poorer children were taught in church schools or by their families, friends, or traveling teachers.

Public education began in the Delaware region after the Revolutionary War. A public school fund was set up by the state legislature in 1792. The legislature established a system of public education in 1829. But education remained under local control until the 1920's.

Today, a seven-member state board of education makes policies for the public school system. The gover-

Population density

More than two-thirds of Delaware's people live in the Wilmington metropolitan area, in the far northern part of the state. The Dover and Lewes areas are also heavily populated.

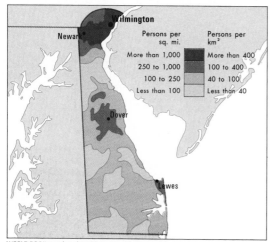

WORLD BOOK map; based on U.S. Bureau of the Census data.

Universities and colleges

Delaware has six universities and colleges that grant bachelor's or advanced degrees and are accredited by the Middle States Association of Colleges and Schools. Locations shown below refer to the schools' mailing addresses. For enrollments and further information, see **Universities and colleges** (table).

Name	Location
Brandywine College of Widener University	Wilmington
Delaware, University of	Newark
Delaware State College	Dover
Goldey Beacom College	Wilmington
Wesley College	Dover
Wilmington College	New Castle

University of Delaware

The Mall at the University of Delaware in Newark

nor appoints members, subject to state Senate approval. The board's president has no definite term. The other members serve six-year terms. The department of public instruction, headed by the superintendent of public instruction, supervises the system. The board of education appoints the superintendent to a one-year term. Children from age 5 through 15 must attend school. For the number of students and teachers in Delaware, see **Education** (table).

Libraries. The first library in the region was established in Wilmington in 1754, when Delaware was still a British colony. In 1788, after Delaware became a state, the Library Company of Wilmington was incorporated. This library still exists as the Wilmington Institute Free Library.

Delaware has about 30 public libraries and many school libraries and special libraries. The Historical Society of Delaware in Wilmington and the state Hall of Records in Dover have excellent collections of materials dealing with the history of Delaware. The Morris Library of the University of Delaware and the Hagley Museum and Library are the other chief research libraries in the state.

Museums. The Corbit-Sharp House and the Wilson-Warner House, both in Odessa, display American antiques. The Old Dutch House, built in New Castle in the 1600's, offers a glimpse into the lives of early Dutch colonists. Wilmington's Old Town Hall, built in 1798, displays material of the Historical Society of Delaware. Other important museums in the state include the Delaware Agricultural Museum in Dover; and the Rockwood Museum, the Nemours Mansion, the Delaware Art Museum, and the Delaware Museum of Natural History, all near Wilmington. See also the *Places to visit* section of this article.

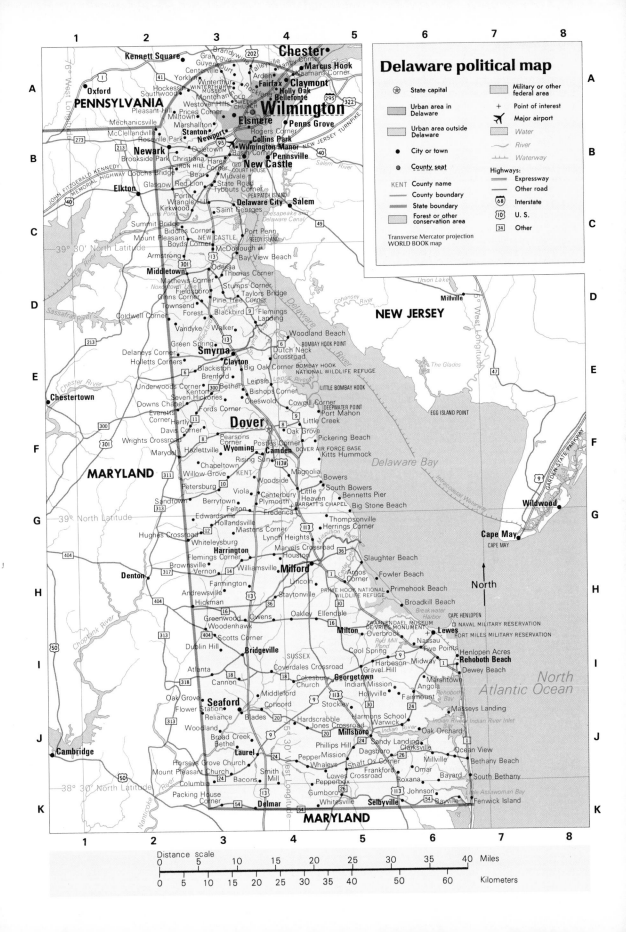

Delaware political map

Legend:

⊛ State capital

▮ Urban area in Delaware

▮ Urban area outside Delaware

● City or town

◉ County seat

KENT County name

County boundary

State boundary

Forest or other conservation area

Military or other federal area

+ Point of interest

✈ Major airport

Water

River

Waterway

Highways:
Expressway
Other road

68 Interstate

10 U.S.

34 Other

Transverse Mercator projection
WORLD BOOK map

Distance scale

0 5 10 15 20 25 30 35 40 Miles

0 5 10 15 20 25 30 35 40 50 60 Kilometers

Visitor's guide

Delaware's many freshwater lakes and ponds, its ocean beaches, and its rivers and streams provide excellent fishing, swimming, and boating. Cultural and historic attractions also bring visitors to the state. Hunters search the salt marshes for small animals and birds.

One of Delaware's most exciting annual events is the Delaware State Fair, which is held in Harrington during the third week in July.

Places to visit

Fort Delaware, a pentagon-shaped fort on Pea Patch Island, was used as a prison during the Civil War. It can be reached by boat from Delaware City.

Great Cypress Swamp, near Laurel, has the northernmost natural grove of bald cypresses to be found in the United States.

Hagley Museum and Eleutherian Mills, on Brandywine Creek near Wilmington, features the original powder mills of Éleuthère Irénée du Pont, and his residence. The site also has indoor and outdoor exhibits that show development of American industry.

Henry Francis du Pont Winterthur Museum, near Wilmington, has a magnificent collection of Early American furniture. More than 100 rooms in the museum are furnished in styles that were fashionable at various times between 1640 and 1840. Beautiful gardens surround the museum.

Houses of worship rank among Delaware's most interesting places to visit. Barratt's Chapel, near Frederica, has been called the Cradle of Methodism in America. The Methodist leaders Francis Asbury and Thomas Coke met in this chapel on Nov. 14, 1784. Their meeting led to the organization of the Methodist Episcopal Church in America. Immanuel Church, an Episcopal church in New Castle, was completed about 1710. In its churchyard are the graves of many people famous in Delaware's early days. Other famous Delaware church buildings, with their completion dates, include Christ Church in Dover (Episcopal, 1734), Christ Episcopal Church on Chipman Pond near Laurel (1771), Old Drawyer's Presbyterian Church near Odessa (1770's), Old Swedes Church in Wilmington (now Episcopal, built as a Swedish Lutheran church in 1698), and Welsh Tract Baptist Church near Newark (1746).

John Dickinson Mansion, near Dover, was the boyhood home of the famous American patriot. The house was built in 1740.

Lewes, on Delaware's northern coast, is the state's oldest settlement. It is the site of many historic buildings and homes. Also located in Lewes is the Zwaanendael Museum. This museum is modeled after a wing of the town hall in Hoorn, the Netherlands. Exhibits include historic documents, Indian relics, and mementos of seafaring days in southern Delaware.

New Castle has many historic buildings. The Amstel House, home of the New Castle Historical Society, features exhibits of colonial arts and handicrafts. It was built about 1730. The Court House, which was built in 1732, served as Delaware's colonial capitol and first state house. The George Read II House and Garden, completed in 1804, is an elegant example of the Georgian style of architecture.

State House, in Dover, was Delaware's state capitol until 1933. It was built in 1792 and features a restored courtroom and legislative chambers. Nearby is the Delaware State Museum.

State parks and forests. Delaware has 11 state parks and 4 state forests. For information on Delaware's state parks, write to Delaware State Parks, 89 Kings Highway, P.O. Box 1401, Dover, DE 19903. For information on state forests, write to the Delaware Division of Fish and Wildlife, 89 Kings Highway, P.O. Box 1401, Dover, DE 19903.

Delaware map index

Source: 1980 census. Places without population figures are unincorporated areas.

*Does not appear on map; key shows general location.
°County seat.

**Fort Delaware on
Pea Patch Island**

Bob Glander, Shostal

Richard C. B. Clark

Barratt's Chapel near Frederica

The Henry Francis du Pont Winterthur Museum

Henry Francis du Pont Winterthur Museum

Delaware Development Office

Fall Regatta on Rehoboth Bay

Annual events

January-April
Delaware Kite Festival at Cape Henlopen State Park in Lewes (Good Friday); Boardwalk Fashion Promenade at Rehoboth Beach (Easter Sunday); Irish Festival at Hagley Museum near Wilmington (last Saturday in April).

May-August
Old Dover Day (first Saturday in May); Wilmington Garden Day in Wilmington (first Saturday in May); Winterthur Point to Point Horse Race in Winterthur (first Sunday in May); World Weakfish Tournament (third week in May); Delaware State Fair in Harrington (July); Bethany Beach-Fenwick Island Arts Festival (August); Laurel Watermelon Festival (mid-August).

September-December
Nanticoke Indian Pow-Wow near Oak Orchard (second week in September); Brandywine Arts Festival in Wilmington (second Saturday in September); Fall Regatta on Rehoboth Bay (mid-September); Delaware "500" stock car race in Dover (third Sunday in September); Fall Harvest Festival at the Delaware Agricultural Museum in Dover (late October); Christmas and Candlelight tours at 9 museums in the Brandywine Valley (December).

Delaware Division of Parks and Recreation

A cypress swamp covers part of southern Delaware. Bald cypress trees and red cedars thrive throughout the region.

Land regions. Delaware has two main land regions: (1) the Atlantic Coastal Plain and (2) the Piedmont.

The Atlantic Coastal Plain stretches along the east coast of the United States from New Jersey to southern Florida. The coastal plain covers all of Delaware but the northern tip. This region is a low, flat plain that seldom rises over 80 feet (24 meters) above sea level. Some sections of the coastal plain have good farmland. A 30,000-acre (12,000-hectare) swamp lies along Delaware's southern boundary.

The Piedmont extends from New Jersey to Alabama. This region crosses the northern edge of Delaware and is about 10 miles (16 kilometers) wide at its widest point in the state. Rolling hills and fertile valleys cover the Piedmont. The highest point in Delaware, 442 feet (135 meters), is in this region near the northern border of the state. Farms and estates occupy much of the Piedmont region.

Coastline of Delaware is 28 miles (45 kilometers) long from Maryland to the mouth of Delaware Bay. If bays, creeks, rivers, and sounds are included, the coastline measures 381 miles (613 kilometers). A long sand reef forms the Atlantic coastline. This dune-covered strip of land is a popular vacation region. An inlet divides the reef near its center, leading into Rehoboth and Indian River bays.

Rivers, bays, and lakes. The broad Delaware River is the state's largest and most important river. It links the Atlantic Ocean with the northern part of Delaware and with parts of New York, Pennsylvania, and New Jersey. The mouth of the Christina River forms Wilmington Harbor. Barges carry cargo up the Christina from Wilmington as far west as Newport. Brandywine Creek is the Christina's chief tributary. Other streams that flow into the Delaware River include Appoquinimink Creek and the Smyrna River.

Many streams in southeastern Delaware empty into Delaware Bay and the Atlantic Ocean. The most important ones include the Broadkill, Indian, Mispillion, Murderkill, and St. Jones rivers. Most of Delaware's streams flow eastward from a long, low ridge near the western boundary. But most of the rivers in southwestern Delaware flow southward and westward across Maryland and into Chesapeake Bay. The Nanticoke is the most important of these rivers.

Ocean ships sail across Delaware Bay to reach the Delaware River. Rehoboth and Indian River bays lie within the great sand reef in southeastern Delaware.

Land regions of Delaware

PIEDMONT

Delaware R.

ATLANTIC

COASTAL

PLAIN

WORLD BOOK map

Many of the state's more than 50 small lakes and ponds have good beaches and provide excellent freshwater fishing.

Plant and animal life. Forests cover about a third of Delaware. The state's most common trees include beech, black tupelo, hickory, holly, loblolly pine, oak, shortleaf pine, and sweet gum. Such smaller trees as magnolia, sassafras, wild cherry, and willow are also common in the state. Bald cypress and red cedar trees thrive in the southern swamps.

Many kinds of wild flowers grow in the state. Water lilies and floating hearts dot the ponds and lakes. Pink and white hibiscus flourish in the sea marshes. Magnolias and pink lady's-slippers bloom in the swamps. In some places, blueberries and cranberries form almost impassable thickets.

Average monthly weather

Wilmington					
	Temperatures				Days of rain or snow
	F.°		C°		
	High	Low	High	Low	
Jan.	42	25	6	−4	13
Feb.	43	25	6	−4	10
Mar.	53	32	12	0	13
Apr.	63	40	17	4	12
May	75	51	24	11	13
June	83	60	28	16	10
July	87	65	31	18	9
Aug.	85	63	29	17	9
Sept.	79	57	26	14	9
Oct.	67	45	19	7	8
Nov.	55	36	13	2	10
Dec.	44	26	7	−3	11

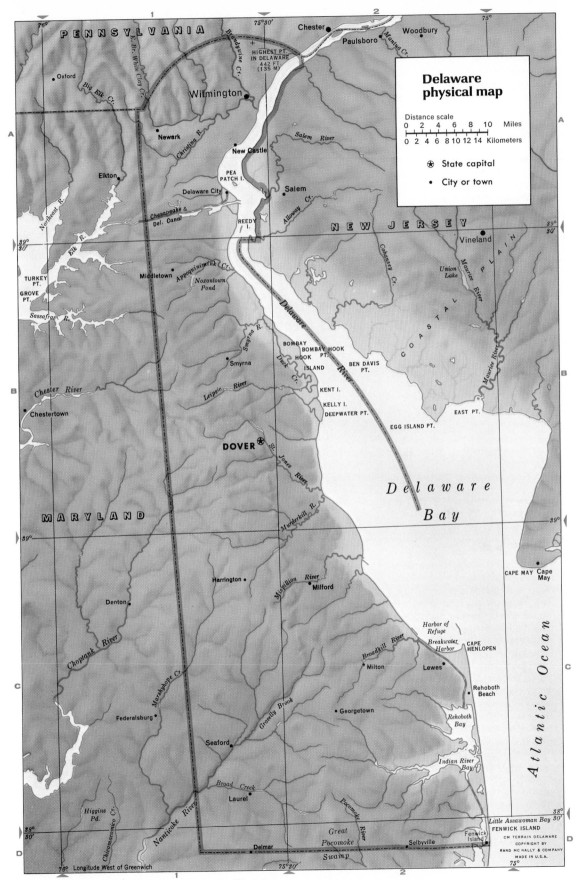

Delaware physical map

Distance scale

0 2 4 6 8 10 Miles

0 2 4 6 8 10 12 14 Kilometers

✳ State capital

• City or town

PENNSYLVANIA

Oxford

E. Br. White Clay Cr.

Brandywine Cr.

HIGHEST PT.
IN DELAWARE
442 FT
(135 M)

Chester

Paulsboro

Woodbury

Mantua Cr.

Wilmington

Big Elk Cr.

Newark

Christina R.

New Castle

Salem River

Elkton

PEA
PATCH I.

Delaware City

Salem

Alloway Cr.

NEW JERSEY

Northeast R.

Chesapeake &
Del. Canal

REEDY
I.

Vineland

39°
30'

39°
30'

TURKEY
PT.

Elk R.

Middletown

Appoquinimink Cr.

Noxontown
Pond

Cohansey Cr.

Union
Lake

Maurice River

GROVE
PT.

Sassafras R.

Smyrna R.

Delaware

C O A S T A L   P L A I N

Maurice River

Chester River

Smyrna

Duck Cr.

BOMBAY
HOOK

BOMBAY HOOK
PT.

BEN DAVIS
PT.

Leipsic River

River

Chestertown

HOOK
ISLAND

KENT I.

KELLY I.

DEEPWATER PT.

EAST PT.

EGG ISLAND PT.

DOVER ✳

St. Jones River

MARYLAND

Murderkill R.

Delaware

Bay

39°

39°

39°

Harrington

Mispillion River

Milford

Denton

CAPE MAY

Cape
May

Choptank River

Harbor of
Refuge

Breakwater
Harbor

CAPE
HENLOPEN

Broadkill River

Milton

Lewes

Marshyhope Cr.

Federalsburg

Gravelly Brook

Georgetown

Rehoboth
Beach

Rehoboth
Bay

A t l a n t i c   O c e a n

Seaford

Indian River
Bay

Broad Creek

Higgins
Pd.

Chicamacomico Cr.

Laurel

Nanticoke River

Great
Pocomoke
Swamp

Pocomoke River

Selbyville

Little Assawoman Bay

FENWICK ISLAND

CM TERRAIN DELAWARE
COPYRIGHT BY
RAND MC NALLY & COMPANY
MADE IN U.S.A.

Fenwick
Island

38°
30'

38°
30'

Delmar

79° Longitude West of Greenwich

75°30'

75°

Specially created for *The World Book Encyclopedia* by Rand McNally and World Book editors

Deer, mink, otter, rabbits, and red and gray foxes live in Delaware's fields and forests. Muskrats are found in the marshes and swamps. Common birds of Delaware include blue herons, cardinals, ducks, hawks, orioles, ruby-throated hummingbirds, sandpipers, snowy egrets, and wrens.

Fishing enthusiasts find bass, carp, catfish, eels, trout, and white perch in the state's lakes, ponds, and streams. Coastal waters have clams, crabs, menhaden, oysters, sea trout, shad, and striped bass. Some diamondback terrapins live along the coast. Snapping turtles are found in the swamps.

Climate. Delaware has a humid climate with hot summers and generally mild winters. On hot summer days, Atlantic breezes cool the beaches. Mountains in Penn-

sylvania protect Delaware from the northwest winds of winter. Temperatures away from the coast vary across the state by about 4° F. (2° C) in summer and 2° F. (1° C) in winter. Temperatures in the state average 76° F. (24° C) in July and 35° F. (2° C) in January. Millsboro had both the highest and lowest temperatures ever recorded in Delaware. On July 21, 1930, the temperature there reached 110° F. (43° C). On Jan. 17, 1893, the temperature there fell to −17° F. (−27° C).

The state averages about 45 inches (114 centimeters) of *precipitation* (rain, melted snow, and other forms of moisture) a year. Snowfall varies from an annual average of about 18 inches (46 centimeters) in the north to 14 inches (36 centimeters) in the south. The coast receives about 12 inches (30 centimeters) of snow a year.

Average January temperatures

Delaware has generally mild winters because mountains in Pennsylvania protect the state from wintry northwest winds.

Average July temperatures

The state has hot, humid summers. The southeastern portion of Delaware has the highest temperature.

Average yearly precipitation

Precipitation is distributed fairly evenly throughout the state. The north and southeast receive the most precipitation.

WORLD BOOK maps

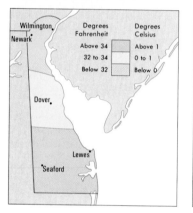

Degrees Fahrenheit		Degrees Celsius
Above 34		Above 1
32 to 34		0 to 1
Below 32		Below 0

Wilmington, Newark, Dover, Lewes, Seaford

Degrees Fahrenheit		Degrees Celsius
Above 77		Above 25
76 to 77		24 to 25
Below 76		Below 24

Wilmington, Newark, Dover, Lewes, Seaford

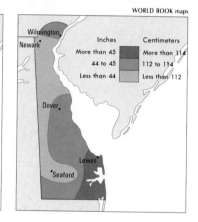

Inches		Centimeters
More than 45		More than 114
44 to 45		112 to 114
Less than 44		Less than 112

Wilmington, Newark, Dover, Lewes, Seaford

Economy

Service industries, taken together, make up about two-thirds of Delaware's *gross state product*—the total value of all goods and services produced in a state in a year. However, manufacturing is Delaware's single most important economic activity. The production of chemicals is the most important manufacturing activity. Farmland is generally good throughout the state.

A state law permits businesses to incorporate in Delaware even if they have nothing but a mailing address in the state. Companies find it easy and inexpensive to incorporate in Delaware. Also, corporate tax rates are lower in Delaware than they are in most other states. For these reasons, many of the nation's largest companies incorporate in Delaware, even though they do almost all their business outside the state.

Natural resources of Delaware include fertile soil and mineral deposits.

Soil. Most of the state is covered by soils that are generally fertile but somewhat sandy. Some of the rocky hills of the Piedmont in northern Delaware are covered by patches of gravel and coarse, red sand and silt. A mixture of clay and loam soils covers the region just south of the Piedmont.

Minerals. Delaware has deposits of clays, sand and gravel, and stone. Brandywine blue granite, a building material used for decorative purposes, is also found in the state.

Service industries account for 65 per cent of Delaware's gross state product. The state's service industries are concentrated in the Wilmington metropolitan area.

Finance, insurance, and real estate form the most valuable service industry in Delaware. Banking in the state has grown rapidly since 1980. During the early 1980's, the Delaware government reduced taxes and fees on banking companies doing business in the state. As a result, many large banks moved some of their operations to Delaware. By the late 1980's, the Wilmington area had become an important national financial center. Several large insurance companies and investment firms are also based in the Wilmington area. The growth of banks and other businesses in northern Delaware has created demand for new office space and homes. This demand has benefited the state's real estate companies.

Next in importance among Delaware service industries are (1) wholesale and retail trade, and (2) community, social, and personal services. Distributors of au-

Production and workers by economic activities

Economic activities	Per cent of GSP* produced	Employed workers Number of persons	Per cent of total
Manufacturing	28	68,700	22
Finance, insurance, & real estate	18	22,900	7
Wholesale & retail trade	14	67,300	22
Community, social, & personal services	14	66,600	21
Government	11	46,100	15
Transportation, communication, & utilities	8	12,700	4
Construction	5	18,900	6
Agriculture	2	8,300	3
Mining	†	100	†
Total	100	311,500	100

*GSP = gross state product, the total value of goods and services produced in a year.
†Less than one-half of 1 per cent.
Figures are for 1986.
Sources: *World Book* estimates based on data from U.S. Bureau of Economic Analysis, U.S. Bureau of Labor Statistics, and U.S. Department of Agriculture.

tomobiles, food products, and minerals play a leading role in the state's wholesale trade. Such retail establishments as discount stores, grocery stores, and restaurants employ many of the state's workers.

Community, social, and personal services consist of a wide variety of economic activities. These activities include the operation of doctors' offices and private hospitals, law firms, hotels, and car rental agencies. Wilmington is the leading health care center. Resort hotels dot the southern Delaware coastline.

Government ranks fourth in importance among service industries in Delaware. Government services include the operation of public schools and hospitals, and military bases. The public school system is a major employer. The federal government operates Dover Air Force Base and Fort Miles Military Reservation. State government offices are in Dover and Wilmington.

Transportation, communication, and utilities rank last in importance among Delaware service industries. Railroad and trucking companies transport the state's manufactured and imported goods to major East Coast markets. Columbia Gas System is Delaware's largest utility. More information about transportation and communication can be found later in this section.

Manufacturing accounts for 28 per cent of Delaware's gross state product. The state's manufactured goods have a *value added by manufacture* of about $3 billion annually. Value added by manufacture represents the increase in value of raw materials after they become finished goods.

Chemicals are Delaware's chief manufactured product. Wilmington is sometimes called the *Chemical Capital of the World.* It is the headquarters of E. I. du Pont de Nemours & Company, Hercules Inc., and ICI (America) Inc. The Du Pont Company has several plants in Delaware. Its research center, near Wilmington, is one of the largest in the world. Other important chemical companies also have factories, offices, and research laboratories in Delaware. Chemical factories in Delaware produce drugs, industrial chemicals, and plastics and other

synthetic materials. Although Delaware does not rank among the leading chemical manufacturing states, it is among the leaders in chemical management and research.

Food processing ranks second in value among Delaware's manufacturing activities. A large plant in Dover makes gelatin, pudding, and other prepared desserts. Sussex County has several large canneries and poultry processing plants. The state's other processed foods include baked goods, fish products, and soft drinks.

Delaware ranks among the leading states in automobile production. It has two automobile manufacturing plants. These plants, located in Newark and Newport, provide a major source of employment in the state. Factories in the Wilmington area manufacture paper products. Other products manufactured in Delaware include plastics products, scientific instruments, and printed materials.

Agriculture accounts for 2 per cent of Delaware's gross state product. Farmland covers about half the state. Delaware's approximately 3,000 farms have an average size of about 200 acres (81 hectares).

Livestock and related products account for about 80 per cent of Delaware's farm income. *Broilers* (chickens from 5 to 12 weeks old) are Delaware's most valuable farm product by far. Delaware ranks as an important broiler-producing state. Most of the broilers come from Sussex County. Farms in Kent and New Castle counties produce the largest amounts of milk in the state. Southern Delaware farms raise most of the state's hogs.

Crops in Delaware provide about 30 per cent of the state's farm income. Soybeans are Delaware's leading crop. They are raised on about two-fifths of the cultivated land in the state. Corn, the second most valuable crop, is grown throughout the state. Delaware's farmers also grow barley and wheat. Potatoes and peas are the largest vegetable crops in Delaware. Apples are the state's leading fruit.

Greenhouse and nursery products are also an important source of agricultural income. These products include flowers, ornamental shrubs, and young plants.

Delaware Department of Agriculture

Workers in a poultry-processing plant in Millsboro prepare broiler chickens for shipment to food stores. Food processing is Delaware's second largest manufacturing activity.

Farm and forest products

This map shows where the leading farm and forest products are produced. The major urban area (shown in red) is the state's important manufacturing center.

WORLD BOOK map

clams, lobsters, oysters, sea bass, and sea trout. The most valuable freshwater fish caught in Delaware include eels and carp.

Electric power. Coal-burning plants generate most of Delaware's electric power. Plants that burn petroleum or gas provide the rest of the state's power.

Transportation. The Delaware River and its tributaries formed the first transportation system in the Delaware region. The state's first railroad, the New Castle and Frenchtown Railroad, was completed in 1831. Delaware's modern highway system began in 1911, when Thomas Coleman du Pont built a paved highway between Wilmington and the Maryland border.

Wilmington is Delaware's chief port for foreign shipping. The Chesapeake and Delaware Canal crosses northern Delaware. Ships traveling between Baltimore, Md., and Philadelphia, Pa., can save about 285 miles (459 kilometers) by using the Chesapeake and Delaware Canal. The Lewes and Rehoboth Canal connects Lewes with Rehoboth Bay.

Nearly all of Delaware's 5,300 miles (8,500 kilometers) of roads and highways are surfaced. The Delaware Memorial Bridge, which crosses the Delaware River near New Castle, connects northern Delaware with New Jersey. The Delaware Turnpike John F. Kennedy Memorial Highway links northern Delaware and northeastern Maryland. The turnpike forms part of a major nonstop highway between Boston and Washington, D.C. The Cape May-Lewes Ferry crosses Delaware Bay and connects southern Delaware with New Jersey.

Greater Wilmington Airport near New Castle is the state's chief air terminal. Four railroad lines in the state provide freight service. Wilmington is the only city in Delaware that is served by passenger trains.

Communication. The *Delaware Gazette* was the first successful newspaper published in the Delaware region. Jacob A. Killen began publishing it in Wilmington in 1785. Delaware's first radio station, WDEL, began broadcasting in Wilmington in 1922. The first television station in Delaware began operating in Wilmington in 1949. Today, the state has 2 daily newspapers and about 15 weeklies. The dailies are Dover's *Delaware State News* and the *Wilmington News Journal.* About 10 periodicals are published in the state. Delaware has about 20 radio stations and 3 television stations.

Mining. Delaware ranks last among the states in annual value of mineral production. Magnesium is the state's leading mineral product. A plant near Lewes processes seawater to obtain magnesium. Sand and gravel provide nearly all of the remaining mining income. All three of Delaware's counties mine sand and gravel.

Fishing industry in Delaware has an annual fish catch of about 2\frac{1}{3}$ million. Crabs are the most valuable catch. Workers in the industry also bring in quantities of

Government

Constitution of Delaware dates from 1897. Earlier constitutions were adopted in 1776, 1792, and 1831. An *amendment* (change) to the Constitution may be proposed by the state legislature or by a constitutional convention. Legislative amendments must be approved by two-thirds of the members of both houses of the legislature. They must then be approved in a similar manner after the next legislature is elected. Delaware is the only state in which legislative amendments do not need approval by the voters. Before a constitutional convention can meet, it must be approved by two-thirds of both houses of two successive legislatures. Then it must be approved by a majority of the people who vote on it.

Executive. Delaware's governor serves a four-year term and may be reelected only once. These terms may

be served in succession. The lieutenant governor, the attorney general, and the insurance commissioner are each elected to four-year terms. The state treasurer and the auditor of accounts are also elected to four-year terms.

The governor appoints the secretary of state, members of an executive department cabinet, judges, and members of the state board of education. Major appointed officials serve terms that range from 3 to 10 years.

Legislature is also called the *General Assembly.* It consists of a 21-member Senate and a 41-member House of Representatives. State senators are elected to four-year terms, and representatives to two-year terms. Regular legislative sessions begin on the second Tuesday in January each year. Regular sessions may not extend beyond June 30. The governor or the presiding officers of both houses may call for special sessions. Special sessions have no time limit.

In 1897, when Delaware's current Constitution was adopted, the state was shifting toward an industrial economy. It tried to protect farmers by giving them greater representation than city areas in the legislature. In 1964, Delaware changed its legislative districts to give better representation to the state's city areas. But in 1967, a federal court ruled that the change did not give enough representation to city areas. Delaware redrew its legislative districts in 1968. The state also redrew the districts in 1971 and again in 1981, following federal censuses.

Courts. All Delaware judges are appointed by the governor, with the approval of the state Senate. The highest court in Delaware is the state Supreme Court. It has a chief justice and four associate justices. The governor selects the chief justice. The Superior Court has 13 judges. It meets in all three counties of the state. Delaware's Court of Chancery has played a major role in developing the state's corporation laws. Other Delaware courts include the Wilmington Municipal Court, family courts and common pleas courts in each county, and justice of the peace courts. Justices of the peace serve four-year terms. All other judges in Delaware serve 12-year terms.

Local government. Delaware has only three counties—Kent, New Castle, and Sussex. The county of New Castle is governed by a six-member council headed by an elected president. Sussex County has a five-member council, with one councilman serving as president. An elected *levy court* (county commission) governs Kent County. The levy court has seven members. All members of the three county governing bodies serve four-year terms. Other elected county officials in Delaware include a comptroller, sheriff, and recorder of deeds.

Delaware is the only state in which counties are divided into *hundreds*. A hundred has no government of its own, but it serves as a basis for property and zoning location.

A state law permits Delaware municipalities of 1,000 or more people to have *home rule* (self-government) to the extent that they may amend their own charters. Most Delaware cities and towns have either a mayor-council or a council-manager form of government.

Revenue. Taxation provides about half of the state government's *general revenue* (income). Income taxes are the main source of tax income. Other sources of revenue include taxes on gasoline, public utilities, tobacco products, and licenses. About a fifth of the state's revenue comes from federal grants and other U.S. government programs. The state has no sales or personal property taxes.

The state governors of Delaware

	Party	Term		Party	Term
John McKinly	None	1777	William Temple	Whig	1846-1847
Thomas McKean	None	1777	William Tharp	Democratic	1847-1851
George Read	None	1777-1778	William H. Ross	Democratic	1851-1855
Caesar Rodney	None	1778-1782	Peter F. Causey	†American	1855-1859
John Dickinson	None	1782-1783	William Burton	Democratic	1859-1863
John Cook	None	1783	William Cannon	Union	1863-1865
Nicholas Van Dyke	None	1783-1786	Gove Saulsbury	Democratic	1865-1871
Thomas Collins	None	1786-1789	James Ponder	Democratic	1871-1875
Jehu Davis	None	1789	John P. Cochran	Democratic	1875-1879
Joshua Clayton	Federalist	1789-1796	John W. Hall	Democratic	1879-1883
Gunning Bedford, Sr.	Federalist	1796-1797	Charles C. Stockley	Democratic	1883-1887
Daniel Rogers	Federalist	1797-1799	Benjamin T. Biggs	Democratic	1887-1891
Richard Bassett	Federalist	1799-1801	Robert J. Reynolds	Democratic	1891-1895
James Sykes	Federalist	1801-1802	Joshua H. Marvil	Republican	1895
David Hall	*Dem.-Rep.	1802-1805	William T. Watson	Democratic	1895-1897
Nathaniel Mitchell	Federalist	1805-1808	Ebe W. Tunnell	Democratic	1897-1901
George Truitt	Federalist	1808-1811	John Hunn	Republican	1901-1905
Joseph Haslet	*Dem.-Rep.	1811-1814	Preston Lea	Republican	1905-1909
Daniel Rodney	Federalist	1814-1817	Simeon S. Pennewill	Republican	1909-1913
John Clark	Federalist	1817-1820	Charles R. Miller	Republican	1913-1917
Jacob Stout	Federalist	1820-1821	John G. Townsend, Jr.	Republican	1917-1921
John Collins	*Dem.-Rep.	1821-1822	William D. Denney	Republican	1921-1925
Caleb Rodney	Federalist	1822-1823	Robert P. Robinson	Republican	1925-1929
Joseph Haslet	*Dem.-Rep.	1823	C. Douglass Buck	Republican	1929-1937
Charles Thomas	*Dem.-Rep.	1823-1824	Richard C. McMullen	Democratic	1937-1941
Samuel Paynter	Federalist	1824-1827	Walter W. Bacon	Republican	1941-1949
Charles Polk	Federalist	1827-1830	Elbert N. Carvel	Democratic	1949-1953
David Hazzard	American Republican	1830-1833	J. Caleb Boggs	Republican	1953-1960
Caleb P. Bennett	Democratic	1833-1836	David P. Buckson	Republican	1960-1961
Charles Polk	Whig	1836-1837	Elbert N. Carvel	Democratic	1961-1965
Cornelius P. Comegys	Whig	1837-1841	Charles L. Terry, Jr.	Democratic	1965-1969
William B. Cooper	Whig	1841-1845	Russell W. Peterson	Republican	1969-1973
Thomas Stockton	Whig	1845-1846	Sherman W. Tribbitt	Democratic	1973-1977
Joseph Maull	Whig	1846	Pierre S. du Pont	Republican	1977-1985
			Michael N. Castle	Republican	1985-

*Democratic-Republican   †Know-Nothing

Politics. During the 1900's, Delaware's electoral votes have been cast for Republican presidential candidates about twice as often as for Democrats. Since 1900, Democrats have been elected governor of the state only five times. But Democrats in Delaware made major gains in the 1960's and 1970's. During this period, three Democratic presidential candidates carried the state and three Democrats won election as governor. For Delaware's electoral votes in presidential elections, see **Electoral College** (table).

History

Indian days. Two tribes of Algonquian Indians lived in the Delaware region when white explorers first arrived. The Lenni-Lenape tribe lived along the banks of the Delaware River. The Nanticoke lived along the Nanticoke River in the southwestern part of the region. By the mid-1700's, white settlers had forced most of the Indians out of the region.

Exploration and early settlement. Henry Hudson, an English explorer, was probably the first white person to visit the Delaware region. He sailed into present-day Delaware Bay in 1609. Hudson was trying to find a trade route to the Far East for the Dutch East India Company. Seeing that the bay led to a river, Hudson left the region and sailed northward. In 1610, Captain Samuel Argall of the Virginia colony sailed into the bay, seeking shelter from a storm. Argall named the bay De La Warr Bay, for Lord De La Warr, the governor of Virginia. The Dutch attempted to establish the first settlement in the region at Zwaanendael (present-day Lewes) in 1631. But trouble developed between the Dutch settlers and the Indians. Within a year, the Indians massacred the settlers and burned their fort.

Swedish settlers came to the Delaware region in 1638. They founded the colony of New Sweden, the first permanent settlement in the region. The Swedes also built Fort Christina at present-day Wilmington. New settlers came to New Sweden from Sweden and Finland, and expanded the colony northward.

The Dutch government believed that New Sweden was in Dutch territory. In 1651, Peter Stuyvesant, governor of the Dutch colony of New Netherland, established Fort Casimir at present-day New Castle. The Swedish colonists captured Fort Casimir in 1654. But the following year, the Dutch captured all New Sweden and made it part of New Netherland.

English rule. In 1664, England captured all New Netherland, including the Delaware region. The English ruled the Delaware settlements as part of the colony of New York. The Dutch recaptured the region in 1673, but returned it peacefully to the English the following year.

William Penn of England founded the colony of Pennsylvania in 1681. He wanted to establish a connection between his colony and the Atlantic Ocean. In 1682, the Duke of York gave the Delaware region to Penn as a territory of his Pennsylvania colony. That same year, Penn established representative government for both the colony and the territory. Both the Pennsylvania and Delaware regions had the same number of delegates in Pennsylvania's legislature.

The Delaware region became known as the Three Lower Counties because it was down the Delaware River from Pennsylvania. Pennsylvania continued to grow in the late 1600's and added new counties. Colonists in the Three Lower Counties began to fear that they would soon have a minority voice in the government. In 1701, delegates from the Three Lower Counties refused to meet with those from Pennsylvania. They asked Penn to give them a separate legislature, and Penn consented. The first separate legislature of the Three Lower Counties met in 1704. Pennsylvania governors continued to govern the Three Lower Counties until the Revolutionary War.

The Revolutionary War. England imposed severe taxes on the American colonies during the 1760's. Colonists in the Three Lower Counties resented these taxes. They sent delegates to Philadelphia to attend the First Continental Congress in 1774.

The Revolutionary War began in 1775. On July 2, 1776, the Three Lower Counties joined other American colonies in voting for independence at the Second Continental Congress. Later that year, the region became the Delaware State, and its people adopted their first constitution. In 1777, John McKinly won election as Delaware's first president (governor). New Castle served as the capital.

Delaware soldiers fought throughout the Revolutionary War. Only one small battle took place on Delaware soil. In August 1777, British troops landed in Maryland and marched across Delaware toward Philadelphia. American troops met the British at Coochs Bridge near

The Landing of the Swedes (early 1900's), an oil painting on canvas by Stanley M. Arthurs; Permanent Collection of the University of Delaware

Swedish settlers arrived in the Delaware area in 1638. They founded the colony of New Sweden and built Fort Christina at what is now Wilmington as their first permanent settlement.

Historic Delaware

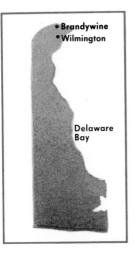

• Brandywine
• Wilmington

Delaware Bay

Henry Hudson, an English explorer, visited Delaware Bay in 1609. He was searching for a trade route to the Far East for the Dutch East India Company and sailed into the bay in hopes of finding a clear passage.

Peter Stuyvesant, a Dutch colonial governor in North America, established Fort Casimir in 1651 at the site of present-day New Castle.

Nylon was developed by research chemists at the Du Pont Company. They combined water, air, and a by-product of coal in a chemical process. Du Pont introduced nylon commercially in 1938.

Delaware became the first state on Dec. 7, 1787. On that date, it ratified the U.S. Constitution, the first of the original 13 states to do so.

Éleuthère Irénée du Pont, a French immigrant, established a powder mill on Brandywine Creek, near Wilmington, in 1802. The mill formed the basis for Delaware's chemical industry.

WORLD BOOK illustrations by Kevin Chadwick

Important dates in Delaware

1609 English explorer Henry Hudson, sailing for the Dutch, visited Delaware Bay.

1610 A ship commissioned by Lord De La Warr, governor of Virginia, entered Delaware Bay.

1631 The Dutch founded Zwaanendael at present-day Lewes.

1638 Swedish colonists founded the colony of New Sweden. They established Fort Christina, Delaware's first permanent settlement, at present-day Wilmington.

1655 The Dutch captured New Sweden.

1664 The English seized Dutch territory on the Delaware River.

1682 William Penn took over the Delaware counties.

1704 Delaware's first separate legislature met.

1777 The British invaded Delaware and won a small battle at Coochs Bridge.

1779 Delaware signed the Articles of Confederation.

1787 (Dec. 7) Delaware became the first state of the Union.

1802 Éleuthère Irénée du Pont founded a powder mill on the banks of Brandywine Creek.

1861-1865 Delaware fought on the Union side during the Civil War.

1897 Delaware adopted its present constitution.

1917 Delaware established a state highway department.

1951 The Delaware Memorial Bridge opened, connecting Delaware with New Jersey.

1957 The state began providing funds for needy students to attend the University of Delaware.

1963 The Delaware Turnpike John F. Kennedy Memorial Highway was opened, completing a nonstop highway between Boston and Washington, D.C.

1968 Delaware redrew its legislative districts.

1971 The Delaware Coastal Zone Act prohibited construction of industrial plants in coastal areas.

Newark on Sept. 3, 1777. The outnumbered Americans retreated, and the British went on to Pennsylvania. There they defeated General George Washington's forces in the Battle of Brandywine, just north of the Delaware border, on September 11. On September 12, the British occupied Wilmington. Delaware moved its capital from New Castle because of the closeness of British troops. The legislature met at several sites before making Dover the capital. The British stayed for about a month in Wilmington, where they treated their wounded. Then they moved on.

Statehood. On Feb. 22, 1779, Delaware signed the Articles of Confederation (the forerunner to the U.S. Constitution). But leaders from Delaware and other colonies were dissatisfied with the Articles of Confederation. They urged the adoption of a stronger body of rules. John Dickinson and George Read of Delaware helped draft a constitution. On Dec. 7, 1787, Delaware voted unanimously to *ratify* (approve) the United States Constitution. It was the first state to do so. In 1792, Delaware adopted a new state constitution and changed its name from the Delaware State to the State of Delaware.

During and after the Revolutionary War, the Wilmington area became the center of the nation's flour-milling industry. In 1802, Éleuthère Irénée du Pont, a French immigrant, established a powder mill on Brandywine Creek near Wilmington. This mill was the beginning of Delaware's great chemical industry.

During the War of 1812, British ships stopped carrying goods to the United States. As a result, new industries sprang up in Delaware and in other states to provide needed goods. British ships bombarded Lewes in 1813, but they caused little damage.

The Civil War and industrial expansion. Delaware was a slave state, but it also was one of the original 13 states of the Union. Because of Delaware's location between the North and the Deep South, Delawareans had strong ties with both the Union and the Confederate states. The state fought on the Union side during the Civil War (1861-1865). But many Delawareans felt that the Confederate States should have been allowed to *secede* (withdraw) peacefully from the Union.

President Abraham Lincoln issued the Emancipation Proclamation in 1863, freeing the slaves in all areas of the Confederate States still in rebellion. But the Emancipation Proclamation did not affect slave states that had remained loyal to the Union. The few slaves left in Delaware were not freed until 1865. That year, Amendment 13 to the U.S. Constitution abolished all slavery in the United States.

Delaware's farms and industries prospered during and after the Civil War. The growth of railroads in the 1850's helped farmers move their crops to market. As a result, the value of farmland in southern Delaware increased. During the late 1800's, Wilmington grew rapidly as an industrial city. Thousands of people worked in the city's shipyards, iron foundries, machine shops, and manufacturing plants. Delaware's present constitution was adopted in 1897.

The early 1900's brought improvements in education, public welfare, and roadbuilding in Delaware. By 1920, the legislature had established an industrial-accident board, a state board of charities (now the state board of welfare), and a state highway department. The legislature also set up a state income tax, and a pension system to help mothers of needy children. In the 1920's, Pierre S. du Pont gave several million dollars to build new schools and to aid public education in the state. Du Pont also served as state tax commissioner.

The Great Depression of the 1930's put thousands of Delawareans out of work. Richard C. McMullen was elected governor in 1936. He was the state's first Democratic governor since 1901. In 1941, the state legislature changed its Sunday blue laws, placing fewer restrictions on Sunday activities (see **Blue laws**).

The mid-1900's. During World War II (1939-1945), many Delaware factories and mills produced materials for the armed services. The state's economy grew rapidly in the 1950's and 1960's. The Delaware Memorial Bridge across the Delaware River opened in 1951, connecting Delaware with New Jersey. New industries came into Delaware, including such giant corporations as Chrysler, General Foods, and General Motors. Many other companies expanded their facilities, and Du Pont became Delaware's largest employer.

Delaware's population increased about 40 per cent during the 1950's and rose another 20 per cent in the 1960's. This growth took place chiefly in cities and suburbs. However, the state constitution, adopted in 1897, favored representation of rural areas in the state legislature. By the 1960's, a minority of the voters was electing a majority of the legislators. Delaware's legislative districts were redrawn in 1964 and 1968 in an attempt to give the voters equal representation.

Delaware State Archives

Fort Delaware became a prison for captured Confederate soldiers during the Civil War (1861-1865). The pentagon-shaped fort is located on Pea Patch Island in the middle of the Delaware River. The fort was originally built for coastal defense in 1859.

Like many other states, Delaware faced racial problems in the 1950's and 1960's. Black groups challenged the state's system of separate schools for white and black children. In 1954, the Supreme Court of the United States ruled that compulsory segregation in public schools was unconstitutional. By the mid-1960's, all of Delaware's public school districts were integrated. In 1963, the state legislature passed a bill banning segregation in public eating and drinking places. In 1969, the legislature approved a bill ending discrimination in the rental or sale of housing in Delaware.

Recent developments. A new state agency, the Department of Natural Resources and Environmental Control, was set up in 1969 to promote conservation and to control air and water pollution in Delaware. In 1971, the Delaware legislature passed the Coastal Zone Act. This act banned construction of industrial plants along the Delaware coastline. The legislature also responded to further pressure from the state's growing urban districts by redrawing Delaware's legislative districts in 1971 and 1981.

The rapid economic growth Delaware experienced during the mid-1900's slowed during the 1970's, but the economy improved in the 1980's. In 1980, the state adopted a constitutional limit that restricted government spending to 95 per cent of the government's expected revenue. The government's unspent revenue helped improve the state's financial base. Many financial institutions began operations in Delaware, and tourism increased.   Barbara E. Benson and Peter W. Rees

Study aids

Related articles in *World Book* include:

Biographies

Bassett, Richard	Dickinson, John	McKean, Thomas
Bedford, Gunning, Jr.	Du Pont, Éleuthère Irénée	Penn, William
Broom, Jacob	Evans, Oliver	Pyle, Howard
Cannon, Annie J.	Hudson, Henry	Read, George
Clayton, John M.	Marquand, John P.	Rodney, Caesar
De La Warr, Lord		Stuyvesant, Peter

Cities

Dover	Newark	Wilmington

History

Colonial life in America	New Netherland
Delaware Indians	New Sweden
Mason and Dixon's Line	Revolutionary War in America

Physical features

Delaware Bay	Piedmont region
Delaware River	

Other related articles

Delaware, University of	Log cabin
Du Pont Company	

Outline

I. People
  A. Population
  B. Schools
  C. Libraries
  D. Museums
II. Visitor's guide
  A. Places to visit
  B. Annual events
III. Land and climate
  A. Land regions
  B. Coastline
  C. Rivers, bays, and lakes
  D. Plant and animal life
  E. Climate
IV. Economy
  A. Natural resources
  B. Service industries
  C. Manufacturing
  D. Agriculture
  E. Mining
  F. Fishing industry
  G. Electric power
  H. Transportation
  I. Communication
V. Government
  A. Constitution
  B. Executive
  C. Legislature
  D. Courts
  E. Local government
  F. Revenue
  G. Politics
VI. History

Questions

Why do so many large corporations have their headquarters in Delaware?
What is a *hundred*?
With what other state did Delaware once share its governor and General Assembly? Why?
Why did the Emancipation Proclamation have no effect in Delaware, a slave state?
How does the Delaware Constitution differ from all other state constitutions?
Why is Delaware often called the First State?
What name was given the Delaware region after it became a territory of Pennsylvania? Why did Delaware receive this name?
When and why was Delaware's capital moved from New Castle to Dover?
How has Delaware tried to promote conservation and to control air and water pollution?
What are Delaware's most important agricultural and manufactured products?

Additional resources

Level I
Bleeker, Sonia. *The Delaware Indians: Eastern Fishermen and Farmers.* Morrow, 1953.
Carpenter, Allan. *Delaware.* Rev. ed. Childrens Press, 1978.
Christensen, Gardell D., and Burney, Eugenia. *Colonial Delaware.* Nelson, 1975.
Fradin, Dennis B. *Delaware in Words and Pictures.* Childrens Press, 1980.
Lyman, Nanci A. *The Colony of Delaware.* Watts, 1975.
Thompson, Kathleen. *Delaware.* Raintree, 1987.

Level II
Delaware: A Guide to the First State. Rev. ed. Scholarly, 1976.
Dolan, Paul, and Soles, J. R. *The Government of Delaware.* Univ. of Delaware, 1976.
Gray, Ralph D. *The National Waterway: A History of the Chesapeake and Delaware Canal, 1769-1965.* Univ. of Illinois Press, 1967.
Hancock, Harold B. *The Loyalists of Revolutionary Delaware.* Univ. of Delaware Press, 1977.
Hoffecker, Carol E. *Delaware: A Bicentennial History.* Norton, 1977. *Corporate Capital: Wilmington in the Twentieth Century.* Temple Univ. Press, 1983.
Munroe, John A. *Colonial Delaware: A History.* KTO Press, 1978. *History of Delaware.* 2nd ed. Univ. of Delaware Press, 1984.
Weslager, Clinton A. *The Delaware Indians: A History.* Rutgers, 1972.

Delaware, Lord. See De La Warr, Lord.

Delaware, University of, is a coeducational university at Newark, Del. It has colleges of arts and science; agricultural sciences; business and economics; education; engineering; human resources; marine studies; nursing; physical education, athletics and recreation; and urban affairs and public policy. The university grants associate degrees and bachelor's, master's, and doctor's degrees. In cooperation with two museums and a botanical garden, it offers graduate programs in early American decorative arts, industrial history, and ornamental horticulture. The university first opened as an academy in 1743. It became Newark College in 1833, and was renamed Delaware College in 1843. In 1921, it became the University of Delaware. For enrollment, see **Universities and colleges** (table).

Critically reviewed by the University of Delaware

Delaware Bay is a large inlet of the Atlantic Ocean. It separates New Jersey and Delaware. The deep channel of the bay connects with the Delaware River, enabling oceangoing vessels to reach the ports of Wilmington, Del., and Philadelphia. Delaware Bay is about 50 miles (80 kilometers) long and about 35 miles (56 kilometers) wide at its widest point. The channel is from 30 to 60 feet (9 to 18 meters) deep through its entire length. At Cape Henlopen, near the bay entrance, a breakwater provides shelter for ships. See also **Delaware** (physical map); **Delaware River.**   Peter W. Rees

Delaware Indians is the English name of a tribe that lived in what are now Delaware, New Jersey, New York, and Pennsylvania. These Indians called themselves *Lenni-Lenape,* which means *genuine people.* Their English name came from the Delaware River, which flowed through their land. The tribe farmed, hunted, and fished. The Delaware were divided into three major groups— the Munsee, the Unalachtigo, and the Unami. Each group spoke a different dialect of a language that belonged to the Algonquian language family.

In 1682, the Delaware signed a treaty of friendship with the English colonial leader William Penn. Despite the treaty, however, Europeans began to take the Indians' land and gradually pushed them westward.

During the 1760's, a religious leader known as the Delaware Prophet preached that Indians should abandon the use of firearms, steel, and other European inventions. He told the Indians they could gain the power to expel the Europeans from their land by returning to traditional tribal ways of life. The Delaware Prophet influenced an Ottawa Indian leader named Pontiac, who tried to unite the Delaware and other Indians in an attempt to drive out the intruders. The British defeated Pontiac in 1763.

In 1818, the Delaware surrendered all their land east of the Mississippi River to the government. Most of the Delaware moved to Missouri and then to Kansas. In the 1860's, they moved to Oklahoma, where about 300 of them now live, many as farmers. Others live in Wisconsin or in Ontario, Canada.   Merwyn S. Garbarino

See also **Munsee Indians.**

Delaware River rises in southern New York and flows southward for about 300 miles (480 kilometers) before emptying into Delaware Bay. It passes through the Delaware Water Gap near Stroudsburg, Pa. (see **Delaware Water Gap**). The Delaware forms the boundary be-

tween New York and Pennsylvania, Pennsylvania and New Jersey, and New Jersey and Delaware. The Schuylkill and Lehigh rivers are its main tributaries.

The Delaware serves as a water transportation route for Philadelphia, Trenton and Camden, N.J., and Wilmington, Del., which lie in one of the great industrial areas of the United States. The Chesapeake and Delaware Canal connects the river with Chesapeake Bay. In 1961, the Delaware Basin Compact created a regional administrative agency to develop and control the water resources of the Delaware River Basin.   Peter W. Rees

See also **Delaware Bay; Pennsylvania** (picture).

Delaware Water Gap is a deep, narrow *gorge* (valley) cut through the Kittatinny Mountains east of Stroudsburg, Pa. The Delaware River carved the winding path out of solid rock millions of years ago. The gap is about 3 miles (5 kilometers) long and has steep walls that rise more than 1,200 feet (360 meters) on each side. Highways follow the river's path through the gorge. Mount Tammany stands on the New Jersey side of the

Shostal

The Delaware Water Gap is a scenic gorge that separates New Jersey from Pennsylvania. The Delaware River carved this gorge in the Kittatinny Mountains millions of years ago.

gap, and Mount Minsi is on the Pennsylvania side. The gap and the area around it form the Delaware Water Gap National Recreation Area.   William C. Rense

De La Warr, Lord (1577-1618), became the first governor of the Virginia colony. He was also known as *Lord Delaware.* Delaware River, Delaware Bay, the colony of Delaware, and the state of Delaware were named for him. His given and family name was Thomas West. De La Warr became a member of the Privy Council of Queen Elizabeth I and was a member of the Virginia Company Council.

He arrived with supplies at Jamestown in June 1610, in time to prevent the discouraged settlers from deserting the colony. He returned to England in 1611 and died on a trip to America in 1618.   Joseph Carlyle Sitterson

See also **Delaware; Jamestown.**

Delbrück, Max. See Nobel Prizes (table: Nobel Prizes for physiology or medicine—1969).

Del Cano, Juan Sebastián. See Magellan, Ferdinand (The end of the voyage).

Delegate is a representative chosen by a group to speak or act in its interests. National governments send delegates to international meetings. Delegates to a national political convention are chosen by the states they represent. The states determine the method of selection. They generally use either the primary (popular election) or the state party convention. More delegates may be chosen than the state has votes, in which case there are fractional votes.   Ned A. Shearer

De León, Juan Ponce. See Ponce de León, Juan.

De Lesseps, *duh LEHS ehps,* **Ferdinand Marie** (1805-1894), was a French canal builder and diplomat. In 1854, Said Pasha, ruler of Egypt, invited him to start preparatory work on the Suez Canal. De Lesseps' plans provided for a canal without locks, extending from Port Said to Port Tewfik, connecting the Mediterranean Sea with the Gulf of Suez and the Red Sea. The company he organized started work on the Canal in 1859, and completed it 10 years later (see **Suez Canal**).

De Lesseps was born in Versailles. From 1825 until his resignation in 1849, he worked in the French consular and diplomatic service. He was a member of the French Academy and the Academy of Science. At 74, De Lesseps reluctantly agreed to head the French company formed to build the Panama Canal (see **Panama Canal** [The French failure]).   Robert W. Abbett

Delft (pop. 86,278) is a Dutch town located near The Hague. For location, see **Netherlands** (map). Many of Delft's old buildings and picturesque canals have been preserved. One famous building, the Prinsenhof, now a museum, is the place where William I of Orange was assassinated in 1584. The Nieuwe Kerk (New Church), built in the 1400's, contains the tombs of William I and other rulers of the House of Orange. Many painters, including Jan Vermeer and Pieter de Hooch, lived and worked in Delft.

The manufacture of blue pottery was once Delft's most famous industry. Only a few craftspeople continue the tradition. Today, Delft produces metal and electrical machinery. It is the home of Delft University, a large technical university.   Jan de Vries

Delft is a type of earthenware that was made in the late 1500's and flourished into the mid-1700's. It is named for the town of Delft in the Netherlands, a center of production. About the same time, potters in England made a similar pottery also called delft. Delft was glazed with tin oxide to produce a creamy white surface. Designs were painted with other metallic oxides that turned various colors when the pottery was *fired* (baked). Delft resembles pottery called *faïence* and *majolica.* The three types differ in the style of their decoration. See **Faïence; Majolica.**

Delft of the early 1600's imitated Chinese porcelain. By the 1700's, potters had adopted European stylistic

Corcoran Gallery of Art, Washington, D.C.,
William A. Clark Collection

A delft vase

characteristics and subject matter. Dutch delft often shows historical events, landscapes, or scenes of daily life. Much English delft is decorated with simple mottoes or portraits of monarchs. Some delft is still produced today.   John W. Keefe

Delgado, *dehl GAH doh,* **José Matías,** *hoh SAY mah TEE ahs* (1767-1832), a Salvadoran priest and patriot, is called the father of his country. He led the people of El Salvador in three revolutions for their freedom and became the nation's hero.

Many Latin-American countries revolted against Spain in 1810. Father Delgado directed the revolt in El Salvador in 1811. The Spaniards quickly put it down. The Central American countries finally won their independence from Spain in 1821. When Mexico tried to include them in its empire in 1822, Father Delgado headed the resistance movement in El Salvador. He was president of the congress that drew up a constitution for the United Provinces of Central America, a union of nations that existed from 1823 to the late 1800's. Disappointed in the union, Father Delgado began a campaign against neighboring countries but died before the battle ended. He was born in San Salvador.   Harvey L. Johnson

Delhi, *DEHL ee* (pop. 4,884,234; met. area pop. 5,729,283), is the second largest city in India. Only Bombay has more people. Delhi lies on the Jumna River in northern India (see **India** [political map]). It was India's capital from 1912 until 1931, when the present capital, New Delhi, was established just south of Delhi.

The city. The central section of Delhi is within the ruins of walls that were built in the mid-1600's. Three of the city's original 14 gates are still standing.

Delhi is an old, crowded city with many narrow streets and slum dwellings. These features contrast sharply with the wide boulevards and modern buildings in some parts of the city and in New Delhi. Many of Delhi's industries are in heavily populated residential areas. The location of these industries is partly responsible for the city's crowded living conditions.

The busiest street in Delhi is Chandni Chowk, a name that means *silver street.* It is lined with tiny shops, in which silversmiths and other craftworkers produce a wide variety of exquisite products. The many beautiful landmarks in Delhi stand out against their dingy surroundings. The Red Fort, one of the city's most impressive monuments, was built in 1648 by the Mogul Emperor Shah Jahan. This red sandstone structure covers several blocks. The remains of the imperial palace and other Mogul structures lie within its walls.

Another famous monument of the mid-1600's is the Jama Masjid, a majestic marble and sandstone mosque with three marble domes. Between Delhi and New Delhi is a shrine called the Rajghat. It marks the place where the body of the Indian leader Mohandas K. Gandhi was cremated in 1948. Delhi is the home of the University of Delhi and a number of colleges.

Economy. Delhi is a major center of government and finance in India. It is also an important manufacturing and transportation center. The city's leading manufactured products are electrical machinery and equipment, metal products, and rubber. Railroads are the most valuable part of the city's transportation industry.

History. The Delhi area has been the site of many cities from ancient times to today. Much of the present city

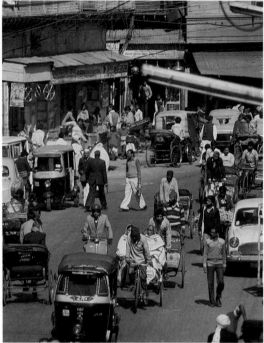

Erwin and Peggy Bauer, Bruce Coleman, Inc.

Delhi, India's second largest city, is old and crowded. Its residential areas are also the site of many of the city's industries, which adds to the congestion.

was built by Shah Jahan and other Mogul emperors during the 1600's. The British captured the city in 1803 and moved the Indian capital from Calcutta to Delhi in 1912. They soon began to build New Delhi, which replaced Delhi as the capital in 1931.

Great industrial growth took place in Delhi after India gained independence from Great Britain in 1947. The city's population began to increase greatly at the same time. This increase resulted partly from the arrival of thousands of Indian refugees from the newly independent nation of Pakistan nearby. Delhi's population has quadrupled since 1951.

In 1955, the government started a program to direct the growth of Delhi. New residential and industrial areas have been created, but the city still faces many problems caused by its rapid growth.   Robert LaPorte, Jr.

See also **New Delhi.**

Delhi Sultanate, *DEHL ee SUHL tuh nayt,* was a Muslim empire that controlled much of what is now Bangladesh, India, and Pakistan from 1206 to 1526. The sultanate's boundaries shifted, depending on its military strength, but it centered in the Ganges Valley and Punjab. Delhi was the capital. The sultans brought much of India under Muslim rule for the first time. Trade routes opened and commerce flourished.

In the late 1100's, Muhammad of Ghor, a Turkish Muslim king, seized much of northern India. In 1206, a sultanate was established at Delhi. During the 1200's, the sultans successfully defended their territory from the remaining Hindu and Buddhist kings. They also prevented the Mongols, who had already conquered China and the Middle East, from conquering India.

During the 1300's, the sultanate temporarily extended its power far into southern India. In 1398, the conqueror Tamerlane looted and destroyed Delhi and massacred most of its people. Although the sultans regained Delhi after Tamerlane left that same year, their former territory was split into regional kingdoms. Babar, a descendant of Tamerlane, defeated the last sultan in 1526 and established the Mogul Empire.

During the sultanate, many Muslims migrated to India to serve as soldiers, government officials, priests, or merchants. Muslim holy men converted many Indians to Islam, the religion of the Muslims. Other Indians switched religions to improve their economic position. Most of the converts lived in the northwest and northeast, now Pakistan and Bangladesh.   J. F. Richards

Delibes, *duh LEEB,* **Léo** (1836-1891), was a French composer. During his lifetime, he was best known for his light operas. Today, his reputation rests on three works—the ballets *Coppélia* (1870) and *Sylvia* (1876) and the opera *Lakmé* (1883). Music from both ballets has been adapted into popular orchestral suites. *Lakmé* contains the famous "Bell Song," an aria for coloratura soprano. The three compositions reflect Delibes's brilliant orchestral writing, rhythmic subtlety, and easily remembered melodies. His other works include music for an 1882 revival of Victor Hugo's play *Le Roi s'amuse* and a collection of 15 songs, published in 1885 or 1886. The collection includes the popular "The Girls of Cadiz."

Delibes was born in St. Germain du Val, near Le Mans. His full name was Clément Philibert Léo Delibes. He studied composition at the Paris Conservatory from 1848 to 1852 and composed his first work, an operetta, in 1855. Delibes also worked as an organist for several years. He became a professor of composition at the Paris Conservatory in 1881.   Mary Vinquist

Delilah, *dih LY luh,* in the Old Testament, was the Philistine mistress of Samson, the Israelite folk hero famed for his tremendous strength. The Philistines, who were enemies of the Israelites, bribed Delilah to find out the secret of Samson's power so that they could take him prisoner. After much coaxing, Samson told Delilah that his strength lay in his long, thick hair which, because of a vow, he had never cut. Delilah had his head shaved while he was asleep. He became weak and helpless. The Philistines easily captured him, blinded him, and made him work as a slave. The story of Samson is told in Judges 16.   J. Maxwell Miller

Delinquency, Juvenile. See Juvenile delinquency.

Delirium tremens, *dih LIHR ee uhm TREE muhnz,* often called the *DT's,* is a nervous and mental disturbance that results from acute alcoholism. It occurs after withdrawal from alcohol or other depressant drugs and may last 3 to 10 days. People often become markedly disturbed after unusually prolonged or heavy drinking of alcoholic beverages. They develop insomnia and a dislike for food, and become irritable and restless. They may then have visual illusions and hallucinations. These visions may be brief but terrifying. In some cases, they may last several days. Death sometimes results, often because pneumonia or heart failure develops. Doctors usually treat DT's by taking alcohol away from patients and giving them sedative and tranquilizing drugs.

Kenneth Blum and Ronald W. McNichol

See also **Alcoholism.**

Delius, *DEE lee uhs,* **Frederick** (1862-1934), was an English composer. He wrote in many forms but is best known for compositions that combine chorus, vocal soloists, and orchestra. These works include *Sea Drift* (1906), based on the poetry of the American poet Walt Whitman; and *A Mass of Life* (1908-1909), based on texts by German philosopher Friedrich Nietzsche. Delius also composed chamber music, concertos, operas, songs, symphonic tone poems, and incidental music for plays. Delius's finest music generates emotional power by blending simple melodies with rich and subtle harmonies.

Delius was born in Bradford. His given and family name was Fritz Theodore Albert Delius. In 1884, he moved to Florida, where he was influenced by black folk music. After living in Virginia in 1885, he returned to Europe in 1886, and entered the Leipzig Conservatory. In his mature style, he combined this influence with elements from such European composers as Claude Debussy, Edvard Grieg, and Richard Wagner.

Vincent McDermott

Della Chiesa, Giacomo. See Benedict XV.
Della Francesca, Piero. See Piero della Francesca.
Della Robbia, Andrea. See Della Robbia, Luca.
Della Robbia, *DEHL uh ROH bee uh,* **Luca** (1399?-1482), was an Italian sculptor of the early Renaissance. Della Robbia created works in bronze and marble, but he is best known for his sculpture in terra cotta, which is a type of hard, durable earthenware. Della Robbia covered his terra cottas with glazes of bright colors, usually

white against a blue background. These glazed terra cottas were less expensive to make than marble and they were also more durable than paint.

The first work known to be by della Robbia—and one of his most famous—is the *Cantoria,* or *Singing Gallery* (1431-1438). The *Cantoria* consists of 10 panels that portray children in relief sculpture singing and playing musical instruments. The panels are framed by delicately carved neoclassical architecture. The work illustrates the Biblical text of Psalm 150. The *Cantoria* was originally located over a doorway in the Cathedral of Florence and is now in the Cathedral museum. A detail of the *Cantoria* appears in **Classical music** (Highlights in the history of classical music). Della Robbia was born in Florence.

Luca della Robbia's nephew Andrea della Robbia was a pupil of his uncle and inherited the family workshop in Florence. Andrea continued to make glazed terra cottas, though he lacked Luca's originality and power. An example of Andrea della Robbia's work appears in **Terra cotta.** Five of Andrea della Robbia's sons were trained in the della Robbia workshop and became recognized sculptors. David Summers

Dello Joio, *DEHL oh JOY oh,* **Norman** (1913-), is an American composer. He won the 1957 Pulitzer Prize in music for his *Meditations on Ecclesiastes* (1957) for orchestra. Dello Joio's style reflects the influence of American jazz, Italian opera, and a movement of the early 1900's called *neoclassicism.* His music features highly developed rhythms and lyrical melodies.

Dello Joio has composed for orchestra, band, chamber groups, chorus, piano, and solo voice. He has written operas, ballets, and music for television. Two of Dello Joio's most impressive compositions are *The Mystic Trumpeter* (1943) and *A Jubilant Song* (1946). He adapted these choral works from the poetry of the American poet Walt Whitman. A number of Dello Joio's pieces are variations on a single theme. Examples of such variations include *Variations, Chaconne, and Finale* (1948) for orchestra.

Dello Joio was born in New York City. He has worked as an organist and choirmaster in several Roman Catholic churches. From 1972 to 1979, he was Dean of Fine Arts at Boston University. Leonard W. Van Camp
Dells. See Dalles.
Deloria, Vine, Jr. (1933-), is a leader in the fight for Indian rights in the United States. He is a principal spokesman in the struggle of Indians to gain greater control over their own affairs. Deloria, a Sioux Indian, supports a return to tribal religions and certain other Indian attitudes toward life. He has written several books about current Indian life. His best-known work, *Custer Died for Your Sins* (1969), deals with the treatment of Indians by whites and the goals of Indian leaders.

From 1964 to 1967, Deloria directed the National Congress of American Indians. This private organization serves the economic and legislative interests of

Glazed terra cotta statue (about 1450); Museo Nazionale, Florence (SCALA/Art Resource)
Luca della Robbia created *Madonna and Child Jesus.*

George Janoff
Vine Deloria, Jr.

Indians. In 1971, he co-founded a law firm called the Institute for the Development of Indian Law. The institute
defends treaty rights of various tribes.

Vine Victor Deloria, Jr., was born in Martin, S. Dak.,
and graduated from Iowa State University in 1958. He
earned a master's degree at the Lutheran School of Theology in 1963 and a law degree at the University of Colorado in 1970. His other books include *We Talk, You Listen* (1970), *God Is Red* (1973), and *Behind the Trail of
Broken Treaties* (1974).   Beatrice Medicine

De los Angeles, Victoria (1923-   ), a Spanish lyric
soprano, won international acclaim as an opera singer, a
recitalist, and an orchestral soloist. She became famous
for her performances in such operatic roles as Mimi in
La Bohème and Manon in *Manon.* Critics consider de
los Angeles one of the finest performers of French
songs and a distinguished interpreter of Spanish folk
songs. Her voice is light and flexible and has a slightly
melancholy tone.

De los Angeles' real name is Victoria de los Angeles
Lopez Garcia. De los Angeles was born in Barcelona and
studied at the Barcelona Conservatory. De los Angeles
made her operatic debut in Barcelona in 1945, and her
Metropolitan Opera debut in 1951 as Marguerite in
Faust.   Ellen Pfeifer

Delphi, *DEHL fy,* was a town situated on the southern
slope of Mount Parnassus. The town had the oldest and
most influential religious sanctuary in ancient Greece. It
was in the district of Phocis.

The ancient Greeks believed that the site of Delphi
was sacred to the god Apollo. It gained importance as
early as the 1100's B.C. Later, the site of Delphi became
an international Greek shrine. The sanctuary of Delphi
contained the main temple of Apollo, a stadium, and a
theater. It also included many small buildings and monuments. The ancient Greeks held the Pythian Games in
Delphi.

The temple contained the famous *oracle,* or prophet
(see **Oracle**). A woman oracle, called Pythia, would utter
weird sounds while in a frenzy. People believed these
were the words of Apollo. Temple priests interpreted
these to the public.

Cities, as well as private individuals, sought the oracle's advice. As a result, the oracle greatly influenced
Greek religion, economics, and politics. This influence
gradually waned in later Greek and Roman times. The
Christian Roman emperor Theodosius closed the sanctuary in A.D. 390.

French scholars began excavations in 1880. The present-day village of Delphi, formerly called Kastri, is near
the site of ancient Delphi.   Ronald P. Legon

See also **Apollo.**

Delphinium. See Larkspur; Flower (picture: Garden
perennials).

Delta is a low plain composed of clay, gravel, sand,
and other sediments deposited at the mouth of a river.
Deltas are named for the Greek letter *delta* (Δ) because
many have a roughly triangular shape. They form when
rivers flow into large bodies of standing water, where
their speed and ability to carry sediments are suddenly
reduced.

The chief factors that affect the formation of deltas include climate, geological features, river size and flooding patterns, and the strength of ocean waves. Dams and

Eric Carle, Shostal

The delta of the Mississippi River, *above,* grows into the Gulf
of Mexico at the rate of about 1 mile (1.6 kilometers) every 16
years. The Mississippi's slow current continuously deposits fertile soil in the delta.

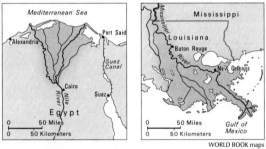

WORLD BOOK maps

The Nile Delta   **The Mississippi Delta**

other structures also influence the development of deltas. For example, construction of the Aswan High Dam in
Egypt during the 1960's decreased the amount of sediments that the Nile River carries to its delta. As a result,
waves may wear away parts of the Nile Delta through
the years.

Deltas have fertile soil that makes them excellent agri-
cultural areas. The rich land of the Mississippi Delta in
Louisiana produces fruits, vegetables, and other crops.
The Nile Delta has been farmed since ancient times.
Some deltas, such as the Irrawaddy Delta in Burma and
the Mekong Delta in Vietnam, support vast rice fields.

J. M. Coleman

See also **Erosion** (How erosion occurs); **Louisiana**
(picture: Mississippi Delta).

Deluge, *DEHL yooj,* according to the Bible, was a great
flood that covered the earth thousands of years ago. The
Deluge destroyed all living things except those that God
permitted to go aboard a huge ark that was built by
Noah.

The Deluge is described in two accounts combined in
Genesis 6 to 8. In one version, God instructs Noah to

save one male and one female of every animal. In the other, God tells Noah to take seven pairs of animals considered "clean" according to ancient dietary laws and one pair of "unclean" animals. Both accounts agree that God sent the flood to punish the wickedness of humanity.

Stories about great floods occur in the religious tradition of many peoples. A famous account is found in the Epic of Gilgamesh from Mesopotamia. Many scholars believe the Mesopotamian and Biblical accounts are related.   H. Darrell Lance

See also **Ararat; Ark; Deucalion; Noah.**

Delusion, dih LOO zhuhn, is a false belief. Persons with mental illness often have delusions. A common delusion is that of *grandeur,* in which people have an exaggerated idea of their importance. Other delusions include those of *persecution,* in which people believe they are being mistreated, and of *reference,* in which they falsely believe they are being talked about.

Paula J. Clayton

Demand. See Supply and demand.

Demarcation, Line of. See Line of Demarcation.

De Maupassant, du moh pah SAHN, **Guy,** GEE (1850-1893), a French author, is considered one of the world's great short-story writers. De Maupassant wrote clearly and simply. His tales are realistic, and reflect his often brutally sarcastic and pessimistic attitude toward people. De Maupassant wrote with sympathy only about the poor and outcasts of society.

De Maupassant's stories deal with many subjects— the middle class, peasants, government officials, the Franco-Prussian War, outdoor life, animals, and ghosts. He wrote about 250 stories, most of them between 1880 and 1890. He published them in several collections. The best known include *The Tellier House* (1881), *Yvette* (1885), *Toine* (1886), and *The Horla* (1887). His most famous stories include "Ball-of-Fat," "The Diamond Necklace," "The Umbrella," and "The Piece of String."

De Maupassant's novels have the same qualities his short stories have. *A Woman's Life* (1883) is a portrait of an unhappy country wife. *Bel-Ami* (1885) describes the rise of an unprincipled journalist. *Peter and John* (1888) is a psychological study of two brothers.

De Maupassant was born in Normandy, in northern France. He learned much of his literary technique and philosophy of life from his godfather, the famous French novelist Gustave Flaubert. De Maupassant died in an insane asylum.   Thomas H. Goetz

Demeter, dih MEE tuhr, in Greek mythology, was the goddess of the earth, agriculture, fertility, and grain. The ancient Romans had a similar goddess whom they called Ceres.

The most famous myth about Demeter tells of her search for her daughter Persephone, whom the Romans called Proserpina. The girl had been kidnaped by Hades, the god of the dead, and taken to his kingdom in the underworld. For details of this myth, see the *World Book* article on **Persephone.**

The Greeks believed that people learned farming through Demeter. She gave Triptolemus, a Greek hero, a bag of seeds and sent him throughout the world in a magic chariot to teach people how to farm.

The most important center of Demeter's worship was in Eleusis, near Athens. There, the Greeks held secret rit-

uals called the Eleusinian Mysteries in her honor. The ceremonies were based on Demeter's search for her daughter. The Greeks also based these ceremonies on a belief in the immortality of the soul, and reward or punishment in a life after death.   Robert J. Lenardon

See also **Mysteries; Ceres.**

De Mille, Agnes (1909-   ), is an American *choreographer* (dance composer), dancer, and author. She began her career as a dancer in 1929, and gave concerts in the United States and Europe until 1940. She then began creating ballets based on American themes. The first was *Rodeo* (1942). In 1943, she created and staged the dances for the musical play *Oklahoma!* This landmark musical was one of the first to successfully blend dancing, story, and music into a unified work. Many of her ballets are regularly performed by the American Ballet Theatre, including *Fall River Legend* (1948).

De Mille was born in New York City. She is the author of the autobiographies *Dance to the Piper* (1952), *And Promenade Home* (1958), and *Where the Wings Grow* (1978).   Selma Landen Odom

Fred Fehl

Agnes De Mille danced in the 1942 première of her ballet *Rodeo* with Casimir Kokitch, *left,* and Frederic Franklin, *right.*

De Mille, Cecil Blount (1881-1959), a motion-picture producer and director, became famous for his spectacular films based on the Bible. His first Biblical film was *The Ten Commandments* (1923). His final film as a director was a remake of this picture in 1956. A shrewd showman, De Mille balanced religion with romance in such films as *The Sign of the Cross* (1932) and *Samson and Delilah* (1949). His striking drama of Christ, *The King of Kings* (1927), was one of the few De Mille Biblical films to win praise from both critics and the clergy. He also made romantic adventures, including *The Plainsman* (1937), *Union Pacific* (1939), and *Unconquered* (1947). His circus spectacle, *The Greatest Show on Earth,* won the 1952 Academy Award for best picture.

De Mille was born in Ashfield, Mass., and went to Hollywood in 1913. His early silent films, including *Male and Female* (1919) and *Forbidden Fruit* (1921), generally dealt with romantic entanglements in high society.

Howard Thompson

Demobilization. See Army, United States (World War II).

Democracy is a form of government, a way of life, a goal or ideal, and a political philosophy. The term also refers to a country that has a democratic form of government. The word *democracy* means *rule by the people.* United States President Abraham Lincoln described such self-government as "government of the people, by the people, for the people."

The citizens of a democracy take part in government either directly or indirectly. In a *direct democracy,* also called a *pure democracy,* the people meet in one place to make the laws for their community. Such democracy was practiced in the ancient Greek city-state of Athens, and exists today in the New England town meeting (see **Town meeting**).

Most modern democracy is *representative democracy.* In large communities—cities, states, provinces, or countries—it is impossible for all the people to meet as a group. Instead, they elect a certain number of their fellow citizens to represent them in making decisions about laws and other matters. An assembly of representatives may be called a council, a legislature, a parliament, or a congress. Government by the people through their freely elected representatives is sometimes called a *republican government* or a *democratic republic.*

Most voting decisions in democracies are based on *majority rule*—that is, more than half the votes cast. A decision by *plurality* may be used when three or more candidates stand for election. A candidate with a plurality receives more votes than any other candidate, but does not necessarily have a majority of the votes. In some countries, elections to legislative bodies are conducted according to *proportional representation.* Such representation awards a political party a percentage of seats in the legislature in proportion to its share of the total vote cast.

Throughout history, the most important aspects of the democratic way of life have been the principles of individual equality and freedom. Accordingly, citizens in a democracy should be entitled to equal protection of

Famous Quotations About Democracy

The views below explain the meaning of democracy as a form of government, a way of life, and a goal or ideal. Views on the benefits of rule by law have been expressed since democracy began to develop in ancient Greece as early as the 600's B.C.

The basis of a democratic state is liberty.

Aristotle

As I would not be a *slave,* so I would not be a *master.* This expresses my idea of democracy. Whatever differs from this, to the extent of the difference, is no democracy.

Abraham Lincoln

The measure of a democracy is the measure of the freedom of its humblest citizens.

John Galsworthy

I believe in democracy because it releases the energies of every human being.

Woodrow Wilson

Never in the history of the world has a nation lost its democracy by a successful struggle to defend its democracy.

Franklin D. Roosevelt

Government of the people, by the people, for the people, still remains the sovereign definition of democracy.

Sir Winston Churchill

My political ideal is democracy. Everyone should be respected as an individual, but no one idolized.

Albert Einstein

Democracy is the recurrent suspicion that more than half of the people are right more than half of the time.

E. B. White

Democracy...is the only form of government that is founded on the dignity of man, not the dignity of some men, of rich men, of educated men or of white men, but of all men.

Robert Maynard Hutchins

Each person quoted above has a biography in WORLD BOOK.

©David R. Frazier

Free elections are held regularly in a democracy. The people use a secret ballot to elect officials to represent them and to run the government on all levels.

their persons, possessions, and rights; have equal opportunity to pursue their lives and careers; and have equal rights of political participation. In addition, the people should enjoy freedom from undue interference and domination by government. They should be free, within the framework of the law, to believe, behave, and express themselves as they wish. Democratic societies seek to guarantee their citizens certain freedoms, including freedom of religion, freedom of the press, and freedom of speech. Ideally, citizens also should be guaranteed freedom of association and of assembly, freedom from arbitrary arrest and imprisonment, and the freedom to work and live where and how they choose.

Some people in democratic states have been eager to increase the role of government in society in order to make material conditions more equal for everyone. But other people have been concerned that the extension of government's role in such areas as welfare, education, employment, and housing may decrease the freedom of the people and subject them to too much government regulation. The supporters of more government involvement are known as *liberals*. The critics of more government involvement are known as *conservatives*. The division between these groups has helped furnish one of the main themes of controversy and discussion in modern democratic societies.

Applying democratic principles in everyday life can be challenging. In the United States, for example, freedom of speech, press, religion, and assembly are protected by the First Amendment to the Constitution. In guarding these freedoms, the U.S. judiciary has tried to balance the interests of individuals against possible injury and damage to other people and the community. Thus, the right of free speech does not allow people to falsely damage reputations of others. It also does not allow one to shout "Fire!" in a crowd when there is no fire.

This article presents a broad survey of democracy—what it is, how it works, and how it has developed. For more information on democracy and other forms of government, see the article on **Government.**

Features of democracy

The characteristics of democracy vary from one country to another. But certain basic features are more or less the same in all democratic nations.

Free elections give the people a chance to choose their leaders and express their opinions on issues. Elections are held periodically to ensure that elected officials truly represent the people. The possibility of being voted out of office helps assure that these officials pay attention to public opinion.

In most democracies, the only legal requirements for voting or for holding public office have to do with age, residence, and citizenship. The democratic process permits citizens to vote by secret ballot, free from force or bribes. It also requires that election results be protected against dishonesty. See **Election.**

Majority rule and minority rights. In a democracy, a decision often must be approved by a majority of voters before it may take effect. This principle, called majority rule, may be used to elect officials or decide a policy. Democracies sometimes decide votes by plurality. Most democracies go beyond a simple majority to make fundamental or constitutional changes. In the United States, constitutional amendments must be ratified by the legislatures of three-fourths of the states or by special conventions called in three-fourths of the states.

Majority rule is based on the idea that if all citizens are equal, the judgment of the many will be better than the judgment of the few. Democracy values freely given consent as the basis of legitimate and effective political power. But democracies are also concerned with protecting individual liberty and preventing government from infringing on the freedoms of individuals. Democratic countries guarantee that certain rights can never be taken from the people, even by extremely large majorities. These rights include the basic freedoms of speech, press, assembly, and religious worship. The majority also must recognize the right of the minority to try to become the majority by legal means.

Political parties are a necessary part of democratic government. Rival parties make elections meaningful by giving voters a choice among candidates who represent different interests and points of view.

The United States and Great Britain have chiefly two-party systems. Many democratic countries have multiparty systems, which have more than two major parties. Often in these countries, no single party gains a majority in the legislature. As a result, two or more parties must join to make up such a majority. These parties form a *coalition government.* In democratic countries, the party or parties that are out of power serve as the "loyal opposition." That is, they criticize the policies and actions of the party in power. In various dictatorships, criticism of the party in power may be labeled as treason. Often, only the "government party" is allowed to exist. The people have no real choice among candidates, and no opportunity to express dissatisfaction with the government. See **Political party.**

Controls on power. Democracies have various arrangements to prevent any person or branch of government from becoming too powerful. For example, the U.S. Constitution divides political power between the states and the federal government. Some powers belong only to the states, some only to the federal government, and some are shared by both.

The Constitution further divides the powers of the U.S. government among the President, Congress, and the federal courts. The power of each branch is designed to check or balance the power of the others. See **Checks and balances.**

In all democratic countries, government officials are subject to the law and are accountable to the people. Officials may be removed from office for lawless conduct or for other serious reasons. The communications media help keep elected officials sensitive to public opinion. See **Government** (The organization of government).

Constitutional government. Democratic government is based on law and, in most cases, a written constitution. Constitutions state the powers and duties of government and limit what the government may do. They also say how laws shall be made and enforced. Most constitutions have a detailed bill of rights that describes the basic liberties of the people and forbids the government to violate those rights. See **Bill of Rights.**

Constitutions that have been in effect for a long time may include certain unwritten procedures that have become important parts of the operation of government. Such procedures are a matter of custom rather than written law. Britain has no single written document called "the constitution." In that country, however, certain customs and convention, as well as certain major documents and many laws, are widely accepted as the "basic rules of the system." See **Constitution.**

An essential characteristic of democratic government is an independent judiciary. It is the duty of the justice system to protect the integrity of the "rules" and the rights of individuals under these rules, especially against the government itself.

Occasionally, dictatorships establish very elaborate constitutions and extensive lists of basic rights of citizens. For example, the 1977 constitution of the Soviet Union contains more detailed rights supposedly guaranteed to citizens than does the U.S. Bill of Rights. In practice, however, Soviet courts were not known to defend individuals' rights against the government. But in the late 1980's, legal reform in the Soviet Union focused on strengthening the rights of the individual.

Private organizations. In a democracy, individuals and private organizations carry on many social and economic activities that are, for the most part, free of government control. For example, newspapers and magazines are privately owned and managed. Labor unions are run by and for the benefit of workers, not the state. Democratic governments generally do not interfere with religious worship. Private schools operate along with public schools. The people may form groups to influence opinion on public issues and policies. Most businesses in democratic societies are privately owned and managed. Britain, Sweden, and other democracies have government ownership and control of certain basic industries and services.

In dictatorial societies, the government alone may organize and control most associations. The people are not permitted to establish or join most groups without the permission of the state. In some countries, the government almost completely owns and manages the economy.

Why democracy?

The Declaration of Independence adopted by the American patriots in 1776 expressed the belief that "all men are created equal, that they are endowed by their Creator with certain unalienable rights, that among these are Life, Liberty, and the pursuit of Happiness." The Declaration said that the people may change or abolish the government if it interferes with those rights.

People once thought that the greatest obstacles to individual freedom and equality were political. They believed they could preserve freedom simply by changing the form of government from a monarchy to a republic. They claimed that the government that governs least governs best. But in time, many people became convinced that some government regulation of society and the economy was necessary to make personal freedom more meaningful and to promote equality, as well as to improve the welfare of the nation.

In today's democracies, there are extensive programs to provide economic security, to ease suffering, and to develop human potential. Such programs include unemployment insurance, minimum wage laws, old-age pensions, health insurance, civil rights laws, and aid to education. Many democracies aim to provide a minimum standard of living and adequate medical care for all.

Making democracy work

Citizen participation. Democracy calls for widespread participation in politics by the people. It is believed to be the duty of all adult citizens to vote in local, state or provincial, and national elections. Qualified individuals should be willing to run for public office, to serve on juries, and to contribute to the welfare of their country. Citizens should help shape public opinion by speaking out on important issues and by supporting the political party of their choice. An active citizenry is thought to be one of the best guarantees against corrupt and inefficient government.

Education and democracy. Faith in the power of education is a characteristic of democracy. According to democratic ideals, widespread participation in politics does not necessarily ensure good government. The quality of government depends on the quality of partici-

pation. Well-informed and well-educated citizens are able to participate more intelligently.

A democracy needs educated citizens who can think for themselves. Citizens have a duty to take part in public affairs, to keep informed on public issues, and to vote intelligently. Democratic institutions must produce leaders worthy of public trust and responsibility. For this reason, democratic governments support education for their citizens.

Voluntary action. An important quality of democratic government is its emphasis on trying to get people to act on the basis of understanding and agreement instead of force. Although all governments use force sometimes, democracies usually emphasize dialogue, negotiation, bargaining, and ultimately, voluntary citizen cooperation. This approach is closely linked to the widely held democratic belief that people are generally rational and well disposed toward the common welfare.

Economic development and agreement on fundamentals. Most successful democracies have existed in developed societies. In such societies, literacy rates are high, *per capita* (per person) incomes are moderate to high, and there are few extremes of wealth and poverty. Some scholars believe democracy works best in countries with a large middle class.

Many democratic governments have collapsed during economic crises. The basic problem involved in the failures of such democracies has been the inability to maintain sufficient agreement among either the people or their political leaders on the purposes of government. Crises have often aggravated and sharpened divisions and suspicions among various classes, groups, parties, and leaders. Excessive divisions have helped block action by freely elected governments, often resulting in widespread public frustration and disorder.

Democratic governments are likely to be unstable whenever people become deeply divided and suspicious of one another. Sometimes racial, ethnic, or religious differences make democracies difficult to operate. In such instances, the people may not see one another as legitimate and trustworthy partners in the enterprise of government.

The development of democracy

Origins of democracy. Democracy began to develop in ancient Greece as early as the 500's B.C. The word *democracy* comes from the Greek words *demos,* meaning *people,* and *kratos,* which means *rule* or *authority.* Greek political thinkers stressed the idea of rule by law. They criticized dictatorship as the worst form of government. Athens and some other Greek city-states had democratic governments.

Democracy in ancient Athens differed in important ways from democracy today. Athenian democracy was a direct democracy rather than a representative one. Each male citizen had the duty to serve permanently in the assembly, which passed the laws and decided all important government policies. There was no division between legislative and executive branches of the government. Slaves made up a large part of the Athenian population, and did most of the work. Neither the slaves nor women could vote.

The ancient Romans experimented with democracy, but they never practiced it so fully as did the Athenians.

Roman political thinkers taught that political power comes from the consent of the people. The Roman statesman Cicero contributed the idea of a universal law of reason that is binding on all people and governments everywhere. He suggested that people have natural rights which every state must respect.

The Middle Ages. Christianity taught that everyone is equal before God. This teaching promoted the democratic ideal of brotherhood among people. Christianity also introduced the idea that Christians are citizens of two kingdoms—the Kingdom of God and the kingdom of the world. It held that no state can demand absolute loyalty from its citizens because they must also obey God and His commandments. During the Middle Ages (A.D. 400's to the 1500's), the conflict between these two loyalties helped lay the foundation for constitutional government.

The Middle Ages produced a social system known as *feudalism.* Under feudalism, persons pledged their loyalty and services to one another. Individuals had certain rights which other persons were required to recognize. A feudal court system was established to protect these rights. Such courts later led to kings' councils, representative assemblies, and modern parliaments. See **Feudalism.**

The Renaissance and the Reformation. The great cultural reawakening called the Renaissance spread throughout Europe during the 1300's, 1400's, and 1500's. A new spirit of individual thought and independence developed. It influenced political thinking and hastened the growth of democracy. People began to demand greater freedom in all areas of life.

The new independence of the individual found religious expression in the Protestant Reformation. The Reformation emphasized the importance of individual conscience. During the early 1500's, Martin Luther, a leader of the Reformation, opposed the Roman Catholic Church as an intermediary between God and people. A number of Protestant churches were established during the period. Some of these churches practiced the congregational form of government, which had a democratic structure. During the 1500's, both Catholics and Protestants defended the right to oppose absolute monarchy. They argued that the political power of earthly rulers comes from the consent of the people.

Democracy in England. In 1215, English nobles forced King John to approve the Magna Carta. This historic document became a symbol of human liberty. It was used to support later demands for trial by jury, protection against unlawful arrest, and no taxation without representation.

English democracy developed slowly during the next several hundred years. In 1628, Parliament passed the Petition of Right. The petition called on King Charles I to stop collecting taxes without the consent of Parliament. It also provided that Parliament should meet at regular intervals. Charles refused to agree to limits on the royal power, and civil war broke out in 1642. The Puritans, led by Oliver Cromwell, fought the followers of the king. Charles was beheaded in 1649, and the Puritans established a short-lived *commonwealth* (republic). See **England** (The Civil War).

The English revolution of 1688 finally established the supremacy of Parliament. John Locke, the philosopher of the revolution, declared that final authority in political matters belonged to the people. The government's main purpose, he said, was to protect the lives, liberties, and property of the people. Parliament passed the Bill of Rights in 1689, assuring the people basic civil rights.

Modern democracy was still far off. The larger factory towns were not represented in Parliament until after the adoption of the Reform Bill of 1832. Property qualifications for voting disappeared only gradually. In 1918, for the first time, all men were permitted to vote. Not until 1928 could all women vote.

French contributions to democracy were made in the 1700's by such political thinkers as Montesquieu, Voltaire, and Jean Jacques Rousseau. Their writings helped bring about the French Revolution, which began in 1789. Montesquieu argued that political freedom requires the separation of the executive, legislative, and judicial powers of government. Voltaire spoke out against government invasion of individual rights and freedoms. Rousseau declared in his book *The Social Contract* (1762) that people "have a duty to obey only legitimate powers." The only rightful rulers, he added, were, ultimately, the people.

The French Revolution, an important event in the history of democracy, promoted the ideas of liberty and equality. It did not make France a democracy, but it did limit the king's powers. See **French Revolution.**

American democracy took root in traditions brought to North America by the first English colonists. The Pilgrims, who settled in Massachusetts in 1620, joined in signing the Mayflower Compact to obey "just and equal laws." The American Revolution began more than 150 years later, in 1775. The colonists wanted self-government and no taxation without representation. The Declaration of Independence, adopted by the Continental Congress in 1776, is a classic document of democracy. It established human rights as an ideal by which government must be guided.

Most of the Founding Fathers distrusted the Athenian version of direct democracy. They wanted to establish a republic because they feared that giving the people too much power would lead to mob rule. For this reason, the men who wrote the Constitution of the United States adopted a system of dividing power between the federal government and the states. They also provided that the federal powers be divided among the legislative, executive, and judicial branches. In addition, they provided that the President be elected by an electoral college rather than by the direct vote of the people (see **Electoral college**).

Thomas Jefferson favored a government that would pay more attention to the common citizen. After he became President in 1801, he spoke of his election as a "revolution." In 1828, the election of Andrew Jackson to the presidency further advanced American democracy. The pioneer spirit of the settlers in the West encouraged self-reliance, promoted individual liberty, and gave meaning to the promise of equal opportunity.

The long-term trend in the United States has been to give almost all adult citizens the right to vote. By 1850, white males could vote in all the states. The 15th Amendment to the Constitution, adopted in 1870, gave black men the right to vote. In 1920, the 19th Amendment gave women the vote. In 1964, the 24th Amendment prohibited poll taxes as voting requirements in national elections (see **Poll tax**).

The spread of democracy. During the 1800's, democracy developed steadily. Many countries followed the American and British examples. Such democratic institutions as elections and legislatures became common. Where kings still ruled, they lost much of their power and performed mainly ceremonial duties.

The Industrial Revolution brought political changes of great importance. During the second half of the 1800's, the working classes demanded and received greater political rights. New laws gave more citizens the right to vote. The freedoms of speech, the press, assembly, and religion were extended and enlarged.

Democracy did not take root everywhere. Some countries that adopted constitutions modeled after that of the United States later became dictatorships. These nations found that a constitution alone did not guarantee democracy. In Russia, a group of revolutionists set up a Communist dictatorship in 1917 and halted Russia's progress toward democracy. Germany adopted a democratic government in 1919, but Adolf Hitler's rise to power brought a fascist dictatorship in 1933.

Democracy today. Most governments today claim to be democratic, but many lack some essential freedoms usually associated with democracy. In some countries, for example, the people are not allowed certain basic freedoms, such as those of speech and of the press, or competitive elections.

Many modern nations have a long history of democratic government. These countries include Australia, Belgium, Canada, Denmark, Great Britain, the Netherlands, New Zealand, Norway, Sweden, Switzerland, and the United States. Other nations—including India, Israel, Italy, and Japan—have been democracies since the mid-1900's. The structure of French government has changed many times since the French Revolution. The present government is a democracy. Several newly independent nations in Africa and Asia are trying to develop democratic institutions. But inexperience with self-rule and other problems make democratic government difficult to achieve.　Alexander J. Groth

Related articles in *World Book* include:

Great documents of democracy

Bill of rights	Human Rights, Universal Declaration of
Constitution of the United States	Magna Carta
Declaration of Independence	Petition of Right
Emancipation Proclamation	Rights of Man, Declaration of the
Gettysburg Address	

Tools of democracy

Ballot	Freedom	Political party
Citizenship	Habeas corpus	Recall
Civil rights	Initiative and referendum	Trial
Constitution		Voting
Due process of law	Jury	Voting machine
Election	Majority rule	Woman suffrage
Fifteenth Amendment	Plebiscite	

Other related articles

Aristocracy	Federalism
Communism	Liberalism
Conservatism	Monarchy
Fascism	Power

Propaganda	Socialism
Public opinion	Town meeting
Republic	

Reading and Study Guide

See *Democracy* in the Research Guide/Index, Volume 22, for a *Reading and Study Guide*.

Additional resources

Level I
Archer, Jules. *Police State: Could It Happen Here?* Harper, 1977.
Lawson, Don. *Democracy.* Watts, 1978.

Level II
Barber, Benjamin R. *Strong Democracy: Participatory Politics for a New Age.* Univ. of California Press, 1984.
Democratic Theory and Practice. Ed. by Graeme Duncan. Cambridge, 1983.
Held, David. *Models of Democracy.* Stanford, 1987.
Pennock, James R. *Democratic Political Theory.* Princeton, 1979.
Tocqueville, Alexis de. *Democracy in America.* First published 1835-1840; available in many editions.

Democratic-Farmer-Labor Party. See Farmer-Labor Party.

Democratic Party is one of the two major political parties of the United States. The Republican Party is the other.

The Democratic Party, the nation's oldest existing party, has played a vital role in the history and politics of the United States. From 1828 through 1988, Democrats won 18 of the 41 presidential elections. They dominated U.S. politics from 1828 through 1856, winning 6 of the 8 presidential elections. From 1860 through 1928, they won only 4 of the 18 presidential elections. But the Democratic candidate won 8 of the 15 presidential elections held from 1932 through 1988. Traditionally, the Democratic Party has drawn support from several groups, including many immigrants, Southerners, wage earners, and—since the 1930's—blacks.

The policies of the Democratic Party, like those of other parties, have changed with the flow of history. Until Woodrow Wilson became President in 1913, the Democrats generally approved a strict interpretation of the U.S. Constitution and favored a limitation on government powers. As President, Wilson expanded the role of government and mobilized the nation to help defeat Germany in World War I (1914-1918). Franklin D. Roosevelt boldly took government action to pull the nation through the Great Depression of the 1930's. During World War II (1939-1945), Roosevelt again expanded government powers to fight Germany and Japan.

Some Democrats thought Roosevelt extended the government's powers too far. Others believed these powers had not been extended far enough. Ever since Roosevelt's presidency, Democrats have disagreed on how extensive the role of government should be.

This article chiefly describes the history of the Democratic Party. For information about the party's national convention and organization, see the articles on **Political convention** and **Political party**.

Origin of the Democratic Party is uncertain. Some historians trace its beginnings to the Democratic-Republican Party that Thomas Jefferson created during the 1790's (see **Democratic-Republican Party**). Most historians, however, regard Andrew Jackson's presidential campaign organization, formed in 1828, as the beginning of the Democratic Party as it is known today.

Jefferson served as President from 1801 to 1809, and other Democratic-Republicans held the presidency from 1809 to 1825. After 1816, the Democratic-Republican Party split into several groups and fell apart as a national organization. Jackson became the favorite of one of these groups and gained great popularity. He lost a bid for the presidency in 1824. But he easily won election in 1828 and swept to reelection in 1832. By about 1830, Jackson and his followers were called Democrats.

By the late 1830's, top Jacksonian Democrats had turned Jackson's loose organization into an effective national political party—the Democratic Party. One of these men, Martin Van Buren, became President in 1837. Other leading Jacksonians included newspaper editor Francis P. Blair, Sr.; presidential adviser Amos Kendall; and state politicians Thomas Hart Benton of Missouri and James Buchanan of Pennsylvania.

Jacksonian policies appealed to a wide variety of voters. Small farmers, large plantation owners, city laborers, and state bankers joined in their support of the Democratic Party. They had in common a strong belief in states' rights and a firm faith in limited government (see **States' rights**). But Democrats also disagreed frequently. For example, they argued over banking policies, slavery, and tariff rates.

In spite of their differences, Democrats won the presidential election of 1844 with James K. Polk. In 1852, they won with Franklin Pierce and in 1856 with James Buchanan. They also controlled Congress during most of the 1840's and 1850's.

The slavery issue, more than any other, divided the Democrats. During Polk's Administration, from 1845 to 1849, vast new territories in the West became part of the United States. Southerners wanted to extend slavery into the new lands, but many Northerners urged Congress to prohibit it. Southerners replied that Congress had no authority to stop citizens of any state from taking slaves anywhere in the United States.

Fierce debates led to division within the party and to sectional hostility between North and South. Congressional leaders, such as Stephen A. Douglas of Illinois, worked for legislation that would satisfy both Northerners and Southerners. They favored the Compromise of 1850, which, for a time, quieted both party and sectional differences (see **Compromise of 1850**).

Hostility flared again after Congress passed the Kansas-Nebraska Act in 1854. In this act, Douglas had provided for "popular sovereignty," which let settlers decide for themselves whether a new state would permit slavery. The act pleased few people. It led to renewed hostility between North and South and caused the Democratic Party to split apart.

In 1860, Northern Democrats nominated Douglas for President. Southern Democrats chose John C. Breckinridge. Both Democratic candidates lost to Abraham Lincoln, the candidate of the new Republican Party. In 1860 and 1861, 11 Southern states took the idea of states' rights as far as it could go when they seceded from the Union. In April 1861, shortly after the seventh state had withdrawn, the Civil War began.

During the Civil War, the Northern Democrats divided. The "War Democrats" supported Lincoln and the war. The "Peace Democrats," especially those known as "Copperheads," opposed Lincoln and the war. In the

"A LIVE JACKASS KICKING A DEAD LION"
And such a Lion! and such a Jackass!
From *Thomas Nast* by Albert Bigelow Paine, permission of Harper & Bros.

The donkey was used as a political symbol by Andrew Jackson after his opponents called him a "jackass" during the 1828 election campaign. By the 1880's, such cartoons as the one above by Thomas Nast had caught the public eye and established the donkey as the symbol of the Democratic Party.

election of 1864, many War Democrats supported Lincoln. They joined the Republican Party to form the National Union Party. Andrew Johnson, a War Democrat, became Lincoln's vice presidential running mate. The Peace Democrats nominated General George B. McClellan. Lincoln won the election. Following Lincoln's assassination in April 1865—just five days after the war ended—Vice President Johnson became President.

After the Civil War. Republicans condemned the Democrats as disloyal to the Union during the Civil War. Unable to win the presidency or to gain control of Congress, the Democratic Party reached its lowest point.

Under Johnson's leadership, the Democrats attacked the Reconstruction plans of the Radical Republicans for the defeated South (see **Reconstruction**). Among other actions, the Republicans (1) denied the vote to Southerners who had fought against the Union and (2) gave the vote to Southern blacks. Enraged white Southerners deprived blacks of the vote after regaining power later. These white Southerners believed that the Republicans were opposed to most Southern beliefs. Thus, the Democratic "Solid South" was born. During the 1870's, meanwhile, Democrats demanded reforms that would end dishonest practices in business and in government.

A business depression swept the nation during the 1870's and helped change the party's fortunes. Many voters blamed the Republicans for the depression and voted Democratic in the congressional elections of 1874. As a result, the Democrats gained control of the House of Representatives. This victory brought hope to the Democrats. They worked hard to win the presidency in 1876 and made reform the central issue of their campaign. The Democratic candidate, Samuel J. Tilden, received more popular votes than did his Republican opponent, Rutherford B. Hayes. But Hayes won the election by a margin of one electoral vote.

During the 1880's and 1890's, the Democratic and Republican parties received almost equal popular support. There seemed to be little difference between the two, except that Democrats wanted lower tariffs and demanded reforms in the civil service. In 1884, Grover Cleveland became the first Democrat to be elected President since 1856. Cleveland narrowly lost the presidency to Benjamin Harrison in a close race in 1888, but regained it in another close race in 1892.

Tremendous changes had reshaped the nation's economy since the Civil War. Railroads had expanded to carry manufactured goods to farmers and farm products to city workers. Vast business and industrial empires had appeared.

Politicians knew little about business growth, depressions, or economic theories. The Democrats and the Republicans both favored a policy of *laissez faire* (nonregulation), and the government left business largely in the hands of businessmen. Neither party seemed aware of

the hardships that industrialization brought to many farmers and city workers. These groups demanded reforms to gain a larger share of the nation's wealth.

In 1893, shortly after Cleveland began his second term as President, a major economic depression struck the nation. Farmers cried out against high railroad charges to send their goods to market. Many city workers demanded jobs, and others called for higher wages. Confused by the problems of an increasingly industrialized society, Cleveland hoped the economy would adjust itself. He followed a laissez-faire policy at the same time that farmers faced ruin, city workers went on strike, and the unemployment rate went up.

As President, Cleveland stood for a national currency backed by gold. By the election of 1896, many Democrats favored government action to increase the money in circulation by allowing the free coinage of silver. They believed that free coinage of silver would help solve the nation's economic problems. The money question became the major campaign issue. Most Democrats supported silver, but most Republicans favored gold.

In 1896, William Jennings Bryan won the Demo-

Democratic presidential and vice presidential candidates

Year	President	Vice President	Year	President	Vice President
1828	*Andrew Jackson*	*John Calhoun*	1912	*Woodrow Wilson*	*Thomas R. Marshall*
1832	*Andrew Jackson*	*Martin Van Buren*	1916	*Woodrow Wilson*	*Thomas R. Marshall*
1836	*Martin Van Buren*	*Richard M. Johnson*	1920	James M. Cox	Franklin D. Roosevelt
1840	Martin Van Buren	Richard M. Johnson	1924	John W. Davis	Charles W. Bryan
1844	*James K. Polk*	*George M. Dallas*	1928	Alfred E. Smith	Joseph T. Robinson
1848	Lewis Cass	William O. Butler	1932	*Franklin D. Roosevelt*	*John Nance Garner*
1852	*Franklin Pierce*	*William R. D. King*	1936	*Franklin D. Roosevelt*	*John Nance Garner*
1856	*James Buchanan*	*John C. Breckinridge*	1940	*Franklin D. Roosevelt*	*Henry A. Wallace*
1860	Stephen A. Douglas	Herschel V. Johnson	1944	*Franklin D. Roosevelt*	*Harry S. Truman*
1864	George B. McClellan	George H. Pendleton	1948	*Harry S. Truman*	*Alben W. Barkley*
1868	Horatio Seymour	Francis P. Blair, Jr.	1952	Adlai E. Stevenson	John J. Sparkman
1872	Horace Greeley	B. Gratz Brown	1956	Adlai E. Stevenson	Estes Kefauver
1876	Samuel J. Tilden	Thomas A. Hendricks	1960	*John F. Kennedy*	*Lyndon B. Johnson*
1880	Winfield S. Hancock	William H. English	1964	*Lyndon B. Johnson*	*Hubert H. Humphrey*
1884	*Grover Cleveland*	*Thomas A. Hendricks*	1968	Hubert H. Humphrey	Edmund S. Muskie
1888	Grover Cleveland	Allen G. Thurman	1972	George S. McGovern	Sargent Shriver
1892	*Grover Cleveland*	*Adlai E. Stevenson*	1976	*Jimmy Carter*	*Walter F. Mondale*
1896	William Jennings Bryan	Arthur Sewall	1980	Jimmy Carter	Walter F. Mondale
1900	William Jennings Bryan	Adlai E. Stevenson	1984	Walter F. Mondale	Geraldine A. Ferraro
1904	Alton B. Parker	Henry G. Davis	1988	Michael S. Dukakis	Lloyd M. Bentsen, Jr.
1908	William Jennings Bryan	John W. Kern			

Names of elected candidates are in italics.   Each candidate has a biography in World Book.

Administrations in office

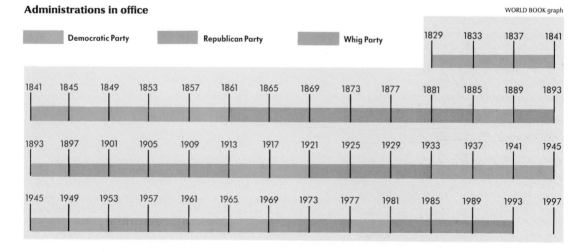

WORLD BOOK graph

Democratic Party   Republican Party   Whig Party   1829 1833 1837 1841

1841 1845 1849 1853 1857 1861 1865 1869 1873 1877 1881 1885 1889 1893

1893 1897 1901 1905 1909 1913 1917 1921 1925 1929 1933 1937 1941 1945

1945 1949 1953 1957 1961 1965 1969 1973 1977 1981 1985 1989 1993 1997

Deng Xiaoping, *duhng shyow pihng* (1904-   ), also spelled *Teng Hsiao-p'ing,* is the most influential leader in China. In theory, the Communist Party's general secretary is China's most powerful official. But China's official leaders consult Deng on all major issues and decisions, and he continues to be a leader of great importance. His influence has enabled him to bring about major changes in China. Deng no longer holds a post in the Chinese government, but he remains influential through his prestige and political connections.

His leadership. Mao Zedong, who had been China's top leader, died in 1976. Deng then emerged as the moving force behind cultural, economic, and political changes that began to occur in the country. These changes were a response to the radical Communist policies of Mao. Under Deng's leadership, cultural contacts and trade between China and other countries increased. Deng also decreased the Communist Party's regulation of business activity.

As a result of Deng's economic changes, China's economy grew and living conditions improved. However, the changes led to inflation and created more social inequality. Also, some of China's Communist Party leaders opposed Deng's policies, thus threatening the unity of the party.

AP/Wide World
Deng Xiaoping

Deng's policies also brought some political openness to Chinese society. But many citizens called for a greater degree of democracy. In 1989, large numbers of people, especially students, demonstrated for more democracy. Large numbers of them were killed by the military. Deng had backed a strong response against the demonstrators. This position weakened the respect that he had commanded.

Deng has used ideas from both Communism and other systems of government to modernize China's economy. In 1962, Deng demonstrated his political flexibility by his statement: "It does not matter whether a cat is black or white so long as it catches mice."

His life. Deng was born Deng Xixian in the province of Sichuan, also called Szechwan, into a family of landowners. He became engaged in revolutionary activities while working and studying in France during the early 1920's. Deng joined the Chinese Communist Party in 1924.

In 1927, fighting began between the Chinese Communists and the ruling Nationalists. Deng commanded Communist soldiers against Nationalists. The Communists won control of China in 1949. Deng had been elected to the Central Committee of the Communist Party in 1945. In 1955, he became a member of the party's Politburo—China's chief policymaking body. In 1956, he was appointed general secretary of the Communist Party—then one of the highest posts.

In the early 1960's, Deng came into conflict with party leader Mao Zedong over the amount of control the Communist Party should have in China. Deng believed that Mao's strict allegiance to Communist principles had damaged the economy. Deng and many others who opposed Mao were removed from office during China's Cultural Revolution (see **China** [The Cultural Revolution]). Deng returned to politics in 1973, only to be deposed again in early 1976. After Mao's death in September 1976, Deng gradually emerged as the top leader in China.   Arif Dirlik

Dengue, *DEHNG gay,* also called *breakbone fever,* is a disease that causes fever, headaches and eye aches, and pain in the muscles and joints. It may also cause a runny nose, sore throat, and skin rash. Dengue is caused by four distinct viruses that are carried by mosquitoes. Symptoms appear three to six days after a disease-bearing mosquito bites the victim. The rash breaks out on the fifth day of the illness. The fever subsides and then usually rises again.

Dengue is found in the tropics and subtropics. It is seldom fatal, but it can trigger a fatal illness—called *dengue hemorrhagic fever*—chiefly in young children. In severe cases, patients experience *shock syndrome* (very low blood pressure and a weak pulse). Dengue hemorrhagic fever with shock syndrome is widespread in Southeast Asia. The illness occurs primarily in children who have had a previous dengue infection.

Thomas P. Monath
See also **Virus.**

Denim is a sturdy fabric made from cotton, synthetic fibers, or a blend of both. The cloth is woven in the *twill weave* pattern (see **Weaving** [The twill weave]). Denim was first woven in Nîmes, France, about A.D. 300 and was called *serge de Nîmes.* In the late 1800's, the American clothing manufacturer Levi Strauss produced the first blue denim jeans.   Phyllis Tortora

See also **Strauss, Levi.**

De Niro, *duh NEER oh,* **Robert** (1943-   ), is an American motion-picture actor. He is best known for his portrayals of intense, psychologically troubled characters. De Niro received the 1980 Academy Award as best actor for his portrayal of boxer Jake LaMotta in *Raging Bull.* He also won the 1974 Academy Award as best supporting actor for his performance as gangster boss Vito Corleone in *The Godfather, Part II.* In addition, De Niro received Academy Award nominations as best actor for his roles as a mentally disturbed killer in *Taxi Driver* (1976) and as a Vietnam War veteran in *The Deer Hunter* (1979).

De Niro was born in New York City. He studied under the famous acting teachers Lee Strasberg and Stella Adler. De Niro appeared in a number of plays in New York City before making his motion-picture debut in 1968 in *Greetings.* De Niro's other motion pictures include *Mean Streets* (1973), *Bang the Drum Slowly* (1973), *The King of Comedy* (1983), *Once Upon a Time in America* (1984), *Falling in Love* (1984), *Midnight Run* (1988), *Jacknife* (1989), and *We're No Angels* (1989).   John F. Mariani

Paramount Pictures Corporation
Robert De Niro

© Travelpix from FPG

Denmark's charm and prosperity are evident in the well-maintained old buildings and fashion-able cafés of Copenhagen's Nyhavn Canal. Copenhagen is the capital and largest city of Denmark, as well as the country's cultural, economic, and political center.

Denmark

Denmark is a small kingdom in northern Europe that is almost surrounded by water. It consists of a peninsula and 482 nearby islands. The peninsula, called Jutland, shares a 42-mile (68-kilometer) border with Germany. Greenland, off the northeastern coast of Canada, is a province of Denmark even though it lies 1,300 miles (2,090 kilometers) away. The Faeroe Islands, north of Scotland, are a self-governing part of the Danish kingdom. Denmark, along with Norway and Sweden, is one of the Scandinavian countries.

More than half of the Danes (people of Denmark) live on the islands near the peninsula. Copenhagen, the capital and largest city of Denmark, is on the largest island. About a fourth of all Danes live in the Copenhagen area, and almost half of the country's manufacturing industries are located there.

Denmark has one of the world's highest standards of living. The Danes have achieved prosperity even though their land is poor in natural resources. They sell their products to other countries to pay for the fuels and metals they must import for their industries.

Denmark is famous for its butter, cheese, bacon, ham, and other processed foods. It is also known for its beautifully designed manufactured goods, including furniture, porcelain, and silverware. Since the Viking era, the Danes have been a seafaring people, and Denmark is still known as a great shipping and fishing nation.

Denmark is a land of small green farms, blue lakes, and white coastal beaches. The carefully tended farmlands make up about three-fourths of the country. In the

M. Donald Hancock, the contributor of this article, is Professor of Political Science at Vanderbilt University.

farm areas, the roofs of most houses are made of red or blue tiles, or are thatched. Storks, which the Danes believe bring good luck, build nests on some rooftops. Castles and windmills rise above the rolling landscape. Visitors can enjoy Denmark's charm even in the busy, modern cities, with their well-preserved sections of colorful old buildings and cobblestone streets.

Government

National government. Denmark is a constitutional monarchy with a king or queen, a prime minister and

Facts in brief

Capital: Copenhagen.
Official language: Danish.
Official name: *Kongeriget Danmark* (Kingdom of Denmark).
Area: 16,632 sq. mi. (43,077 km²). *Greatest distances*—east-west, 250 mi. (402 km); north-south, 225 mi. (362 km). *Coastline*—1,057 mi. (1,701 km).
Elevation: *Highest*—Yding Skovhøj, 568 ft. (173 m) above sea level. *Lowest*—sea level along the coasts.
Population: *Estimated 1991 population*—5,122,000; density, 308 persons per sq. mi. (119 persons per km²); distribution, 86 per cent urban, 14 per cent rural. *1981 census*—5,123,989. *Estimated 1996 population*—5,131,000.
Chief products: *Agriculture*—barley, beef and dairy cattle, eggs, hogs, milk, potatoes, poultry, sugar beets, wheat. *Fishing*—cod, sand lances, trout. *Manufacturing*—bacon, butter, cheese, diesel engines, electrical and electronic equipment, furniture, ham, machinery, porcelain, ships, silverware.
National holiday: Constitution Day, June 5.
National anthems: "Kong Christian stod ved højen mast" ("King Christian Stood by Lofty Mast") and "Der er et yndigt land" ("There Is a Lovely Land").
Money: *Basic unit*—krone. See **Money** (table: Exchange rates). See also **Krone.**

Christiansborg Palace is the home of Denmark's parliament, the *Folketing*. It also houses the Supreme Court and the Queen's Audience Chambers, where formal functions are held.

© Thomas Nebbia, Woodfin Camp, Inc.

cabinet, and a parliament. The government is based on the Danish constitution of 1953, which divides the government into three branches—executive, legislative, and judicial. The monarch serves as head of state but has little real power.

The monarch appoints the prime minister of Denmark. The prime minister must have the support of a majority of the members of the Danish parliament. If one political party controls a clear parliamentary majority, the leader of that party normally becomes the prime minister. However, the large number of parties in Denmark makes it almost impossible for any single party to win a majority. If no party has a majority, the person who can gain the support of the strongest *coalition* (combination of parties) becomes the prime minister. A prime minister who receives a vote of no confidence from the parliament must either (1) resign, along with the rest of the cabinet; or (2) ask the monarch to dissolve the parliament and ____ ____ national election.

The prime minister ____ ____ cabinet. The cabinet consists of a variable numb__ ____ ministers, each of whom normally heads a govern____ ____ department. The monarch selects the members of the ____ ____ based on the prime minister's recommendations. ____ ____ in executive powers are exercised by the cabinet in t__ ____ monarch's name. However, the cabinet remains in pow__ only as long as it has the support of a majority of the members of parliament.

Other high officials in Denmark, including judges, are named by the monarch on the advice of the cabinet. The parliament appoints an official called an *ombudsman,* who investigates citizens' complaints against actions or decisions by the government (see **Ombudsman**).

The Danish parliament, called the *Folketing,* consists of one house. It has 179 members, who are elected to four-year terms. One hundred seventy-five are elected from Denmark, 2 from Greenland, and 2 from the Faroe Islands. Of the seats from Denmark, 135 are filled by elections in voting districts and 40 are divided among the various political parties according to their share of

the total votes in the election. All Danish citizens at least 18 years old may vote.

Members of the Folketing discuss and vote on proposed legislation. Certain kinds of bills passed by the Folketing are subject to approval by the Danish voters. The people of Denmark also must be given the opportunity to vote on a bill if one-third of the Folketing's members call for such action.

Courts. Denmark's highest court is the Supreme Court. It consists of 15 judges, at least 5 of whom must hear each case. There are also two High Courts, with a total of about 50 judges. At least 3 High Court judges and a jury of 12 persons hear serious criminal cases. A jury verdict of innocent is final, but the judges may reverse a verdict of guilty. The judges and jurors act together to set the length of prison sentences. There are more than 100 lower courts.

Local government. Denmark is divided into 14 counties and 2 large municipalities—Copenhagen and Frederiksberg. The 14 counties are subdivided into almost 300 smaller municipalities. In most cases, a municipality consists of an urban center and a rural area. Each county and municipality in Denmark has a council elected by the people. Each council selects a mayor to head the local government.

Politics. Denmark has many political parties. The two largest parties are the Social Democratic Party and the Conservative People's Party. The Social Democrats sup-

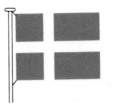

H. E. Harris & Co.

The Danish flag was probably first used in the 1200's, after King Valdemar II led a military crusade to Estonia.

Denmark's coat of arms dates from the 1100's. The lions of the Valdemar arms stand among water lilies.

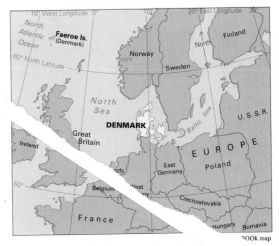

ROOK map

Denmark is a small country in northern Europe. I__ the peninsula of Jutland and hundreds of nearby islan__

Denmark map index

*Population of municipalities, which may include rural as well as the urban center.
†Population of metropolitan area, including suburbs.
‡Does not appear on map; key shows general location.
Source: 1986 official estimates for municipalities; 1985 official estimates for counties and Copenhagen metropolitan area.

port strong social welfare programs, full employment, and public ownership of the means of production. They formed alliances with various smaller parties and dominated Danish politics from the 1930's through the 1970's. The Conservatives favor limited government involvement in the economy. A radical party called the Progress Party opposes immigration into Denmark and favors eliminating income taxes and most of the civil service. Other Danish political parties include the Center Democratic, Christian People's, and Liberal parties.

Armed forces. A total of more than 30,000 people serve in Denmark's army, navy, and air force. Men from 20 to 25 years of age may be drafted for nine months' service in the armed forces.

People

Population and ancestry. Denmark has about 5 million people. Copenhagen, the largest city, has about 470,000 people. About a fourth of all Danes live in Copenhagen or its suburbs. Three other Danish cities have populations of more than 100,000. They are, in order of size, Århus, Odense, and Ålborg. See the articles on the Danish cities listed in the *Related articles* at the end of this article.

The Danes are closely related to the Norwegians and the Swedes. Denmark's only ethnic minority group consists of about 40,000 people of German ancestry. They live in southern Jutland, along Denmark's border with Germany.

Language. Danish, the official language of Denmark, is closely related to the Norwegian and Swedish languages. Regional dialects abound and are especially noticeable in northern Jutland and on the island of Bornholm. German is spoken by the ethnic German minority. Virtually all adult Danes also speak English.

Way of life

City life. More than four-fifths of all Danes live in urban areas. The principal cities of Copenhagen, Arhus, Odense, and Ålborg feature a striking combination of medieval structures, such as castles and cathedrals, and modern office buildings and homes. Denmark's high standard of living and extensive social welfare services ensure that the cities have virtually no slums or substandard housing. Most city dwellers live in apartment buildings. Many suburban residents live in single-family houses. Service industries employ most people in urban areas.

Danish cities are served by an extensive network of public transportation. Modern trains whisk people from the suburbs to the city centers. Trains also link cities to one another. Bicycles, buses, and automobiles provide the chief means of transportation within the cities. The growth of the urban population and the resulting increase in the number of cars and trucks have led to problems of traffic congestion and pollution, especially in Copenhagen. Industrial pollution, however, has decreased, as many urban factories that once burned coal for power now rely on natural gas.

Rural life. Less than a fifth of the Danish people live in rural areas. But although cities dominate Denmark's economic and social life, the nation's many farms and rural villages show the continuing importance of agriculture. Danish farms are not large, and most are owned

© Harvey Lloyd, The Stock Market
Colorful shops and restaurants cluster in an area of Copenhagen called Strøget, which is closed to motor traffic.

and operated by the people who live on them. Most rural residents live in modernized single-family homes.

Food and drink. Most Danes eat four meals a day—breakfast, lunch, dinner, and a late-evening supper. Breakfast generally consists of cereal, cheese, or eggs. Dinner, which includes fish or meat, is usually the only hot meal. A favorite traditional Danish dinner consists of roast duckling stuffed with apples and prunes, served with red cabbage and boiled potatoes.

The chief part of the other Danish meals consists of open-faced sandwiches called *smørrebrød.* One sandwich may be a pyramid-shaped pile of about 20 small shrimps on thin bread. The Danes often prepare a plate of smørrebrød almost as a work of art, with many attractive sandwiches.

Denmark is famous for rich, flaky raised sweet rolls that are often called *Danish pastries.* Danes especially enjoy a nut-filled coffee cake called *kringle.* Typical des-

© Elvig Hansen, Biofoto
Danish farmers use modern equipment, such as this harvesting combine. Most Danish farms are family-owned and operated.

serts eaten by Danes include berry puddings and rice pudding.

The Danish people typically drink coffee with breakfast and during morning and afternoon breaks from work. Many Danes drink beer with meals. On special occasions, they also may drink *aquavit*, a strong liquor slightly flavored with caraway.

About 97 per cent of the Danish people be~~long to~~ ~~Lu~~theran Church, the official church of Den. ~~~~~~~~ ~~re~~quired by law to belong to the church, but the p~~eople have~~ complete freedom to worship as they please. The church is supported largely by a national tax paid only by members. The Evangelical Lutheran Church has no supreme spiritual leader. Ten bishops manage church affairs. The Danish parliament has control of the church but does not interfere in its religious practices. Roman Catholics make up Denmark's second largest religious group.

Education. Almost all adult Danes can read and write. Danish law requires children to attend nine years of school. Elementary school consists of the first seven grades, and high school lasts from three to five years. A five-year high school education makes a student eligible to enter a university. Denmark has three universities. The University of Copenhagen is the oldest and largest. It was founded in 1479 and has about 24,000 students. The other universities are those of Århus and Odense.

The famous Danish folk high schools operate separately from the public educational system. They are private schools, but are supported largely by government funds. These schools provide young adults with a general education in Danish government, history, and literature. Courses last up to six months, and the students live at the schools. Denmark has about 20 folk high schools. The first ones were founded in the mid-1800's to help young farmers take a more active part in Denmark's political and social life. Today, the schools also attract many young adults of the cities and towns.

Libraries and museums. The chief libraries include the Royal Library in Copenhagen, founded in the mid-1600's. It is Denmark's national library, and has about $2\frac{1}{2}$ million books. Other leading libraries in Denmark include the University Library in Copenhagen, and the State and University Library in Århus. The Danish government supports a nationwide system of about 250 public libraries.

Denmark also has about 280 museums. Many important museums are located in Copenhagen. The National Museum houses exhibits that document Danish history from prehistoric through modern times. Fine paintings and sculptures by Danish and other European artists are on display in the State Museum of Art. The New Carlsberg Glyptotek features ancient Egyptian, Etruscan, Greek, and Roman art. The Louisiana Museum, south of Helsingør, is noted for its collection of modern art. The Viking Ship Museum in Roskilde houses five Viking ships dating from the A.D. 1000's.

Arts. Many Danes have won fame in the arts, especially in literature. Ludvig Holberg is known as the father of modern Danish literature. During the early 1700's, he wrote poems and plays that poked fun at Danish society (see **Holberg, Ludvig**). Johannes Ewald, who did much of his writing during the 1770's, became one of Denmark's greatest lyric poets.

Important literary works of the 1800's include the romantic poems of Adam Oehlenschläger and the hymns of N. F. S. Grundtvig. Hans Christian Andersen won world fame for his fairy tales and is probably Denmark's best-known writer (see **Andersen, Hans Christian**). The books of Søren Kierkegaard strongly influenced the development of the modern philosophy called *existentialism* (see **Kierkegaard, Søren**).

Henrik Pontoppidan and Johannes V. Jensen rank among the most important Danish novelists of the early 1900's. Each won the Nobel Prize for literature, as did Karl Gjellerup. Other noted Danish writers include Thorkild Bjørnvig, Isak Dinesen, Martin A. Hansen, and Martin Andersen Nexø. See **Dinesen, Isak.**

Carl A. Nielsen is considered Denmark's greatest musical composer. He wrote six symphonies and many other works, including the comic opera *Maskarade* (see **Nielsen, Carl A.**). In the field of dance, the ballet master August Bournonville made the most significant Danish contribution. The Royal Danish Ballet flowered under his direction during the mid-1800's, and today it enjoys a worldwide reputation.

Noted Danish painters include Michael Ancher, C. W. Eckersberg, Oluf Høst, Christen Købke, P. S. Krøyer, Theodor Philipsen, and William Scharff. Denmark's leading sculptor was Bertel Thorvaldsen. His statue of Christ in the Church of Our Lady in Copenhagen is one of his most famous sculptures (see **Thorvaldsen, Bertel**).

The Danish film director Carl Dreyer is regarded as a major figure in cinema history. His film *The Passion of Joan of Arc* (1928) is considered a masterpiece. In recent years, two Danish films have won the Academy Award for best foreign-language film: *Babette's Feast* (1987), directed by Gabriel Axel, and *Pelle the Conqueror* (1988), directed by Bille August.

Outstanding works of Danish design include the silverware of Georg Jensen and the furniture of Kaare Klint and Arne Jacobsen. As an architect, Jacobsen became known for his precise grouping of simple structural elements. Jørn Utzon designed the famous sail-like vaults of the Opera House in Sydney, Australia.

Recreation. Soccer is the most popular sport in Denmark. Other favorite sports include bicycling, gymnastics, rowing, sailing, swimming, and tennis. Danes have won Olympic and other world championships in most

© Shinichi Kammo, FPG

Tivoli Gardens is a world-famous amusement park in Copenhagen. Its exotic, lighted grounds attract many visitors at night.

of these sports, and also in archery, boxing, diving, fencing, riding, weightlifting, and wrestling.

Copenhagen is world famous for its Tivoli Gardens amusement park, which opened in 1843 in the heart of the city. The park offers ballet and pantomime, rides and shooting galleries, restaurants, circus acts, concerts, and fireworks displays.

Social welfare. Since the 1890's, Denmark has developed many social welfare programs. The country has social insurance plans that cover accidents, handicapping injuries, illness, old age, unemployment, and the death of husbands. Any person living in Denmark may join these programs. Most plans are managed by private, government-approved organizations, with costs shared by insured persons, employers, and the government. The government manages some plans, including aid for the aged and for widows, and pays the total cost.

The land

The peninsula of Jutland accounts for almost 70 per cent of the land in Denmark. However, most Danes live

Danish Tourist Board

The Western Dune Coast is an area of sandy beaches and dunes that extends along most of Jutland's western coast.

© Søren Koustrup, Biofoto

The East-Central Hills, covering much of Jutland and the nearby islands, have gently rolling lands and narrow fiords.

on about 100 nearby islands. The land is low throughout Denmark. The highest point, the hill of Yding Skovhøj on Jutland, rises only 568 feet (173 meters) above sea level. The land is covered mainly by *moraine,* the earth and stone deposited by melting glaciers thousands of years ago. The underlying rock can be seen in only a few areas.

Land regions. Denmark has five main land regions: (1) the Western Dune Coast, (2) the Western Sand Plains, (3) the East-Central Hills, (4) the Northern Flat Plains, and (5) Bornholm.

The Western Dune Coast consists chiefly of great sandy beaches that extend along almost the entire western coast. These beaches close off many long, narrow

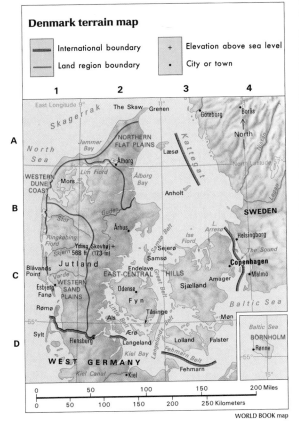

Denmark terrain map

▬▬▬ International boundary	⊞ +	Elevation above sea level
─── Land region boundary	⊡ •	City or town

1   **2**   **3**   **4**

WORLD BOOK map

Physical features

Ålborg Bay	.B	2
Als (island)	.D	2
Baltic Sea	.C	4
Bornholm (island)	.D	4
Falster (island)	.D	3
Fyn (island)	.C	2
Great Belt (strait)	.C	3
Guden River	.B	2
Jutland (peninsula)	.C	1
Kattegat (channel)	.A	3
Lake Arresø	.C	3
Langeland (island)	.D	2

Langelands Belt		
(strait)	.D	2
Lim Fiord	.A	2
Little Belt		
(strait)	.C	2
Lolland (island)	.D	3
Samsø (island)	.C	2
Sjælland (island)	.C	3
Skagerrak		
(channel)	.A	1
The Sound		
(Øresund)	.C	4
Yding Skovhøj		
(hill)	.C	2

inlets called *fiords* that once were connected to the sea. In the southwest are marshes that the tide covers regularly.

The Western Sand Plains are almost flat. Water from ancient melting glaciers flowed over this region and deposited much sand, forming the plains.

The East-Central Hills make up Denmark's largest land region. This gently rolling region includes much of Jutland and almost all the nearby islands. Long, narrow fiords form natural harbors along the coastlines of the region.

The largest inlet is Lim Fiord, which winds across northern Jutland for 112 miles (180 kilometers). This fiord forms an inland lagoon 15 miles (24 kilometers) wide. A beach on the Western Dune Coast closes off the fiord's outlet to the North Sea. Small vessels use the Thyborøn Canal to travel between Lim Fiord and the sea.

The islands in the region lie close together. Their deep moraine soils are the best farmlands in Denmark. The largest island, Sjælland, is 2,713 square miles (7,027 square kilometers). Sjælland is the most thickly populated part of Denmark. On this island stands most of Copenhagen, Denmark's capital and largest city. The rest of the city is on the island of Amager. Falster, Fyn, and Lolland are other important islands.

The Northern Flat Plains were once a part of the sea bottom. The region rose from the water when the weight of ancient glaciers was removed by melting. Many farms are in this region.

Bornholm and nearby small islands lie much closer to southern Sweden than to the rest of Denmark. Granite rock covers most of this region.

Lakes and rivers. Denmark has many small lakes. They formed in small hollows left in the ground by melting ice from the glaciers. Lake Arresø, the largest lake, covers 16 square miles (41 square kilometers). Denmark also has many short rivers. The longest one, Guden River, is 98 miles (158 kilometers) long.

Climate

Denmark has a mild, damp climate, chiefly because it is almost surrounded by water. In winter, seas are not so cold as land, and in summer they are not so warm. As a result, west winds from the seas warm Denmark in winter and cool it in summer. These winds affect Denmark's weather throughout the year. Also in winter, west winds bring some warmth from the North Atlantic Current of the Gulf Stream (see **Gulf Stream**). Denmark is small, so the climate does not differ much from area to area.

Winter temperatures average about 32° F. (0° C) in Denmark, with the coldest days from 15° to 20° F. (−9° to −7° C). The waters on the east may freeze over during especially cold winters. At these times, the waters cannot warm the cold winds and the weather may become bitterly cold. Summer temperatures average 63° F. (17° C). The warmest weather usually varies from 75° to 82° F. (24° to 28° C). Winds from eastern Europe may cause higher temperatures in especially hot summers.

Denmark receives a yearly average of about 24 inches (61 centimeters) of *precipitation* (rain, melted snow, and other forms of moisture). Western Denmark gets a little more precipitation than eastern Denmark because the moisture-bearing west winds reach it first. Rain falls throughout the year, with the most during August and

October. Snow falls from 20 to 30 days a year, but usually melts quickly. Fog and mist occur frequently, especially on the west coast in winter.

Economy

Denmark has a strong economy, even though the country is poor in natural resources. Denmark obtains some natural gas and petroleum from wells in the North Sea. However, it still must import petroleum. Other mineral products of Denmark include chalk and industrial clays. Coal, as well as iron and most other metals, must be imported. Much of the soil in Denmark lacks nutrients, so it requires heavy use of fertilizers to make it productive. The land is flat or gently rolling, so the rivers cannot be used to generate hydroelectric power. Forests cover only about a tenth of the land and supply less than half of Denmark's wood. The seas that almost surround the country provide an inexpensive means of

Denmark's gross domestic product

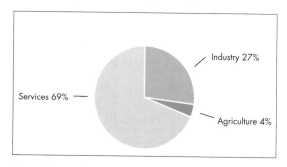

Services 69%

Industry 27%

Agriculture 4%

Denmark's gross domestic product (GDP) was $107,510,000,000 in 1988. The GDP is the total value of goods and services produced within a country in a year. *Services* include community, government, and personal services; finance, insurance, real estate, and business services; transportation and communication; utilities; and wholesale and retail trade. *Industry* includes construction, manufacturing, and mining. *Agriculture* includes agriculture, forestry, and fishing.

Production and workers by economic activities

Economic activities	Per cent of GDP produced	Employed workers	
		Number of persons	Per cent of total
Community, government, & personal services	28	947,000	36
Manufacturing	20	519,000	19
Finance, insurance, real estate, & business services	18	259,000	10
Wholesale and retail trade	13	386,000	14
Transportation & communication	8	197,000	7
Construction	6	182,000	7
Agriculture, forestry, & fishing	4	153,000	6
Utilities	2	19,000	1
Mining	1	3,000	*
Total	100	2,665,000	100

*Less than half of 1 per cent.
Figures are for 1988.
Sources: Nordic Council of Ministers and Nordic Statistical Secretariat; Organization for Economic Cooperation and Development.

transportation by which Denmark can import its industrial needs and export its products. The seas are also rich in fish.

Service industries employ about 60 per cent of the Danish labor force. Service industries are those economic activities that produce services, not goods. They include schools, hospitals, shops, hotels, restaurants, and government services. Banking, real estate, transportation, and communication are also service industries.

Manufacturing in Denmark has expanded rapidly since the mid-1900's and has replaced agriculture as the nation's second largest economic activity. The government has done much to promote manufacturing by expanding educational programs to train engineers, technicians, and skilled workers.

Nearly half of all Danish manufacturing is concentrated in the Copenhagen area. Danish factories produce high-quality goods, including stereos, television sets, furniture, porcelain, and silverware. Among Denmark's other products are diesel engines, machinery, pharmaceuticals, ships, textiles and clothing, and processed foods, which include bacon, butter, cheese, ham, and beer.

Agriculture. Farmland makes up about three-fourths of Denmark's total land area. Farms cover an average of about 100 acres (40 hectares). Until the 1880's, wheat was Denmark's most important farm product. Then wheat prices fell, and Danish farmers began to stress the production of eggs, hogs, and milk. They organized cooperative dairies and slaughterhouses, and shared equipment and profits. Today, cooperatives cover all branches of farming.

Raising hogs and beef or dairy cattle is the major activity on most Danish farms. Most crops are used for livestock feed. They include barley, potatoes, sugar beets, and *rape* (a leafy herb). Barley is grown on more of the nation's farmland than any other crop. About 60 per cent of the country's farm production is exported as meat and dairy products.

Fishing. Danish fishing ships catch about 2 million short tons (1.8 million metric tons) of fish each year. Important fish include cod, herring, Norway pout, sand lances, sprat, and whiting. More than half the catch is taken from the North Sea. Esbjerg is Denmark's major fishing port.

Transportation. Denmark has an excellent road system. There are about $1\frac{1}{2}$ million automobiles in Denmark, or about one car for every four people. At least half of the people use bicycles for transportation, and many roads have separate bicycle lanes.

A government-owned railroad provides fast passenger service to most cities and towns. Train-carrying ferries connect many Danish islands with each other and with the mainland. The islands of Sjælland and Falster are linked by the 10,535-foot (3,211-meter) Storstrøm Bridge.

Denmark has many busy seaports, of which Copenhagen is the most important. Kastrup Airport, near Copenhagen, is one of Europe's largest air terminals. It handles about 12 million passengers a year.

Communication. Denmark has about 50 daily newspapers. The largest dailies include the *Berlingske Tidende, B.T., Ekstra Bladet,* and *Politiken,* all of Copenhagen.

Bang & Olufsen

Danish electronic products are known for their high quality and attractive design. This photograph shows a Danish factory worker assembling a television set.

Almost all Danish families own at least one radio and one television set. All radio and television broadcasting is handled by Radio Denmark, a public organization responsible to the Danish Ministry of Cultural Affairs. No advertising is allowed on the programs. The Danish people pay a yearly license fee for each radio and television set.

The government owns and operates the Danish telegraph system and long-distance telephone service. Most local telephone service is privately owned.

History

Early days. As long as 100,000 years ago, people lived in what is now Denmark. Great changes in the climate occurred, and the region became too cold for human life. The climate started to become warmer about 14,000 years ago, and continuous settlement began. Farming developed in the region about 3,000 B.C.

By the time of Christ, trade by sea had brought the people into close contact with leading civilizations. The contact expanded for hundreds of years. During this period, the Danes lived in small communities governed by local chieftains. About A.D. 950, all Denmark was united by King Harald Bluetooth. Harald fostered the spread of Christianity in Denmark.

About 800, Danish seafarers began raiding European coastal towns and sailing away with slaves and treasure. The Danish Vikings spread terror throughout much of western Europe for about 300 years. The Vikings gained control of England in 1016, and Danish kings ruled that country until 1042. See **Vikings** (The Danish Vikings).

A great power. During the late 1100's and early 1200's, Danish power expanded along the southern coast of the Baltic Sea to Estonia, which Denmark conquered in 1219. But a long period of civil wars and struggles with north German cities, beginning in the 1240's, greatly weakened the country.

Denmark regained its power under Queen Margaret, who became ruler of Denmark as regent for her young son in 1375. Margaret was also the wife of King Haakon VI of Norway. After he died in 1380, Margaret became

A sculpture adorns the tomb of Queen Margaret, who united Denmark, Norway, and Sweden in the Union of Kalmar in 1397. Under her skillful leadership, Scandinavia enjoyed 20 years of peace and economic growth.

Roskilde Museum

regent of Norway as well as Denmark. In 1388, during political confusion in Sweden, Swedish nobles elected her to rule that country, too. In 1397, Margaret united Denmark, Norway, and Sweden in the Union of Kalmar, with power centered in Denmark. Sweden broke away from the union in 1523.

In 1536, during the Reformation, King Christian III established Lutheranism as the official religion of Denmark. That same year, Christian made Norway a province of Denmark.

Wars with Sweden. During the 1600's and 1700's, Sweden defeated Denmark in several wars fought for control of the Baltic Sea. During the Danish-Swedish War (1657-1660), Sweden won a great deal of Danish and Norwegian territory in what is now Sweden. Only pressure from England, France, and the Netherlands prevented Sweden from dividing Denmark itself. During the Great Northern War (1700-1721), Denmark tried unsuccessfully to win back the territory it had lost to Sweden.

In 1788, Denmark began freeing its serfs. These peas-

ants had been bound to the land on which they worked. Educational reforms were begun during the early 1800's. Denmark sided with France in the Napoleonic Wars of that period and was defeated by Sweden in 1813. By the terms of the Treaty of Kiel in 1814, Denmark gave Norway to Sweden but kept Greenland and other Norwegian colonies.

The Schleswig wars. In 1848, the pressure of public opinion forced King Frederik VII to accept a democratic constitution for Denmark. The constitution was adopted in 1849. It granted the highest power of government to an elected two-house parliament.

Also in 1848, a revolt broke out in Holstein and Schleswig, two Danish duchies that were located just south of Denmark. These regions were ruled by the Danish king, though they were not part of Denmark. A revolutionary government of Schleswig-Holstein was established. This government wanted to throw off Danish control and join the German Confederation, of which Holstein was already a member. Danish troops defeated the rebels in 1850. In 1863, Schleswig was made a part of Denmark. Prussia and its ally, Austria, invaded Denmark in 1864. They won a quick victory and took over Schleswig and Holstein.

Social and political reforms. During the late 1800's, education, industry, and trade were expanded in Denmark. The Danes also developed cooperatives and improved their farming methods. At this time, the upper classes had special rights that gave them control of the upper house of the parliament. The small farmers and industrial workers formed political parties and struggled for political equality. A new constitution was adopted in 1915 during the reign of Christian X, who served as king from 1912 to 1947. By the terms of the constitution, the special rights of the upper classes were abolished, and Denmark became a parliamentary democracy.

Denmark remained neutral during World War I (1914-1918). After the war, Denmark granted independence to Iceland, a Danish colony. However, Iceland stayed united with Denmark until 1944, when it became a republic. In 1920, the Allies transferred North Schleswig to Denmark from Germany. Most people of the region had voted for the transfer.

World War II began in 1939. On April 9, 1940, German forces invaded Denmark, and the Danes surrendered after a few hours of fighting. The Germans allowed the Danish government to continue as long as it met their demands. But resistance groups developed and blew up factories and transportation facilities. The

Important dates in Denmark

c. 950 King Harald Bluetooth united Denmark and encouraged the spread of Christianity in the country.
1013-1042 Denmark ruled England.
1380 Denmark and Norway were united under Queen Margaret.
1388 Queen Margaret was elected ruler of Sweden as well.
1397 Denmark, Norway, and Sweden were united in the Union of Kalmar.
1536 Lutheranism became the official Danish religion.
1657-1660 Denmark lost much territory to Sweden in the Danish-Swedish War.
1788 The government began freeing the Danish serfs.
1814 Denmark lost Norway to Sweden in the Napoleonic Wars.
1849 Denmark adopted its first democratic constitution.
1864 Denmark lost Schleswig and Holstein to Prussia and Austria.
1918 Denmark granted independence to Iceland, which remained under the Danish king until 1944.
1920 North Schleswig was returned to Denmark.
1940-1945 Germany occupied Denmark during World War II.
1944 Iceland ended its union with Denmark.
1949 Denmark and 11 other nations formed the North Atlantic Treaty Organization (NATO).
1953 Denmark adopted a new constitution that ended the upper house of parliament.
1959 Denmark and six other countries formed the European Free Trade Association (EFTA).
1973 Denmark became a member of the European Community.
1982 A Conservative-led coalition government replaced the government of the Social Democrats.

Germans took over the government of Denmark in August 1943.

In September 1943, the Danes organized the secret Freedom Council to lead the resistance movement. They also helped about 7,000 Danish Jews escape to Sweden. On May 5, 1945, after the fall of Germany, Allied troops entered Denmark and the Germans there surrendered. See **World War II.**

Denmark became a charter member of the United Nations in 1945 and of the North Atlantic Treaty Organization (NATO) in 1949. During the late 1940's, the United States gave Denmark much aid. The Danes rebuilt industries that had been damaged during the war, and the nation's economy became strong again.

Postwar years. Political reform and economic expansion in Denmark continued during the 1950's and 1960's. In 1953, a majority of Danish voters approved a new constitution that abolished the upper house of parliament. The constitution also made Greenland a province of Denmark, rather than a colony. In addition, Danish voters approved a law that permitted both males and females to inherit the throne.

In 1960, Denmark and six other European countries, including Great Britain, Norway, and Sweden, formed the European Free Trade Association (EFTA). The EFTA regulates and promotes trade among its members (see **European Free Trade Association**). Denmark resigned from the EFTA in 1972. In 1973, the country entered the European Community, an economic association of Western European nations (see **European Community**).

In 1966, Denmark launched a massive economic development program in Greenland. The program called for the expansion and modernization of Greenland's towns and of its fishing and food-processing industries. In 1979, the Danish parliament granted *home rule*—that is, the power of local self-government—to Greenland.

King Frederik IX died in 1972. His oldest daughter, Margrethe, succeeded him to the throne.

Recent developments. During the 1970's and early 1980's, Denmark—like many countries—faced an economic recession. Economic growth slowed, and unemployment and inflation increased sharply. A number of political parties gained support as many voters expressed their frustration over the condition of Denmark's economy. In 1982, a Conservative-led coalition government replaced the government of the Social Democrats. This center-right coalition has worked to encourage economic recovery, but Denmark still faces problems of environmental pollution, unemployment, and the high cost of welfare services.

M. Donald Hancock

Study aids

Related articles in *World Book* include:

Biographies

Andersen, Hans Christian	Christian IV
Anne (Anne of Denmark)	Christian IX
Bering, Vitus	Christian X
Bohr, Niels	Dinesen, Isak
Brahe, Tycho	Holberg, Ludvig
Bruhn, Erik	Kierkegaard, Søren A.
Canute	

Margrethe II	Oersted, Hans C.
Nielsen, Carl A.	Thorvaldsen, Bertel

History

Anglo-Saxons	Seven Weeks' War
Europe, Council of	Sweden (History)
European Community	Vikings
Jutes	World War II
Norway (History)	

Physical features

Baltic Sea	North Sea
Faeroe Islands	Skagerrak

Other related articles

Århus	Krone
Copenhagen	Scandinavia
Greenland	Theater (Scandinavia)
Iceland	Virgin Islands

Outline

I. Government
    A. National government
    B. Courts
    C. Local government
    D. Politics
    E. Armed forces
II. People
    A. Population and ancestry
    B. Language
III. Way of life
    A. City life
    B. Rural life
    C. Food and drink
    D. Religion
    E. Education
    F. Libraries and museums
    G. Arts
    H. Recreation
    I. Social welfare
IV. The land
    A. Land regions
    B. Lakes and rivers
V. Climate
VI. Economy
    A. Service industries
    B. Manufacturing
    C. Agriculture
    D. Fishing
    E. Transportation
    F. Communication
VI. History

Questions

What do Denmark's folk high schools offer students?
What is Denmark's official church?
What is the major farm activity in Denmark?
Which area has about a fourth of Denmark's total population and almost half the country's manufacturing industries?
What does the *ombudsman* do?
How did Denmark, Norway, and Sweden become united during the late 1300's?
Why can Denmark's rivers not be used to generate hydroelectric power?
How is the Danish broadcasting system supported?
Who united Denmark? When?
Who is known as the father of modern Danish literature?

Additional resources

Anderson, Robert T. *Denmark: Success of a Developing Nation.* Schenkman, 1975.
Baedeker's Denmark. Prentice-Hall, 1987.
Fitzmaurice, John. *Politics in Denmark.* St. Martin's, 1981.
James, Alan. *Let's Visit Denmark.* Burke Pub. Co., 1984. For younger readers.

Lauring, Palle. *Denmark: A History.* 7th ed. Nordic Bks., 1986.
MacHaffie, Ingeborg S., and Nielsen, M. A. *Of Danish Ways.*
    Barnes & Noble, 1984. First published in 1976.

Denominate number, *dih NAHM uh niht,* tells the amount of a quantity by giving the number of units and the kind of units that make up the quantity. A denominate number includes a number, which may be written as a numeral or as a word, and the name or symbol of a unit of measurement. For example, *six meters, 90 pounds, $500 million, 18½ miles, 23° C,* and *four days* are all denominate numbers. See also **Unit.**

Karen Connors Fuson

Denominator. See Fraction (In symbols); **Arithmetic** (Working with fractions).

Density is the *mass*—that is, the amount of matter—in a unit volume of any substance. The density of a substance is found by dividing its mass by its volume. The density of a liquid or solid is measured in grams per milliliter or in pounds per cubic foot. The density of a gas is measured in grams per liter or in pounds per cubic foot. The equation for density is:

Density = mass ÷ volume, or d = m/V.

The concentration of a substance in a solution can be determined by measuring the density of the solution. Density measurements are useful in identifying minerals and other solids. In addition, the *molecular weight* of a gas can be calculated from its density (see **Molecule** [Individual molecules]).

The density of a liquid can be determined by measuring the mass needed to fill a container of a known vol-

ume. In most cases, a device called a *pycnometer,* which has a precisely known volume, is used to determine the density of a liquid. An instrument called a *hydrometer* is also used to determine the density of a liquid (see **Hydrometer**).

The density of a regularly shaped solid is determined by simply measuring the object's mass, calculating its volume, and dividing the mass by the volume. The density of an irregularly shaped solid is determined by submerging the solid in a known quantity of liquid and measuring the volume of the liquid displaced. The volume of the displaced liquid equals the volume of the solid. The mass of the object is then determined and is divided by the volume.

The density of a gas is difficult to measure because it is extremely low and changes greatly with variations in temperature and pressure. The mass of a gas is determined by subtracting the mass of an empty container

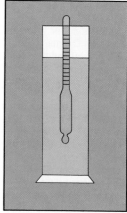

WORLD BOOK illustration by Arthur Grebetz

The density of a liquid can be determined with a hydrometer. This device is placed in the liquid and allowed to sink. How deep it sinks indicates density.

WORLD BOOK illustration by Arthur Grebetz

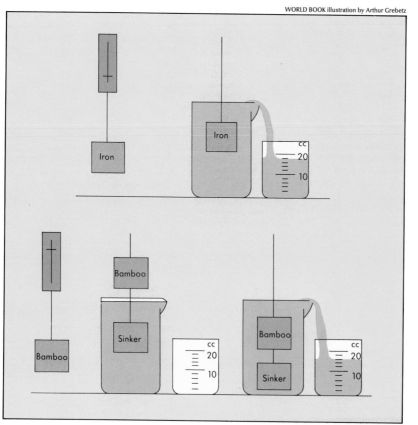

The density of a solid is determined by measuring the object's mass, calculating its volume, and dividing the mass by the volume. The volume can be determined by submerging the object in water, *top left.* The object's volume is equal to the volume of the water that overflows. When this method is used for a solid that floats, *bottom left,* a sinker is attached to the object to submerge it. The volume of the sinker is then subtracted from the total volume of water displaced, to determine the object's volume.

from the mass of the same container filled with the gas. The volume of the container can be found by measuring the amount of water that the container holds.

The *specific gravity* of a substance is related to its density. Specific gravity is the ratio of the mass of a given volume of the substance to the mass of an equal volume of water. It is found by dividing the density of the substance by the density of water at either 4° C (39° F.) or 20° C (68° F.).   Kenneth Schug

For the density of all the elements, see **Element, Chemical** (table).

Density of population. See **Population** (World population); **World** (People of the world).

Dent, John Charles (1841-1888), was a Canadian journalist and historian. He is best known for *The Last Forty Years,* a history of Canada from 1841 to 1881. He also wrote *The Canadian Portrait Gallery* and *The Story of the Upper Canadian Rebellion.*

Dent was born at Kendal, England, but came to Canada as an infant with his parents. He became a lawyer, but practiced for only a short time. He returned to England and served as a journalist with the *London Daily Telegraph.* He became editor of the *Evening Telegram* in 1876, and later joined the editorial staff of the *Globe* of Toronto.   David Jay Bercuson

Dental Association, American, is a national organization of dentists. Its purpose is to promote oral health care and the art and science of dentistry. The association has more than 500 local dental societies in the United States and its possessions. It has more than 148,000 members. The American Dental Association was founded in 1859. Headquarters are at 211 E. Chicago Avenue, Chicago, IL 60611.

Critically reviewed by the American Dental Association

Dental hygiene is the science and practice of preventing diseases of the teeth, gums, and other parts of the mouth. A dental hygienist is a licensed professional who provides services to help children and adults maintain good oral health.

What dental hygienists do. The dental hygienist cleans and polishes the teeth to help prevent gum disease and tooth decay. The hygienist also examines the mouth for signs of disease. The examination may include X rays of the teeth and jaws to locate dental decay or bone abnormalities. The hygienist may apply fluorides and plastic *sealants* to the teeth to help prevent cavities. The hygienist also may provide instruction to individuals and groups in the proper care of the mouth.

Education. Accredited schools of dental hygiene require that applicants have at least a high school education. People who enter schools of dental hygiene may choose either of two kinds of programs. They may take a two-year course, which leads to a certificate or diploma, or they may take a four-year course to earn a bachelor's degree. Subjects studied include anatomy, chemistry, and microbiology. They also include such special subjects as dental anatomy, dental health education, and the clinical practice of dental hygiene skills.

All states require dental hygienists to have a license to practice. In every state except Alabama, applicants must pass both national board examinations and state or regional board examinations to get the license. Alabama allows *preceptor training* of dental hygienists, an apprenticeship program under the supervision of a den-tist. People who complete a preceptorship are still required to complete a dental hygiene program at an accredited school if they wish to apply for a license in another state.

Career. Most dental hygienists work with dentists in private dental offices. Others work in industrial and hospital clinics, do public health work in government and private health agencies, or teach in schools of dental hygiene. For information about a career in dental hygiene, write to the American Dental Hygienists' Association, 444 N. Michigan Avenue, Chicago, IL 60611.

Critically reviewed by the American Dental Hygienists' Association

See also **Teeth** (Care of the teeth and gums).

Dental school. See **Dentistry** (Careers in dentistry).

Dentistry is the art and science of diagnosing, treating, and preventing diseases of the teeth, jaws, and surrounding soft tissues of the mouth. Dentists care for their patients in many ways, but mainly through their skill at recognizing, correcting, and preventing problems of the teeth and the tissues that support them.

Dental treatment includes a wide range of dental services. Some of these services focus on correcting problems of the teeth caused chiefly by dental decay. Such treatment, called *restoration,* often involves the use of some kind of dental filling. Other dental services deal with the prevention and treatment of diseases of the teeth and their supporting tissues and nerves. Still others concentrate on the position of the teeth in relation to each other and to the jawbones. Sometimes teeth require removal. This process, usually performed using an *anesthetic* (painkilling drug), is called *extraction.* Dentists may also treat injuries, infections, tumors, and various other conditions of the teeth, jawbones, and related tissues.

Dentistry is also practiced in dental offices where one or a number of dentists treat patients. Dental schools, in addition to training future dentists, also conduct research. This research provides improvements in the diagnosis and treatment of dental disorders. In addition, dentistry is practiced in large clinics, in hospitals, and in dental schools.

Branches of dentistry

A number of branches of dentistry have been established. They include (1) general dentistry, (2) orthodontics, (3) oral surgery, (4) periodontics, (5) prosthodontics, (6) oral pathology, (7) pediatric dentistry, and (8) endodontics.

General dentistry involves all phases of dental practice. Much dental practice is concerned with the prevention of mouth diseases. Dentists teach patients techniques for cleaning teeth correctly at home. They help patients establish nutritious eating habits that help keep teeth and gums healthy. Dentists also may clean the patient's teeth and gums. In many dental offices, specially trained *dental hygienists* help dentists with these activities (see **Dental hygiene**).

General dental treatment includes filling cavities, extracting teeth, and replacing lost teeth with *bridges* or *dentures* (see **Teeth** [Dental decay]). Difficult problems are sometimes cared for by specialists in other branches of dentistry.

Orthodontics specializes in the correction and prevention of irregularities of the position of teeth. These ir-

Dentistry involves diagnosing, treating, and preventing diseases of the teeth, gums, and jaws. Regular checkups are part of good dental care. In this photo, a dentist examines a patient's teeth during an office visit.

Northwestern University (Paul Baker)

regularities usually happen as the teeth grow during early childhood and may produce *malocclusion* (bad bite). The majority of malocclusions occur because the teeth are too large for the amount of jaw space available. As a result, the teeth become crowded. Orthodontists correct malocclusions with braces or other mechanical devices that move the teeth into a better position. See **Orthodontics.**

Oral surgery is concerned with the surgical correction of oral problems. Many of these problems are associated with the *third molars,* also called *wisdom teeth.* These teeth may be too difficult to remove in a regular dental office if they are *impacted* (heavily wedged) in the jawbone. Oral surgeons remove tumors and cysts from the mouth and treat fractures of the teeth and jaws caused by injuries. They also correct cosmetic problems of the jaws and face, using methods similar to plastic surgery.

Periodontics deals with diseases of the tooth-supporting tissues—the bones surrounding the teeth, the

ligaments between bones and teeth, and the gum tissue. Periodontal diseases are responsible for more tooth loss in adults than any other dental problem. These diseases can be prevented by proper home dental care.

Prosthodontics deals with the replacement of missing or damaged teeth. Replacement often involves the construction of complete or partial dentures, which are removable devices. Sometimes missing teeth are replaced by bridgework cemented to the remaining teeth. Replacements are made of plastic, porcelain, gold or other metals, or combinations of these materials.

Oral pathology deals mainly with the diagnosis of mouth diseases using laboratory procedures. Soft or hard tissues from the patient's mouth may be examined with the aid of a microscope to identify tumors or other disorders. Some oral pathologists also specialize in *forensic dentistry,* which applies oral pathology to legal cases. These specialists are frequently called upon to identify dead people by comparing dental records with the teeth and tissues of the deceased.

Pediatric dentistry specializes in the dental problems of children. Dentists who practice pediatric dentistry are called *pedodontists.* Children sometimes require special attention in treating dental decay and other problems. Pedodontists also care for other special patients, such as adults who have mental or physical disabilities.

Endodontics involves prevention, diagnosis, and treatment of diseased *pulp* and other dental tissues. The pulp is the central portion of the tooth that contains nerves and blood vessels. Severe dental decay and other injuries may cause infection or death of the pulp. This pulp can be removed by a process known as *root canal treatment.* Once removed, the pulp can be replaced with special filling material. Such treatment saves many teeth that would otherwise be extracted.

History

Early dentistry. Human beings have always experienced dental problems. The ancient Greeks, Romans,

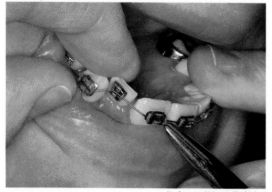

Northwestern University (Paul Baker)

Braces for teeth consist of metal bands, *above,* that are placed around each tooth and connected by wires. Orthodontists use braces to correct irregular positioning of the teeth and jaws.

and Egyptians used various remedies for toothaches, including tooth extraction. People in early civilizations even developed gold dental bridges. In the Middle Ages, dentistry was practiced by such craftworkers as jewelers and barbers.

In 1728, Pierre Fauchard, a French dental scientist, published *The Surgeon Dentist.* This book detailed complex dental devices, instruments, and methods and is considered a landmark in the history of dentistry. Dentistry emerged as a profession in the mid-1800's. In 1840, the world's first dental school, the Baltimore College of Dental Surgery, was founded in Baltimore by the American dentists Horace Hayden and Chapin Harris.

The teeth of the American colonists of the 1600's and 1700's were considered the worst in the world. Poor diet and inadequate dental cleaning and maintenance caused many colonists to lose at least half of their teeth before the age of 20. The founding of the first dental schools in the United States marked the beginning of the solution of this problem for Americans. The United States then became the world's leading center for dental learning and practice.

Modern dentistry began during the mid-1800's with the introduction of *general anesthetics* to relieve discomfort during dental procedures. General anesthetics make patients unconscious and unable to feel pain throughout the body. Nitrous oxide was first used as a general anesthetic by the American dentist Horace Wells in 1844. Two years later, another American dentist, W. T. G. Morton, gave the first formal demonstration of the use of ether as an anesthetic (see **Morton, William T. G.**).

In 1884, the American physician William Halsted used cocaine to block pain sensations in the lower jaw. Cocaine was the first *local anesthetic*—that is, a drug that blocks pain in only part of the body and does not cause unconsciousness.

By 1900, the use of dental drills had become widespread in the United States. In addition, principles for filling cavities had been established through the work of the American dentist G. V. Black. These important developments, along with the discovery of X rays in 1895 and the use of silver filling materials, helped revolutionize dentistry.

Since the 1950's, the addition of *fluorides* to water supplies and toothpastes has greatly reduced tooth decay (see **Fluoridation**). The development of high speed dental drills has lessened the pain involved in dental procedures. In addition, the development of plastic filling materials has made it possible for dentists to cover up unsightly discolorations, cracks, or gaps in teeth.

Careers

Dentistry in the United States and Canada is a large and well-organized profession. There are about 135,000 dentists in the United States and about 13,800 dentists in Canada. The great majority of these dentists have a private dental practice. Most of the remaining dentists work in the military, in public health, in various government organizations and dental societies, as consultants, or as teachers or researchers in dental schools. People who want to become dentists must first attend a school of dentistry. There are about 60 dental schools in the United States and about 10 in Canada.

Educational requirements. All dental schools require a high level of scholastic achievement before admission. Applicants must have at least two years of college education, but most dental students are college graduates. Prospective dental students must also take a dental aptitude test. This test identifies those students who are most likely to succeed in dental subjects.

The usual course of study in dental school lasts four years. The first two years are devoted to studying basic medical and dental sciences, as well as dental laboratory techniques. Clinical aspects of dentistry are emphasized in the final two years of dental school. During that time, students perform dental procedures on patients. Upon graduation, students receive either a Doctor of Dental Surgery (D.D.S.) degree or a Doctor of Dental Medicine (D.M.D.) degree.

Licensing. All U.S. states and Canadian provinces require that dentists be licensed to practice. To obtain a license, a person must have a D.D.S. or D.M.D. degree from an approved school and must also pass a special examination. State and local dental societies work with state governments in administering licensing examinations.

Organizations. The main professional organization of dentists in the United States is the American Dental Association. Some functions of this organization are to promote dentistry in matters of legislation, to inspect and approve dental schools, and to produce educational material for the public. Its headquarters are at 211 E. Chicago Avenue, Chicago, IL 60611. The Canadian Dental Association, performs a similar function in Canada. It has headquarters at 1815 Alta Vista Drive, Ottawa, ON K1G 3Y6.   John P. Wortel

See also **Teeth; Dental Association, American; Hypnotism** (Uses of hypnotism); **Prosthetics; Orthodontics.**

Additional resources

Peterson, Shailer A. *Preparing to Enter Dental School.* Prentice-Hall, 1979.
Ring, Malvin E. *Dentistry: An Illustrated History.* Abrams, 1985.
Ward, Brian R. *Dental Care.* Watts, 1986. For younger readers.

Granger Collection

A traveling tooth-puller, like the one shown above, was one of many untrained people who practiced dentistry in the 1700's. Dentistry became a recognized profession during the 1800's.

Downtown Denver is the commercial center of the Rocky Mountain region. The Colorado Capitol, *center,* stands near the modern business district.

Milt and Joan Mann

Denver is the capital of Colorado, and the distribution, manufacturing, and transportation center for the Rocky Mountain region. The city is also a central point for snow sports and serves as a gateway to nearby mountain vacation spots. Denver lies on the South Platte River, 10 miles (16 kilometers) east of the Rocky Mountains. It is called the *Mile High City* because the Capitol stands on land 1 mile (1.6 kilometers) above sea level.

When gold prospectors founded Denver in 1858, it formed part of the Kansas Territory. The town was named for James W. Denver, the governor of the territory. From 1860 to 1945, Denver was a mining and agricultural community. After World War II ended in 1945, the city became known for its industries. Denver's continued expansion in industry and population has made it one of the nation's fastest growing cities.

The city covers 114 square miles (295 square kilometers) and has the same boundaries as Denver County.

Facts in brief

Population: 492,365. *Metropolitan area population*—1,428,836. *Consolidated metropolitan area*—1,618,461.
Area: *City*—114 sq. mi. (295 km²). *Metropolitan area*—3,778 sq. mi. (9,785 km²). *Consolidated metropolitan area*—4,528 sq. mi. (11,727 km²).
Altitude: 5,280 ft. (1,609 m) above sea level.
Climate: *Average temperature*—January, 30° F. (−1° C); July, 73° F. (23° C). *Average annual precipitation* (rainfall, melted snow, and other forms of moisture)—15 in. (38 cm). For the monthly weather in Denver, see **Colorado** (Climate).
Government: Mayor-council. *Terms*—4 years for the mayor and the 13 council members.
Founded: 1858. Incorporated as a city in 1861.
City flag: The blue, red, white, and yellow design symbolizes the sky, soil, mountains, and sun.
City seal: The black and gold circular seal has an eagle, a shield with a key, a smokestack, the state Capitol, the sun setting over the mountains, and the words *City and County of Denver Seal.*

Denver and nearby Boulder form part of a consolidated metropolitan area that covers 4,528 square miles (11,727 square kilometers).

Broadway, Colfax Avenue, and Larimer Street form a triangle around Denver's main business district. Cherry Creek joins the South Platte River northwest of the triangle. Skyscrapers with banks and investment firms make 17th Street the "Wall Street of the West."

The 16th Street Mall, a 14-block-long pedestrian mall, is located in downtown Denver. During the day, downtown office workers and shoppers mingle among the mall's colorful pushcarts, street musicians, and old-fashioned horse-drawn carriages. Many high-rise apartment buildings have been constructed near the west end of the mall.

Southeast of the city's main business district, the Civic Center includes the City and County Building, the Colorado State Capitol, the Denver Art Museum, and the Denver Public Library. The City Auditorium and Theater, Mile High Stadium, and the Currigan Exhibition Hall stand west of the business district.

Military installations that are located in the Denver area include the Air Force Accounting and Finance Center, Fitzsimons General Hospital, and Lowry Air Force Base.

The people. About 12 per cent of Denver's people are of Mexican ancestry. Blacks form about 12 per cent of the city's population. Denver also has a small number of American Indians and people of Oriental descent.

Economy. More of Denver's people work for the federal and state governments than for any other employer. Denver is the national or regional headquarters of more federal agencies than any other U.S. city except Washington, D.C. The Denver mint, near the Capitol, makes millions of coins every year.

The Denver metropolitan area has more than 1,500 manufacturing plants. Food processing ranks as the city's chief manufacturing activity. Other Denver products include defense, high-technology, and transportation equipment. The Denver Union Stockyards are one of the nation's major livestock centers.

A large number of warehouses help make Denver the distribution center of the Rocky Mountain region. The city also serves as the region's transportation center. Many commercial airlines use Stapleton International Airport, one of the world's busiest airports. Railroad passenger trains, six freight lines, and several highways also serve the city.

Seven television stations and about 40 radio stations serve Denver. The city has three daily newspapers—the *Daily Journal,* the *Post,* and the *Rocky Mountain News.*

Education. Denver's public school system has about 100 elementary schools and 25 secondary schools. The city also has almost 60 church-supported schools. A seven-member board of education runs the public schools. Board members are elected to serve six-year terms.

More than 80 per cent of the public school students are white or of Mexican ancestry, and most of the rest are black. Several thousand children are bused to achieve a balance among these groups in certain Denver schools. The busing program began in 1974.

Colleges and universities in Denver include the University of Colorado Medical School, the Denver Conservative Baptist Theological Seminary, the University of Denver, Iliff School of Theology, Loretto Heights College, Metropolitan State College, Regis College, and St. Thomas Seminary.

Cultural life and recreation. The Denver Art Museum owns one of the world's finest collections of Western Indian art. The Colorado Heritage Center has a collection of articles from early cliff dwellers of the Colorado area.

The Denver Public Library, the largest in the Rocky Mountain region, operates 18 branches. The Denver Symphony Orchestra performs in the Denver Center for the Performing Arts. The Elitch Summer Theater, the nation's oldest theater with a permanent group of performers, was established in Denver in 1891.

Denver

Denver, the "Mile High City," lies near the center of Colorado. It is the largest city in the state and the commercial and industrial center of the Rocky Mountain Region. The map below shows the city and its main points of interest. Denver and Denver County have the same boundaries.

▬▬▬ City boundary	┼┼┼ Railroad
– – – County boundary	▪ Point of interest
▬▬ Major road	Federal area
─── Other road	Park or cemetery

WORLD BOOK map

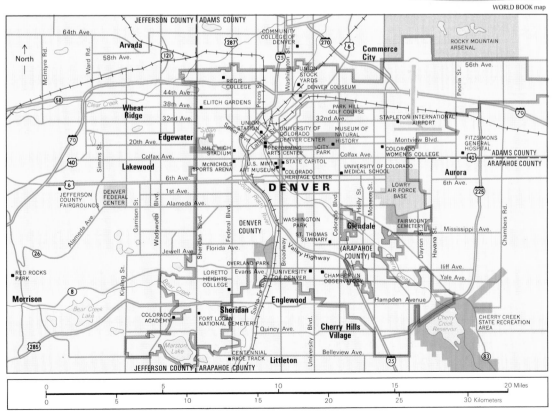

Denver maintains about 100 parks within the city and about 32 square miles (83 square kilometers) of parkland in the Rocky Mountains. Winter Park, a ski resort owned by the city, is located in the mountains. The Denver Broncos of the National Football League play their home games in Mile High Stadium. The Denver Nuggets of the National Basketball Association play in McNichols Sports Arena.

Government. Denver has a mayor-council form of government. The people of Denver elect a mayor and 13 city council members—all to four-year terms. In 1902, Denver led a home-rule movement among the cities of Colorado. As a result of this movement, an amendment to the state constitution made Denver both a city and a county. Denver gets most of its income from taxes that are placed on personal property, real estate, and general sales.

History. Denver was founded in 1858, after prospectors found gold at Cherry Creek. The community became a supply point for mining settlements during the "Pikes Peak or Bust" gold rush of 1859. Denver and nearby Auraria merged in April 1860. The next year, Denver was incorporated as a city. The city became capital of the Colorado Territory in 1867 and the capital of Colorado when it became a state in 1876.

Denver expanded with completion of the Denver Pacific Railroad in 1870. A silver-mining boom gave the city additional wealth during the 1880's and 1890's.

During the early 1900's, Denver changed from a prairie town to a beautiful city. It established many parkways and planted trees throughout the city. By 1910, it had become the commercial center of the Rocky Mountain region. The Moffat Tunnel, a mountain railway route from Denver through James Peak, was completed in 1927.

The population of the Denver area soared during and after World War II (1939-1945). Many members of the U.S. armed forces who had been stationed in the area moved there after the war. Between 1950 and 1960, Denver's population rose from 612,128 to 929,383.

During the 1970's, Denver faced the problem of preserving its natural beauty while continuing to expand the city's industry. In 1968, Denver prohibited all open burning of wastes by city agencies in an effort to lessen air pollution. Since 1968, the South Platte Area Development Council has worked with the city to reduce industrial pollution on the South Platte River.

The Denver Urban Renewal Authority began the Skyline Project in 1968 to replace and restore old, run-down buildings in the city's downtown area. This project includes apartment and office buildings, the Japanese Cultural Center, and the Denver Center for the Performing Arts. The Skyline Project was completed in 1985. In 1990, the huge Denver Convention Complex was completed in downtown Denver.

One of Denver's most successful suburban business developments is the Denver Technological Center (DTC), an office park located southeast of the city. Development of the center began in the 1960's, and new buildings continue to be built in the early 1990's. Today, the DTC is the home of more than 1,000 national, regional, and local companies.   Clark Secrest

See also **Colorado** (pictures).

Deodorant is a consumer product or an ingredient designed to reduce, prevent, or cover up unpleasant body odors. Most external body odor occurs when bacteria react with perspiration and secretions on the skin. Perspiration itself has no odor. Deodorants generally contain chemicals that stop the growth of bacteria. Many deodorants contain a fragrance that masks odor. Some deodorants called *antiperspirants* also reduce the amount of perspiration.

The word *deodorant* is most frequently associated with personal products that act against underarm odor. However, deodorants are also made for the feet and genital area, and to reduce odors from surgical openings and other disorders. Deodorants and antiperspirants are manufactured in the form of creams, roll-on liquids or lotions, sticks, and sprays. Common antibacterial ingredients in deodorants include zinc or magnesium salts, benzethonium chloride, and triclosan. Aluminum, zirconium, or aluminum-zirconium compounds in most antiperspirants act to reduce perspiration.

Antiperspirants alter a body function and so are classified as drugs by the United States Food and Drug Administration (FDA). They must meet FDA regulations for safety and effectiveness. Underarm deodorants that do not contain an antiperspirant ingredient are not subject to these regulations.   Clarence R. Robbins

Deodorizer is a substance or device that eliminates or reduces disagreeable odors. Such odors are sometimes called *malodors.*

Most deodorizers are *masking deodorizers,* which emit fragrances to cover malodors. Masking deodorizers include incense, scented candles, fragrant sprays, and fragrant gels. Deodorizers called *disinfectants* are applied to surfaces on which bacteria that cause malodors live. The disinfectants eliminate odor by killing the bacteria. Many disinfectants also contain a fragrance. *Chemical deodorizers,* such as the chemical compounds *potassium permanganate* and *hydrogen peroxide,* eliminate malodors by means of *oxidation.* In this process, oxygen from the compounds eliminates the odors by combining with chemicals that cause the odors.

To eliminate malodors in large buildings, *mechanical deodorizers* are typically used. Most mechanical deodorizers are *air cleaners.* These devices remove from the air impurities that cause malodors. The air is drawn through the devices by means of fans. In air cleaners called *electrostatic precipitators,* wires in the device give a positive electric charge to airborne particles that cause malodors. The positively charged particles are then captured on negatively charged metal plates in the device. Other air cleaners use a *scrubbing* process. In one form of scrubbing, air that contains malodorous particles is forced through water or some other liquid. The particles dissolve in the liquid and so are removed from the air. See **Air cleaner.**   Patricia Ann Mullen

De Oñate, Juan. See **Oñate, Juan de.**

Deoxyribonucleic acid. See **Nucleic acid.**

De Palma, *duh PAHL muh,* **Ralph** (1883-1956), was a pioneer American automobile race driver. He won the Indianapolis Speedway 500-mile (805-kilometer) race in 1915 and the national driving title in 1912 and 1914. De Palma set a world record of 149.875 mph (241.2 kph) in 1919. He claimed 2,557 victories in 2,889 races. Many of these were match races against another driver, rather than open competition. De Palma was born in Italy.   Sylvia Wilkinson

Department of . . . See the articles on the executive departments of the United States government listed under their key word, as in **Labor, Department of.**

Department store is a large store that sells many kinds of goods in separate departments under one management. It also provides a variety of services. Most department stores occupy a single building and cover at least two floors. In a typical department store, perfumes, jewelry, and similar articles are located on the first floor, and clothing, furniture and appliances are on the upper floors. Many department stores also sell bargain merchandise in the basement.

A typical department store is organized into five divisions: *merchandising, operations, promotion, finance,* and *personnel.* Merchandising involves the buying of merchandise for the store and the selling of it to customers. Operations includes security, customer service, maintenance, and general housekeeping. Promotion deals with advertising and displaying merchandise, and with public relations. Finance covers accounting, credit management, and similar financial matters. Personnel deals with the hiring and training of employees and the keeping of certain records on them.

Many historians believe that Aristide Boucicaut, a French merchant, established the first department store. Boucicaut managed a store in Paris called *Bon Marché* (French for *good bargain*). Bon Marché originally sold only fabrics, but in the 1850's, it began to sell a large variety of goods, arranged by department.

Boucicaut's retailing practices were quickly copied by such American businessmen as Marshall Field, Eben Jordan, Rowland H. Macy, Benjamin L. Marsh, Alexander T. Stewart, and John Wanamaker. By the early 1900's, department stores had spread throughout the United States.

Early department stores differed from those of today in a number of ways. For example, the first department stores were established in downtown areas, but many are now located in suburbs. The early department stores were one-store operations. Today, the majority of department store organizations have several stores within a metropolitan area—or even in different cities (see **Chain store**). Originally, department stores provided a high level of personal service to their customers in all departments. Many modern stores, however, have some departments that are largely self-service. The first department stores occupied several stories and offered a great variety of merchandise. Today's newer department stores occupy only a few floors and sell a smaller variety of goods. In addition, many department stores now sell merchandise through direct-mail activities and other methods (see **Mail-order business**).

Department stores in the United States sell more than $100 billion of merchandise annually. The best known of these stores include Marshall Field & Company and Sears, Roebuck and Company, both with headquarters in Chicago; J. L. Hudson Company of Detroit; Jordan Marsh of Boston; R. H. Macy and Company of New York City; Neiman-Marcus of Dallas; and John Wanamaker of Philadelphia. Among the leading Canadian department stores are the Hudson's Bay Company of Winnipeg, Man., and T. Eaton Company, Ltd., and Simpson's, Ltd., of Toronto, Ont.   William H. Bolen

Depilatory. See **Hair** (Disorders).

Deportation is the action a government takes when it forces an alien to leave the country and return to the place where the alien was born or had lived. A government may deport an alien because the person entered the country illegally, or because it is believed he or she may harm the nation's interests in some way.

In the United States, the attorney general has the power to deport aliens as part of his responsibility to enforce immigration laws. Aliens may be deported if they become public charges, stay longer than their visas permit, or engage in subversive or criminal activities. Naturalized citizens who lose their citizenship may be deported by the Department of Justice.

Deportation also means banishing, or sending a convict to a penal settlement outside the country as punishment for a crime.   Robert J. Pranger

Deposit, in geology. See **Coal** (Where coal is found); **Rock** (Sedimentary rock).

Deposition, *DEHP uh ZIHSH uhn,* in law, is a witness's testimony that is taken outside of court. Lawyers generally obtain depositions from a person who is unable to appear in court. Lawyers may also take a deposition before a trial to discover existing evidence or leads to new evidence. In a deposition, the witness testifies under oath before a notary public or other judicial officer. The testimony consists of a statement in answer to questions, either oral or written, asked by the officer.

When one party in a lawsuit arranges for a deposition, all other involved parties must be notified. They must have the opportunity to be present at the deposition and to question the witness.   Sherman L. Cohn

Depreciation, *dih PREE shee AY shuhn,* is the loss of value. Buildings, machines, vehicles, and other property *depreciate* (lose value) through use or accident, because they grow older, or because a new, better product replaces them. In accounting, depreciation is figured as a normal cost of doing business.

The term *depreciation* is also used to mean the loss of value or purchasing power resulting from an increase in the level of domestic prices. In this sense, the term refers to the currency of a country becoming worth less relative to currencies of other countries. See also **National income** (Determining national income).

Irving Morrissett

Depressant is the former name for a group of drugs that slow the activity of the nervous system. Today, physicians call these drugs *antianxiety and hypnotic drugs.* They are used to ease pain, cause sleep, or reduce tension. Many are either habit-forming or addictive. If a person takes such a drug daily for several weeks, a physical or psychological dependence on it may develop. An overdose can be fatal.

Antianxiety and hypnotic drugs include alcohol, sedatives, and tranquilizers. Alcohol decreases most brain functions. Sedatives, such as barbiturates, calm a patient or bring on sleep. Tranquilizers lessen tension without decreasing mental or physical activity.

Christopher A. Rodowskas, Jr.

See also **Drug** (Antianxiety and hypnotic drugs); **Alcoholism** (Effects); **Sedative; Tranquilizer.**

Depression is a deep, extended slump in total business activity. Buying and selling drop during a depression, causing a decline in production, prices, income, and employment. Money becomes scarce. Many businesses fail, and many workers lose their jobs. A depression can hit an industry, a region, a nation, or the world.

A depression might develop if sales drop in a number of stores. Because of the fall in sales, the stores order less merchandise from manufacturers. The manufacturers, in turn, lower production, cut orders from suppliers, and invest less money in new equipment and factories. As sales drop, prices tend to fall, further reducing business income. Employers lay off workers as business income falls. Bankruptcies may follow.

The depression cycle occurs again and again as unemployment rises. Unemployed workers have less money to spend, leading to further drops in sales, production, income, and employment. The slump feeds on itself, becoming progressively worse until business activity picks up.

Not all business slumps grow into depressions. A milder slowdown in business activity is called a *recession.* Some depressions last several years, but most recessions last only a year or less. In the United States and other industrial nations, depressions and recessions alternate with business expansions. This alternation is called the *business cycle.*

Severe depressions occurred in the United States in 1837, 1873, 1893, 1907, and 1929. Financial panics at the start of these depressions sharply reduced the amount of money available for spending. Depressions have also occurred after wars, when wartime spending suddenly stops. The worst depression in history was the Great Depression, which struck the world in 1929 and continued through the 1930's.

Effects

Effects on individuals. Depressions hurt great numbers of people, especially workers who lose their jobs. Bank failures wipe out the savings of depositors if such funds are not insured. Many people cannot meet rent or mortgage payments and lose their homes.

During a depression, some people must live on charity to survive. They may feel angry and humiliated because they cannot support themselves.

Depressions cause marriage and birth rates to decline. Young people who cannot find jobs delay marriage. Couples uncertain about the future may have fewer children than they would like.

Long periods of unemployment cause people to lose faith in themselves and in the future. After a depression, many people value security above all else.

Some people profit from a depression. For example, those who have enough money can buy businesses, stocks, and other property at low prices. Salaried workers may live better as prices drop and their income buys more and more.

Effects on society. Society suffers as a depression spreads mass unemployment, poverty, and despair. Depressions also change certain beliefs. These changes can affect society. The Great Depression caused many people to distrust business and led the government to regulate business and economic affairs. This increased regulation led to the widespread belief that the government should maintain high employment and guarantee citizens a good life. After the Great Depression, many people no longer trusted employers to protect workers. As a result, labor unions gained more members and

Culver

Lines of jobless Americans were a common sight in many large cities during the Great Depression of the 1930's. Men in this bread line in Brooklyn were waiting for free food.

greater public acceptance than ever before.

A depression makes some people lose faith in their system of government. They may come to believe any leader who promises a change. Leaders who took power during a depression include Adolf Hitler, who ruled Germany as dictator from 1933 to 1945, and Benito Mussolini, dictator of Italy from 1922 to 1943.

Relations between nations suffer during a depression. Each country tries to protect its own interests without concern for other nations.

Causes and prevention

Economists disagree on what causes depressions and how they can be prevented. Some economists believe that psychological factors, such as people's optimism or pessimism, determine decisions to save or spend.

Several theories maintain that population changes or inventions cause periods of expansion and *contraction* (depression or recession). When immigration or higher birth rates cause a population to grow, demand tends to increase. When population growth slows down, demand drops. Such inventions as the automobile and color television spur business investment and consumer spending, causing expansion. After demand for these products has been satisfied, spending drops off, resulting in contraction.

Still other theories suggest that during an expansion, businesses invest too heavily in buying equipment and constructing plants and offices. Then, for some time, they have no need to buy or build, and a contraction results.

Most experts believe that another severe depression can be prevented in various ways. For example, insurance provided by the United States government guarantees that bank depositors will not lose their savings. Social security and unemployment insurance guarantee that people will have some money to spend. In addition, economists can predict swings in the economy, enabling the government to take preventive action.

A government's chief methods of preventing a depression are by its *fiscal policy* and its *monetary policy.* Fiscal policy refers to a government's taxing and spending programs. Monetary policy refers to how a government manages the nation's *money supply*—that is, the total quantity of money in the country, including cash and bank deposits. Most economists stress either fiscal policy or monetary policy as the best means of preventing a depression.

Fiscal policy. John Maynard Keynes, a British economist who published his theories during the 1930's, explained a depression as the result of a drop in *effective demand*—that is, total spending by consumers, business, and government. He believed that increased savings slow the rate of economic growth. According to Keynes, people's decisions to save or spend depend on what they expect the economy to do. If they expect bad times ahead, they may decide to save their money. Similarly, if businesses do not foresee future sales, they will not invest money in new products or equipment.

According to Keynes, a government can prevent depressions by encouraging spending. Tax cuts, for example, give people more money to spend. A government can increase its own spending in such activities as public works and aid to the poor. In addition, Keynes believed that lower interest rates encourage people and businesses to borrow money, which they will either spend or invest.

Monetary policy. Milton Friedman, an American economist, became the main spokesman of a group of economists called *monetarists.* He received the Nobel Prize in 1976 for his research in economics.

Monetarists stress the role of monetary policy and the Federal Reserve System in preventing depressions. They point out that the Federal Reserve System deepened the Great Depression by allowing the money supply to shrink in the 1930's. The Federal Reserve System is a United States government agency that controls the nation's money supply.

According to monetarists, severe swings in the nation's economy could be prevented if the Federal Reserve increased the money supply at a steady rate. They

U.S. prosperity and depressions since 1790   The United States has gone through many periods of prosperity and depression. This graph shows how much business activity has been above or below the long-term economic trend each year. Since 1902, business activity has been measured by industrial production, including manufacturing and mining. Before 1902, such things as exports, government receipts, and canal freight were also used to measure business activity.

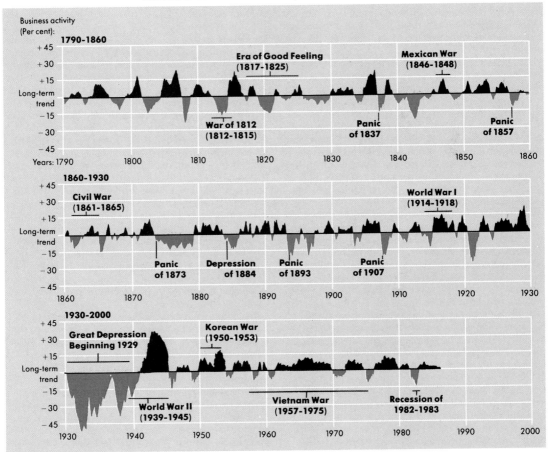

Source: AmeriTrust Company, Cleveland, Ohio.

recommend a rate of 3 to 5 per cent, the approximate rate at which production increases. Monetarists oppose Keynesian proposals to use government spending and taxation to control the economy.   Clair E. Morris

Related articles in *World Book* include:

See also *Depression* in the Research Guide/Index, Volume 22, for a *Reading and Study Guide.*

Additional resources

Glassman, Bruce. *The Crash of '29 and the New Deal.* Silver Burdett, 1986. For younger readers.
Hoffmann, Charles. *The Depression of the Nineties: An Economic History.* Greenwood, 1970.
Kindleberger, Charles P. *Manias, Panics, and Crashes: A History of Financial Crises.* Rev. ed. Basic Bks., 1989.
McElvaine, Robert S. *The Great Depression.* Times Bks. 1984.

Depression is a serious mental disorder in which a person suffers long periods of sadness and other negative feelings. The term *depression* also describes a normal mood involving the sadness, grief, disappointment, or loneliness that everyone experiences at times. This article discusses depression as a mental disorder.

About 10 million to 14 million people in the United States suffer depression. Depressed people may feel fearful, guilty, or helpless. They often cry, and many lose interest in work and social life. Many cases of depression also involve aches, fatigue, loss of appetite, or other physical symptoms. Some depressed patients try to harm or kill themselves. Periods of depression may occur alone, or they may alternate with periods of *mania* (extreme joy and overactivity) in a disorder called *bipolar disorder*, also known as *manic-depressive disorder.*

Psychiatrists do not fully understand the causes of depression, but they have several theories. Some psychiatrists believe that depression follows the loss of a relative, a friend, a job, or a valued goal. Many psychiatrists believe that experiences that occur during early childhood may make some people especially subject to depression later in life.

According to another theory, disturbances in the chemistry of the brain occur during depression. Brain cells communicate with one another by releasing chemicals called *neurotransmitters.* Some experts think that certain neurotransmitters become underactive during depression and overactive during mania. These changes in brain chemistry may be related to disturbances in the body's internal rhythms.

Treatments for depression include hospitalization, psychotherapy, drugs, and *electroconvulsive* (electroshock) therapy. Hospitalization is an essential treatment for depressed patients who are suicidal. In psychotherapy, the psychiatrist tries to understand (1) the childhood events that make a person subject to depression and (2) the events that preceded the patient's current depression. The most commonly prescribed antidepressant is a drug called *fluoxetine.* Fluoxetine is marketed under the name *Prozac. Lithium carbonate* is a drug used in treating manic-depressive persons. Electroconvulsive therapy is generally used only for patients

who fail to respond to other treatment.   Philip A. Berger

See also **Mental illness** (Mood disorders).

Additional resources

Gordon, Sol. *When Living Hurts.* Dell, 1989. First published in 1985. Suitable for younger readers.
Klein, Donald F., and Wender, P. H. *Do You Have a Depressive Illness? How to Tell, What to Do.* NAL, 1988.
Papolos, Demitri F. and Janice. *Overcoming Depression.* Harper, 1987.

Depth charge is a weapon designed to destroy submarines. Depth charges explode underwater, creating shock waves that cause submarines to collapse.

Depth charges that were used during World Wars I and II (1914-1918 and 1939-1945) consisted of light metal cases filled with TNT or other explosives. Ships laid a series of these depth charges in a pattern, rolling some off the deck and firing others to the side.

In the mid-1950's, the United States Navy developed atomic depth charges, to be dropped by antisubmarine planes. These bombs contain a core of fissionable material surrounded by heavy casing (see **Fission**). Each charge has a mechanical device to control its firing time and can be preset to explode at varying depths. Atomic depth charges eliminate the need to know the exact location of a submarine. They can destroy targets within 1 square mile (2.6 square kilometers), and are particularly effective against submarines at great depths. Today, the U.S. Navy uses B57 nuclear depth bombs, which were introduced in 1964.   Jack Sweetman

See also **Torpedo.**

De Quincey, *dih KWIHN see,* **Thomas** (1785-1859), was an English essayist. He wrote a rare kind of imaginative prose that was highly ornate, full of subtle rhythms, and sensitive to the sound and arrangement of words.

At the age of 19, De Quincey started to take opium to ease the pain of severe neuralgic headaches. He was addicted to the drug until he died. He told the story of his addiction in his most famous work, *Confessions of an English Opium Eater* (1821). De Quincey is also known for his imaginative essays describing his visions under the influence of opium. The visions were gorgeous and lofty, as well as tortured and terrible. They have a sense of fearful reality, as in "Vision of Sudden Death" (part of the essay "The English Mail-Coach," 1849).

De Quincey wrote a variety of critical essays, including "On the Knocking at the Gate in *Macbeth"* (1823), "On Murder Considered as One of the Fine Arts" (1827), and "The Literature of Knowledge and the Literature of Power" (1848). His autobiographical works include important essays on writers of his time, such as William Wordsworth, Samuel Taylor Coleridge, and Charles Lamb.

De Quincey was born in Manchester. He lived in Edinburgh from 1828 until his death.   Karl Kroeber

Derain, *duh RAN,* **André,** *ahn DRAY* (1880-1954), was a French artist. He and his friends Henri Matisse and Maurice de Vlaminck were leaders of the fauves, a group of painters of the early 1900's.

Derain's fauve paintings, his most significant works, feature vivid colors, particularly blues, oranges, and reds. He applied paint with short, broken brushstrokes. Derain's paintings are flat in design, with little use of perspective. Many of them show the influence of the artists Paul Gauguin and Vincent van Gogh. Derain's

London Bridge is reproduced in the **Fauves** article. His works after about 1913 are more traditional than his fauve paintings. Derain was also noted for his book illustrations and his costume and set designs for ballets and plays. He was born in Chatou.   Willard E. Misfeldt

Derby, *DUR bee* or (British) *DAHR bee,* is a stiff felt hat with a dome-shaped crown. The British usually call it a *bowler.* The name derby may come from England. The Earl of Derby, who established the Derby horse races in Epsom in 1780, often wore such hats. They were popular among men who attended the races. Derbies were first made in the United States in 1850 at South Norwalk, Conn.   Lois M. Gurel

Derby, *DAHR bee,* is a famous horse race begun in 1780 by the Earl of Derby in Epsom, England. The race, called "the Epsom Derby" in England, is known as "the English Derby" in other countries. The horse race at Churchill Downs, Louisville, Ky., was copied after the Derby (see **Kentucky Derby**).

Derby, Kentucky. See Kentucky Derby.

Dermaptera. See Insect (table); **Earwig.**

Dermatitis, *DUR muh TY tihs,* is an inflammation of the skin that itches or burns. It shows redness, swelling, blisters, oozing, crusting, or scaling. It may be produced by friction, heat, cold, or the sun's rays. However, chemical agents most frequently cause dermatitis. These may be strong poisons that affect anyone's skin, or chemicals that irritate the skin of a person who is especially sensitive to the chemicals. These chemicals may be found in certain plants, foods, fabrics, dyes, cosmetics, and medications. See also **Allergy; Eczema.**   Yelva Liptzin Lynfield

Dermatology, *DUR muh TAHL uh jee,* is the branch of medicine that deals with the prevention, diagnosis, and treatment of skin diseases. Physicians who specialize in this field are called *dermatologists.*

Skin ailments treated by dermatologists include blisters, burns, infections, inflammations, tumors, and warts. Dermatologists also treat many children and teen-agers who have acne or certain allergies. Dermatologists are trained to recognize changes in the skin that indicate a disease in other parts of the body. For example, a certain type of facial rash may be a symptom of *systemic lupus erythematosus,* a disease that affects many internal organs as well as the skin (see **Lupus**).

Dermatology includes research on the structure and function of skin. Some dermatologists perform surgery to correct certain conditions.   David T. Woodley

See also **Skin** and its list of *Related articles.*

Dermis. See Skin.

Derrick. See Crane.

Derringer. See Handgun (Early handguns; picture: Some historic handguns).

Dervish, *DUR vihsh,* is a member of one of the mystical religious orders of the Islamic religion. Most dervishes lead wandering lives of self-denial. They live by begging. The word *dervish* comes from Persian, and means *beggar* or *religious mendicant.* In the A.D. 1000's and 1100's, Muslim mystics organized the first dervish orders. Each order lived in a center resembling a monastery and had its own ritual. One order is known commonly as the *whirling dervishes* because they whirl and dance to the music of a reed pipe as part of their worship. Other orders give special prayers or practice unusual forms of devotion, such as wearing rough cloth-ing, fasting, and keeping vigils. Many Muslims consider dervishes holy, and often think them capable of miracles or predicting the future. Others criticize the dervish orders and practices for introducing changes to fundamental Islam. Dervishes are sometimes called *fakirs.*   Richard C. Martin

DES is a synthetic sex hormone used as a drug. It has the properties of natural *estrogens,* a type of hormone produced by the ovaries of women during their childbearing years. DES is an abbreviation of the hormone's chemical name, *diethylstilbestrol.*

The use of DES has become controversial because the hormone has been linked to the development of cancer. Nonetheless, DES has many properties that make it a useful drug. High doses of DES can slow the growth of certain cancers, particularly cancer of the prostate gland and of the breast. If taken by a woman after sexual intercourse, it can prevent the further development of a fertilized egg. Therefore, DES is sometimes used as an emergency birth control drug. Some physicians also prescribe DES to relieve the symptoms of menopause (see **Menopause**).

Beginning in the late 1940's, doctors in the United States prescribed DES to at least 500,000—and perhaps as many as 2 million—pregnant women threatened with miscarriages. It was believed that DES helped prevent miscarriages, but later studies failed to support this belief. In addition, further research has linked the use of DES by pregnant women to the development of medical problems in some of their daughters. Several studies have indicated that the daughters have an increased risk of experiencing problems during their own pregnancies. Other research has shown an increase in the development of certain vaginal cancers in the daughters. However, the occurrence of these cancers is rare. In 1971, the U.S. Food and Drug Administration (FDA) withdrew its approval of the use of DES during pregnancy.

For many years, farmers in the United States used DES to stimulate growth in cattle and sheep. In 1979, the FDA banned this use of DES because slight traces of the hormone remained in the meat of slaughtered animals.   Eugene M. Johnson, Jr.

See also **Hormone** (Agricultural uses).

Desalination. See Water (Fresh water from the sea).

Descartes, *day KAHRT,* **René,** *ruh NAY* (1596-1650), was a French philosopher, mathematician, and scientist. He is often called the father of modern philosophy. Descartes invented analytic geometry and was the first philosopher to describe the physical universe in terms of matter and motion. He was a pioneer in the attempt to formulate simple, universal laws of motion that govern all physical change.

Descartes wrote three major works. The first was *Discourse on the Method of Rightly Conducting One's Reason, and Seeking Truth in the Sciences* (1637), commonly known as the *Discourse on Method.* The other two books were *Meditations on First Philosophy* (1641), perhaps his most important work, and *Principles of Philosophy* (1644). His philosophy became known as *Cartesianism.*

His life. Descartes was born at La Haye, near Châtellerault, and was educated at a Jesuit college. He served in the armies of two countries and traveled widely. Money from an inheritance and from patrons enabled him to devote most of his life to study. From 1628 to 1649, Descartes led a quiet, scholarly life in the Netherlands and produced most of his philosophical writings. Late in 1649, he accepted an invitation from Queen Christina to visit Sweden. He became ill there and died in February 1650.

Oil portrait (about 1649) by Frans Hals; the Louvre, Paris (EPA/SCALA)

René Descartes

His philosophy. Descartes is called a *dualist* because he claimed that the world consists of two sorts of basic substances—matter and spirit. Matter is the physical universe, of which our bodies are a part. Spirit is the human mind, which interacts with the body but can, in principle, exist without it.

Descartes believed that matter could be understood through certain simple concepts he borrowed from geometry, together with his laws of motion. In Descartes's view, the whole world—including its laws and even the truths of mathematics—was created by God, on whose power everything depends. Descartes thought of God as resembling the mind in that both God and the mind think but have no physical being. But he believed God is unlike the mind in that God is infinite and does not depend for His existence on some other creator.

In *Meditations on First Philosophy,* Descartes first considered the strongest reasons that might be used to show that he could never be certain of anything. These so-called "skeptical" arguments included the idea that perhaps he might be dreaming, so that nothing he seemed to perceive would be real. In another argument, Descartes reflected that perhaps God or some evil spirit was constantly tricking his mind, causing him to believe what was false. Descartes then responded to these arguments. He began with the observation that even if he were dreaming, or constantly deceived, he could at least be certain that he had thoughts, and therefore existed as a thinking being. This, he wrote, was a "clear and distinct" perception of the mind. Nothing could make him doubt it. In another work, Descartes created the famous Latin phrase *cogito ergo sum,* which means *I think, therefore I am.*

Descartes then argued that he could also clearly and distinctly perceive that an infinitely powerful and good God exists. This God would not allow Descartes to be deceived in his clearest perceptions. Through this conception of God, Descartes sought to establish that the physical world exists with the properties the philosopher assumed in his theories of physics.

Margaret D. Wilson

See also **Age of Reason** (The worship of reason); **Philosophy** (Modern philosophy); **Psychology** (Beginnings); **Science** (The scientific revolution).

Additional resources

Grene, Marjorie G. *Descartes.* Univ. of Minnesota Press, 1985.
Pearl, Leon. *Descartes.* Twayne, 1977.
Rée, Jonathan. *Descartes.* Pica Press, 1974.
Vrooman, Jack R. *René Descartes: A Biography.* Putnam, 1970.

Deschutes River. See Oregon (Rivers).
Description. See Literature (Kinds of discourse).
Desegregation. See Segregation.
Deseret, *DEHZ uh reht,* is a word meaning *honey bee* in the *Book of Mormon.* The Mormons adopted the honey bee as the symbol of hard work necessary for the success of their Salt Lake Valley settlement. In 1849, they organized the State of Deseret. Congress refused to admit it as a state, and created instead the Territory of Utah.   Harold W. Bradley

See also **Mormons.**

Desert is generally thought of as a hot, barren region that receives little rainfall. Rainfall is scarce in all desert regions, but deserts are not wastelands. Deserts have varied landscapes and types of soil, and many deserts have at least one permanent stream. Deserts cannot support the wide variety of plant and animal life found in humid climates. However, many kinds of plants and animals thrive in deserts.

Scientists do not agree on a single definition for deserts. Some classify a desert as any region where the amount of moisture lost each year—mainly by evaporation—exceeds the moisture that falls as precipitation. Other scientists use the type of soil or plant life to determine whether a region is a desert. Others consider all these factors. No matter how it is defined, a desert is a region that can support little plant life because of insufficient moisture and dry soil.

Some regions near the North and South poles are also considered deserts. These areas are so cold that moisture freezes and cannot stimulate plant growth. This article discusses deserts in warm regions.

Deserts cover about a fifth of the earth's land area. The largest desert in the world is the Sahara in northern Africa. The Sahara occupies about $3\frac{1}{2}$ million square miles (9 million square kilometers), an area roughly

Fritz Prenzel

Deserts have highly varied landscapes. This photograph of the Australian Desert shows some of the different types of plant life and surface features found in desert regions.

Deserts cover about a fifth of the earth's land surface. Most deserts lie near the Tropic of Cancer and the Tropic of Capricorn. These regions are high-pressure zones in which cool air descends. The descending air becomes warm and absorbs moisture instead of releasing it as precipitation. Other deserts are in (1) regions separated from the ocean by mountains and (2) coastal areas.

 Desert

WORLD BOOK map

equal to that of the United States. In North America, deserts cover about 500,000 square miles (1.3 million square kilometers).

Deserts cannot support large numbers of people. Residents must adjust to the dry climate. Farming is generally restricted to river valleys or areas where water for irrigation can be obtained from wells or springs. Large areas of some deserts are thinly covered with grass and shrubs and are used for grazing cattle, sheep, and goats. Most towns and cities in deserts obtain water from wells or nearby rivers. Some cities bring in water by canal or pipeline from distant sources. Cities often compete for the limited amount of water available in desert regions.

People who live in deserts must protect themselves from high temperatures in summer, and, in some cases, from cold temperatures in winter. In North American deserts, many residents live in adobe or mud houses that provide insulation from the heat and cold. Herders in Africa and Asia live in tents and wrap themselves in long robes for protection against the scorching sun and blowing sand. Air conditioning makes life comfortable for many city dwellers in hot desert regions.

Desert land and climate

Sand covers about 10 to 20 per cent of most deserts. The rest of the land consists of gravel-covered plains, rocky hills and mountains, dry lake beds, and dry stream channels. Many desert soils are rich in salt, uranium, and other minerals. In addition, large deposits of oil and natural gas lie under some deserts.

A desert landscape includes various kinds of surface features created by water and wind erosion and by deposits of silt, sand, and other *sediments*. The drainage system is made up of normally dry streams. These streams are called *arroyos* in the Southwestern United States and northern Mexico. After a rainfall, water fills the stream channels. The rapidly flowing water cuts away the rocks of desert mountains and carries sediments to the mouth of mountain canyons. There, deposits of sediments create fanshaped forms known as *alluvial fans*. Sometimes, the streams carry water into low

WORLD BOOK illustration by Jean Helmer

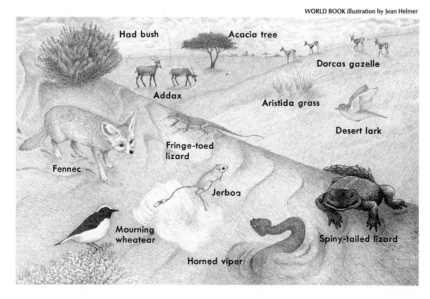

Many kinds of plants and animals live in desert regions. The illustration at the left shows some plant and animal life of the Sahara. These organisms have developed various ways to survive the extremely hot, dry climate of the desert.

Derek Bayes, Photri

Irrigation provides the water needed to raise crops in a desert. An irrigation project in the Sahara, *above*, enables farmers to grow alfalfa in that desert.

areas in the desert plains and form temporary lakes. The water that collects in these lakes either evaporates or seeps into the ground. Water erosion also creates big flat-topped hills known as *mesas* and smaller flat-topped hills called *buttes.* Parts of deserts are covered by mounds and ridges of windblown sand called *dunes.* Vast regions covered by sand and dunes are called *sand seas.* Sand seas cover large areas in desert regions of Africa, Asia, and Australia.

An *oasis* is a fertile area in the desert where underground water comes close enough to the surface for wells and springs to exist. Oases occur throughout a desert and serve as sites for settlement and irrigated farming. Streams that contain water the year around flow through many deserts. Their water comes from streams that begin in mountains outside the desert region.

Most deserts average less than 10 inches (25 centimeters) of precipitation each year, but the amount of precipitation may vary greatly from year to year. A desert may receive no rainfall for several years, but large amounts of rain might fall within a few hours.

Deserts include the hottest places in the world because they absorb more heat from the sun than does land in humid climates. In summer, desert temperatures often reach 100° F. (38° C) or higher during the day. At night, however, temperatures may drop to 45° F. (7° C) or lower. Many deserts have mild winters, but some have freezing temperatures and snow in winter.

Life in a desert

Desert plants tend to be widely scattered. The plants that survive compete for the small amount of water available, and so they cannot grow close together.

Some desert plants obtain water from deep beneath the ground surface. For example, the mesquite tree has roots that extend as deep as 263 feet (81 meters). Other plants store large amounts of water in their leaves, roots, or stems. The stem of a barrel cactus swells with water after a rainfall and shrinks as the plant uses the

water. Other plants survive by reducing their water loss. Most of this loss occurs through the leaves, and so some plants shed their leaves in dry periods.

After a rainfall, colorful flowers cover parts of a desert. This dramatic change occurs because many desert plants do not grow in dry periods. After a rainfall, these plants quickly sprout, flower, and die.

Desert animals include many kinds of insects, spiders, reptiles, birds, and mammals. Deer, foxes, wolves, and other animals may visit a desert after a rainfall in search of food. Most desert animals avoid the extreme midday heat by feeding at night after the temperature has dropped. Many small animals dig burrows underground and stay there during the day. Some of them are *dormant* (inactive) in the summer. Larger desert animals try to stay in shady areas during the day. They obtain water from the food they eat and from the few water holes that exist in a desert.

How deserts develop and change

Most deserts lie between the latitudes of 15° and 35° on each side of the earth's equator. These latitudes are in zones of high atmospheric pressure—that is, areas in which cool air descends and becomes warm. These high pressure zones are created by the way the air moves over the earth. At the equator where temperatures are high, air becomes warm and rises. As the air rises, it cools and releases moisture over regions near the equator. In time, the air descends over areas that extend between 15° and 35° both north and south of the equator. As it descends, it becomes warm and dry. This warm air causes desert conditions. The Sahara and several other great deserts lie in this region.

Regions separated from an ocean by mountains also tend to be dry. A moist wind blowing inland from an ocean loses its moisture as it rises over mountains and becomes cool. As the wind descends on the side of the mountains facing land, it becomes warm and dry. This warm air creates a *rain shadow,* or dry area. The North American deserts developed partly because of the rain-shadow effect.

Cold ocean currents flowing next to a continent can cause deserts to form in areas along the coast. Deserts form because the cool winds that blow across the cold water and onto the land can carry little moisture. The Atacama Desert in South America is an example of such a desert.

A change in climate can cause changes in the location and extent of deserts. During the last few thousand years, many deserts have formed as the world's climate has changed from cool and wet to warm and dry. Human activities have also caused desert regions to expand. This expansion occurs because of the continual loss of fertile land on the outskirts of deserts. This loss occurs chiefly from *overgrazing*—that is, from so much grazing by livestock that plant life is destroyed. Without the protective cover of plant life, wind and water increase soil erosion. This change of fertile land into a desert is called *desertification.* Other activities that cause desert expansion include mining, improper farming methods, and destruction of trees.

Desertification is a serious problem because the loss of productive land can lead to famine. Some steps have been taken to prevent further desertification and to reclaim some of the barren land. For example, trees have been planted in certain desert areas to reduce the wind at ground level. This procedure prevents sand from being blown onto the crops. Scientists believe that improving farming methods and limiting the amount of livestock in areas close to deserts will also help check desert expansion. Wayne Lambert

Related articles in *World Book* include:

Deserts

Atacama Desert	Kara Kum
Australian Desert	Kyzyl Kum
Colorado Desert	Mojave Desert
Death Valley	Negev
Gobi	Painted Desert
Great Basin	Sahara
Great Salt Lake	Sahel
Desert	Syrian Desert
Great Victoria Desert	Thar Desert
Kalahari Desert	

Desert animal life

Animal (pictures: Animals of the deserts)	Dromedary
	Horned lizard
Camel	Kangaroo rat
Chuckwalla	Lizard
Courser	Tortoise

Desert plant life

Cactus	Mesquite
Century plant	Plant (Where plants live)
Creosote bush	Sagebrush
Date palm	Saguaro
Flower (pictures: Flowers of the desert)	Succulent

Other related articles

Alluvial fan	Dune	Sand
Arabs	Irrigation	Sandstorm
Basin	Mesa	World (graph:
Bedouins	Mirage	Largest desert
Butte	Nomad	on each conti-
Caravan	Oasis	nent)
Climate	Rain	

Additional resources

Level I

Carson, James. *Deserts and People.* Silver Burdett, 1982.
Dixon, Dougal. *Deserts and Wastelands.* Watts, 1984.
Graham, Ada and Frank. *The Changing Desert.* Sierra Club, 1981.

Level II

Hyde, Philip. *Drylands: The Deserts of North America.* Harcourt, 1987.
MacMahon, James. *Deserts.* Knopf, 1985.
Nabhan, Gary P. *The Desert Smells like Rain: A Naturalist in Papago Indian Country.* North Point Press, 1982.
Wagner, Frederic H. *Wildlife of the Deserts.* Abrams, 1980.

Desertion is the military crime of running away from a military unit, organization, or place of duty with the intention of staying away permanently. Leaving the armed forces for only a short time to avoid hazardous duty or important work is also desertion. During wartime, deserters may be punished by death. Someone who runs away from military service but intends to return is not a deserter. That person is guilty of the military crime of absent without leave (AWOL).

Desertion occurs in civil law when a married person intentionally leaves his or her spouse, and stays away for a certain length of time without consent or adequate reason. In many states in the United States, desertion is a ground for divorce. A person who forces the spouse

to run away by making their home unsafe or unbearable may also be treated as a deserter. Robert C. Mueller

See also **Abandonment**.

De Seversky, *duh suh VEHR skee,* **Alexander Procofieff,** *pruh KAWF yuhf* (1894-1974), was a pilot, aircraft designer, and military authority. His fighter plane designs were among the most advanced of the 1930's. He invented an automatic bombsight, amphibian landing gear, and hydraulic shock absorbers for aircraft. His theories about the use of air power drew wide attention.

De Seversky was born in Tbilisi, Russia, and received his education at Russia's Imperial Naval Academy. He lost a leg in aerial combat in World War I. He came to the United States in 1918, after the Russian Revolution, and became a U.S. citizen in 1927. De Seversky established an aircraft manufacturing firm in the United States. Robert B. Hotz

De Sica, *duh SEE kuh,* **Vittorio,** *vih TOHR ee OH* (1902-1974), an Italian motion-picture director and actor, became noted for his realistic portrayals of life among the poor. His best films include *Shoeshine* (1946), about war orphans, and *The Bicycle Thieves* (1948), about postwar unemployment. In these and other motion pictures, he presented a grim view of life. De Sica's films won critical acclaim, but the hopelessness they implied became unpopular with audiences. After *Umberto D* (1952), De Sica found it difficult to find backing for the type of film he wanted to make.

De Sica was born in Sora, Italy. A popular actor, he turned to directing in 1939 and had his first success with *The Children Are Watching* (1942). His other films include *Miracle in Milan* (1951), *Two Women* (1961), *Marriage, Italian Style* (1964), and *The Garden of the Finzi-Continis* (1971). Gene D. Phillips

Design is the intended arrangement of materials to produce a certain result or effect. Design plays an important role in all the fine arts and in the creation of many industrial products. This article discusses the basic design principles used in the visual arts.

Painters and other visual artists work with *lines, shapes,* and *colors.* They are concerned with the *direction* of lines, the *size* of shapes, and the *shading* of colors. Visual artists try to arrange these elements into a pattern that will seem emotionally satisfying to the spectator. If this effect is obtained, the design will have *unity.*

Repetition consists in the repeating of lines or shapes. Japanese color prints are noted for their handling of repetition. Many of them have fine slanting lines of rain, or scenes with reflections on water repeated over and over.

Harmony, or balance, can be obtained in many ways in design. It may be either *symmetrical* (in balance) or *asymmetrical* (out of perfect balance, but still pleasing to the eye). Or a small area may balance a large area if the small area has an importance to the eye (because of treatment or color) that equals that of the larger area.

Contrast, or discord, is the opposite of harmony. The colors red and orange harmonize, since orange contains red. A circle and an oval harmonize, because they both are made up of curved lines. However, a short line does not harmonize with a long line. It is in contrast.

Rhythm and movement are obtained by the use of wavy lines, or motifs placed in contrast to *static* (set) patterns which give interest to a design.

Some principles of design

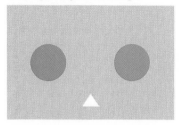

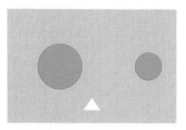

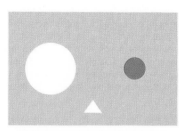

Symmetrical balance is achieved if identical shapes are placed an equal distance from the center of a composition.

Asymmetrical balance results if the larger of two objects is placed closer to the center than the smaller one.

Visual balance is created if a small, bright form is placed opposite a larger but less colorful form.

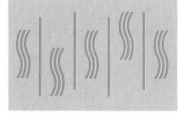

WORLD BOOK illustrations

Repetition of lines, shapes, and colors can help produce an overall appearance of harmony in a composition.

Rhythm provides variety. The repetition of straight and wavy lines gives this design rhythm and a sense of movement.

Unity is a satisfying overall effect. Asymmetrical balance, repetition, and harmonious colors help unify this design.

Unity occurs when all the elements in a design combine to form a consistent whole. Unity resembles balance. A design has unity if its masses are balanced, or if its tones and colors harmonize. But unity differs from balance because it implies that all these balanced elements work together to form harmony in the design as a whole.   Harry Muir Kurtzworth

Related articles in *World Book* include:

Airplane	Furniture	Opera (The de-
Architecture	Geometric style	signers)
Automobile (Build-	Industrial arts	Painting
ing an automobile)	Industrial design	Sculpture
Clothing (Ready-to-	Interior decoration	Theater (Scene de-
wear clothes)	Moiré pattern	sign)
Drawing	Motion picture (Pre-	
Engineering	production; pic-	
Fashion	tures)	

Additional resources

Concepts of Design Series. 10 vols. Davis Pubns., 1974-1975. Each book in this series focuses on one design element or principle, such as *Space: A Design Element* (1974) and *Pattern: A Design Principle* (1975). Suitable for younger readers.
Malcolm, Dorothea C. *Design: Elements and Principles.* Davis Pubns., 1972.

Design, Interior. See Interior decoration.

De Sitter, *duh SIHT uhr,* **Willem,** *WIHL uhm* (1872-1934), was a noted Dutch astronomer. From his studies of Jupiter's satellites and his calculation of their elements and masses, he contributed to the theoretical understanding of satellites. He is most famous for his work on the age, size, and structure of the universe, and for his early realization of the importance of the Einstein theory of relativity in cosmology. In 1917, he proposed an extension of the theory. He suggested that distant galaxies might be receding rapidly from us and that, as a result, space might be expanding. His ideas were later proved by observation. De Sitter was born in Sneek in the Netherlands.   Helen Wright

De Smet, *duh SMEHT,* **Pierre Jean** (1801-1873), was a Roman Catholic missionary who worked in the American West. His success as a missionary and as a peacemaker between Indians and white settlers became legendary. De Smet argued that just and honest treatment of Indians was the surest way to keep peace with them.

De Smet was born in Termonde, also called Dendermonde, Belgium. He came to the United States in 1821 and was ordained a Jesuit priest in 1827. In 1841, he founded St. Mary's Mission among the Flathead Indians near present-day Missoula, Mont. De Smet later started other Indian missions in the Rocky Mountains and in Oregon. He also worked to gain support for missions.

The U.S. government often used De Smet to negotiate with Indians angered by the coming of white settlers. In 1851, he took part in a treaty council at Fort Laramie, Wyo. This council agreed to reserve lands for the Plains tribes. In 1868, he negotiated a temporary peace with Chief Sitting Bull, whose Sioux warriors had vowed to kill the next white person they saw. De Smet wrote several books about Indian life and mission work that are important sources for historians.   James A. De Jong

Des Moines, *duh MOYN* (pop. 191,003; met. area pop. 367,561), is the capital, largest city, and chief manufacturing center of Iowa. The city lies in south-central Iowa, where the Des Moines and Raccoon rivers meet (see **Iowa** [political map]).

The city takes its name from the Des Moines River. According to tradition, the river had been called *Moingona,* meaning *river of the mounds,* because Indians had built mounds in the area. However, French explorers changed the name to *Moin* and called the stream *la rivière des moines.*

In 1843, the Army built Fort Des Moines on the site of what is now Des Moines. The government established the post to protect the Indians of the area. The Army viewed these Indians as "untaught children" and took charge of all their affairs. By 1845, the Indians had given up their rights to the territory.

Description. Des Moines, the county seat of Polk County, covers 66 square miles (171 square kilometers). The State Capitol is the city's most famous downtown landmark. Other attractions include the Des Moines Art Center; the Civic Center; the Center of Science and Industry; the State Historical Museum; and Living History Farms, a collection of working farms demonstrating rural life. The city is the home of Drake University, Grand View College, a public community college, and several religious and trade colleges.

Economy. Des Moines is Iowa's main commercial center. Many workers in the area are employed in wholesale or retail trade. More than 50 insurance companies have their headquarters in Des Moines. There are also approximately 400 manufacturing plants in the area. Printing and publishing is a leading industrial activity. Other industries produce nonelectrical machinery, food products, fabricated metal goods, and glass products. About 100 exporting or importing firms operate in the area. Five freight railroads and the Des Moines International Airport serve the city.

Government and history. Des Moines has a council-manager form of government. The council consists of seven members, including the mayor, all of whom serve four-year terms. The voters of the entire city elect the mayor and two other council members. The four remaining council members are elected from the city's various wards. The council hires a city manager to carry out its policies.

The Sauk and Fox Indians lived in the area before white settlers arrived. Fort Des Moines, built in 1843, was later abandoned. The surrounding settlement was incorporated as the town of Fort Des Moines in 1853. *Fort* was dropped from the name in 1857. Des Moines became the state capital that same year. The Iowa legislature chose the city as the capital because of its central location. Des Moines grew rapidly after it became the capital. Its population jumped from 3,965 in 1860 to 50,093 in 1890.

Des Moines later developed as a military training center. In 1898, during the Spanish-American War, the city had a National Guard camp. In 1902, a cavalry post called Fort Des Moines was established there. It served

as a training camp during World War I (1914-1918) and World War II (1939-1945). The Women's Army Corps (WAC) was founded there in 1942, and Fort Des Moines was its training center through the end of World War II. By 1950, Des Moines had a population of 177,965.

In the early 1980's, Des Moines renovated its central business district. Major construction projects included new office skyscrapers, shopping malls, high-rise apartment buildings, and convention and entertainment centers. A network of elevated walkways called *skywalks* was built to connect most major downtown buildings. In addition, a historic area known as the Court Avenue district was extensively remodeled.   Laurence M. Paul

For the monthly weather in Des Moines, see **Iowa** (Climate). See also **Iowa** (pictures).

De Soto, *dih SOH toh,* **Hernando** (1500?-1542), a Spanish explorer, led the first European expedition to reach the Mississippi River. His group arrived at the river in 1541 during a search for gold. De Soto also took part in the Spanish conquest of the Inca empire in South America during the 1530's.

Early expeditions. De Soto was born in the Estremadura region of Spain, but historians disagree on his exact birthplace. He sailed to Panama while in his teens. De Soto took part in explorations in Central America and helped lead the conquest of Nicaragua, which began in 1524. He later was a well-known resident of Nicaragua after it became a Spanish colony.

From 1531 to 1536, De Soto served as a leader in the conquest of the Inca. This expedition was headed by Francisco Pizarro, another Spanish explorer. De Soto was the first Spaniard to meet Atahualpa, the last Inca emperor, and later opposed the execution of the Indian leader. In 1534, De Soto was appointed lieutenant governor of Cusco, the Inca capital. He became rich from treasures collected during the Inca conquest but desired even greater wealth and power. De Soto returned to Spain in 1536 seeking a governorship in the New World and the leadership of a new expedition.

Journey to the Mississippi. In 1537, King Charles I of Spain appointed De Soto governor of Cuba. The king also gave De Soto the right to explore and conquer a region of North America that included many present-day Southern States. De Soto hoped to find gold there.

De Soto landed near Tampa Bay, off the coast of Florida, in May 1539. His expedition included about 600 soldiers and more than 100 servants. The group headed north and reached Apalache, an Indian area in what is now northeastern Florida. A band of explorers sent by

Des Moines Civic Center

Des Moines Civic Center is a performance hall where such events as dance recitals, concerts, and plays are presented. *Crusoe Umbrella*, a huge sculpture by the American artist Claes Oldenburg, stands at the left.

De Soto's expedition 1539-1543

This map shows Hernando de Soto's explorations in the American Southeast. While searching for gold, he found the Mississippi River. He died in 1542, and Luis de Moscoso completed the journey in 1543.

——— Route of De Soto

------- Route of De Moscoso

○   Indian village

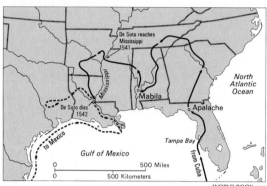

WORLD BOOK map

De Soto from Apalache reached Pensacola Bay in western Florida. The expedition continued north to the Savannah River in Georgia and followed the river to the Blue Ridge Mountains. After crossing the mountains, the explorers followed the Alabama River south to Mabila, near present-day Mobile, Ala. They defeated Indians in a battle there, but they suffered heavy losses.

De Soto continued his unsuccessful search for gold through what became the state of Mississippi. He first sighted the Mississippi River in May 1541. De Soto crossed the river into what is now Arkansas and explored to the west and south. He then returned to the Mississippi, where he died of fever. De Soto's men weighted his body and buried it in the river.

Luis de Moscoso took command of the expedition after De Soto's death and led the explorers as far west as present-day Texas. They then returned to the Mississippi River, built crude boats, and sailed to the Gulf of Mexico. The men were continually attacked by Indians. But they sailed along the Gulf Coast and found refuge at Tampico, Mexico, a Spanish settlement.

Through the centuries, De Soto became known as a courageous explorer. However, his primary goals were riches and power, for which he and his followers killed and tortured many Indians. De Soto also enslaved Indian men and women, stole their belongings, and held Indian chiefs for ransom.   Charles Gibson

See also **Exploration** (picture).

Additional resources

Maynard, Theodore. *De Soto and the Conquistadores.* AMS, 1969. First published in 1930.
Syme, Ronald. *De Soto: Finder of the Mississippi.* Morrow, 1957. For younger readers.

Despotism, *DEHS puh tihz uhm,* is a form of government in which the ruler has unlimited power over the people. Despots are not necessarily harsh or cruel. They may be kindly and considerate, and they may even put the welfare of the people above their own wishes. But usually, despots do not feel bound by the preferences of their subjects, and they sometimes use force to maintain their power.

The late 1700's are often called the Age of the Enlightened Despots. During this period, Frederick the Great of Prussia, Catherine the Great of Russia, and Joseph II of Austria did their best to reform the laws, to promote education and the arts, and to conduct the affairs of the country efficiently. Charles III of Spain, Leopold of Tuscany, Joseph of Portugal, and Gustavus III of Sweden also deserved the name of "enlightened despots." Some of these rulers learned that freedom and education make rebellious subjects, and gave up enlightenment. Nearly all were followed by rulers who undid whatever good the "enlightened despots" had accomplished.
          Alexander J. Groth

See also **Catherine (II); Frederick II** (of Prussia).

Hernando De Soto arrived at the Mississippi River on May 8, 1541. William H. Powell's painting, *Discovery of the Mississippi,* shows De Soto and his group approaching the river's edge.

Desprez, *duh PRAY* or *day PRAY,* **Josquin,** *ZHUHS
kan* or *zhaws KAN* (1440?-1521), was one of the greatest
composers of the Renaissance period. He has been
highly praised for his ability to express words through
music. He was also known for his command of musical
techniques, especially his skillful use of the *canon,* a musical device in which the melody is repeated in one or
more other parts.

Josquin usually wrote music for four voices. Many of
his pieces are love songs. For the church he wrote
about 100 unaccompanied choral works known as *mo-
tets,* and 18 Masses. Beginning in 1502, several of the
earliest books of printed music were devoted to his
works. Many pieces by lesser composers were attributed to him.

Josquin was born in northern France but lived in Italy
for many years. He was a singer at Milan Cathedral and
at the Papal Chapel in Rome. He also served the dukes of
Milan and Ferrara. After his death, Josquin's music was
long neglected, but it is widely admired today. Other
spellings of his name include *Deprés* and *Des Prés.*

Joscelyn Godwin

Dessalines, *DAY SA LEEN,* **Jean Jacques,** *zhahn
zhahk* (1758?-1806), is the national hero of Haiti. He was
an illiterate slave who freed Haiti from France and became the country's emperor. He was born on a plantation at Grande Rivière, Haiti, and took the name of his
French master. He joined the 1791 black revolt that led
to the abolition of slavery in 1793. He fought under
Toussaint L'Ouverture against the British and became a
general (see **Toussaint L'Ouverture**).

After Toussaint was seized and sent to France, Dessalines led a successful rebellion against the French. This
made Haiti the second independent nation in the Western Hemisphere, the United States being the first. Dessalines became president of Haiti on Jan. 1, 1804, but soon
proclaimed himself emperor. He was murdered two
years later.   Donald E. Worcester

See also **Haiti** (History); **Christophe, Henri.**

Destouches, Henri-Louis. See Céline, Louis-Ferdi-
nand.

Destroyer is a warship. Navies use destroyers chiefly
to defend larger warships and amphibious and merchant ships from enemy attack. Destroyers also bom-
bard enemy shores, participate in searches and rescues
at sea, and support amphibious landings.

A destroyer measures about 375 to 560 feet (112$\frac{1}{2}$ to
171 meters) long. Sailors in the United States Navy call
destroyers "tin cans" because they have light steel hulls
with no armor plating. All United States destroyers have

David R. Frazier

Destroyers are used chiefly to defend larger warships. The
U.S.S. *Elliott, above,* is in the *Spruance* class of U.S. Navy destroyers, which are used largely for antisubmarine warfare.

at least one 5-inch (127-millimeter) gun that can be fired
against air, land, or sea targets. These ships can also fire
rockets and torpedoes against submarines. Destroyers
use radar, sonar, and electronic intercept equipment to
detect enemy aircraft, surface ships, and submarines.

The United States Navy has several classes of destroyers, including the *Charles F. Adams, Coontz, Kidd,* and
Spruance classes. The *Spruance* destroyers are used
primarily for antisubmarine warfare, and each destroyer
is capable of carrying two large antisubmarine helicop-
ters. The *Charles F. Adams, Coontz,* and *Kidd* ships have
guided missiles for use against missiles and planes.

In the 1980's, the United States Navy began building a
class of destroyers called *Arleigh Burke.* These destroyers are guided missile ships with a special electronics
and weapon control system known as AEGIS.

Destroyers can reach a maximum speed of about 30
knots (nautical miles per hour). Traveling at 20 knots, the
ships can cover 6,000 miles (9,700 kilometers) without
refueling. Destroyers have turbine engines.

During World War II (1939-1945), the Navy built

WORLD BOOK illustration by George Suyeoka

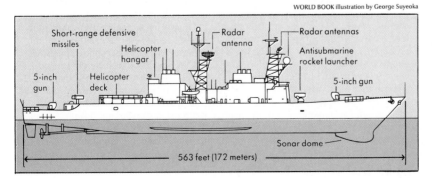

Spruance **class destroyers**
of the United States Navy are
used largely for antisubmarine warfare. A *Spruance* destroyer is shown in the diagram at the left.

Short-range defensive
missiles

Helicopter
hangar

Radar
antenna

Radar antennas

Antisubmarine
rocket launcher

5-inch
gun

Helicopter
deck

5-inch gun

Sonar dome

563 feet (172 meters)

ships called *destroyer escorts.* They were smaller than destroyers and were used mainly for convoy duty. The Navy no longer uses the destroyer escorts built during the war, though some serve in other navies. In 1975, the Navy started to use the term *frigate* for destroyer escorts built after the war.   Norman Polmar

See also **Frigate; Navy, United States** (table: Names of naval ships).

De Sucre, Antonio J. See Sucre, A. José de.

Detective. See Police (Investigations of crimes).

Detective story is a work of fiction about a puzzling crime, a number of clues, and a detective who solves the mystery. In most detective stories, the crime is murder and the clues lead to or away from the solution.

The pattern of most detective stories is the same, whether the tale is a novel, a novelette, or a short story. The author presents the crime, the detective, and several clues and suspects. The detective follows the clues and may even discover additional crimes. The climax of the story comes when the detective reveals the criminal and tells how the mystery was solved.

Certain conventions have developed from the detective story pattern. The author is expected to "play fair" with the reader. That is, the reader should be given exactly the same information that the detective uses to find the criminal. Readers can treat the story as a battle of wits between themselves and the detective.

The detective in most of these stories is not a professional police officer but a private consultant. For example, G. K. Chesterton's Father Brown is a priest, Rex Stout's Nero Wolfe is a gourmet and intellectual, and S. S. Van Dine's Philo Vance is a sophisticated socialite. Fictional professional detectives include Wilkie Collins' Sgt. Cuff, John Creasey's Inspector Gideon (written under the name of J. J. Marric), and Georges Simenon's Inspector Maigret. Romance or financial gain may be a factor in a detective story, but the main theme is the mystery and its solution.

History of the detective story began with Edgar Allan Poe's "The Murders in the Rue Morgue" (1841). With this story and "The Mystery of Marie Rogêt" and "The Purloined Letter," Poe single-handedly created the literary tradition of detective fiction. His detective was C. Auguste Dupin, a brilliant amateur who uses logic to solve mysteries.

Charles Dickens tried the new form in *Bleak House* (1852-1853) and in his unfinished novel, *The Mystery of Edwin Drood.* Wilkie Collins' *The Moonstone* (1868) was one of the most important early detective novels. Sherlock Holmes and his comrade, Dr. John Watson, appeared in 1887 in Sir Arthur Conan Doyle's *A Study in Scarlet.* Holmes is the most famous character in detective fiction—and perhaps in all fiction.

The early 1900's were a period of excitement and originality in detective fiction. In *The Singing Bone* (1912), the English author R. Austin Freeman introduced the *inverted* detective story, in which the criminal is known from the beginning. The mystery is whether—and how—the criminal will be uncovered. The American writer Jacques Futrelle created a character called the Thinking Machine, and the Hungarian-born Baroness Orczy introduced the Old Man in the Corner. The period from 1925 to 1935 brought the publication of the first or major works by such masters as Margery Allingham, Nicholas

Blake, John Dickson Carr, Dame Agatha Christie, Erle Stanley Gardner, Dashiell Hammett, Michael Innes, Msgr. Ronald Knox, Ngaio Marsh, Ellery Queen, Dorothy Sayers, Georges Simenon, Rex Stout, and S. S. Van Dine.

In the 1920's, *Black Mask* magazine introduced a distinctly American style of mystery, often called "private eye" or "hard-boiled" mysteries. These stories focused on a tough detective hero and featured action and violence and a colorful narrative style. Dashiell Hammett was the leader of this style in the 1920's, followed a decade later by Raymond Chandler. The style continues to enjoy great popularity today.

During the mid and late 1900's, a new generation of detective-story writers gained popularity. They included the American writers Emma Lathen, Ross Macdonald, John D. MacDonald, Ed McBain, and Robert B. Parker; the English writers Dick Francis, P. D. James, James McClure, and Ruth Rendell; Janwillem Van de Wetering of the Netherlands; and the Swedish team of Maj Sjöwall and Per Wahlöö.   David Geherin

Related articles in *World Book* include:

Chandler, Raymond	MacDonald, John D.
Chesterton, G. K.	McBain, Ed
Christie, Dame Agatha	Orczy, Baroness
Collins, Wilkie	Poe, Edgar Allan
Creasey, John	Queen, Ellery
Doyle, Sir Arthur Conan	Rinehart, Mary R.
Francis, Dick	Sayers, Dorothy
Gardner, Erle Stanley	Simenon, Georges
Hammett, Dashiell	Stout, Rex
Holmes, Sherlock	Van Dine, S. S.
James, P. D.	

Additional resources

Encyclopedia of Mystery and Detection. Ed. by Chris Steinbrunner and Otto Penzler. McGraw, 1976.

Haining, Peter. *Mystery! An Illustrated History of Crime and Detective Fiction.* Stein & Day, 1981.

Symons, Julian. *Bloody Murder: From the Detective Story to the Crime Novel—a History.* Rev. ed. Viking, 1985. Originally titled *Mortal Consequences.*

Détente. See International relations (New patterns of international relations).

Detergent and soap. A detergent is a substance that cleans soiled surfaces. Soap is a type of detergent. But the word *detergent* usually refers only to synthetic detergents, which have a different chemical makeup than soap.

Soap and detergent products are produced in the form of bars, flakes, *granules* (grains), liquids, and tablets. People use soap to wash their bodies. They shampoo their hair with soaps and detergents. Daily bathing with soap prevents dirt and natural body oils from clogging the pores of the skin. Doctors clean sores and wounds with soap to kill germs that cause infections.

Detergents and soaps have many household and industrial uses. People use these products to wash their dishes and laundry, to scrub floors, to clean windows, and to do many other household jobs. Industries use detergents and soaps as cleaners, lubricants, softeners, and polishers. For example, tire manufacturers apply soap to hot tires to prevent them from sticking to the molds used in *vulcanizing* (hardening) rubber. Some motor oils contain detergents that break down soot, dust, and other particles that can harm engine parts. In addition, soap is used to polish jewelry and to soften leather.

Detergents and soaps contain a basic cleaning agent called a *surfactant* or *surface active agent.* Surfactants consist of molecules that attach themselves to dirt particles in soiled material. The molecules pull these particles out of the material and hold them in the wash water until they are rinsed away.

The chemical industry manufactures a wide variety of synthetic surfactants, each of which has a different chemical composition. Most detergents contain a synthetic surfactant plus other chemicals. These chemicals may improve a detergent's cleaning ability or make it easier to use. All soaps consist of basically the same kind of surfactant. Detergents and soaps may also contain such ingredients as perfumes and coloring agents.

Detergents have certain advantages over soaps. For example, the most important feature of detergents is their ability to clean effectively in *hard water.* Hard water contains certain minerals, and many soaps cannot be used to launder in it. Such soaps react with the minerals to form a substance called *lime soap* or *soap curd.* Lime soap does not dissolve, and so it is difficult to remove from fabrics and other surfaces. It also causes "bathtub ring." Detergents do not leave such deposits, and they also penetrate soiled areas better than soap does. In addition, detergents dissolve more readily in cold water.

How detergents and soap work

Detergents and soaps clean soiled material in much the same way. The cleaning process consists of (1) wetting the soiled material, (2) removing particles of dirt from the material, and (3) *suspending* (holding) the dirt particles in the water until they are rinsed away.

Wetting the material. The surfactants in detergents and soaps increase the wetting ability of water by lowering its *surface tension.* Surface tension holds the molecules of water together and causes water to form in drops.

Molecules of surfactant gather at the water's surface and force the water to expand and spread out. With its surface tension reduced, water penetrates the soiled material more completely. Lowering the surface tension also causes surfactants to form bubbles and suds. However, bubbles and suds do not affect the cleaning ability of the product.

Removing the dirt. The surfactants in detergents and soaps also help remove dirt. A surfactant has two distinct parts with different characteristics. One part of each surfactant molecule is *hydrophilic* (attracted to water), but the other part is *hydrophobic* (repelled by water). The hydrophobic parts of surfactant molecules attach themselves to any surface other than water. Many hold on to and surround the particles of dirt in the soiled material. At the same time, the hydrophilic parts pull away from the material and toward the wash water.

The mechanical *agitation* (motion) of a washing machine, or the movement caused by rubbing by hand, helps break up the dirt. The agitation also helps the hydrophilic parts of the surfactant molecules pull the dirt particles from the material and into the water.

Suspending the particles. After the dirt particles are in the water, the thin layer of surfactant molecules around the particles keeps them separated. These molecules prevent the dirt from settling on the washed material again. The dirt particles remain suspended in the water until they are rinsed away.

How soap is made

The chief ingredients of soap are (1) fats and (2) chemicals called *alkalis.* Manufacturers may use animal fats or such vegetable oils as coconut oil and olive oil. Most soapmakers use sodium hydroxide (often called *lye* or *caustic soda*) as the alkali. Potassium hydroxide is the alkali in liquid soaps and in some bar soaps. Manufacturers use two chief methods to make soap, the *kettle method* and *continuous processing.*

The kettle method. Until the early 1940's, soap companies made most soap in large kettles. Some soap is still made by this method. Manufacturers use steel tanks that stand three stories tall and hold more than 100,000 pounds (45,000 kilograms) of ingredients. Steam from coils in the tanks heats the mixture of fats and alkali for several hours.

Conner Prairie, Indiana

Soap making by American pioneers was performed outside the home in iron kettles. This woman recreates the process as it might have occurred on the Midwestern frontier in the 1800's.

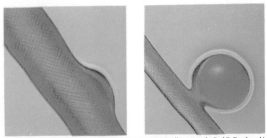

Adapted courtesy of Procter and Gamble (WORLD BOOK illustrations by Paul D. Turnbaugh)

Detergents and soaps clean in much the same way. In the enlarged illustrations, a detergent attacks an oil drop on a strand of cloth, *left.* It pulls the oil out and forms a thin layer around it, *right.* The detergent and oil are then rinsed away.

The heat triggers a chemical reaction called *hydrolysis* or *saponification.* This reaction causes a creamy soap to form within the mixture. Salt is added to the soap, causing the mixture to separate into two layers. The soap, called *neat soap* at this stage, rises to the top of the mixture. A solution of excess alkali, salt, and a liquid called *glycerol* remains beneath the layer of soap (see **Glycerol**).

Other ingredients are added in a huge mixer called a *crutcher.* They include perfumes, colors, *germicides* (germ killers), and *builders* (substances that help remove dirt). The soap mixture is then hardened into bars or made into flakes or granules.

Continuous processing makes as much soap in a few hours as can be made in several days by the kettle method. In continuous processing, soap manufacturers use a stainless-steel tube called a *hydrolyzer.* The tube measures about 3 feet (91 centimeters) in diameter and about 80 feet (24 meters) in height. Water under high pressure and heated to a temperature of 500° F. (260° C) is pumped into the top of the hydrolyzer. At the same time, a machine pumps in hot fat at the bottom. The fat splits into fatty acids and glycerol. The fatty acids rise to the top. They are removed from the hydrolyzer, purified, and mixed with alkali to make soap. The soap is then mixed with other ingredients in a crutcher and made into bars, flakes, or granules.

Bar soaps are made for bathing and for laundry use. Manufacturers use several methods to make bars of soap. They make *floating soaps* by mixing the warm soap solution with air in a machine equipped with cooling coils. The machine cools the soap and squeezes it out in the form of a long continuous bar.

In another method, several sets of rollers called *mills* mix and squeeze soap flakes to make *milled soap.* The milling operation produces a hard soap that lathers better than floating soaps.

Modern continuous *finishing machinery* makes soap bars of better quality than those produced by other methods. A machine sprays hot liquid neat soap into a vacuum chamber, where excess moisture and impurities are removed from the soap. Then the dried soap is cut into the shape of noodles and fed into one or two *kneading units.* Perfume is added to the soap, which comes out of the kneading units in a long bar called a *log.*

Soap made by any of the above methods is cut into small bars of the desired size, called *blanks.* A *press* or *stamper* forms the bars into various shapes and presses the brand name into the finished soap.

Bar soaps used for bathing are usually called *toilet soaps.* These soaps consist entirely of soap or of a mixture of soap and synthetic surfactants. The synthetic surfactants break up lime soap and prevent the formation of bathtub ring and other deposits. *Deodorant toilet soaps* contain a small amount of a germicide.

Granules and flakes. Almost all soap used for home laundering is produced in the form of granules or flakes. Manufacturers make soap granules by pumping warm soap from a crutcher to the top of a tall *drying tower.* The soap is sprayed into a stream of hot air that dries it into bubblelike granules. The granules fall to the bottom of the tower. A filter removes extremely fine particles, and coarse particles are screened out, leaving only granules of about the same size.

Soap flakes are made by pouring soap from a crutcher between two steel rollers, one hot and the other cold. A thin sheet of soap sticks to the cold roller. As the roller turns, the soap is cut into ribbons. A blade scrapes the soap ribbons off the roller. Then the ribbons enter a dryer, where they either break or are cut into flakes.

How detergents are made

The manufacture of detergents involves several complicated chemical processes. First, the synthetic surfac-

Lever Brothers Company

The manufacture of bars of soap begins by making liquid neat soap, *far left,* from fats and chemicals. The neat soap is dried and then cut into soap noodles, *center.* The noodles are formed into long logs, which are then cut into blanks, *far right,* and pressed into bars of soap.

tant is made in a chemical plant. A variety of substances may be used, including by-products of petroleum, as well as the same vegetable oils and animal fats used to make soap. For example, many manufacturers use beef fat, called *tallow,* in the first step of the process. The tallow is made to react chemically with methyl alcohol. The resulting product is treated with hydrogen gas to produce *hydrogenated tallow alcohol.* This liquid is treated first with sulfuric acid and then with an alkali. The resulting product is a synthetic surfactant.

Other ingredients are mixed with the synthetic surfactant in a crutcher. They include bleaches, builders, fabric brighteners, suds stabilizers, and substances called *antiredeposition agents,* which help prevent removed dirt from returning to cleaned material. The detergent mixture is then processed into granules, flakes, tablets, or a liquid.

Detergent granules and flakes are produced in much the same way as soap granules and flakes. Manufacturers make detergent tablets by adding special ingredients to detergent granules and then pressing the mixture into tablet form. Liquid detergents are made by adding various ingredients to the surfactant so that it remains a liquid at normal temperatures.

History

Early soap. No one knows when or where people first made soap. The ancient Romans may have used soap 3,000 years ago. People in France used a rough kind of soap about A.D. 100. By about 700, soapmaking had become a craft in Italy. Spain was a leading soapmaker by 800, and soapmaking began in England about 1200.

In the late 1700's, Nicolas Leblanc, a French scientist, found that lye could be made from ordinary table salt. Following Leblanc's discovery, soap began to be made and sold at prices that almost everyone could afford.

Many early settlers in North America made their own soap. They poured hot water over wood ashes to make an alkali called *potash.* Then they boiled the potash with animal fats in large iron kettles to make soap. The soap cleaned well, but much of it was harsh and had a bad odor.

The soap industry in North America began in the early 1800's. Some people collected waste fats from others and made soap in large iron kettles. They poured the soap into large wooden frames for hardening. Then they cut the hardened soap into bars that were sold from door to door. Since the early 1900's, manufacturers have made big improvements in the mildness, color, fragrance, and cleaning ability of soaps.

The development of detergents. Fritz Gunther, a German scientist, is usually credited with developing in 1916 the first synthetic surfactant for use in detergents. Industries used his product, but it was too harsh for household use. In 1933, the first household detergents based on synthetic surfactants were introduced in the United States. The shortage of fats and other chemical raw materials during World War II (1939-1945) slowed the further development of such products. After the war, several soap companies began to produce detergents based on synthetic surfactants. Since then, the detergent industry has developed a variety of detergents for almost every cleaning job.

Before 1965, detergents in sewage sometimes caused surface foam on rivers and streams. Most detergents contained a synthetic surfactant called *alkylbenzene sulfonate* (ABS), which did not break down completely in sewage treatment systems. In 1965, after more than 10 years of research, the detergent industry developed a surfactant called *linear alkylbenzene sulfonate* (LAS). Bacteria quickly break down LAS molecules, and so detergents that contain LAS do not cause foam.

In the early 1970's, scientists observed that chemicals called *phosphates,* which were used as detergent builders, contributed to water pollution. When phosphates and other chemicals enter rivers and lakes, they overfertilize simple water organisms called *algae.* Overfertilization increases the growth of algae, which causes the oxygen supply in the water to be used up. Fish cannot live in such water, and so they die. Their bodies pollute the rivers and lakes, which also become choked by the algae. See **Eutrophication; Water pollution.**

To help solve the problem, several state and local governments banned the sale of detergents that contained phosphates. Manufacturers reduced the amount of phosphates in many detergents. They also developed several phosphate substitutes, which enabled them to produce phosphate-free detergents.   Myron E. Feinstein

Determinant, in mathematics, is a single number related to a square *array* (arrangement) of numbers called *elements.* For example, the array

$$\begin{vmatrix} 3 & 1 \\ 2 & 6 \end{vmatrix}$$

is related to the single number 16. You can compute the value of this determinant in three steps. (1) Multiply the upper left element *3* by the lower right element *6: 3×6=18.* (2) Multiply the lower left element *2* by the upper right element *1: 2×1=2.* (3) Subtract the product of step 2 from the product of step 1: *18−2=16.* The word *determinant* is also used for the square array itself.

Mathematicians use determinants to state formulas for the solution of many problems. Such problems include the solution of equations and the calculation of certain areas and volumes.

Using 2 by 2 determinants. The array above is called a *2 by 2* determinant because it has two *rows* (3,1 and 2,6) and two *columns* (3,2 and 1,6).

In general, the symbols a_1, b_1, a_2, b_2 can be used to represent the numbers of any 2 by 2 determinant. The value of the determinant is stated as follows:

$$\begin{vmatrix} a_1 & b_1 \\ a_2 & b_2 \end{vmatrix} = a_1b_2 - a_2b_1$$

The 2 by 2 determinant can be used to solve linear equations in two variables (see **Algebra** [Solving linear equations in two variables]). For example, suppose you wanted to solve the following equations:

$$3x + 1y = 5$$
$$2x + 6y = 14$$

To find the value of the variable *x,* eliminate the variable y by multiplying the first equation by 6, and then subtracting the second equation:

$$18x + 6y = 30$$
$$-2x - 6y = -14$$
$$\overline{16x \quad = \quad 16}$$

$$x = \frac{16}{16} = 1$$

The above operations could also be written as follows:

$$6 \times 3x + 6 \times 1y = 6 \times 5$$
$$-2x - \quad 6y = -14$$
$$\overline{(6 \times 3 - 1 \times 2)x = 6 \times 5 - 1 \times 14}$$

$$x = \frac{6 \times 5 - 1 \times 14}{6 \times 3 - 1 \times 2}$$

The last expression can be written as the ratio of two determinants:

$$x = \frac{\begin{vmatrix} 5 & 1 \\ 14 & 6 \end{vmatrix}}{\begin{vmatrix} 3 & 1 \\ 2 & 6 \end{vmatrix}} = \frac{5 \times 6 - 14 \times 1}{3 \times 6 - 2 \times 1} = \frac{30 - 14}{18 - 2} = \frac{16}{16} = 1$$

You could solve the original equations in a similar way for y and get

$$y = \frac{\begin{vmatrix} 3 & 5 \\ 2 & 14 \end{vmatrix}}{\begin{vmatrix} 3 & 1 \\ 2 & 6 \end{vmatrix}} = \frac{3 \times 14 - 2 \times 5}{3 \times 6 - 2 \times 1} = \frac{42 - 10}{18 - 2} = \frac{32}{16} = 2$$

Note that the same determinant appears as the denominator in the formulas for both x and y. This determinant is called the *determinant of the system*. It is made up of the coefficients of x and y in the original equations (3,1,2,6). The numerator in the formula for x is the determinant of the system with the coefficients of x replaced by the constants in the original equations (5,14). Similarly, these constants replace the coefficients of y in the numerator of the formula for y.

In general, equations in x and y can be written as

$$a_1x + b_1y = c_1$$
$$a_2x + b_2y = c_2$$

You can solve these equations for x as follows: (1) multiply the first equation by b_2; (2) multiply the second equation by b_1; (3) subtract the product of step 2 from the product of step 1. The result is:

$$(a_1b_2 - a_2b_1)x = c_1b_2 - c_2b_1$$

$$x = \frac{c_1b_2 - c_2b_1}{a_1b_2 - a_2b_1} = \frac{\begin{vmatrix} c_1 & b_1 \\ c_2 & b_2 \end{vmatrix}}{\begin{vmatrix} a_1 & b_1 \\ a_2 & b_2 \end{vmatrix}}$$

You could solve for y in a similar way and get:

$$y = \frac{a_1c_2 - a_2c_1}{a_1b_2 - a_2b_1} = \frac{\begin{vmatrix} a_1 & c_1 \\ a_2 & c_2 \end{vmatrix}}{\begin{vmatrix} a_1 & b_1 \\ a_2 & b_2 \end{vmatrix}}$$

Using higher order determinants. The order of a determinant is the number of rows or columns it has. A 2 by 2 determinant is of the *second* order, a 3 by 3 of the *third,* and so on. Determinants of an order higher than the second appear, for example, in the solution of three or more simultaneous equations.

You can use third order determinants to solve the following three equations:

$$3x + 2y + z = 10$$
$$4y - z = 5$$
$$5x + y - 2z = 1$$

The formulas for x, y, and z are similar to the ones used to solve only two equations. The denominator of each formula is the determinant of the system. The numerators are the determinant of the system with the coefficients of x, y, or z replaced by the constants. For example, the formula for x is:

$$x = \frac{\begin{vmatrix} 10 & 2 & 1 \\ 5 & 4 & -1 \\ 1 & 1 & -2 \end{vmatrix}}{\begin{vmatrix} 3 & 2 & 1 \\ 0 & 4 & -1 \\ 5 & 1 & -2 \end{vmatrix}}$$

Third order determinants such as the one above can be computed in several ways. One method is to reduce the determinant to a series of 2 by 2 determinants. With this method, the denominator in the above formula can be reduced as follows:

$$\begin{vmatrix} 3 & 2 & 1 \\ 0 & 4 & -1 \\ 5 & 1 & -2 \end{vmatrix} = 3\begin{vmatrix} 4 & -1 \\ 1 & -2 \end{vmatrix} - 2\begin{vmatrix} 0 & -1 \\ 5 & -2 \end{vmatrix} + 1\begin{vmatrix} 0 & 4 \\ 5 & 1 \end{vmatrix}$$

$$= 3(-7) - 2(5) + 1(-20)$$
$$= -21 - 10 - 20 = -51$$

In this operation, each 2 by 2 determinant is multiplied by a number that appears in the first row of the 3 by 3 determinant (3,2,1). The 2 by 2 determinants are called *minors* of these first row elements. For example, the determinant

is the minor of 3. It consists of the elements that remain in the 3 by 3 determinant after the row and column in which 3 appears are crossed out. Similarly, the minor of 2 includes the elements that remain after the first row and second column are crossed out.

This series of 2 by 2 determinants is called an *expan-*

sion in terms of the minors of the first row. It consists of the products of the first row elements and their respective minors. The value of the 3 by 3 determinant is computed by alternately adding and subtracting these products. In general terms, the formula for expanding a 3 by 3 determinant in this way is

$$\begin{vmatrix} a_1 & b_1 & c_1 \\ a_2 & b_2 & c_2 \\ a_3 & b_3 & c_3 \end{vmatrix} = a_1 \begin{vmatrix} b_2 & c_2 \\ b_3 & c_3 \end{vmatrix} - b_1 \begin{vmatrix} a_2 & c_2 \\ a_3 & c_3 \end{vmatrix} + c_1 \begin{vmatrix} a_2 & b_2 \\ a_3 & b_3 \end{vmatrix}$$

Determinants can be expanded similarly in terms of the minors of any row or column if the signs of the minors are properly chosen.

Determinants of orders higher than the third also can be computed by reducing them to 2 by 2 determinants. However, the minors of these determinants are not 2 by 2 determinants. (The order of a minor is always one less than the order of the determinant from which it is formed.) The minors themselves must be repeatedly expanded until 2 by 2 determinants are finally obtained. Mathematicians may use other methods to simplify high order determinants.   Jeffrey C. Barnett

Determinism. See Free will; Taine, Hippolyte A.
De Tocqueville, Alexis. See Tocqueville, Alexis de.
Detonator, *DEHT uh NAY tuhr,* is a small metal or plastic capsule that contains an easily explodable charge. It is used to *detonate* (set off) larger explosive charges, such as dynamite, mines, and bombs. It contains a heat-sensitive *priming charge,* such as lead azide, and a *base charge* of some more powerful explosive, such as RDX. Flame from a fuse or heat from an electric wire ignites the priming charge, which ignites the base charge. The base charge explosion sets off the dynamite, mine, or bomb. Electric detonators need careful handling because many kinds may be set off by a spark of static electricity from the body. Detonators for dynamite are called *blasting caps.* They can cause serious injury and should be handled only by experts.   James E. Kennedy

Detoxification. See Drug addiction.
Detroit, *dih TROYT,* Mich., is one of the world's greatest industrial centers. More automobiles are produced in the Detroit area than anywhere else in the United States. Detroit is often called the *Automobile Capital of the World* or *Motor City.*

Detroit is Michigan's largest city and the sixth largest

Facts in brief

Population: *City—*1,203,339. *Metropolitan area—*4,488,072. *Consolidated metropolitan area—*4,752,820.
Area: *City—*143 sq. mi. (370 km²). *Metropolitan area—*4,589 sq. mi. (11,885 km²). *Consolidated metropolitan area—*5,312 sq. mi. (13,758 km²).
Altitude: 581 ft. (177 m) above sea level.
Climate: *Average temperature—*January, 26° F. (−3° C); July, 73° F. (23° C). *Average annual precipitation* (rainfall, melted snow, and other forms of moisture)—31 in. (79 cm). For the monthly weather in Detroit, see **Michigan** (Climate).
Government: Mayor-council. *Terms—*4 years for the mayor and the nine council members.
Founded: 1701. Incorporated as a city in 1815.

in the United States. It lies on the southeastern border of the state, where the Detroit River separates the United States and Canada. Like a strait, the river connects Lakes Erie and St. Clair. The French word *Detroit* means *strait.* The Detroit River carries more shipping than almost any other river in North America, and Detroit is a chief U. S. port. The city also serves as a center of transportation.

Antoine de la Mothe Cadillac, a French colonist, founded Detroit in 1701. Much of its early development resulted from fur trading and agriculture. The automobile industry grew rapidly in the 1900's, and the population boomed. During World War II (1939-1945), the city manufactured huge amounts of military equipment and became known as the *Arsenal of Democracy.*

The city

Detroit covers 143 square miles (370 square kilometers), or about a fourth of Wayne County. Downtown Detroit lies along the Detroit River. Because of a bend in the river, Detroit is directly north of the Canadian city of Windsor, Ont.

Detroit's Civic Center borders the river at the foot of Woodward Avenue. Gardens set off its handsome buildings. These structures include the Veterans Memorial Building, a meeting place for veterans and civic groups; the 20-story City-County Building, which houses government offices and courtrooms; and the Henry and Edsel Ford Auditorium, with a seating capacity of nearly 3,000. They also include the Cobo Conference/Exhibition Center. This center includes the circular Cobo Arena, which can seat about 12,000 people; and Cobo Hall, which has about 700,000 square feet (65,000 square meters) of exhibition space. The arena and hall were named for Albert E. Cobo, who was mayor of Detroit from 1950 to 1957. Near Cobo Arena and Cobo Hall is the Joe Louis Arena,

Ford Motor Company

Automobile manufacturing is Detroit's chief industry. The city is one of the world's greatest manufacturing centers.

Cameramann International, Ltd.

Downtown Detroit lies on the north bank of the Detroit River. The Renaissance Center, *center,* includes a circular 73-story hotel and four 39-story office buildings.

which can seat 19,275. This sports arena was named for heavyweight boxing champion Joe Louis, who grew up in Detroit. The 73-story Westin Hotel in the riverfront Renaissance Center complex is Detroit's tallest building. It rises 750 feet (229 meters).

Inland from the waterfront, downtown Detroit spreads over more than 40 square blocks. Located within this area is Greektown, a district of restaurants, shops, and entertainment spots.

Detroit's residential areas spread outward from the downtown section. About 60 per cent of the residential units are single-family homes. Like many other large industrial cities, Detroit has slums. These areas stand in sharp contrast to the clean, modern, and relatively wealthy suburbs that surround the city.

The Detroit metropolitan area covers 4,589 square miles (11,885 square kilometers) in Lapeer, Livingston, Macomb, Monroe, Oakland, St. Clair, and Wayne counties. About half of Michigan's people live in this area. Three Detroit suburbs—Livonia, Sterling Heights, and Warren—have more than 100,000 people each. Other suburbs include Dearborn, East Detroit, Pontiac, Royal Oak, Southfield, St. Clair Shores, Taylor, Wyandotte, and five cities with Grosse Pointe as part of their names. The cities of Hamtramck and Highland Park are entirely surrounded by Detroit. The metropolitan areas of Detroit and of Ann Arbor, Mich., form the Detroit-Ann Arbor Consolidated Metropolitan Area.

The people

About 94 per cent of Detroit's people were born in the United States. Blacks make up more than 60 per cent.

Other groups include those of Canadian, English, German, Irish, Italian, Mexican, and Polish descent. About half of Hamtramck's people are of Polish ancestry.

Racial tension has been a major problem in Detroit since the 1940's. Competition between the city's blacks and whites for jobs and housing led to a race riot in 1943. During the 1960's, blacks began to push harder for equal rights, and racial tension increased. In 1967, a riot broke out in a largely black area. After this riot, many civic organizations were formed to ease racial tension and help improve education, housing, and job opportunities for blacks. These organizations included New Detroit Inc., the Economic Development Corporation, and the Inner City Business Improvement Forum.

Economy

Industry. The more than 4,000 factories in the Detroit metropolitan area produce billions of dollars' worth of

Symbols of Detroit. The city flag shows French fleurs-de-lis, British lions, and American stars and stripes to represent the three nations that have controlled Detroit. The city seal symbolizes the Detroit fire of 1805 and the city's rebirth. It bears the city's mottoes, *Speramus Meliora* (We hope for better things) and *Resurget Cineribus* (It shall rise again from the ashes).

goods yearly. More than 20 per cent of the workers in metropolitan Detroit are employed in manufacturing, including more than 10 per cent in the automobile industry. The automobile companies not only assemble cars and trucks, but they also manufacture many parts for these vehicles.

Detroit ranks as one of the nation's leading producers of business machines, chemicals, hardware, machine tools, and plumbing fixtures. One of the largest salt mines in the United States lies under the city. This salt mine, which covers nearly 2 square miles (5 square kilometers), contains corridors and large rooms hollowed out of what was once solid salt. See **Salt** (picture: A salt mine).

Manufacturing has brought prosperity to Detroit, but the city's many factories have also created problems. For example, Detroit is usually one of the first cities to suffer during major slumps in the nation's economy. A sharp drop in automobile production may also cause hardship for thousands of Detroit workers. In addition, long labor strikes—especially in the automobile industry—can hurt Detroit's economy. Many of the factories in the area also contribute heavily to the city's air and water pollution problems.

Shipping. Detroit, Michigan's largest port, handles about 25 million short tons (23 million metric tons) of cargo yearly. The city is a gateway for commerce between eastern and western Great Lakes ports. The open-

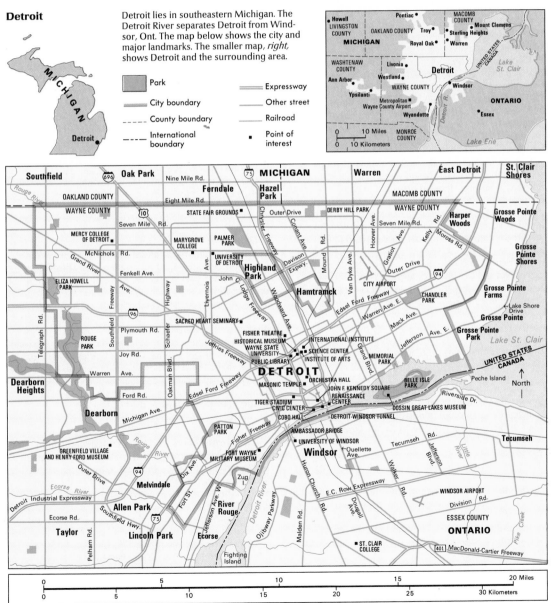

Detroit

Detroit lies in southeastern Michigan. The Detroit River separates Detroit from Windsor, Ont. The map below shows the city and major landmarks. The smaller map, *right*, shows Detroit and the surrounding area.

WORLD BOOK map

ing of the St. Lawrence Seaway in 1959 made Detroit an international seaport. The seaway permits oceangoing ships to sail from the Atlantic Ocean to the Great Lakes. About 30 shipping lines use the Port of Detroit, and over 130 foreign ships dock there annually.

The Detroit River ranks as one of the busiest inland waterways in the world. Every year, ships carry more than 100 million short tons (91 million metric tons) of cargo on the Detroit River.

Transportation. The Detroit Metropolitan Wayne County Airport, located 18 miles (29 kilometers) west of the city, provides air service for the Detroit area. Railroad passenger trains, freight rail lines, and 200 trucking lines also serve the city.

The Detroit People Mover, an elevated rail vehicle, makes a 2.9 mile (4.7 kilometer) loop of Detroit's central business district. It connects hotels, convention halls, shopping areas, and office buildings. Detroit has more than 75 miles (121 kilometers) of freeways that connect with major highways.

Communication. Detroit's two daily newspapers are the *Free Press* and the *News.* More than 40 radio stations and 11 television stations serve the Detroit area. Radio station WWJ, which began operating in Detroit in 1920, made one of the nation's first regular commercial broadcasts.

Education

Detroit's public school system consists of about 260 schools. About 170,000 students attend these schools. Property taxes and state aid provide the chief sources of income for the public schools. About 110 parochial and private schools serve about 22,000 students. An 11-member school board heads the city's public school system. The members of the board are elected to four-year terms.

Universities and colleges in Detroit include the College of Art and Design—Center for Creative Studies, Marygrove College, Mercy College of Detroit, Sacred Heart Seminary College, the University of Detroit, and Wayne State University. The University of Michigan is in nearby Ann Arbor.

The Detroit Public Library has almost 30 branches. The main library owns more than 2 million books.

Cultural life

The arts. The Detroit Symphony Orchestra presents concerts in Orchestra Hall. The orchestra gives outdoor concerts every summer in downtown Detroit and in other sections of the city. The Michigan Opera Theatre performs at the Fisher Theatre. The Detroit Institute of Arts owns a fine collection of sculptures and paintings. The collection includes murals by the Mexican artist Diego Rivera.

Museums. In addition to the Institute of Arts, Detroit's Cultural Center includes four large museums. The Detroit Historical Museum has exhibits on the city as it looked during the 1800's. The Children's Museum of the Detroit Public Schools has a bird room and a planetarium.

The International Institute in Detroit displays arts and crafts from more than 40 nations. The Detroit Science Center offers science demonstrations and many exhibits on the space program. Other museums in the Detroit

area include the Dossin Great Lakes Museum, featuring models of historic ships, and the Fort Wayne Military Museum, one of the best-preserved forts in the United States.

Recreation

Parks. Detroit's park system covers about 6,000 acres (2,400 hectares) and includes more than 200 parks, playfields, and playgrounds. The largest of the parks, 1,172-acre (474-hectare) River Rouge Park, has a golf course, swimming pools, and tennis courts. Belle Isle, a 982-acre (397-hectare) park located in the Detroit River, features an aquarium, a conservatory, a beach, and a children's zoo. The Detroit Zoological Park covers 122 acres (49 hectares) in Royal Oak. The Michigan State Fair is held every August and September at the State Fairgrounds in Detroit.

Sports. The Detroit Tigers of the American League play baseball in Tiger Stadium. The Detroit Red Wings of the National Hockey League play in the Joe Louis Arena. The Detroit Pistons of the National Basketball Association play in the Palace of Auburn Hills. The Detroit Lions of the National Football League play in the Pontiac Silverdome.

Other interesting places to visit include:

Cranbrook, in Bloomfield Hills. This 300-acre (120-hectare) educational center includes three private schools, an art museum, and a science institute.

Greenfield Village and Henry Ford Museum, in Dearborn. The village has nearly 100 restored Early American homes, schools, and stores. The museum, which stands next to the village, features the world's largest collection of antique cars. See **Greenfield Village.**

Government

Detroit has a mayor-council form of government. The people elect the mayor and the nine members of the Common Council—all to four-year terms. These elections are nonpartisan—that is, party labels do not appear on the ballots.

Detroit's mayor has broad powers. For example, the mayor can veto acts of the Common Council and can appoint most key officials, including the police commissioner. The council is the city's legislative body. It passes laws, holds public hearings, and provides money for city services. The government's main sources of revenue are a property tax and a city income tax. The income tax, adopted in 1962, applies to all Detroit residents and to suburbanites who work in the city.

History

Early settlement. The Wyandot Indians lived in the Detroit region before the first white people arrived. In 1701, a group of French settlers led by Antoine de la Mothe Cadillac built Fort Pontchartrain on the north bank of the Detroit River. The fort became an important fur-trading post.

The British gained control of the fort in 1760, during the French and Indian War. Pontiac, an Ottawa chief, led an Indian attack on the fort in 1763 but could not capture it (see **Pontiac**). The British began to build Fort Lernoult on the site in 1778, during the Revolutionary War in America. The war ended in 1783, but the British wanted to keep their valuable fur trade in the Michigan region and refused to surrender Fort Lernoult until 1796.

Lieutenant Colonel John Francis Hamtramck became the fort's first American commander. Also in 1796, the surrounding area was named Wayne County, and Detroit became the county seat. The county was named after General "Mad Anthony" Wayne, who had won fame for his reckless courage during the Revolutionary War.

The 1800's. Detroit was incorporated as a town in 1802. Fire destroyed the entire settlement in 1805. In rebuilding their community, the people followed a street plan suggested by the layout of Washington, D.C.

British forces captured the city during the War of 1812 and held it briefly. In 1815, Detroit was incorporated as a city. Detroit served as Michigan's first capital from 1837 until 1847, when Lansing became the capital. The opening of the Erie Canal in 1825 provided a cheap water route between the East and Northwest. Thousands of settlers moved to Detroit from New York and New England, and the city became a commercial center.

In 1855, the Soo Canals were completed on the United States-Canadian border, and shipping on the Great Lakes increased. This traffic aided the growth of industry in Detroit, and the city's population climbed to 45,600 by 1860. At that time, Detroit served mainly as a marketing center for the farm products of the area. After the Civil War ended in 1865, manufacturing became the city's chief activity. By 1880, Detroit had 116,000 people and more than 900 factories.

The 1900's. During the early 1900's, a group of Detroit business executives helped make the city the center of the U.S. automobile industry. They included Henry Ford, John and Horace Dodge, and Ransom E. Olds. The automobile industry grew rapidly in Detroit, partly because the city had a large labor supply. In addition, land and lake routes made it easy and cheap to bring raw materials to Detroit. Between 1900 and 1910, the city's population rose from 285,704 to 465,766.

During World War I, Detroit produced airplane motors, armored vehicles, and trucks for the Allies. Detroit's population soared and reached over $1\frac{1}{2}$ million by 1930. The city suffered widespread unemployment during the Great Depression of the 1930's. In 1935, the United Automobile Workers (UAW) was organized in Detroit. A UAW strike in 1937 caused General Motors to recognize the union and greatly strengthened the labor movement in the United States.

During World War II, the city's automobile plants switched to the manufacture of military products, including artillery, jeeps, and ships. The war created thousands of jobs in Detroit. Many people from other parts of the United States, including great numbers of blacks from the South, came to the city seeking work. In 1943, fighting between blacks and whites led to a riot. Thirty-four people were killed and more than 1,000 were injured in the outbreak. By 1950, the city's population had reached 1,849,568.

Recent developments. Detroit's rapid population growth created several problems. Schools became overcrowded, crime increased, and race relations grew more tense. Detroit began many urban renewal projects during the 1950's and 1960's. Slums were cleared in 17 areas, and the city erected nine large, low-rent housing developments and a medical center. The $106-million Civic Center was built along the waterfront.

A trend toward suburban living developed in the 1950's, and thousands of white middle-class families moved from Detroit to new developments outside the city. Detroit's population fell to 1,670,144 by 1960.

In July 1967, rioting broke out in a chiefly black section of Detroit. Rioters burned buildings, looted stores, and shot at police officers and fire fighters. National Guard and U.S. Army troops helped restore order. The riot lasted a week and resulted in 43 deaths and property damage of $45 million.

Renaissance Center, one of the largest renewal projects in United States history, opened on the Detroit riverfront in 1977. The $500-million development included four 39-story office buildings, two 21-story office buildings, a circular 73-story hotel, and shopping malls.

In 1973, Coleman A. Young was elected mayor. Young, a Democrat, became the first black mayor of Detroit. He was reelected in 1977, 1981, 1985, and 1989. The city's economy suffered in 1974 and 1975 because of a nationwide recession and a sharp drop in automobile production. After a brief recovery, declining sales caused further drops in production. By 1980, Detroit's automobile industries were sustaining record losses. The city's population had fallen to 1,203,339. But by the mid-1980's, Detroit's auto industries had recovered strongly.

In the mid- to late-1980's extensive development began along the route of Detroit's People Mover transportation system, which began operating in 1987. Cobo Hall doubled its exhibition space. The construction of new buildings along the People Mover route continued into the early 1990's.   William C. Tremblay

See also **Cadillac, Antoine de la Mothe; Ford, Henry; Ford, Henry II; General Motors Corporation; Michigan** (pictures).

Detroit River is one of the most important inland waterways in North America. A strait, it connects Lake St. Clair and Lake Erie. It also forms part of the boundary between the state of Michigan in the United States and the Canadian province of Ontario. The river carries much of the grain shipped from the Canadian Prairie Provinces and the U.S. northern Great Plains. Ships also use the river to carry iron ore from Minnesota and northern Michigan ports and coal, potash, and forest products from Thunder Bay, Ont.

The Detroit River is about 25 miles (40 kilometers) long and from $\frac{1}{2}$ mile to 3 miles (0.8 to 5 kilometers) wide. Warehouses, factories, office buildings, homes, and parks line its banks. Boating is popular. The river has several island parks, including Michigan's Belle Isle and Ontario's Peche Island Provincial Park and Bois Blanc (also called Bob Lo). Grosse Ile, Mich., the largest island, is a residential area. The Ambassador Bridge over the river and an automobile tunnel under the river link Detroit, Mich., and Windsor, Ont.   Richard A. Santer

Deucalion, *doo KAY lee uhn,* was the "Noah" of Greek mythology. He was the son of Prometheus, who was a member of the earliest race of gods, called Titans. When Zeus decided to destroy all human beings by a flood because of their wickedness, Prometheus warned Deucalion and Deucalion's wife, Pyrrha. He told them to build a wooden ark. They floated in this ark for nine days until they landed on the top of Mount Parnassus. When the water went down, they were the only living creatures left on the earth.

Deucalion and Pyrrha asked the oracle at Delphi how they might restore humanity. The oracle told them to "throw the bones of their mother." They guessed this to mean stones, the bones of mother earth. The stones Deucalion threw became men, and those that Pyrrha threw became women. Deucalion and Pyrrha became the ancestors of the Greeks through their son Hellen, for whom the Hellenes (Greeks) were named. The grave of Deucalion was said to be visible in the city of Athens in the ancient temple of Zeus.　William F. Hansen

Deuterium, *doo TIHR ee uhm* or *dyoo TIHR ee uhm,* also called *heavy hydrogen,* is a stable isotope of hydrogen (see **Isotope**). Its chemical symbol is D or ^{2}H. Deuterium is an essential part of the hydrogen bomb, and is used in research in atomic physics, biochemistry, and chemistry. About 1 part in 6,700 parts of all normal hydrogen is deuterium.

Properties. The mass of an atom of deuterium is about twice that of a normal hydrogen atom. The nucleus of an ordinary hydrogen atom contains only a proton. A hydrogen atom has the atomic mass 1.0079. The nucleus of a deuterium atom, called a *deuteron,* contains a proton and a neutron. Deuterium has an atomic mass of 2.01410. Deuterium atoms and ordinary hydrogen atoms have one electron. Chemically, deuterium reacts in the same way as ordinary hydrogen. But it generally reacts more slowly and less completely. Deuterium combines with oxygen to form *deuterium oxide* (D_2O), commonly called *heavy water* (see **Heavy water**). Deuterium oxide is used as a *moderator* in heavy water nuclear reactors to reduce the speed of the neutrons released in a nuclear chain reaction.

Uses. Scientists frequently use deuterium to study organic and biochemical reactions. In a process known as *deuterium labeling,* the heavy hydrogen atom serves as an *isotopic tracer* by acting as a substitute for one or more of the regular hydrogen atoms in a molecule. After the reaction is completed, the deuterium can be located by spectroscopic studies. This technique gives scientists important clues as to how the reaction takes place.

Scientists use deuterons as bombarding particles in particle accelerators. One such device, called a *cyclotron,* can accelerate deuterons to energy levels of millions or even billions of electron volts. When these particles hit the target material, they alter the composition of its atoms and form another element or a new isotope of the original element (see **Cyclotron; Transmutation of elements**).

Another isotope of hydrogen, called *tritium,* has an atomic mass of about 3. It contains one proton plus two neutrons, and is unstable. When a mixture of deuterium and tritium is triggered by an atomic explosion, a *thermonuclear* (heat-induced) chain reaction takes place. The atoms of the hydrogen isotopes fuse with each other and release energy (see **Fusion; Nuclear weapon**).

Discovery. Harold C. Urey, an American chemist, announced his discovery of deuterium in 1932. Urey applied Niels Bohr's theories of the atom to the hydrogen atom (see **Bohr, Niels**). He distilled liquid hydrogen and detected deuterium in the liquid remaining. Urey won the Nobel Prize in 1934 for his discovery. Gilbert N. Lewis, an American chemist, first separated deuterium oxide from ordinary water in 1932.　Peter A. Rock

See also **Hydrogen; Isotope; Tritium; Urey, Harold C.**

Deuteron. See Deuterium.

Deuteronomy, *DOO tuh RAHN uh mee,* is the name of the fifth book of the Bible, and the last book of the Pentateuch, or Five Books of Moses. The book is written as if it were Moses' farewell speech to the Israelites before they entered the Promised Land, though the book does not claim that Moses was the author. Scholars agree that some parts may date back to the time of Moses but that the book as a whole is probably from the 700's B.C. During the reign of Josiah (639 B.C. to 608 B.C.), a book of law usually identified as an early form of Deuteronomy was found in the Temple in Jerusalem. It became part of a sweeping reform of Israelite life.

Deuteronomy is presented in the style of a sermon. It contains history, laws, a *covenant* (solemn agreement between the people and God), and poetry. It presents these materials in a personal way, calling on the people to obey God.

Deuteronomy can be divided into five main sections. (1) *The introductory speeches* (1: 1-4: 43) review the historical basis of the Israel's obligation to accept God's rule. (2) *The laws* (4: 44-26: 19) deal with all areas of life. Many of them, including the Ten Commandments (5: 6-21), repeat or expand laws that appear earlier in the Pentateuch. (3) *The covenant section* (27-30) ends with a vivid description of the blessings for the people if they are loyal to God and the curses if they are not. (4) *Moses' farewell* (31-33) includes two well-known poetic songs about his death, the *Song of Moses* (32) and *the Blessing of Moses* (33). (5) *Moses' death* (34) is a moving account of that event.

In addition to obedience to God, Deuteronomy is concerned with justice and equality for all members of society, especially the weaker ones. The book also emphasizes God's great love for the people. The ideas in Deuteronomy had a strong influence on the next six Biblical books, which are sometimes called the *Deuteronomic History.* Deuteronomy is also one of the works most frequently quoted in the New Testament.
　Carol L. Meyers

See also **Josiah; Moses; Pentateuch; Ten Commandments.**

Deutsche mark. See Mark.

Deutschland. See Germany.

Deutschland über Alles, *DOYCH lahnt OO bur UHL uhs,* or *Germany Over All,* became Germany's national anthem in 1922. Germany was divided into west and east sections at the end of World War II. In 1952, the third stanza of *Deutschland über Alles* (*Das Deutschlandlied*) became West Germany's anthem. East Germany chose a different song as its anthem (see **Germany** [Facts in brief]). Hoffmann von Fallersleben composed *Deutschland über Alles* in 1841.

Deutzia, *DOOT see uh,* is a shrub related to the hydrangea. It has clusters of white, pink, or purplish flowers. They bloom in spring or early summer, and usually have five pet-

WORLD BOOK illustration
by Carol A. Brozman

Deutzia

als. The leaves, which are new each year, have small teeth along the edges and are covered with a rough fuzz. Deutzias came from Asia, but grow well in North America and other northern regions. They make fine garden borders. See also **Saxifrage.**

Scientific classification. Deutzia belongs to the saxifrage family, Saxifragaceae. One dwarf variety of deutzia is classified as genus *Deutzia gracilis.*   J. J. Levison

De Vaca. See Cabeza de Vaca, Álvar Núñez.

De Valera, *DEHV uh LAIR uh,* **Eamon,** *AY muhn* (1882-1975), a leader in Ireland's fight to win independence, served three times as prime minister after 1937, and was elected president in 1959 and 1966. He was president of the Irish Free State from 1932 to 1937.

UPI/Bettmann Newsphotos
Eamon de Valera

De Valera was born in New York City, of a Spanish father and an Irish mother. He spent his childhood in Ireland and became a leader in the unsuccessful Easter Rebellion in 1916. A British court sentenced him to death, but the sentence was changed to life imprisonment because he was American-born. He was released in 1917, and was elected to the British Parliament. The Sinn Féin convention in 1917 elected him "President of the Irish Republic," a paper organization. He was sent to prison in 1918. He escaped in 1919 and went to the United States.

In 1921, De Valera took part in negotiations with the British government that established the Irish Free State. But this settlement divided Ireland, and he opposed it. In 1926, De Valera quit as president of Sinn Féin because the party refused to recognize the Dáil Éireann (Assembly of Ireland), whose members had to take an oath of allegiance to the British Crown. He then formed the Fianna Fáil (Soldiers of Destiny) party, which won control of the government in 1932. He served as prime minister from 1937 to 1948, from 1951 to 1954, and from 1957 to 1959.   Alfred F. Havighurst

See also **Ireland** (History); **Sinn Féin.**

De Valois, *duh VAL wah,* **Dame Ninette,** *nih NEHT* (1898-   ), founded Great Britain's Royal Ballet and served as its director until her retirement in 1963. She was born in County Wicklow, Ireland, and trained to be a dancer. In 1926, she opened a school in London and began producing dances for the plays of Shakespeare. The group was first called the Vic-Wells, then the Sadler's Wells Ballet, after the theaters where the company danced. In 1956, the company became The Royal Ballet under a charter granted by Queen Elizabeth II.

Dame Ninette *choreographed* (composed) several dramatic ballets, including *Job* (1931), *The Rake's Progress* (1935), and *Checkmate* (1937). She was made a Dame of the British Empire in 1951.   Dianne L. Woodruff

Devaluation is a measure that a government may take to reduce the value of its currency in terms of foreign currencies. It is used under certain conditions when a country has a *pegged* exchange rate—that is, when it specifies the value of its currency in terms of the curren-

cies of other nations. Such conditions include a deficit in the country's balance of payments and insufficient international reserves to support its exchange rate. A balance of payments is a record of a country's business transactions with other countries and includes exports and imports of goods and services. The goal of devaluation is to improve a country's balance of payments by making exported goods cheaper to foreigners and imported goods more expensive to domestic residents.

Since the early 1970's, many nations have been *floating* their currencies. This means they permit their exchange rate to rise and fall more or less automatically in response to world demand for it. Such changes in turn affect a country's exports and imports in a manner similar to devaluation.   Robert M. Stern

See also **Balance of payments.**

Developing country is any of the world's poor, or "have-not," nations. Such nations were once called *underdeveloped countries,* but most economists now prefer the terms *developing country, less developed country,* or *L.D.C.* A typical developing nation has a shortage of food, few sources of power, and a low gross national product (GNP). GNP is the value of all the goods and services a country produces during a year. Economists often classify nations on the basis of *per capita* (for each person) GNP—that is, the GNP divided by the population. The average per capita GNP in developing countries was $660 in 1988. This amount compared to an average of $13,100 in developed countries, and $19,800 in the United States.

Most developing countries have an increasing population, chiefly because death rates are decreasing and birth rates remain high. These population increases put new pressures on scarce resources. *Physical capital,* such as machinery and efficient transportation systems, is scarce in developing countries. So is *social capital,* such as good education and health systems and stable government. Disease, illiteracy, and inadequate equipment keep agricultural and commercial production low. These factors are most harmful in rural areas, where most of the people live. The people depend on one or two main crops, and suffer if these crops fail.

Richer nations are helping some developing countries conquer poverty, but progress is uneven. Some countries, especially in Africa, are becoming poorer. About three-fourths of the world's people still live in developing countries.   W. Scott Thompson

Related articles in *World Book* include:

Agriculture (Recent developments)	Industry (In developed and developing nations)
Colonialism	Peace Corps
Economics (Developing economies)	Technical assistance
HOPE, Project	Third World
	United Nations

Reading and Study Guide

See *Developing country* in the Research Guide/Index, Volume 22, for a *Reading and Study Guide.*

Developmental psychology is the study of changes in behavior during a lifetime. Many developmental psychologists study only a part of the lifespan. Most are chiefly interested in childhood and adolescence, the period between birth and the early 20's.

There are four main theories of child development that psychologists use in research on the behavior of children: (1) maturational theory, (2) psychoanalytic theory, (3) learning theory, and (4) cognitive theory.

Maturational theory states that the chief principle of developmental change is *maturation,* which means physiological "ripening," especially of the nervous system. Arnold L. Gesell, the leading American supporter of this theory, found that the growing child's behavior seems to follow a set developmental pattern. He believed differences among people result more from heredity than from environment.

Psychoanalytic theory is based on a theory by the Austrian psychiatrist Sigmund Freud. According to Freud, children are driven by impulses of sex and aggression. Children develop through an interaction between their needs, based on sexual impulses, and the demands of their environment. Environmental demands are represented first by loving and restricting parents, and later by the children's own version of their parents' demands. See **Libido; Psychoanalysis.**

Freud's daughter Anna, the American psychologist Erik Erikson, and others have modified Freud's theory and applied it to child behavior. In the psychoanalytic view of development, children change through conflicts, chiefly between their own impulses and the demands of reality. Successful solutions of these conflicts bring normal development, and unsuccessful solutions may lead to mental illness.

Learning theory says a child's development depends mainly on experience with reward and punishment. The child must learn certain responses—such as speech, manners, and attitudes—from adults. Children learn these responses primarily through their association with *reinforcement* (pleasant consequences following certain behavior). If a mother smiles at her child each time the child is polite to adults, her smile reinforces the learning of manners. The task of the adult is to arrange the environment so that it provides suitable and effective reinforcements for desired behavior.

Learning theorists base their ideas on two types of learning—*classical conditioning,* discovered by the Russian physiologist Ivan P. Pavlov; and *instrumental conditioning,* studied by the American psychologists E. L. Thorndike and B. F. Skinner (see **Learning** [How we learn]; **Thorndike, Edward L.**). Maturation and heredity have relatively little importance in the learning theory.

Cognitive theory regards the child as an active solver of problems. Cognitive theorists emphasize the role of a child's natural motivation as a key factor in development. This motivation can include the desire of children to satisfy their curiosity, master challenging tasks, or reduce the inconsistencies and ambiguities they find in the world about them. According to cognitive theory, children form their own theories about the world and the relationships among its different aspects. The theories are primitive at first, but become more realistic after being tested against the child's experience.

There are two dominant types of cognitive theories of development. These types are derived from the theory of Swiss psychologist Jean Piaget and from an analogy to information processing in computers. Piaget described how growing children change their ideas about number, cause, time, space, and morality. First, the children represent the world in terms of their own activities. Then they move to a limited set of generalizations based on their knowledge of specific cases. Finally, they gain the ability to make valid and abstract generalizations about reality. The computer-analogy theories emphasize the development during childhood of more complex *strategies* for organizing information, understanding phenomena, and solving problems. Some psychologists believe the development of such strategies becomes possible with advancing age and experience.

Maturity and old age. Scientists have established that sensory *acuity* (keenness), speed of response, productivity in art and science, and the ability to process new information decline with age, particularly after the late 50's. Less well documented are declines in memory and in the ability to solve familiar kinds of problems. Little is known about the most remarkable fact of old age—that some people decline with the passage of years, and others remain capable and active.   S. M. Kosslyn

Related articles in *World Book* include:

Adolescent	Freud, Sigmund	Personality
Baby	Koffka, Kurt	Piaget, Jean
Behavior	Motivation	Psychology
Child		

Devil, according to many religions, is an evil spirit that opposes God or good spirits. Devils tempt people to be wicked. The chief Tempter is called the Devil and may command many lesser devils. In Judaism and Christianity, the Devil is also known as *Satan.* In Islam, the religion of the Muslims, the Devil is known as *Iblis.*

Sometimes the religious belief in devils is combined with folklore about ghosts and demons. Most Oriental religions do not accept a single supreme Devil, such as Satan or Iblis. These religions teach that countless devils of equal rank try to harm human beings.

In the Old Testament, the Devil is a *shatan,* a Hebrew word that means *opponent.* The Devil serves as a kind of accuser or prosecutor in God's heavenly court. In the Book of Job, which dates from about the 600's to the 400's B.C., God permits the Devil to test the faith of Job by overwhelming the man with misfortunes. Through the centuries, the Devil became an increasingly evil figure. By the time of the New Testament, he had become the opponent of God and had been expelled from heaven because of his rebellious pride. Since then, the Devil has spitefully tempted humanity to turn against God. In Christianity, the Devil also rules hell, where he and his followers punish the damned.

In many works of art and literature, Satan and other devils are portrayed with animal features, particularly bat's wings, split hooves, and a barbed tail. These features probably symbolize the beastly lust and passion that the Devil represents. Many modern theologians consider the Devil to be a symbol of the power of evil, of the worst qualities of human nature, or of the destructive forces in the universe.   Robert S. Ellwood, Jr.

See also **Beelzebub; Devil worship; Exorcism; Lucifer; Mephistopheles; Witchcraft.**

Additional resources

Blumberg, Rhoda. *Devils & Demons.* Watts, 1982. For younger readers.

Cohen, Daniel. *Dealing with the Devil.* Dodd, 1979. Examines Biblical and mythological bases, as well as legends and stories about conjuring the devil. Suitable for younger readers.

Russell, Jeffrey B. *The Prince of Darkness: Radical Evil and the Power of Good in History.* Cornell Univ. Press, 1988.

Devil worship is the practice of worshiping demons or other evil spirits. Only a few groups actually worship devils or other beings they consider evil. Members of a Brazilian religious group worship evil spirits called *Exus,* who they believe will harm their enemies. An anti-Christian movement called *Satanism* has a small number of followers in Europe and North America. Satanism involves elements of magic and witchcraft. Its chief ceremony is the *Black Mass,* a distorted version of a Christian church service in which the worshipers praise Satan and ridicule God.

The term *devil worship* is sometimes used by people to describe a religion other than their own. Individuals who consider their religion the only true one may regard the gods of others as devils—especially if the gods are portrayed as fierce. People also may use the term *devil worship* for practices they misinterpret. For example, some groups offer gifts to evil spirits to calm the spirits' anger. Such offerings may seem like devil worship to other people.

A Middle Eastern religious group called the Yazidis acquired the name *devil worshipers* through a misunderstanding. Like early Christians, the Yazidis believe the Devil was once the chief angel but was expelled from heaven because of his rebellious pride. According to the Yazidis, however, the Devil repented and was restored to his former position by God. The Yazidis worship the Devil as the chief angel, who rules the world on behalf of God.   Robert S. Ellwood, Jr.

Devilfish. See Octopus.

Deville, Henri Étienne Sainte-Claire. See Aluminum (History).

Devils Island. See French Guiana.

Devil's paintbrush is a wild flower also called *orange hawkweed.* Orange-red flower heads grow on a leafless stem, sometimes 28 inches (71 centimeters) high. Oblong leaves grow around the bottom of the stem. The paintbrush appearance comes from a row of bristles on the seeds. The devil's paintbrush grows in Europe and eastern North America.

Scientific classification. Devil's paintbrush belongs to the composite family, Compositae. It is *Hieracium aurantiacum.*   Julian A. Steyermark

WORLD BOOK illustration by Christabel King

Devil's paintbrush

Devils Postpile National Monument is in the Sierra National Forest in east-central California. The monument contains a spectacular mass of blue-gray basalt, columns that resemble a pile of posts. They tower 60 feet (18 meters) above the San Joaquin River. The monument was established in 1911. For its area, see **National Park System** (table: National monuments). See also **Basalt** (picture).   Critically reviewed by the National Park Service

Devil's snuffbox. See Puffball.

Devils Tower National Monument is in northeastern Wyoming. It contains a tower of volcanic rock that rises 865 feet (264 meters) from the hills bordering the Belle Fourche River. The monument, established in 1906, was the first national monument in the United States. For its area, see **National Park System** (table: National monuments). See also **Wyoming** (picture: Devils Tower).
Critically reviewed by the National Park Service

Devil's Triangle. See Bermuda Triangle.

Devolution. See Great Britain (Britain today).

Devonian Period, *duh VOH nee uhn,* in geology, is a period of the earth's history. It began approximately 410 million years ago and lasted for 50 million years. During this time, seas covered large areas of the continents, laying down thick sediment that became rock. The Devonian Period has been called the Age of Fishes.

See also **Earth** (table: Outline of the earth's history); **Fish** (The Age of Fishes); **Prehistoric animal** (Animals with backbones).

Devonshire, Duke of (1868-1938), was governor general of Canada from 1916 to 1921. He served during World War I (1914-1918), when French-Canadian opposition to Canada's military draft divided the nation. Devonshire worked to reestablish national unity (see **Borden, Sir Robert L.** [Conscription crisis]).

Devonshire was born in London. His given name was Victor Christian William Cavendish. He was elected to the British Parliament in 1891. He was treasurer to the household of Queen Victoria in 1900, and of King Edward VII from 1901 to 1903. Cavendish became Duke of Devonshire on the death of his uncle in 1908. From 1922 to 1924, he served as secretary of state for Britain's colonies.   Jacques Monet

De Voto, Bernard Augustine (1897-1955), an American editor and critic, became well known for his histories of the western frontier. He won the Pulitzer Prize for *Across the Wide Missouri* in 1948. He also wrote a history, *The Year of Decision: 1846,* and *Literary Fallacy,* a criticism of fiction writing. He wrote fiction under the name John August. He wrote his books like a straight-talking frontiersman. De Voto promoted conservation in a column, "The Easy Chair," in *Harper's* magazine. He served as editor of *The Saturday Review of Literature* from 1936 to 1938. De Voto was born in Ogden, Utah, on Jan. 11, 1897.   Edwin H. Cady

De Vries, *duh VREES,* **Hugo** (1848-1935), a Dutch botanist and student of organic evolution, was known primarily as the author of the *mutation theory* (see **Mutation**). This theory states that new species of plants and animals arise by *mutations* (sudden transformations) which might appear at any time and are then continued from generation to generation. De Vries' work stimulated research on heredity and evolution. However, mutations as conspicuous as those he described in the evening primrose were later proved to be the exception, not the rule. Born in Haarlem, the Netherlands, de Vries became famous with the publication of *The Mutation Theory* (1901-1903).   Rogers McVaugh

Dew is the name given to the glistening beads of water that often appear on blades of grass, leaves, and car tops early on clear mornings. Dew forms when air near the ground cools to the point where it cannot hold all its water vapor. The excess water vapor then *condenses* (changes to liquid) on objects near the ground.

During the day, objects absorb heat from the sun. At night, they lose this heat through a process known as *thermal radiation.* As objects near the ground cool, the temperature of the air immediately surrounding them is also reduced. Colder air cannot hold as much water vapor as warmer air can. If the air continues to cool, it will eventually reach the *dew point.* The dew point is the temperature at which the air contains as much water vapor as it possibly can hold (see **Dew point**). If the air cools further, some of the vapor condenses on the nearest available surface.

Dew forms best on calm, clear nights. When the wind is blowing, air cannot stay in contact with cool objects as long and it needs more time to cool to the dew point. When it is cloudy, objects cool more slowly because the clouds radiate heat back to earth. Dew also forms better when the humidity is high.

Dew evaporates as the sun rises. The sunshine heats the ground, which in turn warms the air. This warmer air is able to hold more water vapor, and dew evaporates into this air.

When ordinary dew forms at the dew point and then freezes, it is called *frozen dew* or *white dew. Frost* forms when the dew point is below freezing, causing excess water vapor to freeze directly onto objects near the ground.   Alexis B. Long

See also **Air** (Moisture in the air); **Frost; Humidity.**

DEW line, which stands for *D*istant *E*arly *W*arning line, is a long-range radar network. It has provided the United States and Canada with warning of a possible air attack from the north since its completion in 1957. The DEW line extends from northwest Alaska to the east coast of Greenland and has 31 radar stations. In 1985, the United States and Canada agreed to replace the DEW line's aging radars and build additional stations. The upgraded system, renamed the North Warning System, was scheduled to replace the DEW line by the end of 1992. See **North Warning System; Radar** (In the military; map).

Dew point is the temperature at which moisture in the air begins to condense. The dew point is either lower than the air temperature, or the same as the air temperature, when the relative humidity is 100 per cent. Dew forms when a thin film of air, in contact with the surface, is cooled to below the dew point. This cooling of the air causes dew on the surface or fog in the air, when the dew point is above the freezing temperature. If the air temperature and dew point are below freezing, frost may form on the surface, or ice crystals may form in the air. Fog and clouds occur when large volumes of air are cooled to a temperature below the dew point.

Phil E. Church

See also **Dew; Fog; Frost; Humidity.**

Dewberry is a small, oval fruit that grows on a trailing blackberry plant. Unlike other blackberries, which grow on erect bushes, dewberries develop on long, slender branches that spread along the ground. They are black or various shades of red. Each fruit consists of a cluster of tiny fruits called

WORLD BOOK illustration by Stuart Lafford, Linden Artists Ltd.

Dewberries

drupelets. Dewberries are eaten fresh or used to make pies, jelly, jam, or wine.

Dewberries grow wild throughout much of North America. They are also grown commercially in some states, including Arkansas, California, and Oregon. British Columbia is the leading dewberry-producing province in Canada. Commercially grown varieties of dewberries include boysenberries and loganberries.

Growers produce dewberry plants by burying sections of stems or roots in mounds of earth. As the plants grow, they are tied to stakes or wire frames to ensure their proper development and to allow growers to care for them easily. The dewberry plants produce new stems each year, but only two-year-old stems bear fruit. After the dewberries are harvested, growers remove the two-year-old stems to make room for new stems to develop.

Scientific classification. Dewberries belong to the rose family, Rosaceae. The southern dewberry is *Rubus trivialis;* the western dewberry, *R. ursinus.*   Paul Eck

See also **Blackberry; Boysenberry; Loganberry.**

Dewey, George (1837-1917), an American naval officer, won fame as the *hero of Manila.* He was the only American ever to become Admiral of the Navy.

Dewey was in Hong Kong in command of the Asiatic Squadron when war broke out between Spain and the United States in 1898. He received orders on April 25 to go to the Philippine Islands and capture or destroy the Spanish fleet. Late on April 30, Dewey's six ships, led by the U.S.S. *Olympia,* approached Manila Bay. Early the next day Dewey gave the captain of the *Olympia* the famous command, "You may fire when you are ready, Gridley," and attacked the Spanish fleet of 10 cruisers and gunboats. By noon, Dewey's force had destroyed the Spanish fleet without the loss of a single American life. This victory made the United States an important power in the Pacific Ocean, and inspired the confidence of the American people in the U.S. Navy. After his victory, Dewey remained in Manila Bay until troops arrived to capture Manila. When Dewey returned to New York City in 1899, he received a great welcome. People donated funds to buy a home for him in Washington, D.C. The Congress presented Dewey with a sword, and all his men were awarded medals.

Brown Bros.

Admiral George Dewey

Dewey was born in Montpelier, Vt. He studied at Norwich Military Academy and at the United States Naval Academy at Annapolis. Dewey saw his first wartime naval service in the Civil War. As a lieutenant, he became the executive officer of the U.S.S. *Mississippi* in David Farragut's fleet in 1861. He took part in the famous run past the forts that guarded New Orleans. Later, Dewey served on Farragut's flagship (see **Farragut, David G.**).

Dewey became president of the newly created General Board of the Navy Department in 1900, and the next year he served as president of the Schley court of inquiry (see **Sampson, William T.**). He served as an honored adviser on all naval matters until his death. In 1925, Dewey's body was placed in the Washington Cathedral in Washington, D.C.   Donald W. Mitchell

See also **Spanish-American War.**

Dewey, John (1859-1952), was an American philosopher and educator. He helped lead a philosophical movement called *pragmatism* (see **Pragmatism**).

Dewey was strongly influenced by the then-new science of psychology and by the theory of evolution proposed by the English scientist Charles R. Darwin. Dewey came to regard intelligence as a power that people use when they face a conflict or challenge. He believed that people live by custom and habit. In most situations, it is sufficient to think and act as we have done in the past, but some physical and social situations present problems calling for new responses. According to Dewey, we cannot solve such problems by habitual action and thought. We must use intelligence as an instrument for overcoming any obstacles. Dewey's philosophy is thus called *instrumentalism.*

Dewey believed that knowledge is a means of controlling the environment, hopefully to improve the quality of human life. He wrote widely on art, democracy, education, philosophy, and science. In his writings, Dewey always focused on the same problem—how to close the gap between thought and action. Dewey's interpretation of science shows how thought and action are united. He considered science as a method for inquiring into the behavior of things. The results of such inquiry are the joint products of thought and activity. Dewey regarded *activity* as conducting experiments under controlled situations and *thought* as those theories that guide our experiments.

In every area of life, Dewey called for experimenting and trying out new methods. As an educator, he opposed the traditional method of learning by memory under the authority of teachers. He believed that education should not be concerned only with the mind. Students should develop manual skills. Learning must be related to the interests of students and connected with current problems. Dewey declared that education must include a student's physical and moral well-being as well as intellectual development.

In *Art as Experience* (1934), Dewey connected works of art with the experiences of everyday life. He wrote that daily experience can be glorious, joyous, sad, tedious, terrifying, and tragic. These, he said, are the qualities that architects, composers, painters, and writers seek to capture and express in their works. Dewey regarded education as incomplete if it ignores these experiences.

Dewey was born in Burlington, Vt. He had a distinguished teaching career at several universities, especially at Columbia University from 1904 until his retirement in 1930. His works include *Democracy and Education* (1916), *Reconstruction in Philosophy* (1920), and *Experience and Nature* (1925).   John E. Smith

See also **Progressive education.**

Additional resources

Bernstein, Richard J. *John Dewey.* Washington Square, 1966.
Bullert, Gary. *The Politics of John Dewey.* Prometheus, 1983.
Coughlan, Neil. *Young John Dewey: An Essay in American Intellectual History.* Univ. of Chicago Press, 1975.
Dykhuizen, George. *The Life and Mind of John Dewey.* Southern Illinois Univ. Press, 1973.

Dewey, Melvil (1851-1931), an American librarian, began the decimal library-classification system (see **Dewey Decimal Classification**). He founded the American Library Association and the *Library Journal* in 1876 (see **American Library Association**). He became chief librarian of Columbia University in 1883, and established the first library school there in 1887. He served as the director of the New York State Library from 1889 to 1906. Dewey was born in Adams Center, N.Y.   R. B. Downs

Dewey, Thomas Edmund (1902-1971), a prosecuting attorney and Republican politician, served as governor of New York from 1943 to 1954. He ran unsuccessfully for President of the United States on the Republican ticket in 1944 and 1948. Dewey's running mates for Vice President were John Bricker and Earl Warren.

Dewey was born on March 24, 1902, in Owosso, Mich. He graduated from the University of Michigan, and finished his law course at Columbia University in two years. In 1933, he became United States attorney for the southern district of New York state. Governor Herbert Lehman appointed him special prosecutor for vice and racket investigations in New York City in 1935. Dewey's vigorous and successful prosecution of organized crime brought him wide recognition.

United Press Int.

Thomas E. Dewey

Dewey was defeated for the New York governorship in 1938, but was elected in 1942, the first Republican governor of the state in 20 years. He was reelected in 1946 and 1950, but did not run for reelection in 1954. Dewey's loss to President Harry S. Truman in the 1948 presidential election was considered a major political upset. Dewey returned to his private law practice in 1955.   Richard L. Watson, Jr.

Dewey Decimal Classification is the most widely used method of classifying books in a library. It is named for Melvil Dewey, who developed it in 1876 (see **Dewey, Melvil**). This system classifies books by dividing them into 10 main groups, each represented by figures, as in the table with this article.

Each of these 10 main classes is broken up into more specialized fields. For example, class 600-699, Technology, is subdivided into 10 special classes. Each of these divisions is further subdivided. The numbers 630-639, for example, represent Agriculture, and are subdivided into such classes as Field Crops, Garden Crops, and Dairy and Related Technologies. When the classification becomes very fine, decimals are used to represent specific areas. For example, books on useful insects, such as bees and silkworms, are grouped under the number 638. Books on beekeeping are in 638.1, and those on silkworms in 638.2.

Some libraries do not use the Dewey Decimal Classi-

Main Dewey Decimal Classification groups

000-099	Generalities (encyclopedias, bibliographies, periodicals, journalism)
100-199	Philosophy and related disciplines (philosophy, psychology, logic)
200-299	Religion
300-399	Social sciences (economics, sociology, civics, law, education, vocations, customs)
400-499	Language (language, dictionaries, grammar)
500-599	Pure sciences (mathematics, astronomy, physics, chemistry, geology, paleontology, biology, zoology, botany)
600-699	Technology and applied sciences (medicine, engineering, agriculture, home economics, business, radio, television, aviation)
700-799	The arts (architecture, sculpture, painting, music, photography, recreation)
800-899	Literature (novels, poetry, plays, criticism)
900-999	Geography, history, and related disciplines

fication. They have their own systems for classifying books. Deanne B. Holzberlein

See also **Library of Congress Classification.**

Additional resources

Comaromi, John P. *The Eighteen Editions of the Dewey Decimal Classification.* Forest Press, 1976.
Melvil Dewey: The Man and the Classification. Ed. by Gordon Stevenson and Judith Kraemer-Greene. Forest Press, 1983.

Dexedrine. See Amphetamine.

Dextrin, *DEHKS trihn,* is a sticky substance formed during the chemical breakdown of starch. Some dextrins are used as a *mucilage* (glue) on postage stamps and envelopes. Dextrins are also used in *sizing* (stiffening) paper and textiles. Such commercial dextrins are produced by treating starch with heat or acid or both. Dextrins are also produced in the human body. During digestion, starch-containing foods are broken down into dextrins and other products. Starch is also converted into dextrins during the baking of foods. See also Starch. James Nelson Rieck

Dextrose, *DEHKS trohs,* is the name used in industry for pure, crystalline glucose sugar. It is usually sold in the form of fine, white *granules* (grains). Dextrose is produced commercially by treatment of starch with the enzyme *amylase* or by putting starch in water mixed with dilute hydrochloric acid. When the starch-acid mixture is heated under steam pressure in a converter, it changes to glucose. Glucose can be purified and dried to fine granules called dextrose. As a pure white sugar, dextrose is used mainly in candy, baked goods, and canned fruit. As a syrup, dextrose is used to produce *high-fructose corn syrup,* a sweetener in many foods and beverages. Dextrose is not as sweet as *sucrose* (common table sugar). See also **Glucose.** Kay L. Franzen

Dhaka, *DAK uh* (pop. 2,365,695; met. area pop. 3,430,312), is the capital, largest city, and commercial and industrial center of Bangladesh. Dhaka, formerly spelled *Dacca,* lies on the Buriganga River. For location, see **Bangladesh** (map).

The old section of Dhaka, called the Sadarghat, includes the city's main shopping district and a busy outdoor market known as the Chauk. The Sadarghat has many *mosques* (Muslim houses of worship), some of which are hundreds of years old. Large numbers of poor families live in crowded slums in the Sadarghat. Middle-

class and wealthy people make up most of the population of Ramna, one of the city's fastest growing areas. Ramna lies on the northern edge of Dhaka. It is the home of the University of Dhaka and has many tree-lined streets, a park, and a shopping district.

The central location of Dhaka helped it become the nation's commercial and industrial center. Factories operate in many parts of the city and its suburbs. The Dhaka area's major products include cotton fabrics, glass, leather, metals, sugar, and *jute,* a plant fiber used in making rope and certain fabrics.

Settlers from South Asia founded Dhaka in the A.D. 600's. In 1608, the city became the capital of Bengal, a province of the Mogul Empire (see **Mogul Empire**). Dhaka came under British control in the mid-1700's as part of India. India gained independence from Great Britain in 1947, and part of it—including what is now Bangladesh—became the independent nation of Pakistan. Dhaka was named the capital of the Pakistani province of East Pakistan. In 1971, civil war in Pakistan led to the establishment of East Pakistan as an independent nation, Bangladesh, with Dhaka as the capital. P. P. Karan

See also **Bangladesh** (pictures).

Dharma, *DAHR muh,* is the moral and religious law of Buddhism and Hinduism. Each of these religions has its own dharma.

In Buddhism, the dharma is reflected in the teachings of Buddha, who founded the religion. The principles of the Buddhist dharma govern daily life and show the way to salvation. Buddha preached that life is a continuing cycle of death and rebirth. He taught that by following Buddhist ways of life called the *Middle Way* and the *Noble Eightfold Path,* a person could overcome suffering and achieve *nirvana,* a state of peace and happiness. Buddha's followers compiled his teachings in a scripture called the *Tripitika.*

In Hinduism, the dharma establishes rules of duty and ethical conduct for all people. The Hindu dharma also sets forth the responsibilities of the four major *castes* (classes) that make up Hindu society. Writings called the *Dharma Sutras* and the *Dharma Commentaries* explain these principles. Frank E. Reynolds

See also **Buddha; Buddhism; Hinduism; Nirvana.**

Diabetes, *DY uh BEE tihs* or *DY uh BEE teez,* is the name of two diseases that have the same symptom, excessive urination. *Diabetes* usually refers to *diabetes mellitus,* by far the more common disease, in which the body cannot use sugar normally. In the other disease, *diabetes insipidus,* the pituitary gland or the *hypothalamus,* a part of the brain, functions abnormally.

Diabetes mellitus ranks among the leading causes of death in the United States. Approximately 11 million Americans have diabetes, but about half of them do not know they are diabetic. The body of a diabetic person is slow in using *glucose* (sugar), and so glucose builds up in the blood. The kidneys discharge some of the excess glucose into the urine. In severe cases of diabetes, fats and proteins also cannot be used normally.

Most physicians once believed that all cases of diabetes were caused by a lack of the hormone *insulin.* Insulin, which is produced by the pancreas, enables the body to use and store glucose quickly. Some diabetics do lack insulin. This form of the disease is called *Type I diabetes* (also known as *insulin-dependent diabetes* or juvenile-type diabetes). However, many diabetics—especially those who become diabetic after the age of 40—have normal or even above-normal production of insulin. Their bodies do not respond efficiently to the insulin. Doctors call this form of the disease *Type II diabetes* (also known as *non-insulin-dependent diabetes* or *adult-type diabetes*). In North America and Europe, about 80 per cent of all diabetics have Type II, which is a milder form of the disease. In other parts of the world, more than 95 per cent of all diabetics have Type II.

Symptoms of diabetes include excessive urination, great thirst, hunger, and loss of weight and strength. These symptoms may appear gradually—and even be unnoticed—in Type II diabetes, which is most common in overweight individuals over the age of 40.

In Type I diabetes, the more serious form of the disease, the symptoms may occur suddenly. Type I diabetes usually strikes young people but also occurs in adults of any age. It hits some people so suddenly that the lack of insulin causes an emergency condition called *diabetic ketoacidosis.* The symptoms of this condition are excessive urination and thirst, loss of appetite, nausea, vomiting, and rapid deep breathing. If the victim does not receive immediate treatment, he or she may go into a state of *diabetic coma,* which can lead to death.

Cause of diabetes is unknown. The disease is common in some families, but many diabetics have no known family history of diabetes. Many researchers suspect that certain people inherit a tendency for developing Type II diabetes. Additional factors, such as obesity or severe stress, may trigger the onset of the disease in such people. Some physicians believe that Type I diabetes also involves hereditary traits. These traits possibly cause the body's disease-fighting immune system to respond to certain viral infections by mistakenly attacking the insulin-producing cells of the pancreas.

Treatment. Diabetes cannot be cured, but proper treatment can improve a patient's condition. Many diabetics live almost as long as people of normal health.

Type I diabetics need to receive daily doses of insulin. Some patients need more than one dose of insulin each day. To be effective, insulin must be absorbed into the bloodstream. It cannot be administered orally, because it is destroyed in the digestive system. Most diabetics who use insulin receive it by hypodermic injections. A small number of diabetics use portable pumps to inject insulin. During the early 1980's, some diabetics began using an experimental pump that can be implanted within the body.

The dosage of insulin prescribed by the physician depends on the patient's diet and exercising habits. If a diabetic stops taking needed insulin, the amount of glucose in the blood may become excessive. This excess can result in diabetic ketoacidosis, and the patient may go into a diabetic coma.

Most Type I diabetics follow carefully planned diets consisting of planned amounts of carbohydrates, fats, and proteins. Most also test their urine or blood daily for glucose and for *acetone*, a substance produced when the effect of insulin is inadequate. A diabetic follows the planned diet strictly—except if he or she has an *insulin reaction,* or *insulin shock.* This condition occurs when the effect of insulin is so great that the level of sugar in the blood becomes too low. The patient may perspire greatly and become nervous, weak, or even unconscious. The condition can be treated quickly by having the patient eat food that is rich in sugar. Many diabetics carry candy or table sugar with them in case of an insulin reaction.

Many cases of Type II diabetes can be controlled by a diet that is low in calories. Some Type II diabetics whose condition cannot be controlled by diet alone use insulin or take oral drugs that reduce the level of glucose in the blood. But studies in the 1960's and 1970's indicated that such oral drugs might have harmful side effects.

Complications. Diabetes can lead to serious complications. For example, it may cause changes in the blood vessels of the retina. This condition is called *diabetic retinopathy.* In advanced form, it is a major cause of blindness (see **Blindness** [Diseases]). Diabetes may cause similar changes in the blood vessels of the kidneys. This condition, called *diabetic nephropathy,* may lead to kidney failure. Various treatments can control many cases of diabetic retinopathy and diabetic nephropathy.

The nerves may also be affected by diabetes. This complication, known as *diabetic neuropathy,* can result in loss of feeling or abnormal sensations in different parts of the body. Diabetes can also lead to *arteriosclerosis* (hardening of the arteries), which may cause a stroke, heart failure, or gangrene (see **Arteriosclerosis**).

Research. Scientists are continually searching for ways to control, prevent, and cure diabetes. Since the 1960's, physicians have been experimenting with transplants of the *islets of Langerhans,* the part of the pancreas that produces insulin. Since the 1970's, bioengineers have been working to develop and miniaturize an artificial pancreas. Such a device could measure the amount of glucose in the blood and release either insulin or glucose into the body to maintain a normal level of blood glucose. Other researchers are working to identify the hereditary traits that might contribute to diabetes and the viruses that might be responsible for triggering Type I diabetes.

Many organizations sponsor research and conduct public education in the field of diabetes mellitus. These organizations include the American Diabetes Association, the Juvenile Diabetes Foundation, and the National Institutes of Health.

Diabetes insipidus is a disease in which the kidneys cannot retain water that passes to them from the blood. A patient with diabetes insipidus urinates excessively and becomes extremely thirsty. The disease is caused by a lack of *vasopressin,* a hormone that controls the amount of water leaving the body as urine. Vasopressin is made by the hypothalamus and is stored in and released by the pituitary gland. A disease or injury that affects the hypothalamus or the pituitary gland can cause this condition. Most cases of diabetes insipidus cannot be cured. However, the disease can be controlled by taking vasopressin.   Jesse Roth

See also **Insulin; Hodgkin, Dorothy C.; Hypoglycemia.**

Additional resources

Diabetes in the Family. Ed. by the American Diabetes Association. Rev. ed. Prentice-Hall, 1987.
Silverstein, Alvin and V. B. *The Sugar Disease: Diabetes.* Lippincott, 1980.
Tiger, Steven. *Diabetes.* Messner, 1987. For younger readers.

Diacritical mark, DY uh KRIHT uh kuhl, is a sign used with letters of the alphabet to show pronunciation or meaning of words. Diacritical marks are a regular part of spelling in many foreign languages (see the Key to Pronunciation at front of the A volume). In English, some words borrowed from other languages also use diacritical marks, but the marks are mainly used in dictionaries to show how words are pronounced. Diacritical marks in English include the *circumflex* (which is written ˆ as in ôrder); the *dieresis* (¨ as in fär, rüle); the *macron* (¯ as in āge, ēqual, īce, ōpen, ūse); the *tilde* (˜ as in cãre); the *single dot* (˙ as in tèrm, pu̇t); and the *breve* (˘ as in bĕd, pĭt).   Marianne Cooley

Diaghilev, DYAH gih lehf, **Sergei Pavlovich,** sehr GAY pah VLAW vihch (1872-1929), was one of the most important artistic directors in dance history. He established ballet as a modern theatrical art, creating an audience comparable to that for symphonic music.

From 1909 to 1929, Diaghilev directed and produced ballet performances by his own company, the *Ballets Russes*. At first, he used Russian dancers and *choreographers* (dance composers). Later, he drew from the artistic communities elsewhere in Europe as well. Diaghilev persuaded great composers, choreographers, dancers, and artists to collaborate on ballets. These included dancers Vaslav Nijinsky and Tamara Karsavina, composer Igor Stravinsky, artist Pablo Picasso, and choreographers Michel Fokine and George Balanchine. Among Diaghilev's best-known ballets are *Les Sylphides* (1909), *Petrouchka* (1911), and *The Rite of Spring* (1913). Diaghilev directed about 80 ballets and operas. He was born in the province of Novgorod in Russia.   Dianne L. Woodruff

See also **Ballet** (Russian ballet).

Diagnosis. See **Disease** (Diagnosing disease); **Medicine** (Diagnosis).

Diagraming, in grammar. See **Sentence.**

Dialect is a variation of a language used by a particular group of speakers. All living languages change through time. Variations in a once uniform speech arise from geographical and social factors. A geographical factor might be a large body of water that separates two groups who originally spoke a language in the same way. For example, the Atlantic Ocean separates the speakers of English in Great Britain and the United States, leading to American and British dialects of that language. Social factors might include levels of education, economic status, and, sometimes, ethnic background. All three of these factors can produce separate dialects in a large American city.

Dialects involve differences in pronunciation and vocabulary. On the basis of such differences, it is possible to identify certain dialects of American English. The eastern United States would include (1) the Eastern New England dialect, (2) the Western Pennsylvania dialect, and (3) the Eastern Virginia dialect. In the first area, one might hear *idea* pronounced *idear* and the word *buttonwood* used for *sycamore*. In the second area, the words *cot* and *caught* might be pronounced in the same way and a *chipmunk* could be called a *grinnie*. In the third area, people may pronounce *afraid* as *afred* and call a *peanut* a *goober*.

Frequently, the term *dialect* implies that there is a standard form of a language that speakers of a dialect do not follow. For example, the French spoken in Paris is considered the standard form of that language. Those people who do not speak Parisian French are said to speak a dialect of that language. But as a variation of the language, Parisian French must also be considered a dialect.   Robert J. Kispert

See also **Grammar** (Grammar and usage); **Idiom; Language** (Development of language); **Pronunciation** (English dialects in the United States); **Slang; Speech.**

Dialectic. See **Hegel, G. W. F.** (Hegel's dialectic).

Dialectical materialism. See **Materialism; Philosophy** (Modern philosophy).

Dialysis machine. See **Kidney** (Kidney diseases).

Diameter, in geometry, is the length of any straight line segment that passes through the center of a circle or a sphere and touches the figure's boundaries at opposite points. *Diameter* is also the name of such a line segment.

The diameter of a circle or sphere is twice as long as the figure's *radius*. The radius is the length of any line segment that runs from the center of a circle or a sphere to any point on the figure's boundary. *Radius* is also the name of such a line segment.

The degree of magnification achieved by a microscope or telescope is expressed in *diameters*. For example, a microscope that doubles the apparent size of an object is said to magnify the object two diameters.   Philip S. Marcus

See also **Circle; Microscope; Sphere.**

Diamond is the hardest naturally occurring substance, and also one of the most valuable natural substances. Because of its hardness, the diamond is the most lasting of all gemstones. In Europe, America, and Japan, the diamond is widely used for engagement and wedding rings. Diamonds are also used in industry for cutting, grinding, and boring other hard materials. About half of the world's natural diamonds are suitable only for industrial use. A small percentage of all diamonds mined are set in jewelry.

What diamonds are. Diamonds are crystals made up almost entirely of carbon. Some diamond crystals have six faces, but most form *octahedrons,* which have eight faces (see **Octahedron**). Other crystal shapes also occur, some of which are very complex. Natural diamonds probably form in the earth's *upper mantle*—the zone beneath the crust—where high temperature and pressure cause the diamonds to crystallize. The diamonds are later brought to the earth's surface by volcanic activity.

A diamond must be used to cut another diamond. However, a diamond can be cleanly broken with a sharp, accurate blow because of its *cleavage*. Cleavage is a property some minerals have of splitting in certain directions and producing flat, even surfaces. A diamond will not dissolve in acid. But it can be destroyed when it is subjected to intense heat. If a diamond is heated in the presence of oxygen it will burn and form carbon dioxide. If it is heated without oxygen, a diamond will turn to graphite, a form of carbon so soft that it is used as a lubricant.

Where natural diamonds are found. The first diamonds were found thousands of years ago in the sand and gravel deposits of stream beds. Diamonds found in such deposits are called *alluvial diamonds*. The diamond fields of South Africa were discovered in 1867,

John Reader

Diamonds have been prized throughout history for their beauty and for their extreme hardness. Skilled cutters and polishers can transform rough diamonds, such as those shown above, into brilliant jewels. Some of the world's most famous diamonds are pictured at the right. Each of these diamonds is shown at about three-fourths its actual size.

The Louvre, Paris

Regent
The Louvre, Paris
140.50 carats
Found in India

Tiffany & Company

Tiffany
Tiffany & Company, New York City
128.51 carats
Found in South Africa

Orloff
Diamond Treasury, Moscow
189.60 carats
Found in India

Arnaud de Rosnay from Peter Schub

Baumgold Brothers

Earth Star
Baumgold Brothers, New York City
111.59 carats
Found in South Africa

Giraudon

Condé
Condé Museum, Chantilly, France
50 carats
Found in India

©By kind permission of the Controller of Her Majesty's Stationery Office, from Colorific

Cullinan I, or Star of Africa
British Crown Jewels, London
530.20 carats
Found in South Africa

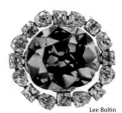

Lee Boltin

Hope
Smithsonian Institution, Washington, D.C.
45.52 carats
Found in India

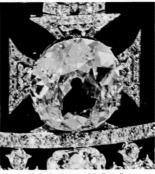

©By kind permission of the Controller of Her Majesty's Stationery Office, from Colorific

Koh-i-noor
British Crown Jewels, London
108.93 carats
Found in India

when a farmer's child found "a pretty pebble" near the banks of the Orange River. The "pebble" proved to be a diamond worth $2,500. In 1870, diamonds were discovered for the first time in *kimberlite*. This rare rock forms pipe-shaped bodies, which once filled the throats of some volcanoes. A huge diamond deposit was found in 1979 in Western Australia. The Australian diamonds occur in a kind of rock called *lamproite.*

Even in the richest deposits, tons of rock must be mined and crushed to produce one small diamond. Some diamond mines produce about 1 carat (200 milligrams, or .007 ounce) of diamonds for every 3 short tons (2.7 metric tons) of rock mined. By the late 1980's, the world's diamond mines produced about 90 million carats each year. Australia outranks all other countries in the annual production of natural diamonds. Zaire ranks second. Other leading producers include Botswana, South Africa, and the Soviet Union.

The United States has no commercial diamond mines. However, kimberlite has been found in Arkansas, Colorado, Michigan, and Montana, and single alluvial diamonds have been discovered in a number of states.

How diamonds are cut to make jewels. Diamonds have great power to reflect light, bend rays of light, and break light up into the colors of the rainbow. But to produce the greatest possible brilliance in a diamond, many little *facets* (sides) must be cut and polished on it. Each tiny facet must be exactly the right size and shape and must be placed at exactly the right angle in relation to other facets.

During the 1400's, diamond cutters learned how to shape and polish a stone by using an iron wheel coated with diamond dust. As people learned more about diamonds, they discovered the shapes that give the greatest brilliance. The style of cut often seen today is the round shape with 58 facets, which is called the *brilliant*

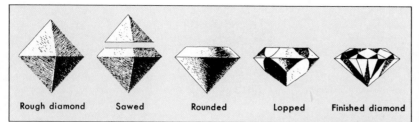

De Beers Consolidated Mines, Ltd.

Diamond cutting begins when skilled craftworkers saw a rough diamond in two. They use a thin circular saw that holds diamond dust. The corners are then rounded by rubbing together a spinning diamond and a stationary one. Later, cutters use the *lopping* process to grind *facets* (sides) on the stone. Lopping, *right,* involves carefully pressing the diamond against a rotating wheel coated with diamond dust. Most finished diamonds have 58 facets.

Gemological Institute of America

cut. This style of cutting was begun in the 1600's. Diamond saws cut diamond crystals with great accuracy, and so help prevent waste. See **Gem** (illustration: Types of gem cuts).

How diamonds can be judged. Gem diamonds are graded according to weight, clarity, color, and cut. The weight of a diamond is measured by the carat. The clarity of a diamond can be lessened by various kinds of flaws. Among these flaws are *inclusions* (other substances enclosed in the crystals), small bubbles, and small *fissures* (cracks), which jewelers sometimes call *feathers.* The best-quality diamonds—and the most valuable ones—are completely colorless. Very few diamonds reach this standard. Many diamonds have a yellowish tint. Other diamonds are black, blue, brown, green, pink, purple, or red. Red is the rarest color in natural diamonds. The way a diamond is cut may affect its value because a stone that is not properly proportioned lacks the brillance of a well-cut stone.

In buying a diamond, the buyer should have the advice of a reliable dealer. Terms used to describe gem diamonds vary considerably. A *flawless diamond* should have no physical defects, such as cracks, inclusions, scratches, blemishes, or a cloudy appearance. But a flawless diamond may not be colorless. Some people consider a diamond to be perfect if it is colorless as well as flawless, has high clarity, and is correctly cut.

Cutting and polishing a rough diamond is a slow and costly process. It must be done by highly trained workers, who take many years to learn their trade.

Famous diamonds. Many large diamonds of rare quality are the property of royalty or of a government. The largest stone ever discovered was the *Cullinan.* This diamond, found in 1905 in the Premier mine of South Africa, weighed 3,106 carats, or about $1\frac{1}{3}$ pounds (0.6 kilo-

gram). It was purchased by the Transvaal government and presented to King Edward VII of Britain. Transvaal was a British colony in what is now South Africa. Amsterdam cutters *cleaved* (split), cut, and polished the Cullinan into 9 large gems and 96 smaller stones. The largest cut diamond in the world came from the Cullinan. It is the 530-carat *Cullinan I* or *Star of Africa.*

In 1934, the *Jonker* diamond was found. It weighed 726 carats, and was said to be unequaled in purity. Between 1935 and 1937, the Jonker was cut into 12 flawless stones. The largest stone weighed 125 carats. The *Orloff* is a magnificent Russian crown jewel bought by Prince Orloff for the Empress Catherine II. This huge diamond is said to have been stolen from the eye of an idol in a Hindu temple. The *Koh-i-noor,* now in the British crown jewels, was for many centuries possessed by Indian and Persian rulers. Great Britain acquired it when the British annexed the Punjab in 1849.

The *Regent* diamond, once known as the *Pitt* diamond, is an Indian gem regarded as one of the most beautifully cut of the world's large diamonds. It is owned by the government of France and is on display in the Louvre Museum in Paris. The blue *Hope* diamond became the property of the Smithsonian Institution in the United States in 1958.

Industrial uses. Diamonds unsuitable for cutting into gemstones are widely used in industry. Industrial-grade diamonds include stones that are imperfectly formed, contain many inclusions or other flaws, or have poor color. Manufacturers need these diamonds to shape, with great accuracy, hard metals that are used in making automobiles, airplanes, and various types of engines and other machinery. Diamonds are used in such work because of their extreme hardness. They can cut, grind, and bore very hard metal quickly and accurately. Some-

| ½ carat | 1 carat | 1½ carats | 2 carats | 2½ carats | 3 carats | 3½ carats | 4 carats |

McCaffery & Co. (WORLD BOOK photo by Steinkamp/Ballogg)

The size of a diamond is determined by its weight in carats. One carat equals 200 milligrams. The picture above shows round diamonds of different carats and the approximate difference in their diameters. However, not all diamonds of these weights would have exactly these diameters. For example, a 4-carat diamond deeper than the one shown would have a smaller diameter.

times whole rough diamonds are set into industrial tools. Sometimes the diamonds are crushed and then baked onto cutting tools. Occasionally, diamonds are cut into special shapes before they are set into tools. Diamonds are set in the ends of drills used in mining. Very fine wire is drawn to size through diamonds in which tapering holes have been cut. A diamond *stylus* (needle) is used in most record players.

Synthetic diamonds. The demand for industrial diamonds cannot be met by the supply of natural diamonds. For this reason, industry now depends on synthetic diamonds. The world's first synthetic diamond was produced in 1954 at the General Electric Research Laboratory. Scientists at the laboratory made the diamond by compressing carbon under extremely high pressure and heat. Today, several companies manufacture industrial diamonds.

In 1970, the General Electric Company produced the first synthetic diamonds of gem quality and size. Scientists use these diamonds to research new uses for diamonds. For example, researchers have found that adding small amounts of the chemical element boron to synthetic diamonds turns them into *semiconductors.* Semiconductors are materials with special electrical properties. They are used to make transistors and other electronic equipment. Synthetic diamonds are not sold as jewelry because they cost so much to produce that, as gems, they would cost more than natural diamonds.

Imitation diamonds are gems that resemble genuine diamonds. Some are natural gemstones, such as colorless varieties of spinel and zircon. Others do not occur in nature and are manufactured from substances that are similar to diamonds in appearance. These substances include glass, strontium titantate, yttrium aluminum garnet (YAG), and cubic zirconia. A cubic zirconia is difficult to distinguish from a genuine diamond. Jewelers must use scientific tests to tell them apart. Imitation diamonds are softer than genuine diamonds and may show scratches and other signs of wear.   Robert I. Gait

See also **Arkansas** (Places to visit); **Borazon; Gem; Hardness.**

Diamond Head. See Honolulu (The city; picture).

Diana was a goddess in Roman mythology. She was the daughter of Jupiter, the king of the gods, and the goddess Latona. Diana and the god Apollo were twins. She was born on the island of Delos, and so the ancient Romans sometimes called her the Delian goddess, or Delia. She resembled the Greek goddess Artemis.

Diana was a moon goddess and the goddess of various aspects of women's life, including childbirth. She also was the goddess of young living things, particularly young animals, and of hunting. Diana symbolized chastity and modesty. She was a virgin and demanded that all her attendants be virgins. Artists showed the goddess wearing hunting clothes, carrying a bow and quiver of arrows, and accompanied by forest nymphs and hunting dogs.   Paul Pascal

See also **Artemis.**

Diana, Princess. See Charles, Prince.

Diaphragm, *DY uh fram,* the large muscle attached to the lower ribs, separates the chest from the abdomen. Only human beings and other mammals have complete diaphragms. The diaphragm is the chief muscle used in breathing. It is shaped like a dome.

When a person takes a breath, the diaphragm contracts and moves downward. This increases the space in the chest. At the same time, muscles attached to the ribs cause the ribs to move outward. This expands the chest, and together with the downward motion of the diaphragm, creates a slight vacuum in the chest. The vacuum causes air to enter the lungs through the windpipe. This action is called *inspiration* or *inhalation.*

During *expiration,* also called *exhalation,* air moves out of the lungs as the diaphragm and rib muscles relax. When a person breathes normally, expiration is passive and muscles do no work. The expanded lung contains elastic fibers that were stretched during inspiration. This elastic tissue behaves like stretched rubber bands, causing the lung to contract like a collapsing balloon. This forces air out of the chest. The lung gets smaller until it reaches the size at which the breath started. The lungs do not empty completely during expiration because the chest wall holds them in a partially expanded state. In hard breathing, as occurs during exercise, expiration is

General Electric

Synthetic diamonds are produced in a press, *left,* developed by scientists in the early 1970's. Synthetic-diamond powder, *center,* is placed in the press along with a metal catalyst. The mixture then is subjected to extreme heat and pressure. The diamonds that result, *right,* have the quality and size of natural gems.

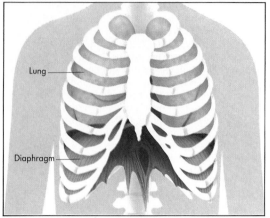

The diaphragm is a large, dome-shaped muscle that plays a major role in respiration. It is attached to the ribs on each side and to the breastbone in front and the lower spine in back, *above.* When a person inhales, *below left,* the diaphragm contracts and its dome flattens. This action increases the volume of the lungs, thereby creating a slight vacuum that pulls air into the lungs. When a person exhales, *below right,* the diaphragm and rib muscles relax. The stretched elastic fibers in the lung contract and cause the lung to become smaller, forcing air out.

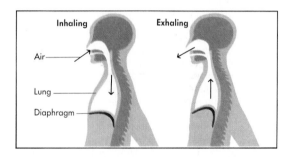

active. Another set of rib muscles helps to make the chest smaller. Muscles in the abdominal wall also contract to push the abdominal organs upward against the diaphragm, helping force air out of the lungs.

The *phrenic nerve* carries the electrical signals to the diaphragm that stimulate it to contract. This nerve arises from the spinal cord high in the neck and extends into the chest down to the diaphragm.   Robert A. Klocke

See also **Abdomen; Chest; Lung; Respiration.**

Diarrhea, *DY uh REE uh,* is a condition characterized by loose and frequent bowel movements. The stools are usually watery and soft, and may contain mucus, pus, or blood. Nausea, loss of bowel control, and abdominal cramps frequently accompany diarrhea.

Diarrhea is usually a symptom of an intestinal disorder and not a disease itself. The most frequent cause of diarrhea is infection from food or water contaminated by viruses, bacteria, or protozoans. The body usually develops a defense against the invading agent, and diarrhea then disappears. However, diarrhea may become chronic and lead to dehydration, malnutrition, vitamin deficiencies, and a weakened immune system. Such infectious diarrhea is epidemic in many developing countries. Every year, dehydration resulting from infectious

diarrhea kills millions of children worldwide. Other causes of diarrhea include *colitis* (inflammation of the colon) and intestinal cancer. Emotional disturbances, such as nervousness or fear, can also bring on diarrhea.

Treatment of diarrhea consists primarily of replacing lost body fluids and salts. A doctor should be consulted if diarrhea persists for more than a few days, or if it afflicts infants or young children, the elderly, or the severely ill.   André Dubois

See also **Cholera; Colitis; Dehydration; Dysentery.**

Diary is a written account of a person's experiences and thoughts, recorded each day or every few days. Many people keep diaries as a personal record. Most do not intend that other people read their diaries.

Diaries resemble journals, and the two words are often used interchangeably. However, journals are generally less personal than diaries, and many journals are written for other people to read.

Throughout history, people have kept diaries. Some diaries provide insight into the events and customs of a particular period. One of the most famous historical diaries was written by Samuel Pepys, a British government official. Pepys's diary, written in a personal code, covers the period from 1660 to 1669. Pepys was a sociable, prosperous Londoner who made keen observations about public events. His diary includes information on the Great Plague of 1665 and the Great Fire of London, which occurred in 1666. Pepys's diary was not decoded until the early 1800's. The complete diary was first published in nine volumes during the 1970's.

The diary of William Byrd II, a wealthy landowner in colonial Virginia, vividly portrays the lives of well-to-do colonists during the 1700's. Perhaps the best-known diary of the 1900's was written by Anne Frank, a young German-Jewish girl. She and her family hid from the Nazis during World War II to avoid persecution. From 1942 to 1944, Frank kept a record of her experiences in *The Diary of Anne Frank* (1947).

Many authors of fiction have written novels and short stories in the form of diaries. Such tales have a highly personal quality because the reader can become closely involved with the personality of the central character. The Russian author Nikolai Gogol wrote "The Diary of a Madman" (1835), a short story in the form of the diary of a clerk. In the novel *Dangling Man* (1944), the American author Saul Bellow portrays the hero of the story in the act of writing a diary. The novel consists largely of the hero's diary entries.   Marcus Klein

See also **Bellow, Saul; Burney, Fanny; Byrd** (William II); **Evelyn, John; Frank, Anne; Pepys, Samuel.**

Dias, Bartolomeu (1450?-1500), also spelled *Diaz,* was a Portuguese sea captain and explorer. His discovery of a sailing route around Africa helped establish travel between western Europe and Asia.

Little is known about Dias' early life. In 1481 and 1482, he commanded one of the ships in an expedition to the Gold Coast in Africa. This region now makes up the nation of Ghana.

In 1487, King John II of Portugal ordered Dias to try to sail to the southern end of Africa. The king wanted to know if ships could reach Asia by sailing around Africa. He had earlier ordered land and sea expeditions to travel to Asia, but those attempts at the journey failed.

Dias commanded a fleet of three ships that left Portugal in the summer of 1487. After reaching the mouth of the Orange River in southern Africa, a storm blew the ships out to sea. Dias and his crews did not see land for 13 days. When the storm ended, he realized that the ships had been blown around the southern tip of Africa. He sailed along the southeast shore of the continent, hoping to continue on to India. However, the men were exhausted by their long voyage, and their food supply was running low. They persuaded Dias to return to Portugal. As the expedition sailed around the tip of Africa toward Portugal, Dias sighted what is now called the Cape of Good Hope. According to tradition, he named it the *Cape of Storms.* However, King John later renamed it the Cape of Good Hope because its discovery indicated that a sea route to India would soon be found. The expedition reached Portugal in December 1488.

In 1494, Dias directed the construction of two ships for what became the first successful expedition around Africa to India. Vasco da Gama, another Portuguese explorer, led the voyage in 1497. In 1500, Dias commanded four ships in an expedition led by Pedro Álvares Cabral, also a Portuguese adventurer. Cabral's expedition consisted of 13 ships. He tried to follow da Gama's route to India, but the fleet drifted off course and reached what is now Brazil. Dias died during the voyage from Brazil when a storm sank his ship.　　　John Parker

See also **Da Gama, Vasco; Exploration** (map: The great age of discovery).

Diaspora. See **Jews** (Invasions and conquests).

Diathermy, *DY uh* THUR *mee,* is a method of treating muscle and joint disorders and other diseases by creating heat energy in tissues beneath the skin. Diathermy is used chiefly to relieve such conditions as muscle aches, muscle strain, and pain and inflammation in the joints.

In diathermy, an electric current is passed through the body, generating an electromagnetic field. The tissues of the body have different resistances to the flow of electric current. This resistance causes a temperature rise in the tissues. At the same time, the tissues absorb the electromagnetic field, causing molecules in the tis-

sues to *oscillate* (move back and forth). The oscillation of the molecules generates heat energy. It is this energy that affects the tissues, resulting in healing, relaxation of the muscles, or other therapeutic effects.

The electric current used in diathermy is an oscillating current with very high frequencies. The current oscillates so rapidly that the patient does not feel any shock. There are several forms of diathermy, each having a different range of frequencies. All forms of diathermy used for therapeutic purposes are known as *medical diathermy. Short-wave diathermy,* with frequencies in the range of radio waves, is the most commonly used form of medical diathermy. This diathermy is usually applied with two insulated metal plates, which fit against the part of the body treated. *Surgical diathermy* is used to destroy tumors and other abnormal growths. The current is concentrated at the point of a fine wire, with sufficient heat generated to kill the tissue.

Mary T. Moffroid

Diatom, *DY uh tahm,* is a microscopic, single-celled organism. Diatoms are found in the ocean, in freshwater lakes, rivers, and streams, and on moist soil. In water, diatoms live attached to rocks, sand, or plants, or they may float freely. Diatoms are probably best known as part of the mass of drifting organisms in oceans called *plankton.*

Diatoms belong to a group of simple plantlike organisms called *algae.* Like green plants, diatoms can live and grow using only sunlight, water, carbon dioxide, and certain minerals.

Diatom cells contain both green and yellow-orange pigments that enable them to trap the sun's energy. This combination of pigments gives diatoms a golden-brown color. For this reason, they are sometimes called *golden-brown algae.*

Diatoms differ from other algae in that their cells are enclosed in a hard, glasslike shell made of opal. The shell, also called the *frustule,* consists of two parts that fit one inside the other, like a box with its lid. Most diatoms are either circular or oblong in shape. Diatoms

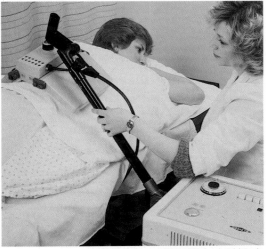

WORLD BOOK photo by Ralph Brunke

A diathermy machine uses electric current to create heat energy in tissues beneath the skin, producing therapeutic effects.

Eric Gravé, Science Photo Library

Diatom shells show some of the possible shapes of these one-celled organisms. The edgewise view above illustrates how the halves of a diatom shell fit together. The photographs below show flat views of a square and a five-pointed diatom.

Gene Cox, Science Photo Library　　　　　Eric Gravé, Science Photo Library

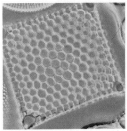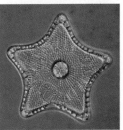

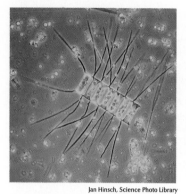

***Chaetoceros* diatoms link** themselves together into chains.

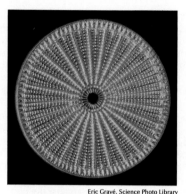

An Arachnoidiscus diatom is flat and has a circular shape.

Freshwater *meridion* diatoms join and form a delicate fanlike pattern.

usually multiply through cell division—that is, one cell divides into two cells. After a diatom cell divides, each new cell retains one part of the parent shell and builds a new part to fit into it. Some diatoms stay linked after cell division, forming chain- or ribbon-shaped colonies.

Some scientists have estimated that there may be more than 12,000 species of diatoms. Scientists identify species by examining the shells.

Planktonic diatoms are especially plentiful in certain regions of the oceans, where they serve as an important source of food for fish and other marine animals. When diatoms die, their hard shells remain intact. Eventually the shells sink to the bottom of the sea. Over thousands of years, the layer of diatom shells may become very deep. On land, the accumulation of diatom shells from ancient seabeds is mined as *diatomaceous earth,* also called *diatomite.* This substance is used as a polishing powder, abrasive, insulator, or filter. Diatomaceous earth is also used as a filler in paints and in rubber and plastic products.

Scientific classification. Diatoms have traditionally been classified in the plant kingdom, Plantae. Many scientists now classify diatoms in the kingdom Protista.   David L. Garrison

See also **Algae; Plankton.**

Diaz, Bartolomeu. See Dias, Bartolomeu.

Díaz, *DEE ahs,* **Porfirio,** *pawr FEE rih oh* (1830-1915), served as president of Mexico from 1877 to 1880 and from 1884 to 1911. Díaz gained fame as a general in the war against French invaders that lasted from 1863 to 1867. Overthrowing President Lerdo de Tejada in 1876, Díaz acted as provisional president until his election in 1877. His policies encouraged railroads, large-scale agriculture, banking, and industry. However, conditions improved little for most people. A popular uprising in 1910 forced Díaz into exile in France, where he died. Díaz was born in Oaxaca, Mexico.   Harold Eugene Davis

See also **Mexico** (The dictatorship of Porfirio Díaz).

Dice are small cubes used in such games of chance as craps. Dice are also used in playing backgammon, Monopoly, and other board games. A single cube is called a *die.* Each die has six sides, with each side imprinted with one to six dots. In most games, two dice are used. Players roll the dice on a craps table or other flat surface. When the dice stop rolling, the total number of dots on the top side of both dice determines the number used for that particular turn. Random chance decides which numbers appear on the dice and skill is not involved.

Craps is a popular gambling game in which a player rolls the dice, trying for a certain number from 2 to 12, depending on the situation. There are 36 combinations of numbers that will produce one of the 11 numbers from 2 to 12.   Leonard Miller

Dichloro-diphenyl-trichloroethane. See DDT.

Dick, Philip K. (1928-1982), was an American science-fiction writer. His novels and stories often feature common science-fiction elements, such as alien beings, alternate universes, and humanlike machines called androids. But his best works reflect his philosophical ideas and his concern with character rather than with action or gadgetry.

Dick's most popular novel, *The Man in the High Castle* (1962), is an alternate history in which the Germans and Japanese have won World War II and occupied the United States. In *Do Androids Dream of Electric Sheep?* (1968), a bounty hunter hired to kill escaped androids begins to feel sympathy for them. Later novels reflect Dick's concern with religion. In *VALIS* (1981), a character resembling the author believes he has received enlightenment from a godlike source. His other major fiction includes the novels *Dr. Bloodmoney* (1965) and *Ubik* (1969) and *The Collected Stories of Philip K. Dick* (1987).

Philip Kendred Dick was born in Chicago. His essay "Man, Android and Machine" (1976) takes up key themes in his fiction, such as reality versus illusion.

Neil Barron

Dickcissel, *dihk SIHS uhl,* is a bunting of the finch and sparrow family (see **Bunting**). The dickcissel is a bird

Dice are used in games of both chance and skill. In many games, they determine the number of moves a player may take.

Hans Reinhard, Bruce Coleman Ltd.

Dickcissels are small birds that live along railroads and roadsides, primarily in the central United States. The birds have grayish-brown feathers and a yellow breast.

about 6 inches (15 centimeters) long. Its plumage is a streaked grayish-brown, varied by a yellow breast and bright chestnut wing patches. There is a conspicuous black crescent on the throat. Dickcissels are common in the central United States, and are sometimes seen in the eastern states. They live along railroads and roadsides. The birds eat insects and seeds. The female lays from 3 to 5 eggs. The nest is built of leaves, grass, and hair, and is on or near the ground.

   Scientific classification. The dickcissel belongs to the New World seedeater family, Fringillidae. The bird is *Spiza americana.*   George J. Wallace

   See also **Bird** (picture: Birds of grasslands).

Dickens, Charles (1812-1870), was a great English novelist and one of the most popular writers of all time. His best-known books include *A Christmas Carol, David Copperfield, Great Expectations, Oliver Twist, The Pickwick Papers,* and *A Tale of Two Cities.* Dickens created some of the most famous characters in English literature. He also created scenes and descriptions of places that have long delighted readers. Dickens was a keen observer of life and had a great understanding of humanity, especially of young people. He sympathized with the poor and helpless, and mocked and criticized the selfish, the greedy, and the cruel.

   Dickens was also a wonderfully inventive comic artist. The warmth and humor of his personality appear in all his works. Perhaps in no other large body of fiction does the reader receive so strong and agreeable an impression of the person behind the story.

Dickens' life

   Charles John Huffam Dickens was born in Portsmouth on Feb. 7, 1812. He moved with his family to London when he was about two years old. Many of the events and people in his books are based on events and people in his life. Dickens' father, John Dickens, was a poor and easygoing clerk who worked for the navy. John served in some respects as the model for Wilkins Micawber in *David Copperfield.* He spent time in prison for debt, an event Charles re-created in *Little Dorrit.*

   Even when John was free, he lacked the money to support his family adequately. At the age of 12, Charles worked in a London factory pasting labels on bottles of shoe polish. He held the job only a few months, but the misery of that experience remained with him all his life.

   Dickens attended school off and on until he was 15, and then left for good. He enjoyed reading and was especially fond of adventure stories, fairy tales, and novels. He was influenced by such earlier English writers as William Shakespeare, Tobias Smollett, and Henry Fielding. However, most of the knowledge he later used as an author came from his observation of life around him.

   Dickens became a newspaper reporter in the late 1820's. He specialized in covering debates in Parliament, and also wrote feature articles. His work as a reporter sharpened his naturally keen ear for conversation and helped develop his skill in portraying his characters' speech realistically. It also increased his ability to observe and to write swiftly and clearly. Dickens' first book, *Sketches by Boz* (1836), consisted of articles he wrote for the *Monthly Magazine* and the London *Evening Chronicle.* These descriptions, fictional portraits, and short stories surveyed manners and conditions of the time.

   Literary success. Dickens won his first literary fame with *The Posthumous Papers of the Pickwick Club.* Published in monthly parts in 1836 and 1837, the book describes the humorous adventures and misadventures of a group of slightly eccentric characters in London and the English countryside. After a slow start, *The Pickwick Papers*—as the book is usually called—gained a popularity seldom matched in the history of literature. At 24, Dickens suddenly found himself famous. He remained so until his death.

   Dickens founded and edited two highly successful weekly magazines. He edited *Household Words* from 1850 to 1859 and *All the Year Round* from 1859 to his death. As a public figure, Dickens was constantly in the news, and was recognized and honored wherever he went. He was famous in America as well as in Britain, and he toured the United States in 1842 and in 1867 and 1868.

   Personal life. Personal unhappiness marred Dickens' public success. In 1836, he married Catherine Hogarth. Catherine had a sister Mary, who died in 1837. Dickens' grief at Mary's death has led some scholars to believe that he loved Mary more than his wife. Catherine was a good woman but lacked great intelligence. She and Dickens had 10 children. The couple separated in 1858.

   Dickens had remarkable mental and physical energy. He recorded his activities in thousands of letters, many of which make delightful reading. He spent much of his crowded social life with friends from the worlds of art and literature. Dickens enjoyed drama and went to the theater as often as he could. When he was rich and famous, he made a hobby of producing and acting in amateur theatrical productions. He had great success giving public readings of his works. Dickens' gift for creating dramatic scenes in his novels can be traced to his love for the theater.

   Besides writing, editing, and touring as a dramatic reader, Dickens busied himself with various charities. These charities included schools for poor children and a loan society to enable the poor to move to Australia. Dickens often walked for hours to work off his remain-

Charles Dickens, the most famous English writer of his time, enchanted audiences with dramatic readings from his novels.

ing energy. He came to know the streets and alleys of London better, perhaps, than any other person of his time.

Dickens' health began to decline about 1865 and he died of a stroke on June 9, 1870.

Dickens' books

Dickens wrote 20 novels (including 5 short Christmas books), and many sketches, travel books, and other non-fiction works. Not all of his books were best sellers, but the most popular ones broke all sales records for the time. Most of his novels were published in sections.

The first phase. After the success of *The Pickwick Papers,* Dickens turned to more serious themes and plots. However, he always introduced enough humor to keep his books entertaining.

Oliver Twist (1837-1839) describes the adventures of a poor orphan boy. The book was noted for its sensational presentation of London's criminal world and for its attack on England's mistreatment of the poor.

In *Nicholas Nickleby* (1838-1839), Dickens criticized greedy proprietors of private schools, who treated students brutally and taught them nothing.

The Old Curiosity Shop (1840-1841) is less respected today than when it was first published, largely because the death scene of Little Nell seems sentimental to modern tastes.

Barnaby Rudge (1841) is a historical novel that deals with a series of riots in London in 1780. *Martin Chuzzlewit* (1843-1844) is one of two books that Dickens based on his first trip to America. The other is the travel book *American Notes* (1842). Dickens intended *Martin Chuzzlewit* to be a study of many forms of selfishness. But it is best known for its unflattering picture of the crudeness of American manners and for its comic characters. Two of its finest creations are the hypocrite Pecksniff and the chattering, alcoholic midwife Sairey Gamp.

Dickens wrote his five "Christmas books" during the

1840's. The first, *A Christmas Carol* (1843), is one of the most famous stories ever written. In the book, three ghosts show the old miser Ebenezer Scrooge his past, present, and future. Realizing that he has been living a life of greed, Scrooge changes into a warm and unselfish person. The other Christmas books are *The Chimes* (1844), *The Cricket on the Hearth* (1845), *The Battle of Life* (1846), and *The Haunted Man* (1848).

The second phase. During the 1840's, Dickens' view of Victorian society, and perhaps of the world, grew darker. His humor became more bitter, often taking the form of biting satire. His characters and plots seemed to emphasize the evil side of human experience.

At the same time, Dickens increasingly refined his art. The range of his tone widened and he paid more attention to structure and arrangement. He turned to symbolic themes to help express and expand his observations on topical political and social issues and on larger matters of morality and values. The unhealthy London fog in *Bleak House,* for example, symbolizes the illness of society, especially its lack of responsibility toward the downtrodden and the unfortunate.

Dombey and Son (1846-1848) deals primarily with a selfish egotist whose pride cuts him off from the warmth of human love. The book stresses the evils of the Victorian admiration for money. Dickens believed that money had become the measure of all personal relations and the goal of all ambition.

With *David Copperfield* (1849-1850), Dickens temporarily lessened the role of social criticism to concentrate more on semiautobiography. The novel describes a young man's discovery of the realities of adult life. David's youth is clearly patterned after Dickens' youth.

Bleak House (1852-1853) is in many respects Dickens' greatest novel. It has a complex structure and many levels of meaning, mixing melodrama with satire and social commentary. The book deals with many social evils, chiefly wasteful and cruel legal processes. It also attacks the neglect of the poor, false humanitarians and clergymen, and poor sanitation.

This long novel was followed by the much shorter and simpler *Hard Times* (1854). *Hard Times* attacks philosopher Jeremy Bentham's doctrine of *utilitarianism.* Bentham believed that all human ideas, actions, and institutions should be judged by their usefulness. Dickens was convinced that Bentham reduced social relations to problems of cold, mechanical self-interest.

In *Little Dorrit* (1855-1857), Dickens continued his campaign against materialism and snobbery, which were represented by the rich Merdle family and their social-climbing friends. He also ridiculed government inefficiency in the form of the "Circumlocution Office." The prison, like the fog in *Bleak House,* is symbolic. It stands for the painful conditions of life in a materialistic, decaying society.

A Tale of Two Cities (1859) was the second of Dickens' two historical novels. It is set in London and Paris and tells of the heroism of fictional Sidney Carton during the French Revolution.

In *Great Expectations* (1860-1861), Dickens returned to the theme of a youth's discovery of the realities of life. An unknown person provides the young hero Pip with money so that Pip can live as a gentleman. Pip's pride is shattered when he learns the source of his "great expectations." Only by painfully revising his values does Pip reestablish his life on a foundation of sympathy, rather than on vanity, possessions, and social position.

Our Mutual Friend (1864-1865) was Dickens' final novel of social criticism. Dickens again attacked the false values of the newly rich. He satirized greed, using the great garbage heaps of the London dumps as a symbol of filthy money. The novel is also notable for its suggestive use of London's River Thames.

Dickens had completed about one-third of his novel *The Mystery of Edwin Drood* when he died. Nobody knows how Dickens intended the story to end. Scholars and readers throughout the years have proposed many possible solutions for the mystery.

Dickens' place in literature

Dickens is now considered one of the major figures in English literature, but his position was not always so high. His reputation declined between 1880 and 1940. This was partly due to the psychological emphasis that became fashionable in novels after Dickens' death. Critics valued Dickens chiefly as an entertainer and, above all, as a creator of a huge gallery of comic, pleasant, and villainous characters. They recognized him as a master creator of plot and scene, and as a sharp-eyed observer of London life. But they considered his outlook simple and unrealistic. They believed he lacked artistic taste and relied too much on broad comedy, dramatic effects, sentimentality, and superficial psychology.

However, since 1940, numerous books and essays have described Dickens as a writer of considerable depth and complexity. He has also been praised as a sensitive and philosophic observer of human struggles within social institutions. In this sense, Dickens has been associated with such authors as Herman Melville, Franz Kafka, and Fyodor Dostoevsky.

Recent criticism has demonstrated that Dickens can no longer be regarded only as an entertainer, though his ability to entertain is probably the major reason for his popularity. Whatever his other claims to greatness may be, Dickens ranks as a superbly inventive comic artist. His characters have been compared to those of Shakespeare in their variety, color, energy, and life. Dickens was aware of human evil, but he never lost his perspective. His art was sustained by an awareness and appreciation of the human comedy.   K. K. Collins

See also *Dickens, Charles,* in the Research Guide/Index, Volume 22, for a *Reading and Study Guide.*

Additional resources

The Charles Dickens Encyclopedia. Comp. by John M. D. Hardwick and M. G. Hardwick. Scribner, 1973.
Kaplan, Fred. *Dickens: A Biography.* Morrow, 1988.
Johnson, Edgar. *Charles Dickens: His Tragedy and Triumph.* Rev. ed. Viking, 1977. Abridgment of original 1952 edition.
Wilson, Angus. *The World of Charles Dickens.* Academy Chicago, 1984. First published in 1970.

Dickey, James (1923-   ), is an American poet and novelist. He is known chiefly for works that portray people testing their survival instincts against other people and nature. Some of his writings explore people's animal instincts, which include killing for enjoyment. Dickey writes in a clear, matter-of-fact style that shows people learning about the brutal side of human nature.

Dickey's novel *Deliverance* (1970) tells about a middle-class businessman who must struggle to survive in the wilderness. In his fight to survive, he has to kill another man. This experience teaches him that cruelty is part of people's nature. Many of Dickey's writings are based on episodes from his own life. Some of his works, particularly the poem "The Firebombing" (1964), reflect his experiences as a combat pilot. The pilot in this poem feels a sense of power at killing, but no sorrow.

Oliver Twist* and *David Copperfield contain many popular Dickens characters. In *Oliver Twist, left,* an original illustration by the artist George Cruikshank shows Oliver watching in alarm as the Artful Dodger and Charley Bates pick Mr. Brownlow's pocket. In *David Copperfield, right,* David, Betsy Trotwood, and Mr. Dick watch the joyful reunion of Wilkins Micawber and his family. Hablot Knight Browne, popularly known as Phiz, drew this illustration for the first edition of the novel.

Collection of Mr. and Mrs. David Bradford, Chicago

Dickey was born in Atlanta, Ga. He won the National Book Award for poetry in 1966 for his collection *Buck-dancer's Choice* (1965). His other collections include *Poems 1957-1967* (1967) and *The Strength of Fields* (1980). A number of his prose pieces were published in *Sorties: Journals and New Essays* (1971). Dickey also wrote a second novel, *Alnilam* (1987). Marcus Klein

Dickinson, Anna Elizabeth (1842-1932), was an orator of the Civil War period who spoke on abolitionism and women's rights. Woman orators were a novelty at that time, and she became known as the North's "Joan of Arc." She attracted large crowds with her emotional pleas to end slavery.

Dickinson was born in Philadelphia. She gave her first important speech in 1860, the year before the Civil War began, when she addressed the Pennsylvania Anti-Slavery Society. Dickinson was then only 18 years old. The next year, she spoke on the "Rights and Wrongs of Women." In 1864, she denounced the

Dictionary of American Portraits
Anna E. Dickinson

South in a speech to members of the U.S. Congress and President Abraham Lincoln.

After the Civil War, Dickinson frequently lectured on feminism and blacks' rights. She spoke for organizations called *lyceums,* which sponsored adult education programs. During some years, she earned as much as $20,000, a large income for anyone of her day.

Dickinson's speaking career declined in the early 1870's. She campaigned for the Democratic Party in 1872, and for the Republicans in 1888. She spent her last 40 years in seclusion. Nancy Spelman Woloch

Dickinson, Emily (1830-1886), was an American poet. Dickinson and Walt Whitman are considered the two most gifted poets in American literature. Like Whitman, she was influenced by the writings of American author Ralph Waldo Emerson. In her verses, Dickinson expressed Emerson's late pessimism. Many of her poems reflect the alienation of American intellectuals after the Civil War (1861-1865).

Her life. Emily Dickinson was born in Amherst, Mass., on Dec. 10, 1830. She was reclusive, and much about her is unknown. She never married, and after turning 30, seldom saw anyone other than her immediate family.

Dickinson's seclusion from society has fascinated her readers. Scholars believe that she chose to think and write in, as she wrote, "her own Society," rather than in the narrow-minded literary establishment of her time. This establishment expected female writers to confine themselves to domestic subjects and sentimental observations. Furthermore, an unmarried professional woman in America had few opportunities in the 1800's. Therefore, Dickinson chose to remain in her comfortable, upper-middle-class home. Although her choice no longer seems so strange, people in her town viewed her as a curiosity and finally resented her unavailability.

Dickinson always wrote as what she called the "supposed person." This person never tired of examining the unique facts of existence. Hidden away on the second story of her parents' home, she analyzed practically every aspect of nature in poems that she began to bind into small books that were called *fascicles.*

Emily Dickinson

At about the age of 30, Dickinson began to look intensely at life itself, rather than looking for the normal expectations of life. While the Civil War raged, she produced the most and best of her poems. The poet continued to write in the 1870's but at a much slower pace. Probably one of her best poems, however, was written in this period of decline. Called "A Route of Evanescence," it describes the fluttering ascent of a hummingbird. For Dickinson, this erratic ascent was also the route of experience. Life was finally inscrutable, and its joy was to be found in studying its paradoxes.

Her poems. Dickinson wrote over 1,700 poems, but scholars generally agree she did not wish to publish any of them. But at least 10 of her poems appeared in print during her lifetime without her permission. One of them, "Success Is Counted Sweetest," teaches that experience resides in the ratio between success and failure rather than in either of the two exclusively.

The mere experience of being alive dominates Dickinson's poetry. Her poems show how Dickinson was sensitive to both the ecstasy and the anguish of everyday experience. In "A Narrow Fellow in the Grass" her crisp imagery conveys the sudden and flashing fear of coming upon a snake in the tall grass:

> Yet when a Boy, and Barefoot—
> I more than once at Noon
> Have passed, I thought, a Whip lash
> Unbraiding in the Sun

Dickinson daily dressed in white, as if to mock the traditions of marriage. She often pondered the consequences of her life style:

> I'm "Wife"—I've finished that—
> That other state—
> I'm Czar—I'm "Woman" now—
> It's safer so—

The "lover" in many of her poems is not a potential husband and "master" but death and eternity. In what many critics believe is her greatest poem, "Because I Could Not Stop for Death," a carriage that brings her gentleman caller holds "but just Ourselves/And Immortality."

The point of view of most of her poems reinforces her theme that our most important moments are over as soon as they begin. Dickinson's "I Heard a Fly Buzz" reflects this theme, describing with beauty and simplicity a dying person's impressions at the moment of death. This poem appears in the **Poetry** article.

Often her poems open with a clear story line, but quickly fade at their close into silence, as if to suggest her inquiry continues in the subconscious. As she wrote in another poem, it was the poet's job to distill "amazing sense/from ordinary meaning."   Jerome Loving

See also **American literature** (Individualists).

Additional resources

Barth, Edna. *I'm Nobody! Who Are You? The Story of Emily Dickinson.* Clarion, 1979. First published in 1971. For younger readers.

Ferlazzo, Paul J. *Emily Dickinson.* Twayne, 1976.

Dickinson, John (1732-1808), represented Delaware at the 1787 Constitutional Convention in Philadelphia and played an important role in drafting the Constitution of the United States. Illness forced Dickinson to leave the convention early, but he authorized another delegate to sign the Constitution for him. At the convention, Dickinson supported a strong national government. However, he also defended the rights and powers of the states against those of the federal government. He was among several delegates who first raised the idea of a dual legislature that would give states both equal and population-based representation.

Dickinson was born in Talbot County, Md. He studied law in Philadelphia and London. In 1767 and 1768, Dickinson wrote a series of newspaper articles that expressed the American Colonies' resistance to British taxation. The series was published later in a pamphlet titled *Letters from a Farmer in Pennsylvania to the Inhabitants of the British Colonies.* Dickinson's writings earned him the nickname "Penman of the Revolution."

Dickinson opposed the Declaration of Independence and was among the members of the Second Continental Congress who refused to sign it. However, he proved his patriotism by joining the American army in the Revolutionary War in America (1775-1783) and by helping write the Articles of Confederation. Dickinson was prominent in both Delaware and Pennsylvania. He was president of Delaware in 1782 and 1783 and of Pennsylvania from 1782 to 1785.   Barbara E. Benson

See also **Delaware** (Places to visit).

Dickson, Brian (1916-   ), served as chief justice of the Supreme Court of Canada from 1984 to 1990. He was appointed by the government headed by Prime Minister Pierre Trudeau and had served as a *puisne* (associate) judge of the court since 1973. On constitutional issues, he showed concern for maintaining a well-balanced federal system in Canada.

Robert George Brian Dickson was born in Yorkton, Sask. He earned a law degree from the University of Manitoba. During World War II, he served in Europe with the Royal Canadian Artillery from 1940 to 1945. He lost most of his right leg in battle. After the war, Dickson practiced law in Winnipeg. He was appointed to the Manitoba Court of Queen's Bench in 1963 and to the Manitoba Court of Appeal in 1967.

Under Dickson, the Supreme Court decided the first cases on the basis of the Canadian Charter of Rights and Freedoms. This bill of rights took effect in 1982. As chief justice, Dickson took a liberal approach. In 1988, he was among the five-judge majority that rejected Canada's restrictive abortion law.   Peter H. Russell

See also **Supreme Court of Canada.**

Dicotyledon, *dy КАНТ uh LEE duhn,* is a type of flowering plant that has two *cotyledons* (leafy parts within each seed). Dicotyledon plants have leaves with netted veins. Their flower petals usually grow in multiples of 4 or 5. Common dicotyledons include beans, peas, squashes, and tomatoes. See also **Cotyledon.**

Dictating machine is a business machine that records speech on a magnetic disk, tape, or other device. The recording can then be played back and copied, generally in typed form. Dictating machines save time because a person can dictate at any time without calling a stenographer. Some machines are lightweight and small enough to be carried easily on business trips.

A dictating machine has either a built-in microphone or a separate microphone that plugs into it. The person dictating speaks into the microphone. The speech is recorded on a variety of materials, including plastic belts, cartridges, disks, and tapes. Cassette tapes are most widely used. To play back the dictation, a typist places the recording in a device called a *transcriber* and listens to it through earphones. Some dictating machines have a built-in transcriber. Others use a separate unit.

A centralized dictating system allows people to dictate from different locations to a central office. With this system, the person dictating may use a regular telephone or a special microphone that is connected to telephone lines.   Eileen Feretic

Dictatorship is a form of government in which an individual, a committee, or a group holds absolute power. The term *dictator* originated in ancient Rome. The Roman Senate often appointed individuals as temporary "dictators" who could handle national emergencies without the approval of the people or the Senate. But the Roman dictator did not have the absolute power of modern dictators. Today, many countries are ruled by dictatorships, including some Communist nations.

Dictatorship is similar to *absolute monarchy,* another system of government in which the rulers have no legal restrictions on their power. However, the two systems differ. Throughout history, most people have accepted monarchies as a form of government. Once established, monarchies tended to become hereditary. Most monarchs respected the established customs and institutions of countries they ruled and often shared power with other government officials and nobles. Dictatorships, on the other hand, generally lack the approval of the people and are almost never hereditary. Dictators also maintain exclusive control over the government.

Most dictatorships are established through violence, force, and sometimes political trickery. Joseph Stalin used these methods while serving as general secretary of the Communist Party in the Soviet Union, and he became dictator of the country in 1929. Dictators must continue to use force to maintain their power. Thus, most dictators outlaw or limit freedom of speech, assembly, and the press. Many dictators also forbid elections entirely. Many others change the votes or force people to vote for candidates chosen by the government. In spite of denying their citizens numerous basic freedoms, however, many dictatorships call themselves "people's republics" or "people's democracies."

Some dictatorships develop after a country has been conquered by a foreign power. The Soviet Union controlled much of Eastern Europe following World War II (1939-1945), and Stalin established Communist dictatorships in Poland, Czechoslovakia, and other nations in that region. A dictatorship may also take over a democratic nation during a period of crisis. The crisis may divide the government and limit its ability to maintain domestic order, security, and prosperity. Dictators who came to power under such circumstances included Benito Mussolini of Italy in 1922, Adolf Hitler of Germany in 1933, Francisco Franco of Spain in 1939, and Augusto Pinochet of Chile in 1973.   Alexander J. Groth

See also **Autocracy; Government.** For a *Reading and Study Guide,* see *Dictatorship* in the Research Guide/Index, Volume 22.

Additional resources

Marrin, Albert. *Stalin.* Viking, 1988. *Hitler.* 1987. Both suitable for younger readers.
Rubin, Barry M. *Modern Dictators: Third World Coup Makers, Strongmen, and Populist Tyrants.* McGraw, 1987.

Dictionary is a book that contains a selected list of words arranged in alphabetical order. It explains their meanings and gives information about them. In a dictionary, a person can look up a word quickly, discover what it means, and learn how it is pronounced. Most modern dictionaries describe the facts of a language as educated speakers and writers use it. They are called *descriptive dictionaries* because a dictionary editor does not change the facts of a language. Many older dictionaries tried to prescribe rules, some of which did not agree with the way people commonly talked or wrote. These books are called *prescriptive dictionaries.*

What dictionaries contain

Dictionaries give the meanings of many kinds of words. Most general dictionaries include (1) the ordinary words of everyday life, such as *bread, run,* and *with;* (2) literary words used in formal writing, such as *aggregation, despoil,* and *incontrovertible;* (3) technical words, such as *starboard, gene,* and *ratio;* (4) words used chiefly on informal occasions, such as *gab* and *wimp;* (5) words used in writing to give an old-fashioned flavor, such as *aweary* and *avaunt;* (6) words not used today but found in the writings of some authors, such as *plaister* for *plaster;* (7) words or phrases from other languages, such as *coup d'état* from French, *tofu* from Japanese, and *barrio* from Spanish; (8) idioms (groups of words with meanings different from their literal meanings), such as *split hairs* and *under the thumb of;* (9) abbreviations, such as *U.S.A., Kans.,* and *p.;* and (10) important proper names, such as *Buddha* and *Jupiter.*

No dictionary records all the words of our language. In fact, no one knows exactly how many English words there are. Besides ordinary words used in everyday speech, the English language includes thousands of geographical names. There are thousands of words that are no longer used. And there are hundreds of thousands of technical terms, including more than 750,000 names of insects alone. New words are coined for new scientific and technical discoveries, and slang words and special vocabularies constantly spring up. As nations draw closer together through trade and travel, satellite communication, and sharing of technology, languages tend to borrow more and more words from each other. That is why dictionary editors must be selective in the words they decide to include.

Most dictionaries tell us much more than just the meanings of words. Many list pronunciations, derivations, prefixes and suffixes, illustrative quotations, synonyms and antonyms, usage notes, and other information. The illustration with this article shows in detail what dictionaries tell us.

Kinds of dictionaries

Dictionaries may be classified as *general dictionaries* and *specialized dictionaries.* A general dictionary contains information on everyday words such as *it* and *the.* But it also defines many technical terms such as *chromatography* and *columella.* A specialized dictionary omits most everyday terms, and limits itself to information on words used in a particular field, such as biology.

General dictionaries range in size from small pocket dictionaries to large multivolume or table dictionaries. The number of entries in a general dictionary depends on its purpose. Each dictionary is designed to answer the questions of a certain type of reader. A sixth-grade student, for example, would not want all the information given in a dictionary a college professor would use. For this reason, dictionary editors work hard to design their products to suit the needs of their intended audiences. They know that the usefulness of any dictionary depends on the education of the user and the kind of information the user wishes to find.

A general dictionary may be designed for use by elementary-school students, high-school students, or college students. It may also be designed for use by the general reader, or even by the entire family. *The World Book Dictionary* is an example of a dictionary designed for family use.

The largest general dictionaries may contain over 400,000 entries. When a dictionary has this many entries, many obsolete and technical terms are included. Other general dictionaries may have from 15,000 entries to 200,000 entries.

Specialized dictionaries are designed to give more information in particular fields than general dictionaries can. A *gazetteer* (geographical dictionary) lists the names of cities, countries, islands, lakes, and other places. It gives the pronunciation of each name and a brief description. A *biographical dictionary* lists and gives the pronunciation of the names of important people. Each entry includes birth and death dates, nationality, and why the person is remembered. A *thesaurus* contains lists of synonyms and antonyms. Other specialized dictionaries are devoted to usage; idioms; pronunciations; slang; spelling; new words and meanings; and various aspects of science and technology. Research or scholarly dictionaries may cover the vocabulary of earlier periods of a language, such as Old English or Late Latin. Some are also devoted to various dialects, such as Scottish or South African English. There are dictionaries of all the major languages. *Bilingual dictionaries* translate the words of one language into another.

How to use a dictionary

Before using a dictionary, one should become familiar with the methods, principles, and scope of the book because various dictionaries are arranged in different ways. Many American dictionaries arrange all entries in a single alphabetical list. Others put abbreviations, geographical and biographical names, and foreign words and phrases in separate lists, usually at the end of the

What a dictionary tells you

In addition to defining words, a dictionary provides much useful information about them. You can get the most out of a dictionary by learning what its abbreviations and symbols stand for. These examples come from *The World Book Dictionary*.

Word entries begin in bold black type. Only proper nouns are capitalized. The first letter of the entry extends into the margin for easy location. This dictionary uses an asterisk to indicate that the entry is accompanied by an illustration.

Illustrations clarify the definitions. Labels show which meaning of the word is illustrated.

Pronunciations are given in phonetic symbols. This dictionary has a key to its phonetic symbols at the bottom of each right-hand page, with more detailed information at the front of the book.

Parts of speech labels show the word's grammatical use. Any word used as more than one part of speech is defined accordingly. The parts of speech are abbreviated, as in *adj.* for *adjective* and *n.* for *noun*. Verbs are shown as transitive (*v.t.*) or intransitive (*v.i.*).

Phrases that include the key word but have special meanings of their own are explained separately.

Synonyms that have the same or nearly the same meaning as the defined words appear immediately after the definition.

Synonym studies explain in detail the various shades of meaning of some synonyms. All these studies include examples.

Usage notes explain points of spelling or grammar and advise how to use the word in speaking or writing.

* ab|do|men (ab′də mən, ab dō′-), *n.* **1a** the part of the body containing the stomach and the intestines; belly. In man and other mammals the abdomen is a large cavity between the chest (thorax) and the pelvis, and also contains the liver, pancreas, kidneys, and spleen. **b** a corresponding region in vertebrates below mammals. **2** the last of the three parts of the body of insects and many other arthropods, including spiders and crustaceans. [< Latin *abdōmen*]

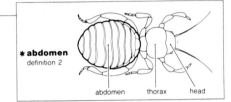

* abdomen
definition 2

abdomen   thorax   head

ab|dom|i|nal (ab dom′ə nəl), *adj.* of the abdomen; in the abdomen; for the abdomen: *Bending the body exercises the abdominal muscles.* **SYN:** ventral, visceral. — **ab|dom′i|nal|ly,** *adv.*
abdominal brain, = solar plexus.
ab|dom|i|nous (ab dom′ə nəs), *adj.* = potbellied.

a|bide¹ (ə bīd′), *v.,* **a|bode** or **a|bid|ed, a|bid|ing.**
— v.t. 1 to put up with; endure; tolerate: *A good housekeeper can't abide dust. She can't abide him.* **SYN:** bear, stand. **2** to await submissively; submit to; sustain: *He must abide his fatal doom* (Joanna Baillie). **3** to await defiantly; withstand: *He soon learned to abide … terrors which most of my bolder companions shrank from encountering* (Hugh Miller). **4** *Archaic.* to wait for; await: *I will abide the coming of my lord* (Tennyson).
— v.i. 1 to stay; remain; wait: *Abide with me for a time. I'll call upon you straight: abide within* (Shakespeare). *He within his ships abode the while* (William Cowper). **2** to continue to live (in a place); reside; dwell: *No martin there in winter shall abide* (John Dryden). **3** to continue (in some state or action): *… ye shall abide in my love* (John 15:10). **4** to continue in existence; endure: *Thou hast established the earth, and it abideth* (Psalms 119:90). **SYN:** last. **5** *Archaic.* to be left. **6** *Obsolete.* to stay behind.
abide by, a to accept and follow out; be bound by: *Both teams will abide by the umpire's decision.* **b** to remain faithful to; stand firm by; be true to; fulfill: *Abide by your promise.*

a|bil|i|ty (ə bil′ə tē), *n., pl.* **-ties. 1** the power to do or act: *the ability to think clearly. The old horse still has the ability to work.* **SYN:** capability, capacity. **2** skill: *Washington had great ability as a general.* **3** power to do some special thing; natural gift; talent: *Musical ability often shows itself early in life.* [< Middle French *habilité,* learned borrowing from Latin *habilitās* aptness < *habilis* able]
— Syn. 2, 3 Ability, talent mean special power to do or for doing something. **Ability** applies to a demonstrated physical or mental power to do a certain thing well: *She has developed unusual ability as a dancer.* **Talent** applies to an inborn capacity for doing a special thing: *a child with a remarkable talent for painting.*
► After **ability** the infinitive of a verb preceded by *to* is used, rather than the gerund preceded by *of: A lawyer needs the ability to think clearly,* not *of thinking clearly.* The preposition used after *ability* and before a noun is *in: ability in music.*
A|bim|e|lech (ə bim′ə lek), *n.* a son of Gideon who was set up as king of Israel by the people of Shechem (in the Bible, Judges 9).
ab init., ab initio.
ab in|i|ti|o (ab′ i nish′ē ō), *Latin.* from the beginning: *The decree was not a nullity in the sense of being void ab initio* (London Times).

Definitions give the precise meanings of words. If a word has more than one meaning, the definitions are numbered. This dictionary lists the most common meanings first. Some dictionaries present definitions in historical order, with the earliest meanings first.

Examples point out how the word is used in phrases or sentences.

Cross-references show that the form consulted is less widely used than some other form, which has its own main entry.

Other forms of the word include the principal parts of verbs, unusual plural forms, and comparative forms for adjectives.

Quotations from well-known authors or publications illustrate the meaning of the word. The sources of quotations are identified.

Usage labels, such as *Slang, Informal, Archaic,* and *Obsolete,* indicate when and where the word is acceptable in current English usage. Each label is defined in a list at the front of the dictionary.

Etymologies tell what language or languages a word comes from, usually with its meaning in the original language. The symbol < means *comes from.*

Foreign words and phrases in common use in English have entries that give their pronunciation and translation, often with examples or illustrative quotations.

book. All good dictionaries today have introductory sections that explain what the book contains and how it is arranged.

The first thing a dictionary entry shows is how to spell a word and how to divide it into syllables. Accent marks and symbols that are explained in the book tell how to pronounce the word. Many dictionaries also tell what part of speech the word is. For example, they list *boy* as a *noun,* and *speak* as a *verb.*

Definitions of the word usually follow. Some dictionaries list the most commonly used meaning of the word first. Others arrange the meanings historically, so that the first meaning listed is the one that occurred first in the language. Some dictionaries also use the word in a sentence or phrase to help define it. Sometimes pictures or drawings are added to provide more information about the entry.

After the definitions, many dictionaries include a list of *synonyms,* or words with about the same meaning as the words being defined. Other information is often included about *etymology* (the history or origin of a word). Many dictionaries also have usage labels, such as *Slang* and *Dialect;* subject labels, such as *Biology* or *Electronics;* and regional labels, such as *British* or *U.S.* In addition, usage notes explain important points about the way a word is commonly used.

History

The word *dictionary* comes from the medieval Latin word *dictionarium,* which in turn came from the Latin *dictio,* meaning *word* or *saying.* The ancient Greeks and Romans were the first to produce these works. But most Greek and Latin dictionaries were either lists of rare and difficult words or specialized lists of words.

During the Middle Ages, scholars made much use of Latin dictionaries which explained hard Latin words in easier Latin. Toward the end of the Middle Ages, as Latin began to lose ground to English, French, German, and other national languages of Europe, scholars began to rely on *glossaries* to understand Latin manuscripts. The glossaries usually gave the meanings of hard Latin words in the words of the national language. As these languages became accepted in each country, people needed new dictionaries to explain the hard words of their own language in terms of simpler words in the same language.

Early English dictionaries. In 1604, Robert Cawdrey, a schoolmaster, prepared the first English dictionary. Called *The Table Alphabeticall of Hard Words,* it defined about 3,000 English words that had been taken from other languages. Larger dictionaries that offered more information about the words they contained were produced in the 1600's. In 1721, Nathan Bailey published a dictionary containing about 60,000 words. This was the first English dictionary that tried to include most English words instead of hard words only.

In the early 1700's, Jonathan Swift, Alexander Pope, Joseph Addison, Samuel Johnson, and other literary men of England wanted to prepare a dictionary that would set the standard for good usage in English. French and Italian scholars had already published such presriptive dictionaries in their languages, and this success influenced the literary men of England.

Samuel Johnson undertook the task of preparing an English dictionary. He spent several years selecting quotations from the best writers to illustrate the meanings of words. He came to the conclusion that language could not be "fixed" or prescribed, only described to the best of one's ability. Johnson finally published his great work, *A Dictionary of the English Language,* in 1755. With John Walker's *Critical and Pronouncing Dictionary and Expositor of the English Language* (1791), it served as the standard for information about English words until the mid-1800's.

In 1806, Noah Webster published a small school dictionary in the United States. Webster wanted to set up an American standard of good usage to compare with the British standard set by Johnson and Walker. In his dictionary, Webster simplified many older spellings, such as *music* for *musick.* In 1828, Webster published a dictionary containing 70,000 entries. Since then, Webster's dictionaries have been frequently revised and are widely used today.

Modern dictionaries. The period of national dictionaries gave way to scholarly dictionaries in the mid-1800's. In Germany, the brothers Jakob and Wilhelm Grimm began work on a historical dictionary of the German language. In France, Emile Littré compiled a dictionary of modern French. In England, John Ogilvie edited a dictionary that later served as the basis of *The Century Dictionary.* Various current English dictionaries trace their development back to *The Century Dictionary.*

Probably the greatest scholarly dictionary to appear in any language is *A New English Dictionary on Historical Principles.* It appeared in parts from 1884 to 1928 and has almost 415,000 entries. In 1933, it was published in 12 volumes, with a one-volume supplement, as the *Oxford English Dictionary (O.E.D.).* This dictionary gives a historical record of each word in written English. No other dictionary in any language approaches the *O.E.D.* in wealth and authority of historical detail. In 1989, a 20-volume second edition of the *O.E.D.* was published that integrated the 1928 edition with four supplementary volumes issued between 1972 and 1986. The historical method used to compile the *O.E.D.* was also used in making *A Dictionary of Canadianisms* (1967) and the *Dictionary of Jamaican English* (1967).

Current dictionaries sold in the United States and Canada include *Webster's Third New International Dictionary,* with about 450,000 entries, the most complete modern American dictionary of the English language. *The World Book Dictionary,* which is a Thorndike-Barnhart work that consists of more than 225,000 entries, is designed for family use. It was the first dictionary especially designed to be used with a specific encyclopedia. Many dictionary publishers offer basic, intermediate, and high school dictionaries that contain from as few as 18,000 to as many as 100,000 entries. College dictionaries have about 150,000 entries. Some publishers have also adapted dictionaries for computer use.

Robert K. Barnhart

Related articles. See the separate articles in *World Book* on each letter of the alphabet. See also:

Abbreviation	Johnson, Samuel	Punctuation
Antonym	Language	Spelling
Barnhart, Clarence L.	Linguistics	Synonym
Capitalization	Parts of speech	Syntax
Etymology	Pronunciation	Webster, Noah
Grammar		

Diderot, *DEE duh roh,* **Denis,** *duh NEE* (1713-1784), was one of the major philosophers of an intellectual movement called the Age of Reason. His work extended beyond philosophy and included writings in fiction, drama, and art and literary criticism. Diderot was also a satirist and a brilliant conversationalist. He spent much of his life compiling, editing, and writing the French *Encyclopedia,* a reference work that reflected revolutionary political views and antireligious sentiment. Diderot's major works are *Philosophical Thoughts* (1746) and *Thoughts on the Interpretation of Nature* (1754).

Diderot strongly supported experimental methods in philosophy and science. He believed that nature was in a state of constant change and no permanently adequate interpretation of it was possible. Diderot was also a philosophical materialist, believing that thought developed from the movements and changes of matter. His views on this subject were vague, as were his religious opinions. At one time, he was an atheist. At another time, Diderot was a deist, believing that God existed independently of the world and had no interest in it. But he later suggested that all of nature was God. Diderot was born in Langres, France, near Chaumont.

Stephen A. Erickson

See also **Encyclopedia** (An age of experiment); **Drama** (European drama [France]).

Didion, *DIH dih ahn,* **Joan** (1934-   ), is an American essayist and novelist. She was born in Sacramento, Calif., and often has used California's culture and geography and the lives of its residents as topics and symbols, especially in her earlier writings. Didion writes her essays and fiction in a spare and intense style that conveys a lack of roots and a sense of social disintegration.

In the title essay of her collection *Slouching Towards Bethlehem* (1968), Didion examines the drug culture of the mid-1960's in the Haight-Ashbury section of San Francisco. Her collection *The White Album* (1979) similarly explores such California phenomena as exotic religious groups and Los Angeles freeways. Her nonfiction

© Jill Krementz
Joan Didion

book *Miami* (1987) analyzes the impact of Cuban exiles on the city of Miami.

Didion's novels include *Run River* (1963), *Play It As It Lays* (1970), *A Book of Common Prayer* (1977), and *Democracy* (1984). Didion concentrated on political subjects in such nonfiction books as *Salvador* (1983), which is based on a trip that she took to El Salvador.

Marcus Klein

Dido, *DY doh,* also called Elissa, *ih LIHS uh,* was the legendary founder and queen of Carthage. She was the daughter of King Belus of Tyre, and the wife of Sychaeus, or Acerbas. She fled to Africa with many devoted followers after her brother, Pygmalion, murdered her husband. There she was offered as much land as might be surrounded by a bull's hide. She cut a hide into thin strips, pieced them together, and laid them out to surround a large area. This area became the site of Carthage (see **Carthage**).

In the original legend, Dido committed suicide to escape the African prince Iarbas, or Hiarbas, who wished to marry her. But in the Roman epic poem the *Aeneid,* Dido killed herself after the Trojan hero Aeneas, whom she had treated as her husband, deserted her. Aeneas later saw Dido when he visited the Underworld, but she had been happily reunited with Sychaeus there and would not look at Aeneas (see **Aeneid**).   Elaine Fantham

Didrikson, Babe. See Zaharias, Babe Didrikson.

Didymus. See Thomas, Saint.

Die and diemaking. A die is a precision tool used to shape or cut metals or other materials. Diemaking is the process of producing dies. Diemakers, who are usually called *tool and diemakers,* rank among the most highly skilled industrial workers. The diemaker's product ranges from small diamond dies, used to draw metal into fine wire, to huge metal dies that form automobile parts from sheet metal.

Materials used for making dies include alloy steels, rubber, plastics, and certain combinations of materials. The materials are shaped by basic machine tools or by newer methods, including the use of electricity (see **Machine tool** [Advanced machine tool operations]). After shaping, most dies are *heat treated* (carefully heated and cooled) to make them more resistant to wear.

When in use, certain dies must be lubricated. Common lubricants include oils and greases, soap solutions, and various chemical compounds. Dies used at high temperatures require such lubricants as graphite in oil or water, or molybdenum disulfide.

Dies are used in several industrial processes, including die casting, drawing, extrusion, forging, and stamping. Some of these processes use pairs of dies, one called a *male* die, or *punch,* and the other a *female* die.

In die casting, metals are melted in a machine that forces the liquid metal into steel dies. These dies replace the molds used in other casting. The metal hardens into the design of the die and comes out solid. See **Cast and casting.**

In drawing and extrusion, a hot or cold solid material, usually metal, is forced through an opening in a die (see **Extrusion**).

In forging, metal is often heated and put into two dies. The dies are pressed together and shape the metal. See **Forging.**

In stamping, a machine uses dies to stamp sheets, plates, or strips of metal or other materials, including plastics. Some stamping dies punch a hole in metal or cut it to a desired shape. Others form and shape the metal. Still other stamping dies do both jobs.

I. Melvin Bernstein

See also **Toolmaking.**

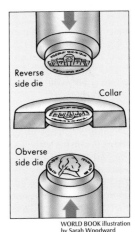
WORLD BOOK illustration by Sarah Woodward

Coin-stamping dies are used to stamp both sides of a coin in one operation. A collar holds the smooth disk of coin metal, called a *blank,* as it is fed into a stamping press.

Reverse side die

Collar

Obverse side die

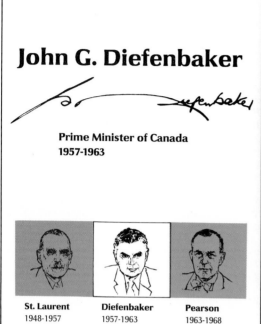

John G. Diefenbaker

Prime Minister of Canada
1957-1963

St. Laurent	Diefenbaker	Pearson
1948-1957	1957-1963	1963-1968

John Evans

Diefenbaker, *DEE fuhn* BAY *kuhr,* **John George** (1895-1979), served as prime minister of Canada from 1957 to 1963. One of the reasons for the defeat of Diefenbaker's Progressive Conservative government was his refusal to accept atomic warheads for defense missiles supplied by the United States. The Liberals won the election of April 1963, and Liberal leader Lester B. Pearson became prime minister.

The Progressive Conservatives elected Diefenbaker as party leader in 1956. Diefenbaker led his party to victory in the 1957 election, and became the first Progressive Conservative prime minister in 22 years. In 1958, Canadians reelected the party with the largest parliamentary majority in the nation's history. The party won again in the 1962 election, but did not have an absolute majority in Parliament. Diefenbaker's government stayed in power only with the support of the small Social Credit Party.

As prime minister, Diefenbaker increased Canada's social welfare programs and speeded development of the nation's rich northland. Canada faced serious economic problems in the early 1960's, and Diefenbaker adopted austerity measures to fight them. Under Diefenbaker, Canada increased its trade with Communist countries. The St. Lawrence Seaway was completed, and Georges P. Vanier became the first French-Canadian governor-general of Canada.

Tall and thin, with gray, curly hair and piercing blue eyes, Diefenbaker won friends and made enemies with his strong personality and fighting spirit. Diefenbaker made strong appeals to the national feeling of Canadians. "We are an independent country," he declared, "and we have the right to assert our rights and not have them determined by another country." Some people called

Diefenbaker's attitude "anti-American," but he disagreed. "The very thought is repugnant to me," Diefenbaker said. "I am strongly pro-Canadian."

Early life

Boyhood and education. John Diefenbaker was born on Sept. 18, 1895, in the village of Neustadt, Ont. The family of his father, William, had come to Canada from Germany. His mother, Mary Florence Bannerman Diefenbaker, was a granddaughter of George Bannerman, one of Lord Selkirk's Scottish settlers in the Red River Colony of Manitoba. John had a younger brother, Elmer.

John's father taught school for 20 years, then became a civil servant. As prime minister, Diefenbaker recalled: "My father was a person who had a dedicated devotion to the public service. Throughout the schools he taught, there were a great many who went into public life, because of his feeling that it was one field in which there was a need."

In 1903, the family moved to a homestead in Saskatchewan. John loved stories of the early days on the prairie. He was fascinated by tales about Gabriel Dumont, Louis Riel's right-hand man during the North West Rebellion of 1885 (see **North West Rebellion**). John also studied the lives of such men as Abraham Lincoln, William Gladstone, and Napoleon.

John's interest later shifted to Canadian history. One night, according to a family legend, he looked up from reading a biography of Prime Minister Sir Wilfrid Laurier and announced: "I'm going to be premier (prime minister) of Canada." But John most admired former Prime Minister Sir John A. Macdonald.

In 1910, the Diefenbakers moved to Saskatoon, Sask.,

so John could attend high school there. John went on to the University of Saskatchewan, where he was active in campus politics. The college magazine predicted that someday he would lead the opposition in the House of Commons. He received his bachelor's degree in 1915 and a master's degree in 1916.

Diefenbaker was commissioned a lieutenant in the Canadian Army during World War I. He arrived in France in 1916, but was returned to Canada the next year after being injured in training camp.

Young lawyer. Diefenbaker had always planned to be a lawyer. "There was no member of my family who was a lawyer," he said, "but I never deviated from that course from the time I was 8 or 9 years of age." He studied law at the University of Saskatchewan and received his law degree in 1919. That same year, he opened a small office in the nearby town of Wakaw.

Diefenbaker developed an outstanding reputation as a defense lawyer. Some people who heard him in court claimed he could hold a jury spellbound with his oratory. "I just chat with the jury," said Diefenbaker.

In 1923, Diefenbaker moved to Prince Albert, Sask. He became a King's Counsel in 1929, and was a vice president of the Canadian Bar Association from 1939 to 1942.

Diefenbaker married Edna May Brower in 1929. She died in 1951. Two years later, he married Mrs. Olive Freeman Palmer, an old friend from Wakaw. Mrs. Palmer, a widow with a grown daughter, was assistant director of the Ontario Department of Education.

Member of Parliament

In 1925 and 1926, Diefenbaker ran as a Conservative Party (called Progressive Conservative Party after 1942) candidate for the Canadian House of Commons. He lost both times. He ran for the Saskatchewan legislature in 1929 and 1938, and was defeated each time. He also ran for mayor of Prince Albert in 1934, and lost.

Diefenbaker's repeated defeats did not discourage him. He became leader of the Saskatchewan Conservative Party in 1936 and served until 1940. That year, he won election to the House of Commons from Lake Centre. Diefenbaker was reelected to Parliament from Lake Centre in 1945 and 1949. He won election to the House of Commons from Prince Albert in 1953.

As a lawyer, Diefenbaker had made a reputation by defending individual civil rights. As a member of Parliament, he argued for a national bill of rights. Canada's first bill of rights was adopted in 1960 when Diefenbaker was prime minister.

The first bill Diefenbaker introduced in Parliament provided for Canadian citizenship for Canadians. They were then British subjects. Diefenbaker denounced what he called "hyphenated citizenship." He meant that every Canadian was listed in the census by the national origin of his father, such as French or Italian.

In 1948, the Progressive Conservatives met to choose a leader to succeed John Bracken. Some members suggested Diefenbaker, but the party chose George Drew. In 1956, Drew became ill and gave up politics. Diefenbaker was chosen leader in December 1956.

The Progressive Conservatives, discouraged after a long period of Liberal rule, held little hope for a victory in the 1957 election. But Diefenbaker waged a vigorous campaign. He charged that the Liberals had grown too powerful. Diefenbaker seemed to radiate vitality as

Important dates in Diefenbaker's life

1895 (Sept. 18) Born in Neustadt, Ont.
1929 Married Edna May Brower.
1936 Became leader of Saskatchewan Conservative Party.
1940 Elected to Parliament.
1951 Mrs. Edna Diefenbaker died.
1953 Married Mrs. Olive Freeman Palmer.
1956 Chosen leader of Progressive Conservative Party.
1957 (June 21) Became prime minister of Canada.
1958 Progressive Conservatives won largest parliamentary majority in Canadian history.
1962 Progressive Conservatives won reelection.
1963 Liberals defeated Progressive Conservatives. Diefenbaker resigned as prime minister on April 22.
1967 Succeeded as party leader by Robert L. Stanfield.
1979 (Aug. 16) Died in Rockcliffe Park, Ont.

WORLD BOOK illustration by Tom Doresett

Important events during Diefenbaker's Administration

AP/Wide World

St. Lawrence Seaway was opened in 1959. Taking part in the ceremony were, *second, third, and fourth from left,* Queen Elizabeth II, Diefenbaker, and U.S. President Dwight D. Eisenhower.

Hospitalization insurance for all Canadians was set up by the government in 1961.

Canadian dollar was devalued to 92.5 cents during an economic crisis in 1962.

Atomic weapons dispute with the United States led to the downfall of Diefenbaker's government in early 1963.

he told of his plans for developing northern Canada.

In the 1957 election, the Progressive Conservatives won more seats in Parliament than any other party, though they did not win a majority. Diefenbaker became the first Conservative prime minister since Richard B. Bennett, who served from 1930 to 1935.

Prime minister (1957-1963)

John G. Diefenbaker, the first prime minister of Canada to come from a prairie province, took office on June 21, 1957. He succeeded Louis S. St. Laurent.

Parliament passed several bills sponsored by Diefenbaker's government. One bill increased old-age pensions. Other legislation provided loans to economically depressed areas. Another bill gave financial aid to expand hydroelectric power in the Atlantic provinces.

In 1958, Diefenbaker asked for a new election. He wanted more supporters in Parliament to help him pass his legislative program. His party won 208 of the 265 seats in the House of Commons—the largest parliamentary majority in Canadian history.

Much of Diefenbaker's social legislation soon became law. Parliament increased pensions for the blind and disabled, and approved a program of federal hospital insurance. In 1958, the government began to build roads into Canada's rich but undeveloped northland.

Economic problems. During the early 1960's, Diefenbaker's government faced major economic problems. Canada imported far more from the United States than it sold there. In an effort to improve the trade balance, Diefenbaker urged Canadians to increase their trade with nations of the British Commonwealth. The government set up restrictions to discourage Canadians from investing abroad. It wanted such investment to take place in Canada, where it would aid the economy. But these measures did not solve the problem. Canada also faced major unemployment—up to 11 per cent of the work force in 1961 and 1962.

By the middle of 1962, Diefenbaker was forced to adopt austerity measures to boost the economy. The government lowered the value of the Canadian dollar. It reduced spending, raised tariffs on imports, and borrowed about $1 billion from foreign banks. In the election of June 1962, the Progressive Conservatives won the most seats in Parliament, but not an absolute majority. Diefenbaker remained prime minister only because the Social Credit Party supported him.

Nuclear controversy. In 1961, it was announced that the United States would supply Canada with missiles essential for the defense of North America. However, the Canadian government was not ready to accept atomic warheads for missiles received from the United States. By 1963, Canada had still not equipped the missiles with atomic warheads.

On Jan. 30, 1963, the United States charged that Canada had failed to propose a practical plan for arming its forces against a possible Soviet attack. Diefenbaker angrily answered that the U.S. statement was "an unwarranted intrusion in Canadian affairs." He opposed acquiring nuclear warheads, saying that U.S. control of the missiles would threaten Canadian sovereignty. But Liberal leader Lester B. Pearson declared Canada should live up to its agreement and accept nuclear warheads. On Feb. 5, the House of Commons passed a motion of no-confidence in Diefenbaker's government, and the government fell from power.

In the election of April 1963, the Liberals won 129 seats in the House of Commons. This was just short of an absolute majority of the 265 seats, but more than any other party won. The Progressive Conservatives won only 95 seats. Pearson succeeded Diefenbaker as prime minister on April 22, 1963.

Later years

Diefenbaker led the opposition in Parliament until 1967, when the Progressive Conservatives chose Robert L. Stanfield to succeed him. Diefenbaker continued to represent Prince Albert in the Canadian House of Commons. He served as chancellor of the University of Saskatchewan from 1969 until his death.

Diefenbaker died of a heart attack at his home in the Ottawa suburb of Rockcliffe Park on Aug. 16, 1979. He was buried in Saskatoon, Sask.   G. F. G. Stanley

See also **Canada, History of; Pearson, Lester B.; Prime minister of Canada.**

Additional resources

Diefenbaker, John G. *One Canada: Memoirs of the Right Honourable John G. Diefenbaker.* 3 vols. Macmillan (Toronto), 1975-1977.

Stursberg, Peter. *Diefenbaker: Leadership Gained, 1956-1962.* Univ. of Toronto Press, 1975. *Diefenbaker: Leadership Lost, 1962-1967.* 1976.

Diego Garcia, *dee AY goh gahr SEE uh,* is an island in the Indian Ocean. It is part of the Chagos Archipelago, an island group. The United States maintains a naval base on Diego Garcia that serves as a communications center and a refueling stop for ships and airplanes.

Diego Garcia is a U-shaped coral island called an *atoll.* It is about 15 miles (24 kilometers) long, and about 7 miles (11 kilometers) wide at its widest point.

Diego Garcia came under Great Britain's control in 1814, and until 1965 was administered as a dependency of the British Colony of Mauritius. In 1965, Diego Garcia became part of a newly formed British dependency called the British Indian Ocean Territory. For the location of this dependency, see **World** (political map).

In 1966, Britain agreed to allow the construction of the U.S. naval base on Diego Garcia. The base was built during the 1970's. By 1972, British authorities had moved all of the island's inhabitants to Mauritius. Today, about 1,300 American naval workers and 25 British naval representatives live on Diego Garcia. In 1982, a dispute arose when Mauritius claimed the right to govern Diego Garcia.   Robert I. Crane

See also **Rapid Deployment Force.**

Diem, Ngo Dinh. See Ngo Dinh Diem.

Diemaking. See Die and diemaking.

Dien Bien Phu, *dyehn byehn FOO,* **Battle of,** was fought between Vietnamese Communists, called *Vietminh,* and France in 1954. It was the decisive battle of the Indochina War (1946-1954). The French were defeated, and they gave up their colonies in Indochina.

In November 1953, France began building an army base around the village of Dien Bien Phu (also called Dien Bien), in what is now northwestern Vietnam. For the village's location, see **Vietnam** (map). The base was intended to disrupt Vietminh army movements. On March 13, 1954, about 50,000 Vietminh soldiers began attacking the French force of more than 10,000 troops at the base. They quickly destroyed the base's airfield, leaving the French without adequate supplies. The outnumbered French resisted the Vietminh attack for 56 days, but were forced to surrender on May 7, 1954. The fighting ended early the next day.   David P. Chandler

Diesel, *DEE zuhl,* **Rudolf** (1858-1913), a German mechanical engineer, developed an internal-combustion machine that used oil as fuel. Because of its simplicity of design and the economy of its fuel, the diesel engine is frequently preferred to the gasoline engine. It has greatly increased the efficiency of industry and transportation. See **Diesel engine.**

Diesel was born in Paris of German parents, and received his technical education in Munich. He became interested in designing an engine more efficient than steam and gas engines. He based his work on the theory of heat engines and on the designs of other engineers. He patented his design in 1892, and had completed and operated the first successful diesel engine by 1897. He also founded a factory to make diesel engines. In 1913, Diesel mysteriously disappeared from a German ship bound for London.   Robert E. Schofield

See also **Ship** (Increasing power and speed).

Diesel engine, *DEE zuhl* or *DEE suhl,* is a type of internal-combustion engine used chiefly for heavy-duty work. Most of the locomotives in the United States are diesel powered. Diesel engines drive huge freight trucks, large buses, tractors, and heavy roadbuilding equipment. They are also used to power submarines and ships, the generators of electric-power stations in small cities, and emergency electric-power generators. Some automobiles are powered by diesel engines.

How a diesel engine works. There are two main types of internal-combustion engines—gasoline engines and diesel engines. The gasoline engine, found in most cars, is a *spark-ignition* engine. It uses electricity and spark plugs to ignite the fuel and air mixture in the engine's cylinders (see **Gasoline engine**). The diesel engine is a *compression-ignition* engine. It compresses the air in the cylinders, causing the temperature of the air to rise. Fuel injected into the hot, compressed air immediately ignites.

During the combustion process, the stored chemical energy in the fuel is converted to *thermal,* or heat, energy. The temperature in each cylinder rises as high as 4500° F. (2480° C) and creates pressures of 1,500 pounds per square inch. The pressure pushes against the tops of the pistons, forcing them to the other end of their cylinders. The pistons are connected by a rod or other suitable connecting mechanism to a crankshaft that they turn. In this way, a diesel engine supplies rotary power to drive vehicles and other machines.

To ignite the fuel, the compressed air must have a certain temperature. The degree to which the temperature of the air rises depends on the amount of work done by the piston in compressing it. This work is measured as a ratio between the volume of uncompressed air and the volume of the air after compression. The compression ratio necessary to ignite the fuel depends on the size of the engine's cylinders. In large cylinders, the compression ratio is about 13 to 1. For small cylinders, it may be as high as 22 to 1.

Near the end of the piston's compression stroke, the fuel is injected into a cylinder. In order for the fuel and air to mix well, the fuel is injected under high pressure as a spray. Combustion usually starts just before the piston ends its compression stroke. The power of diesel engines can be increased by *supercharging,* or forcing air under pressure into the cylinders. See **Fuel injection.**

Diesel engines have a high *thermal efficiency,* or ability to convert the stored chemical energy in the fuel into *mechanical energy,* or work. In the spark-ignition engine, the amount of power produced is determined by a throttle that regulates how much air enters the cylinder. The throttle may operate in a partly closed position much of the time, thereby reducing the engine's air intake and efficiency. Diesel engines do not require a throttle, making them more efficient than gasoline engines.

How a four-cycle diesel engine works

A cycle begins with the intake stroke when the piston moves down and draws air into the cylinder. The piston rises and compresses the air. During the compression stroke, the air temperature rises to about 900° F. (480° C). When fuel is injected into the cylinder, it mixes with the hot air and burns explosively. Gases produced by this combustion push the piston down for the power stroke. During the exhaust stroke, the piston moves up and forces the burned gases out of the cylinder.

WORLD BOOK diagram

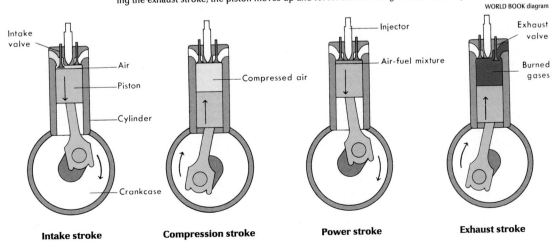

| Intake stroke | Compression stroke | Power stroke | Exhaust stroke |

Diesel engines are suited for heavy-duty work because they are larger and heavier than gasoline engines of equal power and therefore can better withstand heavy loads. In addition, diesel engines burn fuel oils, which require less refining and are cheaper than higher-grade fuels such as gasolines.

Kinds of diesel engines. There are two main types of diesel engines. They differ according to the number of piston strokes required to complete a cycle of air compression, power, exhaust, and intake of fresh air. A *stroke* is the distance a piston travels in one direction. These engines are (1) the four-stroke cycle engine and (2) the two-stroke cycle engine.

In a four-stroke cycle engine, each piston moves down, up, down, and up to complete a cycle. The first downstroke draws air into the cylinder. The first upstroke compresses the air. The second downstroke is the power stroke. The second upstroke exhausts the gases produced by combustion. A four-stroke engine requires exhaust and air-intake valves.

In a two-stroke cycle engine, the intake and exhaust processes occur near the end of the piston downstroke, or power stroke. The two-stroke cycle engine does not need valves. As the piston rises during the upstroke, it compresses the air and closes the intake and exhaust ports. The fuel is injected near the end of this compression stroke. Because the two-stroke cycle engine has twice as many power strokes as the four-stroke cycle engine, it provides more power.

History. The diesel engine is named for Rudolf Diesel, the German engineer who invented it. Diesel patented his design for the engine in 1892 and built his first engine in 1893. The engine exploded and almost killed him, but it proved that fuel could be ignited without a spark. He operated his first successful engine in 1897. Later, Sir Dugald Clerk of Great Britain developed the two-stroke diesel. William H. Haverdink

See also **Diesel, Rudolf; Engine analyzer; Locomotive; Starter.**

Diet. See Japan (Government).

Diet is the food and drink that a person takes regularly day after day. The word *diet* also refers to the amounts or kinds of food needed under special circumstances, such as losing or gaining weight. Diet needs vary according to age, weight, condition of health, climate, and amount of activity. *Dietetics* is the science of feeding individuals or groups. The money that is available and health and nutritional needs affect the type of feeding prescribed.

Normal diet, or *balanced diet,* contains all the food elements needed to keep healthy. A person needs *proteins* to build tissues, and *fats* and *carbohydrates* to provide energy and heat. *Minerals* and *vitamins* are needed for growth and to maintain tissues and regulate body functions. In the United States, calcium and iron are the minerals most often lacking in the diet. Vitamins A and C, and Folacin, a B-vitamin, are often eaten in smaller amounts than are recommended. A diet that lacks any needed food element may cause certain *deficiency diseases.* For example, lack of vitamin A causes night blindness, and lack of vitamin C causes scurvy (see **Scurvy**).

Diets for losing or gaining weight. Both the energy value of food and the energy spent in daily activity are measured in units of heat called *kilocalories.* These measurements are usually referred to as *food calories,* or simply *calories* (see **Calorie**). Diets for gaining or losing weight are based on the amount of calories taken into the body in food and the amount of calories used up in activity. If people take in more calories than they use up, they will gain weight. They will lose weight if they take in fewer calories than they use up. A diet aimed toward losing or gaining weight should include all the food elements. People should seek the advice of a doctor before beginning such a diet.

Special diets may be prescribed for people suffering from certain diseases. For example, the healthy body needs sugar, but a person with diabetes must limit the use of sugar. Doctors may prescribe low-salt diets for patients with certain heart or kidney diseases.

Some people suffer allergic or skin reactions from certain food products, such as milk, tomatoes, strawberries, wheat, potatoes, eggs, fish, nuts, chocolate, or pork. These people should avoid such foods and consult a physician.

Certain groups of people, such as young children or older people, have special dietary needs. Because children grow rapidly, they need food not only to replace worn-out tissues and provide energy, but also to build new tissue. A well-balanced diet for a child or an adult should include milk and milk products; eggs, lean meat, poultry, fish; or nuts, seeds, and *legumes,* such as peas and soybeans; fruits and vegetables; and cereals or bread products. Older people need as many nutrients as children and young adults. But if their activity is reduced, they need fewer calories. Expectant or nursing mothers and babies also need special diets (see **Baby** [The expectant mother; Feeding procedures]).

Mary Frances Picciano

Related articles in *World Book* include:

Allergy	Fat	Metabolism
Calorie	Food	Nutrition
Carbohydrate	Fruit (introduction)	Protein
Cooking	Health	Vitamin
Digestive system	Lipid	Weight control

Diethylstilbestrol. See **DES.**

Dietrich, Marlene (1904-   ), a German-born actress and singer, became a famous Hollywood motion-picture star. Her charm, famous figure, expressive eyes, and husky voice have made her an international favorite for over 40 years.

United Press Int.

Marlene Dietrich

Marlene Dietrich first attracted attention for her performance in the German film *The Blue Angel* (1930). Then she made such American films as *Morocco* (1930), *Shanghai Express* (1932), *The Garden of Allah* (1936), and *Destry Rides Again* (1939). Since World War II her films have included *A Foreign Affair* (1948), *Witness for the Prosecution* (1958), and *Judgment at Nuremberg* (1961). Marlene Dietrich was born Maria Magdalene Dietrich in Berlin.

Howard Thompson

See also **Von Sternberg, Josef.**

Dietrich of Bern. See Theodoric.

Diffraction is the spreading out of waves—water, sound, light, or any other kind—as they pass by the edge of an obstacle or through an opening. Diffraction explains why water waves spread out in all directions after passing through a narrow channel in a breakwater. It also explains why sound can be heard around a corner even though no straight path exists from the source to the ear.

Diffraction of light differs from diffraction of sound because diffraction is most evident when the obstacle is about the same size as the wavelength diffracted. The sound waves we hear have wavelengths of about a yard and are diffracted by ordinary objects. But visible light waves have wavelengths of less than $\frac{1}{35,000}$ of an inch (0.00007 centimeter). Thus, light waves can be diffracted noticeably only by extremely small objects.

How diffraction occurs. Diffraction takes place among all waves at all times. To understand why it becomes noticeable only when the obstacle is about the size of the diffracted wavelength, one must understand both diffraction and *interference.*

Christiaan Huygens, a Dutch scientist, developed the principle that explains why diffraction occurs. This principle states that each point on the surface of a wave is the source of small waves. These wavelets move outward in all directions. To find the total wave reaching an area, all the wavelets that strike the area must be considered. If the crests of two wavelets reach a point at the same time, they reinforce each other. This condition is called *constructive interference,* and the resulting wave is large. If the crest of one wave reaches a point at the same time as the low point of another, the two waves cancel each other. This condition is called *destructive interference,* and the resulting wave is small or nonexistent. See **Interference.**

A beam of light moves in a straight line because effects of diffraction outside the beam are canceled by destructive interference. The wavelets at the edge of the beam spread, but most of the light travels in a straight line with the beam. When light travels through a tiny opening, interference occurs only among the wavelets coming from the opening. These wavelets produce a diffraction pattern because most of the destructive interference has been eliminated.

Diffraction of light from a tiny source can likewise be observed if some of the light—and thus its interference—is removed. A disk placed in the path of such a source blocks out the wavelets that originate behind the disk. At points beyond the disk, these eliminated wavelets are missing not only in the shadow of the disk but also outside of the shadow, where they would have interfered constructively. The shadow pattern on a screen beyond the disk consists of a series of rings, alternately light and dark, in and surrounding the shadow area. A bright spot occurs at the center of the shadow because at that point all waves interfere constructively. They do so because they have all traveled the same distance from the edge of the disk.

Uses of diffraction. The occurrence of diffraction has been used as a test of whether various things are waves. For example, diffraction of X rays by crystals convinced scientists that X rays are waves.

The pattern of X-ray diffraction depends on the type

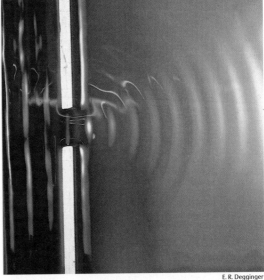

E. R. Degginger

A diffraction pattern results when waves of water pass through a small opening, as in the wave tank above. The pattern is similar to the one made by dropping a pebble into water.

and distribution of atoms in the diffracting substance. This fact has been used to study the structure of crystals by X-ray diffraction and to discover the structure of proteins and nucleic acids.

A *diffraction grating* is a glass plate with lines ruled on it at small, equal intervals. Light can pass only between the lines, and the slits are about as far apart as a wavelength of light. If a parallel beam of white light strikes the grating, a pattern of light of various colors appears on a screen beyond the grating. The colors appear because white light consists of different colors. These colors have different wavelengths, and the longer wavelengths are diffracted at greater angles. Scientists can identify a substance by the pattern of colors it produces through a diffraction grating.   Gerald Feinberg

See also **Light** (How light behaves); **Molecule** (Studying molecules; picture); **Sound** (Diffraction); **Spectrometer; Waves.**

Diffusion, *dih FYOO zhuhn,* in chemistry, is the mixing of the atoms or molecules of one substance with those of another. It is caused by the natural movements of atoms and molecules. It differs from the mixing caused by stirring or shaking or the blowing of wind.

Diffusion occurs readily in gases and liquids because of the constant and random motion of their atoms and molecules. The process takes place more rapidly in gases than in liquids. Molecules of gases are farther apart and collide less frequently than those of liquids—and collisions among molecules hinder diffusion. In solids, the molecules are arranged in rigid patterns and move very little. Therefore, diffusion does not occur in solids except under special conditions.

Diffusion can be demonstrated by adding ink to a glass of water. Each molecule of ink has its own constant and random motion. The motion of the ink molecules causes them to spread through the water. The water molecules also move about and become mixed with the

How diffusion occurs

The diagrams at the right show how diffusion occurs in gases. The molecules of two different gases in a container are separated by a divider, *top*. After the divider is removed, the molecules begin to mix together because of their constant movement, *bottom*. As the molecules move at random, some of them bump into one another and slow down the mixing process.

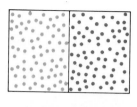
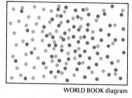

WORLD BOOK diagram

ink molecules. After being mixed completely, the molecules of ink and water each continue to move individually. But as a result of diffusion, the color of the mixture becomes the color of the ink.

Many common occurrences involve diffusion. For example, water boiling in an uncovered pot produces steam that disappears. The disappearance results from the diffusion of steam molecules with air molecules. Odors from flowers, food, perfume, and other sources are produced by the diffusion of special gaseous odor molecules with molecules of air.   John B. Butt

Digestion. See Digestive system.

Digestive system is the group of organs that break down food into smaller particles, or molecules, for use in the human body. This breakdown makes it possible for the smaller digested particles to pass through the intestinal wall into the bloodstream. The particles are then distributed to nourish all parts of the body.

The digestive system consists primarily of the *alimentary canal*, a tube that extends from the mouth to the rectum. As food moves through this canal, it is ground and mixed with various digestive juices. Most of these juices contain *digestive enzymes*, chemicals that speed up reactions involved in the breakdown of food. The stomach and the small intestines, which are parts of the alimentary canal, each produce a digestive juice. Other digestive juices empty into the alimentary canal from the salivary glands, gall bladder, and pancreas. These organs are also part of the digestive system.

The fats, proteins, and carbohydrates (starches and sugars) in foods are made up of very complex molecules and must be digested, or broken down. When digestion is completed, starches and complex sugars are broken down into simple sugars, fats are digested to fatty acids and glycerol, and proteins are digested to amino acids and peptides. Simple sugars, fatty acids and glycerol, and amino acids and peptides are the digested foods that can be absorbed into the bloodstream. Such foods as vitamins, minerals, and water do not need digestion.

From mouth to stomach. Digestion begins in the mouth. Chewing is very important to good digestion for two reasons. When chewed food is ground into fine particles, the digestive juices can react more easily. As the food is chewed, it is moistened and mixed with saliva, which contains the enzyme *ptyalin*. Ptyalin changes some of the starches in the food to sugar.

After the food is swallowed, it passes through the esophagus into the stomach. In the stomach it is thor-

Digestion

Digestion is the process that breaks food down into simple substances the body can use. The digestive system includes all the organs and tissues involved in this process.

Parts of the digestive system

WORLD BOOK illustrations by Colin Bidgood

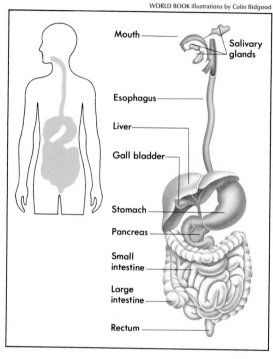

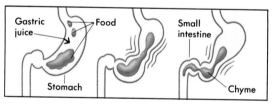

The stomach churns food and adds gastric juice, which breaks down proteins. Food exits the stomach as *chyme,* a thick liquid.

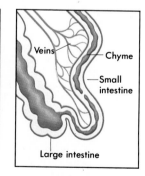

Bile and pancreatic juice act on the chyme in the upper small intestine. Pancreatic juice digests proteins, fats, and sugars and starches. Bile helps break down fats.

Digested foods are absorbed into the bloodstream from the small intestine. The indigestible remains pass into the large intestine and are eliminated from the body.

oughly mixed with a digestive juice by a vigorous, to-and-fro churning motion. This motion is caused by contractions of strong muscles in the stomach walls.

The digestive juice in the stomach is called *gastric juice*. It contains hydrochloric acid and the enzyme *pepsin*. This juice begins the digestion of protein foods such as meat, eggs, and milk. Starches, sugars, and fats are not digested by the gastric juice. After a meal, some food remains in the stomach for two to five hours. But liquids and small particles begin to empty almost immediately. Food that has been churned, partly digested, and changed to a thick liquid is called *chyme*. Chyme passes from the stomach into the small intestine.

In the small intestine, the digestive process is completed on the partly digested food by pancreatic juice, intestinal juice, and bile. The pancreatic juice is produced by the pancreas and pours into the small intestine through a tube, or duct. The pancreatic juice contains the enzymes *trypsin, amylase,* and *lipase*. Trypsin breaks down the partly digested proteins, amylase changes starch into simple sugars, and lipase splits fats into fatty acids and glycerol. The intestinal juice is produced by the walls of the small intestine. It has milder digestive effects than the pancreatic juice, but carries out similar digestion. Bile is produced in the liver, stored in the gall bladder, and flows into the small intestine through the bile duct. Bile does not contain enzymes, but it does contain chemicals that help break down and absorb fats.

When the food is completely digested, it is absorbed by tiny blood and lymph vessels in the walls of the small intestine. It is then carried into the circulation for nourishment of the body. Food particles are small enough to pass through the walls of the intestine and blood vessels only when they are completely digested.

Almost no digestion occurs in the large intestine. The large intestine stores waste food products and absorbs small amounts of water and minerals. The waste materials that accumulate in the large intestine are roughage that cannot be digested in the body. Bacterial action produces the final waste product, the *feces,* which are eliminated from the body.   André Dubois

Related articles in *World Book* include:

Alimentary	Carbohydrate	Indigestion	Pancreas
canal	Cellulose	Intestine	Pepsin
Amino acid	Dyspepsia	Liver	Starch
Assimilation	Enzyme	Lymphatic sys-	Stomach
Beaumont,	Esophagus	tem	Sugar
William	Fat	Mastication	Teeth
Bile	Gland		

See also *Digestive system* in the Research Guide/Index, Volume 22, for a *Reading and Study Guide.*

Additional resources

Jackson, Gordon, and Whitfield, Philip. *Digestion: Fueling the System.* Torstar, 1984.
Simon, Seymour. *About the Food You Eat.* McGraw, 1979. For younger readers.
Ward, Brian R. *Food and Digestion.* Watts, 1982.

Digit. See Arabic numerals; Decimal system.
Digital computer. See Computer.
Digitalis, *DIHJ uh TAL ihs,* is a powerful drug made from the dried leaves of the purple foxglove, a common garden flower. It takes its name from the scientific name of the foxglove (see **Foxglove**).

In 1785, a British physician, William Withering, intro-

duced digitalis for the treatment of certain heart diseases. Doctors use digitalis when the action of the heart muscles is too weak to force blood out of the heart normally. They also use it to make the heart beat more regularly. It can be given as a powder, in tablets, as a liquid, or in a solution called a *tincture*. Digitalis is very powerful and should be taken only under a doctor's direction.
N. E. Sladek

Dik-dik is one of the smallest antelopes. Dik-diks live in dense wooded areas. Four species live in eastern Africa and one species in southwestern Africa. The tallest dik-diks are about 15 inches (39 centimeters) high at the shoulder. Females are somewhat larger than males but have no horns.

Dik-diks are delicate, slender animals with tiny hoofs, short tails, and long hairy muzzles. They live alone or in groups of two or three. Dik-diks warn each other of danger with high-pitched whistles.

Scientific classification. Dik-diks belong to the bovid family, Bovidae. They are genus *Madoqua.*   Anne Innis Dagg

See also **Antelope** (with picture).

Dike. See Irrigation (Surface irrigation; picture: Flood irrigation); **Levee; Netherlands** (introduction; pictures).

Dill is a plant used in making pickles and as a flavoring in other foods, including fish, sour cream, and vinegar. Dill is widely grown for its bitter seeds and its small green leaves. These leaves are called *dill weed*. In addition, a flavoring oil is distilled from the plant. Dill is related to such plants as anise, caraway, celery, and parsnip.

Eric Crichton, Bruce Coleman Ltd.

Dill

Scientific classification. Dill is a member of the parsley family, Apiaceae or Umbelliferae. It is classified as *Anethum graveolens.*   J. B. Hanson

Dillinger, *DIHL ihn juhr,* **John Herbert** (1903-1934), was one of the most notorious criminals in United States history. In 1933 and 1934, he and his gangs attracted national headlines for a series of Midwestern bank robberies and narrow escapes from the law.

Dillinger was born in Indianapolis, Ind., and raised in nearby Mooresville. He attempted his first robbery, in Mooresville, in 1924. He was caught and imprisoned until 1933. Soon afterward, Dillinger helped some prison inmates escape, and they formed a robbery gang.

In January 1934, Dillinger was arrested in Arizona and sent to Indiana to face charges of killing a policeman. He soon broke out of a supposedly escape-proof jail in Crown Point, Ind., by using what he claimed was a carved wooden pistol. His flight across state lines in a stolen car violated federal

Federal Bureau of Investigation

John Dillinger

law, making him a fugitive from the FBI, then called the Bureau of Investigation. After recruiting a new gang, Dillinger resumed robbing banks. He twice escaped capture in gun battles with federal agents in Minnesota and Wisconsin. By mid-1934, he had been involved in at least 10 bank robberies in Indiana, Ohio, Wisconsin, and South Dakota.

Dillinger was hiding in Chicago when he was betrayed by Anna Sage, an acquaintance, on July 22, 1934. Sage told federal agents she would be wearing a red dress when she and a girlfriend accompanied Dillinger to the Biograph theater that night to see the Clark Gable crime movie *Manhattan Melodrama*. Federal agents fatally shot Dillinger as he left the theater, and Sage became famous as the "woman in red."   William J. Helmer

Additional resources

Cromie, Robert A., and Pinkston, Joseph. *Dillinger: A Short and Violent Life*. McGraw, 1962.
Toland, John. *The Dillinger Days*. Random House, 1963.

DiMaggio, *duh MAH jee oh,* **Joe** (1914-   ), was one of the greatest outfielders in baseball history. He played his entire career, from 1936 through 1951, with the New York Yankees. DiMaggio was nicknamed "the Yankee Clipper" because of his graceful fielding and "Joltin' Joe" because of his powerful hitting. DiMaggio hit safely in 56 straight games in 1941, a major league record. He had a lifetime batting average of .325 and hit 361 home runs in 1,736 games. DiMaggio played in 10 World Series and in 11 All-Star games. He was voted the American League's most valuable player in 1939, 1941, and 1947. In 1948, he led the league with 39 home runs and 155 runs batted in.

AP/Wide World

Joe DiMaggio

Joseph Paul DiMaggio was born in Martinez, Calif. Two of his brothers, Dominic and Vincent, also played major league baseball. DiMaggio was briefly married to movie star Marilyn Monroe in 1954. He was elected to the National Baseball Hall of Fame in 1955.

Dave Nightingale

See also **Baseball** (picture).

Dime is a United States coin worth 10 cents, or one-tenth of a dollar. The word dime comes from the Latin *decimus* (tenth). Until 1933, the dime was only legal as

WORLD BOOK photo by James Simek

A dime portrays Franklin D. Roosevelt. On the reverse side, the torch of liberty appears between sprigs of laurel and oak.

payment in amounts of $10 or less. Then, Congress made the dime legal tender in any amount. Dimes were made almost completely of silver until 1965. That year, Congress ruled that dimes should be made of a solid copper center between two layers of a copper-nickel alloy.   R. G. Doty

See also **Fasces; Money.**

Dimethyl sulfoxide. See **DMSO.**

Dine, Jim (1935-   ), is an American artist. Dine is sometimes associated with the pop art movement, which emerged in the United States during the 1960's.

Like the pop artists, Dine has painted realistic pictures of familiar everyday objects, such as articles of clothing and gardening equipment. But Dine's style tends to be more personal than theirs. Sometimes he has added ac-

black bathroom #2

Art Gallery of Ontario, Toronto, Gift of Mr. and Mrs. M. H. Rapp, 1966

Jim Dine's *Black Bathroom No. 2* consists of a bathroom sink projecting from a partially painted canvas. Many of Dine's works combine everyday objects with painting.

tual objects to his paintings or placed real objects in front of his paintings. For example, in *Black Bathroom No. 2* (1962), Dine attached a sink to a canvas painted black to represent a bathroom wall. Dine repeats certain images in many of his works. These images include a bathrobe and a necktie. In some paintings, he features the tools and equipment of professional house painters, such as brushes and color paint charts.

James Dine was born in Cincinnati, Ohio. He has won recognition as a printmaker, especially in lithography and silk-screen printing. He has also created sculptures, collages, and book illustrations, and designed sets and costumes for plays.   Ann Lee Morgan

Dinesen, *DEE nuh suhn,* **Isak,** *EE sak* (1885-1962), was the pen name of Baroness Karen Blixen-Finecke, a Danish author who wrote in English and Danish. Like Gothic fiction, her stories deal with fantastic, unreal, often grotesque people and situations. She had a deep concern for the supernatural, and she preferred to portray life in exotic settings of the past. Her volumes of short stories include *Seven Gothic Tales* (1934), *Winter's Tales* (1942),

Last Tales (1957), *Anecdotes of Destiny* (1958), and *Ehrengard* (1963).

Born Karen Christence Dinesen in Rungsted, Denmark, she was married to Baron Bror Blixen-Finecke in 1914. Dinesen was divorced in 1921. She owned a coffee plantation in eastern Africa, and lived there from 1914 to 1931. Then she returned to Denmark. Dinesen recorded her years in Africa in two books of memoirs, *Out of Africa* (1937) and *Shadows on the Grass* (1961).

Niels Ingwersen

Dingo, *DIHNG goh,* is the wild dog of Australia. Dingoes were brought to Australia by *Aborigines,* the first people to live in Australia.

Dingoes are about as large as English setters. They have alert faces; sharp, erect ears; and brushlike tails. Most dingoes have yellowish-brown fur, but the animal's colors range from yellowish-white to black. Din-

Warren Garst, Atoz Images

The dingo is a wild dog that lives in Australia.

goes rarely bark, but howl instead. If dingoes are caught as puppies, they make good pets. They may interbreed with dogs.

Dingoes hunt alone or in family groups. Their most important food is the *wallaby* (small kangaroo), but they also kill sheep. As a result, the Australian government has spent much money to fence out dingoes and to poison them.

Scientific classification. The dingo belongs to the dog family, Canidae. It is *Canis dingo.* Anne Innis Dagg

Dinka, *DIHNG kah,* are a cattle-herding people of central Africa. They make up the largest black ethnic group in the Sudan. Most of the approximately 2 million Dinka live on the plains of the southern Sudan. Besides herding cattle, they also fish and grow crops. Their main crop is a grain called *millet.* Their diet also includes fish, milk, and vegetables. The Dinka obtain milk from their cattle but do not kill the animals for meat.

The Dinka religion includes belief in a supreme god called *Nhialic* and many spirits. Ritual leaders called *masters of the fishing spear* lead religious ceremonies and settle disputes. The masters of the fishing spear trace their descent to a leader called Awiel Longar. Longar was the original spear master. The Dinka believe that the masters of the fishing spear have spiritual

power, which the masters use to provide health and prosperity for their people. Some of the Dinka have become Christians or Muslims and do not practice their traditional religion.

The Dinka language belongs to the Nilotic family of African languages. Many Dinka also speak English.

Great Britain and Egypt made the Sudan a protectorate in 1899 and ruled the country until it won independence in 1956. Arabic-speaking Muslims from northern Sudan controlled the new government. The Dinka and other southern peoples have rebelled several times against northern control. John W. Burton

Dinkins, David Norman (1927-), became the first black mayor of New York City. In 1990, he replaced Edward I. Koch as mayor of the largest city in the United States. Dinkins, a Democrat, defeated Rudolph W. Giuliani in the 1989 general election. Dinkins got about 50 per cent of the total vote. He won support from about 90 per cent of the city's black voters and about 30 per cent of the white voters. Dinkins is a liberal who became known for his skill in resolving conflicts.

Joan Vitale Strong

David Dinkins

Dinkins was born in Trenton, N.J. He earned a bachelor's degree in mathematics from Howard University in Washington, D.C. In 1956, he graduated from Brooklyn Law School. Dinkins was elected to the New York Legislature in 1965 and served one term. He was city clerk of New York City from 1975 to 1985. He then was elected president of Manhattan, one of the five boroughs of New York City. Guy Halverson

Dinoflagellate, *DIH nuh FLAJ uh layt,* is a kind of single-celled organism found throughout the oceans and in freshwater lakes and ponds. Dinoflagellates make up part of the drifting mass of water organisms known as *plankton* (see **Plankton**). Some dinoflagellates need only sunlight and inorganic nutrients for growth. Others engulf bacteria and other tiny organisms.

Dinoflagellates have two *flagella* (long, hairlike projections) that enable them to swim. Some dinoflagellates produce a chemical light called *bioluminescence.* Some also are toxic and can kill fish and poison shellfish. When dinoflagellates become abundant, they may discolor the water, producing red tides (see **Red tide**).

Scientific classification. Dinoflagellates have traditionally been classified in the animal kingdom, Animalia, or the plant kingdom, Plantae. Today, many scientists consider dinoflagellates to be protists and classify dinoflagellates in the kingdom Protista.

David L. Garrison

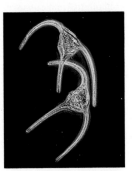

Eric Gravé, Photo Researchers

Dinoflagellates

Dinosaurs of the Jurassic Period (205 million to 138 million years ago) included the longest known dinosaur, the 90-foot (27-meter) diplodocus, *above right.* Other dinosaurs included the plated stegosaurus, *upper left,* the allosaurus, *center,* and the camptosaurus, *lower right.*

Dinosaur

Dinosaur is the name of a kind of reptile that lived millions of years ago. The word *dinosaur* comes from two Greek words meaning *terrible lizard.* Dinosaurs were not lizards. But the size of some dinosaurs was terrifying. The biggest ones were the largest animals ever to live on land. They weighed more than 10 times as much as a full-grown elephant. Only a few kinds of whales grow to be larger than these dinosaurs.

The first dinosaurs appeared on the earth around 220 million years ago. For about 150 million years, they ruled the land. They lived in most parts of the world and in a variety of surroundings, from swamps to open plains. Then about 63 million years ago, dinosaurs died out rather suddenly.

Dinosaurs varied greatly in size, appearance, and habits. But the most famous kinds include such giants as the

Peter Dodson, the contributor of this article, is Associate Professor of Anatomy at the School of Veterinary Medicine of the University of Pennsylvania. The paintings and diagrams were prepared for World Book *by Alex Ebel.*

apatosaurus, diplodocus, and tyrannosaurus rex. Apatosaurs, also called brontosaurs, grew about 80 feet (24 meters) long. The diplodocus grew even longer—to about 90 feet (27 meters). Both the apatosaurus and the diplodocus were plant-eaters. They had a tiny head and an extremely long neck and tail. Tyrannosaurs were fierce meat-eaters. They stood almost 10 feet (3 meters) tall at the hips and had an enormous head and long, pointed teeth. But not all dinosaurs were giants. The smallest kind was about the size of a chicken.

In some ways, dinosaurs were like most present-day reptiles. For example, some had teeth, bones, and skin like those of crocodiles and other reptiles living today. Many probably were also about as intelligent as crocodiles. But dinosaurs differed from present-day reptiles in other ways. For example, no modern reptiles grow as large as large dinosaurs. Another important difference is in posture. The legs of lizards, turtles, and most other reptiles are pushed out to the sides of the body. The structure of the legs gives the animals a sprawling posture. But a dinosaur's legs were under the body like the legs of a horse. This leg structure lifted the dinosaur's body off the ground and enabled some kinds to walk on their hind legs.

Dinosaurs of the Cretaceous Period (138 million to 63 million years ago) included the tyrannosaurus rex, *upper left,* and the horned triceratops. Two anatosaurs stand in the foreground. Flowering plants appeared during this period, and opossums, snakes, and lizards were common.

Dinosaurs lived during a time in the earth's history called the *Mesozoic Era.* This era lasted from about 240 million to 63 million years ago. The Mesozoic Era is also called the *Age of Reptiles* because reptiles ruled the land, sea, and sky during that time. The most important reptiles belonged to a group of animals called *archosaurs* (ruling reptiles). In addition to dinosaurs, this group included *thecodonts,* the ancestors of the dinosaurs; crocodiles; and flying reptiles. By the close of the Mesozoic Era, all archosaurs except crocodiles had died out, and the Age of Reptiles ended.

Scientists do not know why dinosaurs disappeared. For many years, they thought that dinosaurs had left no *descendants* (offspring). But scientists now believe that certain small meat-eating dinosaurs were the ancestors of birds.

Scientists learn about dinosaurs by studying dinosaur *fossils*—that is, the preserved bones, teeth, eggs, and tracks of dinosaurs. They also study living reptiles and other animals that resemble dinosaurs in some ways.

The world of the dinosaurs

When dinosaurs lived, the earth was much different from the way it is today. For example, the Alps, the Him-alaya, and many other surface features had not yet been formed. The first flowering plants did not appear until late in the Mesozoic Era. The mammals of the Mesozoic Era were extremely small, and many of the plants and animals that were common then are now rare or extinct.

The land and climate. Scientists believe that the continents once formed a single land mass surrounded by an enormous sea. During the Mesozoic Era, this land mass began to break up into continents. The continents slowly drifted apart toward their present locations (see **Continental drift**). But for many centuries, dinosaurs could wander freely over the land connections between continents.

As the continents moved apart, their surface features and climate changed. For a time, shallow seas covered much of North America, Europe, and southern Asia. Thick forests bordered drier plains, and swamps and deltas lined the seacoasts. Later in the Mesozoic Era, the Rocky Mountains began to form, and the seas drained from North America.

Throughout much of the Mesozoic Era, dinosaurs probably lived in an almost tropical climate. Areas near the seas may have had mild, moist weather all year. Inland regions probably had an annual dry season. Toward the end of the Mesozoic Era, the climate grew cooler and drier.

Plant and animal life also changed during the Mesozoic Era. During the first half of the era, cone-bearing trees were the most common plants. Other plant life consisted mainly of cycads, ferns, mosses, and tree ferns. Land animals, in addition to dinosaurs, included crocodiles, frogs, insects, lizards, turtles, and a few kinds of small mammals. Reptiles called *ichthyosaurs* and *plesiosaurs* lived in the seas, along with such animals as clams, corals, jellyfish, snails, sponges, squids, starfish, and sharks and other fish. *Pterosaurs* were reptiles that had wings and could fly.

By the end of the Age of Reptiles, flowering plants had become common. Trees of the forests included cypresses, ginkgoes, maples, oaks, palms, poplars, and redwoods. Birds had developed, and the first snakes appeared. Sea animals included modern fish, plus 12-foot (3.7-meter) sardines, huge turtles, and gigantic lizards called *mosasaurs*.

Kinds of dinosaurs

Scientists divide the dinosaurs into two major groups: (1) saurischians and (2) ornithischians. The two groups differed in the structure of the hips. Saurischians, whose name means *lizard-hipped,* had a hip structure much like that of lizards. Ornithischians, whose name means *bird-hipped,* had a birdlike hip structure. Each of the groups consisted of several basic kinds of dinosaurs.

Some kinds of dinosaurs lived throughout the Mesozoic Era. Other kinds lived during only one or two of the three *periods* into which the era is divided. The periods are the *Triassic,* the *Jurassic,* and the *Cretaceous.* The Triassic Period lasted from about 240 million to 205 million years ago. The Jurassic Period lasted from about 205 million to 138 million years ago. The Cretaceous Period lasted from about 138 million to 63 million years ago.

Saurischians included the largest and fiercest dinosaurs. There were three basic kinds of saurischians: (1) prosauropods, (2) sauropods, and (3) theropods. Each of these groups included many variations.

Prosauropods, such as the plateosaurus, grew about 20 feet (6 meters) long and had a long neck and a small head. Prosauropods walked on their two hind legs sometimes and on all four legs at other times. They were the first common plant-eating dinosaurs. They appeared about 220 million years ago and apparently died out early in the Jurassic Period.

Sauropods were the giants of the dinosaur world. They averaged about 70 feet (21 meters) long and stood 12 to 15 feet (3.7 to 4.8 meters) tall at the hips. Most adults weighed from 10 to 30 short tons (9 to 27 metric tons). Sauropods walked on four heavy legs like those of an elephant. A typical sauropod had a long neck, a small head, a long tail, and a huge, deep chest. Sauropods were the main plant-eaters of the Jurassic Period. During the Cretaceous Period, other plant-eaters became more important.

One of the best-known sauropods is the apatosaurus, or brontosaurus. For many people, the word *dinosaur* brings to mind the image of an apatosaurus. The animal's front legs were shorter than its hind legs, and its back sloped down toward the base of the neck. The diplodocus, the longest dinosaur known, looked much like an apatosaurus but was slimmer and lighter. The diplodocus grew as long as 90 feet (27 meters). Both the apatosaurus and the diplodocus lived during the Jurassic Period in what is now North America.

The largest known dinosaur was the brachiosaurus, another type of sauropod. Brachiosaurs lived in many parts of the world during the Jurassic Period. Brachiosaurs stood 40 feet (12 meters) tall or more, and weighed up to 85 short tons (77 metric tons). Their front legs were longer than the back ones. The animals stood

Kinds of dinosaurs   Scientists divide dinosaurs into two major groups—*ornithischians* and *saurischians*—according to the structure of the hips. Ornithischians, such as the corythosaurus, had a birdlike hip structure. Saurischians, such as the allosaurus, had a hip structure much like that of lizards.

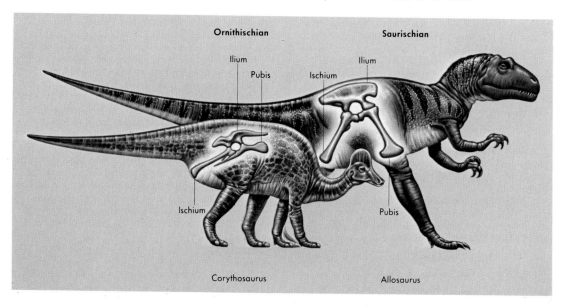

Ornithischian

Saurischian

Ilium

Pubis

Ischium

Ilium

Ischium

Pubis

Corythosaurus

Allosaurus

like giraffes, with the back sloping down toward the tail.

Theropods were the only meat-eating dinosaurs. The animals walked upright on two hind legs. Typical theropods had a long, muscular tail, which they carried straight out behind them for balance. Their forelimbs were slender. Large theropods had a short neck and a large, long head. Small theropods had a long neck and a smaller head. Theropods had strong jaws and bladelike teeth. They lived throughout the Mesozoic Era.

The fierce tyrannosaurus rex is the best-known theropod. The name *tyrannosaurus rex* means *tyrant-lizard king,* and the tyrannosaurus was the most feared meat-eater of its time. Tyrannosaurs stood nearly 10 feet (3 meters) high at the hips and grew about 40 feet (12 meters) long. Their head measured up to 4 feet (1.2 meters) in length, and their teeth were about 6 inches (15 centimeters) long. The animals had very short forelimbs, which probably were almost useless. Each forelimb had two fingers. Tyrannosaurs ruled the land near the end of the Age of Reptiles. A few tyrannosaurus fossils have been discovered in North America.

About 140 million years ago, long before tyrannosaurs appeared, allosaurs were the main meat-eating dinosaurs. They resembled tyrannosaurs but were not quite as large. Allosaurs also had longer forelimbs with three fingers on each. Smaller theropods included the deinonychus and the ornithomimus. The deinonychus was about 3 feet (0.9 meter) tall. On each foot, it had a large curved claw, which was probably used to slash at prey. The ornithomimus looked much like a featherless ostrich and was about the size of an ostrich. Theropods also included the smallest known dinosaur, the compsognathus. It was about the size of a chicken.

Ornithischians were plant-eaters. They had a beaklike bone in front of their teeth, and many had bony plates in their skin. During the Cretaceous Period, ornithischians became the most important plant-eating dinosaurs. There were four basic kinds of ornithischians. They were, in order of their appearance on the earth: (1) ornithopods, (2) stegosaurs, (3) ankylosaurs, and (4) ceratopsians. Each group included numerous variations.

Ornithopods could walk either on four legs or on two hind legs. The first dinosaur fossil discovered was that of an iguanodon, a kind of ornithopod. Iguanodons measured about 30 feet (9 meters) long. The animals had a bony spike on the thumb of each forelimb. Ornithopods lived throughout the Age of Reptiles.

Ornithopods reached their greatest development in duckbilled dinosaurs, or hadrosaurs. Duckbills were the most numerous dinosaurs of the Cretaceous Period. They lived in what are now Asia and North America. They had a flat beak like the bill of a duck at the front of the mouth and jaws with hundreds of teeth farther back in the mouth. They had strong hind legs, and long, slender front legs with webbed toes. Duckbills grew up to 9 feet (2.7 meters) tall at the hips and more than 30 feet (9 meters) long.

Some kinds of duckbills, such as the anatosaurus, had a low, flat skull. Other kinds, such as the corythosaurus, had a showy, bony *crest* (growth) on the top of the head. Air passages from the animal's nose traveled through the crest. Some scientists believe that the crested duckbills may have made honking sounds by using the air passages much like a trumpet.

Stegosaurs were large plant-eaters with huge, upright bony plates along the back. They lived about 140 million years ago. One of the best-known stegosaurs is the stegosaurus, which lived in what is now North America. Stegosaurs walked on four legs. They were about 20 feet (6 meters) long and about 8 feet (2.4 meters) tall at the hips. They had a small head and a short neck. Their hind legs were much longer than the front ones. As a result, the animals carried the head close to the ground and looked bent over.

Stegosaurs had one or two rows of vertical, bony plates down the back. Their tail was armed with two pairs of bony spikes. The plates and spikes may have helped protect the animals from enemies. The plates may also have served as part of a system to cool the body. Blood warmed in the body probably flowed through the thin plates. Air moving around its back may have cooled the blood flowing through the plates.

Ankylosaurs are known as the armored dinosaurs. They were low, broad animals and walked on four legs. Most kinds of ankylosaurs grew 15 to 20 feet (4.8 to 6 meters) long and had a skull more than 2 feet (0.6 meter) long. Heavy, bony plates covered the body and head of most ankylosaurs. Many of the plates had ridges or spikes. Commonly, large spikes also grew at the shoulders or at the back of the head. Some kinds of ankylosaurs had a large mass of bone at the end of the tail, which could be used as a powerful club against enemies. Ankylosaurs lived in many parts of the world during the Cretaceous Period.

Ceratopsians were horned dinosaurs. The animals walked on four feet and resembled rhinoceroses somewhat. They ranged in length from about 6 to 25 feet (1.8 to 8 meters) and had a huge head.

Ceratopsians had a bony frill on the back of the head. The frill spread out over the neck. In one kind of ceratopsian, the styracosaurus, the frill had spikes. Most kinds also had horns on the face. The triceratops had three facial horns, a short one on the nose and one over each eye. The horns over the eyes grew up to 3 feet (0.9 meter) long. The monoclonius had one large horn on the nose. The pentaceratops had five facial horns. One kind of ceratopsian, the protoceratops, was hornless. Ceratopsians were the last major group of dinosaurs. They lived in what are now Asia and North America.

How dinosaurs lived

For many years, people thought that dinosaurs were clumsy, slow-moving creatures that lived much like modern reptiles. However, fossil evidence shows that some kinds of dinosaurs—especially small theropods—probably were much more active than most present-day reptiles. In addition, most dinosaurs resembled birds, rather than modern reptiles, in their leg and foot structure and upright posture. Scientists generally agree that dinosaurs are closer ancestors of birds than of present-day reptiles. They believe that the study of birds can help us learn about the life of dinosaurs.

How dinosaurs lived depends partly on whether they were *ectothermic* (cold-blooded), like modern reptiles, or *endothermic* (warm-blooded), like birds. The body temperature of ectothermic animals changes with the temperature of their surroundings. For example, a lizard's body temperature rises as the air becomes

When dinosaurs lived

Dinosaurs lived during the Mesozoic Era, which lasted from about 240 million to 63 million years ago. The era is divided into three periods—the Triassic, the Jurassic, and the Cretaceous. Some kinds of dinosaurs lived throughout the era. Others lived during only one or two periods.

Corals and mollusks were common. Fish appeared. Land was bare.

Algae were plentiful.

Spore-bearing plants appeared on land.

Forests developed, and insects and amphibians appeared.

Mosses developed. Reptiles appeared.

Paleozoic Era (570 million to 240 million years ago)

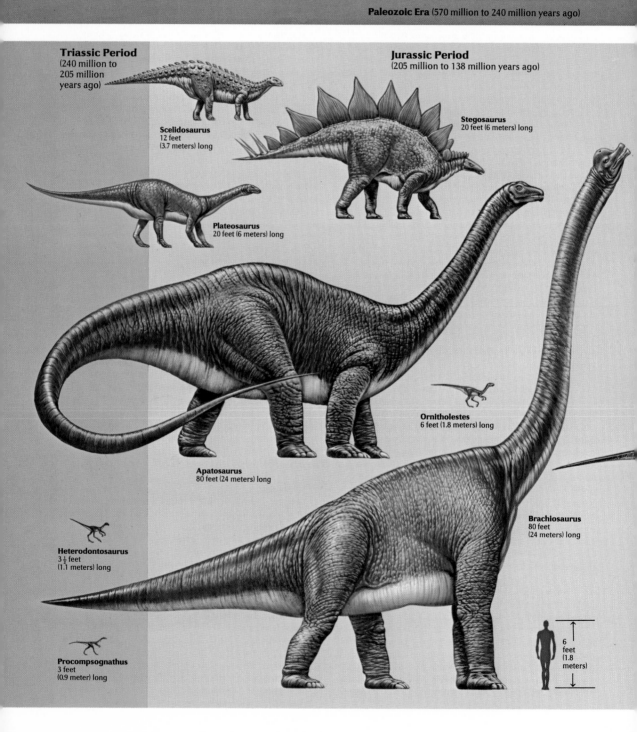

Triassic Period
(240 million to 205 million years ago)

Jurassic Period
(205 million to 138 million years ago)

Scelidosaurus
12 feet
(3.7 meters) long

Stegosaurus
20 feet (6 meters) long

Plateosaurus
20 feet (6 meters) long

Ornitholestes
6 feet (1.8 meters) long

Apatosaurus
80 feet (24 meters) long

Brachiosaurus
80 feet
(24 meters) long

Heterodontosaurus
3½ feet
(1.1 meters) long

Procompsognathus
3 feet
(0.9 meter) long

6 feet
(1.8 meters)

Seed plants developed.	Dinosaurs and mammals appeared.	Birds appeared.	Flowering plants developed.	Dinosaurs died out.	Fruits, grains, and grasses developed.	Early human beings appeared.

	Mesozoic Era (240 million to 63 million years ago)	**Cenozoic Era** (63 million years ago to the present)

Cretaceous Period
(138 million to 63 million years ago)

Camptosaurus
15 feet (4.8 meters) long

Ankylosaurus 15 feet (4.8 meters) long

Corythosaurus
30 feet (9 meters) long

Iguanodon
30 feet (9 meters) long

Compsognathus
2 ½ feet (0.8 meter) long

Torosaurus
30 feet
(9 meters) long

Deinonychus 9 feet (2.7 meters) long

Allosaurus
30 feet (9 meters) long

Tyrannosaurus rex
40 feet (12 meters) long

Ornithomimus
14 feet (4.3 meters) long

warmer. If the air cools, the lizard loses body heat. Endo-thermic animals have a constant, fairly warm body temperature. Such animals tend to be more active than those whose temperature varies.

Scientists disagree on whether dinosaurs were ecto-thermic or endothermic. Traditionally, dinosaurs were considered to be ectothermic. But many scientists now believe that they must have been endothermic to keep up their level of activity. Other experts point out, how-ever, that large animals lose body heat very slowly. Di-nosaurs could therefore have had a warm, constant body temperature and been fairly active even if they were ectothermic.

Reproduction and growth. Scientists do not know how all dinosaur species reproduced. However, fossil dinosaur eggs have been discovered. Therefore, at least some kinds of dinosaurs laid eggs, as do most other reptiles. The female may have scratched a nest in the soil and deposited several eggs in it. Some dinosaurs may have cared for their young after they hatched. Oth-ers probably left them to survive as best they could.

Scientists can only guess how old dinosaurs lived to be. But they can estimate the time it took for dinosaurs to grow to adult size. The growth rate depends on whether dinosaurs were endothermic or ectothermic. Endothermic animals grow more rapidly than do ecto-thermic ones. If apatosaurs were endothermic, it proba-bly took them about 50 years to reach their adult weight of about 30 short tons (27 metric tons). If the animals were ectothermic, however, it may have taken them 200 years or longer to grow that large.

Group life. Fossil evidence shows that more than 20 kinds of dinosaurs may have occupied a particular area at the same time. Many kinds, including ceratopsians, duckbills, and stegosaurs, lived in herds. Other kinds, such as apatosaurs and tyrannosaurs, probably spent most of their life alone.

Some experts think that dinosaurs, like many modern birds and reptiles, were colorful animals. Some kinds of dinosaurs perhaps attracted mates by displaying brightly colored body parts. For example, a duckbill's head crest and a ceratopsian's neck frill may have been vividly colored and so served to attract mates.

Getting food. Sauropods may have waded into shal-low lakes and swamps to eat water plants. Or they may have eaten tree leaves, as did duckbills. Ankylosaurs, ceratopsians, and stegosaurs fed on low plants that grew along shorelines or on open plains.

Allosaurs, tyrannosaurs, and other large theropods may have been hunters that preyed mainly on the huge plant-eating dinosaurs. Or these giant meat-eaters, like some other theropods, might have been *scavengers* and picked meat from dead animals they found. Some small theropods ate insects or eggs. Others hunted mammals or small dinosaurs and other reptiles. These small thero-pods were probably very active and could run quickly. Some of them, including the fierce deinonychus, may have hunted in packs as wolves do today.

Protection against enemies. Plant-eating dinosaurs had many forms of protection against theropods. The huge size of sauropods probably protected them from most predators. Ankylosaurs had bony plates for protec-tion, and ceratopsians and stegosaurs probably used their horns and spikes to fight off enemies. Duckbills could swim into deep water to avoid being attacked by theropods.

Why dinosaurs died out

For about 150 million years, dinosaurs ruled the land, and other large reptiles ruled the sky and sea. Then about 63 million years ago, these huge reptiles died out and mammals took over the earth.

Scientists have developed many theories to explain the disappearance of dinosaurs and the other great rep-tiles. Probably the most widely accepted theory involves a change in the earth's climate. Toward the end of the Cretaceous Period, the climate cooled and may have be-come too cold for the dinosaurs. Dinosaurs were too large to hibernate in dens, and they had no fur or feath-ers for protection against the cold. Smaller animals could hibernate during cold periods. Mammals and birds had fur or feathers for protection, and some could migrate to warmer places to avoid the cold weather. In these ways, such animals could survive the cold that may eventually have killed off the dinosaurs.

Another theory also involves changes in the climate. Some scientists believe that the explosion of a nearby star gave off dangerous radiation and caused cold, unfa-vorable weather on the earth for thousands of years. Di-nosaurs could not avoid the radiation and the cold and probably were killed off by them.

Some experts believe that plant-eating dinosaurs could not eat the new kinds of plants that developed during the Cretaceous Period and thus starved. As they died off, so did the meat-eaters that preyed on them. Other experts think that the dinosaurs could not com-pete successfully with mammals for food and so lost the struggle for existence.

Another theory suggests that a large asteroid hit the earth at the end of the Cretaceous Period. According to this theory, the impact of the asteroid threw billions of tons of dust—or ice crystals, if the asteroid had hit the ocean—into the atmosphere. The debris blocked out sunlight for three to six months. The seeds and roots of land plants survived this lightless period, but the plants themselves stopped growing. The lack of plant growth killed off many of the plant-eating dinosaurs. As the plant-eaters died, so also did the meat-eating dinosaurs that fed on them. The darkness caused land tempera-tures to drop below freezing for six to twelve months. This change in climate further damaged the dinosaur populations. Scientists theorize that small mammals and birds were protected from the cold by fur or feathers and survived by feeding on seeds, nuts, and rotting veg-etation. After the worldwide darkness ended, land plants regrew from dormant seeds and roots.

Many scientists feel that no one theory completely ex-plains why dinosaurs died out. They suggest that dino-saurs simply could not keep up with the changes that were occurring on the earth toward the end of the Cre-taceous Period. Thus, a combination of causes may have contributed to the end of the Age of Reptiles.

Learning about dinosaurs

Scientists have many ways of learning about dino-saurs. One important way is by studying dinosaur fos-sils. For example, a dinosaur tooth can tell an expert whether the animal ate plants or meat. Scientists who

University of Nebraska State Museum

Dinosaur fossils include the preserved bones, teeth, and eggs of dinosaurs. Dinosaur bones and teeth can be fitted together to form a skeleton, such as the one of the apatosaurus at the left. The eggs shown above were laid about 80 million years ago by a protoceratops. They measure about 6 inches (15 centimeters) long.

Field Museum of Natural History (WORLD BOOK photo)

study fossils are called *paleontologists*. Scientists also learn about dinosaurs by observing animals that have traits similar to those of dinosaurs. For example, they might study elephants and hippopotamuses in the wild to learn about the lives of large land animals.

Dinosaur discoveries. Before the 1800's, no one knew that dinosaurs had ever existed. People who found a dinosaur tooth or bone did not realize what it was. Then in 1822, the wife of an English physician named Gideon Mantell found a large tooth partly buried in a rock. She showed the tooth to her husband, who collected fossils. Mantell learned that the tooth resembled that of a South American lizard called an *iguana*. He suggested that the tooth came from a huge, iguanalike reptile, which he named *iguanodon* (iguana tooth).

Within a few years, the remains of several other kinds of large, extinct reptiles had been discovered. In 1841, Sir Richard Owen, an English scientist, suggested that these reptiles belonged to a group of reptiles that were unlike any living animals. Owen called the group *Dinosauria*. Its members came to be known as dinosaurs.

During the late 1800's and early 1900's, large deposits of dinosaur remains were discovered in western North America, Europe, Asia, and Africa. One of these deposits lies in the Morrison Formation, a series of rock layers that extends across part of Colorado, Utah, and Wyoming. Perhaps the world's richest deposit of dinosaur remains is in the Red Deer River Valley of southern Alberta. Deposits also lie in Belgium, Mongolia, Tanzania, and other parts of the world.

Working with dinosaur fossils. Museums and other educational institutions sponsor scientists who search for and study dinosaur fossils. Paleontologists look for fossils in areas where wind and water have worn away the land and exposed deep, fossil-bearing layers of rock. After they locate a skeleton, paleontologists remove the rock above it. In many cases, they dig out the portion of rock that contains the fossil. Then they cover the rock and fossil with cloth and plaster of Paris. The plaster dries into a hard, protective coating, and the fossil is shipped to a laboratory.

At the laboratory, workers clean the bones and teeth and repair broken ones. Specialists may then rebuild the skeleton by putting the bones together on a metal frame. In some cases, missing bones may be replaced with pieces made from fiberglass, plaster, or plastic. Scientists rarely discover all the bones of a large dinosaur, and so they estimate the animal's length based on the bones that have been found.

Some museums make models of dinosaurs for display. Experts study the skeleton and try to imagine how it looked covered with muscles and skin. They then build a metal frame that resembles the skeleton and mold wire and screen around it to shape the dinosaur's body. Finally, they cover the model with "skin" and paint it to look realistic.   Peter Dodson

Related articles. For additional information and pictures of dinosaurs, see **Prehistoric animal.** See also:

Outline

I. **The world of the dinosaurs**
   A. The land and climate   B. Plant and animal life
II. **Kinds of dinosaurs**
   A. Saurischians   B. Ornithischians
III. **How dinosaurs lived**
   A. Reproduction and growth   C. Getting food
   B. Group life   D. Protection against enemies
IV. **Why dinosaurs died out**
V. **Learning about dinosaurs**
   A. Dinosaur discoveries
   B. Working with dinosaur fossils

Questions

What are some theories that scientists have developed to explain why dinosaurs died out?
How did sauropods get food?
What were some dinosaurs that probably lived in herds?
In what kind of area do paleontologists look for dinosaur fossils?
What were the two major groups of dinosaurs? How did they differ?
Which dinosaurs were meat-eaters?
Which was the largest known dinosaur?

Where have some of the most important dinosaur fossil deposits been discovered?

What kinds of animals besides dinosaurs lived during the Age of Reptiles?

Reading and Study Guide

See *Dinosaur* in the Research Guide/Index, Volume 22, for a *Reading and Study Guide.*

Additional resources

Level I

Arnold, Caroline. *Dinosaur Mountain: Graveyard of the Past.* Clarion, 1989.

Cohen, Daniel. *Dinosaurs.* Doubleday, 1987.

Lauber, Patricia. *The News About Dinosaurs.* Bradbury, 1989.

Level II

Horner, John R., and Gorman, J. *Digging Dinosaurs.* Workman, 1988.

The Macmillan Illustrated Encyclopedia of Dinosaurs & Prehistoric Animals. Ed. by Dougal Dixon and others. Macmillan, 1988.

Russell, Dale. *An Odyssey in Time: The Dinosaurs of North America.* NorthWord, 1989.

Dinosaur National Monument, located in Utah and Colorado, is a scenic region with spectacular canyons cut by the Green and Yampa rivers. Its deposits of fossil remains of prehistoric reptiles are of scientific interest. For its area, see **National Park System** (table: National monuments). It was established in 1915.

Dinwiddie, *dihn WIHD ee,* **Robert** (1693-1770), was lieutenant governor of Virginia from 1751 to 1758. He served as the acting governor of the colony, because the governors usually lived in England. Greatly interested in the Ohio region, he decided to keep that area from the French. In 1753, he sent George Washington to demand that the French withdraw from western Pennsylvania, claimed by Virginia. In the war that followed, Dinwiddie urged the colonies to help the English drive the French from the Ohio Valley. He aided the expedition sent against Fort Duquesne in 1755. He quarreled with the Virginia Assembly because of its reluctance to vote funds for the war. Dinwiddie returned to England in 1758. He was born near Glasgow, Scotland. See also **Washington, George** (Early military career).

Joseph Carlyle Sitterson

Diocese. See **Archbishop; Bishop; Roman Catholic Church** (Dioceses and parishes).

Diocletian, *DY uh KLEE shuhn* (A.D. 244?-311), ruled Rome as emperor from 284 to 305. In 303, he began a persecution of Christians that is often called the *Great Persecution.* He shared the rule with three other men.

Diocletian's official name was Gaius Aurelius Valerius Diocletianus. He was born in Illyricum (now Yugoslavia). Diocletian became commander of the bodyguard of Emperor Numerianus. Diocletian was proclaimed emperor by his troops in 284, after Numerianus' death. Diocletian soon made Maximian his co-emperor. In 293, Diocletian appointed Constantius I and Galerius *caesars* (junior emperors), creating a four-man rule that lasted until 305. Diocletian and Maximian then gave up their power. The shared rule, though effective, was unpopular because it increased the number of government officials and led to more efficient collection of taxes.   Timothy David Barnes

Diode. See **Electronics** (Switching; The first commercial vacuum tubes); **Vacuum tube** (Kinds).

Diogenes, *dy AHJ uh NEEZ* (412?-323 B.C.), belonged to the Cynic school of ancient Greek philosophy. The Cynics may have taken their name from the Greek word for "the dog," which was Diogenes' nickname. The Cynics taught that a person should lead a life of self-control and be free from all desire for material things and pleasures. Diogenes carried this view to extremes in his own life. According to tradition, he used a tub for shelter and walked the streets barefoot. A widely known legend tells that he carried a lamp in broad daylight, announcing that he was "in search of a human being." Diogenes held up the life of animals as a model for humanity, believing that good birth, riches, and honor did not help people lead a virtuous life.

Diogenes was born at Sinope, in Asia Minor. Pirates captured him during a journey from Athens to Aegina and offered him for sale as a slave. He told his captors he knew no trade except how to govern people. Pointing to a wealthy Corinthian, he said: "Sell me to this man, he needs a master." The Corinthian bought Diogenes and made him tutor to his sons. When Alexander the Great came to see Diogenes, who was sunning himself, he said, "Ask any favor you wish." Legend says that Diogenes replied: "Please move out of my sunlight," to which Alexander commented: "If I were not Alexander, I would like to be Diogenes."   S. Marc Cohen

See also **Cynic philosophy.**

Dionaea. See **Venus's-flytrap.**

Dionysius the Elder, *DY uh NIHSH ee uhs* or *DY uh NY see uhs* (430?-367 B.C.), was a Greek tyrant and military leader who ruled in ancient Sicily for almost 40 years. He became a general at Syracuse, the largest Greek city on Sicily, in 406 B.C., during a war with Carthage. In 405 B.C., he made peace with the Carthaginians and became ruler of Syracuse. Dionysius hired many foreign soldiers, defeated armies from Carthage in 396 and 392 B.C., and extended his control over much of Sicily. He later gained control of much of southern Italy and assisted Sparta in its battles in Greece.

During the 370's B.C., the Carthaginians defeated Dionysius and forced him to give up half of Sicily. Dionysius died of fever during another war with Carthage. He was succeeded as ruler by his son Dionysius the Younger.

Peter Krentz

Dionysus, *DY uh NY suhs,* was the god of wine in Greek mythology. After coming into contact with Greek culture, the Romans adopted Dionysus as their god of wine, but they called him Bacchus. Dionysus' parents were Zeus, king of the gods, and Semele, the mortal daughter of King Cadmus of Thebes. Dionysus married Ariadne, the daughter of King Minos of Crete.

The ancient Greeks associated Dionysus with violent and unpredictable behavior, especially actions caused by drinking too much wine. Most stories about Dionysus tell of his leading sessions of drunken merrymaking. Dionysus' followers at these gatherings included *nymphs* (maidens), creatures called *satyrs* that were half man and half horse or goat, and women attendants called *maenads* (see **Nymph; Satyr**).

Not all the stories about Dionysus concern drunkenness or violent behavior. Many Greeks believed that Dionysus taught people farming techniques, especially those related to growing grapes and making wine. The Greeks also dedicated the great theater in Athens to Dionysus. Their concept of tragedy in drama grew from a ceremony that honored Dionysus. The word *tragedy* comes from the Greek word *tragos,* meaning *goat.* The goat was sacred to and symbolic of Dionysus.

C. Scott Littleton

See also **Bacchus; Drama** (Greek drama).

Diophantus. See **Algebra** (History).

Diopside, *dy AHP syd,* is a widely occurring mineral with a glassy luster. Diopside is sometimes used as a gemstone (see **Gem** [picture]). It belongs to a group of rock-forming minerals called *pyroxenes.* Diopside is a *silicate* rich in calcium and magnesium (see **Silicate**). Its chemical formula is $CaMgSi_2O_6$. Pure diopside is white, and it melts at 1391° C. An impurity of iron may make the mineral light green. Diopside forms when intense heat and pressure are applied during metamorphism to limestone that consists chiefly of dolomite with silica impurities (see **Metamorphism**). Diopside also forms during the crystallization of certain kinds of *magma* (molten rock material).   Robert W. Charles

Diorama, *DY uh RAM uh,* is an exhibit showing modeled figures or objects in front of a painted or modeled background. The models become smaller toward the back of the exhibit and blend so skillfully with the background that the scene looks real. Museums use dioramas to show historical events, industrial methods, and animals and plants in their natural settings. Schoolchildren sometimes make simple dioramas as projects.

The word *diorama* comes from Greek words meaning *a view through.* Louis Daguerre, a French inventor, first used the word about 1822 for transparent paintings he exhibited and for a theater he opened.   C. M. Charles

Dioxin, *dy AHK suhn,* is any of 75 related chemicals, all of which consist of carbon, chlorine, hydrogen, and oxygen. However, the word *dioxin* is most commonly used to refer to only one of these chemicals, the compound *2, 3, 7, 8-tetrachlorodibenzo-p-dioxin* (TCDD). Some scientists consider TCDD to be the most toxic synthetically produced chemical.

TCDD is a useless by-product of the manufacture of certain weedkillers and several other industrial processes. Disposal of the chemical is difficult, because it does not readily *degrade* (break down) in soil or water. One of the most effective methods of disposing of dioxin is burning the material at high temperatures. Soil and water in parts of Canada, Europe, and the United States, however, have become contaminated with dioxin, because of improper disposal of industrial waste products.

The health effects of TCDD are not completely understood. The chemical is extremely deadly to certain animals, but no human deaths have been directly linked to it. However, some people have developed such health problems as headaches, stomachaches, and a severe skin rash called *chloracne* as a result of exposure to dioxin. Some researchers also believe the chemical may cause birth defects and cancer.

TCDD was first identified as a contaminant in 1957. It was present in *Agent Orange,* a weedkiller used by U.S. armed forces in the 1960's and early 1970's, during the Vietnam War. Dioxin was not recognized as a major public health hazard until the mid-1970's.   Gary F. Bennett

See also **Agent Orange; Missouri** (Missouri today).

Diphtheria, *dihf THIHR ee uh* or *dihp THIHR ee uh,* is a severe, contagious infection of the upper respiratory system or the skin. It can involve serious—or even fatal—complications. During the late 1800's, diphtheria epidemics swept the United States and Western Europe. At that time, most victims were under 10 years of age. Today, diphtheria affects children and adults about equally. Widespread immunization with diphtheria vaccines, which first came into use about 1920, has greatly reduced the number of cases of diphtheria.

Cause, symptoms, and complications. Diphtheria is caused by a bacterium called *Corynebacterium diphtheriae.* This organism commonly infects the mucous membranes of the upper breathing passages, particularly the tonsils and the *pharynx* (the back of the mouth and the upper throat). The bacteria produce a *toxin* (poison), which enters the blood and is carried throughout the body. Infected individuals spread the bacteria by coughing or sneezing. People called *carriers* may harbor the bacteria without showing any symptoms of the disease. Although carriers show no symptoms, they can spread the illness to other people.

Symptoms appear about two to five days after infection. They include a sore throat, fever, and swelling of the lymph nodes in the neck. A thick, grayish membrane forms on the surface of the tonsils and pharynx, and may even extend up into the nose or down into the windpipe and lungs. The membrane may interfere with breathing or swallowing. In severe cases, it can completely block the breathing passages.

Diphtheria toxin can affect the heart and nervous system. One severe effect is heart muscle inflammation, called *acute myocarditis,* which may result in permanent heart damage. In some cases, the toxin so weakens the heart that death occurs. Effects of nerve damage include temporary paralysis of muscles in the throat and eyes, and, most seriously, of the muscles used in breathing. Paralysis of the breathing muscles can be fatal.

Diphtheria bacteria also can infect breaks in the skin. Such infections are called *wound diphtheria* or *cutaneous diphtheria.* In most cases of wound diphtheria, a membrane does not form over the infected area. But toxins enter the bloodstream and can produce the same complications as in the respiratory infection.

Treatment. Physicians hospitalize diphtheria patients and give them *diphtheria antitoxin.* This substance neutralizes diphtheria toxin. If administered early enough, the antitoxin can minimize heart and nerve complications. If the membrane that forms in the throat blocks the breathing passages, a doctor may cut a temporary opening through the neck into the windpipe. Heart failure is treated with medications. If the respiratory muscles become paralyzed, a machine called a *respirator* is used to maintain the patient's breathing. Diphtheria patients also receive antibiotics, which kill the diphtheria bacteria and help control secondary infections caused by other bacteria.

Prevention. People can obtain *immunity* (protection) from diphtheria by using vaccines that contain *diphtheria toxoid.* This toxoid is a specially treated form of diphtheria toxin. It does not damage body tissues, but it triggers the production of disease-fighting substances called *antibodies.* Antibodies formed in response to the toxoid will attack diphtheria toxin if it enters the bloodstream. Public health experts recommend that infants receive a series of four diphtheria immunizations. A person should get a "booster" shot of diphtheria vaccine between the ages of 4 and 6, and about every 10 years thereafter. See **Immunization.**   Hugh C. Dillon, Jr.

Diphthong, *DIHP thawng* or *DIHF thawng,* is the sound produced by pronouncing two vowels as a single syllable. Examples are the *ou* in *out* and *oi* in *oil.* One sees how two sounds become a diphthong by pronouncing *ah* and *ee* together slowly, then more rapidly. They become the diphthong heard in *mine,* known as *long i.*   Gary Tate

Diplodocus. See Dinosaur (introduction; Saurischians).

Diplomacy, *duh PLOH muh see,* is the means of conducting negotiations between nations. Some scholars today also apply the term to the strategies and tactics nations use when they negotiate. In this sense, diplomacy involves formulating the policies that nations follow to influence other nations. When diplomacy fails during a major crisis, war often occurs.

Traditionally, however, diplomacy referred to the formal practice that most nations follow of sending representatives to live in other countries. These *diplomats* help carry on day-to-day relationships between their country and the country where they serve. They work to gain political or economic advantages for their country and to promote international cooperation.

Diplomatic representatives observe strict rules about rank and importance. The highest rank is ambassador extraordinary and plenipotentiary, followed by envoy extraordinary and minister plenipotentiary, minister resident, minister-counselor, counselor of embassy, secretary of embassy, and attaché. Most large nations send ambassadors to each other, and to many smaller nations. Smaller countries sometimes send and receive diplomats of lower rank. Most governments also send *consuls* to handle international business.

Each nation handles its diplomatic affairs through a foreign office. In the United States, the office that handles foreign relations is the Department of State.

Diplomatic duties. Diplomatic officers abroad are the accredited spokespersons for their governments. They gather information on everything of value to their governments and transmit it in formal reports, usually in code (see **Codes and ciphers**). Diplomatic officers also protect the rights of fellow citizens who are abroad.

Diplomats maintain their headquarters in an embassy or legation. The only difference between an embassy and a legation is the rank of the diplomat in charge. An ambassador heads an embassy, and a minister heads a legation. A diplomat's staff may include attachés and other special advisers who report on economic, political, and social conditions.

Diplomatic immunity. Diplomats enjoy several important privileges and immunities while serving abroad. These privileges arise partly because diplomats are the direct representatives of sovereign powers. Just as important, diplomats must have complete independence of action to perform their duties. A diplomat's privileges are based on the principle of *extraterritoriality.* This principle, used in international law, includes the guarantee that people living in foreign countries remain under the authority of their own governments. Four important diplomatic privileges and immunities are:

1. Diplomats cannot be arrested for any reason. Their families usually share this exemption.

2. Their residences, papers, and effects cannot be searched or seized.

3. Their personal belongings cannot be taxed by the country in which they serve.

4. Diplomats, their families, and their staffs enjoy complete freedom of worship.

History. Nations have not always used diplomacy to settle international problems. The ancient Romans used diplomatic representatives only for special purposes. But as relations among countries grew more complex, many nations found that they needed permanent representatives in other countries. Embassies first appeared in Italy during the 1200's and 1300's. At that time, they served as headquarters for spies and espionage agents, as well as for diplomats. Many historians believe that Cardinal Richelieu of France started the system of resident representatives during the 1600's.

Through the years, formal diplomatic procedures have changed in various ways. Beginning in the 1950's, for example, U.S. Secretary of State John Foster Dulles became the first major diplomat to engage in extensive *personal diplomacy* around the world. Dulles often bypassed the appointed ambassadors in the countries he visited. In the early 1970's, U.S. Secretary of State Henry Kissinger further enhanced this practice when he engaged in *shuttle diplomacy.* He traveled back and forth among the major capitals of the Middle East in an attempt to solve an ongoing conflict there. Even heads of governments sometimes feel they need personal conferences with leaders of other governments in *summit meetings.*

Some scholars argue that diplomatic representatives are unnecessary today because of the ease of high-level exchanges and long-distance communication. But ongoing personal diplomatic contact has many advantages. Diplomats take great care to make friends with government officials and influential citizens. When they present a formal proposal, they can count on these friendships to help them. Diplomats also can test reaction to ideas their governments are considering by talking with acquaintances.   Michael P. Sullivan

Related articles in *World Book* include:

Ambassador	Foreign policy	Logan Act
Attaché	Foreign Service	Minister
Consul	International rela-	Protocol
Diplomatic corps	tions	State, Department
Extraterritoriality	Legation	of

Additional resources

Eban, Abba S. *The New Diplomacy: International Affairs in the Modern Age.* Random House, 1983.
Jackson, Geoffrey. *Concorde Diplomacy: The Ambassador's Role in the World Today.* Hamish Hamilton, 1981.
Jones, Howard. *The Course of American Diplomacy: From the Revolution to the Present.* Watts, 1985.
Zartman, Ira W., and Berman, M. R. *The Practical Negotiator.* Yale, 1982.

Diplomatic corps, *DIHP luh MAT ihk kawr,* consists of all the heads of diplomatic missions, such as ambassadors and ministers, who represent their governments in a foreign nation. The term may also refer to all the diplomatic personnel of such missions. A diplomatic mission, generally an embassy or a legation, consists of an ambassador, a minister, or a chargé d'affaires; counselors and secretaries; and various attachés.

Diplomats conduct their government's official relations with the host government, including the negotiation of treaties. They also report to their government on economic, financial, military, and political conditions in the host country.   Robert J. Pranger

See also **Ambassador; Diplomacy; Foreign Service.**

Diplura. See **Insect** (table).

Dipper is a small thrushlike bird of Western North America which dives and dips underwater. It is also called the *water ouzel*. It lives in mountain regions and is an active little bird, fearlessly diving into mountain streams for water insects. The dipper builds its nest of moss in a sheltered crack of rock behind waterfalls or under overhanging rocks above mountain streams.

The bird has slate-gray feathers on its back and lighter feathers on its breast. It has short wings, and carries its short tail upward. The female lays three to five white eggs. Relatives of the dipper live in Mexico, Central and South America, and Europe.

Scientific classification. The dipper belongs to the family Cinclidae. It is *Cinclus mexicanus unicolor.*

Donald F. Bruning

WORLD BOOK illustration by Trevor Boyer, Linden Artists Ltd.

American dipper

Dippers. See **Big and Little Dippers.**

Diptera. See **Insect** (table).

Dirac, *dih RAK,* **Paul Adrien Maurice** (1902-1984), a British theoretical physicist, became noted for his mathematical equation describing the behavior of the electron. Dirac also demonstrated the fundamental unity of the two forms of *quantum mechanics,* wave mechanics and matrix mechanics (see **Quantum mechanics**). He shared the 1933 Nobel Prize in physics with the Austrian physicist Erwin Schrödinger for his equation and his other contributions to quantum mechanics.

Dirac introduced his equation, now called the *Dirac equation,* in 1928. It accounts theoretically for the spin of an electron and for other aspects of the particle's behavior. Dirac's theory also predicted that the negatively charged electron should have an antiparticle—a positively charged electron (see **Antimatter**). The American physicist Carl D. Anderson detected this positively charged electron—the *positron*—in 1932.

Dirac was born in Bristol, England. He attended Bristol and Cambridge universities. From 1932 to 1969, he held the Lucasian Professorship of Mathematics at Cambridge, a chair once held by the great English scientist Sir Isaac Newton. In 1971, Dirac became a professor of physics at Florida State University. His book *The Principles of Quantum Mechanics* (1930) is a classic in its field.

Roger H. Stuewer

See also **Anderson, Carl D.; Schrödinger, Erwin.**

Direct current. See **Electric current; Electric generator.**

Direct-mail advertising. See **Advertising** (Direct mail).

Direct primary. See **Primary election.**

Direct Selling Association is a national trade organization of companies that market goods and services through the party plan or person-to-person methods. Products include clothing, food, appliances, toys, housewares, jewelry, cosmetics, and reference books. About 150 companies belong to the organization. The association conducts marketing research and offers seminars and workshops on consumer affairs, marketing, and sales training. It also monitors legislation that affects companies involved in direct selling. The association was founded in 1910. Its headquarters are at 1730 M Street NW, Washington, DC 20036.

Critically reviewed by the Direct Selling Association

Director. See **Theater** (The director); **Motion picture** (How motion pictures are made); **Drama** (Early realism); **Television** (Producing television programs; picture: Rehearsals); also the list of *Directors and producers* in the *Related articles* of **Motion picture.**

Dirigible. See **Airship.**

Dirksen, Everett McKinley (1896-1969), a Republican from Illinois, served as minority leader of the United States Senate from 1959 until his death. A skilled legislator and powerful speaker, Dirksen was probably the most influential senator of the 1960's. He worked closely with every President from Dwight D. Eisenhower to Richard M. Nixon. His deep voice, tousled hair, and theatrical manner made him one of America's best-known public figures.

Dirksen was an isolationist before the United States entered World War II in 1941. He later defended the foreign policies of both Democratic and Republican administrations. Dirksen set his own course concerning problems in America. He opposed some social legislation but supported the civil rights law of 1964.

Dirksen was born in Pekin, Ill., and attended the University of Minnesota. From 1933 to 1949, he served in the United States House of Representatives. Dirksen was elected to the Senate in 1950 and was reelected in 1956, 1962, and 1968.   David S. Broder

Disabled. See **Handicapped.**

Disabled American Veterans (D.A.V.) is an organization of men and women who have been disabled in line of duty during time of war. It was founded in March 1920 by a group of disabled veterans led by Judge Robert S. Marx of Cincinnati, Ohio.

The purpose of the organization is to care for disabled veterans and to help them return to a useful way of living. Money for rehabilitation work comes from two yearly campaigns in which the D.A.V. sends out millions of letters. Enclosed with each letter are 100 name and address labels and a request for contributions. The D.A.V. has more than 1 million members in over 2,500 chapters in the United States and other countries. Headquarters are at 3725 Alexandria Pike, Cold Spring, KY 41076.   Critically reviewed by the Disabled American Veterans

Disarmament means limiting, regulating, reducing, or eliminating a nation's armed forces and weapons. Most disarmament agreements are treaties approved by many nations. Disarmament is also called *arms control.*

Disarmament proposals have ranged from general and complete disarmament to various forms of limited arms control. General and complete disarmament would allow nations to keep only those weapons and forces necessary to provide police services and support international peacekeeping units. No such plan has ever been adopted. Limited arms-control measures call for restrictions on the testing, production, distribution, or possession of certain types of weapons. The restrictions may ban the weapons entirely, or they may only forbid their presence in certain areas. A number of limited arms-control agreements have been approved.

Working out a disarmament agreement is a difficult process. It is almost impossible to conduct successful arms-control negotiations without stable relations between the participants. The United States and the Soviet Union, the world's strongest military powers, are often critical and suspicious of each other and therefore frequently disagree over disarmament proposals. The Soviet Union keeps its society relatively closed to foreigners, and has historically objected to inspections designed to assure that the proposed limitations are being observed. In 1987 and 1988, however, Soviet leaders agreed to such inspections. In addition, it is often hard to compare the military strength of powerful nations because of differences in the types and numbers of weapons. The combined strength of allied nations also makes comparisons difficult.

The current arms-control debate

The argument for disarmament. Today, an increasing number of nations are developing the ability to make nuclear weapons. This trend has led to a growing campaign for arms control. People who favor arms control use the following arguments:

The overwhelming power of modern weapons exceeds any reasonable purpose. Today, one submarine can carry missiles and nuclear warheads that contain more destructive power than all the weapons used during World War II (1939-1945). The use of all existing nuclear warheads in an attack would almost certainly destroy the countries attacked.

A nuclear war might produce enough dust and other debris to cause a major change in the earth's climate. Many scientists believe that such a change would threaten every form of life in part or all of the world.

The threat to use nuclear weapons against a country might itself cause a war. A threatened country might question its ability to survive an attack. As a result, it might attack first if it feared that it was about to be attacked. Arms control is intended to reduce such fears.

Arms control reduces the need for countries to acquire nuclear weapons or increase their supply of other weapons. Arms control thus eases world tension and limits other conditions that might lead to nuclear war.

The argument against disarmament. Some nations want to build nuclear weapons because they regard them as a symbol of technological achievement and prestige. In addition, many people feel more secure if their country is militarily strong. People who oppose arms control use the following arguments:

Armed forces and weapons by themselves do not cause international disputes or tension. They merely reflect political, economic, and other kinds of disputes. These disputes must be settled before nations can agree on disarmament. Nations that first try to agree on arms control raise false hopes that may cause people to oppose spending the money necessary for defense.

Arms-control agreements between an open, free society and a secret, totalitarian society are risky. The totalitarian nation often will not permit adequate inspection to assure that it is keeping its part of the agreement.

Disarmament may damage a nation's military defense. Arms-control agreements may call for the destruction of some existing weapons and may also prevent the replacement or improvement of other weapons systems.

History of disarmament

Until the 1900's, there were only a few limited arms-control agreements. One of these was the Rush-Bagot Agreement of 1817 between the United States and Great Britain. This agreement limited each nation's armed forces along the Great Lakes.

The peace treaty signed after World War I (1914-1918) disarmed Germany and limited the size of its army. In 1922, the Washington Conference led to a disarmament agreement among France, Italy, Japan, Great Britain, and the United States. These nations agreed to destroy some of their battleships and ban construction of others for 10 years. At the London Naval Conference in 1930, Japan, Great Britain, and the United States consented to limit the size and guns of their cruisers, destroyers, and submarines. This agreement lasted only until 1936.

International agreements at the end of World War II (1939-1945), provided for the disarmament of Germany and Japan. In the years following World War II, the United Nations tried to obtain an agreement limiting arms for all nations. In 1952, a 12-nation Disarmament Commission set up by the UN General Assembly began to meet. In 1959, it took in all UN members. That same year, a treaty was signed to keep Antarctica free of military weapons. The treaty took effect in 1961. In 1963, the Limited Test Ban Treaty was signed and ratified by Great Britain, the United States, and the Soviet Union. It prohibited testing of nuclear weapons in the atmosphere, in outer space, or underwater. A treaty commonly called the Outer Space Treaty, which took effect in 1967, limited military activity in outer space. That same year, 21 Latin American states signed the Treaty of Tlatelolco, which banned nuclear weapons in Latin America. In 1968, the UN approved the Treaty on the Non-Proliferation of Nuclear Weapons, which prohibited countries from giving nuclear weapons to other nations. That treaty went into effect in 1970.

Several more UN arms-control treaties won approval during the early 1970's. The Seabed Arms Control Treaty, which took effect in 1972, prohibited countries from putting nuclear weapons on the ocean floor more than 12 nautical miles (23 kilometers) from their coastlines. The Biological Weapons Convention, a UN treaty signed in 1972, banned the production and stockpiling of biological weapons. This treaty went into effect in 1975.

Meetings between the Soviet Union and the United States to discuss the possibility of limiting *strategic* (long-range offensive) nuclear weapons led to two agreements in 1972. The first agreement limited each nation's defensive missile strength. The other agreement restricted United States and Soviet production of certain offensive nuclear weapons. Both agreements went into force in 1972. See **Strategic Arms Limitation Talks.**

In 1979, Soviet and U.S. officials negotiated a treaty that limited long-range bombers and missiles. However, the United States suspended its efforts to ratify this agreement, partly to protest a Soviet invasion of Afghanistan that year. The United States also placed new nuclear missiles in Western Europe in response to technical improvements of Soviet missiles in Eastern Europe.

In the early 1980's, the United States and the Soviet Union began negotiations involving medium-range nuclear weapons in Europe and intercontinental ballistic missiles. However, the Soviet Union suspended these negotiations in 1983 to protest the shipment of new U.S. missiles to Western Europe. In 1988, the two powers concluded a treaty eliminating the medium-range missiles in Europe and prohibiting all missiles of that class. The treaty also provided for the first inspection procedures on national territory to support verification. Following the agreement, the Soviet Union began removing thousands of troops and tanks from East Germany, Hungary, and Czechoslovakia. In addition, U.S. and Soviet leaders sought further cuts in military forces in Europe and a reduction in the number of Soviet and U.S. long-range nuclear missiles.   John D. Steinbruner

See also **United Nations** (Arms control); **Arms Control and Disarmament Agency, United States; Washington Conference.**

Additional resources

Committee on International Security and Arms Control, National Academy of Sciences. *Nuclear Arms Control: Background and Issues.* National Academy Press, 1985.
Krepon, Michael. *Strategic Stalemate: Nuclear Weapons and Arms Control in American Politics.* St. Martin's, 1984.

Disaster is a sudden, extremely unfortunate event that affects many people. Disasters have included natural occurrences, such as earthquakes and floods, as well as accidents involving airplanes and ships. Some of the major disasters are listed in the table on this page.

Related articles in *World Book* include:

Earthquake	Shipwreck	Tornado
Flood	Tidal wave	Volcano (table)
Hurricane (table)		

Disaster relief. See CARE; Civil defense; Coast Guard, United States; National Guard; Red Cross; Salvation Army.

Discharge, Military. See Military discharge.

Disciple. See Apostles.

Disciples of Christ is a Protestant denomination that developed in the United States during the early 1800's. Its full name is the Christian Church (Disciples of Christ). Its founders included three men of Presbyterian background—Thomas Campbell and his son Alexander in Pennsylvania and Barton W. Stone in Kentucky. The church took its present name in 1968.

The church observes two ordinances—Communion or the Lord's Supper, and Baptism. Communion is observed every Sunday as the central part of the worship service. The denomination observes baptism for adults rather than for infants because it considers children too young to fulfill the requirements of a personal decision to follow Christ. Baptism is by *immersion* (submerging in water). The church has about 1,300,000 members. Headquarters are at 221 Ohmer Ave., Indianapolis, IN 46219.   Critically reviewed by the Disciples of Christ

Discount is a term applied in business to a deduction from a stated price or from a payment due at some future date. The discounts most commonly used include *bank discount, trade discount,* and *cash discount.*

Major disasters

Year	Location	Dead	Type of disaster	Year	Location	Dead	Type of disaster
64	Rome	Unknown	City fire	1920	Central China	200,000	Earthquake
365	Crete	50,000	Earthquake	1923	Tokyo-Yokohama	142,800	Earthquake; fire
856	Iran	200,000	Earthquake	1927	Central China	200,000	Earthquake
893	India; Iran	330,000	Earthquake	1932	Central China	70,000	Earthquake
1138	Egypt; Syria	330,000	Earthquake	1935	Western India (now Pakistan)	60,000	Earthquake
1201	Northern Egypt	1,100,000	Earthquake	1939	Central Chile	30,000	Earthquake
1268	Cilicia (now Turkey)	60,000	Earthquake	1960	Western Morocco	12,000	Earthquake
1290	Northeastern China	100,000	Earthquake	1962	Northwestern Iran	10,000	Earthquake
1556	Central China	830,000	Earthquake	1963	Cuba; Haiti	6,700	Hurricane (Flora)
1667	Caucasia (now U.S.S.R.)	80,000	Earthquake	1968	Northeastern Iran	11,588	Earthquake
1669	Sicily	20,000	Mount Etna eruption	1970	Western Peru	66,794	Earthquake; landslide
1693	Sicily	100,000	Earthquake	1970	East Pakistan (now Bangladesh)	266,000	Cyclone; tidal wave
1703	Honshu, Japan	200,000	Earthquake	1972	Nicaragua	5,000	Earthquake
1730	Hokkaido, Japan	137,000	Earthquake	1974	Kashmir (occupied by India and Pakistan)	5,200	Earthquake
1731	Beijing, China	100,000	Earthquake	1976	Guatemala	23,000	Earthquake
1737	Calcutta, India	300,000	Earthquake; tornado	1976	Northeastern China	240,000	Earthquake
1755	Lisbon, Portugal	60,000	Earthquake	1977	Canary Islands	583	Airplane collision
1779	Northern Iran	100,000	Earthquake	1977	Southern India	15,000	Cyclone; tidal wave
1783	Southern Italy	50,000	Earthquake	1978	Eastern Iran	15,000	Earthquake
1815	Sumbawa, Indonesia	92,000	Mount Tambora eruption	1979	West Indies	2,068	Hurricane (David)
1865	Mississippi River	1,653	Ship explosion	1980	Northern Algeria	5,000	Earthquake
1868	Ecuador	70,000	Earthquake	1984	Bhopal, India	3,500	Poisonous gas leak
1883	Southwestern Indonesia	36,000	Krakatoa eruption; tidal wave	1985	Southern Bangladesh	10,000	Cyclone; tidal wave
1887	Eastern China	900,000	Huang He River flood	1985	Central Japan	520	Airplane crash
				1985	Central Mexico	7,200	Two earthquakes
1889	Johnstown, Pa.	2,200	Burst dam; flood	1985	Western Colombia	25,000	Nevado del Ruiz eruption; mudslide
1900	Galveston, Tex.	6,000	Hurricane; storm tide				
1902	Martinique	38,000	Mont Pélée eruption	1987	Ecuador	5,000	Earthquake; landslide
1908	Sicily	75,000	Earthquake	1987	Mindoro Strait, Philippines	1,840	Ship collision; fire
1912	North Atlantic	1,500	Sinking of *Titanic*				
1915	Central Italy	29,970	Earthquake	1988	Armenia, U.S.S.R.	25,000	Earthquake
1917	Halifax, N. S.	1,635	Ship explosion	1990	Northwestern Iran	40,000	Earthquake

Sources: foreign governments; U.S. National Geophysical Data Center.

Bank discount is the deduction that a bank makes from the face value of a note. The bank does this when it cashes a note before it is due. Bank discount is determined in the same manner as simple interest. But it is taken in advance, by being deducted from the face value of the note. The difference between the face value of the note and the discount is called the *proceeds.* For example, the holder of a note may wish to turn it into cash, or have it *discounted,* before it becomes due. This may be done by presenting the note to the bank and receiving for it the amount of its face value, less the interest due during the term of discount. The *term of discount,* or *time to run,* is the period of time following the day the note is presented for payment through the day on which it matures. Bank discount creates a higher effective rate of interest than simple interest. The borrower pays the same amount in either case for the use of the money received. But with bank discount, the borrower receives only the proceeds instead of the face value of the note. Suppose a note for $5,000, dated February 26 and maturing on May 26, were presented to the bank on April 1. The number of days following April 1 through May 26 is 55. If the note bears interest at 12 per cent a year, the interest for this 55-day period would be $91.67 (based on a 360-day year). The bank *deducts* (discounts) this sum from the face value of the note as its charge. Then the bank pays the balance, or $4,908.33, to the person who presents the note for payment. The bank collects the full sum of $5,000 on the date the note matures.

Trade discount is a term used by manufacturers and wholesale merchants when they take off a certain percentage of the price given in a price list. This price is called the *list price.* The list price less the discount is known as the *net price.* Market values may change after price lists are issued. Changes in list prices are often made by varying the trade discount.

Cash discount is a deduction of a percentage of a bill for goods sold on credit. A cash discount is given when the bill is paid within a specific period of time. Such a discount might be expressed as *2/10, n/30,* which is read as *two ten, net thirty.* This means that the buyer may deduct 2 per cent from the bill if it is paid within 10 days, or may wait and pay the whole amount at the end of 30 days. Cash discounts may be used to increase the demand for a product or to speed up the collection of bills.   Joanna H. Frodin

Discount store is a type of store that sells goods to consumers at relatively low prices. To be a discount store, a store must also have sales of at least $500,000 a year and occupy an area of at least 10,000 square feet (900 square meters). Discount stores carry such merchandise as appliances, clothing, and health and beauty aids. Discount stores became an important retail institution during the 1940's. Today, there are more than 8,500 such stores in the United States.   William H. Bolen

Discovery. See Exploration; Invention.

Discrimination. See Segregation; Gray Panthers.

Discus throw is one of the oldest individual sports. It was a popular event with the ancient Greeks in their Olympic Games. The Greeks considered the discus-throwing champion the greatest athlete.

Athletes in ancient times threw a discus that was made of stone or metal. Today's discus is a round plate of wood or other material. It is tapered at the edge and has a smooth metal rim. A men's discus is 219 to 221 millimeters ($8\frac{5}{8}$ to $8\frac{7}{10}$ inches) in diameter and 44 to 46 millimeters ($1\frac{3}{4}$ to $1\frac{13}{16}$ inches) thick at the center. It weighs at least 2 kilograms (4 pounds $6\frac{1}{2}$ ounces). A women's discus is 180 to 182 millimeters (7 to $7\frac{1}{8}$ inches) in diameter and 37 to 39 millimeters ($1\frac{7}{16}$ to $1\frac{9}{16}$ inches) thick at the center. It weighs at least 1 kilogram (2 pounds $3\frac{1}{4}$ ounces).

Athletes throw the discus from a circle 2.5 meters (8 feet $2\frac{1}{2}$ inches) in diameter. The discus thrower holds the discus in the palm of one hand, the ends of the fingers curling around the rim. He or she whirls in a complete turn to gather speed and power, and hurls the discus at the end of another half turn. The fingertips spin the discus as it leaves the athlete's hand, and the discus flies through the air in a fairly flat position.

A throw does not count if the thrower steps on the circle or touches the ground outside the circle before the discus strikes the ground. Judges measure the throw from the inside edge of the circle to the nearest point the discus struck the ground. Under international rules, each athlete gets six throws if eight or fewer contestants enter the competition. If more than eight athletes compete, each one gets three throws. The eight with the longest throws qualify for the finals, where each of the eight gets three more throws.   Bert Nelson

For discus-throwing championship figures, see the tables with **Track and field** and **Olympic Games.**

How to throw a discus
The discus thrower stands in a circle measuring 2.5 meters (8 feet $2\frac{1}{2}$ inches) in diameter. He must not step outside this circle. He holds the discus flat against the palm of his hand, and swings within the circle with his arm outstretched. He releases the discus at the end of $1\frac{1}{2}$ turns. The power comes from his body and the follow-through of his arm.

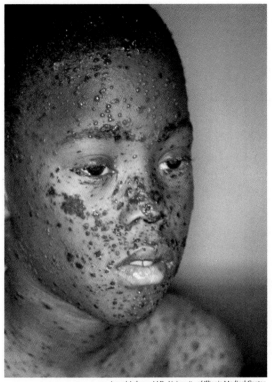

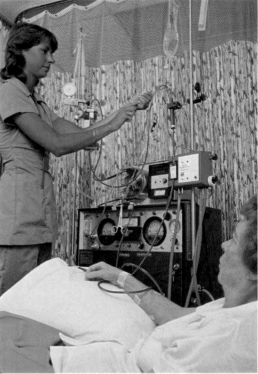

Leon J. Lebeau, M.D., University of Illinois Medical Center   WORLD BOOK photo

Diseases may be either infectious or noninfectious. The child in the picture at the left has chicken pox, an infectious disease. Infectious diseases are caused by germs that invade the body. The photograph at the right shows a patient being treated for a noninfectious kidney disease.

Disease

Disease is a sickness of the body or the mind. A disease can be as mild as a sore throat or as serious as cancer. Diseases can strike almost any part of the body. They can also affect a person's mental and emotional health. This article discusses mainly diseases of the body. For information on mental and emotional diseases, see the article **Mental illness.**

Diseases have killed or crippled more people than all the wars ever fought. Each year, millions of people die from diseases. In the United States alone, diseases kill nearly 2 million people each year. Millions more survive serious diseases, such as heart attacks or strokes, but are left permanently handicapped. Countless others have mild diseases, such as colds or earaches, and recover. But even such mild diseases are costly. In 1984, for example, Americans spent about $550 million on nonprescription drugs to treat colds. In addition, colds resulted in absences of about 28 million days from school and about 26 million days from work in that year.

The contributors of this article are Samuel Lawrence Katz, Chairman of the Department of Pediatrics at Duke University Medical School, and Peter C. English, Associate Professor of Pediatrics and of History at Duke University.

Many diseases are caused by tiny living things, such as *bacteria* or *viruses,* that invade the body. These tiny objects are commonly called *germs,* but scientists refer to them as *microorganisms.* The diseases caused by these objects are called *infectious diseases.*

All other diseases can be grouped together as *noninfectious diseases.* Noninfectious diseases have many causes. Some are caused by substances that harm or irritate the body, such as cigarette smoke or automobile fumes. Others result from not eating a balanced diet. Worry and tension can lead to headaches, ulcers, and other illnesses. Still other noninfectious diseases occur simply because aging affects some of the body's parts.

Nearly everyone gets sick at one time or another. But not everyone is equally likely to get a particular disease. For example, most cases of mumps and chicken pox occur in children. These diseases normally can attack only once. Because most people catch these illnesses as children, they are protected from them as adults. On the other hand, adults are more likely to develop arthritis, heart disease, and other illnesses that involve the gradual breakdown of the body's tissues.

Some illnesses occur chiefly in certain climates and geographical regions. African sleeping sickness, for example, is found mainly in very hot, humid regions of Africa. This disease is carried by an insect called the *tsetse fly,* which lives in such areas. Similarly, people who make their home near swamps are more likely to get malaria than people who live farther from such wet areas. Certain kinds of mosquitoes spread malaria, and swamps serve as breeding grounds for the insects.

Other diseases strike mainly during certain seasons. Most cases of influenza, for instance, occur in winter. Influenza is caused by a virus that spreads directly from one person to another. During cold weather, the crowding of people indoors probably helps the virus to spread more easily.

Diseases have troubled human beings throughout history. Medical researchers have examined the remains of Egyptian mummies more than 2,000 years old. They discovered that the ancient Egyptians suffered from many of the same kinds of diseases as we do today.

However, diseases do change over time. In the United States, Canada, and many other countries, important changes have been brought about by improved living standards and advances in medical science. An improved standard of living means that people have more money to buy good food and to have clean homes. It also enables them to take better care of their health. Advances in medical science make it possible to prevent and treat many diseases that once caused death.

As recently as 1900, such infectious diseases as tuberculosis and typhoid fever were major killers in the United States, Canada, Australia, and Great Britain. These diseases cause few deaths in those countries today. Heart disease, cancer, and other noninfectious diseases now rank as their chief causes of death. Researchers are seeking ways to control these killers.

Infectious diseases

Infections are the most common type of disease. Many kinds of bacteria, viruses, and other microorgan-

Some communicable diseases

Disease	Symptoms	Incubation period	Period of communicability	Preventive measures
AIDS	Swollen lymph glands, fatigue, diarrhea, weight loss, fever, night sweats.	A few weeks to 7 years or more.	Immediately after infection and as long as virus remains in body.	Avoid sexual contact with infected individuals. Avoid sharing hypodermic needles.
Chicken pox	Recurrent skin rashes that form crusts, fever, headache, general discomfort.	14 to 21 days.	From day before symptoms appear until 6 days after first rashes form.	None. Attack gives permanent immunity.
Diphtheria	Sore throat, hoarseness, fever.	2 to 5 days.	About 2 to 4 weeks.	Diphtheria toxoid injections, started at 2 months of age. Repeated doses throughout childhood.
German measles	Headache, enlarged lymph nodes, cough, sore throat, rash.	14 to 21 days, usually 18 days.	From about 7 days before rash appears until about 5 days after.	German measles (rubella) immunization. Attack gives permanent immunity.
Influenza	Fever, chills, muscular aches and pains.	1 to 3 days.	When symptoms appear until 7 days after.	Influenza immunization protects for only a few months.
Measles	Fever, runny nose, cough, red and watery eyes, rash.	10 to 14 days.	From 4 days before rash appears until 5 days after.	Measles immunization.
Mononucleosis (Glandular fever)	Sore throat, enlarged lymph glands, fatigue.	4 to 14 days.	Unknown.	None.
Mumps	Chills, headache, fever, swollen glands in neck and throat.	14 to 21 days, usually 18 days.	From 7 days before until 9 days after symptoms, or until swelling disappears.	Mumps immunization. Gamma globulin protects after exposure.
Poliomyelitis	Fever, sore throat, muscle pain, stiff back, paralysis.	Paralytic, 9 to 13 days. Nonparalytic, 4 to 10 days.	Last part of incubation period and first week of acute illness.	Poliomyelitis immunization.
Scarlet fever	Sore throat, rash, high fever, chills.	2 to 5 days.	Beginning of incubation period until 2 or 3 weeks after symptoms appear.	None. Attack usually gives permanent immunity.
Syphilis	Chancre sore, usually on sex organs; followed in 3 to 6 weeks by sores in mouth and a rash.	10 days to 10 weeks, usually 3 weeks.	Variable and indefinite during 2 to 4 years after infection.	Avoid sexual contact with infected individuals.

Syphilis is covered in the *World Book* article on **Venereal disease.**
Each of the other diseases listed on this table has a separate article in *World Book.*

isms can invade the human body and cause disease. Disease-causing microorganisms are called *pathogens.* Pathogens take over some of the body's cells and tissues and use them for their own growth and reproduction. In the process, they damage or destroy the cells and tissues and so produce diseases.

Infectious diseases can be grouped according to the kind of pathogen that causes them. Bacteria and viruses are the most common pathogens. However, fungi, protozoans, and worms also can produce infections.

Bacterial diseases. Bacteria are microscopic, one-celled organisms. They rank among the most widespread of all living things. A single grain of soil may contain more than 100 million bacteria.

Most bacteria do not cause diseases. Many kinds of bacteria live harmlessly in the human mouth and intestines and on the skin. These "resident" bacteria seldom cause illnesses unless they move to an organ where they are not normally present. For example, bacteria that live harmlessly in the mouth can cause infections if they enter the middle ear. However, most bacterial diseases are caused by microorganisms that are not normally present in the body.

Most bacterial diseases result when bacteria multiply rapidly in living tissue, damaging or killing it. Boils and carbuncles result from the multiplication of bacteria in the skin. Bacterial pneumonia occurs when bacteria invade the lungs and multiply there. Many other serious diseases, including gonorrhea and tuberculosis, result from bacterial multiplication.

Other bacteria cause disease by producing *toxins* (poisons). For example, tetanus, also called lockjaw, is a disease that begins after bacteria that normally live in soil enter the body through a wound. The bacteria produce a poison that affects muscles and nerves far away from the wound. Food poisoning results from eating foods that contain certain bacterial toxins. Botulism, a kind of food poisoning, involves one of the most deadly toxins known. See **Bacteria.**

Viral diseases. Viruses are smaller than bacteria. They are so tiny that scientists can see them only by means of powerful electron microscopes. By itself, a virus seems to be a lifeless particle. But after a virus invades a living cell, it becomes an active organism capable of multiplying rapidly. As a virus multiplies, it damages or destroys the cell. If a number of cells become infected, a disease results.

Viruses cause many common diseases, including chicken pox, German measles, measles, and mumps. Viruses are also responsible for influenza and the common cold. In fact, scientists have identified more than 100 different viruses that cause the common cold. Most cases of diarrhea and vomiting result from viral infections. Viruses also cause many serious diseases, including hepatitis, polio, rabies, and AIDS (Acquired Immune Deficiency Syndrome). See **Virus.**

Other infectious diseases can be caused by fungi, protozoans, and worms that live in or on the human body. These pathogens obtain food by breaking down body tissues or by absorbing digested food from the intestines. They produce diseases ranging from minor skin infections to life-threatening internal disorders.

Fungi resemble green plants but cannot make their own food. Some of the best-known fungi include molds and mushrooms. A few kinds of fungi live on the human skin, where they cause athlete's foot, ringworm, and other infections. Disease-producing fungi also can cause brain inflammations and a lung disease called histoplasmosis. See **Fungi; Fungal disease.**

Protozoans are one-celled organisms. Disease-producing protozoans are found chiefly in tropical areas. They cause such diseases as amebic dysentery, an intestinal infection; malaria; and African sleeping sickness.

Certain flatworms and roundworms cause human diseases. Disease-producing flatworms include flukes, which can invade the blood, intestines, liver, or lungs; and tapeworms, which live in the intestines. Disease-producing roundworms include hookworms and pinworms, which live in the intestines; trichinal worms, which infect the muscles; and filarial worms, which invade the fluids beneath the skin. Worm infections cause many serious tropical diseases, including elephantiasis, river blindness, and schistosomiasis.

Spread of infectious diseases. Most infectious diseases are *communicable*—that is, they can spread from person to person. Occasionally, an infectious disease becomes highly contagious and sweeps through a community. This condition is called an *epidemic.* When an epidemic occurs at several places throughout the world at the same time, it is called a *pandemic* outbreak. Such an outbreak took place during the winter of 1918-1919, when influenza swept the world, killing about 20 million

Major contagious diseases in the United States

This graph shows the number of reported cases of some contagious diseases in the United States. The graph includes only those diseases that doctors are legally required to report to state health officials. Doctors are not required to report less serious diseases, such as the common cold and influenza.

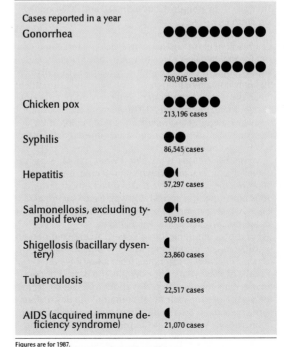

Cases reported in a year

Gonorrhea
780,905 cases

Chicken pox
213,196 cases

Syphilis
86,545 cases

Hepatitis
57,297 cases

Salmonellosis, excluding typhoid fever
50,916 cases

Shigellosis (bacillary dysentery)
23,860 cases

Tuberculosis
22,517 cases

AIDS (acquired immune deficiency syndrome)
21,070 cases

Figures are for 1987.
Source: Centers for Disease Control, U.S. Public Health Service.

How infectious
diseases spread

Most infectious diseases are *communicable*—that is, they can spread from one person to another. Disease-causing microorganisms, called *pathogens,* are spread in three chief ways: (1) by people, (2) by animals, especially insects, and (3) by nonliving sources.

WORLD BOOK illustrations by Roberta Polfus

A sick person can spread pathogens in the tiny droplets released in coughs and sneezes. Diseases spread this way include colds and influenza.

Mosquitoes spread germs that cause encephalitis, malaria, and yellow fever.

Nonliving objects, such as the spout on a public drinking fountain, may carry germs left by a sick individual.

people. Some infectious diseases are always present in a particular geographic region. Such diseases are said to be *endemic* in that region. For example, malaria is endemic throughout much of Africa.

Infectious diseases can be spread in three chief ways. They are (1) by people, (2) by animals, and (3) by nonliving sources.

By people. Many common infectious diseases spread as a result of close contact with a sick person. Such contact frequently takes place through coughing or sneezing. A cough or sneeze expels tiny droplets of moisture that may contain pathogens. If nearby people breathe in these droplets, the pathogens can spread from the sick person to healthy people. Diseases that spread largely through coughing and sneezing include colds, influenza, measles, mumps, pneumonia, tuberculosis, and whooping cough.

Some diseases are transmitted when a healthy person comes into direct contact with an infected area on another person's body. Certain skin infections, such as boils and impetigo, spread this way. So do venereal diseases, which are spread by sexual contact with an infected person. (see **Venereal disease**).

For most communicable diseases, an infected person is contagious only during part of the illness. This *period of communicability* can range from a few days to months or even years. For example, the period of communicability for chicken pox is about one week— from the day before the rash breaks out until the day the last sore crusts over. But the period of communicability for gonorrhea lasts as long as the person has the bacteria within his or her body.

Some people carry infectious organisms within their body but do not show any sign of illness themselves. Many cases of diphtheria, gonorrhea, pneumonia, and typhoid fever result from contact with such *carriers.* The identification and treatment of carriers plays an important role in the control of these diseases.

By animals. Insects spread some of the most deadly infectious diseases. Fleas, mosquitoes, and other insects that feed on blood transmit many serious diseases. These blood-sucking creatures spread infection in a complex way. When such an insect feeds on an infected person or animal, it may at the same time take certain disease-causing microorganisms into its body. The pathogens develop further within the body of the insect. The infection then spreads if the insect bites a healthy person and injects some of the pathogens into the bite wound. Mosquitoes transmit encephalitis, malaria, and yellow fever in this way. In the same manner, fleas spread bubonic plague, and lice carry typhus. Ticks, which are blood-feeding animals closely related to the insects, transmit tick typhus and Rocky Mountain spotted fever in this way.

A few infectious diseases are transmitted by direct contact with infected mammals and birds. Rabies, which is transmitted by the bite of an infected mammal, is probably the best-known example. People catch tularemia, or rabbit fever, by handling infected rabbits and squirrels. Similarly, psittacosis, also called parrot fever, spreads to human beings through direct contact with infected birds.

By nonliving sources. Some pathogens can survive for long periods on nonliving objects. These microorganisms can be transmitted by clothing, bedding, silverware, and other objects handled by sick people. Certain bacterial infections sometimes spread to hospital patients through contact with such contaminated objects.

Some infectious diseases spread through drinking water. For example, mass outbreaks of diarrhea can occur if untreated sewage gets into a community's drinking water. In areas with poor sanitation, impure drinking water may carry pathogens that cause cholera and typhoid fever.

Contaminated foods also transmit infectious diseases. As was previously mentioned, foods contaminated with bacterial toxins can cause food poisoning. In addition, undercooked pork may contain worms that cause trichinosis. Raw cow's milk may contain bacteria that produce bovine tuberculosis and undulant fever in people. Pasteurization, a process that kills bacteria in milk, has made these two diseases uncommon in most industrialized countries.

Noninfectious diseases

Noninfectious disease is a broad term that groups together all illnesses not caused by pathogens. It includes diseases caused by the breakdown of tissues and organs, by birth defects, by poor diet, by environmental and occupational hazards, and by stress and tension.

Chronic, degenerative diseases are long-term disorders that involve the gradual breakdown of tissues and organs. Such diseases affect more adults than children. Common chronic, degenerative diseases include (1) cardiovascular diseases, (2) cancer, and (3) arthritis.

Cardiovascular diseases affect the heart and blood vessels. These diseases, which include arteriosclerosis, high blood pressure, heart attacks, and strokes, are the leading causes of death in the United States.

Arteriosclerosis is a disease of the arteries. It occurs when fatty deposits build up on the inside walls of the arteries, making the vessels hard and narrow. This condition interferes with the flow of blood through the arteries, and can lead to heart attacks and strokes. Hypertension, or high blood pressure, is another disease that contributes to strokes and heart attacks. Doctors often call hypertension "the silent killer," because it seldom produces symptoms until after it has caused widespread damage to the heart and blood vessels. Most cases of hypertension result from unknown causes. See **Arteriosclerosis; Hypertension.**

A heart attack takes place when the heart does not receive enough oxygen-rich blood. The lack of oxygen causes part of the heart muscle to die. If a large part of the heart is affected, the victim may die immediately, or within the next several weeks. Most heart attacks that affect a smaller portion of the heart are not fatal, but the patient may have to restrict his or her activities for months or even years. See **Heart** (Heart attack).

A stroke occurs if part of the brain does not receive an adequate supply of blood. The affected portion of the brain is deprived of oxygen and nutrients, and is permanently damaged. A massive stroke can be fatal. Smaller strokes can leave the victim with various disabilities, depending on what part of the brain is affected. Common problems include paralysis and loss of speech. In some patients, undamaged areas of the brain eventually take over some of the lost functions. However, many victims are left with permanent handicaps. See **Stroke.**

Cancer occurs when certain cells of the body multiply without control. It can affect any type of cell. The cancer cells eventually destroy the surrounding normal cells. In addition, the uncontrolled growth can spread to cells in other parts of the body. If left untreated, most kinds of cancer are fatal. In the United States, only cardiovascular diseases cause more deaths.

Scientists do not know exactly how normal cells are transformed into cancer cells. However, researchers have discovered that many cases of cancer occur after a person has had frequent or extended contact with various chemicals or radiation. See **Cancer.**

Arthritis is a general term for diseases that affect the joints. The most widespread forms of arthritis are rheumatoid arthritis and osteoarthritis. Rheumatoid arthritis causes pain and swelling in many joints throughout the body. It can lead to deformity and crippling. Rheumatoid arthritis strikes people of all ages, but it is most common among middle-aged adults. The cause of the disease is unknown. Osteoarthritis is basically a disease of older adults. It results from wear and tear on the joints, especially those of the knees, hips, and fingers. It seldom causes crippling, but the pain forces many victims to limit their activities. See **Arthritis.**

Hormonal diseases occur if the endocrine glands do not function correctly. These glands produce *hormones,* powerful chemical substances that regulate many body functions. See **Gland; Hormone.**

Perhaps the best-known hormonal disease is diabetes mellitus. It can develop if the pancreas does not work properly. The pancreas produces insulin, a hormone that enables the body to use sugar. Sugar is one of the main products of digestion. If the cells cannot use sugar, the body begins to break down its own tissues for food. Diabetes mellitus leads to death if left untreated.

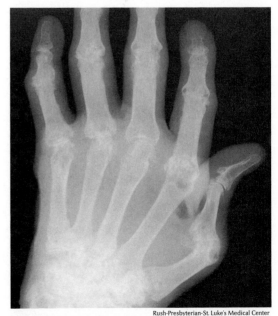

Rush-Presbyterian-St. Luke's Medical Center

Rheumatoid arthritis, a painful disorder of the joints, ranks as one of the most common *chronic, degenerative diseases.* Such diseases involve the gradual breakdown of tissues or organs. The X ray above shows the hand of a rheumatoid arthritis victim.

Addison's disease occurs when the adrenal glands fail to produce sufficient hormones. This disease results in loss of weight, weakness, and, eventually, death. Another endocrine gland, the thyroid, releases hormones that affect the rate at which the body uses food and builds new tissues. If this gland does not produce enough hormones during infancy, a condition known as cretinism results. Cretinism leads to poor physical growth and mental retardation. Various disorders, including gigantism and dwarfism, can occur if the pituitary gland and the hypothalamus, a part of the brain, do not function properly. These endocrine structures produce many hormones.

Congenital diseases are disorders that are present at birth. Many babies are born with serious diseases. In some cases, the disease develops from an infection the mother suffered during pregnancy. For example, if the mother had German measles, the baby may be born with heart defects, mental retardation, or other disorders. Other congenital problems can occur if the mother is exposed to radiation or to certain drugs or other chemicals during pregnancy.

Many serious congenital diseases involve defects that are inherited from one or both parents. Such inherited diseases include hemophilia and sickle cell anemia, which affect the blood; and galactosemia and phenylketonuria (PKU), disorders in which the body cannot properly use certain foods. Most congenital diseases are apparent at birth or in early infancy. Huntington's disease, which affects the nervous system, is an example of an inherited disease that does not produce symptoms until later in life.

Certain other diseases, including hypertension and diabetes mellitus, often run in families. People whose parents have such diseases are much more likely to de-velop these ailments than people whose parents are free of the disorders.

Environmental and occupational diseases. Many environmental factors can produce serious diseases. Air pollution from factories and automobiles can irritate the eyes and nose. It can also contribute to emphysema, bronchitis, and other lung diseases. Wastes from factories and fertilizers from farmlands pollute many waterways. Drinking such polluted water can lead to serious illnesses. Continued exposure to loud noises from machinery, automobiles, and airplanes can result in hearing loss. Such "noise pollution" also causes tensions that contribute to psychosomatic diseases, which are discussed later in this article.

In addition to pollutants, some of the chemicals used in modern products have been linked to diseases. For example, researchers have discovered that certain flavorings and dyes once used in packaged foods could lead to various kinds of cancers.

Exposure to some harmful environmental agents results from an individual's own habits. For example, heavy cigarette smokers expose themselves to substances that have been linked to the development of cancer, emphysema, and heart disease. Similarly, the overuse of alcohol can lead to severe liver and brain damage. The abuse of other drugs—including sedatives, stimulants, and narcotics—also results in many serious physical and emotional diseases. See **Drug abuse.**

Some occupations expose workers to harmful environmental agents. Coal miners and workers in the asbestos, iron, and textile industries may breathe in dust that can lead to lung diseases. People who work in chemical plants risk exposure to poisonous substances. Similarly, farmers frequently handle weed- and insect-killing chemicals. These chemicals can cause serious illnesses if they are inhaled or swallowed, or even if they settle on the skin. Radiation poses a threat to X-ray technicians and to people who work with nuclear materials. Exposure to radiation increases the risk of cancer and can damage the hereditary material of cells.

Nutritional diseases are caused by an improper diet. In many developing countries, poverty forces people to live on an inadequate diet. Undernutrition and deficiency diseases are common among such people. Undernutrition results from an overall lack of food. It is characterized by poor growth, lack of energy, and lowered resistance to infections. Deficiency diseases result from a diet lacking in one or more essential food elements. Protein deficiency leads to kwashiorkor, a serious disease that generally strikes children and can be fatal. Vitamin deficiencies produce such diseases as beriberi, pellagra, rickets, and scurvy. Anemia and goiter result from mineral deficiencies. See **Nutrition** (Results of malnutrition).

Improper eating habits can lead to deficiency diseases in developed countries as well. But in the United States and other developed countries, the most common nutritional problems result from overeating. *Obesity* (extreme fatness) occurs when a person eats more food than the body burns up. Obesity can contribute to a variety of ailments, including cardiovascular diseases and diabetes mellitus. See **Weight control.**

Immunological diseases occur when the *immune system* fails to function properly. The immune system is

© Chuck O'Rear, Woodfin Camp, Inc.

Some occupations expose workers to disease-causing substances. Coal miners who breathe in coal dust over a number of years run a high risk of developing black lung disease.

one of the body's chief defenses against disease. It recognizes and attacks pathogens, cancer cells, and other foreign substances that may be present. For information on the functioning of the body's immune system, see the section *How the body fights disease* in this article.

Allergies, including asthma, hay fever, and hives, are the most common kind of immunological diseases. An allergy may occur if the immune system becomes overly sensitive to a foreign substance. Many people develop allergies to pollen, house dust, animal hair, or various foods. When an allergic person comes into contact with such substances, the immune system reacts. Allergic reactions can range from a runny nose and itching eyes for hay fever victims to fatal reactions for people who are allergic to penicillin or other drugs. See **Allergy.**

Certain serious diseases involve *autoimmune reactions.* Autoimmunity means *self-immunity,* and an autoimmune reaction takes place when the immune system attacks the body's own tissues. In a disease called systemic lupus erythematosus, the immune system attacks the skin and joints and, in severe cases, the kidneys and nervous system. Some physicians suspect that rheumatoid arthritis and multiple sclerosis, a disease of the nervous system, also involve autoimmune reactions.

Some children are born with a defective immune system. They suffer from repeated, serious infections. Many of these children live only a few years unless they receive special drugs, surgical treatment, or bone marrow transplants.

Psychosomatic diseases are physical disorders that result from mental stress and tension. Pressures from work or school, financial burdens, and emotional conflicts are among the many situations that can produce stress. Some people handle stress by "talking out" their problems with other people. Others learn to relieve tensions through relaxation or even by crying. But some people keep tensions bottled up inside, and this unrelieved stress can lead eventually to physical illnesses. Common psychosomatic ailments include tension headaches, pains in the chest or in the arms and legs, and stomach upsets and ulcers. In addition, unrelieved stress lowers the body's resistance to infections and other diseases. See **Stress.**

How the body fights disease

Medical scientists have learned a great deal about how the body defends against illness, especially how it protects itself from infectious diseases. They have discovered that the body uses three chief kinds of defenses: (1) barriers against pathogens, (2) general reactions to infection, and (3) reactions of the immune system.

Barriers. Unbroken skin provides an extremely effective barrier against pathogens. Similarly, few pathogens can penetrate the membranes that line the mouth and nose. These membranes are covered with *mucus,* a sticky fluid that traps many of the pathogens. The body then expels the microorganisms by sneezing or coughing. Mucous membranes also line the tubes that lead to the lungs. Tiny, hairlike *cilia* push mucus from the lungs and windpipe up to the mouth. There, the mucus and its trapped germs are harmlessly swallowed.

The body also has chemical barriers against infection. Tears, for example, not only wash foreign substances

Barriers against infections

The body's first defense against infectious diseases includes mechanical, chemical, and biological barriers against germs. This diagram illustrates some of the body's chief barriers.

WORLD BOOK diagram by Lou Bory

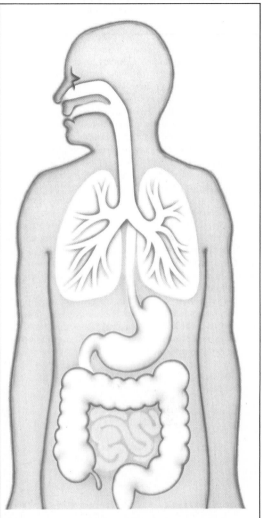

Skin. The tough, dead cells that make up the outer layer of the skin provide an extremely effective mechanical barrier against pathogens.

Tears continually flow over the surface of the eyes, washing out foreign particles and providing chemical protection against many pathogens.

Mucous membranes produce sticky mucus that traps germs. Tiny, hairlike *cilia* push mucus from the lungs and windpipe up to the mouth.

Stomach juices are so high in acid that many microorganisms cannot survive in them. The juices also contain disease-fighting chemicals.

Resident bacteria live harmlessly on the skin and in the mouth and intestines. They crowd out or kill many disease-causing microorganisms.

from the eyes, but also contain chemicals that fight many common pathogens. The mucous membranes also release protective chemicals. The digestive juices of the stomach, which are high in acid, kill many of the pathogens that are swallowed in food or mucus.

Finally, the bacteria that normally live harmlessly on the skin and in the mouth and intestines provide a barrier against infections. These resident bacteria actually crowd out many disease-causing microorganisms that might otherwise establish colonies on or in the body. Resident bacteria also produce substances that kill or damage certain pathogens.

General defense reactions. In spite of the body's barriers against pathogens, some do manage to invade the body. After a foreign substance has entered the body, certain general reactions take place. First, the tiniest blood vessels at the site of the infection begin to leak fluids and cells. The fluids contain various germ-killing chemicals. Most of the cells are white blood cells known as *neutrophils.* Neutrophils can surround and digest invading bacteria—a process called *phagocytosis,* which means *to eat up.*

If the invading pathogen is a virus, the body attempts to counteract the virus by producing a chemical called *interferon.* Interferon is released by cells that have been infected by the virus. It enters the bloodstream and is carried to other cells. Interferon stops viruses from infecting these cells.

Fever is another reaction that accompanies many infections, but its function is unclear. Some researchers believe that fever kills or weakens pathogens that cannot live or reproduce at temperatures higher than the normal body temperature.

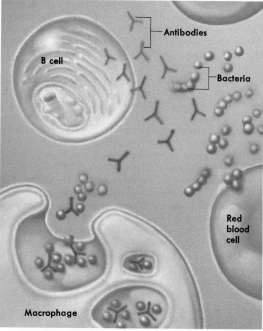

An immune reaction involves a number of different body cells. White blood cells called *B cells* release disease-fighting proteins called *antibodies.* In this illustration, antibodies are attracting clumps of invading bacteria. These clumps are then surrounded and destroyed by large cells called *macrophages.*

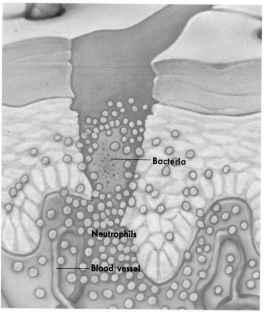

The body's general defenses take over if pathogens manage to slip through the barriers. This illustration shows bacteria entering the body through a break in the skin. Nearby blood vessels have released *neutrophils,* white blood cells that can surround and digest the invading bacteria.

Immune reactions are the most powerful kind of bodily defense against disease. Unlike the body's general defenses, the immune system produces substances that are specifically designed to fight a particular invading substance.

White blood cells called *lymphocytes* play a major role in immune reactions. There are two kinds of lymphocytes, B cells and T cells. Both kinds can recognize and attack pathogens, toxins, and other foreign substances. B cells respond to such invaders by releasing proteins called *antibodies* into the blood. Antibodies attack the invader and either destroy it or make it harmless. For example, antibodies may cause bacteria to clump together. The clumps are then eaten by large scavenger cells called *macrophages,* which are capable of phagocytosis.

T cells protect against viruses and other pathogens that grow inside the cells of the body. T cells attack the infected cells and destroy the intruders. T cells are also responsible for recognizing and destroying cancer cells. In most immune reactions, B cells, T cells, and macrophages all work together to overpower the invader.

An important feature of the immune system is that it can "remember" pathogens after it has encountered them. This feature enables the body to develop long-term protection—called *immunity*—to many infectious diseases. For example, after a person has had measles, the immune system will remember the measles virus. The next time this virus enters the body, it will be attacked immediately by immune system cells specifically designed to combat it. The invading virus will be de-

WORLD BOOK photo

Laboratory tests play an important role in the diagnosis of many diseases. The lab technician pictured above is working to identify bacteria found in samples of patients' body fluids.

stroyed before it can cause illness. For this reason, a person normally gets measles only once. See **Immunity**.

The battle against disease

The fight against sickness is probably as old as humanity. For a detailed history of this battle, from prehistoric times to the age of modern medicine, see the article **Medicine** (History). Today, the struggle to conquer disease involves three chief elements. They are (1) diagnosis, (2) treatment, and (3) prevention.

Diagnosing disease—that is, identifying a disorder—is the first step toward a cure. Many different illnesses produce similar symptoms. Therefore, the physician must carefully identify which disease a patient has to determine the best course of treatment.

The doctor first reviews the patient's medical history and asks the patient to describe the symptoms of the present illness. The doctor also asks about the development of the illness, the health of others in the family, and similar matters that might help pinpoint the disease.

The physician then examines the patient, noting the body temperature, pulse rate, breathing, and blood pressure. The examination is concentrated on those parts of the body involved in the patient's symptoms. The doctor may wish to obtain additional information from laboratory tests. A medical laboratory can provide X rays that show abnormalities in the bones, lungs, heart, and other organs. The laboratory also can test blood, urine, and other body fluids for evidence of certain diseases. After considering all the information, the doctor reaches a diagnosis of the patient's illness.

Treating disease sometimes involves no more than prescribing rest and a healthful diet. The body has great healing powers, and such measures may be all it needs to overcome a mild illness. But more serious diseases may require a specific course of treatment, including drugs, surgery, or other forms of therapy.

Drugs are one of the physician's most important weapons against disease. Antibiotics can cure bacterial infections that once were often fatal. Many fungal and worm infections also can be treated effectively with drugs, but most viral infections cannot.

Drugs also help control many noninfectious ailments. Many cancers can be slowed, or even cured, with drugs. High blood pressure can be controlled with medication, and drugs containing hormones are used to treat hormonal diseases. Aspirin and other pain relievers help arthritic patients lead a more active life.

Surgery enables doctors to remove diseased tissues that threaten the rest of the body. For instance, surgical removal of all or part of a cancerous organ may halt the spread of the disease to other organs. Similarly, surgeons may remove an infected appendix or gall bladder to prevent the infection from spreading to other organs.

Surgeons also can repair or replace diseased organs. For example, many heart defects can be corrected surgically. Surgeons can replace diseased bones and joints with metal or plastic parts. They can even replace a diseased kidney or heart with a healthy organ from another person's body (see **Tissue transplant**).

Other treatments include radiotherapy, special diets, and rehabilitation therapy. Radiotherapy makes use of X rays and other radioactive sources to kill cancer cells. Special diets can control PKU and other hereditary diseases in which the body cannot use certain foods. Diet also plays a major role in treating diabetes mellitus.

Changes in U.S. death rates from diseases

Noninfectious diseases have replaced infectious ones as the leading causes of death from disease in the United States. Medical advances and improved living standards have produced this shift.

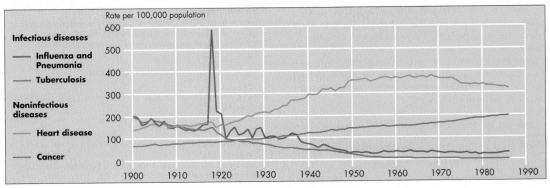

Source: U.S. Public Health Service.

Rehabilitation therapy can help patients regain use of certain parts of their body. Such treatment aids people who have had strokes or other disabling diseases.

Preventing disease involves the cooperation of the individual, the medical profession, and various public agencies.

Individuals can help prevent disease by developing good health habits. Such habits include eating a balanced diet, exercising regularly, getting adequate rest and relaxation, and practicing personal cleanliness. People also can protect their health by not smoking cigarettes and by avoiding excessive use of alcohol and other drugs. For additional information on the basic elements of personal health, see the article **Health.**

The medical profession provides many services that aid in disease prevention. Regular medical examinations play an important role. During such examinations, the physician can check for high blood pressure or other disorders that produce no symptoms until dangerous complications occur. The checkup might also lead to the early diagnosis of cancer, diabetes mellitus, heart disease, or other chronic illnesses. Such diseases can be treated more effectively if detected early. The examination also provides the doctor with an opportunity to advise patients on how to safeguard their health.

Physicians protect patients from many serious diseases through active and passive immunizations. Active immunizations involve the use of *vaccines*, which are drugs that contain dead or weakened pathogens. Vaccines stimulate the body's immune defenses against a particular disease-causing agent. Active immunizations can prevent many serious childhood illnesses, including diphtheria, German measles, measles, mumps, polio, tetanus, and whooping cough. For a recommended schedule of childhood immunizations, see the article **Immunization.**

In passive immunizations, doctors use serums to protect people who already have been exposed to a disease. Serums contain antibodies from a person or animal that is immune to the disease.

Public agencies help prevent disease in a number of ways. In the United States, Canada, and most other developed countries, public agencies purify community water supplies, inspect foods for microorganisms and harmful chemicals, and ensure the safety and effectiveness of drugs. Local health departments oversee the sanitary disposal of sewage and wastes, and conduct programs to control insects, rats, and other animals that spread diseases. The government also protects the public from environmental pollution and inspects workplaces for occupational hazards. Public clinics conduct immunization programs. They may also provide free testing for high blood pressure and for other diseases. Government-sponsored nutrition programs help safeguard the health of poor children and mothers. In addition, community health workers help educate the public about good health habits.

Samuel Lawrence Katz and Peter C. English

Related articles. For articles on specific diseases of organs or parts of the body, see the *Related articles* in such articles as **Blood, Lung,** and **Skin.** See also the following articles:

Symptoms of disease

Backache	Bleeding	Colic	Constipation
Convulsions	Fainting	Indigestion	Nausea
Cough	Fatigue	Inflammation	Pain
Cramp	Fever	Insomnia	Pus
Diarrhea	Headache	Itch	Shock
Dizziness	Hemorrhage	Jaundice	Vomiting
Dyspepsia	Hiccup		

Organs and conditions

Blindness (Diseases)	Heart (Heart diseases)
Birth defect	Kidney (Kidney diseases)
Bone	Liver (Diseases of the liver)
Brain (Disorders of the brain)	Lung (Diseases of the lungs)
Deafness	Senility
Eye (Diseases of the eye)	Teeth (Diseases and defects of the teeth)

Other related articles

Allergy	Heredity (Hereditary disorders)	Microbiology
Bacteria		Parasite
Cell (The cell in disease)	Holistic medicine	Pathology
Centers for Disease Control	Immunity	Plant (Plant enemies)
Drug	Immunization	Prion
Epidemic	Interferon	Quarantine
Fungal disease	Malnutrition	Rickettsia
Gnotobiotics	Medic Alert	Virus
	Medicine	
	Mental illness	

Outline

I. Infectious diseases
  A. Bacterial diseases   C. Other infectious diseases
  B. Viral diseases   D. Spread of infectious diseases

II. Noninfectious diseases
  A. Chronic, degenerative diseases
  B. Hormonal diseases
  C. Congenital diseases
  D. Environmental and occupational diseases
  E. Nutritional diseases
  F. Immunological diseases
  G. Psychosomatic diseases

III. How the body fights disease
  A. Barriers   C. Immune reactions
  B. General defense reactions

IV. The battle against disease
  A. Diagnosing disease   C. Preventing disease
  B. Treating disease

Questions

Which disease is often called "the silent killer"? Why?
Under what conditions do the body's "resident" bacteria sometimes cause diseases?
How can a regular checkup help in disease prevention?
What are *fungi*? What are some diseases they cause?
What is an *autoimmune reaction*? What is an example of disease that involves such a reaction?
What are two of the body's chemical barriers against infections?
What is an *epidemic*?
What are *lymphocytes*? What role do they play in the body?
What are *carriers*? Why is it important to identify them?
What are some of the procedures a physician uses in diagnosing a disease?

Additional resources

Level I
Nourse, Alan E. *Lumps, Bumps, and Rashes: A Look at Kids' Diseases.* Watts, 1976.
Patent, Dorothy H. *Germs!* Holiday House, 1983.

Level II
Archer, Jules. *Epidemic! The Story of the Disease Detectives.* Harcourt, 1977.
Chase, Allan. *Magic Shots: A Human and Scientific Account of the Long and Continuing Struggle to Eradicate Infectious Diseases by Vaccination.* Morrow, 1982.

Goodfield, G. June. *Quest for the Killers*. Birkhäuser, 1985. Discusses the control of several major diseases.
Gregg, Charles T. *A Virus of Love and Other Tales of Medical Detection*. Scribner, 1983.

Dish. See Porcelain; Pottery; Stoneware.

Disinfectant is any substance that destroys germs on nonliving objects. Most common disinfectants are powerful chemicals that people use to sanitize clothes, rooms, and instruments and utensils. Some disinfectants include deodorizers. Detergents are added to many disinfectants to aid cleaning. Substances called *antiseptics* are used to kill germs on living tissue.

Disinfectants are most effective when added to community water and sewage systems to destroy germs and help prevent epidemics. They also help stop the spread of germs in hospitals and other health care institutions. However, general household disinfectants have only limited value in stopping the spread of disease. In most cases, washing with soap and water is as effective as using such a disinfectant.

Important disinfectants include (1) alcohols, (2) formaldehyde and glutaraldehyde, (3) hypochlorites, (4) iodophors, (5) phenols, (6) pine oil disinfectants, and (7) quaternary ammonium compounds.

Alcohols, such as ethyl and isopropyl alcohols, are used to disinfect fever thermometers and previously cleaned plastic and rubber goods.

Formaldehyde and glutaraldehyde are strong and fast acting. Hospitals use them to disinfect surgical instruments and other medical devices.

Hypochlorites, including chlorine bleaches and chlorinated lime, are common ingredients of household disinfectants and deodorizers. They are also used in water and sewage treatment and to disinfect food utensils.

Iodophors are compounds that include iodine. They are used to sanitize large surfaces in hospitals and to disinfect equipment used in food preparation.

Phenols include carbolic acid, creosote, and hexachlorophene. They are used to disinfect floors, garbage cans, toilet facilities, and other surfaces.

Pine oil disinfectants are commonly combined with detergents to clean floors, walls, and bathroom fixtures. They have a pinelike odor.

Quaternary ammonium compounds are in many all-purpose household cleaners. They serve as both disinfectants and detergents.   Velvl W. Greene

Related articles in *World Book* include:

Antiseptic	Cresol
Chlorine	Deodorizer
Creosote	Formaldehyde

Dislocation occurs when any part of the body moves from its normal position. The term usually refers to the movement out of normal position of the bones of a joint (see **Joint**). When bones become dislocated, they do not meet properly at the joint. This usually results in pain and swelling.

Sometimes in dislocation the bones of a joint are pulled out of place only slightly. Physicians call this a *subluxation* or *incomplete dislocation.* In other cases, the bones become completely separated from each other. This is a *complete dislocation.* A physician corrects a dislocation by manipulating the bones to return them to their normal position. This procedure is called *reducing* the dislocation. Some dislocated joints may re-turn to their normal position naturally. In *simple dislocation,* the patient has no external wound. A *compound dislocation* is one accompanied by a wound opening from the body surface. When a dislocation occurs in the same joint many times, physicians say it is *habitual.*

Some types of dislocation are *congenital,* or present at birth. These may be hereditary, or may be caused by some factor before or during birth. An example is congenital dislocation of the hip.   Bruce Reider

See also **First aid** (Fractures and dislocations).

Dismal Swamp is one of the largest swamps in the United States. It covers about 750 square miles (1,940 square kilometers) in northeastern North Carolina and southeastern Virginia. For location, see **North Carolina** (physical map). Dismal Swamp is a tangle of vines and bald cypress, black tupelo, pine, and white cedar trees.

© John M. Hall

Dismal Swamp is a tangle of vines and various kinds of trees. It is one of the largest swamps in the United States.

It contains much partly decayed plant life called *peat.* Its wildlife includes bear, deer, gray fox, opossum, and snakes. Part of the original 2,000 square miles (5,200 square kilometers) of Dismal Swamp was cleared for farming. In 1973, the U.S. Congress established part of the swamp as the Great Dismal Swamp National Wildlife Refuge.   Stephen S. Birdsall

Disney, Walt (1901-1966), was one of the most famous motion-picture producers in history. Disney first became known in the 1920's and 1930's for creating such cartoon film characters as Mickey Mouse and Donald Duck. He later produced feature-length cartoon films, movies about wild animals in their natural surroundings, and films starring human actors. The Disney studio has won more than 50 Academy Awards for its movies and for scientific and technical contributions to filmmaking.

Disney achieved one of his greatest successes in 1955, when he opened Disneyland, a spectacular theme park in Anaheim, Calif. Most of the exhibits, rides, and shows at the park are based on Disney film characters.

Early life. Walter Elias Disney was born in Chicago. His family moved to Missouri, and he spent much of his boyhood on a farm near Marceline. At 16, Disney studied art in Chicago. In 1920, he joined the Kansas City Film Ad Company, where he helped make cartoon advertisements to be shown in movie theaters.

Disney theme parks and expositions attract millions of visitors annually. Walt Disney World, *left,* and Disneyland feature exhibits, rides, and shows partly based on movies by Walt Disney Productions. Walt Disney World's EPCOT Center, *right,* emphasizes displays of future technology.

The first Disney cartoons. In 1923, Disney moved to Los Angeles to become a filmmaker. After he failed, he returned to drawing movie cartoons. He set up his first studio in a garage. For several years, Disney struggled just to pay his expenses. He finally gained success in 1928, when he released the first short cartoons that featured Mickey Mouse. Earlier filmmakers had found that animals were easier to animate than people. Mickey Mouse, drawn with a series of circles, proved ideal for animation.

In 1927, sound had been added to motion pictures, and a process for making movies in color was developed a few years later. Disney and his assistants made imaginative use of sound and color. Disney provided Mickey Mouse's voice. His cartoon *Flowers and Trees* (1932) was the first film in full Technicolor.

From 1929 to 1939, Disney produced a cartoon series called *Silly Symphonies.* Mickey Mouse appeared in these and later cartoons, along with such characters as Donald Duck, Goofy, and Pluto. Throughout his career, Disney actually drew few cartoons. His genius lay in creating, organizing, and directing the films.

Full-length movies. In 1937, Disney issued the first full-length animated film to be produced by a studio, *Snow White and the Seven Dwarfs.* It became one of the most popular movies in history. Disney's later full-length animated films included *Pinocchio* (1940), *Fantasia* (1940), *Dumbo* (1941), *Bambi* (1942), *Cinderella* (1950), *Alice in Wonderland* (1951), *Peter Pan* (1953), *Lady and the Tramp* (1955), and *The Jungle Book* (issued in 1967, after his death). In 1950, Disney released *Treasure Island,* his first full-length movie to use only human actors. *Mary Poppins* (1964), which combines human actors with animation, probably is the most successful of Disney's later films.

During World War II (1939-1945), Disney's studio made educational films for the United States government. After the war, Disney created fewer animated movies. He concentrated on making films that starred real animals or human actors. In 1949, Disney released *Seal Island.* This short movie was the first in a series of "True-Life Adventures" that show how animals live in nature. Disney released his first full-length nature film, *The Living Desert,* in 1953. All his nature movies include scenes of animal life rarely seen by human beings.

After television became popular about 1950, many filmmakers either ignored TV or fought it as a threat to the movie industry. But Disney adjusted easily to the new form of entertainment. He produced a number of movies especially for television and served as the host of a weekly TV show that presented Disney films.

Walt Disney Productions, with headquarters in Burbank, Calif., carried on Disney's work after his death. Walt Disney World, a theme park resembling Disneyland, opened near Orlando, Fla., in 1971. In 1982, the company opened a permanent world's fair called EPCOT Center in Walt Disney World. The center features futuristic technology exhibits. EPCOT is a word made from the first letters of *E*xperimental *P*rototype *C*ommunity *o*f *T*omorrow. In 1983, a Disneyland opened in Tokyo with Japanese sponsors. This park combines the most successful features of the American Disneyland and Walt Disney World with its own attractions.

The parks account for most of the money earned by Walt Disney Productions. The rest of the profits come from movies and the sale of publications, video cassettes, videodiscs, and merchandise based on Disney film characters. The filmmaking division of Walt Disney Productions was not as successful in the 1970's and early 1980's. But the company did make some notable films, including the animated *The Fox and the Hound* (1981), the science-fiction drama *Tron* (1982), and the comedies

© Walt Disney Productions

© Walt Disney Productions

© Walt Disney Productions

Cartoon characters have made Walt Disney famous throughout the world. Mickey Mouse starred in *Steamboat Willie, upper left,* the first cartoon to use sound. Donald Duck, *lower left,* first appeared in a short cartoon in 1934. The full-length motion picture *Bambi* starred Flower, the skunk; Thumper, the rabbit; and Bambi, the deer, *lower left. Pinocchio, right,* is a full-length cartoon about a puppet named Pinocchio. Near the end of the story, a whale swallows Pinocchio and Geppetto, the puppet's father. They escape from the whale's stomach on a raft.

Splash (1984), *Down and Out in Beverly Hills* (1986), *Ruthless People* (1986), and *Three Men and a Baby* (1987). Roy Paul Nelson

See also **Monorail** (picture); **United States** (The arts [picture]).

Additional resources

Finch, Christopher. *The Art of Walt Disney: From Mickey Mouse to the Magic Kingdoms.* Abrams, 1989. First published in 1973.

Shooting Star Archives

Walt Disney opened the Disneyland theme park in 1955. The park was based on many of the cartoon characters that Disney developed in a motion-picture career that began in the 1920's.

Ford, Barbara. *Walt Disney: A Biography.* Walker, 1989. For younger readers.
Thomas, Frank, and Johnston, Ollie. *Disney Animation: The Illusion of Life.* Abbeville, 1984. First published in 1981.

Disney World. See Disney, Walt; **Florida** (Places to visit; picture); **Orlando.**

Disneyland. See Disney, Walt; **Anaheim; California** (Places to visit; picture).

Dispersion. See **Light** (Dispersion).

Displaced person. See Refugee.

Displacement behavior refers to any of a variety of activities that seem inappropriate in the situation in which they occur. For example, some mammals groom their fur when faced with a decision of whether to fight or run away. Most displacement behaviors occur during times of emotional conflict. George B. Johnson

Disraeli, *dihz RAY lee,* **Benjamin** (1804-1881), was one of the most important British political leaders of the 1800's. He served as prime minister of Great Britain in 1868 and again from 1874 to 1880. Disraeli was the first person of Jewish ancestry to become prime minister in Britain.

Disraeli was born in London. His father, Isaac D'Israeli, was a well-known author. D'Israeli had Benjamin baptized into the Church of England at the age of 13. In the 1820's, the younger Disraeli also began a writing career. But in time he decided to enter politics. After several failed attempts to win a seat in Parliament, Disraeli was elected to the House of Commons as a Conservative in 1837.

In Parliament, Disraeli became a leading spokesman of the most conservative interests. He opposed the repeal of the Corn Laws, which taxed British imports of grain. In 1846, Disraeli became a leading figure of the Conservative Party in the House of Commons. In 1852, 1858, and 1866, he became chancellor of the exchequer in Conservative governments that the Earl of Derby headed from the House of Lords.

Disraeli played an important role in the passage of the Reform Bill of 1867. The bill brought greater democracy to Great Britain by giving the vote to many city workers and small farmers. In 1868, Disraeli became prime minister. He lost the position to William Gladstone, the leader of the Liberal Party, later in 1868 but regained it from Gladstone in 1874.

As prime minister, Disraeli followed a strong foreign policy. In 1875, he purchased for Britain a large interest in the Suez Canal, which was a key link in the shipping route that connected Britain and its vast empire in India and the Far East. At the Congress of Berlin in 1878, Disraeli helped prevent Russian expansion in Turkey and won Cyprus for Britain. The Disraeli government also worked to improve living conditions in Britain. It passed important measures affecting health, housing, the environment, trade unions, and working conditions.

National Portrait Gallery, London
Benjamin Disraeli

Disraeli wrote several novels dealing with politics and high society. His major novels include *Coningsby* (1844), *Sybil* (1845), and *Tancred* (1847). He was made Earl of Beaconsfield in 1876.   Richard W. Davis

See also **Conservative Party; Corn Laws.**

Additional resources

Aronson, Theo. *Victoria and Disraeli: The Making of a Romantic Partnership.* Macmillan, 1978.
Blake, Robert. *Disraeli.* St. Martin's, 1966.
Bradford, Sarah. *Disraeli.* Stein & Day, 1982.
Hibbert, Christopher. *Disraeli and His World.* Scribner, 1978.

Dissection. See Anatomy.
Dissociative disorder. See Mental illness (Dissociative disorders).
Distance is the space between two points. It can be measured in miles, rods, feet, inches, meters, kilometers, centimeters, and many other units of measurement. The vast spaces between the stars and planets, or astronomical distances, are measured by the speed of light. Astronomers say, for example, that a star is six *light-years* away, which means that light reaches the earth six years after it leaves the star. Light travels at a speed of 186,282 miles (299,792 kilometers) per second. In one year, light travels 5,880,000,000,000 miles (9,460,000,000,000 kilometers). If a star is 10 light-years away, it is about 60,000,000,000,000 miles (100,000,000,000,000 kilometers) away.

Ordinary distances, such as a few miles, are too small to have meaning in astronomy. But these same distances are extremely large in other sciences. In biology and physics, scientists can measure the distance between two cells, or between atoms in a crystal. Scientists meas-

ure such distances in *microns* (millionths of a meter), or in *millimicrons* (thousandths of a micron).
Leland F. Webb

Related articles in *World Book* include:
Astronomy (Measuring distances in space)
Measurement (Length and distance)
Metric system (Length and distance)
Parallax
Telemetry
Weights and measures (Length)

Distant Early Warning line. See DEW line.
Distemper is a contagious disease of dogs and other animals. In dogs, it is caused by a virus called *paramyxovirus.* This virus affects chiefly young dogs and is often fatal. It also infects such animals as foxes, minks, skunks, raccoons, and wolves. The word *distemper* also refers to different diseases in horses and cats.

A dog with distemper suffers from fever, reddened eyes, loss of appetite, a dry mouth, and discharges containing pus from the nose and eyes. As the disease progresses, pneumonia may occur and bring on coughing and heavy breathing. The virus frequently spreads to the brain and results in jerking motions of the head, jaw, and other parts of the body. This motion is called *chorea.* Brain infection usually leads to death.

Vaccination is the most effective means of preventing distemper. Dogs suffering from this disease require the care of a veterinarian. Drugs can control secondary bacterial infections. Dogs that recover are immune to distemper for several years or for their entire lifetime.

Distemper in horses is caused by *Streptococcus equii* bacteria. In young horses, this disease is called *strangles.* The horse suffers from a sore throat, fever, and swollen lymph glands. Horses treated with penicillin or other drugs frequently recover.

Distemper in cats is called *panleukopenia,* also known as *feline enteritis, cat distemper,* or *feline distemper.* It is caused by a virus called *parvovirus* and infects the bone marrow, intestine, and lymphoid tissue. The cat suffers from diarrhea, a runny nose, and reddened and runny eyes. Many cats with panleukopenia die. Vaccination can protect cats from it. Treatment requires the care of a veterinarian.   Lawrence D. McGill

Distillation, *DIHS tuh LAY shuhn,* is a process that separates a substance or a mixture of substances from a solution through vaporization. Many industrial processes depend on distillation. Distillation usually involves boiling a liquid and condensing the vapor that forms. When water boils, it turns into vapor. Through distillation, the vapor can be collected and condensed to form *distilled water.* The distilled water is purer than the original water because salt and other impurities do not evaporate along with the water.

Distillation is carried out in an apparatus called a *still.* A still consists of a *boiler,* a *condenser,* and a *receiver.* The mixture to be vaporized is heated in the boiler. Whichever substance in the mixture boils at the lowest temperature will be the first to turn into vapor. The vapor enters the condenser, where it cools and becomes liquid again. The distilled liquid, called the *distillate,* then collects in the receiver.

Two general methods are used to distill liquids, *simple distillation* and *rectification.* In simple distillation, all the distillate is removed from the still after collecting in

Types of distillation

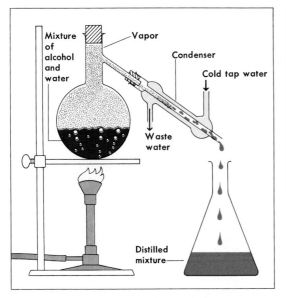

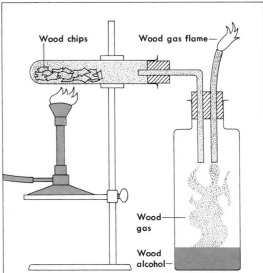

WORLD BOOK diagrams by Arthur Grebetz

Simple distillation separates substances in a liquid. It can be demonstrated by heating a mixture of alcohol and water in a flask. When the mixture boils, it turns into vapor. The vapor has a higher percentage of alcohol than the liquid mixture did, because alcohol boils at a lower temperature than water. The vapor liquefies in the condenser and flows into the receiver.

Destructive distillation, which involves chemical changes in solids, produces new substances. It can be shown by heating wood chips in a closed tube at a temperature high enough for the wood to *decompose* (separate chemically). This decomposition produces wood gas. The gas burns with a luminous flame if lit. When the gas condenses in the jar, it forms wood alcohol.

the receiver. In rectification, part of the distillate flows back into the still. This portion comes into contact with the vapor being condensed and enriches it.

Simple distillation. Two common techniques used in this method of distillation are *fractional distillation* and *flash distillation.*

Fractional distillation, also called *differential distillation,* separates a mixture of liquids that boil at different temperatures. For example, alcohol boils at 172° F. (78° C), and water boils at 212° F. (100° C). When a mixture of these liquids is heated, the alcohol vaporizes faster than the water. But the water vaporizes fairly rapidly at the boiling point of alcohol. As a result, the distillate from a mixture of alcohol and water contains some water. The first distillate collected has a larger proportion of alcohol than the portions that condense later. Therefore, the first distillate is removed before much water distillate has condensed. In the same way, the remaining distillate is collected in *fractions* (portions), which can then be redistilled for a purer product. Fractional distillation is used in making distilled liquors. See **Alcoholic beverage; Distilling.**

Flash distillation involves passing a liquid from a vessel maintained at a high pressure to one kept at a lower pressure. No heating is required to produce vapor by this method. The lower pressure causes part of the liquid to *flash* (turn quickly) into vapor, which is then condensed into distillate. In fractional distillation, the distillate can be processed only in batches. But in flash distillation, a continuous flow of liquid can be distilled. Flash distillation is widely used to turn ocean water into fresh water. See **Water** (Distillation).

Rectification separates many different substances from a solution by using large towers called *fractionating columns.* As the mixture is heated, its vapors rise through these columns. Substances that boil at the lowest temperatures form the first fractions. Their vapors rise highest and are carried off by pipes near the tops of the fractionating columns. Separate pipes carry off different fractions at various levels. The *reflux* (return) of some distillate to the columns produces the most efficient conditions for this method of distillation. Rectification plays a role in chemical processing, including petroleum refining. See **Petroleum** (Refining petroleum).

Destructive distillation. No new substances are formed during simple distillation or rectification. Each of these processes simply separates substances that have been mixed together. But when some solids are heated in a closed vessel, they *decompose* (separate chemically) and produce new substances. For example, wood heated in an airtight tube decomposes into wood gas, which in turn condenses and forms wood alcohol. This process, which involves chemical changes, is called *destructive distillation.* Manufacturers use destructive distillation to produce coal tar from coal.   John B. Butt

See also **Evaporation.**

Distilling is a process used in manufacturing various alcoholic beverages, including whiskey, brandy, and rum. These beverages, sometimes called *spirits,* are made from a "mash" of grains or from various fruit juices. Sugar in the mash or juice is converted into alcohol by a process called *fermentation* (see **Fermentation**). Distilling begins when the fermented mixture is heated, turning the alcohol into vapors. The vapors are collected and then cooled back into a liquid to produce alcoholic beverages (see **Distillation**).

Distilling is done by a machine called a *still.* There are two main types of stills. The *pot still* distills one batch of liquid at a time. It is used for making Irish whiskey, tequila, and a type of brandy called *cognac.* Other spirits are made in *column stills,* which permit continuous distillation. Column stills are the type most often used by commercial distilleries in the United States.

Most kinds of spirits contain from 40 to 50 per cent alcohol. All spirits are colorless when first made, but some darken naturally during the aging process or are artificially colored by manufacturers. The different kinds and flavors of distilled alcoholic beverages depend on the type of fermented mixture used. Distillers produce brandy from fermented fruit juices. Whiskey and vodka are made from several kinds of fermented grain mash, including corn, rye, and wheat. Rum is made from fermented molasses or sugar cane juice. Tequila comes from the fermented juices of the maguey plant. Manufacturers blend alcohol vapors with additional flavoring materials to make gin and cordials.   F. A. Meister

See also **Alcoholic beverage; Whiskey.**

District attorney is a public official whose chief duties are bringing charges against and prosecuting persons charged with a crime or offense. This official is also called the county attorney, prosecuting attorney, commonwealth attorney, deputy attorney general, or state's attorney. District attorneys are the attorneys for the state, or "people," in criminal trials. They may act as attorney for the government in civil suits to collect taxes or to take property for public use. They may appear for the defense in suits brought against the government. In most states, district attorneys have jurisdiction only in a given county. They are elected in some states and appointed in others.

United States district attorneys are officially called United States attorneys. They are appointed by the President and are responsible to the attorney general. A U.S. attorney is appointed for each federal judicial district for a term of four years. United States attorneys serve as attorney for the government when it prosecutes for federal crimes, sues, or is sued.   Jack M. Kress

District court is the court in which most federal cases are first heard in the United States. The district court ranks below the court of appeals. In a district court, questions of fact are decided by a jury, or, if the parties wish, by a judge. The first full hearing of a case is called a trial, and the district court is called a *trial court.* The district court decides on the truth of contested events, and its decision on the facts of a case is final. But the rules of law used by the court may be reviewed by a higher court, on appeal. The appeal is usually to one of the Courts of Appeals. The Supreme Court of the United States may review a Court of Appeals decision.

There are about 95 district courts in the United States and its possessions. Each court has one or more judges, and one United States attorney. There are a total of about 565 permanent district court judges. Each is appointed for life by the President, subject to U.S. Senate approval. The courts hear most federal criminal cases, as well as civil suits arising under postal, patent, copyright, and internal revenue laws.   Jack M. Kress

See also **Court of appeals; Court** (Federal courts).

District of Columbia (D.C.) is the seat of the U.S. government. It covers 69 square miles (179 square kilometers) along the Potomac River between Maryland and Virginia. The city of Washington covers the entire District. For more information, see **Washington, D.C.**

Disulfiram, *dy SUHL fuh ram,* is a drug used to treat alcoholism (see **Alcoholism**). It is commonly known by the trade name Antabuse. Disulfiram does not cure alcoholism, but it discourages people from drinking alcoholic beverages. People who take disulfiram become sick if they drink alcoholic beverages. Symptoms include heavy breathing, dizziness, and vomiting.

People taking disulfiram should avoid any product that contains alcohol. For example, cough syrup, tonics, and even after-shave lotion may result in sickness. When alcohol is avoided, there may be only mild side effects, such as drowsiness, headaches, or skin problems. Disulfiram should be taken only when prescribed by a physician. Two Danish physicians, Jens Hald and Erik Jacobsen, discovered the usefulness of the drug in 1948.
      Kenneth Blum

Diuretic, *DY yu REHT ihk,* is a drug or other substance that increases the secretion of urine by the kidneys. Many substances such as water, glucose solution, tea, coffee, mineral waters, and beer have a diuretic effect on the kidneys. Diuretics are used to treat many diseases in which the secretion and flow of urine are greatly affected, such as when the kidneys are damaged by poisons. They are also used to rid the body of extra fluid, as in edema.   Austin Smith

Diurnal hibernation. See Hibernation.

Diver, a bird. See **Loon.**

Diversified farming. See Agriculture (Mixed farms).

Diverticulitis, *DY vuhr TIHK yuh LY tihs,* is a common disease of the *colon* (large intestine). Its symptoms include pain in the lower left part of the abdomen and a fever. The disease develops from *diverticulosis,* a disorder widespread among middle-aged and elderly people in North America and northern Europe.

Diverticulosis involves the presence of pouches called *diverticula* along the outside of the colon. Diverticula rarely form in people under the age of 30. Most diverticulosis patients have no symptoms.

For many years, physicians believed that a diet low in *roughage* (fruit and vegetable fibers) would help pre-

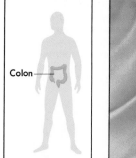
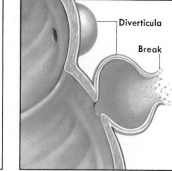

WORLD BOOK illustrations by Robert Demarest

Diverticulitis is a disease of the colon. It occurs when a *diverticulum,* an abnormal pouch on the surface of the colon, is inflamed. An inflamed diverticulum may break open, releasing infectious waste materials.

vent diverticulosis. But today, evidence suggests that the opposite is true. A shortage of roughage in the diet makes the waste material in the colon extremely firm and compact. The waste cannot move easily through the colon, and high pressure results. This pressure can force the inner membrane of the colon to bulge out through several weak points in the lining of the organ. Such action forms small, permanent diverticula that may be seen with an X-ray examination.

In the United States, where most people eat relatively little roughage, nearly half of those over 60 have diverticulosis. The condition rarely occurs in underdeveloped nations, where the standard diet is high in fiber.

Diverticulitis develops in many cases of diverticulosis. It results when one or more of the diverticula are inflamed. The inflamed diverticula may break open. The material that leaks out infects the outer surface of the colon. In most cases, the infection stays in a small area. But it may spread and develop into *peritonitis,* a severe illness that can cause death (see **Peritonitis**).

Doctors treat diverticulitis with antibiotics to control infection, drugs to relax the muscle of the colon, and compounds to help empty the colon. In severe cases, surgeons may remove the inflamed part of the colon. A diet high in roughage may help prevent a recurrence of the disease.   A. William Holmes

Divide is a high place on the land, situated so that the streams on one side flow in the opposite direction to the streams on the other side. These streams then flow into different river systems, which may empty into different oceans. The little streams are called the *headwaters* of the river systems. The divide separates the headwaters of the systems.

A divide may be rather low, like the height of land that runs from east to west across North America. This divide separates the rivers that flow generally northward into the Gulf of Saint Lawrence, Hudson Bay, and the Arctic Ocean from those that flow into the Mississippi basin. Some divides are very high with steep slopes, like the Rocky Mountains. This separates the rivers flowing into the Mississippi and the Gulf of Mexico from those flowing into the Pacific Ocean. The divide that runs north and south through the Rocky Mountains is called the *Great Divide* or the *Continental Divide.*

On Cutbank Pass in Glacier National Park, there are three brooks so close together that a person can pour water into all three at the same time. One brook carries water to Hudson Bay, another to the Pacific Ocean, and the third into the Gulf of Mexico. At several places in the Rocky Mountains, sources of streams flowing to the Pacific and to the Gulf lie only a short distance apart.
          Richard G. Reider

See also **Continental Divide; Great Divide.**

Divider is a drafting instrument used to divide lines into equal parts. It also transfers dimensions from a ruler to a map or a drawing. A divider measures and plots small distances between two points more accurately than a ruler. It can be used on maps to check the distance between two points against the distance scale.

A divider has two needle-pointed legs, joined together at the top. An adjusting screw changes the distance between the two legs. Dividers range in length from about 3 to 8 inches (8 to 20 centimeters). They are a type of caliper (see **Caliper**).   E. B. Espenshade, Jr.

Divination, *DIHV uh NAY shuhn,* is the practice of trying to learn about the unknown by magical or supernatural means. A diviner supposedly can learn about the past, present, or future. Some diviners believe they can learn the causes of past events, such as a person's illness or death. Other diviners, called *dowsers,* claim they can find the location of underground water. Still others believe they can foretell events, such as when a person will die or whom a person will marry.

There are many kinds of divination. For example, *necromancy* involves communicating with the spirits of the dead. *Astrology* is an attempt to predict events by studying the positions of the sun, moon, stars, and planets. Some diviners interpret dreams to foretell events.

Another type of divination, called *palmistry,* involves the prediction of events by reading the lines and marks of the hand. Some fortunetellers claim to read messages in coffee grounds, tea leaves, dried mud, or crystal balls. Others use *tarot cards,* a special deck of pictured playing cards, to tell the future.

Throughout history, people have believed in the powers of divination. In ancient Greece and Rome, prophets known as *oracles* foretold events by interpreting messages from the deities.

At one time, courts used divination to determine the guilt or innocence of criminals. Divination in a trial was called an *ordeal.* For example, in many witch trials of the 1600's in Europe and colonial America, a suspected witch was tied up and thrown into water. If she sank, she was considered innocent. If she floated, she was considered a witch—and was executed.   Alan Dundes

Related articles in *World Book* include:

Astrology	Graphology	Omen	Superstition
Augur	Magic	Oracle	Well
Clairvoyance	Necromancy	Ouija board	(Locating
Fortunetelling	Numerology	Palmistry	wells)

Divine, Father (1880?-1965), was a black American religious leader and the founder of the Peace Mission Movement. The movement worked to end poverty, racial discrimination, and war. Father Divine had a luxurious life style and was often criticized for it. But his goals, spiritual leadership, and generosity attracted support in cities throughout the United States.

Father Divine's real name was George Baker. He was born in Georgia, but little else is known about his early

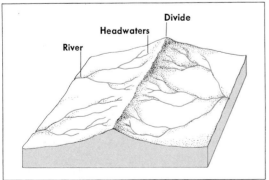

A divide is a high area of land that separates river systems from one another. The headwaters of each system form near the top of the divide. The waters join and form streams and rivers.

Divide

Headwaters

River

WORLD BOOK diagram by Marion Pahl

life. In 1915, he opened his first church in New York City and soon took the name Major J. Devine. His followers, known as *angels,* were encouraged to live together in houses called *heavens* and to contribute their incomes to the Peace Mission Movement. During the Great Depression, grocery stores and other businesses owned by the movement provided food, clothing, and other goods to the poor at little or no cost. Devine's followers began to regard him as God and called him *Father Divine.* After he died, interest in the movement declined sharply.   Fredrick Woodard

UPI

Father Divine

Divine Comedy is a beautiful, long epic poem by the Italian writer Dante Alighieri. Dante began the poem about 1308 and finished it just before his death in 1321. Its main theme is life after death, and Dante himself is the chief character. *The Divine Comedy* is divided into the *Inferno* (Hell); the *Purgatorio* (Purgatory); and the *Paradiso* (Paradise). Dante called the work simply *Commedia* (Comedy) because it ended happily. Later generations added the word *Divine.*

Dante divided each of the three parts of the poem into subdivisions called *cantos. Purgatorio* and *Paradiso* each contain 33 cantos, and *Inferno* has 34. The cantos have a powerful rhythm because of their three-line *terza rima* stanzas. In this verse form, which Dante invented, the first and third lines of each stanza rhyme with the middle line of the preceding stanza.

The poem begins with Dante lost in a dark forest, symbolizing what he felt was his own unworthy life and the evil he saw in society. On Good Friday, after a night of painful wandering, he meets the Roman poet Virgil, who promises to lead him out of the forest and guide him on a journey through the otherworld. They enter hell, a horrible pit shaped like a cone, located deep within the earth. It has nine circles where they find crowds of suffering individuals who are being punished for their sins by monsters, devils, and other creatures. The damned are well-known historical figures, some from the past, but most from Dante's own time.

Dante and Virgil leave hell and reach the mountain of purgatory. From there they climb to bright terraces where the dead, who have gained salvation, seek forgiveness for misdeeds committed on earth. An atmosphere of peace and hope fills this place of purification, in contrast with hell's suffering and despair.

On reaching the earthly paradise, on top of Mount Purgatory, Virgil entrusts Dante to a new guide, Beatrice. *The Divine Comedy* is in many ways a love poem praising Beatrice's moral beauty and her power to lead Dante to a vision of supreme goodness. She guides Dante through the 10 spheres of heaven, where Dante meets the souls of the blessed. They finally arrive at the throne of God, set among hosts of angels. Dante stands in rapture and perceives at last the final truth of life and the meaning of the universe.   Richard H. Lansing

See also **Dante Alighieri.**

Divine proportion. See Golden section.
Divine right of kings is the belief that monarchs get their right to rule directly from God, rather than from the consent or wish of their subjects. According to this belief, it is up to God to punish a wicked king. So far as the people are concerned, "the king can do no wrong" and ought to be obeyed.

This idea was at its height during the 1600's, especially in England during the reign of the Stuarts and in France under Louis XIV. The first blow at divine right was the execution of King Charles I of England in 1649. In the late 1700's, the French Revolution repudiated the belief and asserted that the right to rule came from the people. But the divine-right doctrine lasted long after that time. It was asserted in the early 1900's by the German Emperor Wilhelm II as king of Prussia, and by Czar Nicholas II of Russia.   Roger Howell, Jr.

Diving is an exciting water sport. A skillful diver leaps from a springboard or a platform and performs daring acrobatics in the air before plunging into the water. Unlike swimming, diving emphasizes technique rather than endurance or speed. Talented divers combine strength and grace with great courage while spinning and twisting toward the water.

Some divers perform trick dives at water shows, and others plunge into the water from cliffs. Such divers have great skill and daring, but they perform mostly as entertainers. This article discusses diving as a national and international competitive sport. For information on other forms of diving, see **Diving, Underwater; Skin diving;** and **Spearfishing.**

Types of diving

National and international diving meets consist of two types of competition, *springboard diving* and *platform diving.* In the United States, the National Collegiate Athletic Association (NCAA) holds national competitions in both springboard and platform diving for college divers. In springboard diving, the diver uses the spring from a bouncing board to gain the height necessary to perform a dive. In platform diving, the diver jumps from a high, stationary surface.

Springboard diving. Diving boards used in meets measure 16 feet (5 meters) long and 20 inches (51 centimeters) wide. They extend about 6 feet (1.8 meters) beyond the edge of the pool. Springboard diving competitions are held on boards that are either 1 meter ($3\frac{1}{2}$ feet) or 3 meters (10 feet) above the water.

In the 1960's, the development of aluminum diving boards revolutionized springboard diving. Aluminum springboards are thinner and more flexible than the earlier thick wooden ones. They provide greater spring, making it easier for the diver to spin as well as to gain more height. This increased height and spinning action allows athletes to perform a greater variety of dives, including many more difficult ones. Aluminum springboards introduced during the 1980's enable divers to gain even more height and spinning action.

Platform diving. Diving platforms for meets must be at least 20 feet (6 meters) long and $6\frac{1}{2}$ feet (2 meters) wide. They have a nonskid surface to prevent athletes from slipping. Diving platforms used in competitions are 10 meters (33 feet) above the water. Some platforms have levels that are 5 meters (16 feet) or 7.5 meters (25 feet) high. During the Olympic Games, divers use these lower levels only for practice. However, divers in younger age-group competition may use them in meets.

Diving techniques

Diving is safe for properly trained athletes, but good diving requires proper coaching and equipment. Beginners risk serious injury if they do not learn proper techniques, and so a trained, certified diving instructor is essential. Difficult dives should never be attempted from a backyard or motel pool diving board.

The first movement for many dives consists of the *approach* and the *hurdle*. The approach consists of at least three steps taken by the diver on the board or platform. The hurdle is the last step—actually a short jump—that takes the diver to the edge of the board or platform. The approach steps should be natural and even in length. Steps that are too long or too short may result in shifts in weight that can cause imbalance.

Some platform dives begin with a *standing start*. The diver stands poised at the platform's edge. Other platform dives begin with a handstand at the edge.

All dives involve movements that divers must follow precisely while in the air. Ideally, a diver enters the water vertically, with the body straight and the toes pointed. When the diver enters the water head first, the arms must be extended over the head with the elbows locked and pressed against the ears in line with the body. If the diver enters the water feet first, the arms should be straight and placed firmly against the sides.

Kinds of dives

Springboard and platform dives are categorized into dive groups. In springboard diving, there are five groups. They are (1) forward, (2) back, (3) reverse, (4) inward, and (5) twist. In platform diving, there are six groups. The first five are from the same groups as those performed in springboard diving. In the sixth group, called the armstand group, the diver begins from a handstand position at the end of the platform.

All the groups consist of basic dives and progressively harder variations of them. All the variations in the first four groups and armstand group include at least one somersault. The twist group consists of dives from the first four groups and the armstand group, plus a twisting action. To do a twist, the diver turns his or her body at least one-half revolution in the air.

Divers perform all dives except for some twist dives in one of three positions: (1) straight, (2) pike, and (3) tuck. In the straight position, the diver keeps the body straight. In the pike position, the athlete bends at the hips and keeps the knees straight. In the tuck position, he or she bends at the waist and knees by pulling the knees up toward the chest, and grasping the lower legs with the hands. A fourth position, the *free* position, is used only in certain twist dives. Dives in the free position combine any of the three other positions, depending on the kind of twist dive.

Diving meets

The United States, Canada, and many other countries hold national championship diving meets annually. International meets are held the year around. The meets are held indoors and outdoors. Men and women compete separately, but they perform the same dives and use the same boards and platforms. Every meet consists of required and optional dives. The judging and scoring procedures are the same for men's and women's diving.

The top national and international diving meets are conducted under regulations established by the Fédération Internationale de Natation Amateur (FINA). FINA is the international governing body for diving, competitive swimming, water polo, and a graceful, acrobatic swimming sport called *synchronized swimming*.

Required and optional dives. The FINA assigns each dive a *degree of difficulty.* Difficulty is based on the number of twists and somersaults and whether the dive is performed on the 1-meter or 3-meter springboard or from the 10-meter platform.

In national and international springboard meets, men perform 11 dives. These dives include 5 required dives,

Beginning a springboard dive   A diver must perform a series of movements to begin a dive properly. The most important movements for most dives are the *approach* and the *hurdle.* (1) The approach consists of at least three steps on the springboard. (2) The hurdle is a short jump that takes the athlete to the edge of the board. (3) The diver's arms swing down as the board goes down. (4) They swing up as the board rebounds. (5) The take-off lifts the diver high into the air.

WORLD BOOK illustrations by Robert Keys

1   2   3   4   5

Kinds of dives Five kinds of dives are performed in a springboard meet. These dives, in the order in which they are performed, are (1) forward, (2) back, (3) reverse, (4) inward, and (5) twist. Divers perform the first four dives and certain twist dives in one of three positions: layout or straight, pike, and tuck.

WORLD BOOK illustrations by Robert Keys

Forward (straight position)

Forward 1½ -somersault (tuck position)

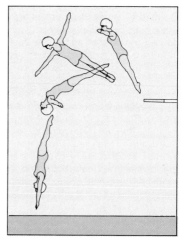

Back (straight position)

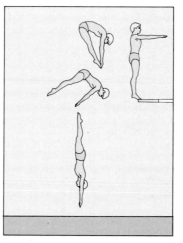

Reverse (straight position)

Inward (pike position)

Half-twist (straight position)

also known as voluntary dives with limit, and 6 optional dives, also called voluntary dives without limit. Women perform 10 dives—5 required and 5 optional. The total degree of difficulty for an athlete's required dives must not exceed a limit assigned by FINA. Optional dives have no such limit. Both men and women must perform one required and one optional dive from each of the five groups of dives—forward, back, reverse, inward, and twist. The men's sixth optional dive may be from any group.

In platform meets at the national and international level, men perform four required and six optional dives. Women perform four required and four optional dives. As in springboard diving, the total degree of difficulty for an athlete's required dives may not exceed a standardized limit. Men platform divers choose one dive from each of the six dive groups. Women platform divers se-

lect four dives from any of the six groups. None of the groups may be repeated.

Scoring and judging. Judges evaluate each diver's approach, take-off, grace and technique in the air, and entry into the water. Each judge awards points and half points on a scale of 0 to 10. A score between 0 to 4½ is unsatisfactory, 5 to 6½ satisfactory, 7 to 8½ good, and 9 to 10 outstanding.

Diving meets use a panel of judges to obtain three impartial scores. In most meets, divers are judged by five to seven judges. But in some meets, divers are judged by as few as two or as many as nine judges. In meets that use five, seven, or nine judges, a diver's highest and lowest scores are dropped. The remaining scores are added and then multiplied by the dive's degree of difficulty. The result is the athlete's score for that dive.

The final meet score is the sum of scores for all dives the athlete did in the competition. The final score is adjusted to make the results comparable to scores obtained in meets using three judges. In competitions that use two judges, no scores are dropped. But the final score is adjusted to make it comparable to those in meets using three judges. Micki King Hogue

See also **Swimming** (Starts and turns; pictures); **Olympic Games** (table: Swimming and diving).

Additional resources

Goldberg, Bob. *Diving Basics.* Prentice-Hall, 1986. For younger readers.
Lee, Sammy, and Lehrman, Steve. *Diving.* Atheneum, 1978. Suitable for younger readers.
Rackham, George. *Diving Complete.* Faber & Faber, 1975.

Diving, Underwater, is the way people reach the strange and beautiful world beneath the surface of oceans, lakes, and rivers. Ancient peoples dived underwater in search of fish, other water animals, and plants for food. With improved skills and equipment, many activities began to be performed underwater.

Today, divers repair ships, recover valuable objects, build and repair various types of structures, and conduct research. Work can be performed at great depths in specially equipped diving vehicles. In the armed services, divers and submarines carry out military missions. Many people enjoy underwater diving as a sport. They dive to study underwater life, to take photographs, to hunt water animals, or simply to explore.

Kinds of underwater diving

There are two basic kinds of diving: (1) *ambient diving,* in which the diver's body is exposed to the pressure of the *ambient* (surrounding) water; and (2) diving in vehicles that protect divers from the water pressure.

Ambient diving. Water pressure on the body increases with water depth. At great depths, this pressure can have dangerous effects on an ambient diver. The three types of ambient diving are (1) breath-hold diving, (2) scuba diving, and (3) surface-supplied diving.

Breath-hold diving is the oldest and simplest form of underwater diving. It is also called *free diving, skin diving,* and *snorkel diving.* Breath-hold divers may use no equipment at all, but most of them use a face mask, foot fins, and a short breathing tube called a *snorkel.* The snorkel allows the diver to swim at the surface and observe underwater before diving.

Breath-hold diving is a popular form of recreational diving. Most breath-hold divers can go only 30 to 40 feet (9 to 12 meters) deep. They must surface to breathe after less than a minute. Some skilled divers can go as deep as 100 feet (30 meters) and stay submerged for as long as two minutes.

Scuba diving gives divers greater mobility and range than breath-hold or surface-supplied diving. The word *scuba* stands for *self-contained underwater breathing apparatus.* A scuba diver wears metal tanks that hold compressed air or a special mixture of breathing gases. The diver breathes from the tanks through a hose. A device called a *demand regulator* supplies the amount of air that is required. Scuba divers also use a mask and fins.

The most common type of scuba equipment, called *open circuit* scuba, uses air. The diver breathes air from the tank, and the exhaled air is released into the water. *Closed circuit* equipment, also called a *rebreather,* uses oxygen or a mixture of oxygen and other gases. It filters out the carbon dioxide and other harmful gases from the exhaled gas. More oxygen is added automatically. This action enables the diver to breathe the same air again and again. Closed circuit equipment usually uses 100 per cent oxygen.

Surface-supplied diving involves wearing a waterproof suit and a helmet. A diver gets air or breathing gas

An underwater diver drives a device into the ocean floor to obtain samples of the ocean bottom for research. The diver descended in a vehicle called a *submersible.* Two cables link the diver to the submersible. One supplies breathing gas, and the other enables the diver to communicate with people in the vehicle.

Surface-supplied diving equipment

In surface-supplied diving, a diver wears a waterproof suit and a helmet for protection against water pressure. Air or breathing gas travels through a hose connected to air pumps on a boat.

WORLD BOOK illustration by David Cunningham

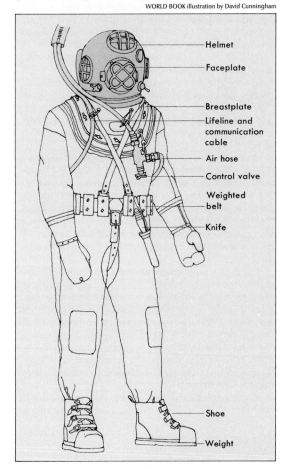

Helmet

Faceplate

Breastplate

Lifeline and communication cable

Air hose

Control valve

Weighted belt

Knife

Shoe

Weight

through a hose connected to air pumps on a boat. Most deep diving is surface supplied. Divers wear many kinds of helmets and suits. Some wear heavy helmets and canvas suits. Lightweight fiberglass helmets and special diving masks are replacing older helmets made of copper. In addition to hoses that supply breathing gas, other hoses and wires may supply hot water to warm the diving suit, electricity or high-pressure air to operate power tools, and gases used for welding torches.

Diving in vehicles. There are several kinds of diving vehicles. These vehicles keep divers dry, warm, and at surface pressure.

Some divers wear metal suits called *articulated armor*. These suits cover the entire body. Like diving vehicles, articulated armor provides protection against pressure, but it enables the diver to move about more freely. Some types of articulated armor permit the diver to descend and ascend without the aid of cables.

Submarines are the largest diving vehicles. Most submarines are warships that carry powerful weapons. For more information about these ships, see **Submarine.**

Submersibles have extremely strong hulls and can descend much deeper than submarines can. Unmanned submersibles, which are operated using a cable, can descend to about 20,000 feet (6,100 meters). Manned submersibles can descend to about 21,000 feet (6,500 meters). Submersibles are used for research and other purposes.

The first submersibles, including the *bathysphere* and the *benthoscope,* were ball-shaped chambers with viewing *ports* (windows). They were lowered on cables from ships. Modern submersibles have motors and propellers and can maneuver independently. Some receive electric power through cables from the surface, but each carries its own supply of air. Some of these vehicles have external mechanical arms called *manipulators,* which can pick up objects from the ocean floor. Submersibles also have cameras and floodlights that enable scientists to photograph objects and organisms at depths where sunlight never penetrates.

Some types of submersibles carry tanks of gasoline, oil, or a foam composed of tiny glass bubbles. Such light substances help make the craft *buoyant* (able to float). Tanks filled with air, such as those used in submarines, would be crushed by the pressure at great depths. To descend, some of the buoyancy substance is released and replaced by water, which gives the craft additional weight. To ascend, the craft is lightened by dropping pieces of iron carried for this purpose. Some types of submersibles also use propellers when descending or ascending. A submersible that is called a *bathyscaph* consists of a steel sphere attached to the bottom of a cigar-shaped hull filled with gasoline. In 1960, the bathyscaph *Trieste* made the deepest dive ever recorded. It descended 35,800 feet (10,910 meters) into the Pacific Ocean. See **Bathyscaph.**

Dangers of underwater diving

There is greater pressure underwater than on land. The pressure increases by almost half a pound per square inch (0.04 kilogram per square centimeter) for each foot (30 centimeters) of depth. For example, the pressure on a diver 33 feet (10 meters) beneath the surface is twice as great as the air pressure at the surface. An ambient diver may be injured if the pressure in the lungs and other air spaces in the body does not equal the water pressure. Such an injury is called *barotrauma* or *squeeze.*

During ascent, the pressure in the lungs must be kept equal to the decreasing water pressure. Otherwise, a serious condition called *air embolism* may result. An ambient diver breathes more molecules of air underwater than on land because the air breathed underwater is compressed. When the diver rises to the surface, the air in the lungs expands because of the lesser pressure. If the air cannot be exhaled, it will tear the lungs and force air bubbles into the blood. These bubbles can block the flow of blood and cripple or even kill the diver. Air embolism can be prevented by breathing naturally and ascending slowly.

A condition known as the *bends* or *decompression sickness* occurs when nitrogen bubbles form in the blood. Nitrogen gas makes up more than three-fourths of the air breathed by human beings. An ambient diver who breathes compressed air absorbs large amounts of nitrogen into the blood. As the diver ascends, this excess nitrogen is exhaled. But if the diver ascends too quickly, bubbles of nitrogen gas form in the blood. The nitrogen bubbles can block the flow of blood and cripple or kill the diver. A diver can avoid the bends by rising slowly enough to allow the excess nitrogen to be eliminated through breathing.

A chart called a *decompression table* tells a diver how long he or she can stay at a certain depth without absorbing a dangerous amount of nitrogen. It also tells how slowly the diver must ascend to avoid the bends. A person who has air embolism or the bends should be put into a *recompression chamber* immediately. In this chamber, the diver is returned to a pressure which compresses the bubbles so that the gas dissolves back into the blood. The pressure is then reduced in stages.

Divers breathing air at extreme depths may also suffer a kind of drugged effect called *nitrogen narcosis.* This condition causes a loss of the ability to reason. Nitrogen narcosis occurs most frequently at extreme depths. To avoid it, divers may breathe a gas mixture that contains helium instead of nitrogen.

A diver who breathes 100 per cent oxygen at great depths may suffer oxygen poisoning. The victim becomes dizzy and vomits and may have convulsions. Gas mixtures with a high oxygen content can also cause oxygen poisoning.

History

Breath-hold divers dived for shells in the Mediterranean Sea as early as 4500 B.C. Ancient Greek and Roman divers sought pearls, sponges, and shells.

Divers in the Persian Gulf used goggles made of polished clear tortoise shell to see clearly underwater as early as A.D. 1300. In the early 1930's, Guy Gilpatric, an American diver, became one of the first to use rubber goggles with glass lenses. By the mid-1930's, face masks, fins, and snorkels had come into use.

The first devices that enabled people to breathe underwater were called *diving bells.* These bell-shaped hulls have been used since ancient times. Diving bells are open to the water at the bottom and get air from the surface through a hose. The air pressure that exists

within the bell keeps water out of the device.

In 1715, an English diver named John Lethbridge designed a wooden and leather diving suit that was used in salvage work. The suits used for helmet diving today are based on a diving suit that was introduced in 1837 by Augustus Siebe, a German engineer who was living in England.

Independent breathing devices for diving appeared during the late 1800's and early 1900's. The first safe and simple device, the *aqualung,* was invented in 1943 by two Frenchmen, Jacques-Yves Cousteau, a naval officer, and Émile Gagnan, an engineer.

The development of enclosed diving vehicles expanded the range of underwater activity. Otis Barton of the United States designed the bathysphere. In 1930, he and William Beebe, an American naturalist, made the first dive in it. The Swiss physicist Auguste Piccard designed the first bathyscaph in 1948.

Experimental underwater *saturation habitats* were developed in the 1960's. These manned stations consist of one or more buildings erected on the ocean floor. They have been tested at depths ranging from 30 to more than 600 feet (9 to 180 meters). Compartments inside the buildings are filled with compressed breathing gas. Divers may live there for weeks. They leave the station daily to explore or work. By staying underwater, the divers avoid the need to undergo decompression every day. The first saturation habitat was built off the coast of France in 1962 by Cousteau. During the 1960's and 1970's, many such structures were built in various locations.   Arthur H. Ullrich, Jr.

Related articles in *World Book* include:

Beebe, William	Marine biology	Skin diving
Bends	Ocean (Exploring the	Spearfishing
Cousteau,	ocean)	Submarine
Jacques-Yves	Piccard (family)	

Additional resources

Earle, Sylvia A., and Giddings, Al. *Exploring the Deep Frontier: The Adventure of Man in the Sea.* National Geographic Soc., 1980.
The Sport Diving Catalog. Ed. by Herb Taylor. St. Martin's, 1982.

Diving bell. See Diving, Underwater (History).
Divining rod. See Well (Locating wells).
Division (military) is a unit in the armed forces. It is the major combat unit of the United States Army. The Army has 16 divisions, each of which has about 15,000 soldiers. There are six kinds of Army divisions: (1) airborne, (2) air assault, (3) armored, (4) mechanized infantry, (5) motorized, and (6) infantry-type, which consists of light infantry and mountain divisions. A division may have from 6 to 15 battalions, depending on its mission. Most divisions have 10 battalions plus artillery, control, engineer, and supply units. In each division, the battalions and other units are organized into three brigades. See **Army, U.S.** (table: Army levels of command).

The division is also a basic ground-fighting unit in the U.S. Marine Corps (see **Marine Corps, U.S.**). A Marine division has about 19,000 marines, organized into three regiments and combat and service support units. A U.S. Air Force air division includes two or more *wings* (see **Air Force, U.S.**). A wing is a mobile unit that can operate independently. In the U.S. Navy, the word *division* refers to a small department on board a ship, such as a boiler room division or a navigation division.   Brooke Nihart

Culver

Diving bells of the 1800's could be used to remove rocks from rivers. These two pictures show a rock being attached to a diving bell and then raised to the surface. Diving bells are open at the bottom. The air pressure within the bell keeps the water out.

WORLD BOOK photo by Ralph Brunke

A division problem at the chalkboard tests a student's knowledge of one of the most basic processes of mathematics.

Division is a way of separating a group of things into equal parts. Suppose you have 18 marbles and you want to share the marbles with two friends. You want each of you to end up with the same number of marbles. To find out how many marbles each of you would get, you can count out the marbles into three equal groups. Each group has six marbles. So each of you would get six marbles as shown below. Separating a group of 18

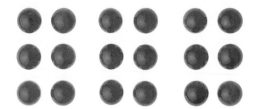

things into three equal parts of 6 things is an example of division.

Division is one of the four basic operations in arithmetic. The others are addition, subtraction, and multiplication. You must learn how to add, subtract, and multiply before you begin to study division.

Learning to divide

Once people learned division only by memorizing. Most teachers now agree that the best way to learn division is by understanding. You can learn to understand division without much difficulty.

Division terms

Dividend. In $32 \div 8 = 4$, 32 is the dividend.

Division fact is a division in which the divisor and quotient are whole numbers not larger than 9. For example, $42 \div 7 = 6$ is a division fact.

Divisor. In $32 \div 8 = 4$, 8 is the divisor.

Long division is a method of dividing numbers in which the work is written out.

Quotient. In $32 \div 8 = 4$, 4 is the quotient.

Remainder is any amount left over after a division operation has been completed. The remainder is always less than the divisor.

Short division is a method of dividing numbers in which much of the work is done mentally.

Writing division. One way of separating a group into equal parts is by counting it out into equal parts. But there is a much easier way to divide. To find how many groups of 3 there are in 12, you can subtract 3 from 12 until nothing is left:

$$\begin{array}{r} 12 \\ -3 \\ \hline 9 \end{array} \quad\Rightarrow\quad \begin{array}{r} 9 \\ -3 \\ \hline 6 \end{array} \quad\Rightarrow\quad \begin{array}{r} 6 \\ -3 \\ \hline 3 \end{array} \quad\Rightarrow\quad \begin{array}{r} 3 \\ -3 \\ \hline 0 \end{array}$$

This shows that there are four 3's in 12.

Each basic operation in arithmetic is indicated by a special symbol. The symbol for division is $\div$. The statement $12 \div 3 = 4$ means that when 12 things are separated into groups of three, there are four such groups. Or, that there are four 3's in 12. It can also mean that when 12 things are separated into three equal groups, there are four things in each group. People who know division usually read $12 \div 3 = 4$ as "12 divided by 3 is 4." A problem in division also may be written this way:

$$3\overline{)12}^{4}$$

The parts of a division problem have special names. The number being divided is called the *dividend*. The number by which the dividend is divided is the *divisor*. The answer, or result, of the division is the *quotient*.

$$\text{Divisor} \longrightarrow 3\overline{)12} \longleftarrow \begin{array}{l}\text{Quotient}\\[4pt]\text{Dividend}\end{array}$$

Another way of writing a problem in division is the form used in writing fractions (see **Fraction**):

$$\frac{12}{3} = 4$$

Division facts. By using subtraction, you discovered that there are three equal groups of 4 things in a group of 12. Or, $12 \div 3 = 4$. This is a *division fact*. You can find all the division facts by using subtraction.

The 64 division facts							
$2\overline{)4}$	$3\overline{)6}$	$4\overline{)8}$	$5\overline{)10}$	$6\overline{)12}$	$7\overline{)14}$	$8\overline{)16}$	$9\overline{)18}$
$2\overline{)6}$	$3\overline{)9}$	$4\overline{)12}$	$5\overline{)15}$	$6\overline{)18}$	$7\overline{)21}$	$8\overline{)24}$	$9\overline{)27}$
$2\overline{)8}$	$3\overline{)12}$	$4\overline{)16}$	$5\overline{)20}$	$6\overline{)24}$	$7\overline{)28}$	$8\overline{)32}$	$9\overline{)36}$
$2\overline{)10}$	$3\overline{)15}$	$4\overline{)20}$	$5\overline{)25}$	$6\overline{)30}$	$7\overline{)35}$	$8\overline{)40}$	$9\overline{)45}$
$2\overline{)12}$	$3\overline{)18}$	$4\overline{)24}$	$5\overline{)30}$	$6\overline{)36}$	$7\overline{)42}$	$8\overline{)48}$	$9\overline{)54}$
$2\overline{)14}$	$3\overline{)21}$	$4\overline{)28}$	$5\overline{)35}$	$6\overline{)42}$	$7\overline{)49}$	$8\overline{)56}$	$9\overline{)63}$
$2\overline{)16}$	$3\overline{)24}$	$4\overline{)32}$	$5\overline{)40}$	$6\overline{)48}$	$7\overline{)56}$	$8\overline{)64}$	$9\overline{)72}$
$2\overline{)18}$	$3\overline{)27}$	$4\overline{)36}$	$5\overline{)45}$	$6\overline{)54}$	$7\overline{)63}$	$8\overline{)72}$	$9\overline{)81}$

The column headers (multipliers) for each column are: 2, 3, 4, 5, 6, 7, 8, 9.

It is important to learn the division facts so well that you can use them automatically. The facts are useful themselves. They are also necessary in learning how to divide larger numbers quickly and accurately.

Long division

Long division is a method that can be used to divide large numbers. In long division, you write out the work carefully.

Suppose you want to find out how many 3's there are in 79, or 79 ÷ 3. Instead of subtracting one 3 at a time, you can shorten your work by subtracting several 3's at once. To begin, you might subtract five 3's, or 15, each time:

$$\begin{array}{c} 79 \\ -15 \\ \hline 64 \end{array} \Rightarrow \begin{array}{c} 64 \\ -15 \\ \hline 49 \end{array} \Rightarrow \begin{array}{c} 49 \\ -15 \\ \hline 34 \end{array} \Rightarrow \begin{array}{c} 34 \\ -15 \\ \hline 19 \end{array} \Rightarrow \begin{array}{c} 19 \\ -15 \\ \hline 4 \end{array} \Rightarrow \begin{array}{c} 4 \\ -3 \\ \hline 1 \end{array}$$

All together, you subtracted 5 + 5 + 5 + 5 + 5 or twenty-five 3's from 79, leaving 4. You cannot subtract five more 3's, but you can subtract one more 3, leaving a *remainder* of 1. Thus, there are 25 + 1 or twenty-six 3's in 79 with 1 left over.

Subtracting five 3's at a time shortened your work. Next, you might try subtracting ten 3's, or 30, each time:

$$\begin{array}{c} 79 \\ -30 \\ \hline 49 \end{array} \Rightarrow \begin{array}{c} 49 \\ -30 \\ \hline 19 \end{array} \Rightarrow \begin{array}{c} 19 \\ -15 \\ \hline 4 \end{array} \Rightarrow \begin{array}{c} 4 \\ -3 \\ \hline 1 \end{array}$$

This time, you subtracted 10 + 10 + 5 + 1 or twenty-six 3's from 79, and had 1 left as a remainder. A better form to use is this:

$$\begin{array}{r} 3\overline{)79} \\ -30 \\ \hline 49 \\ -30 \\ \hline 19 \\ -15 \\ \hline 4 \\ -3 \\ \hline 1 \end{array}$$

10	The number of 3's
10	subtracted are re-
5	corded in this column.
1	
26	The total number of 3's subtracted.

Remainder ➡ 1

After some practice, you might subtract twenty 3's and then six 3's:

26 ⬅ The result is written

$$\begin{array}{r} 3\overline{)79} \\ -60 \\ \hline 19 \\ -18 \\ \hline 1 \end{array}$$

20	above the dividend
6	to complete the form.
26	

To gain further practice in long division, you might now try to find out how many 21's there are in 891, or 891 ÷ 21. First, you must decide how many 21's you will subtract at a time. Ten 21's, or 210, might prove to be

useful. Using 10's, 100's, or 1,000's in multiplying the divisor makes division much easier.

$$\begin{array}{r} 42 \\ 21\overline{)891} \\ -210 \\ \hline 681 \\ -210 \\ \hline 471 \\ -210 \\ \hline 261 \\ -210 \\ \hline 51 \\ -21 \\ \hline 30 \\ -21 \\ \hline \end{array}$$

10	Number of 21's
10	subtracted.
10	
10	
1	
1	
42	

Remainder ➡ 9

When you have subtracted four 210's or forty 21's, you find that the remainder, 51, is too small to subtract ten more 21's. You can, however, subtract one 21 at a time. This finally gives you 10 + 10 + 10 + 10 + 1 + 1 or forty-two 21's in 891, with a remainder of 9.

You could have used twenty 21's, or 420, as your first unit.

$$\begin{array}{r} 42 \\ 21\overline{)891} \\ -420 \\ \hline 471 \\ -420 \\ \hline 51 \\ -42 \\ \hline \end{array}$$

20	Number of 21's
20	subtracted.
2	
42	

Remainder ➡ 9

One last example will illustrate further the process of long division. Suppose you want to know how many 37's there are in 12,526, or 12,526 ÷ 37. Once again you must decide how many 37's to subtract at one time.

$$\begin{array}{r} 338 \\ 37\overline{)12526} \\ -7400 \\ \hline 5126 \\ -3700 \\ \hline 1426 \\ -1110 \\ \hline 316 \\ -185 \\ \hline 131 \\ -111 \\ \hline \end{array}$$

200	Number of 37's
100	subtracted.
30	
5	
3	
338	

Remainder ➡ 20

You may have to experiment on a sheet of scrap paper to find the units that you can use to solve the problem easily. You can use even larger units than 200.

$$\begin{array}{r} 338 \\ 37\overline{)12526} \\ -11100 \\ \hline 1426 \\ -1110 \\ \hline 316 \\ -296 \\ \hline \end{array}$$

300	Number of 37's
30	subtracted.
8	
338	

Remainder ➡ 20

Many persons use a form for long division even shorter than those outlined above. The three steps look like this:

$$
\begin{array}{r} 3 \\ 37\overline{)12526} \\ 111 \\ \hline 14 \end{array}
\qquad
\begin{array}{r} 33 \\ 37\overline{)12526} \\ 111 \\ \hline 142 \\ 111 \\ \hline 31 \end{array}
\qquad
\begin{array}{r} 338 \\ 37\overline{)12526} \\ 111 \\ \hline 142 \\ 111 \\ \hline 316 \\ 296 \\ \hline 20 \end{array}
$$

This form does the same things that have been discussed above, but by a different method. It does not illustrate the process so well to a beginner.

When using this shorter form, it helps to notice that in all these examples you write the answer (quotient) above the proper places in the dividend. That is, when you subtract a number of 100's, you record the number of 100's above the 100's place in the dividend.

Remainders in division. There is often a remainder when you have completed a problem in division. What you do with this remainder depends on the kind of problem. If you want to know how many 3's there are in 79, you might have had 79¢ to spend on three-cent postage stamps. You would find that you could buy 26 stamps and have 1¢ left.

If you wanted to share 79 apples among three persons, you would also find that there are twenty-six 3's in 79 and a remainder of 1. This means that each person gets 26 apples and there is one left to share. If the sharing is to be absolutely equal, you would have to cut the remaining apple into three equal parts. Each person would receive $26\frac{1}{3}$ apples.

These examples show that what is done to a remainder depends on the problem. In some cases, further division into fractional parts is indicated. In other cases, the remainder merely tells how many are "left over."

Division of decimal fractions. You can also use long division to divide numbers that include decimal fractions. The statement 78.35 ÷ 3.6 is this kind of problem. In order to understand division of decimal fractions, you must learn an interesting feature of division.

You know that 15 ÷ 3 = 5 is a division fact. What would happen if both the 15 and 3 were multiplied by 10? That is, what is the result of dividing 150 by 30? Long division will show you that this quotient is also 5. Thus, 15 ÷ 3 = 5, and 150 ÷ 30 = 5. Similarly, 72 ÷ 6 = 12 and 720 ÷ 60 = 12. If the 72 and 6 are multiplied by 100, the quotient of 7,200 ÷ 600 is also 12. These examples illustrate a general rule: *multiplying both the dividend and divisor by 10, 100, 1,000, or any other nonzero number, does not change the quotient.*

This rule can be used to divide 78.35 by 3.6. Both 78.35 and 3.6 can be multiplied by 10. Thus, 78.35 × 10 = 783.5 and 3.6 × 10 = 36. The quotient of 783.5 ÷ 36 will be the same as the quotient of 78.35 ÷ 3.6. But the decimal points now have new positions. A useful device is to use a caret mark (∧) to indicate the new position of the decimal points. The decimal point in the quotient will appear directly above the caret mark in the dividend.

$$3.6_\wedge\overline{)78.3_\wedge5}$$

This shows that 78.35 and 3.6 have both been multiplied by 10. Sometimes it is necessary to multiply the dividend and divisor by 100, 1,000, or some larger multiple of 10. For example, 25.773 ÷ 17.94 should be multiplied by 100:

$$17.94_\wedge\overline{)25.77_\wedge3}$$

You should multiply the dividend and divisor by a multiple of 10 large enough to change the divisor into a *whole number,* or a number that does not include a decimal fraction.

For every division problem with a remainder of zero, there is a corresponding multiplication problem. The two numbers that are multiplied are the quotient and divisor in the division problem. For example:

$$3.25 \div 1.3 = 2.5$$
$$1.3 \times 2.5 = 3.25$$

Experience with such problems has resulted in two rules. In multiplication, the number of decimal places in the *product* (answer to the multiplication problem) is the sum of the number of decimal places in the numbers that were multiplied. In division, the number of decimal places in the quotient is the number of decimal places in the dividend minus the number of decimal places in the divisor. If the divisor is a whole number, you can ignore the decimal point in the dividend while you are working the problem. When you get a number for the quotient, put as many decimal places in the quotient as there are in the dividend. Because the divisor has no decimal places, none must be subtracted from the number in the dividend.

In division problems, you often have to find the quotient to the nearest tenth, hundredth, and so on. You can do this easily. After you have placed the caret marks in the divisor and dividend, use just as many digits to the right of the dividend's caret mark as the number of decimal places wanted in the answer. Sometimes it is necessary to add zeros to the dividend. For example, you must first change $3.6_\wedge\overline{)78.35}$ to $3.6_\wedge\overline{)78.3_\wedge5}$ to make the divisor a whole number. Suppose the quotient must be correct to the nearest hundredth. Then you must add a zero to the dividend, making it $78.3_\wedge50$.

$$
\begin{array}{r}
2\,1\,.\,7\,6 \\
3.6_\wedge\overline{)78.3_\wedge50} \\
-72\,0\ \ 00 \\
\hline
6\,3\ \ 50 \\
-36\ \ 00 \\
\hline
2\,7\ \ 50 \\
-25\ \ 20 \\
\hline
2\ \ 30 \\
-2\ \ 16 \\
\hline
14
\end{array}
\qquad
\begin{array}{r}
2000 \\
\\
\\
100 \\
\\
10 \\
\\
6 \\
\hline
2176
\end{array}
$$

You do not have to do anything with the remainder, because the problem asked you to be accurate only to the nearest hundredth. If the remainder is more than half of the divisor, then the digit in the divisor that is farthest to the right is increased by one. When the remainder is exactly half of the divisor, it is common to add one to the rightmost digit of the divisor if doing so will make it an *even number* (number that can be divided by two without a remainder).

Short division

When dividing by a one-digit number such as 7, you can do some of the work in long division without writing it down. Division of this kind, which is usually done in the mind rather than on paper, is called *short division.* The method is the same as in long division, but you do the work mentally.

Long Division		*Short Division*
$\dfrac{212}{4\overline{)849}}$		212 R(emainder) 1
-800	200	$4\overline{)849}$
$\overline{49}$		
-40	10	
$\overline{9}$		
-8	2	
$\overline{1}$	212	

The only difference between these two examples is that in short division you do the work mentally and indicate the remainder next to the quotient. The letter *R* is often used to mean *Remainder.* In this example, you first see that you can subtract two hundred 4's from 849. You write the 2 in the 100's place over the 8 in the dividend. Next, you can subtract ten 4's from the remaining 49. You write the 1 in the 10's place over the 4 in the dividend. Finally, you can subtract two 4's from the remaining 9. You write the 2 in the 1's place over the 9 in the dividend. You show the remainder to the right of the quotient.

In more difficult problems in short division, you must use a new device. The problem $415 \div 7$ will show this.

$$\dfrac{5}{7\overline{)415}}$$

In solving this problem, your first step is to subtract fifty 7's or 350, which is thirty-five 10's. Write the 5 (for 50 or five 10's) over the 1 in the dividend. You do the subtraction mentally. Thirty-five 10's subtracted from forty-one 10's is six 10's. You write a little 6 to the left of the 5 in the dividend.

$$\dfrac{5}{7\overline{)41^65}}$$

Now you are dividing six 10's and 5, or 65, by 7. You can subtract nine 7's or 63 from 65, leaving a remainder of 2.

$$\dfrac{5\ 9}{7\overline{)41^65}} \qquad \text{R 2} \qquad \text{or } 59\tfrac{2}{7}$$

It is useful to see how this process is derived from long division.

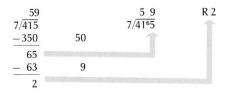

Another example is $7,536 \div 9$. As in the case of long division, you must decide how many 9's you can subtract at one time.

$$\dfrac{8\ 3\ 7}{9\overline{)75^33^66}} \qquad \text{R 3} \qquad \text{or } 837\tfrac{3}{9} \text{ or } 837\tfrac{1}{3}$$

First, you subtract eight hundred 9's, or 7,200. You write the 8 (for eight 100's or 800) over the 5 in the dividend. Mentally you subtract 72 (hundreds) from 75 (hundreds): $75 - 72 = 3$. You write a little 3 to the left of the 3 in the dividend to keep the three 100's in the work. From this new figure of 336, you can subtract thirty 9's or 270. You write the 3 for the thirty 9's over the 3 in the dividend. Next, $33 - 27 = 6$. You write a little 6 to the left of the 6 in the dividend to keep the six 10's in the work. From this new figure of 66, you can subtract seven 9's, or 63. You write the 7 for the seven 9's over the 6 in the dividend. Finally, $66 - 63 = 3$. You indicate the remainder of 3 to the right of the quotient. After you have had some practice, you will be able to leave out the little numbers as reminders of figures that must be included in the work. You will soon be able to remember these numbers in your head.

How to check division

You will be wise to check the answer to a division problem to be sure you have solved it correctly.

Rounding off. One way to check is to see whether or not the quotient is a sensible answer. You can estimate a quotient by rounding off the dividend and divisor. To estimate the quotient of $158 \div 76$, you can round off 158 to 160 and 76 to 80. Because $160 \div 80 = 2$, the quotient of $158 \div 76$ should be about 2. To estimate the quotient of $5,124 \div 36$, you can round off 5,124 to 5,000 and 36 to 50. You can see that $5,000 \div 50 = 100$, and $5,000 \div 25 = 200$. Thus, the quotient of $5,124 \div 36$ should be somewhere between 100 and 200. Estimating the quotient will help you decide whether your answer is sensible.

Checking by multiplication. Another way of checking a quotient is to multiply the quotient by the divisor to see if the product is the dividend. If you have multiplied correctly, this method will catch any error. This is because multiplication is the opposite of division.

$\dfrac{13}{24\overline{)312}}$		$\begin{array}{r} 13 \\ \times 24 \\ \hline 52 \\ 26 \\ \hline 312 \end{array}$

The next example shows how to use the remainder in checking by multiplication:

$\dfrac{42}{21\overline{)889}}$ R 7	$\begin{array}{r} 42 \\ \times 21 \\ \hline 42 \\ 84 \\ \hline 882 \\ +\ 7 \\ \hline 889 \end{array}$ R

The quotient is multiplied by the divisor, and the remainder is added to the product.

Four key division ideas

Here are four important rules to remember for solving division problems.

1. Remember that division means breaking up a number into smaller equal groups. The divisor can show the size of these groups or the number of groups.

2. Learn the division facts so well that you do not have to stop and figure them out each time. You will use the division facts constantly in everyday arithmetic, and will need to know them to divide larger numbers.

3. Remember the method for dividing larger numbers used in long division. In long division, subtract the divisor from the dividend as many times as possible in a single step. In this way, you can reduce the number of steps in long division.

4. Always check the answer after finishing a division problem. You can do this by estimating or by multiplying the quotient by the divisor and adding any remainder.

Fun with division

Space is a game played with cards much like those used in bingo. Each card has a square drawn on it. The square is subdivided into 25 smaller squares. The letters S P A C E are written across the top of the card. The squares are filled in with any arrangement of the numerals from 1 to 9. Each square has one number, except the one in the center which is marked F for "free." Each card should have a different pattern of numerals on it. Each player has a card and a set of small markers. The leader of the game calls out questions on the division facts, for example, "Under A, the 4's in 20." There are five 4's in 20. If the players have the number 5 under A on their card, they cover the number. The first player to completely cover all numbers in a row, a column, or a diagonal calls out "Space!" and wins the game. The leader keeps a record of the division facts called and uses this record to check the winner's card. For a new game, exchange the cards among the players.

S	P	A	C	E
2	1	3	4	5
3	4	5	5	3
5	6	F	6	4
6	8	6	7	6
8	9	8	9	8

Divide-down is an arithmetic version of a spelldown. The players are divided into two teams. Each player is asked one of the division facts, such as "how many 6's in 42?" If the players answer correctly, they stay in the game. If they miss, they must leave the game. When all the members of one team have missed, the other team is declared the winner.   Nadine L. Verderber

Related articles in *World Book* include:

Addition	Fraction
Algebra (Division)	Multiplication
Arithmetic	Numeration systems
Decimal system	Subtraction

Outline

I. **Learning to divide**
    A. Writing division   B. Division facts
II. **Long division**
    A. Remainders in division
    B. Division of decimal fractions
III. **Short division**
IV. **How to check division**
    A. Rounding off   B. Checking by multiplication
V. **Four key division ideas**
VI. **Fun with division**

Practice division examples

1. $4\overline{)56}$	4. $6\overline{)522}$	7. $3\overline{)1008}$	10. $47\overline{)6281}$	13. $3.14\overline{)25.60}$
2. $7\overline{)105}$	5. $9\overline{)387}$	8. $8\overline{)984}$	11. $326\overline{)10457}$	14. $.06\overline{)9.87}$
3. $5\overline{)625}$	6. $2\overline{)1146}$	9. $23\overline{)483}$	12. $29\overline{)1201}$	15. $1.26\overline{).00882}$

16. Miss Smith's class at school is going to visit the local newspaper. Some of the mothers have offered to drive. There are 35 children in the class, and each car can take 5 children. How many cars will be needed for the trip?

17. A certain kind of candy bar costs 6¢ each. How many of these candy bars can Sue buy with 48¢?

18. There are 7 days in a week. How many weeks are there in one year (365 days)?

19. Four boys wish to share equally 64 pieces of candy. How many pieces should each boy get?

20. Tom rides his bicycle at a speed of 6 miles an hour. At this rate, how many hours will it take him to ride 15 miles?

21. Jane's class in school wants to buy some sketchbooks that cost 23¢ each. Her class has $5.85 to spend for books. How many sketchbooks can Jane's class buy?

22. An airplane travels at the rate of 565 kilometers an hour. How long will it take to fly 1,320 kilometers?

23. Bill and his father went on a trip in their car. They traveled 613.9 kilometers in 10 hours, 18 minutes. What was their average rate of speed?

24. Mary's mother rents a house for $2,520 a year. How much rent would she have to pay for one month?

Answers to the division examples

1. 14	5. 43	9. 21	13. 8.15	17. 8 bars	21. 25 books and 10¢ left
2. 15	6. 573	10. 133 R 30	14. 164.5	18. 52 weeks and 1 day	22. 2 hrs. and about 20 min.
3. 125	7. 336	11. 32 R 25	15. .007	19. 16 pieces	23. 59.6 kilometers an hour
4. 87	8. 123	12. 41 R 12	16. 7 cars	20. $2\frac{1}{2}$ hours	24. $210 a month

Divorce is the legal ending of a marriage. The laws of most nations, including the United States and Canada, permit divorce only under certain circumstances. Divorce is restricted chiefly because it breaks up a family, the basic unit of society. Some countries, including Ireland and the Philippines, prohibit divorce.

Most men and women who seek a divorce do so because they cannot solve certain problems in their marriage. Such problems may include differences in goals, financial difficulties, or a poor sexual relationship.

In the United States, a person seeking a divorce generally must appear in court to explain why he or she wants to end the marriage. A judge then decides whether to grant a divorce. A few states prohibit remarriage for a certain period after a divorce. But in general, a man and woman may marry again—each other or someone else—after their divorce becomes final.

Divorce differs from *annulment,* in which a court declares that a marriage has been invalid from its beginning. A person whose marriage has been annulled may remarry. Divorce also differs from *legal separation,* in which a court authorizes a husband and wife to live apart. *Spouses* (a husband and wife) who are legally separated may not remarry.

Divorce is a sizable problem in the United States and many other countries. Experts estimate that about 50 per cent of all U.S. marriages that took place in the 1970's are likely to end in divorce. In more than half these divorces, the couple has children under 18 years old. About a fifth of the children in the United States live with only one parent. Divorce affects many young children deeply. But many experts believe that living with one parent is less harmful to a child than living with both parents in an unhappy environment.

Most divorced men and women remarry, and many such marriages are successful. However, second marriages present special problems of adjustment, especially for couples who have children from a former marriage. Families that include children from one or more previous marriages are called *stepfamilies* or *reconstituted families.* Such families have become more and more common as the divorce rate rises.

The first written divorce regulations were incorporated in the ancient Babylonian *Code of Hammurabi.* Many early societies permitted only the husband to get a divorce. The early Christians taught that marriage was permanent until death, and they abolished divorce in the areas they governed. They also established special church courts to deal with marriage matters. Beginning in the A.D. 1500's, Protestant reformers successfully worked to have matters of marriage and divorce placed under government jurisdiction.

Divorce rarely occurred in the American Colonies. Some colonies made no provision for divorce at all. But by the mid-1800's, almost every state had a divorce law. Today, the U.S. divorce rate is about 16 times as high as it was in 1867, the first year for which the Bureau of the Census published divorce figures. This article deals mainly with divorce in the United States.

Kinds of divorce

Each state of the United States has its own divorce laws. But all the states recognize a divorce granted by the state in which one or both of the spouses are legal residents. State laws set forth the *grounds for divorce*—that is, the reasons for which a divorce may be granted. Depending on the kind of grounds, a divorce can be classified as a *fault divorce* or a *no-fault divorce.*

Fault divorce. Courts traditionally have granted divorces chiefly on *fault grounds.* These grounds vary, but the most common ones are adultery, alcoholism, desertion, drug addiction, failure to support, imprisonment for felony, and mental or physical cruelty.

A person seeking a divorce on a fault ground must prove that his or her spouse committed the fault. For example, a woman seeking a divorce on the ground of desertion must prove that her husband deserted her. The husband may *contest* (argue against) the divorce action. Many divorces are uncontested. If the wife's proof is accepted, the judge grants her a divorce. But if the husband can prove that his wife consented to or encouraged his action, the judge may refuse to grant a divorce. The judge also may rule against the wife if the husband can prove that she committed a legal fault.

No-fault divorce. A person seeking a divorce on a *no-fault ground* does not try to prove that the spouse committed a wrong. The person simply testifies that their marriage has failed. In many cases, the judge grants a divorce even if the person's spouse objects.

In 1969, California became the first state to enact a no-fault divorce law. The California law provides only two grounds for divorce. These grounds are (1) *irreconcilable differences*—that is, disagreements that cannot be settled and have led to the breakdown of the marriage; or (2) the incurable insanity of one spouse. Generally, a person may not tell the judge about any misconduct of the spouse.

Some states have replaced all traditional grounds for divorce with the single no-fault ground of marriage breakdown. Others have added this to their traditional grounds. Several states allow a couple to obtain a divorce on the ground that they have been separated for a certain period. Some states grant divorce on the ground of *incompatibility* (being unable to get along together).

Arguments for no-fault divorce. People who favor no-fault divorce argue that many marriage failures result from causes other than one spouse's misconduct. Therefore, they declare, a divorce should be granted for reasons other than a fault. In addition, these people believe that relations between spouses remain friendlier in no-fault cases than in fault cases.

Supporters of no-fault laws also point out that traditional divorce laws lead many couples to lie in court. For example, a couple may want a divorce because they cannot get along. But they live in a state that grants divorces only on a few fault grounds. To obtain a divorce, the couple might lie to the judge that one spouse has been physically cruel to the other.

A related argument for no-fault laws is that traditional divorce laws lead some people to seek a divorce in another state. For example, a person who lives in a traditional divorce state may go to a no-fault divorce state that has a short residency requirement. After living in this state for the required period, the person might falsely claim to be a permanent resident. The person would then obtain a divorce and return to his or her own state. If the spouse disputes the validity of the divorce, a court may decide that residence was not truly

Annual divorce rate in the United States

Rate

per 1,000 married females ———
per 1,000 total population ———

1989: 21.0

1900: 4.1

1989: 4.7

1900: 0.7

Year	Divorces	Per 1,000 total population	Per 1,000 married females
1900	56,000	0.7	4.1
1905	68,000	0.8	—
1910	83,000	0.9	4.7
1915	104,000	1.0	—
1920	171,000	1.6	8.2
1925	175,000	1.5	—
1930	196,000	1.6	7.5
1935	218,000	1.7	7.8
1940	264,000	2.0	8.8
1945	485,000	3.5	14.4
1950	385,000	2.6	10.3
1955	377,000	2.3	9.3
1960	393,000	2.2	9.2
1965	479,000	2.5	10.6
1970	708,000	3.5	14.9
1975	1,036,000	4.8	20.3
1980	1,189,000	5.2	22.6
1985	1,187,000	5.0	21.7
1989	1,163,000	4.7	21.0

Sources: National Center for Health Statistics; U.S. Bureau of the Census.

established in the state that granted the divorce. As more states liberalize their laws, fewer people seek a divorce in such a state as Nevada, which has a residency requirement of only six weeks.

Arguments against no-fault divorce. Some people oppose no-fault divorces because they believe such divorces can be obtained too easily. They fear that judges may grant a divorce to anyone who says the marriage has broken down, whether it actually has or not. Others believe restrictions should be added to no-fault laws to prevent premature or unnecessary divorces. In some states, courts direct couples planning divorce to consult a marriage counselor. Some states require a waiting period to give a couple time to reconsider their decision.

The divorce process may be simpler under no-fault laws than under fault laws. Therefore, in some no-fault states, some couples can obtain a divorce without hiring lawyers. This method of obtaining a divorce is sometimes called *do-it-yourself divorce.* Some judges oppose this type of divorce because they believe a lawyer is needed to protect the rights of spouses and children.

Divorce provisions

A husband and wife planning a divorce must make arrangements for alimony, child custody and support, and division of their property. They may reach agreement on these arrangements through their lawyers. In some states, courts offer divorce counseling to help couples resolve disagreements. If the judge considers the agreement fair, the judge approves it. If the spouses cannot agree, the judge decides on the arrangements.

Financial arrangements. In the past, the judge ordered many divorced men to pay considerable alimony. They also had to give up some of their property and bear most of the responsibility for supporting their children. There were two chief reasons for this situation. First, large numbers of divorced women had no job outside the home and needed money to support themselves and their children. Second, traditional fault laws provided that the "guilty" spouse could not receive alimony. In many cases, the husband was the legally guilty spouse because his wife filed for the divorce, even though both might have wanted it.

Today, courts base their decisions on financial arrangements primarily on the financial condition of each spouse. Judges realize that many women have the qualifications to work outside the home and need not be fully supported by their former husband. Therefore, if both spouses can earn enough income to support themselves, the court may order that no alimony be paid. If the wife has a higher income than her husband, she may have to pay alimony to him. In addition, the parents may share responsibility for child support.

The court may also divide a couple's property on the basis of financial circumstances. Under the *community property* laws of a few states, property acquired during a marriage belongs equally to both spouses. This property is divided equally in most cases.

Child custody arrangements. In the early and mid-1900's, judges granted custody of the children to the wife almost automatically in the majority of divorce cases. They believed that children should not be separated from the mother. But today, many judges realize that some children might be better off living with the father. Therefore, the court may grant custody to either parent. The judge also determines each parent's rights to visit the children. The judge may ask the children with which parent they would prefer to live.

Some divorced parents return to court several times because one or both of them wants to challenge the child custody decision. If the court changes its decision, the children may have to leave the home of one parent and move in with the other. Such a move can harm children emotionally. As a result, some courts have become reluctant to move children unless they are in danger.

The U.S. divorce rate

The divorce rate is higher in the United States than in almost any other country. Experts have suggested many reasons for this high rate. (1) Divorce is more socially acceptable than ever before. (2) Many people expect more of marriage than earlier generations did, and so they may be more easily disappointed. (3) More high-paying jobs are open to women. These opportunities have made wives less dependent economically on their husbands than women used to be. (4) Changes in divorce laws have made divorce easier to obtain.

In general, cities have a higher divorce rate than rural areas. The rate also varies among different states and regions, partly because divorce laws and court practices differ. But the rates probably also differ because of variances in the cultural, economic, racial, and religious composition of the population. In general, people with nonprofessional jobs and those with low incomes have a higher divorce rate than people with professional jobs and those with high incomes. But one nonprofessional group—farmers—has an extremely low divorce rate.

Most studies show that black couples have a higher divorce rate than white couples. Mixed marriages involving a black and a white apparently have about the same divorce rate as other marriages.

Of the three major religious groups in the United States, Roman Catholics have the lowest divorce rate and Protestants the highest. The Catholic Church holds that valid marriages cannot be dissolved. It allows its members to get a civil divorce to solve financial and child custody problems. But it does not believe such a divorce gives the right to remarry. If the church has annulled a marriage by declaring it invalid, the people involved are once again free to marry (see **Annulment**). Judaism and most Protestant groups permit divorce. Some surveys show that Catholic-Protestant couples and Christian-Jewish couples have a higher divorce rate than couples of the same religion. But one study showed no difference in the divorce rate of Catholic-Protestant couples.   Carlfred B. Broderick

Related articles in *World Book* include:

Abandonment	Alimony	Desertion
Alienation of affections	Community property	Marriage

See also *Marriage and divorce* in the Research Guide/Index, Volume 22, for a *Reading and Study Guide*.

Additional resources

Cherlin, Andrew J. *Marriage, Divorce, Remarriage.* Harvard, 1981.
Friedman, James T. *The Divorce Handbook: Your Basic Guide to Divorce.* Rev. ed. Random House, 1984.

Dix, Dorothea Lynde (1802-1887), led the drive to build state hospitals for the mentally ill in the United States. She also improved prison conditions. She traveled through the United States and Europe for this cause until she was 80. She gained the support of wealthy people, and of such distinguished educators and statesmen as Horace Mann and Charles Sumner.

Dix was born in Hampden, Maine, but grew up in Massachusetts. She visited a Massachusetts house of correction in 1841, and was shocked by the treatment of the mentally ill. She asked the legislature to provide better care, and

Library of Congress
Dorothea Dix

started the reform in that state. During the Civil War (1861-1865), she was superintendent of the U.S. Army nurses.   Audrey B. Davis

Dixie is the name of a famous song especially popular in the South. Daniel D. Emmett, member of a minstrel-show company, wrote the song in 1859 in New York City. He intended it to be a closing number because it permitted a parade of the entire company. The song became an immediate hit. Many publishers printed their own versions. The original first stanza was:

> I wish I was in de land ob cotton,
> Old times dar am not forgotten,
> Look away! Look away! Look away! Dixie Land.

When Abraham Lincoln ran for the presidency in 1860, "Dixie" was used as a campaign song against him. Five years later, after the Civil War, he asked a band at the White House to play "Dixie."   Charles B. Righter

Dixie, also called Dixieland, is a name often given to the southern part of the United States. There are different explanations for this name. A Louisiana bank once printed $10 bills bearing the French word *dix,* which means *ten.* According to one story, people called Louisiana "Dix's Land," and then shortened it to Dixie. In time, *Dixie* came to mean the entire South. In another story, a slaveowner named Dixie, or Dixy, was kind to his slaves. "Dixie's Land" became known as a happy, comfortable place to live. Gradually, the term came to refer to the South.   Ray Allen Billington

Dixie Highway is a series of scenic automobile roads that lead from the Straits of Mackinac, at the northern tip of Lake Michigan, to Miami, near the southern end of the peninsula of Florida. It has two main routes, an east route and a west route. The east route passes through Detroit, Mich.; Cincinnati, Ohio; and Jacksonville, Fla. The west route passes through South Bend, Ind.; Louisville, Ky.; and Atlanta, Ga.

Carl G. Fisher, a pioneer automobile manufacturer, originated the idea of the Dixie Highway to encourage the building of better main roads. Work on the highway began in 1915.   Bruce E. Seely

Dixiecrat Party is the nickname for the States' Rights Democratic Party. In the national election of 1948, many Southern Democrats objected to their party's civil rights program. They formed the Dixiecrat Party and nominated Strom Thurmond for President and Fielding L. Wright for Vice President. The party won the electoral votes of four Southern states (see **Electoral College** [table]).   Donald R. McCoy

Dixon, Joseph (1799-1869), was an American inventor and manufacturer. He founded a factory to make lead pencils and stove polish from graphite at Salem, Mass., in 1827. In 1832, he patented a process of using colored inks to prevent counterfeiting. Dixon also patented and introduced graphite crucibles for making pottery and steel. He was born in Marblehead, Mass.

Dizziness is a condition in which people feel that their surroundings are whirling about, or that they are falling. This type of dizziness is called *vertigo.* Another type of dizziness is characterized by light-headedness, the sensation that comes before fainting. It causes a person to stagger or fall. Often there is nausea and vomiting. Brief periods during which there is a reduced flow of blood to the brain may cause dizziness. It may also be caused by changes in the pressure of the fluid in the semicircular canals of the inner ear. Dizziness often accompanies such disorders as anemia, epilepsy, heart trouble, and diseases of the inner ear. See also **Ear** (Disturbances of the organs of balance).   Richard D. Penn

Djakarta. See Jakarta.

Kay Honkanen

Djibouti, the capital of the country of Djibouti, is the home of more than half of the nation's people. This photograph shows people walking in a public square next to the city's main *mosque* (Muslim house of worship).

Djibouti, *jih BOO tee,* is a small country in eastern Africa. It lies on the western shore of the Gulf of Aden. The gulf and the Red Sea and Suez Canal to the north link the Indian Ocean and the Mediterranean Sea. Djibouti's location has helped make the country's capital, also called Djibouti, a major port. The location also has potential strategic importance. Ships travel freely past Djibouti's coast. But it would be possible for a powerful nation that gained possession of the area to control the passage of vessels traveling between the Indian Ocean and the Mediterranean.

Djibouti is an extremely poor country with almost no natural resources. In 1977, it gained independence from France, which had ruled the area since the late 1800's. The French originally called Djibouti *French Somaliland,* but in 1967 they renamed it the *French Territory of the Afars and Issas.*

Government. Djibouti is a democratic republic. The people elect the nation's legislature, which is called the National Assembly and is made up of 65 members. The National Assembly elects Djibouti's president, who heads the government.

People. Djibouti has about 418,000 people. Two ethnic groups, the *Afars* and the *Issas,* make up most of the country's population. The Afars live in the north and west. The Issas, a Somali people, live in the south. Djibouti also has about 6,000 French and about 3,000 Arab residents.

The Afars and the Issas have traditionally been nomads. Today, many of them still wander over the desolate countryside with herds of goats, sheep, camels, and cattle. Scorching heat, a scarcity of water, and a shortage of grazing lands make life difficult for the nomads. As a result, almost 250,000 Afars and Issas now live in the city of Djibouti. But poverty and an unemployment rate as high as 80 per cent plague the people who live in the capital. Many people throughout the country chew *khat* (also spelled *kat* or *qat*). Khat is a leaf that produces a feeling of well-being when it is chewed. Large numbers of workers spend up to 50 per cent of their income on khat.

The official language of Djibouti is Arabic, but most of the people speak Afar or Somali. A large majority of the people are Muslims. Educational opportunities are limited in Djibouti, and only about 10 per cent of the population can read and write.

Land and climate. The terrain of Djibouti is extremely desolate. A barren plain stretches along the country's coast. Farther inland is a mountain range with several peaks that rise more than 5,000 feet (1,500 meters) above sea level. A rugged plateau lies beyond the

WORLD BOOK map

Djibouti

International boundary
Road
Railroad
✳	National capital
•	Other town
+	Elevation above sea level

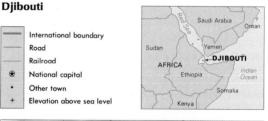

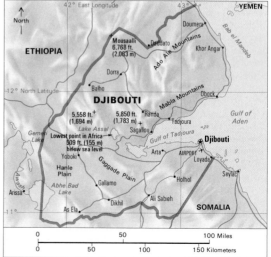

Facts in brief

Capital: Djibouti (city).
Official language: Arabic.
Area: 8,958 sq. mi. (23,200 km²). *Greatest distances*—east-west, 110 mi. (177 km); north-south, 125 mi. (201 km). *Coastline*—152 mi. (245 km).
Elevation: *Highest*—Mousaalli, 6,768 ft. (2,063 m) above sea level. *Lowest*—Lake Assal, 509 ft. (155 m) below sea level.
Population: *Estimated 1991 population*—418,000; density, 47 persons per sq. mi. (18 per km²); distribution, 81 per cent urban, 19 per cent rural. *1961 census*—81,000. *Estimated 1996 population*—388,000.
Chief products: Hides, skins.
Flag: The flag has a blue horizontal stripe at the top, a green horizontal stripe at the bottom, and a red star on a white triangle near the staff. Adopted in 1977. See Flag (picture: Flags of Africa).
Money: *Basic unit*—Djibouti franc.

mountains. Vegetation is scarce throughout the country.

Djibouti, which has been called "a valley of hell," has one of the hottest and driest climates in the world. The temperature averages 85° F. (29° C), and it sometimes rises above 107° F. (42° C) from May to October. The country receives less than 5 inches (13 centimeters) of rain annually.

Economy. Djibouti is an extremely poor and under-developed country. It has no natural resources of any importance and no industry except for two soft-drink plants. Djibouti's only agricultural activity is livestock herding. The nation's economy is based almost entirely on the port of the capital and a railroad that links it with Addis Ababa, Ethiopia. Djibouti serves as a major port for Ethiopian trade. The country has a good harbor and an international airport.

History. People have lived in what is now Djibouti since prehistoric times. During the A.D. 800's, missionaries from Arabia converted the Afars who inhabited the area to Islam. The Afars then established several Islamic states, which fought a series of wars with Christian Ethiopia from the 1200's through the early 1600's. By the 1800's, the Issas had taken over a large part of the Afars' grazing lands, and hostility between the two groups was growing.

France purchased the Afar port of Obock in 1862 and established a coaling station for French ships there in 1881. The French signed agreements in 1884 with the Afar sultans of Obock and nearby Tadjoura. In 1888, the French occupied the uninhabited area that eventually became the city of Djibouti. They then united various small possessions in the area into a single territory and named it French Somaliland.

The French developed good relations with Emperor Menelik II of Ethiopia, who decided to have a railway built from his capital, Addis Ababa, to the city of Djibouti. In 1897, he made Djibouti the official port for Ethiopian trade. The city grew rapidly during the following years, but little development occurred elsewhere in the territory.

After World War II ended in 1945, the Issas and some other groups in French Somaliland began to demand independence from France. However, the French kept these groups under control. Against the opposition of the Issas, the territory voted in 1958 to join the French Community. This organization is an economic and cultural association that links France and its territories.

In 1967, French Somaliland voted to continue its association with France and was renamed the French Territory of the Afars and Issas. But opposition to French rule grew during the 1970's, when the Issa population increased rapidly. In May 1977, the people voted overwhelmingly for independence. As a result, the territory became the independent nation of Djibouti on June 27, 1977.   Richard Pankhurst

See also **Djibouti** (city).

Djibouti, *jih BOO tee* (pop. 290,000), is the capital of Djibouti, a country in eastern Africa. More than half of the nation's people live in the city of Djibouti. The city lies on the Gulf of Aden and has one of the best ports on the eastern coast of Africa (see **Djibouti** [map]). A railroad connects Djibouti with Addis Ababa, the capital of Ethiopia, and many Ethiopian exports and imports pass through Djibouti's harbor.

In 1888, France took control of the Djibouti area, which was then uninhabited. The French founded the city that same year. In 1896, they made it the capital of French Somaliland (now the country of Djibouti). The French developed the city as a well-planned colonial capital with many fine public and commercial buildings. The population of Djibouti has grown rapidly since 1945, and large slums have developed in the city.

Richard Pankhurst

Djugashvili, Iosif. See Stalin, Joseph.

DMSO is a controversial drug used to treat such conditions as arthritis, bursitis, and sprains. When applied externally, the drug is quickly absorbed through the skin into the bloodstream. Supporters of DMSO claim it is remarkably effective in relieving pain and reducing inflammation. But the United States Food and Drug Administration (FDA) has not approved the drug for external use on human beings. The FDA does permit the drug to be used internally to treat a bladder condition called *interstitial cystitis.*

DMSO stands for *dimethyl sulfoxide,* a compound obtained as a by-product of paper manufacturing. DMSO has long been used as an industrial solvent, but scientists did not discover its medicinal properties until the early 1960's. Thousands of people used DMSO until 1965, when the FDA banned it as a human drug. The FDA based its decision on reports that the drug caused eye damage in experiments with laboratory animals. Although eye damage has not been observed in people treated with DMSO, the drug has caused minor side effects, such as garlic-smelling breath, headaches, nausea, and skin rashes.

The FDA later allowed limited testing of DMSO to resume. The drug was approved for cystitis in 1978. However, many Americans obtain and use DMSO for other ailments. Some people treat themselves with industrial DMSO, though it may contain harmful impurities.

Eugene M. Johnson, Jr.

DNA. See Nucleic acid; Heredity (The chemical basis of heredity); **Cell** (The nucleus; The 1900's; The code of life).

DNA fingerprinting, also known as *DNA profiling,* is a technique used to identify criminals through the analysis of genetic material. The technique is also used to settle *paternity* disputes—that is, to determine the biological father of a child. The genetic material used in DNA fingerprinting, called *deoxyribonucleic acid* (DNA), is found in most cells. The technique is based on the theory that it is extremely unlikely that two people would possess identical DNA.

DNA fingerprinting is used to analyze DNA found in such biological materials as blood, semen, bone, and hair. The most common type of DNA fingerprinting is called *restriction fragment length polymorphism* (RFLP). In RFLP, DNA is extracted from biological material found at the scene of a crime. Technicians use a chemical called a *restriction enzyme* to divide the DNA into fragments. The fragments are then separated according to size by a laboratory technique called *electrophoresis* (see **Electrophoresis**). The separated fragments form a pattern of dozens of parallel bands that reflect the composition of the DNA. In principle, the pattern produced will always be the same for the same person. It is estimated that there are more than 10 billion billion, or 10^{19}, possible patterns. Thus, many experts believe it is virtually impossible that the DNA pattern of one person would match that of another.

However, some critics of DNA fingerprinting believe that the technique is not yet reliable enough to be used as evidence in a court of law. They claim that patterns produced in DNA fingerprinting can stretch and shift, making absolute identification difficult or even impossible.   John I. Thornton

Dnepr River, *DNYEH puhr,* is the second longest river in the European section of the Soviet Union. Only the Volga is longer. The Dnepr, also spelled *Dnieper* (pronounced *NEE puhr*), rises in the Valdai Hills, near the city of Smolensk. It flows southward for 1,400 miles (2,200 kilometers) through one of the Soviet Union's most important economic regions. It empties into the Black Sea. Most of the river's course is in the Ukraine, one of the republics of the Soviet Union. Kiev, Ukraine's capital, lies on the river. The northern part of the Dnepr flows through a forested area, and the southern part through farmland and an industrialized region. The Dnepr drains an area of about 195,000 square miles (504,000 square kilometers). For the location of the Dnepr River, see **Union of Soviet Socialist Republics** (terrain map).

The construction of dams and reservoirs has deepened the Dnepr and removed obstacles caused by rapids. As a result, the river is navigable for most of its course. One of the largest dams is the Dneproges Dam (see **Dneproges Dam**). The Dnepr is an important route for the transportation of cargo, including coal and grain from Ukraine and timber from the north. Important tributaries of the Dnepr include the Berezina, Desna, Ingulets, Pripyat, and Psel rivers. Canals connect the Dnepr with several rivers that empty into the Baltic Sea, to the northwest.   Leszek A. Kosinski

Dneproges Dam, *DNYEH prah GEHS,* is a large concrete dam in the Soviet Union. It is located 200 miles (320 kilometers) from the mouth of the Dnepr River. The dam provides hydroelectric power for most of the mines and industries in the southern part of the Soviet Union. The dam is 5,000 feet (1,500 meters) long and 200 feet (61 meters) high, and was completed in 1932. When the Germans invaded Ukraine in 1941, the Soviets blew up the dam and the power plant. They rebuilt both of them after the war. Dneproges Dam holds back 1,600,000 cubic yards (1,220,000 cubic meters) of water.

Its power plant can generate 650,000 kilowatts of electricity.   T. W. Mermel

Dnepropetrovsk, *NEHP roh pih TRAWFSK* (pop. 1,140,000), is a major industrial city in Ukraine, one of the 15 republics of the Soviet Union. It lies in southeastern Ukraine, on the Dnepr River. For the location of Dnepropetrovsk, see **Union of Soviet Socialist Republics** (political map).

Dnepropetrovsk is situated near the Donbas coal fields, the Krivoy Rog iron mines, and the Nikopol manganese mines. These rich mineral resources supply raw materials for the city's huge iron and steel industry. Building materials, chemicals, food products, and heavy machinery are also produced in the city. Dnepropetrovsk has an airport and a large harbor.

Dnepropetrovsk is the home of a state university and a number of specialized technical schools. Shevchenko Park, named for the Ukrainian patriot and poet Taras Shevchenko, is a popular recreation area.

Dnepropetrovsk was founded by Prince Gregory Potemkin of Russia in 1776. At that time, the city was called Ekaterinoslav. It took its present name in 1926.   Jaroslaw Bilocerkowycz

Dnestr River, *DNYEHS tuhr,* also called Dniester, *NEE stuhr,* rises in the Carpathian Mountains in the district of Galicia, in central Europe, and empties into the Black Sea. The Dnestr flows southeast for 875 miles (1,408 kilometers). For much of this distance, it passes through the Soviet Union along the border of Bessarabia. Boats travel the Dnestr to Khotin, a city in western Ukraine.   M. K. Dziewanowski

Doberman pinscher, *DOH buhr muhn PIHN shuhr,* is a breed of dog that originated in Germany. It is named after Louis Dobermann, a German dog breeder. Dobermann first developed the dogs in the late 1800's. Dobermans make good guard dogs and police dogs because of their courage, alertness, and intelligence. They are swift and strong, and their excellent sense of smell enables them to track people. With proper training, Dobermans make affectionate, loyal pets. Most Dobermans have a black coat with rust-colored markings. Some have red, blue, or tan coats. They have short, smooth hair. Most of these dogs have *docked* (cropped) tails

WORLD BOOK photo by Ken Love
The Doberman pinscher is an intelligent watchdog.

and clipped ears. The dogs stand 24 to 28 inches (61 to 71 centimeters) high and weigh from 60 to 75 pounds (25 to 34 kilograms).

Critically reviewed by the Doberman Pinscher Club of America

Dobie, J. Frank (1888-1964), an American author and professor, became famous for his writings on the culture of Texas and the Southwest. In 20 books and hundreds of articles, Dobie collected or retold stories about cowboys, longhorn cattle, and other people and animals of the range country.

James Frank Dobie was born on a ranch in Live Oak County, Texas. For most of the period from 1913 to 1947, he was an English professor at the University of Texas. For many years, Dobie served as secretary and editor of the Texas Folklore Society, which published several of his works. Dobie's first book was *A Vaquero of the Brush Country* (1929), which describes the experiences of a Texas cattleman during pioneer days. Dobie's other works include *Coronado's Children* (1930), *The Longhorns* (1941), *The Mustangs* (1952), and *Tales of Old-Time Texas* (1955).   Arthur R. Huseboe

Dobson fly. See Hellgrammite.

Dock is the water beside a wharf or pier (or between two wharves or piers) in which a ship floats. The term *dock* is also used to mean a wharf or pier. The *wet* dock is a basin with gates to keep in or shut out water, and maintain the same water level while unloading and loading ships. Such docks are used in harbors where the tide rises and falls greatly. See also **Dry dock**.

Wolcott Gibbs, Jr.

Dock is the name of several kinds of plants belonging to the buckwheat family. Three common perennial weeds brought into the United States and Canada belong to this family—*narrow-leaf,* or *yellow,* dock (from the color of the taproot); *sour dock;* and *broadleaf dock.* These weeds infest meadowland, gardens, lawns, and pastures, and are common wayside weeds. They grow from 2 to 4 feet (61 to 122 centimeters) high and have long, large leaves with wavy margins. Their thick, tapering roots are used

E. R. Degginger

The dock plant

medicinally for tonics, astringents, and skin remedies. The leaves of sour dock are eaten as potherbs, or greens, but they may poison animals that have a diet low in calcium. Dock may be controlled with amino triazole sprays. See also **Buckwheat**.

Scientific classification. The dock plants belong to the buckwheat family, Polygonaceae. The narrow-leaf dock is *Rumex crispus.* The broadleaf dock is *R. obtusifolius.* The sour dock is *R. acetosa.*   Louis Pyenson

Doctor. See **Degree, College** (The doctor's degree); **Medicine** (Providing medical care; Careers in medicine).

Doctor Dolittle. See **Lofting, Hugh**.

Doctorfish, one of the surgeonfishes, is a tropical marine fish, found in the East Indies. The doctorfish is grayish-brown to yellow with blue to gray fins. The fish gets its name because it has a sharp erectile spine in a little

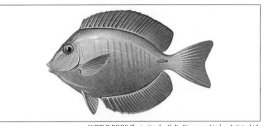

WORLD BOOK illustration by Colin Newman, Linden Artists, Ltd.

The doctorfish lives in the tropical waters of the East Indies. It is grayish-brown to yellow and has blue to gray fins.

groove on each side of the body near the tail. This spine is shaped like a type of knife used by surgeons called a *lancet.*

Scientific classification. The doctorfish is a member of the surgeonfish family, Acanthuridae. It is *Acanthurus bahianus.*

Leonard P. Schultz

Doctorow, E. L. (1931-   ), is an American novelist. His works are noted for their mingling of American history and literary imagination through the interaction of fictional and real-life characters.

Doctorow's first novel, *Welcome to Hard Times* (1960), is set in the late 1800's. It attacks the optimistic belief in the promise of a better life on the Western frontier. *The Book of Daniel* (1971) describes a man's attempt to discover the truth about his parents, who had been executed as Communist spies in the 1950's. *Ragtime* (1975), set in the early 1900's, contrasts economic progress and patriotism with social unrest and inequalities in American life. *Lives of the Poets* (1984) examines the place of the artist in society.

Three of Doctorow's novels are set in the 1930's. *Loon Lake* (1980) tells a "rags to riches" story of a man who is shown to be corrupt. *World's Fair* (1985) is an autobiographical novel about growing up in the Bronx borough of New York City. *Billy Bathgate* (1989) describes a boy's adventures in the gang of a New York City mobster. Edgar Lawrence Doctorow was born in New York City.

Arthur M. Saltzman

Documentary. See **Television** (Commercial television).

Dodd, William Edward (1869-1940), a noted American historian, served as U.S. ambassador to Germany from 1933 to 1937. He resigned in protest against Adolf Hitler's policies, and published the widely read *Ambassador Dodd's Diary*. Dodd made lecture tours in the United States criticizing Nazi Germany. His works include the historical books—*Life of Jefferson Davis, Expansion and Conflict, Statesmen of the Old South,* and *Woodrow Wilson and His Work.*

Dodd was born in Clayton, N.C. He received his Ph.D. degree from the University of Leipzig, Germany. He was a professor of history at Randolph-Macon College in Ashland, Va., and at the University of Chicago.

Eric F. Goldman

Dodder is a destructive weed found over most of the world. It is called a *parasite* because it takes its food from other plants. The dodder grows from seed in the spring and then attaches itself by little suckers to some nearby plant. The root and older part of the stem die, break off, and leave the dodder plant free. Dodder destroys a great deal of alfalfa, clover, and flax.

The stems of the dodder look like yellow, orange, white, and brown threads. The stems twine around other plants and sprawl from one plant to another, forming tangled masses. Dodder flowers are small and white, and they form in dense clusters.

Scientific classification. The dodder plants are members of the morning-glory family, Convolvulaceae. They make up the genus *Cuscuta*.   Arthur Cronquist

See also **Plant** (picture: How nongreen plants get their food).

Dodds, Harold Willis (1889-1980), an American educator, served as president of Princeton University from 1933 to 1957. He stated his educational philosophy in an essay: "We are not put into the world to sit still and know; we are put here to act." He served on the executive board of the United Nations Educational, Scientific and Cultural Organization (UNESCO) in 1946. Dodds was born in Utica, Pa., and was graduated from Grove City (Pa.) College and received his Ph.D. from the University of Pennsylvania. He also taught at Purdue University and Western Reserve University (now Case Western Reserve University).   Douglas Sloan

Dodecanese Islands, *doh DEHK uh NEES,* include about 40 Greek islands and many small reefs in the Aegean Sea. They lie off the southwest coast of Turkey. The islands cover 1,036 square miles (2,682 square kilometers) and have a population of about 145,000. Many of the small islands and reefs are uninhabited. The most important islands are Kalimnos, Karpathos, Kos, Leros, Patmos, Rhodes, and Simi. The chief economic activities include tourism, fishing, sponge fishing, building small boats, farming, and raising sheep and goats. The Dodecanese Islands came under Turkish rule in 1522. Italy took control in 1912 and held the islands until 1947, when they were given to Greece.   John J. Baxevanis

See also **Patmos; Rhodes; Greece** (map).

Dodge, Mary Elizabeth Mapes (1831-1905), an American author, wrote *Hans Brinker, or, The Silver Skates* (1865), a famous children's book about the Netherlands. Within 30 years the book had appeared in more than 100 editions and was translated into six languages. Dodge was recognized as a leader in the field of juvenile literature. She became editor of the magazine *St. Nicholas* when it began in 1873, and got the best authors of the time to contribute to the publication.

She was born in New York City, and grew up in a home that was a center for literary groups. William Cullen Bryant and Horace Greeley were frequent visitors. Her husband died when she was 27, leaving her with two small sons. Because she had to support them, she returned to her father's home in Newark, N.J., and started her literary career.   Jill P. May

Dodge brothers were two pioneers in automobile manufacturing. Both John Francis Dodge (1864-1920) and Horace Elgin Dodge (1868-1920) were born in Niles, Mich.

The Dodge brothers began their business careers making bicycles. In 1901, they opened a machine shop in Detroit. The brothers built parts for the Olds Motor Works and Ford Motor Company.

The Dodge brothers began making their own automobiles in 1914, and produced one of the first American automobiles with an all-steel body. Horace Dodge in-

vented many improvements for automobiles, including an oven for baking enamel on steel bodies. The Dodge Company became part of Chrysler Corporation in 1928.   William L. Bailey

Dodge City, Kans. (pop. 18,001), was a well-known "Wild West" frontier town. It was called the *Cowboy Capital of the World* and, at times, the *Wickedest Little City in the West* and *Queen of Cowtowns.* Dodge City lies on the Arkansas River, in southwestern Kansas (see **Kansas** [political map]). The city is the chief commercial center of the region. It is also a leading beef-slaughtering and meat-packing center. Dodge City is the seat of Ford County, and has a commission government with a city manager. It is the home of St. Mary of the Plains College and Dodge City Community College.

Traders on the Santa Fe Trail traveled through the area in the 1800's. Dodge City was established when the Atchison, Topeka, and Santa Fe Railroad came in 1872. For about 10 years after 1875, it was a major regional shipping point for cattle. Many gunmen lived in Dodge City, and such famous peace officers as Wyatt Earp and Bat Masterson enforced the law. A restoration of Boot Hill and Front Street, the city's old main street, make up a popular tourist attraction. The name *Boot Hill* came from an early cemetery where cowboys and gunmen were buried still wearing their boots.   Lee Finch

See also **Kansas** (picture: Restoration of Front Street).

Dodgson, Charles Lutwidge. See **Carroll, Lewis.**

Dodo, *DOH doh,* is an extinct, flightless bird related to the pigeon. The dodo was about the size of a large turkey. It had short legs, an enormous beak, stubby wings, and a tuftlike tail with curly feathers. The dodo lived on

Illustration by Cyrus Leroy Baldridge; reprinted by permission of Grosset & Dunlap

Mary Dodge's *Hans Brinker, or, The Silver Skates* tells about a Dutch boy, Hans, who competes in an ice skating race. This illustration shows Hans skating with the mayor's daughter.

WORLD BOOK illustration by Trevor Boyer, Linden Artists Ltd.

The dodo had tiny wings that were so small it could not fly. Dodos lived on the island of Mauritius in the Indian Ocean. They have been extinct since about 1680.

the island of Mauritius in the Indian Ocean. It laid a single egg on the ground. Two related species called *solitaires* lived on nearby Reunion and Rodrigues islands.

European sailors killed the birds for food. Pigs and monkeys brought to the island by Portuguese sailors during the 1500's destroyed the eggs and ate the young. The dodo died out about 1680, the Reunion solitaire about 1750, and the Rodrigues solitaire about 1800. Several dodos, and possibly some solitaires, were exhibited alive in Europe and served as models for paintings. The heads and feet of a few dodos are preserved in museums, but the solitaires are known only from pictures,

from accounts written by travelers, and from bones that were found on Reunion and Rodrigues islands.

Scientific classification. The dodo and solitaires belong to the pigeon and dove order, Columbiformes. They are in the dodo and solitaire family, Raphidae. The dodo is *Raphus cucullatus.* The Reunion solitaire is classified as *Raphus solitarius,* and the Rodrigues solitaire as *Pezophaps solitaria.* Alan Feduccia

Dodoma, *DOHD uh мАН* (pop. 45,703), is a city in central Tanzania. In 1973, Tanzanians voted to move the country's capital from the coastal city of Dar es Salaam to Dodoma. The move was scheduled for completion in the 1990's. Dodoma was selected as the new site of the capital primarily because of its central location. For location, see **Tanzania** (map).

Dodoma's business district includes a number of modern commercial buildings. Most of the people live in small brick houses with tin roofs. Dodoma's industries include the manufacturing of bricks, and clay processing. A railroad links Dodoma with Tanzania's east and west coasts, and an airport lies near the city.

Dodoma was a small village when the mainland of what is now Tanzania became a German colony in 1891. In the early 1900's, Great Britain gained control of the colony, and Dodoma became a marketing center. Dodoma's population has more than doubled since the colony gained independence in 1961. L. H. Gann

Doe. See Deer; Goat.

Doenitz, *DAY nihts,* **Karl** (1891-1980), a German admiral, became commander in chief of the German fleet in January 1943, during World War II. Before this appointment, he directed development of the German submarine service. He invented the "wolf pack" technique of submarine warfare to penetrate convoy defenses. With the collapse of Germany in 1945, Adolf Hitler chose Doenitz to succeed him as head of state. Doenitz concluded peace with the Allies.

Doenitz was tried for war crimes in Nuremberg, and he was sentenced to 10 years in prison. He was released in 1956. Doenitz was born in Berlin-Grünau.

Lester B. Mason

Oil painting on canvas; Thomas Gilcrease Institute of American History and Art, Tulsa, Okla.

Dodge City was the scene of many gunfights during the late 1800's. Western artist Charles Marion Russell portrayed one vividly in his painting *When Guns Speak, Death Settles Disputes.*

Dog

Dog is a popular pet throughout the world. At least 12,000 years ago, dogs became the first animals to be tamed. Today, these affectionate and obedient animals can be found almost anywhere there are people to love and serve. About 50 million dogs live as pets in the United States, and about 3 million live in Canada.

Many people recognize only such favorite breeds of dogs as the collie, German shepherd, and poodle. But through careful breeding, human beings have produced hundreds of breeds. Each breed has its own particular abilities and physical features. Some breeds have highly unusual characteristics. For example, the chow chow has a black tongue. The Mexican hairless has no hair except for a small patch on top of its head. The coat of the shar-pei is harsh in texture. A shar-pei puppy's skin is so loose that it appears too large for the dog's body. The basenji, which originated in Africa, is the only dog that cannot bark.

Michael W. Fox, the contributor of this article, is Director of the Institute for the Study of Animal Problems, a division of the Humane Society of the United States. He is also a veterinarian and a psychologist and the author of Understanding Your Dog *and other books on animal behavior.*

Dogs vary greatly in size. The smallest breed is the Chihuahua. On the average, Chihuahuas weigh only about 4 pounds (1.8 kilograms) and stand about 5 inches (13 centimeters) high at the shoulders. The tallest breed is the Irish wolfhound, which may grow 34 inches (86 centimeters) in height. The St. Bernard ranks as the heaviest dog. It weighs as much as 200 pounds (90 kilograms).

Dogs belong to a small family of meat-eating animals that also includes wolves, coyotes, foxes, and jackals. Dogs resemble these animals in body structure and behavior. The dingo of Australia and certain animals that live in other parts of the world are commonly called *wild dogs.* See **Mammal** (picture: Young wild dogs).

Some dogs do important work for people. Dogs are able and willing to learn a wide variety of tasks because they are intelligent and devoted to their owners. Alert watchdogs protect houses and businesses from burglars. Collies, sheepdogs, and some other breeds herd livestock. In some countries, dogs help farmers by hauling vegetables and other produce to market in small carts.

Dogs also use their keen senses to help people. A sharp sense of smell enables beagles and many other hunting dogs to track wild animals. Police rely on the bloodhound's sensitive nose to find criminals and lost people. Law enforcement officers also train German

Some breeds of dogs have extremely unusual characteristics. A shar-pei puppy, *left,* has a wrinkled coat that looks too large for its body. A black tongue is the distinguishing feature of the chow chow, *center.* The puli, *right,* has a coat that becomes tangled into long, ropelike cords.

WORLD BOOK photo by Brent Jones   WORLD BOOK photo   WORLD BOOK photo by Dave G. Wacker

Dogs provide companionship for people of all ages. These children's affectionate friend is a *mongrel* (mixed-breed dog). In general, mongrels have a good disposition and make excellent pets.

WORLD BOOK photo

Specially trained dogs perform many tasks. This German shepherd uses its keen sense of smell to detect drugs being smuggled into the United States.

WORLD BOOK photo

shepherds and other dogs to sniff out illegal drugs and hidden explosives. Guide dogs lead blind people. Other specially trained dogs serve as "ears" for deaf people.

In certain cases, dogs are used in the treatment of emotionally disturbed people. The affection and companionship provided by a dog have helped some patients who failed to respond to any other treatment feel loved and accepted.

Medical researchers use thousands of dogs in experiments every year. In this way, dogs have helped scientists develop new lifesaving drugs and new surgical techniques. However, some people believe that it is cruel to use dogs—as well as other animals—in laboratory experiments.

For hundreds of years, performing dogs have entertained audiences at circuses and in theaters. Highly trained dogs have also starred in many motion pictures and television shows.

The body of a dog

The size, shape, and other characteristics of a dog's body vary widely from breed to breed. But in spite of their differences, all dogs share certain basic physical features.

Coat. Most dogs have two coats—an outer coat of long *guard hairs* and an undercoat of shorter, fluffy hair. The guard hairs protect the dog against rain and snow, and the undercoat keeps the dog warm. Most dogs shed the undercoat in late spring and grow it back in autumn. Dogs also have a number of long, stiff whiskers about the mouth. The whiskers serve as highly sensitive touch organs.

The texture, length, and color of the coat differ greatly among the various breeds. The hair may be curly, as on the poodle, or straight, as on the German shepherd. The collie's coat feels rough, and the Kerry blue terrier's coat is soft. Such breeds as the Afghan hound and the Pekingese have a long, silky coat. The boxer and the whippet have an extremely short coat. The color of the coat may vary even within a breed. For example, a Labrador retriever's coat may be black, yellow, or chocolate-brown.

Body structure is determined mainly by a dog's skeleton. Female dogs have 310 bones. Male dogs have one additional bone, located in the penis. Although all breeds have the same number of bones, the size and shape of the bones differ greatly from breed to breed. For example, the basset hound has very short, thick leg bones. In contrast, the greyhound has unusually long leg bones.

Dogs have four toes on each foot plus an extra thumblike toe called a *dewclaw* on each front foot. Some dogs also have a dewclaw on each hind foot. Dewclaws do not reach the ground. They serve no purpose and can easily be caught on objects and torn. For this reason, a veterinarian should remove the hind dewclaws when a puppy is a few days old. Each of a dog's toes has a blunt toenail, or claw. But unlike cats, dogs cannot pull their claws back. The bottoms of a dog's paws have cushiony pads covered with tough skin.

Some dogs, such as borzois and collies, have an unusually long, narrow skull. The skull shape gives the dogs a long, slender face. Some other breeds, including bulldogs and Pekingeses, have a very short, broad skull, which makes the face look pushed in. Most dogs have a skull shape between these two extremes.

Puppies have 32 temporary teeth, which they begin to lose when they are about 5 months old. Adult dogs have 42 teeth. A dog uses its 12 small front teeth, called *incisors,* to pick up food. The dog tears meat with its 4 large, pointed *canine teeth,* or *fangs.* It uses the 26 other teeth, called the *premolars* and *molars,* to grind and crush food.

Many breeds of dogs have pointed ears that stand straight up. Other breeds have *pendulous* ears, which hang down. Many people have the ears of certain pendulous-eared breeds *cropped* (cut) to make them stand up. Such breeds include Doberman pinschers and miniature schnauzers. Cropping is done at an age when puppies are highly sensitive to pain. Some countries have outlawed cropping as a cruel practice. On terriers and some other breeds, the tail is also *docked* (cut short). Docking is done a few days after birth and so is much less painful than ear cropping.

Body functions of a dog differ only slightly from those of a human being. For example, a dog's heart beats 70 to 120 times per minute. The human heart, on the average, beats 70 to 80 times per minute. A dog's

The sizes of dogs

The Chihuahua is the smallest breed of dog. The St. Bernard is the heaviest breed, and the Irish wolfhound is the tallest. Other breeds of dogs range in size between these extremes. The measurements given for each dog pictured below are the average weight and shoulder height for the breed.

WORLD BOOK illustration by Jean Helmer

Chihuahua
1-6 lb. (0.5-3 kg)
5 in. (13 cm)

Cocker spaniel
22-28 lb. (10-13 kg)
14-15 in. (36-38 cm)

Collie
50-75 lb. (23-34 kg)
22-26 in. (56-66 cm)

St. Bernard
165-200 lb. (75-90 kg)
$25\frac{1}{2}$-30 in. (65-76 cm)

Irish wolfhound
126-145 lb. (57-66 kg)
32-34 in. (81-86 cm)

The body of a dog

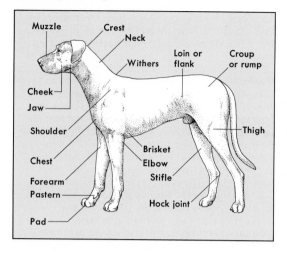

Muzzle · Crest · Neck · Withers · Loin or flank · Croup or rump · Cheek · Jaw · Shoulder · Thigh · Chest · Brisket · Elbow · Stifle · Forearm · Pastern · Hock joint · Pad

The skeleton of a dog

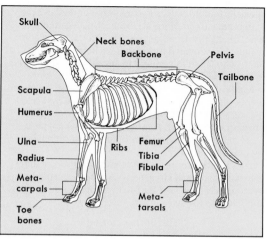

Skull · Neck bones · Backbone · Pelvis · Tailbone · Scapula · Humerus · Ulna · Radius · Ribs · Femur · Tibia · Fibula · Meta-carpals · Meta-tarsals · Toe bones

WORLD BOOK illustrations by Jean Helmer

normal body temperature is 101.5° F. (38.6° C), only a little higher than a person's normal temperature of 98.6° F. (37° C). But unlike human beings, dogs do not cool the body by sweating. Instead, a dog sticks out its tongue and pants. As the dog pants, evaporation of water from the mouth cools its body. Dogs do have sweat glands, but they play only a small role in reducing the body temperature.

Senses. A dog's most highly developed sense is its sense of smell. Dogs recognize objects chiefly by smell, much as people recognize them by sight. Dogs can detect some odors that are millions of times too faint for people to detect. By sniffing a group of objects, a dog can pick out the ones that a particular person touched. Fluid from a gland inside the nose keeps the tip of a dog's nose moist. The moisture helps a dog detect odors. A dog also licks its nose to help keep it moist. In addition, a dog's whiskers may sense the wind direction and so help the dog determine the direction from which an odor is coming.

Dogs also have a much better sense of hearing than people have. Dogs can hear high-pitched sounds far above the limit of human hearing. They can also hear

Dog terms

Bitch is an adult female dog.
Canine is another word for *dog* or *doglike*. The term comes from *canis,* the Latin word for *dog.*
Crossbred means a dog whose parents belong to different breeds.
Dog is an adult male dog. However, the term is generally used for all dogs, regardless of age or sex.
Litter refers to a group of puppies born at one time.
Mongrel is a dog of such mixed ancestry that no one breed can be recognized.
Pedigree is a record of a purebred dog's ancestors.
Puppy is a dog less than 1 year old.
Purebred means a dog whose parents belong to the same breed.
Studbook is a book in which breeders register the pedigrees of dogs.
Whelp is an unweaned puppy—that is, one that still feeds on its mother's milk. The term also means to give birth to puppies.

sounds at much greater distances than people can. In addition, dogs have a highly developed ability to recognize different complicated sounds. For example, many dogs can recognize the sound of their owner's automobile and so tell it apart from other cars.

Dogs cannot see as well as people. Dogs detect movement well, which helps make them good hunters. But they see patterns and forms much more poorly than people do. Dogs also cannot tell certain colors apart. They see green, yellow, orange, and red as the same shade.

The senses of taste and touch are well developed in all breeds of dogs. However, some dogs are much more sensitive to touch and pain than others. Toy breeds are the most sensitive, and breeds used for hunting or attacking game are the least sensitive. Dogs will groom each other and enjoy being stroked and petted by people. But dogs that have been mistreated may show "touch-shyness" and avoid any human contact.

Kinds of dogs

There are hundreds of breeds of *purebred* dogs in the world. A purebred is a dog whose *sire* (father) and *dam* (mother) belong to the same breed. A dog whose parents belong to different breeds is a *crossbred.* A *mongrel,* or *mutt,* is a dog with such mixed ancestry that no one breed can be recognized. Crossbreds and mongrels make up the great majority of all dogs.

The American Kennel Club (AKC) is the chief organization of dog breeders in the United States. It registers 130 breeds in seven groups: (1) sporting dogs, (2) hounds, (3) working dogs, (4) herding dogs, (5) terriers, (6) toy dogs, and (7) nonsporting dogs. The AKC also has a miscellaneous group. The breeds in this group are growing in popularity but have not yet been admitted to one of the seven regular groups. These breeds include the Australian kelpie, the border collie, and the spinoni Italiani. Kennel clubs in other countries recognize many other breeds and use different systems of grouping the breeds. Photographs of many breeds recognized by the American Kennel Club appear on the 10 pages following the table on the next page.

Breeds of purebred dogs recognized by the AKC

Breed*	Place and probable date of origin	Average in lbs.	weight in kg
Sporting group			
American water spaniel	United States, 1800's	25-45	11-20
Brittany	France, 1800's	35-40	16-18
Chesapeake Bay retriever	United States, 1800's	65-80	29-36
Clumber spaniel	England, 1800's	35-65	15-29
Cocker spaniel	England, 1800's	22-28	10-13
Curly-coated retriever	England, 1800's	60-70	27-32
English cocker spaniel	England, 1800's	26-34	12-15
English setter	England, 1500's	50-70	23-32
English springer spaniel	England, 1800's	37-55	17-25
Field spaniel	England, 1700's	35-50	16-23
Flat-coated retriever	England, 1800's	60-70	27-32
German shorthaired pointer	Germany, about 1900	45-70	20-32
German wirehaired pointer	Germany, 1870	55-65	25-29
Golden retriever	Scotland, 1870	55-75	25-34
Gordon setter	Scotland, 1600's	45-80	20-36
Irish setter	Ireland, 1700's	60-70	27-32
Irish water spaniel	Ireland, 1800's	45-65	20-29
Labrador retriever	Newfoundland, 1800's	55-75	25-34
Pointer	Spain, Portugal, eastern Europe, and England, about 1650	45-75	20-34
Sussex spaniel	England, 1800's	35-45	16-20
Vizsla	Hungary, 1000's	50	23
Weimaraner	Germany, 1800's	60-80	27-36
Welsh springer spaniel	Wales, 1700's	40	18
Wirehaired pointing griffon	The Netherlands and France, 1800's	50-60	23-27
Hound group			
Afghan hound	Unknown	50-60	23-27
American foxhound	United States, 1600's	60-70	27-32
Basenji	Africa, 3400 B.C.	22-24	10-11
Basset hound	France, 1600's	45-60	20-27
Beagle	England, Wales, 1600's	18-30	8-14
Black and tan coonhound	United States, 1700's	50-60	23-27
Bloodhound	Middle East, 100 B.C.	80-110	36-50
Borzoi	Russia, 1600's	60-105	27-48
Dachshund	Germany, 1700's	5-20	2-9
English foxhound	England, 1600's	60-75	27-34
Greyhound	Egypt, 4000-3500 B.C.	60-70	27-32
Harrier	France, 1000's	40-50	18-23
Ibizan hound	Balearic Islands, Spain, ancient times	42-50	19-23
Irish wolfhound	Ireland, 400's	126-145	57-66
Norwegian elkhound	Norway, 5000-4000 B.C.	50	23
Otter hound	England, 1300's	65-115	29-52
Pharaoh hound	Egypt, 4000 B.C.	50	23
Rhodesian ridgeback	Africa, 1700's	65-75	29-34
Saluki	Middle East, about 5000 B.C.	60	27
Scottish deerhound	Scotland, 1500's	75-110	34-50
Whippet	England, 1800's	18-23	8-10
Toy group			
Affenpinscher	Europe, 1700's	7-8	3-4
Brussels griffon	Belgium, 1600's	8-10	4-5
Chihuahua	Mexico, 1500's or earlier	1-6	0.5-3
English toy spaniel	Japan or China, ancient times	9-12	4-5
Italian greyhound	Italy, 100 B.C.	6-10	3-5
Japanese chin	China, ancient times	5-9	2-4
Maltese	Malta, 800 B.C. or earlier	4-6	2-3
Miniature pinscher	Germany, 1700's	6-10	3-5
Papillon	Spain, 1500's	5-11	2-5
Pekingese	China, 700's	6-10	3-5
Pomeranian	Pomerania, Poland, 1800's	3-7	1-3
Pug	China, 1700's	14-18	6-8
Shih Tzu	China, ancient times	12-15	5-9
Silky terrier	Australia, about 1900	8-10	4-5
Yorkshire terrier	England, 1800's	4-7	2-3
Working group			
Akita	Japan, 1600's	80-120	36-54
Alaskan malamute	Alaska, 1000 B.C.	75-85	34-39
Bernese mountain dog	Switzerland, 100 B.C.	50-75	23-34
Boxer	Germany, 1800's	60-75	27-34
Bullmastiff	England, 1800's	100-130	45-59
Doberman pinscher	Germany, 1800's	60-75	27-34
Giant schnauzer	Bavaria, 1600-1800	75	34
Great Dane	Germany, 1500's	120-150	54-68
Great Pyrenees	France, 1800-1000 B.C.	90-125	41-57
Komondor	Hungary, 900's	90	41
Kuvasz	Tibet, 1200's	70	32
Mastiff	The Middle East, ancient times	165-185	75-84
Newfoundland	Newfoundland, date unknown	110-150	50-68
Portuguese water dog	Portugal, 700's	35-60	16-27
Rottweiler	Germany, about A.D. 50	80-90	36-41
St. Bernard	Switzerland, 1600's	165-200	75-90
Samoyed	Northern Siberia, 1000 B.C. or earlier	35-60	16-27
Siberian husky	Siberia, about 1000 B.C.	35-60	16-27
Standard schnauzer	Germany, 1400's	35-40	16-18
Herding group			
Australian cattle dog	Australia, 1800's	35-55	16-25
Bearded collie	Scotland, early 1500's	50	23
Belgian Malinois	Belgium, 1800's	50-55	23-25
Belgian sheepdog	Belgium, about 1880	55-60	25-27
Belgian Tervuren	Belgium, about 1880	55	25
Bouvier des Flandres	Flanders, 1800's	70	32
Briard	France, 1100's	70-80	32-36
Cardigan Welsh corgi	Wales, about 1200 B.C.	20-26	9-12
Collie	Scotland, 1600's	50-75	23-34
German shepherd dog	Germany, 1800's	60-85	27-39
Old English sheepdog	England, 1800's	50-65	23-29
Pembroke Welsh corgi	Wales, 1107	18-30	8-14
Puli	Hungary, 1000's	30-35	14-16
Shetland sheepdog	Shetland Islands, 1600's	16-24	7-11
Terrier group			
Airedale terrier	England, 1800's	50-60	23-27
American Staffordshire terrier	United States, early 1900's	35-50	16-23
Australian terrier	Australia, 1885	12-14	5-6
Bedlington terrier	England, 1800's	17-23	8-10
Border terrier	Scottish-English border, 1700's	11½-15½	5-7
Bull terrier	England, 1800's	40-60	18-27
Cairn terrier	Scotland, 1700's	13-14	6
Dandie Dinmont terrier	England and Scotland, about 1700	18-24	8-11
Irish terrier	Ireland, 1700's	25-27	11-12
Kerry blue terrier	Ireland, 1800's	30-40	14-18
Lakeland terrier	England, 1800's	15-17	7-8
Manchester terrier†	England, 1800's	5-22	2-10
Miniature schnauzer	Germany, 1800's	15	7
Norfolk terrier	England, 1880	10-15	5-7
Norwich terrier	England, 1880	10-15	5-7
Scottish terrier	Scotland, 1800's	18-22	8-10
Sealyham terrier	Wales, 1800's	20-21	9-10
Skye terrier	Scotland, 1600's	25	11
Smooth fox terrier	England, mid-1800's	18	8
Soft-coated wheaten terrier	Ireland, 1900's	35-45	16-20
Staffordshire bull terrier	England, 1800's	35	16
Welsh terrier	Wales, 1700's	20	9
West Highland white terrier	Scotland, 1600's	13-19	6-9
Wire fox terrier	England, late 1800's	15-19	7-9
Nonsporting group			
Bichon frise	Mediterranean, 200 B.C.	12-15	5-7
Boston terrier	Boston, Mass., 1870	12-25	5-11
Bulldog	England, 1200's	40-50	18-23
Chow chow	China, 150 B.C.	50-60	23-27
Dalmatian	Dalmatia, Austria, 1700's	40-50	18-23
Finnish spitz	Finland, about 1500 B.C.	30	14
French bulldog	France, 1400's	18-28	8-13
Keeshond	Holland, 1500's	35-40	16-18
Lhasa apso	Tibet, about 1100	15	7
Poodle**	Germany, 1500's	7-55	3-25
Schipperke	Belgium, 1600's	15	7
Tibetan spaniel	Tibet, 200 B.C.	9-15	4-8
Tibetan terrier	Tibet, about 50 B.C.	22-23	10

*Each breed listed in this table has a separate article in *World Book*.†Manchester terriers weighing 12 pounds (5 kilograms) or less are entered in dog shows in the Toy group.**Poodles measuring 10 inches (21 centimeters) or less are entered in dog shows in the Toy group.
Source: American Kennel Club (AKC).

Sporting dogs

Sporting dogs registered by the AKC consist of 24 breeds of pointers, setters, retrievers, and spaniels. Pointers and setters use their sharp eyesight and keen sense of smell to locate birds. They then point their body toward the game to guide the hunter. Retrievers pick up birds that have been shot and bring them back to the hunter. Retrievers can work on land, but they mainly retrieve birds from the water. Most spaniels help hunters by going into bushes or brush to *spring* (scare) birds into the air. Unlike other spaniels, the Irish water spaniel retrieves ducks and other birds from the water.

WORLD BOOK photo

Chesapeake Bay retriever

WORLD BOOK photo by Ken Love

English setter

WORLD BOOK photo by Dave G. Wacker

Golden retriever

WORLD BOOK photo by Dave G. Wacker

Irish water spaniel

WORLD BOOK photo by Brent Jones

Pointer

WORLD BOOK photo by Isac Jo

Labrador retriever

WORLD BOOK photo

Brittany

WORLD BOOK photo by Isac Jo

Vizsla

WORLD BOOK photo by Brent Jones

Weimaraner

WORLD BOOK photo by Brent Jones

English cocker spaniel

WORLD BOOK photo

Cocker spaniel

WORLD BOOK photo by Brent Jones

English springer spaniel

WORLD BOOK photo

Gordon setter

WORLD BOOK photo by Ken Love

German shorthaired pointer

WORLD BOOK photo by Ken Love

Irish setter

Hounds

The AKC registers 21 different breeds of hounds. Hounds hunt either by smell or by sight. *Scent hounds,* such as beagles and foxhounds, run with their nose to the ground to follow an animal's scent. While they are trailing game, coonhounds and some other kinds of scent hounds *bay*—that is, they give out deep, long barks. Tall, slender *gazehounds,* or *sight hounds,* were bred to hunt game by sight. Today, such gazehounds as greyhounds and whippets are used in the sport of dog racing. Other breeds of gazehounds include the Afghan hound and the saluki.

Marshall P. Hawkins

American foxhound

WORLD BOOK photo

Irish wolfhound

WORLD BOOK photo by Ken Love

Norwegian elkhound

WORLD BOOK photo by Ken Love

Rhodesian ridgeback

WORLD BOOK photo by Ken Love

Greyhound

WORLD BOOK photo

Dachshund (wire-haired)

WORLD BOOK photo

Borzoi

Hans Reinhard, Bruce Coleman, Inc.

Beagle

WORLD BOOK photo by Ken Love

Whippet

WORLD BOOK photo by Brent Jones

Basset hound

WORLD BOOK photo by Brent Jones

Saluki

WORLD BOOK photo by Brent Jones

Black and tan coonhound

WORLD BOOK photo by Ken Love

Afghan hound

WORLD BOOK photo

Bloodhound

WORLD BOOK photo
by Brent Jones

Basenji

Working dogs

The American Kennel Club registers 19 different breeds of working dogs. These dogs serve people in various ways. For example, Doberman pinschers and mastiffs make excellent guard and police dogs. Alaskan malamutes, Samoyeds, and Siberian huskies pull sleds, and St. Bernards and Newfoundlands were bred for rescue work.

WORLD BOOK photo

Alaskan malamute

WORLD BOOK photo

Newfoundland

WORLD BOOK photo by Isac Jo

Great Dane

WORLD BOOK photo by Ken Love

Samoyed

WORLD BOOK photo

Boxer

WORLD BOOK photo

Great Pyrenees

WORLD BOOK photo by Brent Jones

St. Bernard

WORLD BOOK photo

Mastiff

Herding dogs

There are 14 breeds of herding dogs recognized by the AKC. Historically, these hardy dogs were used to keep grazing cattle and sheep from straying, and to protect the livestock from wolves. Herding dogs also helped drive cattle and sheep to market. Many of these breeds are still popular as farm animals. This group includes some of the most popular pet breeds, such as the collie and the German shepherd dog.

WORLD BOOK photo by Ken Love

Shetland sheepdog

WORLD BOOK photo

Collie

Robert L. Harris, Briard Club of America

Briard

WORLD BOOK photo by Brent Jones

Pembroke Welsh corgi

WORLD BOOK photo by Brent Jones

German shepherd dog

WORLD BOOK photo by Brent Jones

Old English sheepdog

Roberta Whitesides

Belgian Tervuren

Terriers

There are 24 breeds of terriers recognized by the American Kennel Club. Terriers were originally bred to drive game out of holes in the ground. Their name comes from *terra,* the Latin word for *earth.* Most of the terrier breeds originated in England. The majority of terriers have a wiry coat and a bushy beard. Terriers make fearless watchdogs. They also help people by killing mice, rats, and other pests.

WORLD BOOK photo by Ken Love

Irish terrier

WORLD BOOK photo by Ken Love

Airedale terrier

WORLD BOOK photo by Brent Jones

Manchester terrier

WORLD BOOK photo by Dave G. Wacker

Skye terrier

WORLD BOOK photo by Ken Love

Welsh terrier

WORLD BOOK photo by Isac Jo

Bull terrier

WORLD BOOK photo by William Cripe

Dandie Dinmont terrier

WORLD BOOK photo

American Staffordshire terrier

William P. Gilbert

Miniature schnauzer

WORLD BOOK photo

Bedlington terrier

WORLD BOOK photo by Ken Love

Cairn terrier

WORLD BOOK photo by Brent Jones

Sealyham terrier

WORLD BOOK photo by Ken Love

Scottish terrier

WORLD BOOK photo

Smooth fox terrier

WORLD BOOK photo by Dave G. Wacker

Kerry blue terrier

Toy dogs

Toy dogs consist of 15 small breeds kept as pets. In addition to these breeds, small varieties of poodles and Manchester terriers also compete in the toy group at dog shows.

Toy breeds come from all parts of the world. For example, the Chihuahua was developed in Mexico, the Pekingese in China, and the papillon in Spain. The largest toy dog is the pug, which may weigh up to 18 pounds (8 kilograms).

WORLD BOOK photo by Brent Jones

Yorkshire terrier

WORLD BOOK photo

Maltese

WORLD BOOK photo

Brussels griffon

WORLD BOOK photo

Shih Tzu

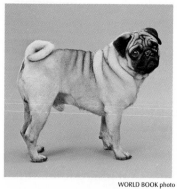

WORLD BOOK photo

Pug

WORLD BOOK photo

Pekingese

WORLD BOOK photo

Miniature pinscher

WORLD BOOK photo

Pomeranian

WORLD BOOK photo

Affenpinscher

WORLD BOOK photo

Chihuahua

Nonsporting dogs

Nonsporting dogs consist of 13 breeds kept chiefly as pets. Many of these breeds were originally bred for work or sport. Poodles, for example, once retrieved ducks for French hunters. People have used Dalmatians for many purposes, including herding cattle and hunting game. The Boston terrier is the only nonsporting breed that originated in the United States. Breeders developed the first Boston terriers by mating bulldogs with terriers.

WORLD BOOK photo by Ken Love
Keeshond

WORLD BOOK photo by Dave G. Wacker
Bulldog

WORLD BOOK photo
Poodle

WORLD BOOK photo
Schipperke

WORLD BOOK photo by Brent Jones
Boston terrier

WORLD BOOK photo by Ken Love
French bulldog

WORLD BOOK photo by Brent Jones
Dalmatian

WORLD BOOK photo
Lhasa apso

WORLD BOOK photo
Tibetan terrier

WORLD BOOK photo

A mother nurses her puppies until they are about 6 weeks old. Most litters consist of 1 to 12 pups, but litters of 15 or more have been reported. These dogs are Chesapeake Bay retrievers.

The life of a dog

Life history. A female dog carries her young for nine weeks before they are born. In most cases, a dog gives birth to a litter of 1 to 12 puppies, though litters of 15 or more have been reported. Dogs are mammals, and so they feed their young on milk produced by the mother's body. A mother dog nurses her pups until they are about 6 weeks old.

Puppies are born with their eyes closed and their ears sealed. Their eyes and ears open about 13 to 15 days after birth. Until that time, they depend entirely on their senses of touch and smell to detect things in their environment. These senses are well developed at or shortly after birth. During the third week of life, puppies begin to walk and to respond to sights and sounds.

Between 4 and 10 weeks of age, a puppy forms emotional attachments to its mother and its littermates. If the puppy is to become a good pet, it must have contact with people during this period. Such contact is the key to developing a close relationship with the dog that will last throughout its life. For this reason, the ideal time to adopt a puppy is when it is about 6 to 8 weeks old.

Dogs become fully grown at 8 months to 2 years of age, depending on the size of the breed. Large dogs develop more slowly than smaller breeds. It is difficult to compare the age of a dog to that of a human being. However, a 6-month-old puppy generally compares in development to a 10-year-old child, and a 2-year-old dog compares to a 24-year-old person. After a dog's second year, each year equals about four or five years of a person's life. On the average, dogs live about 12 to 15 years. Most of the larger breeds have shorter life spans, however.

Communication. By the age of 4 weeks, a puppy can produce a dog's full range of vocal sounds—barks, growls, howls, whines, and yelps. Some of these sounds have different meanings in different situations. A whine,

for example, may mean that the dog is in pain. In other circumstances, the dog may whine simply as a greeting or to indicate that it wants to play. Barking has an especially wide variety of meanings, and dogs may bark in almost any situation.

Barks, whines, and other sounds are not the only way in which dogs communicate their feelings and desires to people or to other dogs. They also use a "body language," which consists of a wide range of body and tail postures combined with various facial expressions. For example, a dog may tell another dog that it wants to play by stretching out its forelegs, bowing, panting, and perhaps pawing at the dog. In contrast, a dog may threaten another dog by standing stiffly, holding its tail up, showing its teeth, and staring. Eye contact is an important part of a dog's body language. A dog uses a direct stare as a threat or challenge. On the other hand, a dog will break eye contact as a sign of surrender to a more *dominant* (commanding) dog.

Dogs also communicate with one another through odors produced by certain glands or given off by urine. For example, the *anal glands,* which lie near the opening to the rectum, produce a distinct, foul odor when a dog is frightened. Male dogs urinate on trees and other objects to mark their territory. A male also marks spots outside its territory to tell other dogs that it has been there. Sometimes a male urinates on the spot where a companion female has urinated. This mark may serve as a sign to other dogs of the friendship between the two.

Behavior. Much of a dog's behavior resembles that of its wild relatives, such as coyotes and wolves. This behavior is *instinctive*—that is, inherited rather than learned. For example, many dogs turn around several times before lying down, much as a wolf or wild dog does in trampling leaves or grass to make a bed.

An important form of instinctive behavior is a dog's defense of its territory. A dog regards its owner's house and yard as its territory. For this reason, it may threaten or attack a strange person or dog that approaches the house or yard. A dog may also consider its owner's car an extension of its territory. While inside the car, such a dog will probably threaten any stranger who comes near. The neighborhood in which a dog lives is known as its *home range.* The home range is a neutral area, and a dog usually will not threaten or attack other dogs it meets there.

A good understanding of dog behavior and communication can help most people avoid dog bites. Never stare at a strange dog because it may consider your stare a threat and attack you. Also, never run past a strange dog. Your flight may trigger its chase response, and you may get bitten. On the other hand, ignoring a dog may make it suspicious of you. If you act friendly and speak to the dog, it will have less reason to challenge you.

As you approach a strange dog, observe how it reacts to you. Even a friendly dog will probably bark at you if you are on its territory. A dog that stays put or backs off when you approach regards you as a dominant intruder and will likely be too scared to attack. A dog that approaches with its tail wagging, even if it is barking, is probably friendly and will not bite. Be on guard, however, if a dog stiffens up, holds its tail high, snarls, and stares at you.

If a dog seems likely to attack, stand your ground. Stare back at it and shout "go home" in a powerful, angry voice. This bluff may scare the dog. Never lean back because any backward movement will suggest you are afraid. Keep your weight forward so you will be ready if the dog jumps at you. If it does jump, thrust your knee upward into the dog's chest. If you are carrying anything, use it as a shield. Always back away slowly as you leave a dog's territory. Never turn and run. The dog may interpret your turning as a sign of weakness and attack you.

Choosing a dog

Before buying a dog, you should consider what type of dog will best fit your needs, personality, and life style. You should decide whether you want a purebred or a mongrel and whether a small dog or a large one would be better for you. You should also determine whether you want a long-haired dog, whose coat requires daily grooming, or a short-haired dog, whose coat needs less attention.

Both purebreds and mongrels make good pets. In general, mongrels are superior to purebreds in disposition and physical vigor. The main advantage of buying a purebred is that you know how the dog will look and how large it will be when fully grown. You also know whether a purebred has any special abilities, such as the ability to guard property or to retrieve game. Visits to dog shows and talks with owners of various breeds can help you decide which particular breed is the right one for you.

Your local humane society or animal shelter should have a variety of healthy mongrel pups from which to choose. The best place to buy a purebred is from an experienced breeder who takes obvious pride in his or her dogs. You can find such breeders at dog shows or through advertisements in local newspapers or national dog magazines. If possible, visit the kennels and see one or both of the parents of the pups. Make certain that the puppy you select is healthy. It should appear lively and playful and have bright, clear eyes, clean skin, and a shiny coat.

Caring for a dog

Feeding. A balanced diet for a dog supplies both calories for energy and nutrients for growth and replacement of body tissues. High-quality commercial dog food provides calories and nutrients in the proportions that your dog requires for good health. Adding extras yourself could upset this carefully formulated balance. Although dogs enjoy table scraps, no more than a quarter of the diet should consist of such leftovers. Never feed your dog only meat because an all-meat diet is nutritionally unbalanced.

Get your puppy used to one or two brands of dog food. If you keep switching brands, your dog may get digestive disturbances. Even worse, the dog may become a finicky eater and "train" you to feed it only what it likes. In time, such feeding probably would harm your pet's health.

Puppies should be fed small amounts four times a day until the age of 3 months. They should eat three times daily from 3 to 6 months of age and two times daily from 6 to 12 months of age. Most adult dogs require only one meal a day, though many like a small snack in addition to their main meal. Whether you feed your dog in the morning or evening is up to you. But after you have chosen a feeding time, stick to it strictly.

Keep fresh, cool drinking water available at all times in a dish that your dog cannot tip over. Food and water bowls should be cleaned thoroughly every day. Many dogs enjoy a little fresh grass and should be allowed to eat it when outdoors. In addition, all dogs should have something safe to chew on to keep their gums and teeth healthy. A large dog biscuit, a rawhide strip, or a raw soupbone is ideal. Never give your dog any other kind of bone because it may splinter and cause serious internal injuries.

Shelter. A dog that lives indoors needs a clean sleeping box lined with blankets or shredded paper. Place the box in a quiet spot out of drafts and away from radiators or other heaters. A dog that lives outdoors should have a well-insulated doghouse with a dry, warm floor. Cover the floor with cedar shavings, sawdust, or blankets. To keep out dampness, raise the doghouse off the ground on bricks or on a foundation of boards 4 to 5 inches (10 to 13 centimeters) wide. Shade should be provided during the summertime and a good windbreak during the winter. In extremely cold weather, a heat lamp may be needed.

Grooming cleans a dog's coat and stimulates the skin. Brushing several times a week will keep a short-haired dog neat and clean. A long-haired dog should have its coat combed daily, and the dog may need clipping in hot weather to make it more comfortable and to prevent skin problems. A dog should be washed as seldom as possible. Too much washing can cause the skin to dry out and flake. If your dog needs a bath, wash it with warm water and mild soap. Then, be sure to rinse and dry the dog thoroughly.

Get your puppy used to being groomed and handled right from the start. Check its teeth, ears, and toenails regularly. The more accustomed a puppy becomes to being handled, the easier it will be to care for the dog later in life.

Exercise and play. All dogs need regular exercise to keep them fit. Dogs that have the run of a large yard may get enough exercise on their own. Dogs kept in the house or in a small area outside should be taken for walks frequently, preferably twice a day. If you like to jog with your dog, do not overdo it with a young puppy or an old dog. Never take a dog of any age on a long run in hot weather.

Playing with your puppy helps it become adjusted to people. Play will give a pup more confidence and also teach it not to be too rough. A puppy should have toys that can be chewed, rolled, and tugged without splintering or breaking into dangerous pieces. A pup can play with these toys by itself, and you can also use them for tugs-of-war and other games with your pet.

In playing with your dog, you might like to try mimicking some of the dog's body language. To tell your dog that you want to play, get down on all fours with your arms stretched out. Then bow in front of the dog with a wide-eyed, smiling face. Combining this bow with a hop forward says to the dog, "I'm going to catch you." The same position with a backward hop means, "Catch me if you can." You may also try panting loudly. Panting does not mean that you are hot or thirsty. Instead, it is the equivalent of laughter in dog language. Try out these signals on your dog with care. Some dogs become defensive or overly excited the first time someone "speaks" to them in their own language.

Medical care is just as important for dogs as for people. Every new pup should be taken to a veterinarian for a thorough checkup. It should also receive a series of shots against such common diseases as canine distemper, hepatitis, leptospirosis, and parvovirus. Adult dogs should also be taken to the veterinarian at least once a year for a checkup and any necessary booster shots, which continue the effectiveness of earlier shots.

If your dog gets sick, do not try to treat it yourself. Take it to a veterinarian. Veterinary care protects your health as well as your pet's because the dog may have a disease that can be transmitted to people. The most dangerous of these diseases by far is rabies. In the United States, every state except Hawaii requires dogs to receive a periodic rabies vaccination. There is no rabies in Hawaii.

All dog owners should learn to recognize signs of illness in dogs. A sick dog may tire easily, drink excessive amounts of water, or refuse to eat. Other signs of sickness include convulsions, fever, a dry cough, runny eyes and nose, or red eyes and a dry nose. Frequent and loose bowel movements for more than 24 hours or repeated vomiting may also indicate a medical problem. You should also seek veterinary care for your dog if it scratches certain areas excessively or yelps when touched in a particular spot.

Parasitic worms cause health problems for many dogs. Most puppies are born with roundworms. All pups should be examined by a veterinarian for these parasites and receive treatment if necessary. A dog's annual checkup should include a blood test for heartworms. These parasites are transmitted by mosquitoes and can cause serious illness and even death. Heartworms are present in all parts of the United States, but they are especially common in the South, along the Atlantic coast, and in Hawaii. Your veterinarian can prescribe medicine that will protect your dog against heartworms. The dog should receive this medicine daily from one month before the mosquito season until one month after the season.

Dogs also suffer from external parasites, chiefly fleas and ticks. Dusting your dog and its sleeping quarters with flea powder once or twice a week should help keep the dog free of fleas. Flea collars may cause skin irritations in some breeds and so should be used only on the advice of your veterinarian.

Social and moral responsibilities. Owning a dog involves a number of social and moral responsibilities. Many communities have laws that deal with some of these responsibilities. For example, anticruelty laws are intended to protect dogs from people who beat, starve, or otherwise mistreat them. However, laws alone cannot ensure that the social and moral obligations of dog ownership are met. Real solutions depend on all owners providing proper care for their dogs and accepting full responsibility for their pets' actions.

Many cities have laws that require dogs to be leashed when they are in public areas. Even in communities without leash laws, owners should never allow their dogs to roam alone. Stray dogs cause a large percentage of the more than 1 million serious dog bites in the United States each year. Many strays are run over by automobiles, and others cause accidents when drivers swerve to avoid them. Free-roaming dogs in rural areas kill livestock and wildlife. In addition, strays may be injured or killed in fights with other dogs.

Inconsiderate owners create unsanitary and unsightly conditions by allowing their dogs to have bowel movements on sidewalks and lawns and in parks. Some cities fine owners who do not clean up after their dogs.

Every year, animal shelters destroy millions of homeless and unwanted dogs. Because of this serious overpopulation problem, it is up to you to make sure that your dog does not father or give birth to unwanted puppies.

Adult male dogs can mate at any time. However, females will mate only when they are in a period of sexual excitement called *estrus* or *heat.* In most females, estrus occurs every six months and lasts about three weeks. If you own a female and do not want her to mate, keep her away from male dogs during estrus. If she is accidentally allowed to mate, a veterinarian may be able to prevent pregnancy by promptly injecting her with certain hormones.

Veterinarians can permanently prevent a dog from reproducing by surgically removing some of its sex organs. This operation is called *spaying* when done on a female and *castration* when done on a male. Most veterinarians recommend that a female should not be spayed until she has had at least one period of estrus, and a male should not be castrated before the age of 6 months. These operations provide the only completely effective means of birth control for dogs.

Training a dog

Almost every dog can be trained to be an obedient, reliable, and well-adjusted companion. But you must establish and maintain a dominant relationship with your puppy to make such training possible. A puppy naturally responds to a strong leader. As soon as you get your puppy, train it to come whenever you call. You should also teach it what "no" means right away. Repeat this command in a stern voice every time the dog does anything that displeases you. Never let your dog misbehave in any way. If you do, it may try to get the upper hand and become uncontrollable.

Never strike a pup for being disobedient or aggressive. However, you may find it helpful to mimic some of the actions that a mother dog uses to discipline a pup. If your puppy plays too rough, for example, growl "bad dog," pin its snout to the ground with one hand, and shake the back of its neck with the other hand. These actions should be effective. In addition, they may help develop deeper understanding between you and your dog.

Housebreaking. Start housebreaking your puppy as soon as you bring it home. Many experts recommend the *den-bed* method to housebreak a puppy. For a detailed explanation of this method, see the article **Pet** (House training).

Obedience training should begin when your puppy is 10 to 12 weeks old. First, get the dog used to wearing a collar and leash, which will be helpful tools in training.

Dave G. Wacker

Field trials test the hunting ability of dogs. This Chesapeake Bay retriever is being rated on how quickly it found a bird that a hunter had shot and whether it returned the bird undamaged.

You can then start to teach your pet such basic commands as "heel," "sit," "stay," and "down."

Give your dog a 10-minute lesson twice a day. Be patient but firm. The dog must understand that a command means instant obedience. Always make sure that your pet has mastered one command before you begin to teach it another. A dog learns by associating an action with your reaction to it. Therefore, you should always praise or correct the dog immediately. In addition, you must always react to a particular action in the same way so that your dog knows what to expect.

Many dog clubs and other organizations hold obedience-training classes for dogs. These classes may be particularly helpful for people with large dogs, especially such guard dogs as German shepherds or Doberman pinschers. The American Kennel Club (AKC) sponsors *obedience trials,* in which dogs are judged on their ability to obey commands.

Dog shows are sponsored by kennel clubs in many countries. In the United States, the American Kennel Club licenses judges and supervises most of the hundreds of dog shows held each year. Some of these shows are called *bench shows* because handlers exhibit the dogs in stalls mounted on benches. A dog must be registered with the AKC to compete in such contests. The Westminster Kennel Club of New York City stages an important bench show each February in Madison Square Garden. This show has been held every year since 1877, which makes it one of the oldest annual sporting events in the United States.

The judges of a dog show rate each dog on how well it fits the AKC standard for its breed. This standard includes such points as the shape and size of the dog's body and the color and condition of its coat. The breed standard also describes an ideal posture and way of moving. The judges first pick the best dog of each breed. They then choose the best dog in each of the seven main groups of dogs. From these winners, the judges name the best dog in the show.

Field trials test the hunting ability of sporting dogs and hounds. Judges rate pointers and setters on their endurance, ability to scent game, and obedience to a handler's commands. In retriever field trials, judges score the dogs on how quickly they find the birds that a hunter has shot down and whether they return them without damage. Field trials for hounds test their skill in tracking game.

History

Scientists believe that the dog gradually developed from a weasellike animal called *Miacis,* which lived about 40 million years ago. They think that *Miacis* was the ancestor not only of dogs but also of such other mammals as bears, cats, raccoons, and skunks. By about 15 million years ago, a descendant of *Miacis* called *Tomarctus* had developed. *Tomarctus* probably looked much like a wolf and had many of the dog's social instincts. From *Tomarctus* came all the members of the dog family—that is, dogs, wolves, coyotes, jackals, and foxes.

Experts disagree on the more recent ancestry of the dog. Some believe that modern dogs developed from small Asian wolves. But distinct differences between the behavior patterns of dogs and wolves indicate that the animals probably have very different recent origins. Other experts suggest that modern dogs may have developed from a dingolike animal that people tamed and perhaps crossbred with wolves.

WORLD BOOK photo by Brent Jones

Obedience-training classes like the one above are conducted by dog clubs and other organizations. With proper training, almost any dog can become an obedient companion.

WORLD BOOK photo

Careful grooming helps keep a dog's coat clean and free of loose hair. The Siberian husky shown above is receiving a final brushing before being exhibited in a dog show.

Authorities agree that the dog was the first animal to be domesticated. The earliest associations between people and dogs began more than 12,000 years ago. At that time, human beings were nomadic hunters and plant gatherers. Many experts think that garbage dumps first attracted dogs to the camps of the hunters and gatherers. Dogs found it easier to feed on garbage than to hunt for themselves, and so they gradually came to depend on people for food. People, in turn, began to tame and value dogs. Dogs kept the campsites clean by eating garbage, and they warned of the approach of strangers and dangerous animals by barking. This theory gains support because dogs perform these same functions for present-day hunting and gathering societies.

After taming dogs, people began to breed them for special physical features and for particular abilities, such as the ability to guard or to hunt. In this way, local varieties and eventually specific breeds of dogs were developed. Several distinct breeds already existed in the Middle East at least 4,000 years ago. One of these breeds was the saluki—probably the oldest of all present-day breeds. Traders and explorers from the Middle East took along their dogs as valuable items of trade and so helped introduce domesticated dogs into other parts of the world.

Many ancient civilizations developed their own special breeds of dogs. The ancient Greeks raised large hunting dogs called mastiffs. The Romans kept dogs as pets. They also used dogs to hunt and to herd sheep. The ancient Chinese bred watchdogs and hunting dogs. American Indians developed their own breeds centuries before Europeans brought their dogs to the New World.

During the Middle Ages (A.D. 400's to 1500's), people throughout Europe used hounds to hunt. In the 1500's, an English scholar named John Caius wrote a description of English dogs. He listed 16 breeds, including hounds, mastiffs, sheepdogs, and terriers.

Nearly all present-day breeds were well established in Europe by the 1800's. At that time, the first kennel clubs were formed. They began to set up specific standards for the recognized breeds. A number of additional breeds, such as the Australian terrier and the Rhodesian ridgeback, have been recognized during the 1900's. Breeders have also developed miniature varieties of

some older breeds, including poodles and Manchester terriers.

Scientific classification. Dogs belong to the dog family, Canidae.   Michael W. Fox

Related articles in *World Book* include:

Recognized breeds of purebred dogs

See the separate articles for each breed listed in the table *Breeds of purebred dogs recognized by the AKC* in this article.

Other dogs

Eskimo dog	Pit bull	Spitz
Foxhound	Police dog	Terrier
Hound	Shar-pei	Toy dog
Mexican hairless	Sheepdog	Wolfhound

Dog family

Coyote	Dingo	Fox	Jackal	Wolf

Other related articles

American Kennel Club	Pedigree
Breeding	Pet
Canine parvovirus	Rabies
Distemper	Reproduction (diagram)
Dog guide	Society for the Prevention of
Dog racing	Cruelty to Animals
Humane society	United Kennel Club

Outline

I. The body of a dog
  A. Coat
  B. Body structure
  C. Body functions
  D. Senses
II. Kinds of dogs
  A. Sporting dogs
  B. Hounds
  C. Working dogs
  D. Herding dogs
  E. Terriers
  F. Toy dogs
  G. Nonsporting dogs
III. The life of a dog
  A. Life history
  B. Communication
  C. Behavior
IV. Choosing a dog
V. Caring for a dog
  A. Feeding
  B. Shelter
  C. Grooming
  D. Exercise and play
  E. Medical care
  F. Social and moral responsibilities
VI. Training a dog
  A. Housebreaking
  B. Obedience training
  C. Dog shows
  D. Field trials
VII. History

Questions

What is a dog's most highly developed sense?
How long do dogs live on the average?
Why does a dog pant?
What is the only dog that cannot bark?
Why should a person never stare at a strange dog?
What is the main advantage of buying a purebred puppy?
When did the earliest associations between dogs and people begin?
What are some signs of illness in dogs?
What are dewclaws?
What abilities do field trials test? Which breeds take part in these trials?

Additional resources

Level I
Cole, Joanna. *A Dog's Body.* Morrow, 1986.
Hess, Lilo. *Life Begins for Puppies.* Scribner, 1978.
Silverstein, Alvin and Virginia. *Dogs: All About Them.* Lothrop, 1986.
Taylor, David. *You & Your Dog.* Knopf, 1986.

Famous dogs in history and legend

Argos, also spelled *Argus,* Ulysses' hunting dog, was the only creature to recognize the Greek hero when he returned home disguised as a beggar after 20 years of adventure.
Balto, an Eskimo dog, led a dog team that carried diphtheria serum 650 miles (1,050 kilometers) through an Alaskan blizzard from Nenana to Nome in 1925.
Barry, a St. Bernard, rescued 40 persons lost in the snows of Switzerland's St. Bernard Pass about 1800.
Caesar, a terrier, was the pet of King Edward VII of Great Britain. He walked ahead of kings and princes in his master's funeral procession in 1910.
Cerberus, the three-headed dog of Greek mythology, guarded the gates to the underworld (see Cerberus).
Igloo, a fox terrier, was the special pet of Admiral Richard E. Byrd. He flew with Byrd on flights over the North and South poles. See also **Antarctica** (picture).
Laika became the world's first space traveler. Soviet scientists sent the small dog aloft in an artificial earth satellite in 1957. See also **Space travel** (picture).

Level II

American Kennel Club. *The Complete Dog Book.* 17th ed. Howell Book Hse., 1985.

The Complete Book of Dog Health. Ed. by William J. Kay and Elizabeth Randolph. Macmillan, 1985.

Morris, Desmond. *Dogwatching.* Crown, 1986.

Pearsall, Milo D. and M. E. *Your Dog: Companion and Helper.* Alpine Pubns., 1981. Includes information for disabled dog owners.

Tortora, Daniel F. *The Right Dog for You.* Simon & Schuster, 1983. First published in 1980.

Volhard, Joachim, and Fisher, Gail. *Training Your Dog: The Step-by-Step Manual.* Howell Book Hse., 1983.

Dog guide is a dog specially trained to guide a blind person or to alert a hearing-impaired person to important sounds. Dogs that guide blind people are called *guide dogs* or *seeing eye dogs,* and those that assist hearing-impaired people are called *hearing dogs* or *hearing ear dogs.* Dogs chosen for either kind of training must show qualities of good disposition, intelligence, physical fitness, and responsibility. Breeds best suited for guide dog work include, in order of importance, German shepherds, Labrador retrievers, and golden retrievers. Hearing dogs are usually mixed breeds selected from animal shelters.

Dog guide users have rights of equal access in almost all states of the United States and in all provinces of Canada. They may be accompanied by their dog guides in all public places, including stores, restaurants, and hotels; and on all forms of public transportation. A guide dog can be recognized by its special harness attached to a U-shaped handle. A hearing dog can usually be recognized by its bright orange or yellow collar and leash.

Guide dogs. For the first year of their lives, most future guide dogs live with families. They learn basic obedience and get used to such experiences as living with people and pets, riding in automobiles and other transportation, and visiting public places. At the age of about 14 months, a guide dog begins an intensive course that lasts from three to five months. It becomes accustomed to the leather harness and the stiff handle it will wear when guiding its blind owner. The dog learns to watch traffic and to cross streets safely. It also learns to obey such commands as "forward," "left," "right," and "sit," and to disobey commands that might lead its owner into danger. For example, a guide dog will refuse to cross a street unless traffic has stopped.

The most important part of the training course is a four-week program in which the dog and its future owner learn to work together. But many blind people are unsuited by temperament to work with dogs. Only about a tenth of blind people find a guide dog useful.

The organized training of guide dogs began in Germany during World War I (1914-1918). The first guide dog school in the United States, The Seeing Eye, Incorporated, was founded in 1929. Other U.S. schools include Guide Dogs for the Blind, Incorporated; Guiding Eyes for the Blind; and Leader Dogs for the Blind.

Hearing dogs begin training between the ages of 8 months and 16 months. In addition to basic obedience, the dogs learn to alert their owners to such common sounds as alarm clocks, doorbells, and telephones, and to sounds that may warn of danger, such as crying babies and smoke alarms. Training is usually completed in three to four months. At the end of the course, the dog's trainer teaches the new owner how to care for the dog and keep it well trained.

The American Humane Association began the first national hearing dog program in 1976. Since then, several

E. James Pitrone, The Seeing Eye, Inc.

A dog guide leads its blind owner. These dogs are trained to avoid obstacles and dangerous situations, such as busy traffic.

© Judy Savage

A hearing dog alerts its owner to common sounds. The dog in this picture is being trained to respond to a cooking timer.

nonprofit organizations and some private organizations in the United States have begun such programs.

Critically reviewed by The American Humane Association

Dog racing, also called *greyhound racing,* is a sport in which greyhounds compete on an oval track. The dogs chase a mechanical lure that may resemble a bone, another greyhound, or a rabbit. Sometimes a wind sock is used. A mechanical lure is effective because greyhounds chase by sight rather than by scent. The lure moves around the track on an electric rail. Dog racing developed from *coursing,* an ancient sport in which two dogs chased a live rabbit over an open field.

Most dog-racing tracks are $\frac{1}{4}$ mile (0.4 kilometer) in diameter. Eight greyhounds compete over a distance of $\frac{7}{16}$, $\frac{3}{8}$, or $\frac{5}{16}$ of a mile (0.7, 0.6, or 0.5 kilometer). Champion greyhounds can run faster than 40 miles (64 kilometers) per hour.

Before each race, the dogs are put into individual stalls in a starting box. The lure is then started. When the lure is opposite the starting box, the doors of the stalls are opened, and the dogs are released. During the race, the lure is kept several yards ahead of the leading dog. The lure is moved out of sight of the dogs after they cross the finish line, and they stop running.

Dog racing is a popular sport in parts of the United States and in several other countries. Fans bet on the greyhounds through the pari-mutuel system. This system is also used in horse racing (see **Horse racing** [Betting]). In the United States, bets on dog races total more than $3 billion yearly.   George D. Johnson, Jr.

Dog show. See **Dog** (Dog shows).

Dog sled. See **Sled; Eskimo** (Transportation).

Dog Star. See **Sirius.**

Dogbane is the name of 11 closely related plants. They grow in the north temperate zone, mostly in the United States and Canada. All the dogbanes are poisonous green plants which contain a milky bitter juice. But they are not very dangerous because most grazing animals dislike the bitter juice and will not eat them.

A common dogbane called the *spreading dogbane,* or *honeybloom,* has light-green leaves and clusters of pale pink flowers. This dogbane has a bitter root which physicians sometimes use to cause vomiting. Another dogbane called the *Canada hemp,* or *Indian hemp,* has greenish-white flowers that grow in clusters. The bark of this dogbane produces a long, strong white fiber that is used to make nets.

Scientific classification. Dogbanes belong to the dogbane family, Apocynaceae. The spreading dogbane is *Apocynum androsaemifolium.* The Indian hemp is *A. cannabinum.*

Harold Norman Moldenke

WORLD BOOK illustration by Christabel King

Spreading dogbane

Doge, *dohj,* was the title of the rulers of Venice from 697 to 1797. *Doge* comes from the Latin word *dux,* meaning *leader.* Genoa also had doges.

The doges of Venice were elected for life from among the richest and most powerful families. They enjoyed almost absolute power in governmental, military, and church affairs until 1032. Then they tried to make the office hereditary but failed. In 1797, French troops led by Napoleon Bonaparte occupied Venice. Napoleon abolished the office of doge.   William H. Maehl

See also **Genoa; Venice** (picture: Venice).

Dogfish is a type of small shark that lives in the ocean. There are about 70 species of dogfish. Most measure

WORLD BOOK illustration by Colin Newman, Linden Artists Ltd.

The spiny dogfish is a member of the shark family.

Mike Serlick

Dog racing is a sport in which greyhounds race around an oval track. They chase mechanical lures, *foreground,* that look like rabbits. Spectators bet on the outcome of the races.

less than 5 feet (1.5 meters) long. However, the largest dogfish, the *Greenland shark,* can reach a length of over 20 feet (6 meters). The smallest, the *pigmy shark,* measures only about $\frac{1}{2}$ foot (0.2 meter) long.

The best-known dogfish is the *spiny dogfish.* This fish has sharp spines in front of its *dorsal* (back) fins. Spiny dogfish can be found along the Atlantic and Pacific coasts of North America, and the Atlantic coast of Europe. In Europe, especially in England, spiny dogfish are an important food.

One type of shark is sometimes called the *smooth dogfish.* However, the smooth dogfish does not belong to the dogfish family. The *bowfin,* a primitive, bony fish, is also occasionally called dogfish. But the bowfin is not a shark (see **Bowfin**).

Scientific classification. Dogfish belong to the family Squalidae. The spiny dogfish is *Squalus acanthias.*

Samuel H. Gruber

Dogtooth violet, also called *adder's tongue,* is an attractive spring wild flower of the Eastern United States

WORLD BOOK illustration by Robert Hynes
The dogtooth violet is a dainty spring wild flower.

and Canada. It is not really a violet, but belongs to the lily family. It breaks through the ground early, and catches the sunshine before leaves appear on the trees and darken the ground. Dogtooth violet has been oddly misnamed because it does not resemble a dog's tooth. The young shoots are sharply pointed. The two smooth, grayish-green leaves, mottled with brown, spring from the bulb. Dogtooth violet has bell-shaped flowers that are yellow, white, or pink. The flower has a faint fragrance. Dogtooth violet may be found in early spring on the banks of brooks. It is sometimes called *trout lily.*

Scientific classification. The common dogtooth violet belongs to the lily family, Liliaceae. It is *Erythronium dens-canis.*

George H. M. Lawrence

Dogwood is the common name for a group of herbs, shrubs, and small trees. About 40 kinds are known. Fifteen of these are native to the United States and Canada.

The best known is the *flowering,* or *American, dogwood.* It has four large whitish *bracts* (modified leaves) beneath its small, greenish-white flowers. The bright-red *drupes* (fruits) usually have two seeds. The leaves have parallel veins that curve upward, and are quite rich in calcium. The polygonal pattern of the bark and the gray, urn-shaped flower buds make the dogwood an attractive winter tree.

Flowering dogwood rarely grows more than 40 feet (12 meters) tall or 18 inches (46 centimeters) in diameter. Its wood is hard and heavy. It is the state flower of North

© Louise K. Broman, Photo Researchers

© Jeffrey W. Myers, FPG
The flowering dogwood is a small North American tree that is covered with large flowers in the springtime. The flower has four large modified leaves called *bracts.*

Carolina. It is also the state tree of Missouri and the state flower and tree of Virginia. The *Pacific dogwood* is the provincial flower of British Columbia.

Scientific classification. Dogwoods belong to the dogwood family, Cornaceae. Flowering dogwood is *Cornus florida.* Pacific dogwood is *Cornus muttallii.*   Jerry M. Baskin

See also **Tree** (Familiar broadleaf and needleleaf trees [picture]).

Doha, *DOH huh,* also called Ad Dawhah (pop. 217,294), is the capital, largest city, and chief port of Qatar, a country on the Persian Gulf. Doha lies on the east coast of this Arab nation. For location, see **Qatar** (map).

Doha was a minor fishing port until the 1950's, when Qatar's rapidly developing oil wealth caused the city to change greatly. Doha became the commercial center of Qatar, and its population grew quickly. Many Arabs from nearby countries moved to Doha.

The city began a modernization program in the 1950's. This program included construction of an international airport and of a new harbor to serve oceangoing ships. Air-conditioned apartment and government buildings, hospitals, hotels, and schools replaced many of Doha's mud-walled houses.   Robert Geran Landen

See also **Qatar** (picture).

Dolbear, *DOHL beer,* **Amos E.** (1837-1910), an American physicist and inventor, might be known today as the inventor of the telephone and radio, if he had only had better luck. In 1864, he made a "talking machine" much like the telephone Alexander Graham Bell patented in 1876. Dolbear insisted the idea was his. After a long, bitter court fight, Bell was declared the true inventor. Dolbear produced radio waves in 1882, but the discovery is usually credited to the German scientist Heinrich R. Hertz in 1888. Dolbear was born in Norwich, Conn.

Ira M. Freeman

Doldrums, *DAHL druhmz* or *DOHL druhmz,* is a belt of calms, light breezes, or sudden squalls near the equator, mainly over the oceans. Sailors first used the term *doldrums,* meaning *listlessness,* for the region because the lack of wind often left their ships unable to sail. Meteorologists call the region the *intertropical convergence zone* because the surface air in the trade winds comes together there. The warm air then rises, causing sudden thunderstorms and gusty winds. The region is one of the rainiest in the world. See also **Calms, Regions of; Trade wind.**   Mark A. Cane

Dole, Elizabeth Hanford (1936-   ), became secretary of labor in the Administration of President George Bush in 1989. She had served as secretary of transportation under President Ronald Reagan from 1983 to 1987.

Dole was born Elizabeth Hanford in Salisbury, N.C. She graduated from Duke University and earned master's and law degrees from Harvard University. In 1975, she married Senator Robert J. Dole of Kansas.

Dole held several important federal posts during the presidency of Richard M. Nixon. From 1969 to 1971, she served as executive director of the President's Committee on Consumer Interests. She was deputy director of the Office of Consumer Affairs from 1971 to 1973. In 1973, Nixon appointed her to the Federal Trade Commission (FTC), and she remained as a member of the FTC until 1979.

From 1981 to 1983, Dole served as President Reagan's assistant for public liaison. In that job, she solicited support from various groups for Reagan's programs and policies.   Lee Thornton

Dole, Robert Joseph (1923-   ), was the Republican nominee for Vice President of the United States in 1976. President Gerald R. Ford and Dole were defeated by their Democratic opponents, former Governor Jimmy Carter of Georgia and Senator Walter F. Mondale of Minnesota.

Dole has been a member of the United States Senate since 1969. He served as majority leader of the Senate from 1985 until 1987. He became minority leader of the United States Senate in 1987, after his party lost the majority in the Senate.

Early life. Dole was born on July 22, 1923, in Russell, Kans. His father, Doran Dole, worked in a grain elevator and later owned a cream and egg business. Dole attended the universities of Kansas and Arizona before he enlisted in the U.S. Army in 1943, during World War II.

© John Chiasson, Gamma/Liaison
Elizabeth H. Dole

In 1945, his right arm was permanently crippled during combat in Italy. Dole graduated from Washburn Municipal University (now Washburn University of Topeka) in 1952 and from the university's law school later that year.

Political career. Dole entered politics in 1950, when he won election to the Kansas House of Representatives. He was elected county attorney of Russell

UPI/Bettmann Newsphotos
Robert J. Dole

County in 1952 and won reelection three times. In 1960, Dole was elected to the United States House of Representatives. He was reelected in 1962, 1964, and 1966. He won election to the Senate in 1968. In Congress, he gained a reputation as a conservative and was especially known for his stinging criticism of Democrats.

In 1971, President Richard M. Nixon appointed Dole national chairman of the Republican Party. As chairman, Dole vigorously defended Nixon's Vietnam War policies and the President's role in the Watergate scandal (see **Watergate**). Dole resigned from the party chairmanship in 1973 and was reelected to the Senate the next year. In 1976, at the request of President Ford, the Republican National Convention nominated Dole as the party's candidate for Vice President.

Dole was an unsuccessful candidate for the Republican presidential nomination in 1980 and 1988. He was chairman of the Senate's powerful Finance Committee from 1981 to 1987. Dole's wife, Elizabeth, was secretary of transportation in the Administration of President Ronald Reagan from 1983 to 1987.   Charles G. Pearson

Dole, Sanford Ballard (1844-1926), led a group that helped make Hawaii a United States territory. In 1893, Dole took part in a movement that deposed Queen Liliuokalani. He then headed the provisional government.

Dole became president of the Republic of Hawaii in 1894 when President Grover Cleveland opposed annexation. The United States annexed Hawaii in 1898, after Cleveland left office. Dole served as the first territorial governor from 1900 to 1903, and as United States district judge in Hawaii from 1903 to 1916. Dole was born in Honolulu.   Pauline N. King

Dolin, *DOH lihn,* **Sir Anton** (1904-1983), became the first internationally famous English male dancer. He was partner to many great ballerinas, particularly Alicia Markova. Together they helped start English ballet. Dolin helped form and develop many companies, including what is now The Royal Ballet, the London Festival Ballet, and the American Ballet Theatre. He also led his own touring companies.

Dolin was born Sydney Francis Patrick Chippendall Healey-Kay in Sussex, England. He became the only English-born male dancer to star with the famous Diaghilev ballet company. Dolin enjoyed his greatest triumphs with Alicia Markova in his version of *Giselle* in the United States. As a *choreographer* (dance composer), Dolin composed his best-known ballet, *Le Pas de Quatre,* for Markova. He was knighted by Queen Elizabeth II in 1981.   P. W. Manchester

The enchanting world of dolls is filled with lovable characters of every description. Some dolls represent babies, children, teen-agers, or brides. Others include costume dolls and cloth dolls.

Doll

Doll is a child's toy made to look like a human being. Dolls vary in size from $\frac{1}{2}$ inch (1.3 centimeters) tall to life-sized or even larger. They may be made of almost any material, including cloth, plastic, porcelain, wax, and wood.

Boys and girls throughout the world enjoy playing with dolls. But dolls also appeal to many adults because of the toys' artistry and historical representation. Many grown-ups collect antique and costume dolls as a hobby and learn about the people of other times and places through these dolls.

Dolls fulfill many needs of children. They serve as playmates and objects for children's affection. Dolls can also provide an outlet for a child's hurt feelings, anger, and other emotions. For example, youngsters upset by a scolding might scold their dolls in turn. How children play with dolls may thus reveal their inner needs, fears, and desires. For this reason, psychologists use dolls to help them identify and treat many problems of children.

Dorothy Coleman and Evelyn Jane Coleman, the contributors of this article, are doll collectors and, with Elizabeth Ann Coleman, authors of The Collector's Encyclopedia of Dolls *and* The Collector's Book of Dolls' Clothes. *Unless otherwise credited, the photographs in the article are courtesy of the Museum of the City of New York.*

Playing with dolls enables children to rehearse the roles they hope to perform after they grow up, such as a parent or a doctor.

Doll-like figures have existed since ancient times. But dolls used mainly as toys for children probably were uncommon in most societies before the 1700's. Most doll-like figures from earlier periods were magical or religious objects, not toys. They were more like pieces of sculpture than toys. Ancient people made human figures as idols or *fetishes* (objects with magic power). Later, Christians made doll-like statues of saints and of figures for Christmas displays, called *crèches*. The figures in crèches showed the scene at Jesus' birth.

The toy dolls that existed before the 1700's served chiefly as playthings for adults as well as for children. At that time, adults and children were more alike in their attitudes and interests than they are today, and childhood as we know it did not really exist. Youngsters were regarded as little adults and were expected to act like them. They shared the work of supporting the family with their parents. People of nearly all ages enjoyed the same simple toys, including dolls and jack-in-the-boxes. Most of the dolls were shaped and dressed like adults.

Adults first came to regard childhood as a special time during the 1700's and especially the 1800's. The first dolls specifically for children probably were made in the 1700's. The dolls themselves looked the same but could be dressed as babies, children, women, or men. In the West, the first doll to be designed as a baby appeared at the London Exhibition of 1851 and came from Japan.

The word *doll* came into general use about 1750. It may have come from the Greek word *eidolon,* meaning *idol,* or from *Dolly,* a nickname for *Dorothy.* Previously, English-speaking people called dolls *puppets* or *babies,* even though most dolls represented adults.

Dolls around the world

Many manufactured dolls, including baby dolls, are the same throughout the world. But other dolls vary from country to country. These dolls include (1) costume dolls and (2) traditional dolls.

Costume dolls are dressed in the national or regional costumes of various countries. Many of the costumes worn by these dolls may represent holiday dress or work uniforms. Some costume dolls, however, wear clothing like that worn every day by many people of a particular country. For example, dolls from India wear a *sari*—a long piece of cloth draped around the body.

Most costume dolls are not toys. Instead, the dolls are made especially for the souvenir market. Dolls in local costume became a commercial item in the late 1800's, when travel became easier and the tourist trade suddenly began to develop. At first, most countries imported dolls from France and Germany, the leading doll-making nations of the time, and dressed the dolls in local costumes. In countries where most people had dark skin, fair-skinned imported dolls sometimes were tinted brown. Over the years, however, a number of countries began to make their own costume dolls.

Traditional dolls, or *folk dolls,* may also be dressed in regional costumes. But unlike most costume dolls, which are made in factories, folk dolls are made by local craftworkers using traditional handicraft skills. Most folk dolls are created from whatever materials are readily available in the area. For example, Eskimos make dolls from sealskin, and people in tropical regions weave dolls from palm leaves. Other materials used for folk dolls include clay, cloth, corncobs, deerskin, flowers, nuts, straw, and wood.

Few peoples or countries outside Europe had traditional dolls until they came into contact with European cultures. But over the years, many people developed their own traditional dolls. For example, the Sioux and other Indians of the Great Plains began to make dolls from deerskin decorated with glass beads and dyed porcupine quills. Indians still make dolls in this way.

African craftworkers make dolls of such native material as clay, feathers, and wood. Some dolls include discarded objects that the doll makers have found and reused. For example, some dolls have been made from various kinds of empty containers or even from old shoes.

Soviet craftworkers use pine cones and twigs to form traditional dolls known as *moss men.* The dolls' name comes from their dried-moss cloaks. Another traditional Soviet doll, the *matreshka,* is a set of four or more hollow wooden dolls that nest within one another. The Russians also made dolls out of triangular pieces of wood that were carved and painted.

Japan is one of the few countries in which children played with dolls before the country came into contact with Western customs. In fact, dolls were being made in Japan in the 1500's. Traditional dolls include round figures with rotating heads and figures of chubby baby boys. Doll making is an art in Japan, and skilled doll makers teach it at schools throughout the country.

Doll festivals and customs

The Japanese celebrate two yearly doll festivals, the Girls' Festival on March 3 and the Boys' Festival on May 5. During these celebrations, families display dolls that have been handed down for generations. Dolls for the Girls' Festival represent Japan's emperor and empress and members of their court. Dolls for the Boys' Festival include figures of heroes and warriors. Through the dolls, the children learn about their country's culture, history, and outstanding men and women.

Many people use doll-like figures in the practice of religion or magic, but such objects are not really playthings. For example, the Pueblo Indians of the Southwestern United States use figures called *kachina dolls* in their religion. The figures are carved from cactus root, cottonwood, and pine. Each is painted to represent one of the hundreds of *kachinas*—powerful spirits of the earth, sky, and water. To honor these spirits, the Indians hold ceremonies in which masked dancers seem to become the kachinas. After the ceremonies, Pueblo children are given the figures as educational toys to help them learn about the kachinas (see **Indian, American** [pictures: Kachina dolls]).

Many peoples practice a type of magic with dolls made in the likeness of their enemies. The *voodoo dolls* of the West Indies are a famous example. The magic involves sticking pins into the dolls or injuring them in

Margaret Woodbury Strong Museum, Rochester, N.Y.

Soviet stacking dolls, painted to look like peasants, are hollow and fit inside one another. Woodcarvers make these dolls, called *matreshka,* in sets of 4, 6, 8, 10, 12, or more.

Margaret Woodbury Strong Museum, Rochester, N.Y.

The Metropolitan
Museum of Art,
New York (Lisa Little)

Japanese festival dolls are displayed on shelves in homes during two yearly celebrations, the Girls' Festival on March 3 and the Boys' Festival on May 5. This pair of dolls, representing the emperor and empress of Japan, occupy the highest shelf during the Girls' Festival.

A fertility doll is carried by Ashanti women of Ghana to bring them beautiful children.

other ways in the hope that these actions will bring harm to the enemy.

In some societies, women carry figures called *fertility dolls,* which they hope will help them bear children, especially beautiful children. Ashanti women of Ghana tuck such a doll into their waistbands. Mfengu women of South Africa carry a fertility doll until their first child is born. The women then give the doll to the baby and get a new doll to carry until their next child is born.

The history of dolls

Ancient times. The earliest known doll-like figures are wooden images found in Egyptian graves dating from about 2000 B.C. The figures are known as *paddle dolls* because they are carved from a flat piece of wood shaped like a paddle. They are painted with patterns to look like clothes and have strings of clay beads to represent hair or a headdress. The paddle dolls resemble dolls, but they were religious figures, not playthings. The Egyptians believed they could enjoy life after death in an *afterlife.* They buried these dolls with the dead to provide them with servants in the afterlife.

Doll-like figures have also been found in Greek and Roman tombs dating from the 300's and 200's B.C. They have jointed, movable arms and legs. Elegant ones are carved from bone or ivory, but most are made of wood or clay. Scholars do not know whether these figures were dolls or religious objects. But they do know that girls in ancient Greece played with dolls until shortly before marriage. They then left their dolls on the altar of Artemis, the goddess of childbirth, to show they had outgrown childish things.

The Middle Ages. Scholars know very little about the toys of the Middle Ages, a period of European history that lasted from about the A.D. 400's to the 1500's. Almost no dolls from this period have survived. But drawings from the period show two boys playing with miniature armored soldiers.

The oldest surviving doll-like figures made of cloth date from the 500's to 600's and come from Akhmim, Egypt. They were found in graves of Copts, members of a Middle Eastern Christian group. The dolls' facial features and costumes are woven into the fabric that forms their bodies.

The Bartholomew Fair, which first took place near London in the 1100's, became famous for its dolls. The fair continued to be held for about 800 years. The use of the word *doll* may have originated with the toymen at this fair.

The Renaissance was a period of great cultural and intellectual activity that spread throughout most of Europe from the 1300's to about 1600. During the Renaissance, the number of dolls increased. An interesting collection of toys from the mid-1400's was discovered in Nuremberg, Germany. The toys are made of fine white clay that had been pressed into molds and baked. The collection includes dolls that represent children in swaddling clothes, little men, and fashionable women of the time. Some of these dolls may have been intended as christening gifts.

In 1485, pictures of Nuremberg doll makers at work were published in the book *Hortus Sanitatis.* Dolls also appear in Renaissance paintings of children, painted mostly by English and French artists.

The 1600's and 1700's saw an increased demand for dolls, both as toys for children and as representations of the fashions at royal courts. Before 1770, there were no fashion magazines. Dolls dressed in the latest fashions were distributed around the world.

The peasants who lived in the wooded areas of Europe often made wooden dolls during the winter months. These dolls, usually sold at fairs, were dressed as children, women, or men. The wooden dolls of about 1700 usually had painted eyes. Later, larger dolls had glass eyes. Most of the dolls had wigs made of either human hair or flax. But painted hair was popular for

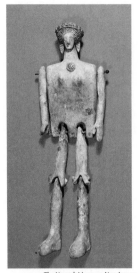

An ancient Greek doll, made about 400 B.C. of clay, is one of the oldest existing dolls.

English wooden dolls from the mid-1700's have dresses made of silk panels sewn together.

Papier-mâché dolls became popular during the early 1800's. These dolls, with molded hairstyles, were made in Germany from the 1820's to the 1840's.

smaller and less expensive wooden dolls. Cloth dolls were popular in this period, and many of them were probably made at home. Some were made of rolled cloth, and features were either embroidered or drawn on the face. Beeswax was another popular material for creating dolls.

Some dolls of the 1600's and 1700's were strictly adult amusements. In the 1700's, for example, French nobles played with dolls called *pantins.* A pantin was a jumping jack—a cardboard or wooden figure made to move by pulling a string attached to its arms and legs. At the end of the 1700's, dolls made of cardboard were mass-produced, especially in France.

The 1800's brought dramatic changes in adults' attitudes toward children, which greatly affected the history of dolls. Adults came to consider play important to children's development and so provided them with more dolls and other toys.

But in the first half of the 1800's, adults themselves found delight in *peddler dolls.* These dolls carried baskets with dozens of miniature items for sale, including buttons, brushes, kettles, and spools of thread. People usually bought the completed doll with its wares. The finished dolls were displayed under glass domes.

Toymakers of the 1800's created many new kinds of dolls using a variety of materials. According to collectors, the material of a doll is designated by the major material of the head. The majority of dolls can be grouped as: (1) wooden dolls, (2) cloth dolls, (3) papier-mâché and composition dolls, (4) wax dolls, (5) rubber dolls, and (6) porcelain dolls.

Wooden dolls from an area of Austria called the Grödner Tal (now part of Italy) were the most common commercial dolls in Europe and the United States during the early 1800's. Some English-speaking people called them *Dutch dolls,* a name that may have come from the German word *Deutsch,* which means *German.* The dolls may also have received their name from the

fact that many were shipped from the Netherlands by Dutch merchants. Some collectors today call them *peg-wooden* dolls because wooden pegs hold the joints together.

The earliest pegwoodens were carefully made, with carved hairstyles and with joints that turned smoothly. Most people bought them without clothes and dressed them at home. The dolls gradually became poorer in quality. The last ones, made in the early 1900's, were splintery and easily broken.

Cloth dolls of the 1800's included soft cloth dolls and dolls with stiffened fabric heads. Beginning in 1831, books offered instructions on how to make cloth dolls at home. Later, magazines such as *Ladies Home Journal* and *Delineator* gave instructions for making dolls. Some of these dolls had needle-sculptured faces, and others had smooth faces. The commercial manufacturers of stiffened fabric cloth dolls in the 1800's were Izannah Walker, George Hawkins, and Martha Chase, all of the United States. Beginning in 1889, Celia and Charity Smith of the United States designed cloth dolls that could be printed on cloth, cut out, and sewed together at home.

Papier-mâché and composition dolls were made by mixing a variety of ingredients. Papier-mâché chiefly consists of paper or wood pulp mixed with glue and clay or flour. Composition is a mixture chiefly of resin, sawdust, starch, and water. These mixtures are easily molded while wet and become hard and strong when dry. With the use of molds, it became easy to produce large quantities of dolls.

German factories began to mass-produce papier-mâché head-and-shoulder units for dolls in the early 1800's. Some of these shoulder-heads were bought by people who attached homemade bodies to them. Most papier-mâché dolls were made in factories as complete dolls with wooden arms and legs and bodies of a thin leather called *kid.* These dolls lacked any joints. Most of them represented females, and many had the fancy hairstyles of the time. Many were sold already dressed as children or adults. A few with simple molded hairstyles were dressed as men in top hats and knee-length, full-skirted frock coats. Papier-mâché dolls became highly popular, and German toymakers produced large quantities of them until the mid-1800's.

French toymakers produced a different type of papier-mâché doll during the 1800's. These French dolls appear cheap and flimsy, but they were actually rather expensive. Some were dressed as fine ladies, and others as clowns, babies in swaddling clothes, or military officers. Few of these fragile dolls have survived.

The first doll patented in the United States had a shoulder-head made of papier-mâché reinforced with cloth. Ludwig Greiner, a German-born toymaker in Philadelphia, patented it in 1858.

Composition dolls replaced papier-mâché dolls by about 1860. Most of the early composition dolls had a thin coating of wax to imitate the more expensive wax dolls.

Wax dolls are among the most fragile dolls. They break easily, and the wax melts or cracks in unsuitable weather. When the wax was reinforced with papier-mâché or composition, the dolls were more durable but not as artistic. Wax was used to cover almost every kind of material to make dolls and improve their appearance. Early in the 1800's, toymakers made waxed dolls' heads. Many of these heads had glass eyes and slits in which to insert hair. The eyes of some of these dolls could be opened and closed by pulling a wire. The early dolls had arms of colored kid representing long gloves. Later ones came with limbs of wood or composition. Some of these dolls had fancy hairdos of human hair or *mohair*

Wax dolls of the 1800's were made in two ways. The German doll, *left,* was made of a substance called *composition* and dipped in wax. The British doll, *right,* was made of poured wax.

(hair from the Angora goat). Others had hairdos and bonnets molded and waxed like the rest of the head.

For hundreds of years, waxworkers had made religious figures by pouring liquid wax into a mold and allowing the wax to harden. Some of the finest wax dolls were made this way in England by two famous doll-making families, the Montanaris and the Pierottis. These expensive dolls had hair inserted strand by strand and faces modeled after real people. For the Great Exhibition of 1851 in London, Montanari made wax dolls that represented the children of the British monarch, Queen Victoria.

The first baby dolls also appeared at the 1851 exhibition. They were made in Japan. Many had a wax head or a head of other material dipped in wax. The head had a few painted wisps of hair. The cloth-covered body contained a squeak box. In 1852, *Harper's New Monthly Magazine* criticized these new baby dolls, saying that they resembled real babies too closely, especially in their crying.

Rubber dolls. In 1839, Charles Goodyear, a Connecticut inventor, developed a process that made rubber stronger and gave it resistance to heat and cold. This process was called *vulcanization.* Dolls made of rubber were most popular in the 1850's and 1860's. They represented both sexes and various ages. When a rubber doll was new, it was an ideal toy because it would not break and was soft to touch. When the doll was old, however, the rubber disintegrated. Very few exist. Because manufacturers used the same molds over long periods of time, experts find it hard to date a rubber doll unless it has its original clothing.

Porcelain dolls. In the 1840's, china factories in Germany and Scandinavia began to make doll heads in glazed porcelain. Most heads were of females with pretty faces, pale skin, and dark hair. Matching porcelain arms and legs were also made. But many of the cloth bodies were made at home. The manufacturers also made complete porcelain dolls, now called *Frozen Charlottes.*

About 1860, French doll makers began to produce costly dolls known today as *fashionable dolls* because of their elaborate clothes. The dolls were then called *poupées* (the French word for *dolls*). Most of them represented elegant young women or older girls and were made with great artistry. They had unglazed or glazed porcelain heads, and some had matching porcelain limbs. Most of them had firmly stuffed kid bodies. More costly dolls had jointed wooden bodies, which were painted or covered with kid. A French doll-making firm called Gesland used a jointed body covered with a padded, knit fabric "skin." Many dolls made by Maison Huret, another French firm, had bodies of a rubberlike substance called *gutta-percha.*

A fashionable doll that was dressed usually cost three times as much as the same doll wearing only its *chemise* (undergarment). European stores sold the clothes and accessories for these dolls. The accessories included combs, fans, furs, and jewelry. Many dolls had trunks or pieces of furniture to hold their belongings.

In Germany in the 1860's, unglazed porcelain became fashionable for dolls' heads. This material was also called *bisque* or *biscuit.* Most bisque shoulder-heads for dolls had elaborate molded braids, curls, and ring-

Bisque dolls, made of unglazed porcelain called *bisque,* became popular in the late 1800's. These French dolls date from 1865 to 1880. The dolls representing children are called *bébés.*

lets decorated with combs, flowers, insects, jewels, or ribbons. Unlike the dark-haired porcelain dolls, most bisque-head dolls with molded hair were blond. Often the same mold was used for both the glazed and unglazed versions of the doll. During the 1890's, a much cheaper doll was made from a coarse bisque called *stone bisque.* Some of these dolls, known as *bonnet dolls,* have hats molded onto their heads.

During the 1870's, French doll makers began to make dolls with the body and facial features of children about 4 years old. These dolls were called *bébés,* a French word meaning *babies.* Most bébés were named after their manufacturer. For example, Bébé Bru was made by a firm founded by Leon Casimir Bru. Bébé Jumeau was manufactured by a company headed by Emile Jumeau. Many bébés had a new kind of body consisting of a hollow trunk and balljointed limbs strung together with elastic. This construction allowed a doll to hold more natural, childlike poses.

Inventions. Many of the doll manufacturers developed mechanisms that allowed the dolls to behave in a lifelike manner. One of the earliest devices made it possible for a doll to say "mama" and "papa." German inventor Johann Maelzel patented the device in 1824. In 1862, several designers—including Americans Enoch Rice Morrison and Joseph Lyon—patented dolls that could walk. In 1878, Elie Martin of France patented a doll that could swim. In 1879, doll maker Casimir Bru of France patented *Bébé Teteur,* a doll that nursed, and *Bébé Gourmand,* a doll that consumed food. In the 1880's, American inventor Thomas Edison reduced the size of

the record player he built so that it could fit inside the body of a doll and make it talk. Other patents included those for dolls with eyes that could wink and flirt.

Rivalry in the doll industry. Most porcelain dolls' heads for the French trade were made in Thuringia, Germany, until the late 1860's. At that time, François Gauthier (later spelled Gaultier), a French porcelain manufacturer, began to make bisque heads for dolls. In the mid-1870's, Frenchman Emile Jumeau, who also had a porcelain factory, created the famous Jumeau bébés. Gaultier and Jumeau made most of the bisque heads used on the French dolls in the late 1800's.

German manufacturers soon copied the Jumeau bébés. They were able to produce dolls that were less artistic but also less expensive. The Germans had learned how to pour *slip* (clay mixture) into the mold rather than press it into the mold as the French were doing. Pressing slip into the mold is a more expensive method. Soon the German manufacturers began to succeed at the expense of the French manufacturers. About 1890, Jumeau had to resort to using the cheaper pouring-slip method for making the heads of his bébés. By 1899, the various French doll makers combined for economic reasons into the Société Française de Fabrication de Bébés & Jouets. Salomon Fleischmann, a German living in France, controlled the group. Germans gained control of most of the doll business in France, England, and the United States.

The early 1900's produced a great variety of new dolls in many different materials. Bisque heads on composition bodies were the favorites. However, doll makers also used various types of composition heads. Composition dolls were often described as unbreakable. But composition cracked in time and was not as durable as bisque.

Before World War I. The emphasis in doll manufacturing during the early 1900's was on realism. Teachers and artists began to criticize the fashionable dolls as unnatural and unappealing to children. In Munich, Germany, a group of artists started a movement called *Puppen Reform* (doll reform). These artists designed all-composition dolls that were simple and natural. German doll makers Kämmer & Reinhardt and other firms manufactured dolls with bisque heads that were called *character dolls* because their faces showed realistic expressions.

Wooden dolls also reflected realism. In China, carved *Door of Hope* dolls had faces and clothes similar to what could be seen in that country. In 1911, Albert Schoenhut, a German-born toymaker of Philadelphia, patented his All-Wood Perfection Art Doll. The doll's joints had steel springs that enabled it to hold lifelike poses. Most Schoenhut dolls represented children or infants with realistic faces.

In 1909, an American illustrator named Rose O'Neill published a drawing of a character with large round eyes, a pug nose, and a curved-line mouth. O'Neill modeled the figure on her baby brother and called it *Kewpie,* a shortened form of the word *Cupid.* In 1913, doll manufacturers began producing Kewpie dolls. Kewpie dolls had small tufts of molded and painted hair, blue wings, and starfish-shaped hands. Millions of Kewpie dolls were made in bisque, Celluloid, composition, and other materials.

The comical kewpie doll came from a drawing by Rose O'Neill, an American illustrator. The dolls were first manufactured in Germany in 1913.

In the first decade of the 1900's, many U.S. businesses offered cloth dolls as advertising premiums. These dolls included Sunny Jim, a premium for Force cereal; Aunt Jemima, for Aunt Jemima pancake flour; and Buster Brown, for Buster Brown shoes.

When World War I broke out in 1914, European doll makers turned to other manufacturing activities, and the United States tried to fill the doll-manufacturing gap. One success appeared in 1915, when a New York City political cartoonist, Johnny Gruelle, obtained a design patent for a cloth doll named Raggedy Ann. Ann's twin brother, Raggedy Andy, appeared later. Both dolls became known by their red-and-white striped legs, red yarn hair, and shoe button eyes. Gruelle wrote a series of books about their adventures, beginning with *Raggedy Ann Stories* (1918). In general, however, U.S. manufacturers lacked skill and experience in producing dolls, and necessary materials were difficult to obtain. The doll-manufacturing gap existed until about 1920.

After the war, artists were especially successful with felt dolls, such as the Lenci dolls from Italy and the Chad Valley dolls made in England. Germany's economic problems in the early 1920's hindered the recovery of the German doll-making industry.

Dolls modeled on a newborn baby became popular in the 1920's. One of the most successful was the Bye-Lo Baby, first copyrighted in 1922 by an American sculptor named Grace Storey Putnam. Putnam used a newborn infant as a model, copying its half-closed eyes and fat neck. The first dolls had heads of wax. The dolls were later made of bisque, Celluloid, composition, rubber, vinyl, and wood. The Bye-Lo Baby became one of the most popular dolls ever and was known as the "million-dollar baby."

Margaret Woodbury Strong Museum, Rochester, N.Y.

A cloth doll from Italy is made of felt that has been molded into shape. An Italian designer named Elena Scavini made this doll in the 1920's under the trade name Lenci.

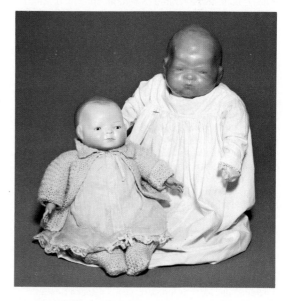

The Bye-Lo Baby was created in 1922 by the American sculptor Grace Storey Putnam. The Bye-Lo Baby on the left has a bisque head. The one on the right has a wax head.

Doll makers produced a number of other newborn baby dolls. The German firm of Armand Marseille made the bisque heads for many of these dolls. They included "My Dream Baby," produced by the U.S. firm of Arranbee; and "Rock-a-Bye Baby," made by the German firm of Cuno & Otto Dressel. Both of these dolls came in either a closed-mouth or open-mouth version.

The rise of motion pictures in the early 1900's led to the popularity of *portrait dolls*. These were dolls made to resemble well-known people or fictional characters. Among the most famous portrait dolls were those representing movie stars Charlie Chaplin, Jackie Coogan, and Shirley Temple.

Modern dolls. Plastic dolls appeared in the late 1940's, and plastic quickly became the most popular material for dolls. It first appeared in a hard form and then later as a soft material called vinyl. One of the earliest vinyl dolls was Sparkle Plenty, a doll with long blond hair and vinyl skin. The doll was based on a character in the "Dick Tracy" comic strip.

Beginning in the 1950's, children's television programs inspired many other portrait dolls. They included Howdy Doody, Yogi Bear, and "Sesame Street" characters.

The most successful dolls of the 1950's were the teenage fashion dolls. The first one was Lilli, a German doll based on a comic strip and produced in 1958. The American Barbie doll appeared in 1959. Like the fashionable dolls of almost 100 years earlier, these dolls have huge wardrobes. Unlike the fashionable dolls, they are play dolls rather than dolls made primarily to show fashions.

Also at this time, U.S. doll manufacturers began to use many technical devices to achieve a high degree of realism. They created dolls that changed expression, dolls with hair that appeared to grow, and dolls that played catch. A large number of dolls were mechanized, powered by batteries, operated by remote control, or run by a tiny computer inside the doll.

In the early 1960's, a soldier doll named G.I. Joe became the first doll designed specifically for boys to achieve worldwide popularity. Like Barbie, he has many clothes and accessories.

The 1970's brought renewed interest in the uncomplicated dolls of the past. As a result, manufacturers began to produce cloth dolls and other simple, homemade-looking dolls that encouraged make believe.

In the 1980's, Cabbage Patch dolls became the most popular dolls among young children. Each doll has its own name and even a birth certificate. Its head is made of vinyl, porcelain, or an elastic cloth called *stockinet*.

Also in the 1980's, ethnic dolls became increasingly popular. For example, some Cabbage Patch dolls and Barbie dolls had dark skin. A number of companies manufactured collections of dark-skinned dolls created primarily for black children.

The doll industry today

The creation of a modern doll begins in a doll manufacturer's design department, where artists sketch ideas for new dolls. After company officials select a design, the design department builds a full-sized clay or wax model of the doll. Mold makers then form metal molds from the model. In most cases, they make separate molds for the body, head, arms, and legs.

Most doll parts are molded from vinyl or other plastics. The chief molding processes are blow molding and rotational molding. In *blow molding,* a machine squeezes hot, softened plastic into a mold. A blast of compressed air forces the plastic outward against the mold's cool walls, where it hardens. In *rotational molding,* a worker squirts powdered plastic resin into a mold. The mold is put in an oven and rotated so the plastic melts and covers the inside walls of the molds. The plastic hardens as it bakes.

After either molding process, the molds are opened and the doll parts removed. Skilled workers add facial features and hair to the heads. Finally, assembly-line workers attach the heads and limbs to the bodies, dress the dolls, and pack them. The dresses may be made in the same factory or purchased from specialists. The clothes have to be redesigned nearly every year to keep them up to date with fashion trends.

Doll manufacturers compete intensely. Most introduce several new dolls every year and take great care to keep their designs secret. Companies spend millions of dollars a year on advertising—especially on television—to create a market for their dolls.

Today, China, Hong Kong, South Korea, and Taiwan are the leading producers of dolls. France, Germany and the United States are also major doll producers.

Doll collecting

Doll collecting is one of the most popular hobbies in the world. Collectors enjoy acquiring beautiful, artistic, rare, and unusual dolls. Depending on the kinds of dolls they collect, they may also learn about the history and customs of other countries through their hobby.

Antique dolls, particularly those more than 50 years old, usually are rare and costly. Many sell for $50 to $5,000 or more. Collectors buy and sell such dolls at auctions, antique shops, and shows, and through personal advertisements.

People who plan to collect dolls should study the subject of dolls before they buy any. They should read about the historical periods when dolls were produced and about the history of fashions and textiles. Above all, they should look at as many dolls as possible in museums, in private collections, and at shows.

What to buy. Collectors should try to buy antique dolls in the original clothing. It is always best if a collector can obtain a doll directly from its original owner. The owner is likely to have all the original clothes and also can tell the collector the doll's *provenance* (history).

Some sellers re-dress dolls to make them look "pretty," but this practice may decrease a doll's value and destroy clues that reveal its history. Many types of dolls were made for a period of 40 years or more. But collectors often can arrive at a more precise date for a doll by examining the style and features of the doll's original clothing. Collectors must remember, though, that more than one generation of children might have played with a doll, and the doll's clothes may belong to several different periods.

Many collectors specialize in dolls of a particular country, manufacturer, material, period or style. A specialized collection need not be costly. For example, you can find cloth dolls nearly everywhere. Or you might

How dolls are made

Doll manufacturers make most dolls from plastic. Separate molds are made for the body, head, arms, and legs. Workers then add facial features and hair and assemble the parts.

Workers spray-paint the dolls' facial features.

A device like a sewing machine adds hair to the heads.

Ideal Toy Corporation (WORLD BOOK photos)

Assembly-line workers put the dolls together.

concentrate on costume dolls. You could even make an interesting collection of dime-store portrait dolls, which are sold briefly and then become rare and possibly valuable. Such dolls include the figures from the 1960's of U.S. President John F. Kennedy and of the Beatles, the noted British musical group. Dime-store dolls include the figures from the 1980's of British royal couple Prince Charles and Princess Diana and U.S. singer and songwriter Michael Jackson. These portrait dolls are called *collectible dolls.*

The rules of good collecting apply as much to dime-store dolls as to antique dolls. Collect and keep only dolls that are complete and perfect. Save all labels and tags on dolls and their original boxes. Store the dolls carefully to protect them from damage and dirt. When you display them, be sure they are not exposed to damaging elements such as light, dust, or fumes. Keep up-to-date records of all your dolls.

Probably the most common mistake collectors make is to buy more dolls than they can afford or arrange in a pleasing display. A small collection of well-chosen and attractively displayed dolls is better than a large, unmanageable collection of poorly selected ones. Often, a collector can replace a poor example with a better example when one becomes available.

Many magazines focus entirely on dolls. These periodicals include the U.S. publications *The Doll Reader* and *Dolls; The Australian Doll Digest;* and magazines published in Germany and South Africa.

Dolls in museums

Many museums throughout the world have doll collections. Peddler dolls and other old dolls may be seen in London's Bethnal Green Museum, a branch of the Victoria and Albert Museum. The Musée Carnavalet and the Musée des Arts Decoratifs in Paris have rare dolls. Fine German collections are exhibited in the Germanic National Museum and the German Toy Museum in Nuremberg and the German Toy Museum in Sonneberg. Both cities are historic toymaking centers, and their museums have many dolls that probably were put away new many years ago.

The Strong Museum in Rochester, N.Y., which opened in 1982, includes the largest doll collection in a museum. The collection, which has about 25,000 dolls, was bequeathed by Margaret Woodbury Strong of Rochester.

Other excellent doll collections in the United States include those of the Museum of the City of New York; the Shelburne Museum in Shelburne, Vt.; the Wenham Museum, Wenham, Mass.; the Children's Museum, Indianapolis; and the Children's Museum, Boston. Many other U.S. museums have fine collections of dolls that are kept in storage and brought out for special displays.

Dorothy Coleman and Evelyn Jane Coleman

Related articles in *World Book* include:

Dollhouse	Puppet
Fetish	Toy
Kachina	United States (The
Play	arts [picture])

Outline

I. Dolls around the world
   A. Costume dolls
   B. Traditional dolls

Questions

What countries are the leading producers of dolls?
Where can you find the largest doll collection displayed in a museum?
When did the first baby dolls appear?
What are some rules of good collecting for beginning doll collectors?
What are *kachina dolls*?
What was the first doll specifically for boys to achieve worldwide popularity?
Where were the oldest known doll-like figures found?
What are some needs of children that dolls fulfill?
In what country do skilled doll makers teach people the art of doll making?
What doll became known as the "million-dollar baby"?

Additional resources

Level I
Brecht, Ursula. *Precious Dolls: A Treasury of Bisque Dolls.* HP Bks., 1984.
Glubok, Shirley. *Dolls, Dolls, Dolls.* Follett, 1975.
Horwitz, Joshua. *Doll Hospital.* Pantheon, 1983.
Lasky, Kathryn. *Dollmaker: The Eyelight and the Shadow.* Scribner, 1981.

Level II
Boehn, Max von. *Dolls.* Dover, 1972. First published in 1932.
Cieslik, Jurgen and Marianne. *German Doll Encyclopedia: 1800-1939.* Hobby Hse., 1985.
Coleman, Dorothy S., and others. *The Collector's Encyclopedia of Dolls.* 2 vols. Crown, 1968-1986. *The Collector's Book of Dolls' Clothes.* 1975.
Earnshaw, Nora. *Collecting Dolls.* Collins Pubs., 1987.
Merrill, Madeline O. *The Art of Dolls: 1700-1940.* Hobby Hse., 1985.

Dollar is the monetary unit of the United States, Canada, and many other countries. The dollars of the United States and Canada are paper bills or coins equal to 100 cents. The U.S. dollar was modeled after a Spanish coin called the *peso* or *piece of eight.* The origin of the dollar sign ($) is unknown. It probably developed from *ps,* an abbreviation of the word *peso.* The use of the dollar sign has become as widespread as the use of the currency it represents.

The term dollar is derived from *Joachimsthaler,* a word originally applied to a large silver coin made from metal obtained from the Joachimsthal mine in Bohemia. Shortened to *thaler,* the name was later applied to many large silver coins of about the same size.

The United States dollar. By the 1760's, the American Colonies used pieces of eight for business. Few British coins were shipped to the colonies. However, many pieces of eight circulated there as a result of illegal trade. By 1767, Maryland was issuing paper money in denominations that were expressed in dollars, and other colonies soon did the same. The American Continental Congress issued *Continental Currency* in order to finance the Revolutionary War in America (1775-1783) against Great Britain. These notes were promises of payment in dollars.

By an act of Congress in 1792, the dollar became the

The **Anthony dollar,** *above,* minted for circulation in 1979 and 1980, honored woman suffrage leader Susan B. Anthony.

WORLD BOOK photo by James Simek

WORLD BOOK photo

The **Canadian dollar coin** shown above was first minted in 1989. A slightly different version was issued from 1987 to 1989.

WORLD BOOK photo by James Simek

The **first U.S. silver dollar,** *above,* was minted in 1794. It had an eagle on the back and a liberty head on the front.

WORLD BOOK photo by James Simek

The **Peace dollar,** *above,* was issued in the United States from 1921 to 1935. The word *Peace* appeared on the back of the coin.

official currency unit of the United States. The values of all other U.S. coins were expressed in terms of the dollar's value. The earliest silver dollars appeared in 1794. Each weighed 27 grams (slightly less than 1 ounce). The amount of pure silver in the coins was just under 90 per cent in early years, and exactly 90 per cent after 1837. Silver dollars never became popular in the Eastern United States, where people preferred paper currency. But the coins circulated widely elsewhere, especially in the far Western states, the Pacific Northwest, and parts of the Southern States. The United States stopped producing silver dollars for circulation in 1935.

In the late 1900's, there were two attempts to revive the dollar coin. The Dwight D. Eisenhower dollar was minted from 1971 to 1978, and the smaller Susan B. Anthony dollar was minted in 1979 and 1980. Both were made of a copper-nickel composition. But neither coin became popular, perhaps because neither looked worth its stated denomination. Paper dollars now circulate widely in the United States, but dollar coins do not.

The dollar in other countries. Canada adopted the dollar in the 1800's, indicating the importance of the U.S. dollar in trading. The first paper dollars issued by the Dominion of Canada appeared in 1870. But Canada did not begin to make silver dollars until 1935, the year the United States stopped minting the coin. In 1987, a new Canadian dollar coin went into circulation. The front of the coin had an image of Queen Elizabeth II of Great Britain as a young woman. In 1989, Canada began minting a revised version of the coin, which showed Elizabeth as an older woman.

Hong Kong has used the dollar since the 1860's. Australia adopted it in 1966 and New Zealand, in 1967. Many former British possessions in the Caribbean adopted the dollar in the late 1960's and early 1970's.   R. G. Doty

See also **Money** (pictures); **Eurodollar; Half dollar.**

Dollar Decade. See Roaring Twenties.

Dollar diplomacy seeks to extend a nation's business interests in other countries through superior economic power instead of war. The term was first applied to United States policy in the Caribbean and other areas during President William Howard Taft's Administration. The period from 1909 to 1913 is generally considered the era of dollar diplomacy. See also **Taft, William H.** (Foreign affairs).   Robert J. Pranger

Dollhouse is a miniature house filled with tiny furniture and other home furnishings. Girls and boys like to play with dollhouses, and many adults enjoy building and furnishing them as a hobby. Old dollhouses also provide valuable information about life in the past.

The first dollhouses were made in the 1600's for wealthy adults. Many stood 6 feet (1.8 meters) tall or taller. They were furnished like the homes of their owners, with fine furniture, pictures, china, and silver. Many Dutch merchants had *cabinet dollhouses,* which were wooden cabinets with tiny rooms instead of drawers or shelves. Famous cabinet dollhouses include the Utrecht Dollhouse, made in 1670, and a dollhouse built in the early 1700's for a Dutch woman named Petronella Brandt. The Utrecht Dollhouse is in the Central Museum in Utrecht, and the Brandt Dollhouse is in the Rijksmuseum in Amsterdam, both in the Netherlands.

Similar dollhouses became popular in Great Britain during the 1700's. Unlike the Dutch dollhouses, the British ones looked like real homes from the outside. They were called *baby houses* because *baby* was an old word for *doll.* The famous designer Thomas Chippendale probably made furniture for one of these houses.

Children's dollhouses appeared in the 1800's. They were smaller than adult dollhouses. Many had only one room and stood about 1 foot (30 centimeters) high.

Fancy dollhouses continued to interest adults, how-

Museum of the City of New York (WORLD BOOK photo)

A furnished dollhouse includes beds, chairs, tables, lamps, and such household articles as books, clothes, dishes, and pictures. This complete six-room dollhouse dates from 1895.

ever. The Stettheimer Dollhouse in the Museum of the City of New York was made in the 1920's by a society woman named Carrie Stettheimer. Well-known artists, including Marcel Duchamp, Gaston Lachaise, and William Zorach, created tiny works especially for this house. Another famous dollhouse was made in the 1930's for the silent film star Colleen Moore. This dollhouse is now in the Museum of Science and Industry in Chicago.

A homemade dollhouse can be made from a wooden or cardboard box. Little rectangles of sandpaper can be used as bricks, and gift-wrap can serve as wallpaper. Furniture for the dollhouse can be made from many everyday materials. For example, a small handbag mirror might become a wall mirror for a dollhouse.

John Noble

Dolmen. See Megalithic monuments.

Dolomite, *DAHL uh myt,* is a mineral that serves as the chief source of magnesium obtained from the earth's crust. It is fairly hard and brittle and consists of calcium carbonate and magnesium carbonate. Dolomite's chemical formula is $CaMg(CO_3)_2$. Pure dolomite may appear white or yellow. Impurities, such as manganese or iron, may make dolomite pink, brown, or some other color. Dolomite and a mineral called *calcite,* which consists only of calcium carbonate, often look alike. Chemical tests may be used to tell the minerals apart.

The term *dolomite* also refers to rock composed principally of dolomite. This rock also is called *dolostone* or *dolomite rock.* Dolostone may form when magnesium carbonate replaces calcium carbonate in limestone or the skeletal remains of animals and plants. The rock also may form from minerals that settle out of seawater, or from hardened deposits of mud and mineral matter. Many mountain ranges in Europe and other parts of the world have great masses of dolomite rock. The rock also occurs in various parts of North America.

Iron and steel manufacturers use dolomite in the smelting process. Finely ground dolomite is used as a filler in paint, putty, and rubber. Marble composed of dolomite crystals is famous for its unusual colors and is used as a building material.   David F. Hess

See also **Marble.**

Dolores, Mission. See San Francisco (Residential districts; Early settlement; map).

Dolphin, *DAHL fuhn,* is a small, toothed whale. Like all whales, dolphins are mammals, not fish. Mammals, unlike fish, feed their young with milk that is produced in the mother's body. Also unlike fish, dolphins have lungs and are *warm-blooded*—that is, their body temperature always stays about the same, regardless of the temperature of their surroundings. Many scientists believe that dolphins rank among the most intelligent animals, along with chimpanzees and dogs.

Dolphins and other whales make up a group of mammals called *cetaceans.* This article deals with *marine dolphins.* Most species of marine dolphins live only in salt water. These animals inhabit nearly all the oceans. Many species remain near land for most of their lives, but some marine dolphins live in the open sea. A different family of cetaceans, called *river dolphins,* live in fresh or slightly salty water. The word *dolphin* also refers to a large game fish. See **River dolphin; Dolphin** (fish).

Marine dolphins are closely related to porpoises, an-

Jim Annan

A trained dolphin, *above,* leaps high out of the water to snatch an object from a trainer's hand. A dolphin can jump through a hoop and use its mouth to catch and throw a ball.

other group of sea mammals. Most zoologists classify marine dolphins and porpoises into one family consisting of about 40 species. The chief differences between dolphins and porpoises occur in the snout and teeth. "True" dolphins have a beaklike snout and cone-shaped teeth. "True" porpoises have a rounded snout and flat or spade-shaped teeth. However, these characteristics are not present in all species. Some scientists distinguish between dolphins and porpoises, but other experts use the term *dolphin* or the term *porpoise* for all members of the family. In this article, the word *dolphin* refers to all members of the family of marine dolphins and porpoises.

Types of dolphins

The various species of dolphins range from 4 to 30 feet (1.4 to 9 meters) long and weigh from 100 pounds (45 kilograms) to 5 short tons (4.5 metric tons). The most familiar types include *bottle-nosed dolphins, common dolphins,* and *common porpoises.*

Bottle-nosed dolphins are the best-known species. Their short beaks give these dolphins an expression that looks like a smile. Most of the performing dolphins in amusement parks, aquariums, and zoos are bottle-nosed dolphins. Members of this species measure up to 15 feet (4.6 meters) long and can weigh as much as 440 pounds (200 kilograms). They are gray, but their backs are darker than their undersides. Bottle-nosed dolphins show apparent great friendliness toward people and often swim alongside ships. They also adapt well to life in captivity.

Bottle-nosed dolphins live in warm or tropical waters. Most of them stay within 100 miles (160 kilometers) of land. Many live in bays and protected inlets, where the water is relatively shallow. Bottle-nosed dolphins frequently appear off the coast of Florida. They range as far north as Japan and Norway and as far south as Argentina, New Zealand, and South Africa.

Common dolphins have several distinct features. For example, a dark band around their eyes extends to the end of their long, narrow beak. Common dolphins also have black backs, white undersides, and prominent gray and yellowish-brown stripes on their sides. These dolphins grow from 6 to 8 feet (1.8 to 2.4 meters) long and weigh up to 165 pounds (75 kilograms).

Common dolphins live in warm or tropical waters. They often swim in large schools and are frequently seen in the open ocean. Common dolphins sometimes follow ships for many miles. As they do so, these playful dolphins may leap out of the water and turn somersaults.

Some kinds of dolphins

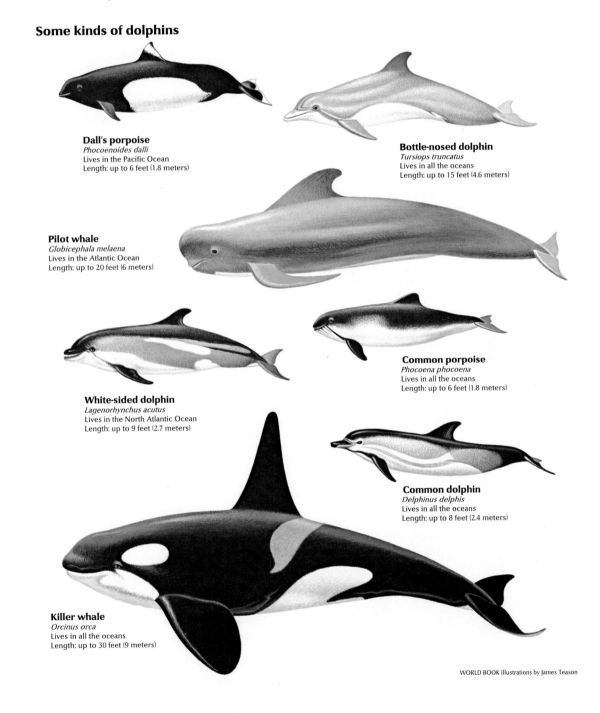

Dall's porpoise
Phocoenoides dalli
Lives in the Pacific Ocean
Length: up to 6 feet (1.8 meters)

Bottle-nosed dolphin
Tursiops truncatus
Lives in all the oceans
Length: up to 15 feet (4.6 meters)

Pilot whale
Globicephala melaena
Lives in the Atlantic Ocean
Length: up to 20 feet (6 meters)

Common porpoise
Phocoena phocoena
Lives in all the oceans
Length: up to 6 feet (1.8 meters)

White-sided dolphin
Lagenorhynchus acutus
Lives in the North Atlantic Ocean
Length: up to 9 feet (2.7 meters)

Common dolphin
Delphinus delphis
Lives in all the oceans
Length: up to 8 feet (2.4 meters)

Killer whale
Orcinus orca
Lives in all the oceans
Length: up to 30 feet (9 meters)

WORLD BOOK illustrations by James Teason

Common porpoises are one of the smallest species of dolphins. They seldom grow longer than 6 feet (1.8 meters), and they weigh from 100 to 120 pounds (45 to 54 kilograms). These dolphins, which are sometimes called *harbor porpoises,* usually travel alone or in small groups. They avoid people and lack the playfulness of some other species.

Common porpoises have black backs and white undersides. Many live in the cool waters of the North Atlantic Ocean and in other oceans, but they are rarely seen in the tropics. Members of this species sometimes swim up rivers in search of food. They have been seen in several major European rivers, including the Thames in England and the Seine in France.

Other species include the largest dolphins, which are called *killer whales.* Killer whales measure as long as 30 feet (9 meters) and may weigh 4 or 5 short tons (3.6 or 4.5 metric tons). Members of another species, known as *pilot whales,* or *blackfish,* grow 15 to 20 feet (4.6 to 6 meters) long. Pilot whales have gray to black backs and sides. They differ from other large dolphins because of their bulging foreheads. Among the most numerous species of dolphins are *spinner dolphins*, which sometimes spin on their sides when they leap out of the water.

Many kinds of dolphins have distinguishing colors or other markings. For example, *Risso's dolphins* are brown and gray, and most of them have many irregular white streaks. *White-sided dolphins* have gray, white, and yellow stripes on their sides. Their colorful markings make them popular attractions at many aquariums and zoos. *Spotted dolphins* are named for their white spots. *Striped dolphins* have black stripes on their undersides. *Dall's porpoises* have black bodies and white sides and are slightly larger than common porpoises.

The bodies of dolphins

All dolphins have torpedo-shaped bodies, which enable the animals to move through the water quickly and easily. They have a pair of paddle-shaped forelimbs called *flippers,* but no hindlimbs. Most species of dolphins also have a *dorsal fin* on their back. This fin, along with the flippers, helps balance the animal when it swims. Powerful tail fins, called *flukes,* propel dolphins through the water.

The skin of dolphins is smooth and rubbery. A layer of fat, called *blubber,* lies beneath the skin. The blubber keeps dolphins warm and acts as a storage place for food. It is lighter than water, and so it probably also helps dolphins stay afloat.

Like all other mammals, dolphins have lungs. The animals must surface regularly to breathe air and usually do so once or twice a minute. A dolphin breathes through a *blowhole,* a nostril on top of its head. The animal seals its blowhole by means of powerful muscles most of the time while underwater.

Dolphins have a highly developed sense of hearing. They can hear a wide range of low- and high-pitched sounds, including many that are beyond human hearing. Dolphins also have good vision, and the entire surface of their bodies has a keen sense of touch. All these senses function well both above and below the surface of the water. Dolphins have no sense of smell and little, if any, sense of taste.

Dolphins have a natural sonar system called *echolocation,* which helps them locate underwater objects in their path. A dolphin locates such objects by making a series of clicking and whistling sounds. These sounds leave the animal's body through the *melon,* an organ on top of the head. The melon consists of special fatty tissue that directs the sounds forward. Echoes are produced when the sounds reflect from an object in front of the dolphin. By listening to the echoes, the animal determines the location of the object.

Most kinds of dolphins have a large number of teeth. Some species have more than 200. Dolphins use their teeth only to grasp their prey, which are chiefly fish and octopuslike animals called *squids.* Dolphins swallow their food whole and usually eat the prey headfirst.

The life of dolphins

Most dolphins mate in spring and early summer. During courtship, the males, called *bulls,* and the females, called *cows,* bump heads and also take part in other rituals. The pregnancy period for most species of dolphins lasts from 10 to 12 months. The females almost always give birth to one baby, called a *calf,* at a time. One or more female dolphins may help the mother during birth. The calf is born tailfirst and immediately swims to the surface, sometimes with its mother's help, for its first breath of air. A newborn dolphin is about a third as long as its mother.

Tom Stack

Many sharp teeth line the dolphin's jaws. A fatty organ called the *melon* causes a bulge on top of the animal's head.

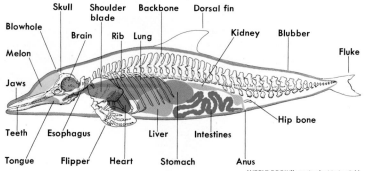

The body of a common dolphin

Skull · Shoulder blade · Backbone · Dorsal fin · Blowhole · Brain · Rib · Lung · Kidney · Blubber · Melon · Fluke · Jaws · Teeth · Esophagus · Liver · Intestines · Hip bone · Tongue · Flipper · Heart · Stomach · Anus

WORLD BOOK illustration by Marion Pahl

Dolphins travel in groups called *schools.* A dolphin swims by moving its tail and the rear part of its body up and down. The animal's streamlined shape and smooth skin reduce friction with the water.

Lewis Wayne Walker

Female dolphins, like all female mammals, have special glands that produce milk. The calf drinks the milk from its mother's nipples. The females nurse and protect their young for more than a year. Male dolphins take no part in caring for the young.

Most species of dolphins live at least 25 years. Some pilot whales reach 50 years of age. Sharks are the chief natural enemies of dolphins.

Some dolphins die after swimming into extremely shallow water and stranding themselves on the shore. The animals cannot live long out of water because their bodies become overheated. Scientists do not know why dolphins beach themselves. Some believe the beachings result from a malfunction in the echolocation system.

Group life. Most knowledge about the living habits of dolphins comes from aquariums and zoos. Killer whales seem to have the closest-knit family groups, most of which consist of from several to 17 or 18 animals. Bottle-nosed dolphins live in groups of about 12. Among some species the family units combine and form schools of 100 to 1,000 dolphins.

Most family groups consist of a dominant male, several females and their young, and a few immature dolphins of both sexes. The animals in such a group play and hunt for food together. They also help other members of the group that are in trouble. Dolphins sometimes use their backs or flippers to keep an ill or injured dolphin near the surface so it can breathe.

Dolphins communicate with one another by means of a complex series of sounds called *phonations.* The animals make these sounds in air-filled sacs connected to their blowholes. Phonations resemble the clicking and whistling sounds of echolocation.

Swimming and diving. Dolphins swim by moving their flukes up and down. This action differs from that of most fish, which propel themselves through the water by swinging their tail fins from side to side. Dolphins use their flippers to make sharp turns and sudden stops. Killer whales and some smaller species of dolphins can swim at speeds of 20 to 25 miles (32 to 40 kilometers) per hour. But they can maintain those speeds for only a short time. Most dolphins swim much slower.

Dolphins do not usually dive deeply, though they have the ability to do so. Some dolphins have been trained to dive more than 1,000 feet (300 meters). When a dolphin dives, its lungs collapse and its heart rate slows down. These actions allow the animal's body to adjust to the increasing pressure as the dolphin dives deeper underwater.

Dolphins and people

The attraction between dolphins and people goes back thousands of years. Ancient Greek artists decorated coins, pottery, and walls with pictures of dolphins, and the animals appear in Greek and Roman mythology. The ancient Greeks considered the common dolphin sacred to the god Apollo. For centuries, sailors have regarded the presence of dolphins near ships as a sign of a smooth voyage.

On the other hand, hunters of several nations, including China and Japan, kill thousands of dolphins annually. The dolphins provide meat eaten by people and animals, and the oil from their bodies is used as a lubricant. In addition, millions of dolphins have drowned in fishing nets that were intended to catch cod, mackerel, salmon, and other kinds of fishes. Tuna fishing crews were responsible for the largest number of these deaths among dolphins. For some unknown reason, dolphins often swim over large schools of tuna. As a result, nets

Wometco Miami Seaquarium

Baby dolphins are born in the water. The mother and other female dolphins push the infant to the surface for its first breath of air. The mother nurses its baby with milk for about a year. Dolphins breathe through a *blowhole* on top of the head.

meant to catch tuna trap many dolphins as well. In 1972, the United States government passed a law limiting the number of dolphins that could be killed yearly by tuna fishing crews. Improved fishing technology also greatly reduced the number of dolphins killed unintentionally by human beings. In 1990, leading U.S. tuna-canning companies announced that they would refuse to accept tuna caught in nets that also kill dolphins.

Since the mid-1900's, thousands of dolphins have been trained to perform tricks and stunts in shows presented by aquariums, zoos, and amusement parks. Scientists conduct various types of research on dolphins to understand their complex communication systems.

Training dolphins. Most trained dolphins in amusement parks, aquariums, and zoos are bottle-nosed dolphins, though many pilot whales, striped dolphins, and killer whales also perform in shows. These playful, intelligent animals sometimes invent stunts by watching other dolphins perform. Trained dolphins jump through hoops, throw balls through nets, or "walk" backwards on the water by using their powerful flukes. Some leap 15 to 20 feet (4.6 to 6 meters) out of the water to ring a bell or to take a fish from a trainer's mouth.

Research on dolphins is simplified by the willingness of the animals to submit to experiments. Most of the research has concentrated on dolphins' echolocation and communication systems. For example, dolphins that have been blindfolded with suction cups use echolocation to detect even small differences in the shape, size, and thickness of objects.

Dolphins communicate with one another by making a wide variety of sounds, and certain sounds apparently are associated with specific situations. For example, some zoologists believe dolphins make a particular sound when they are in trouble, though these distress calls vary. Eventually, researchers hope to learn the exact nature of the information that dolphins apparently transmit among themselves.

Scientific classification. Marine dolphins and porpoises make up the family Delphinidae in the order Cetacea. The bottle-

Biological Systems, Inc.
Dolphins communicate with one another through a series of clicks and whistles. In the picture above, a scientist records these sounds with a device called a *hydrophone*.

nosed dolphin is *Tursiops truncatus,* the common dolphin is *Delphinus delphis,* and the common porpoise is *Phocaena phocaena.*   H. Dean Fisher

See also **Killer whale; Pilot whale; River dolphin; Whale.**

Additional resources

Ellis, Richard. *Dolphins and Porpoises.* Knopf, 1982.
Fox, Michael W. *The Way of the Dolphin.* Acropolis, 1981. For younger readers.
Leatherwood, Stephen, and Reeves, R. R. *The Sierra Club Handbook of Whales and Dolphins.* Sierra Club, 1983.
Stonehouse, Bernard. *A Closer Look at Whales and Dolphins.* Watts, 1978. For younger readers.

Dolphin, *DAHL fuhn,* is a large game fish that lives in warm salt waters. It is also called *dorado* or *mahi mahi.* The largest dolphins are about 6 feet (1.8 meters) long and weigh 75 to 100 pounds (34 to 45 kilograms). They live in all tropical oceans. The dolphin's long body tapers toward a V-shaped tail. It is shimmery bluish-green and silver. A fast swimmer, the dolphin sometimes chases flying fish at sea for food. The dolphin is good to eat.

Scientific classification. The dolphin is a member of the family Coryphaenidae. The most common species is *Coryphaena hippurus.*   William N. Eschmeyer

See also **Fish** (picture: Fish of coastal waters).

Domagk, *DOH mahk,* **Gerhard,** *GEHR hahrt* (1895-1964), a German physician, identified the therapeutic ability of the chemical *prontosil rubrum,* the first of the sulfa drugs. He showed that this drug—commonly known by the trade name Prontosil—effectively destroyed streptococcic bacteria. These bacteria cause a wide variety of infections, including strep throat, scarlet fever, and impetigo. Domagk won the 1939 Nobel Prize in physiology or medicine for his discovery.

Domagk's later publications dealt chiefly with the search for a cancer cure. He was born in Lagow, Germany.   Daniel J. Kevles

See also **Sulfa drug** (Development of sulfa drugs).

Dome is a curved roof erected on a circular base, much like a bowl turned upside down. The earliest domes covered primitive huts and were made of brick or stone. The ancient Romans used domes to top such circular temples as the Pantheon in Rome. The Pantheon has one of the largest masonry domes ever built, with a height and a diameter of 142 feet (43 meters).

In the early A.D. 500's, the invention of *pendentives,* curved triangular supports, allowed architects to place domes over square buildings. Previously, builders could only construct domes on round buildings. One of the first large buildings to use pendentives was the church of Hagia Sophia in Constantinople (now Istanbul), completed in 537.

Renaissance domes, such as those atop St. Peter's Church in Rome and the Cathedral of Florence, are generally taller than earlier domes. The dome on St. Peter's provided the model for the dome on the United States Capitol and many others. Most mosques and Muslim tombs have domed roofs. The Taj Mahal in Agra, India, is a particularly beautiful example. Architects today have used huge domes to cover stadiums such as the Astrodome in Houston, Tex., and the Louisiana Superdome in New Orleans.   William J. Hennessey

For illustrations of domes, see **Architecture; Houston**

SCALA/Art Resource

Domes were an important feature of ancient Roman architecture. A dome covers the Pantheon, *above,* a temple in Rome.

(The Houston Astrodome); **India** (The Taj Mahal); **Milwaukee** (The Mitchell Park Conservatory); **New Orleans** (The Louisiana Superdome); **Washington, D.C.** (The United States Capitol). See also **Cupola; Fuller, Buckminster; Hagia Sophia; Pantheon; Taj Mahal.**

Dome of the Rock. See Jerusalem (Holy places; picture).

Domesday Book, *DOOMZ day* or *DOHMZ day,* was the first official record of the property holders living in England and the amount of land they held. The information was collected and recorded at the command of William the Conqueror in 1086, 20 years after he and his followers from Normandy crossed the English Channel and conquered England. Afterward, the properties of the great English landholders were taken over by William and his followers. William ordered the Domesday survey to discover how much land he owned, how the rest was divided, and how the land was peopled.

The kingdom was divided into districts. Each district supplied census takers who knew the territory. The census and the land survey covered most of the territory William controlled. No survey was held in either London or Winchester, and information about regions in northern England is incomplete. Nevertheless, Domesday Book is viewed as the greatest public record of medieval Europe. It is displayed at the Public Record Office in London.   C. Warren Hollister

See also **Norman Conquest.**

Domestic animal. See Animal (The importance of animals).

Domestic shorthair cat. See Cat (Short-haired breeds).

Domestic system. See Industrial Revolution (The textile industry).

Dominance is a form of behavior among individual animals that shows their ability to win aggressive encounters with other animals. These animals may be members of the same species or members of different species. Dominance determines which individuals have first choice of resources that are needed to survive and reproduce and that are in limited supply. These resources might include food, water, or mates. Individuals that lose the aggressive encounters or give in to domi-

nant individuals without a fight are called *subordinates.* Subordinates that are denied use of scarce resources may be among the first to die or to leave an area.

In a group, a particular individual may be dominant to some members and subordinate to others. This results in a *dominance hierarchy*—that is, a ranking of individuals by their dominance in relation to each other. In many cases, an individual loses to all those ranked above it and wins against all below it. This type of ranking is called *linear dominance hierarchy.* However, dominance hierarchies may be more complicated. For example, in *circular dominance hierarchy,* individual A may be dominant to individual B and B dominant to individual C, but C is dominant to A. Individuals can change their position in the group's dominance hierarchy as their ability to win fights changes with experience or maturity.

Encounters that establish dominance only occasionally include actual fighting. In most cases, these encounters involve only certain signals that indicate an individual's willingness or ability to win a potential fight. An individual's large size or threatening natural weapons, such as the horns of mountain sheep, might be enough to cause subordinates to give up without a fight.

Dominance differs from *territoriality,* a form of animal behavior in which an individual or group claims a certain area as its own (see **Territoriality**). A dominant individual usually can win wherever it is.   Larry L. Wolf

Domingo, *doh MIHNG goh,* **Placido,** *PLAH see doh* (1941-   ), a Spanish tenor, became one of the most popular opera singers of the 1900's. Domingo gained international praise for his performances in lyric and heroic roles in Italian operas. He has also sung a number of major roles in the German operas of Richard Wagner.

Domingo was born in Madrid. He moved with his family to Mexico in 1950 and studied singing at the National Conservatory of Music in Mexico City. Domingo made his opera debut in 1960 in Monterrey, Mexico, as Alfredo in *La Traviata.* Domingo sang in Israel and in the United States before becoming a leading tenor with the New York City Opera from 1965 to 1968. He made his debut with the Metropolitan Opera in 1968 as Maurizio in *Adriana Lecouvreur.*   Reinhard G. Pauly

Dominic, Saint (1170?-1221), was a Spanish religious leader. Dominic founded the Order of Friars Preachers, also called the Dominican Order. He was born in Calaruega in the Old Castile region of Spain. He studied at

WORLD BOOK photo

Dominance affects how wolves behave with one another. Low-ranking wolves retreat at threats from the pack leader, *far left.*

the University of Palencia and became a canon at the cathedral of Osma, near El Burgo. Later, he opposed the heretical teachings of the Albigenses. In 1216, Pope Honorius III gave him permission to establish a new religious order for the purpose of preaching against heresy. By the time of Dominic's death, the order had spread throughout Europe. Saint Dominic's feast day is celebrated on August 4.   William J. Courtenay

See also **Albigenses; Dominicans.**

Dominica, *DAHM uh NEE kuh* or *duh MIHN uh kuh,* is a small island country in the Caribbean Sea. It consists of one island that lies 320 miles (515 kilometers) north of the Venezuelan coast (see **West Indies** [map]). Dominica has an area of 290 square miles (751 square kilometers) and a population of about 86,000.

Dominica became independent in 1978 after being ruled by Great Britain since the 1700's. Its official name is Commonwealth of Dominica. Roseau, which has a population of about 11,000, is the capital and largest city. Dominica's basic unit of money is the East Caribbean dollar. For a picture of the Dominican flag, see **Flag** (Flags of the Americas).

Government. Dominica is a republic. A president is officially the country's chief executive. But a prime minister is the most powerful official. The prime minister is a member of an eight-member Cabinet, which conducts the operations of the government. A legislature called the House of Assembly makes the nation's laws. It consists of 21 members elected by the people and 3 appointed by the government. The legislature elects the president. The prime minister is the leader of the political party with the most seats in the legislature.

People. Most Dominicans have African or mixed African, British, and French ancestry. A small percentage of Dominicans have mostly Carib Indian ancestry. About four-fifths of the people live in rural villages, and the rest live in urban areas. Most of the people of Dominica live in Western-style houses or in thatch-roofed huts. They wear Western-style clothing. Their main foods include bananas, crabs, crayfish, frog legs, lobsters, and sweet potatoes.

The majority of Dominicans who live in cities speak English, the nation's official language. The villagers speak chiefly a kind of language called *French patois,* which is a mixture of African languages and French. About 80 per cent of the people are Roman Catholics,

© Fritz Henle, Photo Researchers, Inc.

Dominica is a small island country in the Caribbean Sea. The village of Soufrière, *above,* lies on the country's southern coast.

and almost all the rest are Protestants. Dominica has about 55 elementary schools and 7 high schools.

Land and climate. Dominica is a mountainous, tree-covered island formed by volcanic eruptions. Some mountains in the north and south rise over 4,000 feet (1,200 meters). Flat land lies on parts of the coast. The country has many rivers, but most are too rough to be used by boats other than canoes. Temperatures in Dominica seldom rise above 90° F. (32° C) or fall below 65° F. (18° C). Annual rainfall ranges from 79 inches (201 centimeters) in Roseau, on the southwest coast, to 400 inches (1,000 centimeters) in the mountains.

Economy of Dominica is based on agriculture. More than 60 per cent of the people work on farms, and most of the rest are employed in processing agricultural products. Bananas are the country's chief product and export. Other products and exports of Dominica include coconuts and coconut by-products. Manufacturing, mining, retail trade, and tourism are minor economic activities.

History. Arawak Indians, Dominica's first inhabitants, settled there about 2,000 years ago. Carib Indians took over the island about 1,000 years later. On Nov. 3, 1493—a Sunday—Christopher Columbus became the first European to sight the island. He named it *Dominica,* the Latin word for *Sunday.*

French and British settlers began to arrive in Dominica in the 1600's. For many years, the Carib, British, and French fought for control of the island. The British gained possession of it in 1763 and shipped African slaves to Dominica as farmworkers. Britain freed the slaves in 1834. From the 1930's to the 1970's, Britain gradually increased Dominica's control over its own affairs. Dominica gained independence on Nov. 3, 1978.

In 1979, a major hurricane struck Dominica. It killed over 50 people and caused much damage. In 1983, Dominica and several other Caribbean nations joined the United States in an invasion of Grenada, another West Indian country, to overthrow a Marxist government there. See **Grenada** (History and government).

Gustavo A. Antonini

See also **Roseau.**

Dominica

WORLD BOOK map

⊛   National capital

·   Other city or town

+   Elevation above sea level

      Road

Dominican Republic

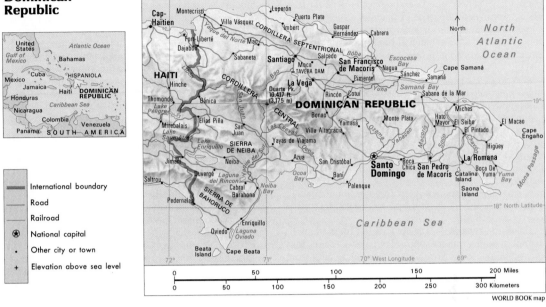

WORLD BOOK map

Legend:

━━━ International boundary

─── Road

─── Railroad

⊛ National capital

• Other city or town

+ Elevation above sea level

Dominican Republic is the country that makes up the eastern two-thirds of the island of Hispaniola. Haiti covers the island's western end. The Dominican Republic is in the West Indies island group, about 575 miles (925 kilometers) southeast of Miami, Fla. The country is a land of fertile valleys and forested mountains.

About half of the Dominicans live on small farms or large plantations. Santo Domingo, a busy port city of about 1,313,000, is the capital and largest city. The country's name in Spanish, the official language, is República Dominicana.

Christopher Columbus landed on Hispaniola in 1492. Some historians believe he is buried on that island in the Cathedral of Santo Domingo. Santo Domingo was the first city in the Western Hemisphere founded by Europeans. The University of Santo Domingo, which was established in 1538, is the oldest university in the Western Hemisphere.

During much of its history, the Dominican Republic has been ruled by dictators and by other countries. United States troops occupied the Dominican Republic twice in the 1900's to halt fighting between political groups there.

Government. A president heads the Dominican Republic. The president appoints a Cabinet. The national legislature consists of a 27-member Senate and a 120-member Chamber of Deputies. The people elect the president and legislators to four-year terms. Only civilians over 18 can vote.

The Dominican Republic is divided into 26 provinces and one national district—the capital and its surrounding area. The president appoints provincial governors and *commune* (county) leaders. The people elect the leaders of the country's 100 *municipios* (townships).

People. Most Dominicans speak Spanish and follow other ways of life brought to their land from Spain. The early Spanish colonists nearly wiped out the Indians who lived on the island before the Spaniards arrived. African influence, which came to the country chiefly by way of Haiti, is strong. In Haiti, most of the people are descendants of slaves from Africa.

About 75 per cent of the people are of mixed black and white descent. About 10 per cent are black, and about 15 per cent white. Some descendants of ex-slaves from the United States live near Samaná Bay in the northeast. A small group of European Jews settled near Puerto Plata in the north about 1940.

About 40 per cent of the people live in rural areas and work on farms. Some own small farms and raise their

Facts in brief

Capital: Santo Domingo.
Official language: Spanish.
Form of government: Republic. *Head of state*—President.
Area: 18,816 sq. mi. (48,734 km²). *Greatest distances*—east-west, 240 mi. (388 km); north-south, 170 mi. (274 km). *Coastline*—604 mi. (972 km).
Elevation: *Highest*—Duarte Peak, 10,417 ft. (3,175 m) above sea level. *Lowest*—Lake Enriquillo, 150 ft. (46 m) below sea level.
Population: *Estimated 1991 population*—7,312,000; density, 389 persons per sq. mi. (150 per km²); distribution, 60 per cent urban, 40 per cent rural. *1981 census*—5,647,977. *Estimated 1996 population*—8,050,000.
Chief products: *Agriculture*—avocados, bananas, cacao, coffee, mangoes, rice, sugar cane, tobacco. *Mining*—gold, nickel. *Manufacturing*—molasses, sugar.
National anthem: "Himno Nacional."
Flag: A white cross divides the *national flag,* flown by the people, into alternately red and blue quarters. Blue stands for liberty, white for salvation, and red for the blood of heroes. The *state flag,* used by the government, has the Dominican coat of arms in its center. See **Flag** (picture: Flags of the Americas).
Money: *Basic unit*—peso. For the price of the peso in U.S. dollars, see **Money** (table: Exchange rates). See also **Peso.**

own food. They sell some of what they raise to buy clothing, household goods, and other items. Other farmers work for wages on large plantations, especially sugar plantations. Many Dominican farmers live in two-room shacks that have thatched roofs and dirt floors. But small bungalows built by the government are slowly replacing these shacks. Most city dwellers earn a living as factory workers, as government employees, or by fishing. Many of them live in crowded, old Spanish-style apartment buildings. Dominicans dress in much the same way as people in the United States.

Dominicans love music that mixes the rhythmic pounding of African drums with the rattle of Spanish *maracas* (dried gourd shells with seeds and lead inside). Dominicans enjoy dancing the *merengue,* the national dance.

Most Dominicans are Roman Catholic. Some people who live near the Haitian border practice voodoo religions (see **Voodoo**).

Children between the ages of 7 and 14 must attend school. The government supplies most of the funds for most schools. About two-thirds of Dominican adults can read and write.

Land. The West Indies lie between the Atlantic Ocean and the Caribbean Sea. Hispaniola is formed by the peaks of two undersea mountain chains, one coming from Cuba and the other from Jamaica.

The Dominican Republic is a mountainous land. The *Cordillera Central* (Central Mountain Range) runs from northwest to southeast through the center of the country. Duarte Peak, which rises 10,417 feet (3,175 meters) above sea level in the Cordillera Central, is the highest point in the West Indies. The land west of the Cordillera Central is mostly dry and desertlike. Mountains in the west include Sierra de Neiba and the Sierra de Bahoruco. Lake Enriquillo, the lowest point in the West Indies at 150 feet (46 meters) below sea level, lies between these mountains.

The *Cibao* lies north of the Cordillera Central. The *Cibao* is an area of pine-covered slopes and a fertile plain called the *Vega Real* (Royal Plain). It is the country's chief agricultural area. The *Cordillera Septentrional* (Northerly Range) is in the far north.

The eastern end of the Dominican Republic is less mountainous. Most of the country's sugar cane is grown along the southern coast east of Santo Domingo and in other eastern areas.

The Dominican Republic has a warm, tropical climate all year. Temperatures vary little and seldom go below 60° F. (16° C) or above 90° F. (32° C). The country averages about 60 inches (150 centimeters) of rainfall a year. The rainy season lasts from May to November in the south and from December to April in the north. Hurricanes sometimes strike the Dominican Republic.

Economy. The Dominican Republic is an agricultural country. About half of the working people are farmers. Most of the farmers work on their own small farms, or as sharecroppers for large landowners. Others rent land from large landowners. Large plantations, most of them owned by wealthy Dominicans and the government, also employ many farm workers. The broad, fertile plains are heavily farmed to produce avocados, bananas, mangoes, oranges, rice, sugar cane, and tobacco. In the forest-covered mountain foothills, coffee and

cacao beans (seeds used to make chocolate) grow in the shade of fruit and mahogany trees.

Most manufacturing in the Dominican Republic is related to the processing of farm products, especially sugar cane. Refineries process about 1 million short tons (910,000 metric tons) of sugar cane annually, and about three-fourths of it goes to the United States. The people consume most of the rest or turn it into molasses and rum. Other manufactured products include cement and textiles.

Gold and nickel rank as the most important mining products of the Dominican Republic. The country also mines clay, gypsum, limestone, and salt. Salt is also produced by the evaporation of seawater.

Less than 2 per cent of all Dominicans own an automobile. Many Dominicans own a radio, and the country has an average of about 1 television set for every 15 people. About 10 daily newspapers are published in the Dominican Republic. Santo Domingo has an international airport.

History. Christopher Columbus landed on Hispaniola on Dec. 6, 1492, on his first voyage to the New World. He ordered Fort Navidad built on the north coast from the ruins of his flagship, the *Santa Maria.* He returned in 1493 with about 1,300 men to seek the island's gold. Columbus found that the Indians had destroyed the fort and killed the men he had left behind. Thousands of Spanish colonists soon came to Hispaniola. They conquered the Indians and established towns on the north

Georgio Ricatto, Shostal

A statue of Christopher Columbus stands in the Piazza Colon in Santo Domingo, the capital of the Dominican Republic.

coast. In 1496, they founded La Nueva Isabela (now Santo Domingo).

By the mid-1500's, the scarcity of gold in Hispaniola sent Spaniards in search of more promising lands. They moved on to Cuba, Mexico, and Peru. Hispaniola had barely 30,000 inhabitants and produced little of value. It was neglected by Spanish trading vessels. Pirates and Dutch, English, and French merchants began trading with the people in the small ports on the northern and western coasts.

In 1606, Spain ordered all Spanish settlers to move to the Santo Domingo area to strengthen the defense of Santo Domingo and increase trade for Spanish merchants there. This plan backfired when non-Spanish settlers moved into the abandoned lands in the interior and on the northern coast. By the Treaty of Ryswick of 1697, Spain turned over the western third of the island (now Haiti) to France.

The French section prospered, but the Spanish section suffered from neglect. Black slaves in Haiti, led by Toussaint L'Ouverture, rebelled against their French masters and conquered the whole island by 1801. France and Spain recovered their colonies for brief periods after 1801, but the Haitians gained control of the island again in 1822.

Dominican heroes Juan Pablo Duarte, Francisco del Rosario Sánchez, and Ramón Mella led a successful revolt against the Haitians in 1844. From 1861 to 1865, at the Dominicans' request, Spain governed the country to protect it from the Haitians. Dictator Ulises (Lilis) Heureaux, who ruled the country from 1882 to 1899, left it in debt to several European nations. The United States took over the collection of customs duties in the Dominican Republic from 1905 to 1941 and used the money to pay the debts. From 1916 to 1924, U.S. Marines occupied the Dominican Republic to keep peace between rival politi-

cal groups and to prevent *anarchy* (complete disorder) in the area during a critical time in world affairs.

Rafael Leonidas Trujillo Molina seized power in a military revolt in 1930. He ruled the Dominican Republic harshly for 30 years, allowing little freedom and imprisoning or killing many of his opponents. Trujillo carried out some beneficial projects, such as rebuilding Santo Domingo after a destructive hurricane in 1930. He ruled efficiently, and the country prospered economically. But the people gained little or no benefits, because all the profits were channeled to the Trujillo family.

Conspirators shot and killed Trujillo in 1961. A power struggle then began among the military, the upper class, the people who wanted a democracy, and those who favored Communism. Juan Bosch, a writer and popular foe of Trujillo who had been exiled, promised land and economic aid to the people. He was elected president in December 1962, but military and upper class leaders ousted him in September 1963. They charged him with allowing too many Communists in the government. Military leaders then formed a three-member *junta* (council) to govern.

Rebels tried to seize power in 1965. They captured parts of Santo Domingo, but met strong military opposition. President Lyndon B. Johnson sent U.S. troops to the Dominican Republic in April 1965 to maintain order. He said he acted to protect U.S. citizens there and to keep Communists from taking over the country. Some members of the Organization of American States also sent troops. A truce was arranged in May 1965. The last foreign troops left the country in September 1966.

In June 1966, Dominican voters elected Joaquín Balaguer president over Juan Bosch. Balaguer had previously served as president from 1960 to 1962, chiefly during the Trujillo dictatorship. Balaguer was reelected in 1970 and 1974. In 1978, Antonio Guzmán was elected president. In 1982, the voters elected Salvador Jorge Blanco president. Guzmán died a month before he was to leave office. Vice President Jacobo Majluta served as president until Blanco's term began. Balaguer was elected president again in 1986. He was reelected in 1990.

In 1979, a hurricane killed more than 2,000 people and destroyed the homes of about 200,000 others in the country. The hurricane caused an estimated $1 billion worth of property damage.   Gary Brana-Shute

Related articles in *World Book* include:

Grant, Ulysses S. (Foreign relations)	Santiago
	Santo Domingo
Haiti	Santo Domingo, University of
Roosevelt, Theodore (Foreign policy)	West Indies

Dominicans are members of a Roman Catholic religious order founded by Saint Dominic of Spain in the early 1200's. Its official name is the Order of Preachers.

Today, the Dominican order consists of about 123,000 men and women throughout the world. It is comprised of friars, priests, nuns, sisters, members of the *secular institutes,* and the *laity.* Members of secular institutes live in regular society but have taken religious vows. Members of the laity follow Dominican teachings but have not taken religious vows. From their founding until 1968, the Dominicans were divided into three orders. The First Order was made up of friars, the Second

© Angelina Max, Photo Researchers

The sugar cane crop is the Dominican Republic's most important product. Plantation workers cut most of the crop by hand.

Order was made up of nuns, and the Third Order, also known as tertiaries, was comprised of sisters and the laity. In 1968, the Dominican order eliminated the distinction between the three orders and adopted the name *the Dominican Family.*

Saint Dominic established the Dominicans to oppose *heresy.* He founded the Second Order in 1206 and the First Order in 1216. Within a generation of their founding, Dominicans staffed theological faculties of major universities. The order included such famous theologians as Saint Albertus Magnus, Saint Thomas Aquinas, Johannes Eckhart, Saint Catherine of Siena, and Saint Martin de Porres. The emphasis on preaching, teaching, and theological study continues today.   Ann Willits

See also **Dominic, Saint; Albertus Magnus, Saint; Aquinas, Saint Thomas; Catherine of Siena, Saint; Eckhart, Johannes; Friar.**

Dominion Day. See Canada Day.

Domino theory. See Vietnam War.

Dominoes, *DAHM uh nohz,* is the name of several games played with small, flat, oblong pieces called dominoes. Dominoes were probably invented in China, and introduced in Europe in the 1300's. Most sets of dominoes are made of bone, ivory, plastic, or wood. A regular set consists of 28 dominoes. A line divides each domino into two sections. Each section of 21 of the 28 dominoes is marked with from one to six dots. Both sections on one domino are blank, and six dominoes have one blank section and one section with dots.

The simplest domino game is called the *block* game. In this game, the players first place all the pieces facedown and mix them well. Then each chooses a certain number, usually seven if there are two playing, or five if there are three or four. The player with the highest *double domino* (piece with matching sections of dots) usually plays first. Suppose it is the 4-4. The player at the left plays next by matching any domino with four dots in one section to the 4-4 domino. For example, the matching domino may be the 4-6. The following player may then match a section with six dots to the 4-6 domino, or a section with four dots to the 4-4. *Single dominoes* (pieces with different sections of dots) are placed end to end. Double dominoes are placed at right angles to the line of pieces. Plays can be made on either end of a single domino. Plays can be made on both sides of a double, but not on the ends.

If the players cannot match from the dominoes they have chosen, they draw from the pile that remains until they find one that will match. After the pile is used, play-

ers who cannot match must miss a turn, or *pass.*

The game ends when one player runs out of dominoes or when no player can match any of the remaining dominoes with those he or she still holds. A player who goes out scores points equal to the number of dots on the other players' pieces. If no one goes out, the player with the fewest dots on his or her unplayed dominoes scores the difference between this number and the total number on the opponents' unplayed dominoes. In most games, the first player to reach 100 points wins.
    R. Wayne Schmittberger

Domitian, *duh MIHSH uhn* or *doh MIHSH ee uhn* (A.D. 51-96), succeeded his brother Titus as Roman emperor in A.D. 81. His father Vespasian had been emperor from A.D. 69 to 79. When he became emperor, Domitian tried to restore old standards of conduct and religion and to control the greed of provincial governors. He settled a war with Dacia (now Hungary and Romania) by compromise and extended the Roman frontier in Germany. During his reign, people of other religions, such as Christians and Jews, were persecuted. His absolute rule made him unpopular with the Roman Senate. He was assassinated in his palace.   F. G. B. Millar

Domus Aurea. See Rome (Other remains).

Don Juan, *dahn JOO uhn,* or, in Spanish, *dohn HWAHN,* is the hero of one of the most famous legends in literature. The legend originated in Europe during the Middle Ages. Its form became established in *The Trickster of Seville* (1630), a play by the Spanish author Tirso de Molina. In this work, the handsome nobleman Don Juan Tenorio seduces many women. But when he tries to seduce the daughter of the knight commander Don Gonzalo, Don Gonzalo challenges him to a duel. Don Gonzalo is killed by the hero. Don Juan visits the commander's tomb and scornfully invites the statue of his victim to dinner. The statue appears at the feast and returns the invitation, which Don Juan accepts. In the graveyard, the statue takes Don Juan's hand and drags him down into hell as apt punishment for his crimes against God and society.

The complex personality of Don Juan has fascinated writers and composers for hundreds of years. He has appeared in plays by Molière and George Bernard Shaw, an opera by Mozart, and a poem by Lord Byron. José Zorrilla's *Don Juan Tenorio* (1844) is the most popular treatment of the theme in modern Spanish literature. Each interprets Don Juan's personality differently.
    Harry Sieber

Don Quixote, *dahn kih HOH tee* or *dahn KWIHK suht,* is a novel by Miguel de Cervantes of Spain. Cervantes published the novel in two parts, in 1605 and 1615. Until the 1800's, *Don Quixote* was thought of as a humorous story of a madman's adventures. Then, it became a model for a new type of fiction with heroes who do not conform to their times.

The hero of *Don Quixote* is a Spanish landowner who enlivens his monotonous life by reading fictional tales about knights of old, which he believes to be true and accurate. Wishing to live like the knights, he takes the name Don Quixote of La Mancha, dresses in armor, and sets out to gain fame by performing heroic deeds. He attacks windmills he thinks are giants and flocks of sheep he mistakes for armies. The peasant Sancho Panza serves as Don Quixote's *squire* (attendant) during the

In playing dominoes, each person matches a section of a domino with an identical section of an opponent's domino.
WORLD BOOK photo by Ralph Brunke

Drawing (1955) by Pablo Picasso (Art Resource)

Don Quixote and Sancho Panza, one of them lanky and the other squat, have been popular subjects in art for centuries.

hero's adventures. Small, round Sancho riding his donkey contrasts with the tall, thin Don Quixote on his scrawny horse Rocinante. Sancho stands for the real in life, Don Quixote for the ideal. Their conversations together make up a large part of the novel.

Although beaten and scorned, Quixote still believes in his heroic destiny. When part two of the novel begins, he is amazed to discover that the first part of his life has been published. He must now live up to his literary fame. He loses faith in his destiny, becomes a prisoner of his imagined reputation, and is forced to behave as if he really believed in himself as a hero. Quixote finally regains his senses before he dies.   Harry Sieber

See also **Spanish literature** (The 1600's).

Don River is an important waterway in the southern part of the Soviet Union. The Don rises from a small lake near Tula. It flows south for 1,220 miles (1,963 kilometers) and empties into the Sea of Azov. Large ships can sail on the Don for about 800 miles (1,300 kilometers). A canal connects the Don and Volga rivers. The northern part of the Don River flows through wooded, swampy land. But most of the river course is through rich farm and timber lands. The river carries shipments of lumber, grain, and cattle. The Don also has valuable fish, especially sturgeon. The city of Rostov is near the mouth of the Don. The chief branch of the Don is the Donets.

Theodore Shabad

Donatello, *DAHN uh TEHL oh* (about 1386-1466), was a great Italian sculptor. He was a master of all the techniques and materials of sculpture, and seemed able to handle any subject in the most striking manner.

Donatello was born in Florence, and served as assistant to sculptor Lorenzo Ghiberti. From 1416 to about 1420, he carved the marble statue of *St. George* and the

relief below it, *St. George Killing the Dragon* (see **Dragon** [picture]). The saint stands relaxed, as if deep in thought—an ideal example of the Christian knight. The remarkably flat relief shows an extensive landscape.

Donatello's effective use of realism appears in the statue of a prophet, known as *Lo Zuccone* (*The Pumpkinhead*), which he created about 1425. Late in life, Donatello began using distortion as he tried to show even more realistic emotional expression.

Donatello did three well-known statues of *David.* One of them is reproduced in the **Sculpture** article. His bronze *David* from the 1430's shows the influence

Marble sculpture (c. 1415); Museo Nazionale, Florence (SCALA/Art Resource)

Donatello's *St. George*

of classical Greek sculpture on his own style (see **Renaissance** [picture: Donatello's *David*]). Donatello's other famous works include the bronze *equestrian monument* (man on horseback) of the Italian general *Gattamelata.* Donatello created the monument in Padua between 1443 and 1453.   Roger Ward

See also **Sculpture** (Early Renaissance).

Donetsk, *dah NEHTSK* (pop. 1,064,000), is the largest city in the Donets River Basin of the Soviet Union. It lies in the Ukrainian Soviet Socialist Republic, about 80 miles (130 kilometers) northwest of Rostov (see **Union of Soviet Socialist Republics** [political map]). Donetsk is in the center of the rich Donets coal fields. The coal is used in the huge iron and steel mills that make Donetsk one of the most important Soviet industrial cities. Machinery and food products are also produced there.

The city was founded in the 1870's under the name Yuzovka. After the Russian Revolution, its name was changed to Stalin. In 1935, it became Stalino. The name was changed to Donetsk in 1961 as part of Soviet Premier Nikita Khrushchev's drive to downgrade Joseph Stalin.   Roman Szporluk

Donizetti, *DAHN ih ZEHT ee,* **Gaetano,** *GAH eh TAH now* (1797-1848), was an Italian opera composer. During his lifetime, he ranked second only to Gioacchino Rossini among Italian opera composers of his day. Donizetti wrote about 65 operas and operettas, and became famous for his beautiful, charming melodies and the dramatic pace and romantic vitality of his operas. He established his reputation with *Anna Bolena* (1830).

Perhaps Donizetti's finest work is the comic opera *Don Pasquale* (1843). However, *L'Elisir d'amore* (*The Elixir of Love,* 1832) and *La Fille du régiment* (*The Daughter of the Regiment,* 1840) have also remained popular. Of his tragic operas, *Lucia di Lammermoor* (1835), with its famous sextet and "mad scene," is best known (see **Opera** [The Opera repertoire]). Donizetti is also known for the high literary quality of his many letters. He was born in Bergamo.   Charles H. Webb

Donjon. See Castle.

Donkey is the name of the domesticated ass. The wild ass of northern and northeastern Africa is the ancestor of the donkey. This wild ass looks like a zebra with no stripes, except occasionally on the legs. It stands about 4 feet (1.2 meters) high at the shoulders. Its coat of hair is gray, with a darker line along its back. Other characteristics of the species are long ears, small feet, and long hair at the end of the tail. Selective breeding has resulted in donkeys that vary in size, color, and the length of their coat of hair.

Thousands of years ago, people tamed the African

American Donkey and Mule Society

The common domesticated donkey, *above,* is used chiefly for riding and for pulling carts and wagons. This breed of donkey makes an ideal pet for children.

wild ass and raised it for their own use. The domesticated donkey is most common in southern Asia, southern Europe, and northern Africa. There are several varieties of the donkey. People use light, speedy donkeys for riding. Those of a larger, heavier breed draw carts or carry loads on their backs. The hardy donkeys do not require as much or as good food as horses do. But they become stubborn and dull if badly treated. Female donkeys give good milk. A female donkey is called a *jenny* or a *jennet.* If a *jack* (male donkey) is mated with a *mare* (female horse), the animal that is born is a *mule* (see **Mule**). A cross between a female donkey and a *stallion* (male horse) is called a *hinny.* Small donkeys called *burros* are often used as pack animals because they are sure-footed. Other kinds of wild asses live on the dry plains of Asia. They include the *kiang, kulan,* and *onager* (see **Onager**). All wild asses are rare and face possible extinction.

Scientific classification. Donkeys are in the horse family, Equidae. Domesticated donkeys and the African wild ass are *Equus asinus.* Geo. H. Waring

Donne, *duhn,* **John** (1572-1631), was one of the greatest English poets and preachers of the 1600's. Donne was scholarly and had a keen, logical mind, but he was also deeply emotional. These qualities are evident in his poems and sermons. During his own time, Donne influenced several other poets. Donne and these poets were called the *metaphysical poets* (see **Metaphysical poets**).

His life. Donne was born in London. A descendant of Saint Thomas More, he was raised as a Roman Catholic. However, sometime during the 1590's, Donne became an Anglican. About 1597, he became secretary to Sir Thomas Egerton, a distinguished government official. In 1601, Donne secretly married Egerton's 16-year-old niece, Ann More. More's father was outraged at the marriage and had Donne dismissed from his position and finally imprisoned.

For the next 14 years, Donne struggled to support himself and his growing family, often living on the generosity of patrons. In 1615, at the urging of King James I, Donne became an Anglican priest. Donne also received a Doctor of Divinity degree from Cambridge. He quickly became famous for his sermons and often preached at the royal court. In 1621, Donne became dean of St. Paul's Cathedral, holding this position until his death.

His poetry. Donne wrote poetry on a variety of subjects and used many different *genres* (poetic types). His early *Satires* and *Elegies* follow classical models but they also have a distinctly modern flavor. In *Songs and Sonnets,* his best-known group of poems, Donne wrote both tenderly and cynically of love. His major love poems include "The Canonization" and "The Extasie."

Later, Donne turned to writing religious poetry. He produced a superb series of *Holy Sonnets,* including "Death be not proud" and "Batter my heart, three person'd God." Donne also wrote a moving meditative poem called "Good Friday, 1613. Riding Westward" and three magnificent hymns. He wrote nearly 200 poems, but only a few were published during his lifetime. The others circulated in manuscript copies and were not published until 1633. Donne's poetry was somewhat ignored during the 1700's and 1800's, but in the early 1900's, interest in his poetry revived. Modern poets, including T. S. Eliot, have praised and imitated his works.

Donne's language is dramatic, witty, and sometimes shocking. He used a variety of imagery and based his rhythms on everyday speech. At times, the complexity of his thought makes his meaning difficult to understand, but his poems always unfold in a logical way. He had a genius for creating extended poetic metaphors called *conceits.* In the metaphysical conceit, the poet developed a lengthy, complex image to express precisely his view of a person, object, or feeling. Donne's lyric, "A Valediction: Forbidding Mourning," contains his most famous conceit. Donne compares the souls of separated lovers to the legs of a compass:

> If they be two, they are two so
>   As stiffe twin compasses are two,
> Thy soule the fixt foot, makes no show
>   To move, but doth, if th' other do.

Gary A. Stringer

See also **English literature** (Metaphysical and Cavalier poets).

Additional resources

Carey, John. *John Donne: Life, Mind, and Art.* Oxford, 1980.
Pinka, Patricia G. *This Dialogue of One: The "Songs and Sonnets" of John Donne.* Univ. of Alabama Press, 1982.
Warnke, Frank J. *John Donne.* Twayne, 1987.

Donnelly, Ignatius (1831-1901), was an American politician, reformer, and author who helped form the Populist Party. He served in the U.S. House of Representatives from 1863 to 1869 as a Republican congressman from Minnesota, then later quit the party.

Donnelly wrote part of the Populist Party platform in 1892 (see **Populism**). This platform called for a federal income tax, government ownership of railroads, an eight-hour work day, and unlimited coinage of silver (see **Free silver**).

Donnelly was born in Philadelphia, and moved to Minnesota in 1857. He wrote several books, including one on his own theory of the earth's collision with a comet and one on Francis Bacon's supposed writing of Shakespeare's plays. Charles B. Forcey and Linda R. Forcey

Donner Pass cuts through the Sierra Nevada, a mountain range in eastern California. The pass was the scene of a great tragedy in the severe winter of 1846-1847. A party of 82 settlers from Illinois and adjoining states, led by George and Jacob Donner, became snowbound there, and only 47 survived. They built crude shelters of logs, rocks, and hides, and ate twigs, mice, their animals, and their shoes. Finally, they ate their own dead.

The party reached the High Sierras in late October, but a snowstorm had already closed the pass. In December, 15 persons tried to get through the snow-blocked pass. Eight of them died, but seven got through and sent back rescue workers. The rescue workers brought the other 40 survivors through the pass.

Donner Pass lies 7,088 feet (2,160 meters) above sea level, about 35 miles (56 kilometers) southwest of Reno, Nev. The first transcontinental railroad system, completed in 1869, went through the pass. Donner Pass is a national historical landmark. The area is now a summer resort and ski resort. Richard A. Bartlett

Doodlebug. See Ant lion.

Dooley, Thomas Anthony, III (1927-1961), an American physician, became famous in the 1950's as the *jungle doctor of Laos.* As a medical officer in the U.S. Naval Reserve, he served on a ship that carried Southeast Asian refugees. He also organized refugee camps in Vietnam. He left the Navy in 1956 to start a private, mobile medical unit in Laos. In 1957, Dooley helped found MEDICO (Medical International Cooperation Organization). He helped finance MEDICO with funds from lecture tours and books he wrote.

Dooley's three books—*Deliver Us from Evil* (1956), *The Edge of Tomorrow* (1958), and *The Night They Burned the Mountain* (1960)—describe his experiences in Southeast Asia. At the age of 34, Dooley died of cancer. After his death, Congress awarded him a gold medal for his humanitarian work. Dooley was born in St. Louis.

Kenneth R. Manning

Doolittle, Hilda (1886-1961), an American poet, was a leader of the imagism movement in poetry during the early 1900's. Doolittle's style reflects imagism's emphasis on the clear, precise, and objective treatment of images, scenes, and events. She was strongly influenced by classical literature, especially Greek verse. Many of her poems deal with Greek mythology. She also wrote three long poems about her experiences in London during World War II (1939-1945). The poems are *The Walls Do Not Fall* (1944), *Tribute to the Angels* (1945), and *The Flowering of the Rod* (1946).

Doolittle was born in Bethlehem, Pa. She moved to Europe in 1911 and lived primarily in London and in

Switzerland until her death. During the early 1930's, Doolittle was psychoanalyzed by the Austrian psychiatrist Sigmund Freud. She provided a fascinating account of her treatment in *Tribute to Freud* (1956). Doolittle also wrote novels and verse plays and translated ancient Greek poetry and drama. She wrote all her works under the initials H.D. Elmer W. Borklund

See also **American literature** (Experiments in poetry).

Doolittle, James Harold (1896-   ), a noted American flier, led the first bombing raid on Tokyo in World War II. He led 16 B-25 twin-engine bombers, normally land-based planes, from the deck of the aircraft carrier U.S.S. *Hornet* in the surprise attack on Tokyo on April 18, 1942. Congress awarded him the Medal of Honor for this daring raid.

A lieutenant colonel when he led his raid, Doolittle rose to lieutenant general during World War II. He commanded the 12th Air Force in the North African invasion in 1942, and later the 15th Air Force in the Mediterranean area. In 1944 and 1945, he was commander of the 8th Air Force, which bombed western Europe. He also commanded the 8th Air Force on Okinawa after Germany surrendered.

Doolittle was born in Alameda, Calif., and graduated from the University of California. He was an Army aviator during World War I. Doolittle left the Army in 1930 to work for the Shell Petroleum Corporation. He returned to military duty in 1940.

Doolittle was chairman of the National Advisory Committee for Aeronautics from 1956 to 1958. He was director of the Space Technology Laboratories, an aerospace firm, from 1959 to 1962. Alfred Goldberg

See also **Airplane** (table: Speed records); **World War II** (The tide turns).

Doom palm. See Doum palm.

Doomsday Book. See Domesday Book.

Doorweed. See Knotgrass.

Doppler effect is the change in frequency of sound, light, or radio waves caused by the relative motion of the source of the waves and their observer. For example, the *pitch* (frequency) of a train whistle seems higher when the train approaches and lower after it passes and begins to move away. The actual pitch of the whistle remains constant. Astronomers study the speed of a star by measuring the apparent change in the frequency of its light waves caused by motion. Christian Doppler, an Austrian physicist, described the effect in 1842.

Thomas A. Griffy

See also **Sound** (The speed of sound); **Log; Radar** (Continuous-wave radar); **Relativity** (General relativity theory).

Dorado. See Dolphin (fish).

Dorchester, Baron. See Carleton, Sir Guy.

Doré, *daw RAY,* **Gustave,** *goo STAV* (1832-1883), a French painter and sculptor, illustrated a large number of literary masterpieces. These include the Bible, the works of Rabelais and Balzac, Dante's *Divine Comedy,* LaFontaine's *Fables,* Tennyson's *Idylls of the King,* Cervantes' *Don Quixote,* Coleridge's "The Rime of the Ancient Mariner," and Poe's "The Raven." His style is dramatic and imaginative, but sometimes repetitious.

Doré was born Paul Gustave Doré in Strasbourg, Alsace-Lorraine. As a boy, he showed a remarkable talent for drawing. His work was in great demand while he

Detail of *Satan's Flight Through Chaos*; illustration from *Masterpieces from the Works of Gustave Doré*. © 1887 Cassell Publishers

A Doré engraving illustrates an edition of *Paradise Lost* by John Milton. Doré's engravings rank among his best works.

was still quite young. His fame outside of France rests chiefly on his illustrations.   Elizabeth Broun

See also **City** (picture: The Industrial Revolution).

Dore metal. See Assaying (Dry process).

Dorians, *DAWR ee uhnz,* were a group of ancient Greeks. They lived in the northwestern part of the Greek mainland before 1200 B.C. According to Greek tradition, the Dorians overran most of the *Peloponnesus* (the southern peninsula of Greece) toward the end of the 1100's. The best-known Greeks of Dorian descent were the Spartans. In addition to Sparta, Dorian cities included Argos, Corinth, Megara, and Rhodes. Dorians also settled in Crete, Sicily, southern Italy, the Sporades Islands, and southwestern Asia Minor (present-day Turkey). Some scholars have questioned whether the Dorians actually existed. Information about them comes mostly from later Greek traditions.   Norman A. Doenges

See also **Achaeans; Aeolians; Corinth; Greece, Ancient** (History); **Ionians; Mycenae; Sparta.**

Dorion, *daw RYAWN,* **Marie** (1790?-1850), an American Indian, became known for her bravery as a member of the Astor Overland Expedition. She was the only woman on this 3,500-mile (5,630-kilometer) trip. The expedition left St. Louis in March 1811 and reached Astoria, a fur-trading post in the Oregon region, in February 1812.

Dorion's husband, Pierre, was an interpreter on the trip, and their two small sons accompanied them. The expedition walked most of the way, and Marie had more endurance than almost all the men. In December, she gave birth on the trail. The next day, she rode about 20 miles (32 kilometers) on horseback to rejoin the group. The infant died nine days later.

During the winter of 1814, Pierre Dorion and the other men were killed by Indians in Oregon. Marie and her two sons escaped into the mountains, where she built a shelter. Because of the severe cold and deep snow, she and the children stayed in the shelter for 53 days. She killed their horse to provide nourishment.

Marie Dorion, a member of the Iowa tribe, was also called *Marie Iowa* or *Marie Aioe*. Historians know little about her early life.   Priscilla Giddings Buffalohead

Dormancy. See Germination.

Dormouse, *DAWR mows,* is a tiny mammal that looks like a small squirrel. Dormice are well known for their sleepy ways. When cold weather arrives, they stock a nest with food and *hibernate* (sleep through the winter). They may wake up on warm winter days and eat some of their food. In *Alice's Adventures in Wonderland,* author Lewis Carroll described a humorous dormouse that could not be kept awake at a tea party.

The dormouse has fine, silky fur, a pointed nose, and big black eyes. Its body is about 3 inches (8 centimeters)

WORLD BOOK illustration by John D. Dawson

The tiny dormouse has a pointed nose and a long tail.

long, and so is its tail. Dormice are rodents, and are related to mice and rats. They live in trees and bushes in parts of Africa, Asia, and Europe. Dormice hunt for food at night, and eat berries, grains, and nuts.

Scientific classification. Dormice belong to the dormouse family, Gliridae. There are several genera.   Clyde Jones

See also **Animal** (picture: Hibernating animals).

Dörpfeld, Wilhelm. See Troy (The archaeological Troy).

Dorr Rebellion was an uprising against the state government of Rhode Island in 1842. It was led by Thomas W. Dorr, a Providence lawyer who thought the state government was undemocratic. The rebellion failed, but it helped bring about a new constitution.

At the time of the rebellion, Rhode Island was still governed by its colonial charter of 1663. Landholding conservatives held all the power because people without land did not have the right to vote. The landless, including many immigrants, could not convince the conservatives to draft a more democratic constitution.

Dorr and other radicals drew up a new constitution, which voters unofficially ratified in 1841. The following April, Dorr and his followers held their own elections, and Dorr was elected governor. But the conservatives refused to recognize the radical government.

The radicals believed in the right of the people to overthrow an unjust government. As a result, Dorr formed an army and attempted to take power by force. But the army suffered two humiliating defeats, and Dorr fled the state. The conservatives, anxious to avoid future uprisings, drafted a new constitution almost as democratic as the radicals' constitution. The constitution took effect in 1843. Dorr returned to Rhode Island. He was convicted of treason and imprisoned in 1844 but was released in 1845.   Marvin E. Gettleman

Dosimeter. See Electroscope (with picture).

Dos Passos, *dohs PAS ohs,* **John** (1896-1970), was an American novelist whose work is dominated by social and political themes. His experiments in fiction earned him distinction as an avant-garde novelist in the 1920's and 1930's (see **Avant-garde**).

Dos Passos first achieved fame with his World War I novels, *One Man's Initiation* (1917) and *Three Soldiers* (1921). *Three Soldiers* protests the impact of war on civilization and art. *Manhattan Transfer* (1925) reveals Dos Passos' disillusioned response to postwar urban America. This novel led to his most famous work, the *U.S.A.* trilogy, which pessimistically surveys the disintegration of U.S. culture that Dos Passos believed took place in the early 1900's. The trilogy consists of *The 42nd Parallel* (1930), *1919* (1932), and *The Big Money* (1936).

U.S.A. brings together many characters in a wide variety of episodes. Dos Passos featured a technique called the Newsreel, which used newspaper headlines, words from popular songs, and advertisements to surround the action and characters. Another technique, called The Camera's Eye, gives the author's view of his subject. Dos Passos regarded his style as providing a social and historical background in which individual actions reflected larger patterns he saw in United States society.

John Roderigo Dos Passos was born in Chicago and attended Harvard University. He was a political liberal in his early years, but moved sharply toward conservatism by the 1940's. His *District of Columbia* trilogy—*Adventures of a Young Man* (1939), *Number One* (1943), and *The Grand Design* (1949)—reveals his conservative attitudes. Dos Passos also wrote *Mr. Wilson's War* (1962), a history of World War I.   Joseph N. Riddel

Dostoevsky, *DAHS tuh YEHF skee,* **Fyodor,** *FYAW dahr* (1821-1881), was one of the greatest writers in Russian literature. Dostoevsky's finest works are novels of ideas, embodied in great characters. His intensely individual and highly complex characters are usually caught up in very dramatic plots. The underlying theme in his books is the struggle between good and evil for dominance of the human soul. Dostoevsky attempts to resolve this struggle by leading his characters to salvation through purifying suffering.

Fyodor Mikhailovich Dostoevsky was born in Moscow. He received a military engineering education in St. Petersburg (now Leningrad), but decided to follow a literary career. Dostoevsky's first novel was *Poor Folk* (1846), a psychological study written in letter form. His next book, *The Double* (1846), is the complex story of an unpopular civil servant who goes mad and sees his own double. During the late 1840's, Dostoevsky wrote many stories about the poor and the downtrodden as well as strange and abnormal residents of St. Petersburg.

In 1847, Dostoevsky joined the Petrashevsky circle, a group of socialists who met to read and discuss political and economic books banned by the government. In 1849, police arrested the members of the circle. Dostoevsky and several others were condemned to death by a firing squad. By order of the czar, they were pardoned moments before they were to die. Dostoevsky was then

sentenced to four years of hard labor in a Siberian prison and then served four years as a common soldier.

After returning to St. Petersburg in 1859, Dostoevsky wrote *Notes from the House of the Dead* (1860-1862). It is a fictionalized version of his prison experiences and one of the great prison works in Western literature. Years of bitter, poverty-stricken existence followed for Dostoevsky. He was plagued by financial difficulties due to poor money management and a gambling habit.

Dostoevsky achieved success with *Notes from Underground* (1864), a psychological study of a spiritual and intellectual misfit. His greatest success came with four novels that rank among the masterpieces of world literature. *Crime and Punishment* (1866) concerns a student who murders because he imagines himself to be superior to most people, but who cannot face the enormity of his crime. In *The Idiot* (1868-1869), Dostoevsky tried to portray a truly good Christian person. *The Possessed* (1871-1872), also published as *The Devils*, is a prophetic portrait of Russian revolutionaries. Dostoevsky's greatest novel is probably *The Brothers Karamazov* (1879-1880). It centers on the murder of the evil Fyodor Karamazov and the effect of this crime on each of his four sons.

His later works show Dostoevsky to be a pioneer in psychological analysis and an important and original religious thinker. As an interpreter of the human

Pictorial Parade
Fyodor Dostoevsky

condition, he anticipated many of the ideas of the philosophical movement called *existentialism.*   Anna Lisa Crone

See also **Russian literature** (The 1860's and 1870's).

Additional resources

Chapple, Richard L. *A Dostoevsky Dictionary.* Ardis, 1983.
Frank, Joseph. *Dostoevsky: The Seeds of Revolt, 1821-1849.* Princeton, 1976. *The Years of Ordeal, 1850-1859.* 1983. *The Stir of Liberation, 1860-1865.* 1986. Multivolume biography, publication in progress.

Douala, *du AH lah* (pop. 1,029,731), is the largest city and chief seaport of Cameroon. It lies along the Wouri River, about 15 miles (24 kilometers) from where the river flows into the Gulf of Guinea, an arm of the Atlantic Ocean (see **Cameroon** [map]).

Busy docks line parts of Douala's waterfront. A bridge that is 5,910 feet (1,800 meters) long spans the Wouri River in Douala. The city has open squares, a cathedral, and a museum. Shipping and related businesses are the chief economic activities. Other activities in the Douala area include banking; cacao processing; and the production of beer, cement, fertilizer, leather, matches, shoes, tobacco goods, and textiles.

The city is named for the Douala people, who have lived in the area for hundreds of years. The Douala established a number of villages there. The Germans, who ruled the area from 1884 to 1916, built the city on the site of the villages. Douala was enlarged by the French, who governed it from 1919 to 1960.   Victor T. LeVine

Douay Bible. See Bible (Early English translations).

Double jeopardy. See Constitution of the United States (Amendment 5).

Double knit. See Textile (Knitted fabrics).

Double star. See Binary star.

Doubleday, Abner (1819-1893), was a United States Army officer who was once considered the inventor of baseball. In order to settle a dispute over the origin of the game, Albert G. Spalding, a sporting-goods manufacturer and former ballplayer, suggested the appointment of a commission to study the matter. The commission's report, published in 1908, credited Doubleday with inventing the game in Cooperstown, N.Y., in 1839. In honor of Doubleday, Cooperstown residents established the National Baseball Hall of Fame and Museum in the town. The Hall of Fame operates under the jurisdiction of professional baseball. Most historians today claim that Doubleday had little, if anything, to do with baseball. They believe the sport probably developed from an English game called *rounders*. See **Baseball** (History [The Abner Doubleday theory]).

Doubleday was born in Ballston Spa, N.Y. He graduated from the United States Military Academy in 1842, and he served in the Mexican War (1846-1848). Doubleday became a major general in the Union Army during the Civil War (1861-1865). He commanded the troops at Fort Sumter that fired the first shots by the North in the Civil War. Doubleday also fought heroically at the Battle of Gettysburg.   Jack Lang

Doublet, in clothing, see **Clothing** (The Renaissance); in jewelry, see **Gem** (Imitation and synthetic gems).

Doubloon, *duh BLOON,* is a Spanish and Spanish-American gold coin that was widely used in America until the 1800's. The name comes from the Latin *duplus,* meaning *double.* The doubloon was equal to four *pis-*

WORLD BOOK photo by James Simek
A Spanish doubloon has a profile of King Charles IV of Spain on one side. This coin was minted in Lima, Peru, in 1801.

toles (16 silver dollars). It was also called *doblón de a ocho* meaning *doubloon of eight,* because it was worth eight gold escudos. It weighed about 27 grams (slightly less than one ounce).   Burton H. Hobson

Doughnut is a round, fried cake with a hole in the center. Dutch settlers brought the fried cake to colonial America. A legend suggests that Hanson Gregory of the United States invented the doughnut hole in 1847 at the age of 15. Gregory supposedly recommended that his mother cut the centers from her fried cakes so they would cook more thoroughly.   Kay L. Franzen

Douglas. See Man, Isle of.

Douglas, Sir James (1803-1877), served as the first governor of the colony of British Columbia, in what is

now Canada. Douglas held the office from 1858 to 1864.

Douglas was born in Demerara, British Guiana (now Guyana), and was educated in Great Britain. In 1820, he went to Quebec as an employee of the North West Company, a British fur-trading firm. The Hudson's Bay Company, a rival organization, took over the North West Company in 1821.

From 1839 to 1858, Douglas served as chief officer in the Columbia territory for the Hudson's Bay Company. In 1843, he founded Fort Victoria (now Victoria) as headquarters for the company. The fort stood on Vancouver Island, which today forms part of British Columbia. Vancouver Island became a British colony in 1849, and Douglas served as governor from 1851 to 1863. He was knighted in 1863.   P. B. Waite

Douglas, Lloyd Cassel (1877-1951), a Protestant minister, wrote the best-selling novels *Magnificent Obsession* (1929), *The Robe* (1942), and *The Big Fisherman* (1948). He also wrote *Forgive Us Our Trespasses* (1932), *Green Light* (1935), and *Invitation to Live* (1940). *A Time to Remember* (1951) is his autobiography. As a novelist, Douglas was mainly interested in inspiring religious teaching, but, to his surprise, his books won great popularity.

Douglas was born in Columbia City, Ind. He graduated from Wittenberg College. He began to preach in Indiana, and then became a pastor in Washington, D.C. Later, he directed religious work at the University of Illinois, and served as a pastor in Ann Arbor, Mich.; Akron, Ohio; and Los Angeles, Calif.   Bernard Duffey

Douglas, Norman (1868-1952), a British novelist and essayist, is best known for his witty and satirical novel *South Wind* (1917). The book is set on an imaginary island called Nepenthe, based on the island of Capri. The word *nepenthe* means a drug capable of banishing sorrow and fear. The central theme of *South Wind* is the nature of truth. Thomas Heard, an Anglican bishop, receives an education in the complexity of truth and a doctrine of individualism. Douglas' books about the Mediterranean region include *Siren Land* (1911), *Fountains in the Sand* (1912), and *Old Calabria* (1915). He wrote two other novels, *They Went* (1921) and *In the Beginning* (1928). George Norman Douglas was born near Aberdeen, Scotland, but lived most of his life abroad, primarily in Italy.   Garrett Stewart

Douglas, Stephen Arnold (1813-1861), was a popular and skillful American orator and political leader just before the Civil War. He is best known for his debates with Abraham Lincoln on the question of slavery. These debates ranked as noteworthy events in the history of the United States. See **Lincoln, Abraham** (The debates with Douglas).

Douglas was born on a farm near Brandon, Vt. Politics interested him and he wanted to become a lawyer. At the age of 20, he went to Illinois. He was admitted to the bar at Jacksonville, Ill. Douglas, a Democrat, was elected prosecuting attorney for his district in 1835. The next year he was elected to the state legislature. He was judge of the Supreme Court of Illinois from 1841 to 1843. Douglas was elected to the United States House of Representatives in 1843, and became a member of the United States Senate in 1847.

Douglas was a short man, with a large head and broad shoulders. Because of his appearance, he received the nickname the *Little Giant.* He won respect in the Senate for his ability, energy, and fearlessness, and became chairman of the Senate committee on territories. More than any other person, Douglas helped win passage of the Compromise of 1850. This compromise was a series of laws that temporarily eased tensions over slavery. See **Compromise of 1850.**

Photograph by Mathew Brady.
National Archives, Washington, D.C.

Stephen A. Douglas

The slavery controversy was the great issue of the mid-1800's. As each territory applied for admission to the Union, a storm of debate arose in Congress as to whether the new state should be free or slave-holding. Douglas believed that the people of the territories should decide for themselves whether they wanted slavery. He called this principle *popular sovereignty.* It was also called *squatter sovereignty* (see **Popular sovereignty**). Douglas' committee reported the famous Kansas-Nebraska Bill in 1854. It included the principle of popular sovereignty (see **Kansas-Nebraska Act**). Douglas' brilliant leadership was responsible for the passage of this much disputed bill.

When Douglas ran for reelection to the Senate in 1858, his Republican opponent was Abraham Lincoln, a man then almost unknown outside Illinois. Douglas and Lincoln held a series of public meetings in which they debated the problem of slavery and its extension. These meetings attracted the attention of the entire country.

Douglas argued that the people must have the right to control slavery. Lincoln said that a nation half-slave and half-free could not exist. Douglas won his reelection to the Senate, but some of his speeches in the debates displeased Southern Democrats. Douglas was a candidate for the Democratic presidential nomination in 1860, but only Northern Democrats supported him. The Democratic Party split its votes among three candidates. Douglas received only 12 electoral votes, though he achieved the second highest popular vote. The Republican candidate, Abraham Lincoln, won the election.

Douglas supported Lincoln and the Union when the Civil War broke out. "There can be no neutrals in this war," he declared, "only patriots—or traitors." Douglas died a few months later. He was buried in a small park at the east end of 35th Street in Chicago.   Gabor S. Boritt

Additional resources

Capers, Gerald M. *Stephen A. Douglas: Defender of the Union.* Little, Brown, 1972. First published in 1959.
Jaffa, Harry V. *Crisis of the House Divided: An Interpretation of the Issues of the Lincoln-Douglas Debates.* Univ. of Chicago Press, 1982. First published in 1959.
Johannsen, Robert W. *Stephen A. Douglas.* Oxford, 1973.
Wells, Damon. *Stephen Douglas: The Last Years, 1857-1861.* Univ. of Texas Press, 1971.

Douglas, Thomas. See Selkirk, Earl of.
Douglas, William Orville (1898-1980), served on the Supreme Court of the United States longer than any other justice. Douglas served as an associate justice

from 1939 to 1975. He gained renown not only because of his work as a member of the Supreme Court, but also because of his wide travels and his books dealing with problems in America's national and international life.

On the Supreme Court, Douglas strongly supported government protection of civil liberties and civil rights. His books include *Of Men and Mountains* (1950) and *Strange Lands and Friendly People* (1951). Douglas also wrote *The Anatomy of Liberty* (1963) and *Points of Rebellion* (1970).

Douglas was born in Maine, Minn., and graduated from Whitman College. He received his law degree from Columbia University. Douglas was chairman of the Securities and Exchange Commission, 1937 to 1939.
     H. G. Reuschlein

Additional resources

Douglas, William O. *Go East, Young Man—The Early Years: The Autobiography of William O. Douglas.* Random House, 1974.
The Court Years, 1939-1975: The Autobiography of William O. Douglas. 1980.
Simon, James F. *Independent Journey: The Life of William O. Douglas.* Harper, 1980.

Douglas-fir is one of the largest and most valuable timber trees in the world. This *conifer* (cone-bearing tree) is the source of more lumber than any other species of tree in North America. It is common in the Western United States and Canada, both in the Pacific Coast region of the Rocky Mountains. The Douglas-fir is not a true fir. It belongs to a separate *genus* (group) in the pine family.

The flat needles of a Douglas-fir are about 1 inch (2.5 centimeters) long. The egg-shaped cones have odd, three pointed *bracts* (leaflike structures). In the Pacific Northwest, Douglas-firs grow from 180 to 250 feet (55 to 76 meters) tall and up to 8 feet (2.4 meters) thick through the trunk.

Douglas-firs may live up to 800 years. Forests of older trees are economically valuable, but they also provide a home for rare plants and animals that cannot live anywhere else. As a result, there is much disagreement

Grant Heilman

The Douglas-fir towers above most other trees in the evergreen forests of the Western United States and Canada. It provides more lumber than any other kind of North American tree.

about how these forests should be managed. The Douglas-fir is the state tree of Oregon.

Scientific classification. The Douglas-fir belongs to the pine family, Pinaceae. It is *Pseudotsuga menziesii.*

Douglas G. Sprugel

See also **Conifer; Pine; Spruce; Tree** (picture: Familiar broadleaf and needleleaf trees).

Douglas-Home, Alexander Frederick. See Home, Lord.

Douglass, Frederick (1818?-1895), was the leading spokesman of American blacks in the 1800's. Born a slave, Douglass became a noted reformer, author, and orator. He devoted his life to the abolition of slavery and the fight for black rights.

Frederick Augustus Washington Bailey was born in Tuckahoe, Md., near Easton. At the age of 8, he was sent to Baltimore to work for one of his master's relatives. There, helped by the wife of his new master, he began to educate himself. He later worked in a shipyard, where he *caulked* ships, making them watertight.

In 1838, the young man fled from his master and went to New Bedford, Mass. To avoid capture, he dropped his two middle names and changed his last name to Douglass. He got a job as a caulker, but the other men refused to work with him because he was black. Douglass then held a number of unskilled jobs, among them collecting rubbish and digging cellars.

In 1841, at a meeting of the Massachusetts Antislavery Society, Douglass told what freedom meant to him. The society was so impressed with his speech that it hired him to lecture about his experiences as a slave. In the early 1840's, he protested against segregated seating on trains by sitting in cars reserved for whites. He had to be dragged from the white cars. Douglass also protested against religious discrimination. He walked out of a church that kept blacks from taking part in a service until the whites had finished participating.

In 1845, Douglass published his autobiography, *Narrative of the Life of Frederick Douglass.* He feared that his identity as a runaway slave would be revealed when the book was published, so he went to England. There, Douglass continued to speak against slavery. He also found friends who raised money to buy his freedom.

Douglass returned to the United States in 1847 and founded an antislavery newspaper, the *North Star,* in Rochester, N.Y. In the 1850's, Douglass charged that employers hired white immigrants ahead of black Americans. He once declared: "Every hour sees the black man elbowed out of employment by some newly arrived emigrant whose hunger and whose color are thought to give him a better title to the place." He accused even some abolitionist business executives of job discrimination against blacks.

Douglass also led a successful attack against segregated schools in Rochester. His home was a station on the underground railroad, a widespread system which helped runaway

J. W. Hurn, Library of Congress
Frederick Douglass

slaves reach freedom (see **Underground railroad**).

During the Civil War (1861-1865), Douglass helped recruit blacks for the Union Army. He discussed the problems of slavery with President Abraham Lincoln several times. Douglass served as Recorder of Deeds in the District of Columbia from 1881 to 1886 and as U.S. minister to Haiti from 1889 to 1891. He wrote two expanded versions of his autobiography—*My Bondage and My Freedom* (1855) and *Life and Times of Frederick Douglass* (1881).   Otey M. Scruggs

Additional resources

Douglass, Frederick. *The Frederick Douglass Papers, Series I: Speeches, Debates, and Interviews.* 2 vols. Yale, 1979-1982. Volume 1 covers 1841-1846; Volume 2, 1847-1854.
Huggins, Nathan I. *Slave and Citizen: The Life of Frederick Douglass.* Little, Brown, 1980.
Preston, Dickson J. *Young Frederick Douglass: The Maryland Years.* Johns Hopkins, 1980.
Santrey, Laurence. *Young Frederick Douglass: Fight for Freedom.* Troll, 1983. For younger readers.

Doukhobors, *DOO kuh bawrz,* also spelled *Dukhobors,* belong to a Christian sect in western Canada. *Doukhobors* is a Russian word meaning *spirit wrestlers.* They believe the "voice within" each person is his or her guide. Therefore, they see no need for churches or governments. Doukhobors are pacifists.

Peasants founded the sect in Russia in the mid-1700's. The Doukhobors adopted many of the ideas of the Russian author Leo Tolstoy in the late 1800's, under the leadership of Peter Verigin. In 1899, Tolstoy and English and American Quakers helped more than 7,000 Doukhobors emigrate to western Canada. There they established communal farms. The group still survives, but its communal life has largely died out. A small group of Doukhobors called the *Sons of Freedom* wishes to restore the communal communities in Canada or in any country that would welcome them.   Ivan Avakumovic

Doum palm, *doom,* also spelled *doom palm,* grows in Arabia, Upper Egypt, and Central Africa. Each branch of the doum palm ends in a tuft of deeply lobed, fan-shaped leaves. The tree bears an irregularly oval fruit about the size of an apple. The fruit has a red outer skin and a thick, spongy, and rather sweet inner substance that tastes like gingerbread. The palm has often been called the *gingerbread tree.* Large quantities of these fruits have been found in the tombs of the Egyptian pharaohs. The seeds are a source of *vegetable ivory.*

Scientific classification. Doum palms are in the palm family, Palmae. They are *Hyphaene thebaica.*   Harold E. Moore, Jr.

Dove is a name that refers to the smaller members of the pigeon and dove family. The name *pigeon* refers to the larger members of the family (see **Pigeon**). Doves live in temperate and tropical regions.

Doves have plump bodies and small heads. They grow from 6 to 12 inches (15 to 30 centimeters) long and weigh from 1 to 9 ounces (28 to 255 grams). They fly rapidly and have low cooing voices. Doves eat a variety of fruits, grains, insects, and nuts.

Scientific classification. Doves belong to the pigeon and dove family, Columbidae.   Edward H. Burtt, Jr.

See also **Mourning dove; Turtledove.**

Dove, Arthur Garfield (1880-1946), was one of the earliest abstract painters in the United States. He created his first symbolic abstract pictures of nature in 1910, long before abstract art was common in America. Most of his compositions involve subjects drawn from nature and landscape. Dove's abstract designs, generally small in size, emphasized areas of solid color, often earthy in tone. During the 1920's, he also made collaged constructions (see **Collage**).

Dove was born in Canandaigua, N.Y., and gained early success as a magazine illustrator. From 1908 to 1909, he lived in Paris, where he absorbed the influences of the new art movements. Dove's advanced work never had great popular success during his lifetime in spite of the support of Alfred Stieglitz, a photographer and art dealer, and of Duncan Phillips, an art collector and patron. Today, however, he is recognized as one of the most significant pioneers in modern American art.

Charles C. Eldredge

Dover, Del. (pop. 23,507), is the state capital and the commercial center of a large rural area. Dover lies in central Delaware on the St. Jones River. The city's main industries include canning, food processing, and the manufacture of latex products. Agricultural products of the area include poultry, soybeans, corn, and potatoes. Delaware State College and Wesley College are in the city. Dover Air Force Base is located near the city. Dover was founded in 1717 and became the capital of Delaware in 1777. It was incorporated as a town in 1829 and as a city in 1929. It has a council-manager government. Dover is the seat of Kent County. See **Delaware** (pictures; map).   Lee Ann Walling

Dover is an English town on the Strait of Dover. It is the chief town in the district of Dover, which has a population of 102,500. It is famous for its white cliffs, which border the strait. These cliffs are made of chalk. On a clear day, a person standing on the cliffs can see the city of Calais, France, 26 miles (42 kilometers) away. The ruins of Dover Castle overlook the town from one of the chalk cliffs. During World War II (1939-1945), Germany shelled and bombed Dover.

Dover is the main port of sea travel between England and France, and the city's port is a major source of local employment. In 1987, construction began on an underwater railway tunnel from a point near Dover to France. See **English Channel** for details.   D. A. Pinder

See also **Citadel** (picture).

Dover, Strait of, is a narrow channel which connects the English Channel and the North Sea and separates

WORLD BOOK map

The Strait of Dover lies between England and France.

England and France at their closest points. The strait is only about 21 miles (34 kilometers) wide and is very shallow, with an average depth of less than 100 feet (30 meters). Chalk cliffs rise high on either side of the strait. The ports of Dover, England, and Calais, France, are opposite each other on the Strait of Dover. Great Britain and France are building a railway tunnel under the strait. Construction on the tunnel began in late 1987 and is expected to be completed by 1993. Many athletes have set records by swimming across the English Channel, usually from Calais to Dover (see **English Channel**).

John W. Webb

Dow, Herbert Henry (1866-1930), was an early leader in the U.S. chemical industry. In 1897, he founded the Dow Chemical Company. Through research, which Dow emphasized, the company has made a variety of products. It mass-produced industrial chemicals, led in developing carbon tetrachloride, introduced a cheap *phenol* (carbolic acid), and developed uses for bromine extracted from seawater (see **Bromine; Carbon tetrachloride**). Dow was born in Belleville, Ont.   J. R. Craf

Dow Jones averages are statistics that show the trend of prices of stocks and bonds. They are averages of selected stocks and bonds traded on the New York Stock Exchange. Dow Jones & Company, a financial publishing firm, computes averages for each trading hour of every business day. There are four kinds of these averages: (1) an average of the common stock prices of 30 industrial firms, (2) an average of the common stocks of 20 transportation companies, (3) an average of the common stocks of 15 utility companies, and (4) an average of the 65 stocks that make up the first three averages. Public interest is centered on these averages.

Grant Heilman

The mourning dove was named for the sad cooing sound made by the male. This North American bird is found from southeastern Alaska and southern Canada to Panama.

The industrial stock average is the one most often used by investors. Its advances and declines, like those of the other averages, are given in *points*. For example, suppose the industrial average at the close of trading on one day is 879.32, and on the following day the average goes up to 882.56. It has then risen 3.24 points.

In 1896, Dow Jones began to publish an industrial average, using the stocks of 12 companies. The average was a simple total of the prices of these stocks, divided by 12. However, some companies whose stocks were used in the average began *splitting* their stocks. That is, they issued two or more shares of stock for each existing share. The price of the stock then dropped in proportion. Suppose, for example, that a stock was selling for $18. If the company *split it two for one* (issued two shares for each existing share), the price would drop to $9. The investor would lose nothing, because two shares of stock would still be worth $18. But the Dow Jones average, if the $9 price were used, would take into account an artificial decline from $18.

Stock averages can be distorted by other causes besides splits. To provide a correction for all these causes, Dow Jones uses a flexible divisor. After a stock split, the total of the prices of all the stocks used in the average is not divided by the number of stocks. Instead, a divisor is used that will make the average equal to what it was before the split. The first flexible divisor, used in 1928, was 16.67. Because of corrections through the years, the divisor for industrials was about 0.55 by the early 1990's. The divisor is changed to correct a distortion of five or more points in the average.   Robert Sobel

See also **Standard & Poor's indexes.**

Dower is a wife's right to a share of her deceased husband's *real property* (real estate). It is sometimes called the *widow's share.* Under English and American common law, the widow is entitled to one-third of her husband's property during her lifetime. The common law bars a husband from transferring ownership of his real property during his lifetime without his wife's consent. This protects the wife's dower right. A husband may also claim a share of his deceased wife's property. This right is called *estate by curtesy.*

Most states in the United States have passed legislation substantially altering the common-law dower right, often increasing the widow's share. Some states have *community property* laws, rather than the law of dower. These laws provide that a couple share ownership of property gained during their marriage.   John W. Wade

See also **Common law; Community property.**

Dowland, John (1563-1626), was an English composer during the Renaissance. He was also considered one of the best lute players of his time. The lute is a stringed instrument with a pear-shaped body and is played like a guitar. Dowland composed many songs for voice accompanied by the lute. "Flow my tears," from his *Second Book of Airs* (1600), was one of the most famous pieces of its time. Dowland's beautiful songs are often on dark and melancholy subjects. He also wrote religious songs, difficult lute solos, and dances for lute and Renaissance bowed instruments called *viols.*

Dowland may have been born in London. He graduated from Oxford University and performed at the court of Elizabeth I. Dowland served various foreign rulers, notably the king of Denmark from 1598 to 1606, when he returned permanently to England. In 1612, he became court lutanist to King James I.   Joscelyn Godwin

Down's syndrome, *SIHN drohm,* formerly called *Mongolism,* is a disorder that is present at birth. It is characterized by mental retardation and such physical features as upward-slanting eyes; a flat nose; a small head; and short, stubby hands. In addition, the ears and teeth are small and abnormally shaped. Down's syndrome may be accompanied by heart disorders, poor vision, and respiratory problems. The degree of mental retardation in children ranges from severe to mild.

Down's syndrome is caused by an abnormality in the number of *chromosomes.* Chromosomes are the parts of a cell that contain tiny structures called *genes,* which determine hereditary traits. People with Down's syndrome have 47 chromosomes instead of the normal 46, or 23 pairs. The extra chromosome occurs as a third chromosome with the pair that has been designated as *chromosome 21.* Researchers have linked this disorder to an abnormality in the genes of the parents. Scientists use special tests to examine chromosomes in an unborn baby and to determine whether the fetus has certain defects (see **Genetic counseling**).

Down's syndrome appears in an average of 1 of every 1,000 births. It can occur in people of every nationality and all social and economic backgrounds. The risk of having a child with Down's syndrome increases greatly after a woman reaches the age of 45.

Children with Down's syndrome can be trained and can develop their full potential within the limits of their disability. Foster homes and various institutions care for the most severely retarded victims. Most experts recommend that less seriously handicapped children live at home. Studies show that, in general, children reared at home have a higher IQ and achieve more than those raised in institutions. Children who live at home can attend special classes in public schools. Many can be trained to do routine tasks and can learn simple skills. Special workshops offer jobs to adults with Down's syndrome, and some adults work in regular industry.

Down's syndrome was named after John Langdon Haydon Down, a British physician who first described the condition in 1866. It was once called Mongolism because the facial features of young victims seemed to resemble those of Orientals.   Anne Christake Cornwell

Additional resources

Down Syndrome: A Resource Handbook. Ed. by Carol Tingey. College-Hill, 1988.
Down Syndrome: Growing and Learning. Ed. by Siegfried M. Pueschel. Andrews and McMeel, 1978.

Dowry. See **Marriage** (Marriage in other cultures).
Dowser. See **Divination.**
Doyle, Sir Arthur Conan (1859-1930), a British writer, created Sherlock Holmes, the world's best-known detective. Millions of readers have followed Holmes's adventures and delighted in his ability to solve crimes by an amazing use of reason and observation. Doyle wrote a story in 1893 in which Holmes was killed. But public demand forced Doyle to bring Holmes back to life in another story. Critic Christopher Morley said of Holmes, "Perhaps no fiction character ever created has become so charmingly real to his readers."

Doyle was born in Edinburgh, Scotland. He began

practicing medicine in 1882, but his practice was not a success. He started writing while waiting for the patients that never came. His early stories earned him little money, but he won great success with his first Holmes novel, *A Study in Scarlet* (1887).

Brown Bros.
Sir Arthur Conan Doyle

Holmes appeared in 56 short stories and three other novels—*The Sign of Four* (1890), *The Hound of the Baskervilles* (1902), and *The Valley of Fear* (1915). Doyle may have been the highest paid short-story writer of his time. He also wrote historical novels, romances, and plays. He eventually abandoned fiction to study and lecture on *spiritualism* (communication with spirits). For his efforts in support of the British cause during the Boer War (1899-1902), Doyle received a knighthood in 1902.   David Geherin

See also **Holmes, Sherlock.**

D'Oyly Carte, *DOY lee KAHRT,* **Richard** (1844-1901), an English theater manager, produced all but the first of the 14 operettas written by Sir William S. Gilbert and Sir Arthur S. Sullivan. D'Oyly Carte's production of Gilbert and Sullivan's second work, *Trial by Jury* (1875), established the team as a success. D'Oyly Carte used the profits from his productions of Gilbert and Sullivan's early operettas to build the Savoy Theatre in London in 1881. Gilbert and Sullivan's last eight operettas had their premières at the Savoy. Their works became known as *Savoy operas,* and performers and other people associated with them became known as *Savoyards.* In the 1880's, D'Oyly Carte founded the D'Oyly Carte Opera Company, to perform Gilbert and Sullivan operettas. D'Oyly Carte was born in London.   James Sykes

See also **Gilbert and Sullivan.**

Drabble, Margaret (1939-   ), is an English novelist. She has become especially popular among women readers for her realistic portrayals of middle-class women struggling with the demands of careers, personal relationships, and other interests. Drabble's works have sometimes been criticized as rambling and plotless. But her best novels, particularly *The Needle's Eye* (1972), contain detailed and perceptive analyses of dilemmas women face in the modern world.

Drabble's early novels, such as *A Summer Bird-Cage* (1963) and *The Garrick Year* (1964), are almost autobiographical studies of conflicts young women experience in their careers, marriages, and family lives. Her later novels, such as *The Realms of Gold* (1975) and *The Ice Age* (1977), include a larger number of characters who represent a cross section of English society.

In her later works, Drabble gave more emphasis to current economic, political, and social concerns. For example, in *The Middle Ground* (1980) and *The Radiant Way* (1987), she focuses on how social change influences her characters. *A Natural Curiosity* (1989), a sequel to *The Radiant Way,* continues the social concern and multiple characters of the earlier work. Drabble has also written historical works and literary criticism and was the editor of the fifth edition of *The Oxford Companion*

to English Literature (1985). Drabble was born in Sheffield.   Cynthia A. Davis

Drachma, *DRAK muh,* is a nickel-brass coin that is the monetary unit of Greece. It is divided into 100 *lepta.* For the price of the drachma in U.S. dollars, see **Money** (table: Exchange rates). The drachma was formerly made of silver. It was one of the standard coins of ancient Greece and was equal to six *obols.*   R. G. Doty

Draco, *DRAY koh,* was a Greek lawmaker who introduced the first written code of law in ancient Athens in 621 B.C. The code was designed to reduce discontent caused by the unfairness of the Athenian justice system. The system had been based on unwritten laws known only to a few aristocratic judges, who often favored the nobility. By putting laws into writing, Draco's code enabled people to find out for themselves what the laws were. Draco's code was said to be "written in blood" because it made almost all crimes punishable by death. Today, the word *Draconian* means *harsh* or *cruel.*

For the first time, the code made the government responsible for punishing a murderer. Previously, punishment was left to the victim's family, and bloody feuds were common. The code placed responsibility for upholding the law in the hands of the government. It helped Athens become one of the first city-states, or independent political units that consisted of a city and its surrounding territory.   Donald Kagan

Dracula, *DRAK yuh luh,* a novel by the English author Bram Stoker, is the most famous vampire story of all time. The main character is a wicked nobleman, Count Dracula of Transylvania, a region of Romania. Dracula is a vampire—a corpse that returns to life at night, attacks innocent people, and sucks their blood.

The novel describes in detail Dracula's horrifying search for new victims. The search leads him to England, where he pursues two young women, Lucy Westerna and Mina Seward. He, in turn, is hunted by Mina's fiancé, Jonathan Harker, and by Abraham Van Helsing, an authority on vampires. The two men finally track down Dracula and destroy him. *Dracula* was based on vampire legends that probably arose from hundreds of savage murders committed in the 1400's by Vlad Tepes, a prince from Walachia, a region south of Transylvania.

Stoker's novel, published in 1897, is probably best known as a motion picture. Film versions include *Nosferatu* (1922) and *Dracula* (1931).   James Douglas Merritt

See also **Stoker, Bram; Vampire.**

Draft is a written order drawn by one party, directing a second party to pay a definite amount of money to a third party. Such a party may be an individual, a corpora-

WORLD BOOK photo by James Simek
The drachma is the monetary unit of Greece.

tion, or a bank. Most drafts are used to finance business transactions when the buyer and seller are in different locations. A draft may also be drawn payable to the party that draws it.

A draft may read *pay at sight* or *on demand.* In such cases, the draft is like a check, and the payer must pay immediately upon accepting the draft. If a *time draft* is used, the payer accepts the draft, agreeing to pay it within a stated period of time. The draft, signed by the payer, becomes legally binding and is then called an *acceptance* or *note.*

A draft is the same as a *bill of exchange* except that the term *draft* usually means a transfer of money between parties in the same country. Bills of exchange are frequently used for the transfer of money abroad. A draft drawn on a bank is a *check.* Checks originate with the buyer, but trade drafts originate with the seller. Sellers of goods and services often use drafts to avoid the credit risk of open book accounts.　　Joanna H. Frodin

See also **Bill of exchange; Commercial paper; Negotiable instrument; Note.**

Draft, Military, also called *conscription,* is a system of selecting men for required military service. A nation's needs for military manpower determine (1) how long a man must serve and (2) the branch of the armed forces in which he serves.

Since ancient times, governments have conscripted men whenever they needed larger military forces than they felt they could get through voluntary enlistments. Many countries use a draft during wartime. Some nations also draft men—and women in a few countries—in peacetime. Other countries have never had a draft.

The U.S. draft system

The United States used a draft during the Civil War (1861-1865), World War I (1914-1918), and World War II

United Press Int.

The first U.S. military draft number for World War I was drawn in 1917 by Secretary of War Newton D. Baker, *right.*

(1939-1945). The government also drafted men from 1948 through 1972 because of its deep involvement in world affairs, the tensions created by the Cold War, and U.S. commitments in the Vietnam War.

In 1973, the U.S. government stopped drafting men and began accepting only volunteers into its armed forces. The government also created a *stand-by draft,* which was administered by the Selective Service System, a federal agency. Under the stand-by draft, men who had reached the age of 18 were required to register with the Selective Service System through local draft boards. The stand-by draft was discontinued in 1975. In 1980, however, Congress passed legislation resuming registration requirements for the draft. Under the new law, men who reached the age of 19 or 20 in 1980 were required to register with the Selective Service System that year. Beginning in 1981, all men were required to register for the draft as they reached the age of 18. Such registration was designed to provide the government with a list of men who could be inducted into the armed services in the event of a national emergency.

The history of conscription

In Europe and Asia. Ancient Greece and Rome conscripted men into their armies at times, but they generally relied on professional troops. In Europe during the Middle Ages, warfare was not part of the ordinary man's life. To bear arms was considered a privilege of the nobility. In addition, rulers often employed *mercenaries* (soldiers who offered their services for hire).

King Gustavus Adolphus of Sweden conscripted men in the 1600's, and France practiced conscription in the 1700's. In the 1800's, Prussia produced a large, skilled army by calling up small groups of conscripts for a year's training and then placing them in the reserves. From the early 1900's to the 1950's, most major European countries staffed their armies through conscription. But since the 1950's, a number of countries have abandoned the draft because of the high cost of maintaining a large army and because modern methods of warfare have generally reduced the need for large ground forces. The British Army is made up of volunteers. India and many other non-Communist Asian countries also rely on volunteer forces. Canada conscripted troops during World War I and World War II. After each war, the Canadian armed services returned to all-volunteer forces.

In the United States, conscription dates back to colonial times, when the colonies drafted men to serve in their militias. Most of the colonies sent militia troops to fight in the Revolutionary War (1775-1783). In 1790, Secretary of War Henry Knox and President George Washington proposed a universal military service plan, but Congress rejected it. Until 1940, the United States maintained only volunteer military forces in peacetime. During the Civil War, both the Union and the Confederacy drafted men.

During World War I, the United States drafted about $2\frac{3}{4}$ million men. About 10 million men were drafted during World War II, and about 2 million men were drafted at the time of the Korean War (1950-1953). During America's heaviest military involvement in the Vietnam War, from 1965 to 1973, about 1,700,000 men were drafted.

In 1940, the Selective Service System was created to administer the draft. Men were called up on the basis of a classification they received from their local draft board. Men classified 1-A were available for induction. Other men received classifications that *deferred* (postponed) their eligibility for induction. These men could not be drafted as long as they held such a classification. A 2-A classification, for example, meant that a man performed a job considered essential to the national interest. Draft boards issued 4-F classifications to men who were physically or mentally unable to serve. During the 1950's and 1960's, many full-time college students got 2-S deferments that let them complete their studies.

Criticism of the draft. During the 1960's, many Americans began to criticize the Selective Service System. Some charged that the draft favored the middle and upper classes. They said that too high a proportion of poor men were being drafted because they could not afford to go to college and so obtain student deferments. Some people also charged that the draft was not run uniformly by the local boards. Other Americans complained that the policy of drafting the oldest men ahead of the youngest ones resulted in a long period of uncertainty for some men classified 1-A. In that period, such men had trouble finding jobs and getting loans.

Also at this time, many Americans began to challenge the morality of the draft itself. A number of them believed that the United States was involved in an immoral war in Vietnam. Some viewed the draft as an unjust and unnecessary restriction of individual liberties. Some persons also believed that the rules governing conscientious objector deferments were too narrow (see **Conscientious objector**). Opposition to the draft system or to the Vietnam War led some men to burn their draft cards and refuse to be inducted. Some left the United States and moved to other countries. A number of draft resisters were imprisoned.

In 1969, the United States adopted a draft lottery to ease some of the problems associated with the draft system. In the lottery system, the order of induction of 1-A men depended on a chance drawing of birth dates. Inductions started with undeferred men whose birth date was paired with the number 1 and ended with the men whose birth date was paired with the highest number needed to fill the draft call. Registrants with numbers higher than the cutoff number remained ineligible for the draft with a 1-H classification.

The ongoing debate. Today, the United States maintains volunteer military forces offering good pay and many benefits to both men and women who enlist. This all-volunteer system tends to produce armed forces with better-trained personnel who serve for longer periods. It also helps remove the opposition to military service that has often accompanied the draft. However, its disadvantages include higher costs and difficulty in attracting enough people for situations requiring higher force levels. Some people consider the draft—and resulting lower military pay—a way of reducing military expenditures. Some also consider it an obligation of American citizenship. Thus, the question of whether or not to reinstitute the draft remains a continuing issue in U.S. public policy debates.   Kenneth M. Dolbeare

See also **Army** (The rise of modern armies); **Canada, History of** (The conscription issue); **Civil War** (The draft); **World War I** (The United States enters the war); **World War II** (On the home front).

Additional resources

Cohen, Eliot A. *Citizens and Soldiers: The Dilemmas of Military Service.* Cornell Univ. Press, 1985.
Davis, James W., and Dolbeare, K. M. *Little Groups of Neighbors: The Selective Service System.* Greenwood, 1981. First published in 1968.
The Military Draft: Selected Readings on Conscription. Ed. by Martin Anderson and Barbara Honegger.
Taylor, L. B., Jr. *The Draft.* Watts, 1981. For younger readers.

Drafter. See **Mechanical drawing.**
Drag. See **Aerodynamics** (Drag); **Streamlining.**
Drag, a means of transportation. See **Travois.**
Drag racing. See **Automobile racing** (Drag racing); **Hot rod.**
Drago, *DRAH goh,* **Luis María** (1859-1921), an Argentine statesman and jurist, supported the principle that became known as the *Drago Doctrine.* Drago was minister of foreign affairs in 1902, when Great Britain, Germany, and Italy aroused Latin America by blockading Venezuelan ports. Drago argued that no European country could use public debt as an excuse for armed intervention or for the occupation of American territory. The Hague Peace Conference of 1907 accepted Drago's doctrine.

Drago was born in Buenos Aires. He studied law, and became a judge of both the civil and criminal courts. Great Britain and the United States asked him to arbitrate the Atlantic fisheries dispute in 1909 and 1910. The Carnegie Endowment for International Peace invited him to visit the United States. It described Drago as the "most eminent exponent of intellectual culture in South America."   Donald E. Worcester

Dragon is a mythical beast in the folklore of many European and Asian cultures. Legends describe dragons as large, lizardlike creatures that breathe fire and have a long, scaly tail. In Europe, dragons are traditionally portrayed as ferocious beasts that represent the evils fought by human beings. But in Asia, especially in China and Japan, the animals are generally considered friendly creatures that ensure good luck and wealth.

Many European legends tell how a hero slew a dragon. For example, Apollo, a god of the ancient Greeks and Romans, once killed a dragon called Python. Saint George, the patron saint of England, rescued a princess from a dragon by slaying the beast with a lance.

Orsanmichele, Florence. SCALA/Art Resource

Saint George Slaying the Dragon is a marble sculpture created in the early 1400's by the Italian sculptor Donatello.

According to some medieval legends, dragons lived in wild, remote regions of the world. The dragons guarded treasures in their dens, and a person who killed one supposedly gained its wealth.

In China, the traditional New Year's Day parade includes a group of people who wind through the street wearing a large dragon costume. The dragon's image, according to an ancient belief, prevents evil spirits from spoiling the new year. Another traditional Chinese belief is that certain dragons have the power to control the rainfall needed for each year's harvest.   C. Scott Littleton

See also **Chen Rong.**

Dragon of Komodo. See **Komodo dragon.**

Dragonfly is a beautiful flying insect. It has four large, fragile wings which look like fine gauze. The wings shimmer and gleam in the sunlight when the insect flies. The dragonfly's long, slender body may be red, green, or blue, with white, yellow, or black markings. Large compound eyes, which look like beads, cover most of the head. The dragonfly can see motionless objects almost 6 feet (1.8 meters) away, and moving objects two or three times that distance. The insect has six legs covered with spines. It can use its legs to perch on a limb, but the legs are not adapted for walking. As it flies through the air, it holds its legs together to form a basket in which to capture insects. The dragonfly grasps its prey with its legs or jaws, and may eat it while flying.

Dragonflies have been known to fly 50 to 60 miles (80 to 97 kilometers) an hour. They fly so swiftly that they usually escape from birds or other animals. Some extinct species of dragonflies had wingspreads of 2½ feet (76 centimeters).

Male and female dragonflies often fly together and sometimes mate while in flight. The female often deposits her eggs in the water or places them inside the stem of a water plant. The *nymph* (young dragonfly) hatches within one to three weeks. It has a thick body, big head and mouth, and no wings. It has a folding lower lip, called a *mask*, which is half as long as its body. The lip has jawlike hooks at the end and can move out to capture victims. The nymph breathes by means of gills.

The dragonfly nymph remains in the water for one to five years. It eats insects and small water animals. Some large dragonfly nymphs feed on young fish. While developing into an adult dragonfly, the nymph *molts* (sheds its skin) about 12 times. For its final molt, the

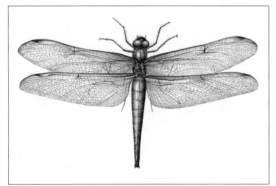

WORLD BOOK illustration by Oxford Illustrators Limited
A dragonfly has four large wings and can fly swiftly. It can attain speeds of up to 60 miles (97 kilometers) an hour.

nymph leaves the water and climbs onto a reed or rock. It then sheds its skin for the last time and emerges as an adult that soon can fly. Adult dragonflies live for only a few weeks to a few months.

Dragonflies are sometimes called *devil's-darning-needles, snake doctors, snake feeders, horse stingers,* and *mule killers.* They help people by feeding on harmful insects such as mosquitoes. Small, graceful *damsel flies* look like dragonflies, but have more slender, fragile bodies.

Scientific classification. Dragonflies and damsel flies belong to the class Insecta. They make up the order Odonata.

Sandra J. Glover

See also **Insect** (illustration: Incomplete metamorphosis).

Dragster. See **Automobile racing** (Drag racing).

Drainage is the removal of excess water from the soil. Plants cannot grow well in soil that is saturated with water. In most areas, water drains naturally from the soil. The water runs off or evaporates, or it is absorbed by the soil or by plants. In areas that do not drain naturally, artificial drainage systems are used to aid plant growth. Drainage systems are also used to make soil suitable for other purposes, including the construction of buildings and highways.

Excess water may accumulate in soil from rainfall, irrigation, or underground sources. Soils require drainage if they have water standing on their surface or if water fills the spaces between the soil particles. Soils also need to be drained if the area has a high *water table.* The water table is the level below which the soil is saturated. In soils that do not drain properly, the water table may rise almost to the surface of the ground. High water tables limit the growth of plant roots or cause them to rot. Drainage systems lower the water table, allowing air to enter the soil so plants can grow normally.

In irrigated areas, drainage systems serve another purpose. Most irrigation water contains salts. After plants use this water, the salts remain in the soil. If allowed to accumulate, salts can reduce or prevent plant growth. Drainage systems carry away these salts.

There are two main types of drainage systems—*surface drainage* and *subsurface drainage.* Both systems carry excess water to a suitable outlet, such as a pond or stream. A third system drains soils by means of wells and pumps. But this system is too costly under most conditions.

Surface drainage removes water before it soaks into the soil. It is used in areas that have flat lands and high rainfall, where water accumulates rapidly. It is also used to drain fine-textured soils, such as silts and clays, which do not absorb water quickly. Surface drainage systems consist of a series of shallow channels or deep ditches. The systems reduce the need for subsurface drainage, which is costlier than surface drainage.

Shallow channels can be dug in a random pattern or along low places in the land where water runs off naturally. Ditches are used chiefly in large, flat areas. They are dug to a depth of 3 to 6 feet (1 to 2 meters), usually in a parallel series. They drain surface and underground water and can be used to control high water tables. But they obstruct the movement of people, machines, and animals, and they take up farmland and accumulate weeds.

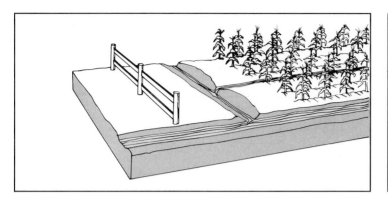

WORLD BOOK illustrations
by Bill and Judie Anderson

Drainage systems remove excess water from the soil. Surface drainage systems, *left,* consist of a series of channels or ditches. These systems carry away water before it soaks into the soil. Subsurface drainage systems use a series of tubes or pipes buried underground. Drainage tubes, *right,* have small holes through which water enters. The water is carried to a pond or other suitable outlet. These systems are costlier than surface drainage systems.

Subsurface drainage is the usual method of lowering high water tables. Most subsurface drainage systems use a series of buried tubes or pipes. Drainage tubes are made of plastic and have small holes through which water enters. Drainage pipes consist of 12-inch (30-centimeter) clay segments called *tiles,* which are laid end to end. Water enters through the spaces between tiles. A layer of gravel, called an *envelope,* may be placed around the tubes or pipes to prevent soil from entering and plugging the system.

The tubes or pipes of subsurface drainage systems measure 4 to 10 inches (10 to 25 centimeters) in diameter, depending on how much water they must carry. They are buried 30 to 600 feet (9 to 183 meters) apart and $2\frac{1}{2}$ to 4 feet (0.8 to 1.2 meters) deep. The cost of laying the system increases with the depth. But the deeper the pipes are laid, the fewer are needed to drain the same amount of soil.   Delmar D. Fangmeier

See also **Irrigation** (Providing artificial drainage).

Draisine. See **Bicycle** (Early bicycles; picture: The draisine).

Drake is the male duck. See **Duck.**

Drake, Edwin Laurentine. See **Petroleum** (Beginnings of the oil industry).

Drake, Sir Francis (1543?-1596), an explorer and military commander, was the first Englishman to sail around the world. His naval warfare against the Spaniards, the chief rivals of the English, helped England become a major sea power.

Drake was the most famous of the sea captains who roved the oceans during the rule of Queen Elizabeth I. The queen encouraged the "sea dogs," as the captains were called, to raid Spanish shipping. She gave them money and ships for such voyages, and she shared in the treasure they brought back. Drake lived in the great age of piracy and became one of the most feared pirates of his time.

Drake had no formal education, but he had great self-confidence and ambition. In battle, he was courageous, quick, and sometimes merciless. He treated his crew kindly but demanded loyalty and respect.

Early life. Drake was born near Plymouth in Devonshire. In 1549, he moved with his family to the county of

Kent, where his father became a chaplain in naval shipyards on the coast. Francis was apprenticed to the master of a ship that sailed to ports on the English Channel and in the mouth of the River Thames.

From 1566 to 1569, Drake sailed on two slave-trading voyages organized by his cousin, Sir John Hawkins, a famous sea dog. Hawkins obtained slaves in Africa and sold them to West Indian plantation owners. These voyages brought protests from both Portugal and Spain.

Oil painting by an unknown artist; National
Maritime Museum, Greenwich, England

Sir Francis Drake, a daring English seaman and pirate, helped England become a mighty sea power. Queen Elizabeth I knighted Drake in 1581 after he had sailed around the world.

Portugal did not want English competition in the slave trade, and Spain objected to English ships sailing in Caribbean waters. The slave-trading voyages gave Drake valuable sailing experience.

In 1567, Drake commanded the *Judith* on the second of the expeditions organized by Hawkins. On the return trip, the ships stopped at the Mexican port of San Juan de Ulúa, near Veracruz. A fleet of Spanish ships approached the harbor, pretending to be friendly. But the Spaniards attacked the English, killing many sailors and sinking several vessels. Only the *Judith* and Hawkins' ship, the *Minion,* escaped. Drake returned to England hating the Spaniards and vowing revenge.

From 1570 to 1572, Drake took part in looting missions to the West Indies. In 1572, he seized several Spanish ships off the coast of Panama. He landed on the coast and captured the port of Nombre de Dios, near Colón. Drake then looted the town and ambushed a mule train carrying Peruvian silver across the Isthmus of Panama.

Voyage around the world. Drake's most famous voyage began on Dec. 13, 1577. He and more than 160 men sailed from Plymouth in the *Pelican,* the *Elizabeth,* and the *Marigold.* Two other ships, the *Swan* and the *Benedict* (also known as the *Christopher*), carried supplies. The original goals of the voyage are not clear, nor is Queen Elizabeth's role in planning the voyage. But Drake hoped to explore the possibilities of trade and co-

The *Golden Hind* was Sir Francis Drake's ship during his voyage around the world from 1577 to 1580. It was about 100 feet (30 meters) long and had 18 guns. Approximately 50 men finished the famous voyage with Drake.

Water color by Gregory Robinson; National Maritime Museum, Greenwich, England

Drake's voyage around the world, 1577-1580

This map shows the route Drake followed on his voyage around the world. After passing the Straits of Magellan, Drake raided Spanish ships along the western coast of South America. The voyage made Drake the first Englishman to sail around the world.

WORLD BOOK map

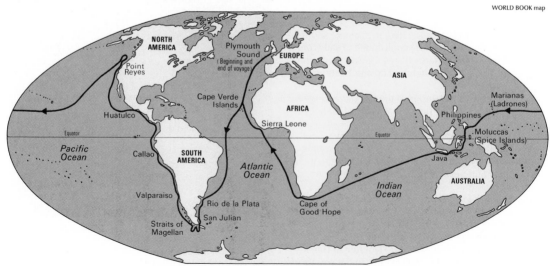

lonial settlement in the Pacific Ocean and to find the western outlet of the Northwest Passage (see **Northwest Passage**). Drake also may have intended to search for an undiscovered continent that was believed to lie in the South Pacific. He probably planned to loot Spanish ships and colonies along the Pacific coast of South America.

After leaving São Tiago in the Cape Verde Islands, Drake's expedition met two Portuguese ships. Drake captured one of the vessels and gave its command to a friend, Thomas Doughty. The ships sailed south along the Atlantic coast of South America and ran into violent storms. The expedition then stopped at San Julián for supplies. There, Drake had Doughty beheaded because he suspected him of planning a mutiny.

Before leaving San Julián, Drake destroyed the supply ships and the captured Portuguese ship because they were in poor condition and he did not think they could complete the voyage. The three remaining ships sailed through the Strait of Magellan. Shortly afterward, violent storms wrecked the *Marigold* and blew the *Elizabeth* off course, forcing it to return to England. The storms also blew the *Pelican,* which Drake renamed the *Golden Hind,* far to the south. Drake then headed north along the Pacific coast of South America. The Spaniards had left their coastal ports unguarded because until then, only Spanish ships had sailed the Pacific. After raiding several Spanish settlements, Drake captured a Spanish ship, the *Cacafuego,* and stole its cargo of gold, silver, and jewels.

Loaded with treasure, the *Golden Hind* sailed north along the Pacific coast of North America, perhaps as far as 48° north latitude. Drake then turned south. He repaired his ship near what is now San Francisco and named the area New Albion. He claimed the land for England.

Drake had planned to return to England through the Strait of Magellan, not to sail around the world. But he feared an attack by the Spaniards if he sailed south again. So he decided to sail home by way of the Pacific and Indian oceans.

Drake stopped for water at the Philippine Islands and for spices at the Molucca Islands. He also visited Sulawesi (Celebes) and Java. After crossing the Indian Ocean, Drake sailed around the Cape of Good Hope. Drake reached Plymouth on Sept. 26, 1580. He had been gone almost three years, and the voyage made him a national hero. Drake's voyage was the second voyage around the world. The first had been made from 1519 to 1522 by an expedition under the command of the Portuguese explorer Ferdinand Magellan.

Drake's voyage increased British interest in the Pacific Ocean and led to many trading ventures in eastern Asia. It broadened English knowledge about the world and paved the way for later exploration. Drake's raids on Spanish possessions angered King Philip II of Spain, and he demanded that Drake be punished. Elizabeth responded in 1581 by making Drake a knight.

From 1580 to 1585, Drake lived at Buckland Abbey, his country home near Plymouth. He bought the home with his share of the wealth from the voyage. In 1581 and 1582, Drake served as mayor of Plymouth. In 1584 and 1585, he represented the town of Bossiney in the House of Commons.

Expeditions against Spain. In May 1585, King Philip ordered an embargo on English goods in Spain and on English ships in Spanish ports. His action angered Elizabeth. In September, she put Drake in command of a fleet of 25 ships and 2,000 men. He left that fall with orders to capture Spanish treasure ships in the West Indies.

On his way, Drake looted the Spanish port of Vigo and burned São Tiago. After landing on the island of Hispaniola, Drake's men burned Santo Domingo. They later occupied the town of Cartagena for six weeks and held it for ransom. On the return voyage, Drake looted and burned St. Augustine. He then sailed north to an English colony on Roanoke Island, in what is now North Carolina, and took some colonists back to England.

Meanwhile, Philip had begun to gather Spain's warships into a fleet called the *Invincible Armada.* The Spaniards gave their fleet this name because they thought it could not be defeated. Philip planned a great attack on England, but Elizabeth learned of his intention. She sent Drake to the Spanish port of Cádiz, where he sank about 30 ships and seized many supplies.

Yet, Drake could not prevent the Armada from sailing in May 1588. He proposed a plan to attack the Armada along the coast of Portugal, but the plan was not approved in time. The queen appointed Drake vice admiral of the English fleet.

In the summer of 1588, in the English Channel, the English and Spanish fleets fought one of history's greatest naval battles. Drake commanded a large group of warships from his ship, the *Revenge.* He played an important part in the Battle of Gravelines, in which the English sank or captured many Spanish ships. The surviving ships of the Armada fled into the North Sea, hoping to find a friendly port in Ireland. But storms wrecked many of the ships and the Irish killed several Spaniards who landed.

Later life. In 1589, Drake led a fleet in a raid on Lisbon, which was then a Spanish port. He seized many merchant vessels at Lisbon but failed to capture the city or carry out other parts of Elizabeth's instructions. Thousands of English sailors died on the voyage, and Elizabeth called it a failure. Drake lost the queen's approval and received no commands for almost six years. Drake retired to Buckland Abbey and, in 1593, he represented Plymouth in the House of Commons.

Drake's last voyage took place in 1595, when he and Sir John Hawkins again sailed to the West Indies. Hawkins died as the fleet reached the islands. Drake went on and destroyed several towns. He captured Nombre de Dios but could not seize Panama City. While still off the coast of Panama, he died of dysentery. His crew buried him at sea.   Helen Delpar

Additional resources

Bradford, Ernle D. S. *The Wind Commands Me: A Life of Sir Francis Drake.* Harcourt, 1965.
Sir Francis Drake and the Famous Voyage, 1577-1580: Essays Commemorating the Quadricentennial of Drake's Circumnavigation of the Earth. Ed. by Norman J. W. Thrower. Univ. of California Press, 1984.
Thomson, George M. *Sir Francis Drake.* Morrow, 1972.
Wilson, Derek. *The World Encompassed: Francis Drake and His Great Voyage.* Harper, 1978.

Drakensberg. See Transvaal.
Dram. See Apothecaries' weight.

William Hutt as Tartuffe, Stratford Festival Theatre

Tartuffe in Molière's _Tartuffe_

Tony Van Bridge as Falstaff (De Wys)

Falstaff in Shakespeare's _Henry IV,_ Part 1

Dustin Hoffman as Willy Loman (Inge Morath, Magnum)

Willy Loman in Arthur Miller's _Death of a Salesman_

Drama

Drama is an art form that tells a story through the speech and actions of the characters in the story. Most drama is performed by actors who impersonate the characters before an audience in a theater.

Although drama is a form of literature, it differs from other literary forms in the way it is presented. For example, a novel also tells a story involving characters. But a novel tells its story through a combination of dialogue and narrative, and is complete on the printed page. Most drama achieves its greatest effect when it is performed. Some critics believe that a written script is not really a play until it has been acted before an audience.

Drama probably gets most of its effectiveness from its ability to give order and clarity to human experience. The basic elements of drama—feelings, desires, conflicts, and reconciliations—are the major ingredients of human experience. In real life, these emotional experiences often seem to be a jumble of unrelated impressions. In drama, however, the playwright can organize these experiences into understandable patterns. The au-

dience sees the material of real life presented in meaningful form—with the unimportant omitted and the significant emphasized.

No one knows exactly how or when drama began, but nearly every civilization has had some form of it. Drama may have developed from ancient religious ceremonies that were performed to win favor from the gods. In these ceremonies, priests often impersonated supernatural beings or animals, and sometimes imitated such actions as hunting. Stories grew up around some rites and lasted after the rites themselves had died out. These myths may have formed the basis of drama.

Another theory suggests that drama originated in choral hymns of praise sung at the tomb of a dead hero. At some point, a speaker separated from the chorus and began to act out deeds in the hero's life. This acted part gradually became more elaborate, and the role of the chorus diminished. Eventually, the stories were performed as plays, their origins forgotten.

According to a third theory, drama grew out of a natural love of storytelling. Stories told around campfires re-created victories in the hunt or in battle, or the feats of dead heroes. These stories developed into dramatic retellings of the events.

This article describes the history of drama. For a discussion of modern theater arts, see the _World Book_ article on **Theater.**

Julius Novick, the contributor of this article, is Professor of Literature at the State University of New York College at Purchase and theater critic for The New York Observer _and_ The Village Voice. _He is the author of_ Beyond Broadway: The Quest for Permanent Theatres.

Among the many forms of Western drama are (1) tragedy, (2) serious drama, (3) melodrama, and (4) comedy. Many plays combine forms. Modern dramatists often disregard these categories and create new forms.

Tragedy maintains a mood that emphasizes the play's serious intention, though there may be moments of comic relief. Such plays feature a *tragic hero,* an exceptional yet flawed individual who is brought to disaster and usually death. The hero's fate raises questions about the meaning of existence, the nature of fate, morality, and social or psychological relationships. Aristotle identified the emotional effect of tragedy as the *"catharsis* [emotional release] of pity and fear."

Serious drama, which developed out of tragedy, became established in the 1800's. It shares the serious tone and often the serious purpose of tragedy and, like tragedy, it concentrates on unhappy events. But serious drama can end happily, and its heroes are less imposing and more ordinary than the tragic hero. Serious drama is sometimes viewed as tragedy's modern successor.

Melodrama involves a villain who initiates actions that threaten characters with whom the audience is sympathetic. Its situations are extreme and often violent, though endings are frequently happy. Melodrama portrays a world in which good and evil are clearly distinguished. As a result, almost all melodramas have a sharply defined, oversimplified moral conflict.

Comedy tries to evoke laughter, often by exposing the pretensions of fools and rascals. Comedy usually ends happily. But even in the midst of laughter, comedy can raise surprisingly serious questions. Comedy can be both critical and playful, and it may arouse various responses. For example, *satiric comedy* tries to arouse

Orion Press

A kabuki play in Japan

scorn, while *romantic comedy* tries to arouse joy.

Farce is sometimes considered a distinct dramatic form, but it is essentially a type of comedy. Farce uses ridiculous situations and broad physical clowning for its humorous effects.

The structure of drama

Aristotle, a Greek philosopher who lived in the 300's B.C., wrote the earliest surviving and most influential essay on drama, called *Poetics.* In it, he identified the parts of a tragedy as (1) plot, (2) character, (3) thought, (4) diction, (5) music, and (6) spectacle. These six elements are fundamental to all types of drama, not just tragedy. In a well-written play, all of the elements combine to form a unified, coherent, and purposeful sequence of incidents.

Plot is a term sometimes used to mean a summary of a play's story. More properly, it means the overall structure of the play. In this sense, it is the most important element of drama. The beginning of a play includes *exposition,* which gives the audience information about earlier events, the present situation, or the characters. Early in most plays, the author focuses on a question or a potential conflict. The author brings out this question or conflict through an *inciting incident* which sets the action in motion. The inciting incident makes the audience aware of a *major dramatic question,* the thread that holds the events of the play together.

Most of the play involves a series of *complications*—discoveries and decisions that change the course of action. The complication leads to a *crisis,* a turning point when previously concealed information is at least partly revealed and the major dramatic question may be answered. The final part of the play, often called the *reso-*

lution, extends from the crisis to the final curtain. It pulls together the various strands of action and brings the situation to a new balance, thus satisfying the expectations of the audience. Writers of modern drama often ignore these traditional aspects of plot.

Character is the principal material from which a plot is created. Incidents develop mainly through the speech and behavior of dramatic characters. The characters must be shaped to fit the needs of the plot, or the plot must be shaped to fit the needs of the characters.

Thought. Every play, even the most light-hearted comedy, involves thought in its broadest sense. In dramatic structure, thought includes the ideas and emotions implied by the words of all the characters. Thought also includes the overall meaning of the play, sometimes called the *theme.* Not all plays explore significant ideas. But every play makes some comment on human experience, either through direct statement or, more commonly, by implication.

Other parts of drama. *Diction,* or *dialogue,* is the use of language to create thought, character, and incident. *Music* involves either musical accompaniment or, more commonly today, the arranged pattern of sound that makes up human speech. *Spectacle* deals with the visual aspects of a play, especially the physical actions of the characters. Spectacle also refers to scenery, costumes, makeup, stage lighting, and props.

Ruins of the ancient Greek theater at Epidaurus; David Seymour, Magnum

Ancient Greek theaters were outdoor amphitheaters that seated thousands of spectators for annual contests in acting, choral singing, and writing comedy and tragedy. Scholars are not sure what the stages looked like. The drawings below show some possible reconstructions of the stage house of the Theater of Dionysus.

Illustration from *Antike Griechische Theaterbauten* by Robert Fiechter, courtesy University of Chicago Library

Drama was born in ancient Greece. Much of our knowledge of Greek theater comes from archaeological studies and historical writings of the time. By the 600's B.C., the Greeks were giving choral performances of dancing and singing at festivals honoring Dionysus, their god of wine and fertility. Later, they held drama contests to honor Dionysus. The earliest record of Greek drama dates from about 534 B.C., when a contest for tragedy was established in Athens. Thespis, who was the winner of the first competition, became the earliest known actor and dramatist. The word *thespian* comes from his name.

The most important period of ancient Greek drama was the 400's B.C. Tragedies were performed as part of an important yearly religious and civic celebration called the *City Dionysia*. This festival, which lasted several days, offered hotly contested prizes for the best tragedy, comedy, acting, and choral singing.

The Greeks staged performances in the Theater of Dionysus, on the slope below the Acropolis in Athens. The theater seated about 14,000 people. It consisted of rows of stadiumlike seats that curved about halfway around a circular acting area called the *orchestra*. Beyond the circle and facing the audience was the *skene* (stage house), originally used as a dressing area and later as a background for the action. This structure eventually developed into a long building with side wings called *paraskenia* projecting toward the audience. The skene probably had three doors. The action may have taken place on a raised platform, or perhaps entirely in the orchestra. See **Europe** (picture: Ancient Greek drama).

Tragedy. Greek tragedy, perhaps because it originally was associated with religious celebrations, was solemn, poetic, and philosophic. Nearly all the surviving tragedies were based on myths. Typically, the main character was an admirable, but not perfect, person confronted by a difficult moral choice. This character's struggle against hostile forces ended in defeat and, in most Greek tragedies, his or her death.

Greek tragedies consisted of a series of dramatic episodes separated by choral odes (see **Ode**). The episodes were performed by a few actors, never more than three on stage at one time, during the 400's B.C. A chorus danced and sang and chanted the odes to musical accompaniment.

The actors wore masks to indicate the nature of the characters they played. Men played women's roles, and the same actor appeared in several parts. The acting style, by modern standards, was probably far from realistic. The poetic language and the idealized characters suggest that Greek acting was dignified and formal. The dramatist usually staged his own plays. A wealthy citizen called the *choregus* provided the money to train and costume the chorus.

Of the hundreds of Greek tragedies written, fewer than 35 survive. All but one were written by three dramatists—Aeschylus, Sophocles, and Euripides.

Aeschylus, the earliest of the three, won 13 contests for tragedy. His plays are noted for their lofty tone and majestic language. He was the master of the *trilogy,* a dramatic form consisting of three tragedies that focus on different phases of the same story. His *Oresteia,* the only surviving Greek trilogy, tells how Clytemnestra killed her husband, Agamemnon, and was then killed by

Roman copy of a Greek marble bas-relief of 100's or 200's B.C., courtesy Vatican Museums (Raymond Schoder, S.J.)

Menander was the most popular Greek playwright of his time. This bas-relief shows him with masks worn in comedies. The woman at the right may represent Thalia, the goddess of comedy.

their son Orestes. This trilogy traces the development of the idea of justice from primitive vengeance to enlightened, impersonal justice administered by the state. This development is portrayed in a powerful story of murder, revenge, remorse, and divine mercy. The chorus is important in Aeschylus' plays.

Sophocles is the playwright whose work served as the primary model for Aristotle's writing on tragedy. Sophocles seems today the most typical of the Greek tragic playwrights. His plays have much of Aeschylus' philosophic concern, but his characters are more fully drawn and his plots are better constructed. He was also more skillful in building climaxes and developing episodes. Aeschylus used only two characters on stage at a time until Sophocles introduced a third actor. This technique increased the dramatic complexity of Greek drama. Sophocles also reduced the importance of the chorus. His most famous play, *Oedipus Rex,* is a masterpiece of suspenseful storytelling and perhaps the greatest Greek tragedy.

Euripides was not widely appreciated in his own day, but his plays later became extremely popular. Euripides is often praised for his realism. His treatment of traditional gods and myths shows considerable doubt about religion, and he questioned moral standards of his time. Euripides showed his interest in psychology in his many understanding portraits of women. His *Medea* describes how a mother kills her children to gain revenge against their father.

Euripides used a chorus, but did not always blend it well with the episodes of his tragedies. He is sometimes criticized for his dramatic structure. Many of his plays begin with a prologue summarizing past events and end with the appearance of a god who resolves a seemingly impossible situation.

Satyr plays. Each playwright who competed in the contests at the City Dionysia had to present three tragedies and then a satyr play. The satyr play, a short comic parody of a Greek myth, served as a kind of humorous afterpiece to the three tragedies. It may be even older than tragedy. The satyr play used a chorus performing as *satyrs* (mythical creatures that were half human and

half animal). The actors and chorus in the tragedies also appeared in the satyr play.

Only one complete satyr play still exists—Euripides' *Cyclops.* It is a parody of Odysseus' encounter with the monster Cyclops. The satyr play was a regular part of the Athenian theater during the 400's B.C. But the form disappeared when Greek drama declined after the 200's B.C.

Old Comedy. Greek playwrights did not mix tragedy and comedy in the same play. Greek Old Comedy, as the comic plays of the 400's are called, was outspoken and bawdy. The word *comedy* comes from the Greek word *komoidia,* which means *merrymaking.*

In the first scene of a typical Old Comedy, a character suggests the adoption of a *happy idea.* For example, in the comedy *Lysistrata* by Aristophanes, the women of Athens figure out a way to stop their men from going to war. After a debate called an *agon,* the proposal, sometimes greatly changed, is adopted. The rest of the play shows the humorous results. Most of these plays end with a *komos* (an exit to feasting and merrymaking).

The only surviving examples of Old Comedy are by Aristophanes. He combined social and political satire with fantasy, robust farce, obscenity, personal abuse, and beautiful lyric poetry. Aristophanes was a conservative who objected to the social, moral, and political changes occurring in Athenian society. In each of his plays, he ridiculed and criticized some aspect of the communal life of his day.

New Comedy. Tragedy declined after 400 B.C., but comedy remained vigorous. Comedy changed so drastically, however, that most comedies written after 338 B.C. are called New Comedy. In spite of its popularity, only numerous fragments and a single play have survived. The play is *The Grouch* by Menander, the most popular playwright of his time. Most New Comedy dealt with the domestic affairs of middle-class Athenians. Private intrigues replaced the political and social satire and fantasy of Old Comedy. In New Comedy, most plots depended on concealed identities, coincidences, and recognitions. The chorus provided little more than interludes between episodes.

Roman drama

After the 200's B.C., Greek drama declined and leadership in the art began to pass to Rome. Today, Greek drama is much more highly regarded than Roman drama, which for the most part imitated Greek models. Roman drama is important chiefly because it influenced later playwrights, particularly during the Renaissance. William Shakespeare and the other dramatists of his day knew Greek drama almost entirely through Latin imitations of it.

In Rome, tragedy was less popular than comedy, short farces, pantomime, or such nondramatic spectacles as battles between gladiators. Roman theaters were adaptations of Greek theaters. The government supported theatrical performances as part of the many Roman religious festivals, but wealthy citizens financed some performances. Admission to theatrical performances was free and audiences were unruly in the brawling, holiday atmosphere.

The Roman stage was about 100 feet (30 meters) long and was about 5 feet (1.5 meters) above the level of the orchestra. The back wall represented a *façade* (building front) and probably had three openings. In comedies, these openings were treated as entrances to houses, and the stage became a street. Scholars disagree on whether the back wall was flat or three-dimensional.

Tragedy was introduced in Rome by Livius Andronicus in 240 B.C. But the dramatic works of only one Roman tragedian, Lucius Annaeus Seneca, still exist. Seneca's plays probably were never performed during his lifetime. His nine surviving plays were based on Greek originals. These plays are not admired today. However, they were extremely influential during the Renaissance.

Later western dramatists borrowed a number of techniques from Seneca. These techniques included the five-act form; the use of elaborate, flowery language; the theme of revenge; the use of magic rites and ghosts; and the device of the *confidant,* a trusted companion in whom the leading character confides.

Comedy. The only surviving Roman comedies are the works of Plautus and Terence. All their plays were adaptations of Greek New Comedy. Typical plots revolved around misunderstandings. These misunderstandings frequently were based on mistaken identity, free-spending sons deceiving their fathers, and humorous intrigues invented by clever slaves. Plautus and Terence eliminated the chorus from their plays, but they added

Marble relief sculpture showing a Roman adaptation of Greek New Comedy; National Museum, Naples, Italy (SCALA/Art Resource)

Roman comedy was usually performed on a stage that represented a public street. The back wall had openings through which the actors entered and exited. Most Roman comedies included musical accompaniment and many songs. Actors wore comic masks.

many songs and much musical accompaniment. Plautus' humor was robust, and his plays were filled with farcical comic action. Terence avoided the broad comedy and exaggerated characters of Plautus' plays. Terence's comedies were more sentimental and more sophisticated and his humor more thoughtful. His six plays had a strong influence on later comic playwrights, especially Molière in France in the 1600's.

Minor forms of drama were popular in Rome, but no examples of these forms exist today. The *mime,* a short and usually comic play, was often satiric and obscene. In the *pantomime,* a single dancer silently acted out stories to the accompaniment of choral narration and orchestra music.

The Roman theater gradually declined after the empire replaced the republic in 27 B.C. The minor dramatic forms and spectacles became more popular than regular comedy and tragedy. Many of these performances were sensational and indecent, and offended the early Christians. In the A.D. 400's, actors were excommunicated. The rising power of the church, combined with invasions by barbarian tribes, brought an end to the Roman theater. The last known performances in ancient Rome took place in A.D. 533.

Medieval drama

Although state-supported drama ended in the A.D. 500's, scattered performances by traveling mimes and troubadours probably continued throughout the Middle Ages. The plays of Plautus, Terence, and Seneca were preserved by religious orders which studied them not as plays but as models of Latin style.

Medieval drama flourished from the 900's to the 1500's, and became increasingly diverse. It was gradually suppressed, however, because of the religious strife associated with the Reformation. By 1600, religious drama had almost disappeared in every European country except Spain.

Liturgical drama. The rebirth of drama began in the 900's with brief playlets acted by priests as part of the *liturgy* (worship service) of the church. The Resurrection was the first event to receive dramatic treatment. A large body of plays also grew up around the Christmas story, and a smaller number around other Biblical events. In the church, the plays were performed in Latin by priests and choirboys.

Mystery plays. Beginning in the 1200's, plays were moved outdoors. Plays written after this time are often called *mystery plays.* These plays, which were written in verse, taught Christian doctrine by presenting Biblical

Mansion stages were popular in medieval Europe. They consisted of separate settings on a long platform. The actors moved from one setting to another, following the action of the play.

Pageant wagons were traveling stages used to present drama in medieval England. Audiences stood in the street or saw the plays from nearby houses. The actors were townspeople.

characters as if they lived in medieval times. Many mystery plays were rich with comedy.

During the 1300's, the performance of mystery plays was taken over by such *secular* (nonreligious) organizations as trade guilds. The *vernacular* (local language) replaced Latin. The short plays had been staged throughout the year. But by the 1300's, they were often given as a group called a *cycle*. A cycle portrayed the entire Christian story of the relationship between God and human beings, from the creation of the world to the final judgment. It included an account of the life, death, and Resurrection of Jesus Christ. Cycles usually were performed during the summer.

Cycles of mystery plays from four English towns—Chester, Lincoln, Wakefield, and York—have been preserved. All date from the 1300's. Plays from France, Italy, Spain, and elsewhere have also survived.

In England, the setting for each play was mounted on a *pageant wagon*. This wagon was drawn through a city to various places where audiences gathered. Because of the limited space, the actors probably performed on a platform beside the wagon. The audience usually stood in the street or watched the performance from nearby houses. The actors were townspeople, and most of them belonged to the trade guilds that financed and produced the plays.

In various cities on the European continent, several *mansions* (miniature settings) were erected on a long platform. The actors moved from one of these settings to another, according to the action of the play. See **Mystery play.**

Miracle plays and morality plays were also popular during the Middle Ages. Miracle plays dramatized events from the lives of saints or the Virgin Mary. The action in most of these plays reached a climax in a miracle performed by the saint. Morality plays used allegorical characters to teach moral lessons. These dramas grew from fairly simple religious plays into secular entertainments performed by professional acting companies. See **Miracle play; Morality play.**

Farces and interludes. Purely secular drama achieved its greatest development in two short forms of drama—the farce and the interlude. Farces were almost entirely comic, and many were based on folk tales. Interludes originally were entertaining skits, probably acted between courses during banquets or at other events. The interlude was especially associated with the coming of professional actors who became regular parts of many noble households.

Italian Renaissance drama

Even before the development of the theater in England and Spain, the Renaissance had begun to transform Italian drama. A new interest in ancient Greece and Rome extended to the drama, and classical plays were studied for the first time as drama, not just as literature. Italian critics of the 1500's wrote essays based on Aristotle's *Poetics* and Horace's *Art of Poetry.* From these essays grew a movement in the arts known later as *neoclassicism.*

The centers of Italian theatrical activity were the royal courts and the academies, where authors wrote plays that imitated classical drama. These plays were produced in small private theaters for the aristocracy. Most of the actors were courtiers, and most performances were a part of court festivities.

There were three types of plays—comedy, tragedy, and *pastoral.* Pastoral drama dealt with love stories about woodland goddesses and shepherds in idealized rural settings. Few Italian Renaissance plays had much real artistic value. But they are important historically because they departed from the shapelessness of medieval drama and moved toward greater control of the plot. Ludovico Ariosto was the first important comic writer. His comedies *Cassaria* (1508) and *I Suppositi* (1509) are considered the beginning of Italian drama. *La Mandragola* (about 1520), a comedy by the statesman and writer Niccolò Machiavelli, is still admired and performed today. The first important tragedy was *Sofonisba* (1515), by Giangiorgio Trissino, who followed the Greeks rather than Seneca.

Intermezzi and operas. To satisfy the Italian love of spectacle, the *intermezzo,* a new form, developed from the court entertainments. The intermezzi were performed between acts of regular plays. They drew flattering parallels between mythological figures and people of the day, and provided opportunities for imaginative costumes and scenery. After 1600, the intermezzi were absorbed into opera, which originated in the 1590's from attempts to reproduce Greek tragedy. By 1650, opera was Italy's favorite dramatic form.

The Italian stage. More important than the plays was the new type of theater developed in Italian courts and academies. Italian scenic designers were influenced by two traditions—the Roman façade theaters and the newly acquired knowledge of perspective painting. In 1545, Sebastiano Serlio published the first Italian essay on staging. He summarized contemporary methods of adapting the Roman theater for use indoors. Serlio's designs show semicircular seating in a rectangular hall and a wide, shallow stage. Behind the shallow stage was a *raked* (tilted) stage on which painted sets created a perspective setting. Serlio's three stage designs—for comedy, tragedy, and pastoral dramas—were widely imitated.

The Roman façade was recreated in the Teatro Olimpico, Italy's first important permanent theater, which opened in 1585. A *perspective alley* showing a view down a city street was placed behind each of seven

Pantaloon Serenading His Mistress, (about 1580), an oil painting on wood panel by an unknown artist showing, *left to right,* the heroine, Harlequin, Pantaloon, and Zanni. Drottningholms Teatermuseum, Stockholm

Commedia dell' arte was a loosely constructed form of comedy that dominated Italian drama from the 1500's through the 1700's. A stock group of characters appeared in all commedia plays.

Serlio's design for comedy from *The First Book of Architecture,* courtesy Newberry Library, Chicago

Scenic designs by Sebastiano Serlio popularized perspective settings in Renaissance drama. His designs for comedy, tragedy, and satire were based on the classical Roman stage.

openings in the façade. A more significant development of the façade appeared in the Teatro Farnese, built in 1618. This theater had the first permanent *proscenium*

arch, a kind of large frame that enclosed the action on stage. It was especially suited for perspective settings. In 1637, the first public opera house opened in Venice. There, earlier developments helped create the proscenium stage that dominated theater until the 1900's.

Commedia dell' arte (pronounced *kawm ME dyah del LAHR tay*) was the name given to boisterous Italian plays in which the actors *improvised* (made up) the dialogue as they went along. Commedia was a truly popular form in Italian, as opposed to the literary drama of the court and academies. Commedia was performed by professional actors who worked as easily on simple platforms in a market square as they did on elaborate court stages.

The commedia script consisted of a *scenario* (outline of the basic plot). Characters included such basic types as Harlequin the clown and Pantaloon the old man. The same actor always played the same role. Most of the lively, farcical plots dealt with love affairs, but the main interest lay in the comic characters. We do not know how commedia originated, but by 1575 the companies that performed it had become extremely popular in Italy. Commedia soon was appearing throughout Europe. It remained a vigorous force in drama until the mid-1600's, and continued to be performed until the end of the 1700's. Commedia had an important influence on much of the comedy written during the 1600's.

Elizabethan, Jacobean, and Caroline drama

The Reformation directly affected the history of drama by promoting the use of national languages rather than Latin. The use of these languages led to the development of national drama. The first such drama to reach a high level of excellence appeared in England between 1580 and 1642. Elizabethan drama was written mainly during the last half of the reign of Queen Elizabeth I, from about 1580 to 1603. Jacobean drama was written during the reign of King James I (1603-1625). William Shakespeare, the greatest dramatist of the age, bridged the Elizabethan and Jacobean periods, but he generally is considered an Elizabethan playwright. Caroline drama was written in the reign of King Charles I (1625-1649).

Elizabethan theaters. The first public theater in England, called The Theatre, was built near London in 1576. By 1642, there had been at least nine others in and around London, including the Globe, Rose, and Fortune.

All Elizabethan public theaters had the same basic design. A large unroofed area called the *yard* was enclosed by a three-storied, gallery-type structure that was round, square, or octagonal. A large, elevated platform stage projected into the yard and served as the theater's principal acting area. The audience stood in the yard or sat in the galleries, watching the play from three sides.

At the rear of the platform stood a two- or three-story façade. On the stage level, the façade had two doors that served as the principal entrances. Another acting area on the second level was used to represent balconies, walls, or other high places. Some theaters had a façade with a third level where the musicians sat. The specific place of the dramatic action was indicated primarily through descriptive passages in the play's dialogue. A

few pieces of scenery were used. This theater design was ideal for Elizabethan plays, which moved at a rapid pace and had many scenes.

Performances began in the early afternoon and lasted until just before dusk. Women never appeared on the professional stage. Boys played women's roles, and some acting companies consisted entirely of boys. All classes of society attended the theater, and refreshments were sold during performances. The audience watched in a boisterous, holiday mood.

Elizabethan playwrights. Elizabethan plays developed from the interludes performed by wandering actors, and the classically inspired plays of schools and universities. These two traditions merged in the 1580's when a new group of playwrights, many of them university-educated, began writing for professional actors of the public theater.

Thomas Kyd is important in the history of drama because he brought classical influence to popular drama. Kyd wrote the most popular play of the 1500's, *The Spanish Tragedy* (1580's). This play established the fashion for tragedy in the theater. It moved freely in place and time, as did medieval drama. But *The Spanish Tragedy* also showed the influence of Seneca in its use of a ghost, the revenge theme, the chorus, the lofty poetic style, and the division of the play into five acts. Most of all, Kyd demonstrated how to construct a clear, absorbing story. He wrote *The Spanish Tragedy* in blank verse and established this poetic form as the style for English tragedy (see **Blank verse**). *The Spanish Tragedy* may seem crude today. However, the play was a remarkable advance over earlier drama and had great influence on later drama.

Detail from a painting (about 1597) by an unknown artist of a wedding masque during a banquet at the house of Sir Henry Unton, National Portrait Gallery, London

Masques were elaborate, colorful spectacles that combined music, dancing, vivid costumes, and symbolic drama. English masques were popular with royalty and nobility.

Christopher Marlowe perfected blank verse in English tragedy. Marlowe wrote a series of tragedies that centered on a strong *protagonist* (main character). Marlowe's work was filled with sensationalism and cruelty, but it included splendid poetry and scenes of sweeping passion.

John Lyly wrote primarily for companies of boy actors that specialized in performing before aristocratic audiences. Most of Lyly's plays were pastoral comedies. He mixed classical mythology with English subjects, and wrote in a refined, artificial style.

Robert Greene also wrote pastoral and romantic comedies. His *Friar Bacon and Friar Bungay* (about 1589) and *James IV* (about 1591) combined love stories and rural adventures with historical incidents. Greene's heroines are noted for their cleverness and charm.

Thus, by 1590, several dramatists had bridged the gap between the learned and popular audiences. Their blending of classical and medieval devices with absorbing stories established the foundations upon which Shakespeare built. William Shakespeare, like other writers of his time, borrowed from fiction, histories, myths, and earlier plays. Shakespeare contributed little that was entirely new, but he developed the dramatic techniques of earlier playwrights. His dramatic poetry is unequaled, and he had a genius for probing character, producing emotion, and relating human experience to broad philosophical issues.

Ben Jonson's comedies are sometimes called *corrective* because he tried to improve human behavior by ridiculing foolishness and vice. He popularized the *comedy of humours.* According to a Renaissance medical concept, everyone had four *humours* (fluids) in his or her body. Good health depended on a proper balance among them. An excess of one humour might dominate a person's disposition. An excess of bile, for example, supposedly made a person melancholy. Jonson also wrote two tragedies on classical subjects, and many elaborate spectacles called *masques.*

Several other playwrights bridged the Elizabethan and Jacobean periods besides Shakespeare and Jonson. They included George Chapman, Thomas Dekker, Thomas Heywood, and John Marston.

Jacobean and Caroline drama. About 1610, English drama began to change significantly. The *tragicomedy,* a serious play with a happy ending, increased in popularity. Many plots were artificially arranged and contained sensational, rather than genuinely tragic, elements. The obsession of much Jacobean and Caroline tragedy with violence, dishonesty, and horror has appalled many critics. But these plays have also been greatly admired for their magnificent poetry, their dramatic power, and their unflinching view of human nature and the human condition.

Important Jacobean playwrights included Francis Beaumont, John Fletcher, Thomas Middleton, Cyril Tourneur, and John Webster. Philip Massinger and John Ford were among the important Caroline playwrights.

After Charles I was deposed in the 1640's and the Puritans gained control of Parliament, theatrical performances were prohibited. The Puritan government closed the theaters in 1642, ending the richest and most varied era of English drama.

The Golden Age of Spanish drama

The late 1500's brought a burst of theatrical activity in Spain as well as in England. The period between the mid-1500's and late 1600's was so productive that it is called the Golden Age of Spanish drama.

During the Middle Ages, religious drama developed only in northeastern Spain. The rest of the country was occupied by the Moors. After the Moors were driven from the country in the late 1400's, Spanish rulers began to re-Christianize the country. Drama became an important means of religious teaching. Religious drama, perhaps because of church control, grew in importance in Spain while being banned in other countries during the Reformation. Until the 1550's, Spanish religious plays resembled those of other European nations. After 1550, the religious plays of Spain assumed various traits of their own.

Religious plays in Spain were called *autos sacramentales*. They combined features of the cycle play and the morality play. Human and supernatural characters were mingled with such symbolic figures as Sin, Grace, and Pleasure. Dramatists took stories from secular as well as religious sources, and adapted them to uphold church teachings. In Madrid, trade guilds staged the plays until the city council took over the job in the 1550's. The council engaged Spain's finest dramatists to write plays and hired professional companies to perform them. The public and religious stages closely resembled each other after 1550, and the same dramatists wrote for both.

Production of the plays varied from community to community, but the staging in Madrid was typical. The autos sacramentales were performed on *carros* (two-storied wagons) that resembled the pageant wagons of the English cycle plays. Carros carrying scenery were drawn through the streets to various points where audiences gathered. A second wagon served as a stage when placed in front of the carro. The second wagons eventually became permanent acting areas at various places, and the carros were drawn up to them. The autos were performed by professionals, but they retained their religious content and their close association with the church. They were performed annually during the Feast of Corpus Christi.

In addition to the autos, the actors performed short farces in the form of interludes and dances. These grew in importance, and gradually the secular elements began to dominate the performances. In 1765, church authorities forbade autos because of their content and the carnival spirit of farce and dancing.

Secular drama. The first permanent theater in Spain opened in Madrid in 1579. Spanish theaters generally resembled Elizabethan theaters in design.

Lope de Rueda, a dramatist, actor, and producer, established the professional theater in Spain during the mid-1500's. However, the professional Spanish theater actually did not flourish until after 1580. The two greatest playwrights of the Golden Age of Spanish drama

Illustration by Juan Comba from *El Corral de la Pacheca* by Ricardo Sepúlveda, courtesy University of Chicago Library

Carros, the Spanish traveling stages, brought religious drama to town audiences during the annual Feast of Corpus Christi.

were Lope de Vega and Pedro Calderón de la Barca.

Lope de Vega may have written as many as 1,800 plays. More than 400 surviving plays are attributed to him. Lope took subjects for his plays from the Bible, the lives of the saints, mythology, history, romances, and other sources. He was inventive and skillful, but his plays lack the depth of Shakespeare's. Like Shakespeare, he often used song and dance and mixed the comic with the serious. Lope influenced almost all future Spanish drama.

Calderón wrote many kinds of plays, but is best known for works exploring religious and philosophical ideas. Most of his works were autos written for the Corpus Christi festivals of Madrid. After Calderón's death in 1681, Spanish drama declined rapidly and never fully recovered its early vitality.

French neoclassical drama

The French theater had its roots in the medieval religious plays produced by guilds. The most important of these amateur groups, the Confrérie de la Passion, established a permanent theater in Paris in the early 1400's. It eventually received a royal monopoly, making it the city's only play-producing organization.

During the late 1500's and 1600's, the Confrérie's theater, called the Hôtel de Bourgogne, was rented to visiting professional companies. The first of these groups to establish itself was Les Comédiens du Roi, sometime after 1598. Alexandre Hardy, the most popular dramatist of the early 1600's, wrote many plays for this company. Hardy mostly wrote loosely constructed tragicomedies filled with adventures of chivalry.

The French theater changed significantly after the neoclassic theories were imported from Italy. In France, these theories took firmer root and were followed more rigidly than elsewhere. The basic beliefs of neoclassicism can be summarized in four parts. (1) Only two types

of drama, tragedy and comedy, were legitimate forms, and tragic and comic elements should not be mixed. (2) Drama should be written to teach a moral lesson by presenting the lesson in a pleasant form. (3) Characters should be universal types rather than eccentric individuals. This principle became known as the doctrine of *decorum*. (4) The unities of time, place, and action should be observed. This rule usually meant that a plot should cover no more than 24 hours, take place in a single locality, and deal with a single action.

Neoclassical playwrights. Although neoclassical ideas were accepted among educated French people in the late 1500's, they made little impression in public theaters until the 1630's. The playwright most closely associated with the change to neoclassic drama in France was Pierre Corneille. His play *The Cid* set off a stormy dispute that ended with the triumph of neoclassicism. *The Cid* is a tragicomedy based on a Spanish story. It follows many neoclassical rules, but violates the doctrine of decorum because the heroine marries her father's murderer. In later plays, Corneille observed the neoclassic rules and helped establish neoclassicism as the standard for French drama. The distinguishing characteristic of Corneille's drama is the hero of unyielding will. The hero gains steadily in power, but his character does not become more complex. Corneille wrote in a form of verse called Alexandrine, which became standard for French neoclassic drama.

The plays of Jean Racine marked the peak of French neoclassic tragedy. His first dramas in the 1660's established his reputation, and he soon surpassed Corneille. Racine used neoclassical rules to concentrate and intensify the dramatic power of his stories. His tragedies contained little outward action. Their drama came from internal conflicts centering on a single fully developed personality. This character usually wants to act ethically, but is prevented by other forces—often by conflicting desires. Racine created simple plots, but he revealed his characters with remarkable truth.

Molière raised French comedy to a level comparable with that of French tragedy. He also was the finest comic actor of his age, and a theater manager and a director. Molière borrowed freely from many sources, including Roman comedy, medieval farce, and Spanish and Italian stories. His most famous plays were comedies that centered around such humorous eccentrics as misers. The ridiculous excesses of the protagonists were exposed by characters of "good sense." Molière's comedies offered much biting social and moral criticism, but were amusing and good-natured. He has achieved wider and more lasting appeal than Corneille or Racine.

By about 1690, the three major French dramatists were either dead or had given up writing. Most of their successors merely repeated the old formulas, and French drama declined.

European drama: 1660-1800

England. In 1660, the Restoration ended the Puritan government. Charles II returned to the throne. Once again the theater became legal in England. But the English theater had lost the broad popular appeal it had enjoyed in Shakespeare's day. It became the pastime of a narrow circle of courtiers. Only gradually did it again become popular with the middle classes.

Soon after the theaters reopened in 1660, new playhouses in the Italian style were built in London. These theaters had a large *apron* (the part of the stage in front of the proscenium arch). Permanent doors opened onto the apron. The auditorium had tiered galleries with some private boxes. Cheaper seats were in a roughly U-shaped flat area called the *pit.* Until 1762, spectators often sat on the stage itself.

Settings in the English theater closely resembled those used in Italy, with scenes painted in perspective. Because of the neoclassic demand for universal themes, most settings were generalized—a palace or a garden, for example. During the later 1700's, settings began to show specific places.

Actresses first appeared regularly on the English stage in the 1660's, and male actors soon stopped playing women's roles. Actors became increasingly important during the 1700's, and audiences often went to see outstanding performers rather than a particular play. Actors apparently based their style on real life, but their acting was undoubtedly more exaggerated than today's audiences would approve. In the 1740's, David Garrick brought greater realism to English acting.

The Restoration period is known especially for the *comedy of manners* and the *heroic drama.* The comedy of manners was the form most identified with the Restoration. It *satirized* (poked fun at) upper-class society in witty prose. Some of these satires tolerated immorality, but the ideal behind them was self-knowledge. Characters in the comedy of manners were ridiculed for deceiving themselves or trying to deceive others. The most common characters included the old woman trying to appear young, and the jealous old man married to a young wife. The ideal characters were worldly, intelligent, and undeceived.

The comedy of manners originated largely in the plays of George Etherege. The form was perfected in the dramas of William Congreve, whose *The Way of the World* (1700) is often called the finest example of the form. In the works of William Wycherley, the tone was coarser and the humor more robust.

English comedy enjoyed a period of extreme liberty during the reign of Charles II. But Puritan elements reappeared in the early 1700's as the merchant class grew more powerful. Middle-class disapproval of the comic tone was reflected in the change from the mocking Restoration plays to the more sentimental comedies of

David Garrick and Mrs. Pritchard in *Macbeth,* detail from a painting (about 1770) by Johann Zoffany; Garrick Club, London

David Garrick was the leading English actor of his day. Garrick's realistic style of acting had a great influence on the English theater.

The School for Scandal by Richard Brinsley Sheridan is one of the greatest English comedies of the 1700's. This print shows a scene from the play at the famous Drury Lane Theatre in London in 1778.

School of Drama Library, Yale University

George Farquhar. Farquhar put emphasis on emotion and good-hearted behavior.

The heroic play flourished from about 1660 to 1680. It was written in rhymed couplets and dealt with the conflict between love and honor. These plays featured elaborate rhetoric, many shifts in plot, and violent action. Such dramas seem absurd today, but they were popular in their time.

A more vital strain of tragedy developed alongside heroic drama. These tragedies were written in blank verse that imitated Shakespeare's. Notable examples were John Dryden's *All for Love* (1677), which reshaped the story of Antony and Cleopatra according to neoclassical rules, and Thomas Otway's *Venice Preserv'd* (1682).

The term *sentimental* is often applied to most drama of the 1700's. It indicates an overemphasis on arousing sympathy for the misfortunes of others. Plots dealt with the ordeals of characters with whom the audience sympathized. The humorous portions of plays featured such minor characters as servants. Today, the characters seem too noble and the situations too artificial to be convincing. But audiences of the 1700's liked them, believing that emotional displays were spiritually uplifting.

Sentimental comedy had its first full expression in *The Conscious Lovers* (1722) by Sir Richard Steele. In the 1770's, when this type of comedy dominated the English stage, two dramatists tried to reform public taste with comedies that avoided excessive sentimentality. Oliver Goldsmith attempted to reestablish what he called *laughing comedy* in the tradition of Ben Jonson. Richard Brinsley Sheridan's plays have the satire of Restoration comedy, but lack its questionable moral tone.

Domestic tragedy substituted middle-class characters for the kings and nobles of earlier tragedy. It is an ancestor of serious drama. Domestic tragedy showed the horrifying results of yielding to sin, while sentimental comedy showed the rewards of resisting sin. George Lillo's *The London Merchant* (1731) popularized domestic tragedy. This drama became a model for playwrights in France and Germany as well as England.

Several minor dramatic forms also developed. The *ballad opera* was a prose comedy with lyrics sung to popular tunes. The most famous one was John Gay's *The Beggar's Opera* (1728). The *burlesque* was a parody of well-known dramas or literary practices. The *pantomime* combined dance, music, acting without dialogue, and elaborate scenery and special effects.

France. By the end of the 1600's, France had become the cultural center of Europe. The standard for European drama was set by the neoclassic tragedies of Corneille and Racine and the comedies of Molière. The effort to obey the rules of neoclassicism tended to freeze dramatic invention during the 1700's. Voltaire was the only notable French tragic dramatist. The first important French writer of domestic tragedy was Denis Diderot. His plays enjoyed little popularity during his lifetime. However, his proposed reforms in staging, acting, and playwriting—all designed for greater realism—greatly influenced dramatists of the 1800's.

For most of the 1700's, the French government permitted only one theatrical company, the Comédie-Française, to produce regular comedy and tragedy. Minor forms, including comic opera, short plays, and burlesques, were staged by the Comédie-Italienne, an Italian group, and at Paris fairs.

Pierre Marivaux wrote comedies in a sophisticated style that had some sentimental touches but were primarily revelations of human psychology. Sentimental comedy appeared in the works of Pierre de La Chaussée. His play *The False Antipathy* (1733) established the popularity of *comédie larmoyante* (tearful comedy). True comedy in the form of brilliant social satire appeared in the plays of Pierre Beaumarchais.

Italy. During the 1700's, commedia dell'arte underwent changes in form. Carlo Goldoni was the greatest Italian dramatist of the century. He departed from the commedia style by creating several fully written plays in the mid-1700's that gained great popularity. During this time, Carlo Gozzi opposed Goldoni's changes in commedia, and attempted reforms of his own by writing imaginative fantasies with some improvised scenes. Commedia dell'arte declined in popularity, and by the end of the 1700's, was no longer a significant form. The only important Italian tragic dramatist of the 1700's was Vittorio Alfieri.

Germany. A crude type of drama developed in various German states during the 1500's and 1600's. German theater had a low reputation until about 1725. At that time, the actress-manager Caroline Neuber and the dramatist Johann Gottsched made serious efforts to reform both playwriting and play production. Their work marked a turning point in German theater.

The dramatist and critic Gotthold Ephraim Lessing also made important contributions. His plays and his influential critical work *The Hamburg Dramaturgy* turned attention from French neoclassicism to English dramatic models. By the end of the 1700's, the German theater had been revolutionized. All major German states supported theaters modeled on the Comédie-Française, and German playwrights won recognition outside Germany. The neoclassical ideal was giving way to the romantic movement.

Asian drama

Drama in Asia developed independently of European drama. Not until the 1800's did Western playwrights generally become aware of Oriental drama and begin to borrow from its rich heritage.

India. Indian drama is one of the oldest in the world. Its exact origins are uncertain, but sometime between 200 B.C. and A.D. 200, the wise man Bharata wrote the *Natyasastra,* an essay which established traditions of dance, drama, makeup, costume, and acting.

By the mid-A.D. 300's, flourishing drama in the Sanskrit language had developed. In technique, Sanskrit plays resembled epic poems. Each play was organized around one of nine *rasas* (moods). The goal was to produce harmony, so authors avoided clashing moods and all plays ended happily. The most important of the surviving plays are *The Little Clay Cart* (probably A.D. 300's) and *Shakuntala* by Kalidasa (late 300's or early 400's).

China. The drama of China probably originated in ancient ceremonies performed in song, dance, and mime by priests at Buddhist shrines. Professional storytellers became common by the A.D. 700's, but not until the 1200's did performances become truly dramatic.

The first formal Chinese drama appeared during the Yuan dynasty (1279-1368). Since the 1800's, *Peking opera* (also called *Beijing opera*) has been the major form. The plays of the Peking opera are based on traditional stories, history, mythology, folklore, and popular romances. The play is merely an outline for a performance. Performers often make changes in the script.

The Chinese stage is simple, permitting rapid changes of location. These changes are indicated by speech, actions, or symbolic props. A whip, for example, indicates that a performer is on horseback. Musicians, and assistants who help the performers with their costumes and props, remain on stage during the performance. But by tradition they are considered invisible. The performer is the heart of Chinese theater. Richly and colorfully costumed, the performer moves, sings, and speaks according to rigid conventions. Each type of role has a definite vocal tone and pitch, and delivery follows fixed rhythmic patterns.

Japan. The *no* plays are the oldest of the three traditional forms of Japanese drama. They developed during the 1300's from dances performed at religious shrines. The no theater reached its present form in the 1600's, and it has remained practically unchanged since then.

No plays are poetic treatments of history and legend, influenced by the religious beliefs of Buddhism and

Edward B. Harper, University of Washington, Seattle

Scene from *The White Serpent;* Prof. Josephine Huang Hung, National Taiwan University, Taipei, Taiwan

Indian and Chinese drama emphasize national legends, myths, and history. Indian folk theater, *left,* dramatizes stories from Indian epics and sacred Hindu writings. Peking opera, *right,* is the leading dramatic tradition of China. Peking opera is noted for its richly costumed performers.

Japanese kabuki plays, *above,* are violent and melodramatic. These plays, traditionally performed by male casts, dramatize historical or legendary events.

Shintoism. Many of these plays are shorter than Western one-act plays, and they may seem undramatic. Like ancient Greek tragedy, a no drama is accompanied by music, dance, and choral speaking, and the actors playing women and demons wear masks. The no performance is probably the most carefully controlled in the world. Every detail of the traditional stage, every movement of the hands and feet, every vocal intonation, and every detail of costume and makeup follows a rule.

Japanese *doll* or *puppet* theater enjoyed great popularity in the 1600's and 1700's. Today, only one theatrical company performs these plays. Like the no plays, the puppet dramas originally were religious. The puppets stand 3 to 4 feet (0.9 to 1.2 meters) high and look realistic, with flexible joints and movable eyes, mouth, and eyebrows. The puppet handlers work quietly on the stage in view of the audience. A narrator recites the story to music and expresses each puppet's emotions.

The *kabuki* play is the most popular traditional form in Japan today, and the most sensitive to changing times. It is also the least pure of the three traditional forms, having borrowed freely from other types of theater. Kabuki, the last of the forms to develop, appeared about 1600. It competed with the puppet theater for popularity during the late 1700's and also took over many puppet theater plays and techniques.

The earliest kabuki were performed by a single female dancer. An all-male cast later became traditional. Although kabuki borrowed much from the no drama, it differs greatly from the formality of the no plays. Kabuki theater is violently melodramatic. It features colorful costumes and makeup, spectacular scenery, and a lively and exaggerated acting style. See **Japan** (The arts [Theater; picture]).

Romanticism

Many elements made up romanticism, a European literary movement of the late 1700's and early 1800's. The most important was a growing distrust of reason and a new belief that people should be guided by their feelings and emotions. The romantics tended to rebel against traditional social and political institutions. Romantic playwrights rebelled against the rules of neoclassical tragedy, taking Shakespeare as their model. Variety and richness became the standard for judging drama, replacing the unity and simplicity admired by the classicists. See **Romanticism.**

By 1800, a productive romantic movement had become established in Germany. Two important dramatists of the period, Johann Wolfgang von Goethe and Friedrich Schiller, wrote plays in the romantic style, but both denied being romantics. In many ways, Goethe's *Faust* showed the romantic outlook in the protagonist's unending search for fulfillment. Many of Schiller's plays dramatized moments of crisis in history.

After Germany's defeat by Napoleon's armies in 1806, some Germans became increasingly interested in their national past and less hopeful about human nature. This skeptical attitude appeared in the work of two of the best German dramatists of the day, Heinrich von Kleist and Georg Büchner.

The intentions of French romantics were clearly established with the publication of Victor Hugo's preface to his play *Cromwell* in 1827. Romanticism triumphed in the French theater with the production of Hugo's *Hernani* in 1830. *Hernani* revolved around the conflict between love and honor, and was filled with exciting episodes, suspense, and powerful verse. French romantic plays were less philosophical than German romantic plays. In addition, they depended more on such devices as disguises and narrow escapes. Probably the most out-standing French romantic dramatist was Alfred de Mus-set, who explored the psychological motives of his pro-tagonists.

Melodrama appeared along with romantic drama at the beginning of the 1800's. It helped stimulate the de-velopment of realistic scenery. Many melodramatic scenes of breathtaking escapes and such natural disas-ters as floods required clever, detailed settings. Melo-drama appealed to a much wider audience than roman-tic drama, and remained popular long after the romantic movement had ended.

Early realism

By the mid-1800's, Europe was being transformed by the development of an industrial society creating new and complex social conditions. Many people believed these conditions should be studied to determine their effect on human behavior. They also felt that literature should reflect real life. As these attitudes spread throughout literature and the theater, they were re-flected in the style known as realism. Realistic play-wrights tried to portray the real world, which they stud-ied by direct observation. These playwrights found their subjects in daily life and wrote dialogue in conversa-tional prose. See **Realism.**

The popularity of melodrama stimulated the develop-ment of realistic settings and elaborate special effects. The development of the *box set* was an important step toward stage realism in the 1800's. Scenery enclosed the acting area at the back and sides, imitating the shape of a room with one wall removed. Actors tried to create the illusion of real people in a real room.

Realism was soon followed by *naturalism,* a more ex-treme but less influential movement. The naturalists be-lieved that drama should become scientific in its meth-ods. They argued that drama should either demonstrate scientific laws of human behavior or record case histo-ries. Naturalists also placed greater emphasis on hered-ity and environment in determining behavior. Natural-ism as a self-conscious movement declined after 1900, but by emphasizing the need for copying the details of daily life, it strengthened the realist movement. See **Nat-uralism.**

Directors appeared in the late 1800's, partly as a result of the growing complexity in staging. In earlier periods, a leading actor took the responsibility of staging most plays. As the demand for greater realism increased, so did the need for more careful rehearsals and better co-ordination of all elements. The history of the modern di-rector is usually traced from the work of Georg II, Duke of Saxe-Meiningen. His well-rehearsed German acting company toured Europe between 1874 and 1890. This group demonstrated the value of integrating all aspects of a theatrical production into an artistic whole.

The independent theater movement developed in most European countries because commercial theaters refused to present realistic drama. Commercial theater managers feared the controversy it aroused, leading to the possibility of government opposition. Independent theaters began to appear in the 1880's. They were pri-vate organizations open only to members and could perform works that otherwise would not have been pre-sented. The first important independent theater was the Théâtre Libre, founded in Paris in 1887 by André An-toine. The Freie Bühne was established in Berlin by Otto Brahm in 1889. The Independent Theatre Society, founded by Jacob T. Grein in London in 1891, intro-duced the witty plays of George Bernard Shaw to audi-ences in England.

Modern drama: Ibsen to World War II

Ibsen. The strongest influence in the development of realistic drama came from Henrik Ibsen, Norway's first important dramatist. Ibsen is often called the founder of modern drama. His plays were both the high point of re-alism and the forerunner of movements away from real-ism. Ibsen broke with tradition not only in technique but also in his fearless treatment of human problems. He portrayed the environment in his plays realistically. His characters reveal themselves as they would in real life—through their words and actions rather than by a state-ment by the author.

Ibsen's *The League of Youth* (1869) was the first of a series of plays that handled social problems realistically, though his realistic plays contain important elements of symbolism as well. *A Doll's House* (1879) and *Ghosts* (1882) were explosive attacks against the conventional morality of Ibsen's time. In *Hedda Gabler* (1891) and *The Master Builder* (1893), Ibsen intensified his focus on the mind and spirit of the individual. In his late plays, espe-cially in *When We Dead Awaken* (1900), Ibsen increased his emphasis on symbols and mysterious forces beyond human control.

Russian drama and Chekhov. The realistic plays of the Russian writer Anton Chekhov became nearly as in-fluential as those of Ibsen. The principal playwrights in Russia before Chekhov included Nikolai Gogol, Alexan-der Ostrovsky, and Ivan Turgenev. Gogol's farce *The Inspector-General* (1836) satirized small-town officials. Ostrovsky portrayed the everyday life of the merchant class in such plays as *The Storm* (1860). Turgenev's play *A Month in the Country* (completed in 1850) was a realis-tic study of boredom, jealousy, and compromise, ele-ments that appear in Chekhov's plays.

Chekhov took his subjects from Russian society of his day. He skillfully created action that reflects the apparent aimlessness of life itself. As in life, comic incidents often intermingle with pathetic or tragic ones. Chekhov's greatest masterpieces are his last four plays—*The Seagull* (1896), *Uncle Vanya* (1898), *The Three Sisters* (1901), and *The Cherry Orchard* (1904).

English drama. The realistic spirit gradually influ-enced dramatists throughout Europe. Until the last quar-ter of the 1800's, the British theater was dominated by sentimental romances and melodrama. Henry Arthur

Courtesy of the Theatre Collection, New York Public Library at Lincoln Center, Astor, Lenox and Tilden Foundation

Expressionism distorts the outside world to reveal the tortured minds of the characters in the grip of fear or other violent emotions. This scene is from *The Adding Machine* by Elmer Rice.

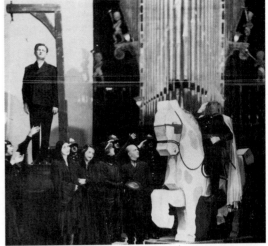

Deutsches Theatermuseum

Epic theater largely consists of the work of a single playwright, Bertolt Brecht of Germany. Brecht's most popular work is the satirical musical drama *The Threepenny Opera* (1928).

Jones and Arthur Wing Pinero, the most popular British dramatists of the late 1800's, moved toward realism.

The plays of Sir James M. Barrie have some realism, but they are basically romantic and many are overly sentimental. Oscar Wilde is remembered chiefly for his brilliant comedy *The Importance of Being Earnest* (1895). Novelist John Galsworthy wrote powerful realistic plays, including *Strife* (1909), a drama about labor strikes.

George Bernard Shaw was an influential critic as well as dramatist. He supported the social and artistic ideals of Ibsen, and was chiefly responsible for their spread in England. Most of Shaw's plays are examples of the comedy of ideas, in which the theater is used as a forum for social, political, and moral criticism.

Irish drama. A remarkable period of theatrical activity developed in Ireland during the late 1800's and extended into the 1900's. It was part of a general nationalistic revival of Irish literature known as the Irish Literary Revival. Irish drama centered around the Abbey Theatre in Dublin. It staged the plays of most major Irish dramatists, including Lady Gregory, Sean O'Casey, John Millington Synge, and William Butler Yeats.

French drama. Jean Giraudoux was probably the leading French playwright between World War I and World War II. He often used Greek myths, Biblical stories, and fantasy to make sympathetic and witty comments about humanity. Jean Cocteau also used Greek myths as the basis of his plays, but he was much more experimental in his style. Paul Claudel became famous for his religious verse plays. Jean Anouilh's many plays vary in form, but they usually take the side of youthful purity against the corrupting forces of age and greed.

United States drama. Until the early 1900's, American drama closely followed the European theater. Few American dramatists of distinction appeared until the 1800's, and none gained international recognition until Eugene O'Neill, who began writing in 1913. O'Neill's plays are a record of persistent experimentation with various styles and dramatic devices. His power is proba-

bly best revealed in his drama of tortured family relationships, *Long Day's Journey into Night*.

Other significant American dramatists of the 1920's and 1930's were Lillian Hellman; Clifford Odets, whose best plays express the political and social radicalism of the Great Depression years; Elmer Rice; and Thornton Wilder. Popular comic playwrights included the team of George S. Kaufman and Moss Hart. In this period, American musical comedy developed into an art form capable of a wide range of expression. Much of its appeal resulted from the music of composers George Gershwin, Jerome Kern, Cole Porter, and Richard Rodgers.

Italian drama. Since the late 1700's, few important Italian dramatists have appeared. A noteworthy exception is Luigi Pirandello, the leading Italian playwright of the 1900's. His plays are based on the idea that there is no single truth—only the conflicting views of individuals. Another dramatist, Ugo Betti, became famous for his tragedies about guilt and justice.

Symbolism in drama developed in France during the 1880's. The symbolists believed that appearance is only a minor aspect of reality. They believed that reality could be found in mysterious, unknowable forces that control human destiny. They argued that truth could not be portrayed by logical thought, but could only be suggested by symbols. Their plays tended to be vague and puzzling. The settings and the performers' movements and speaking style were deliberately unrealistic in an attempt to stimulate the audience to look for deeper meanings in the action. The most celebrated symbolist dramatist was Maurice Maeterlinck.

Expressionism is difficult to define because the term was used in Germany between 1910 and 1925 to describe almost any departure from realism. Most German expressionists believed that the human spirit was the basic shaper of reality. Surface appearance, therefore, was important only as it reflected an inner vision. To portray this view, expressionist playwrights used distorted sets, lighting, and costumes; short, jerky speeches; and machinelike movements. Expressionistic techniques can be seen in Georg Kaiser's *From Morn to Midnight* (1916), a symbolic story of humanity's misguided search for happiness through wealth.

Expressionism appeared in Germany about 1910. The dramatic techniques of expressionism owed much to the Swedish dramatist August Strindberg. In such plays as *To Damascus* (parts I and II written in 1898, part III written in 1901), *A Dream Play* (written in 1901), and *The Ghost Sonata* (1908), time and place shift freely. Characters multiply and merge and objects change in appearance. See **Expressionism.**

Epic theater. The discontent of the post-World War I era appeared in much drama of the 1920's and 1930's.

The most fruitful attempt to focus the attention of theatergoers on political, economic, and social realities was epic theater, developed by the German dramatist Bertolt Brecht.

Brecht adopted the name *epic* to distinguish his aims from those of the traditional *dramatic* theater. He used techniques of the epic poem, including episodic action and narrative mixed with dialogue. In such plays as *Mother Courage and Her Children* (1941) and *Life of Galileo* (1943), Brecht tried to make spectators think critically and relate his plays to real-life conditions. In this way, he hoped to inspire them to change those conditions. Brecht wrote all his major works before 1945, but his greatest influence came later.

Modern drama since World War II

Theater of the absurd, which emerged in France during the 1950's, was probably the most influential new movement in drama after the end of World War II in 1945. The absurdists rejected conventional notions of plot, character, dialogue, and logic in favor of dreamlike metaphors that did not try to imitate surface reality. They hoped to express the disorientation of living in a universe they saw as unfriendly, irrational, and meaningless, and therefore absurd.

The most famous play of the theater of the absurd was *Waiting for Godot* (1953) by Samuel Beckett. In this work, two tramps pass the time uncomfortably while waiting for someone named Godot, who never arrives. The plays of Eugène Ionesco, particularly *The Bald Soprano* (1953), also violated conventional dramatic form. Jean Genet portrayed human behavior as a series of ceremonies expressing sexual and political desires for violence and domination.

Experimental theater. Many theater artists were influenced by the writings of French director and dramatist Antonin Artaud. He demanded an intense, rigorous theater free from the domination of playwrights.

Americans Julian Beck and Judith Malina established the Living Theater in 1951. The Living Theater worked to abolish the conventional boundaries between theater and politics, between actors and spectators, and be-

tween stage and auditorium. Joseph Chaikin, a former Living Theater actor, later founded the Open Theater in New York City. It staged such works as *The Serpent* (1968), with a text by American dramatist Jean-Claude van Itallie. The productions and writings of the Polish director Jerzy Grotowski also influenced experimental theater. In the 1970's, experimental theater lost much of its crusading energy and determination to change the world.

Later German-language drama reflects the influence of both epic and absurdist theater. Swiss dramatist Friedrich Dürrenmatt's *The Visit* (1956) and *The Physicists* (1962) are dark parables about crime, guilt, responsibility, and justice. German playwright Peter Weiss' powerful *Marat/Sade* (1964) features an anguished reconsideration of the French Revolution (1789-1799) by inmates of a mental institution. Austrian dramatist Peter Handke and German playwright Heiner Müller wrote plays in the absurdist tradition. German dramatist Franz Xaver Kroetz wrote harsh, naturalistic plays of stinging social criticism.

Later English drama. In England after World War II, interest in verse drama was revived briefly by T. S. Eliot and Christopher Fry. A new period in English drama began with John Osborne's *Look Back in Anger* (1956). This realistic play gave a voice to the rebellious spirit of a group of writers eventually called the "angry young men." Along with the plays of Brecht and Beckett, *Look Back in Anger* stimulated a new generation of English playwrights.

Harold Pinter is Beckett's most important follower. Pinter's plays create a menacing atmosphere from everyday events and seemingly realistic dialogue. John Arden, Edward Bond, Caryl Churchill, David Hare, and Arnold Wesker wrote specifically as political radicals. Tom Stoppard attacked political radicals in his plays. Despite their differences, all of these dramatists expressed discontent with the quality of life in modern Great Britain. Other later British playwrights include Alan Ayckbourn, Michael Frayn, Peter Nichols, Joe Orton, and Peter Shaffer.

Later United States drama. Tennessee Williams and Arthur Miller became the leading American dramatists of the 1940's and 1950's. Both playwrights combined realistic dialogue with expressionistic staging. Both were also accurate observers of American life, Williams in

Bert Lahr, *left,* and E. G. Marshall, *right,* in a scene from *Waiting for Godot* by Samuel Beckett; Elliot Erwitt, Magnum

Theater of the absurd was a broad movement that included many important new playwrights of the 1950's. Samuel Beckett wrote about helpless characters who lead meaningless lives.

James Earl Jones, *second from right,* in a scene from *Fences* (William B. Carter)

Madonna, *left,* and Joe Mantegna, *right,* in a scene from *Speed-the-Plow* (© Brigitte Lacombe, Gamma/Liaison)

Modern American playwrights have expressed a variety of concerns. August Wilson won acclaim for *Fences, left,* and other plays about black life in the United States. In *Speed-the-Plow, right,* David Mamet portrayed the Hollywood film industry in a harshly humorous manner.

the South and Miller in the North. But Williams demanded compassion for the doomed dreamers in his plays, while Miller dealt judgment to guilty strivers. In such plays as *The Glass Menagerie* (1945) and *A Streetcar Named Desire* (1947), Williams wrote of faded Southern belles who were not equipped to function in the turbulent United States of the 1900's. In *Death of a Salesman* (1949), Miller used a common man's personal failure to criticize society's focus on material success.

In the 1950's, small theaters sprang up in several neighborhoods of Manhattan in New York City. These theaters became known collectively as *off-Broadway.* They introduced many American playwrights, notably Edward Albee. Albee's successful play *Who's Afraid of Virginia Woolf?,* a wry, grim drama of domestic discord, was first produced on Broadway in 1962.

During the 1960's, the Broadway comedies of Neil Simon became tremendously popular. But in general, the Broadway theater, the traditional arena for American plays, declined. Meanwhile, performances of new plays by new dramatists flourished in lofts, basements, and cafes. These productions formed the basis of what has become known as the *off-off-Broadway* movement.

Also around the 1960's, new voices in the American theater expressed various ethnic, sexual, political, and aesthetic concerns. A number of important black playwrights found a place in the postwar American theater during this period. Lorraine Hansberry's *A Raisin in the Sun* (1959) was the first play by a black dramatist to achieve major success on Broadway.

During the late 1900's, noncommercial theaters took up the functions that Broadway had performed, especially the presentation of new plays. For example, Sam Shepard's hallucinatory family plays *Curse of the Starving Class* and *Buried Child* (both 1978) were first presented at the New York Shakespeare Festival in New York and the Magic Theater in San Francisco, respectively. David Mamet, a harsh critic of dishonesty in American life, began his career in Chicago, where his *American Buffalo* was first produced in 1975. Lanford Wilson, author of three plays about the Talley family of

Lebanon, Mo., was a founder of the Circle Repertory Company in New York City. David Rabe, best known for his plays about the Vietnam War (1957-1975), was sponsored by the New York Shakespeare Festival. August Wilson became the leading black American dramatist of the 1980's. He is writing a cycle of plays that reflect black life in the 1900's. The cycle includes *Ma Rainey's Black Bottom* (1984), *Fences* (1985), *Joe Turner's Come and Gone* (1986), and *The Piano Lesson* (1987), all first produced by the Yale Repertory Theater in New Haven, Conn. Today, Broadway functions mainly as a showcase for plays produced elsewhere.

Drama in other countries often expresses anger at political and social injustice. South African dramatist Athol Fugard writes somber, realistic plays about *apartheid* (South Africa's policy of racial segregation). Dario Fo of Italy writes broadly comic but pointedly satiric plays. Czechoslovakian dramatist Václav Havel explores the breakdown of communication. The plays of Wole Soyinka of Nigeria reveal his belief in the importance of individual freedom.   Julius Novick

Study aids

Related articles. See **Theater** and its list of *Related articles.* See also such literature articles as **American literature** and the following articles:

American playwrights

Albee, Edward	Hart, Moss
Anderson, Maxwell	Hecht, Ben
Baraka, Amiri	Hellman, Lillian
Barry, Philip	Herne, James A.
Behrman, S. N.	Howard, Bronson C.
Cohan, George M.	Howard, Sidney
Connelly, Marc	Inge, William
Dunlap, William	Kaufman, George S.
Fitch, Clyde	Kelly, George E.
Gillette, William	Kingsley, Sidney
Glaspell, Susan	Lindsay, Howard
Green, Paul E.	Luce, Clare Boothe
Hansberry, Lorraine	Mamet, David

McCullers, Carson
Miller, Arthur
Moody, William Vaughn
Odets, Clifford
O'Neill, Eugene G.
Payne, John Howard
Rice, Elmer
Saroyan, William
Shaw, Irwin

Shepard, Sam
Sherwood, Robert E.
Simon, Neil
Tyler, Royall
Van Druten, John W.
Wilder, Thornton N.
Williams, Tennessee
Wilson, August
Wilson, Lanford

British playwrights

Barrie, Sir James M.
Beaumont, Francis
Behn, Aphra
Bulwer-Lytton, Edward
Chapman, George
Congreve, William
Coward, Sir Noel
Davenant, Sir William
Dekker, Thomas
Dryden, John
Eliot, T. S.
Etherege, Sir George
Farquhar, George
Fletcher, John
Ford, John
Fry, Christopher
Galsworthy, John
Gascoigne, George
Gay, John
Gilbert and Sullivan
Goldsmith, Oliver
Granville-Barker, Harley

Greene, Robert
Heywood, Thomas
Jonson, Ben
Kyd, Thomas
Lyly, John
Marlowe, Christopher
Marston, John
Massinger, Philip
Maugham, W. Somerset
Osborne, John
Pinero, Sir Arthur Wing
Pinter, Harold
Priestley, J. B.
Shakespeare, William
Shaw, George Bernard
Sheridan, Richard Brinsley
Stoppard, Tom
Vanbrugh, Sir John
Webster, John
Wilde, Oscar
Williams, Emlyn
Wycherley, William

French playwrights

Anouilh, Jean
Beaumarchais, Pierre
Beckett, Samuel
Brieux, Eugène
Camus, Albert
Claudel, Paul
Cocteau, Jean
Corneille, Pierre
Dumas, Alexandre, *pere*
Dumas, Alexandre, *fils*
Genet, Jean
Giraudoux, Jean

Hugo, Victor
Ionesco, Eugène
Marivaux, Pierre
Molière
Musset, Alfred de
Racine, Jean
Rostand, Edmond
Sardou, Victorien
Sartre, Jean-Paul
Scribe, Augustin Eugène
Voltaire

German language playwrights

Brecht, Bertolt
Büchner, Georg
Dürrenmatt, Friedrich
Frisch, Max
Goethe, Johann W. von
Hauptmann, Gerhart
Hofmannsthal, Hugo von
Kaiser, Georg

Kleist, Heinrich von
Lessing, Gotthold
    Ephraim
Schiller, Johann von
Schnitzler, Arthur
Sudermann, Hermann
Wedekind, Frank

Irish playwrights

Boucicault, Dion
Dunsany, Lord
Gregory, Lady

O'Casey, Sean
Synge, John Millington
Yeats, William Butler

Italian playwrights

Alfieri, Vittorio
D'Annunzio, Gabriele

Goldoni, Carlo
Pirandello, Luigi

Russian playwrights

Chekhov, Anton
Gogol, Nikolai

Gorki, Maxim
Pushkin, Alexander

Scandinavian playwrights

Bjørnson,
    Bjørnstjerne

Holberg, Ludvig
Ibsen, Henrik

Lagerkvist, Pär F.
Strindberg, Au-
    gust

Spanish playwrights

Benavente, Jacinto
Calderon de la Barca, Pedro
García Lorca, Federico

Tirso de Molina
Vega, Lope de

Ancient Greek and Roman playwrights

Aeschylus
Aristophanes
Euripides

Menander
Plautus
Seneca, Lucius A.

Sophocles
Terence
Thespis

Other playwrights

Čapek, Karel
Fugard, Athol

Maeterlinck, Maurice
Molnár, Ferenc

Other related articles

Burlesque
Comedy
Masque
Miracle play
Morality play

Musical comedy
Mystery play
Opera
Passion play

Pulitzer Prizes
    (table: Drama)
Tragedy
United States (The
    arts [pictures])

Outline

I. Forms of drama
II. The structure of drama
III. Greek drama
IV. Roman drama
V. Medieval drama
VI. Italian Renaissance drama
VII. Elizabethan, Jacobean,
    and Caroline drama
VIII. The golden age of
    Spanish drama
IX. French neoclassical
    drama

X. European drama:
    1660-1800
XI. Asian drama
XII. Romanticism
XIII. Early realism
XIV. Modern drama:
    Ibsen to World
    War II
XV. Modern drama
    since World War
    II

Questions

What are three leading theories about the origin of drama?
What was the influence of Thomas Kyd on Elizabethan drama?
What is the function of the plot of a play?
What were the major theories that shaped French neoclassi-
    cism?
What were some differences between Old Comedy and New
    Comedy?
What was the comedy of manners? What was emphasized in a
    sentimental comedy?
What contribution did the Greek playwright Sophocles make to
    dramatic form?
What role did the church play in the rebirth of drama during the
    Middle Ages?
What is the theme of most absurdist drama?
What are the three most important traditions in Japanese
    drama?
What were Victor Hugo's contributions to the rise of romanti-
    cism in drama?

Reading and Study Guide

See *Drama* in the Research Guide/Index, Volume 22, for a *Reading and Study Guide.*

Additional resources

Bigsby, C. W. E. *A Critical Introduction to Twentieth-Century
    American Drama.* 3 vols. Cambridge, 1982-1985.
Bordman, Gerald M. *The Oxford Companion to American Thea-
    tre.* Oxford, 1984.
Esslin, Martin. *An Anatomy of Drama.* Hill & Wang, 1977.
Matlaw, Myron. *Modern World Drama: An Encyclopedia.* Dut-
    ton, 1972.
Nicoll, Allardyce. *The Theatre and Dramatic Theory.* Green-
    wood, 1978. First published in 1962.
Nicoll, Allardyce, and others. *World Drama: From Aeschylus to
    Anouilh.* 2nd ed. Harper, 1976.
The Reader's Encyclopedia of World Drama. Ed. by John Gassner
    and Edward Quinn. T. Y. Crowell, 1969.
Shipley, Joseph T. *The Crown Guide to the World's Great Plays:
    From Ancient Greece to Modern Times.* Rev. ed. Crown, 1984.

Dramamine is the G. D. Searle Company's trade name for a drug used to prevent motion sickness, and to control nausea and vomiting in certain illnesses. Dramamine is one of the antihistaminic drugs. It acts as a mild sedative to reduce the activity of the central nervous system. Large doses may cause drowsiness. Its generic name is *dimenhydrinate.*　　N. E. Sladek

See also **Antihistamine; Motion sickness.**

Draughts. See Checkers.

Dravidians, *druh VIHD ee uhnz,* were among the earliest known inhabitants of India. Their descendants now live mainly in southern India and trace their ancestry back at least 4,500 years. Dravidians and Indo-Aryans form the two major ethnic groups of India.

The term *Dravidian* also refers to a family of about 20 languages. Four of the languages are spoken by over 240 million Indians, about 30 per cent of the country's population. The Indian government has formed separate states based on these four languages. Tamil is spoken in the state of Tamil Nadu, Telugu in Andhra Pradesh, Kannada in Karnataka, and Malayalam in Kerala.

The origin of the Dravidians remains unknown. But ruins of the cities of Harappa and Mohenjo-Daro in the Indus Valley Civilization, which began about 2500 B.C., revealed an advanced culture thought to be Dravidian. About 1500 B.C., a people of central Asia called the Aryans invaded northern India and forced the Dravidians south. From about the A.D. 300's to 600's, Dravidian kings valued *Brahmans* (Hindu priests and scholars) from northern India for their literary skills and adopted much of their heritage.

Since the early 1900's, however, Dravidians have organized movements against remaining aspects of the Brahman heritage. During the 1960's, Tamil-speaking Indians were especially violent in protesting against a ruling that would have made Hindi, an Indo-European language, India's only official language. Today, 4 of the country's 16 official languages are Dravidian.

Robert Eric Frykenberg

See also **India** (People; History).

Drawbridge. See Bridge (Drawbridges); **Castle.**

Drawing is the act of making a design or image, using line or tone, on any suitable surface. The design or image itself is also called a drawing. Drawings can be made for artistic or technical purposes. This article discusses drawing as a fine art. For information on technical drawing, see **Mechanical drawing.**

Purposes. Artists create drawings for a variety of purposes. Many make preliminary drawings to help them develop the composition of a painting or sculpture. They also produce drawings as finished works of art. Artists may use drawings to record information for future use. For example, an artist may draw a detailed sketch of a tree and refer to the drawing later when incorporating the tree into a painting. Art students draw figures and objects to gain skill with line and form.

Materials and techniques. Artists draw with chalk, charcoal, crayon, or pencil. They may use a liquid, such as ink, applied with a brush or pen. Artists also scratch drawings into a surface. For example, a *silverpoint drawing* is made by scratching into specially coated paper with a silver instrument or silver wire.

Manufacturers produce chalk and ink in a wide range of colors. Brushes, pencils, and pens are made in a vari-

Portrait of Isabella Brant (about 1625); The British Museum, London

A chalk drawing can be as delicate and realistic as a painting. The Flemish artist Peter Paul Rubens used black, red, and white chalk to draw this expressive portrait of his wife.

Color Intervals at Provincetown (1943); Addison Gallery of American Art, Phillips Academy, Andover, Mass.

A crayon drawing may have a forceful, dramatic quality. The German artist Hans Hofmann drew his forms in crayon and outlined them in ink to create this almost abstract picture of a town.

ety of widths to create different kinds of lines. Artists can add tone to a drawing by applying a thin layer of liquid color called a *wash.* They also may combine several materials and techniques in one drawing.

Almost any surface can be used for a drawing. Prehistoric people drew on clay and stone, and the ancient Chinese used silk cloth. In the Middle Ages, many artists drew on parchment. Since the 1400's, paper has been

Landscape with Satyr (early 1500's) attributed to Titian;
© The Frick Collection, New York City

A pen-and-ink drawing shows how forms can be developed by the combination of lines and blank areas. Artists often choose pen and ink to create a drawing with many details.

the most popular surface because it is inexpensive and easy to carry. Drawing paper is made in many colors and textures, and in various degrees of absorbency.

History. People have made drawings since prehistoric times. This art form first gained popularity among European artists during the 1400's, when paper became generally available. Since then, each century has produced artists who have created great drawings.

Masters of drawing in the 1400's and 1500's included Leonardo da Vinci, Albrecht Dürer, Michelangelo, and Raphael. During the 1600's, Claude, Nicolas Poussin, Rembrandt, and Peter Paul Rubens created important drawings. In the 1700's, great drawings were produced by Jean Honoré Fragonard, Francisco Goya, Giovanni Battista Tiepolo, and Antoine Watteau. The masters of drawing during the 1800's included Paul Cézanne, Jacques Louis David, Edgar Degas, Théodore Géricault, Jean Ingres, Odilon Redon, Henri de Toulouse-Lautrec,

Preliminary study for the portrait *Comtesse d'Haussonville* (1845);
© The Frick Collection, New York City

A drawing is often used as a preliminary study for a painting. The finished painting of this sketch by the French artist Jean A. D. Ingres appears in the *World Book* article on **Painting.**

Making a drawing

By following the steps shown below, an artist can create a drawing that is lifelike and has the proper proportions. This method can be used for a single figure or a complete composition.

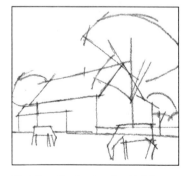

WORLD BOOK illustrations by David Cunningham

First, the artist sketches the chief elements of the drawing in a series of simple curved and straight lines.

Next, the artist refines the lines to make the drawing more realistic. Details and shading are added to show solid forms.

Finally, the artist completes the drawing by adding textures and tones to the figures. Unwanted lines can then be erased.

The Locomotive (1923); Philadelphia Museum of Art, the Harrison Fund

A charcoal drawing can effectively portray large, solid forms. The American artist Edward Hopper emphasized dark, heavy shapes to show a massive locomotive in front of a dark tunnel.

and Vincent Van Gogh. Great drawings in the 1900's have been created by Max Beckmann, Willem De Kooning, Arshile Gorky, Edward Hopper, Paul Klee, Oscar Kokoschka, Käthe Kollwitz, Henri Matisse, Jules Pascin, and Pablo Picasso.   Critically reviewed by Reed Kay

See also **Da Vinci, Leonardo** (pictures); **Painting** (Water color painting); **Cartoon; Comics.**

Additional resources

Ashwin, Clive. *Encyclopaedia of Drawing: Materials, Technique, and Style.* Batsford, 1982.
Eisler, Colin. *The Seeing Hand: A Treasury of Great Master Drawings.* Harper, 1975.

Drawing, Mechanical. See **Mechanical drawing.**

Drayton, Michael (1563-1631), was an English poet who experimented with many literary forms. He wrote a number of love sonnets, but he concentrated on English patriotic themes in his works.

Drayton was born in Warwickshire and settled in London about 1591 to pursue a literary career. His first works included the sonnets *Idea, the Shepherd's Garland* (1593) and *Idea's Mirror* (1594). Drayton's major work was his long poem *Poly-Olbion* (1612-1622), a geographical and historical survey of England's counties. It was influenced by Edmund Spenser's epic poem *The Fairie Queene.* Drayton's poem *Nymphidia* (1627) pays homage to Geoffrey Chaucer, Spenser, and William Shakespeare in a mythological setting.   John N. King

Dreadnought, *DREHD nawt,* is a type of battleship first launched by the British Navy in 1906. It is also spelled *dreadnaught.* It had heavy armor plate, and batteries of big guns in turrets. Shipbuilders later developed the more powerful superdreadnought. See also **Warship; Navy** (Engineering advances).

Dream is a story that a person "watches" or appears to take part in during sleep. Dream events are imaginary, but they are related to real experiences in the dreamer's life. They seem real to the dreamer while they are taking place. Some dreams are pleasant, others are annoying, and still others are frightening (see **Nightmare**).

Everyone dreams, but some people never recall

dreaming. Others remember only a little about a dream they had just before awakening and nothing about earlier dreams. No one recalls every dream and, in general, dreams are very easily forgotten.

What dreams consist of. The events of a dream form a story. In some dreams, the dreamer takes part in the story. In others, the dreamer merely "watches" the tale unfold. Dreams involve little logical thought. In most dreams, the dreamer cannot control what is happening. The story may be strange or confusing, and things happen that would not happen in real life.

People see in most dreams, and they may also hear, smell, touch, and taste in them. Most dreams occur in color, though the color is often recalled only vaguely.

The biology of dreams. Dreaming, like all mental processes, is a product of the brain and its activity. Whether a person is awake or asleep, the brain continuously gives off electrical waves. Scientists measure these waves with an instrument called an *electroencephalograph* (see **Electroencephalograph**). At most times during sleep, the brain waves are large and slow. But at certain times, they become smaller and faster. During periods of fast brain waves, the eyes move rapidly as though the sleeper were watching a series of events. This stage of sleep, called *REM* (*Rapid Eye Movement*) *sleep,* is when dreams occur. If awakened during REM sleep, the person is likely to recall details of the dream. Most adults dream from three to five times during eight hours of sleep. The dreams occur every 90 to 100 minutes and last from 5 to 30 minutes each.

During REM sleep, the pathways that carry nerve impulses from the brain to the muscles are blocked. Therefore, the body cannot move during dreams. Also, the *cerebral cortex*—the part of the brain involved in higher mental functions—is much more active during REM sleep than during nondreaming sleep. The cortex is stimulated by *neurons* (nerve cells) that carry impulses from the part of the brain called the *brain stem.*

The meanings of dreams. Dreams include events and feelings that the dreamer has experienced. Most dreams are related to events of the day before the dream, and many minor incidents of the hours before sleep appear in dreams.

Many experts who study dreams also feel that they are related to deep wishes and fears of the dreamer, and several theories explaining the meaning of dreams have been developed. During the 1890's, Sigmund Freud, an Austrian physician who originated psychoanalysis, developed one of the best-known theories of dream interpretation. Freud suggested that dreams are fulfillments of wishes, usually in disguised form. The disguise—or "dream language"—involves *condensation* (combining several ideas into one image), *displacement* (shifting a feeling from one idea or person to another), and *symbolism* (the use of symbols to represent what cannot be pictured directly).

In 1977, two Harvard University scientists, Robert W. McCarley and J. Allan Hobson, developed a theory of dreaming that appeared to contradict Freud's views. They suggested that biological processes in the brain can completely explain the content of dreams. Thus, according to McCarley and Hobson, there is no need for any psychological explanations of dream content. They maintain that the brain stem's stimulation of the cortex during dreaming sleep occurs in a chance manner. The cortex, attempting to make sense of this random stimulation, brings forth the confused images and story plots that make up dreams. This theory has been criticized, and most psychiatrists and psychologists still consider dreams to be psychologically meaningful.

Functions of dreams. The function of dreaming is not completely understood. Dreaming sleep may play a role in restoring the brain's ability to handle such tasks as focused attention, memory, and learning. Also, despite the McCarley-Hobson theory, most psychiatrists still believe that a person's hidden feelings often surface in dreams. Psychiatrists therefore analyze patients' dreams in an effort to help the patients understand themselves better. Ernest Hartmann

Additional resources

Freud, Sigmund. *The Interpretation of Dreams.* Various editions available. First published in German in 1900.
Mayle, Peter. *Sweet Dreams and Monsters: A Beginner's Guide to Dreams and Nightmares and Things That Go Bump Under the Bed.* Harmony Bks., 1986. For younger readers.
Sleep & Dreams: A Sourcebook. Ed. by Jayne Gackenbach. Garland, 1987.
The Variety of Dream Experience: Expanding Our Ways of Working with Dreams. Ed. by Montague Ullman and Claire Limmer. Continuum, 1987.

Dred Scott Decision was an important ruling by the Supreme Court of the United States on the issue of slavery. The decision, made in 1857, declared that no black—free or slave—could claim United States citizenship. It also stated that Congress could not prohibit slavery in United States territories.

The ruling aroused angry resentment in the North and led the nation a step closer to civil war. It also influenced the introduction and passage of the 14th Amendment to the United States Constitution after the Civil War (1861-1865). This amendment, adopted in 1868, extended citizenship to former slaves and gave them full civil rights.

The background of the case. Dred Scott was the slave of a U.S. Army surgeon, John Emerson of Missouri, a state that permitted slavery. In 1834, Scott went with Emerson to live in Illinois, which prohibited slavery. They later lived in the Wisconsin Territory, where slavery was forbidden by the Missouri Compromise (see **Missouri Compromise**). In 1838, Scott returned to Missouri with Emerson. Emerson died there in 1843, and three years later Scott sued the surgeon's widow for his freedom.

Missouri Historical Society
Dred Scott

Scott based his suit on the argument that his former residence in a free state and a free territory—Illinois and Wisconsin—made him a free man. A state circuit court ruled in Scott's favor, but the Missouri Supreme Court later reversed the decision. Meanwhile, Scott had become legally regarded as the property of John F. A. Sanford (spelled Sandford in the U.S. Supreme Court records) of New York. Because Sanford did not live in Missouri, Scott's lawyers were able to transfer the case to a federal court. This court ruled against Scott, and his lawyers then took the case to the Supreme Court.

The Supreme Court ruling. By a majority of 7 to 2, the Supreme Court ruled that Scott could not bring a suit in a federal court. Chief Justice Roger B. Taney, speaking for the majority, declared that Scott could not do so because blacks were not U.S. citizens.

The court could have simply dismissed the case after ruling on Scott's citizenship. But there was a growing national desire for a ruling on the constitutionality of such laws as the Missouri Compromise. Therefore, the court discussed this issue as part of its decision in the Dred Scott case. By a smaller majority, it ruled that the Missouri Compromise, which had been repealed in 1854, was unconstitutional. Taney argued that because slaves were property, Congress could not forbid slavery in the territories without violating a slaveowner's constitutional right to own property.

Dred Scott himself was sold shortly afterward. His new owner gave him his freedom two months after the Supreme Court decision. Stanley I. Kutler

See also **Taney, Roger B.**

Additional resources

Ehrlich, Walter. *They Have No Rights: Dred Scott's Struggle for Freedom.* Greenwood, 1979.
Fehrenbacher, Don E. *The Dred Scott Case: Its Significance in American Law and Politics.* Oxford, 1978.

Dredging, *DREHJ ihng,* is the work of clearing out the bottom of rivers, harbors, and other bodies of water so that ships can use them. The machines that do the work are called *dredges.* They work somewhat as a *power shovel* does on land. Dredges usually are run by steam or diesel engines.

The *dipper dredge* has a large scoop shovel, or *dipper,* shaped like a box which hangs on a chain from a long steel beam. The steel beam, or *derrick,* is attached to a strong mast which can swing the beam and dipper in a wide semicircle. The chain can be wound and unwound to raise and lower the dipper, and the derrick also can be raised and lowered.

When the dredging begins, the dipper is lowered to the bottom of the river or harbor. The derrick arm is swung in a semicircle to drag the dipper across the bottom so that it scoops up dirt and mud. Then the dipper is raised above the water and swung above a barge nearby. The bottom of the dipper has a door which is pulled open by a long cord to dump the dirt into the barge. Then the dipper is again lowered beneath the water to dig more mud.

The first steam dredge was used in England in 1796. It had a long endless chain with several buckets hanging from the chain. One end of the chain was lowered to the bottom. The chain was revolved until one of the buckets caught in the mud and was filled. The chain was revolved again and the bucket was raised while other buckets were lowered on the chain to dig. The buckets were emptied into barges alongside the dredge.

The *hydraulic dredge* is most efficient for moving large quantities of beach or river sand. A suction pipe carries the sand and water to a pump. A discharge pipe leads from the pump to a barge or to a disposal area.

Dredging requires powerful equipment called *dredgers* that operate like steam shovels. Dredging is necessary to remove silt from the bottom of rivers, harbors, and other waterways so that ships can navigate through them safely. The dredging unit shown above is clearing the shipping lanes in the port area of the Savannah River in Georgia.

Earth deposited by this process for dams, dikes, or building sites is called *hydraulic fill.* Robert G. Hennes

See also **Gold** (The dredge); **Mining** (picture).

Dreiser, *DRY suhr,* **Theodore** (1871-1945), ranks as the foremost American writer in the *naturalism movement* (a somber and pessimistic form of realism). Dreiser's characters are victims of apparently meaningless incidents which result in pressures they can neither control nor understand. He based such novels as *Sister Carrie* and *An American Tragedy* on events from real life. He condemned not his villains, but the repressive, hypocritical society that produced them. Dreiser's style lacks grace, but his best stories are powerful and sobering.

Dreiser was born in Terre Haute, Ind. His older brother was Paul Dresser, who wrote the song "On the Banks of the Wabash, Far Away." Dreiser's family was very poor, and he soon saw a profound difference between the promise and the reality of American life. This realization was a major source of Dreiser's discontent and an important influence on his works.

Dreiser attended Indiana University for a year. In the 1890's, he worked as a newspaperman in Chicago and St. Louis. By 1907, he was the successful editor of the very sort of woman's magazine whose sentimentality and superficiality he despised.

Dreiser's first novel, *Sister Carrie,* was partly based on the experiences of one of his sisters. The novelist Frank Norris, an editor at Doubleday, Page, and Co., enthusiastically accepted the manuscript for publication. But Neltje Doubleday, wife of the president of the company, was shocked by the manuscript's amorality, and the publisher tried to cancel the contract to publish the book. Dreiser insisted the agreement be honored. Doubleday printed the book in 1900, but did not advertise or distribute it. The novel became generally available in 1912, after another publisher issued it.

Sister Carrie is the story of Carrie Meeber, a poor girl alone in Chicago. She lives with a traveling salesman and then runs off to New York with George Hurstwood, a prosperous married man. Hurstwood's fortunes de-

cline, and he becomes a bum and commits suicide. Carrie finds success, but not happiness, as an actress.

Dreiser wrote *Jennie Gerhardt* (1911), another novel of desire and fate. However, his reputation was assured with the publication of *The Financier* (1912), the most purely naturalistic of his works. It is the story of an industrial tycoon who claws his way to great power. Dreiser intended the novel as the beginning of a "Trilogy of Desire." But the second volume, *The Titan* (1914), was a failure, and the third volume, *The Stoic,* was not published until two years after his death.

An American Tragedy (1925) is possibly the most impressive of Dreiser's books. It concerns a weak young man who is executed for the murder of his pregnant girl friend. Again, Dreiser did not condemn his villain, but the society that produced and destroyed him. See **Naturalism.** Joseph N. Riddel

Dresden (pop. 519,860) is one of the largest cities in Germany and a major European art center. The city lies on both banks of the Elbe River in east-central Germany. For location, see **Germany** (political map).

Dresden was one of the most beautiful cities in Europe before World War II (1939-1945). In February 1945, Allied bombing raids killed thousands of people in Dresden and destroyed much of the city, including most of its architectural monuments. Restoration of these historic buildings has been underway since the 1950's. The first historic building to be restored was the Zwinger, a museum complex that is an outstanding example of the decorative Baroque architectural style. The Zwinger, which was built during the 1700's, houses a magnificent art collection. Its treasures include many porcelain artworks, priceless jewels, and paintings by famous old masters.

Much of Dresden has been rebuilt in a modern style since 1945. The city has many broad streets lined with boxlike concrete buildings. Dresden's main shopping area lies along Pragerstrasse, a street reserved for pedestrians. The city is the home of Dresden Technical University and several other schools.

Dresden is more important as an area of industrial research and development than as a manufacturing center. Its products include drugs, electronics equipment, furniture, optical and precision instruments, and machinery. The world-famous Dresden china is produced in nearby Meissen (see **Dresden china**).

German settlers from Meissen founded Dresden in the early 1200's. In the 1400's, the city became the capital of Saxony, the kingdom of a people called Saxons. During the next 400 years, Saxon rulers established and enlarged Dresden's art collection and made the city an important art center. After Saxony became part of the German Empire in 1871, Dresden also gained importance as a commercial center.

The German government hid Dresden's art treasures outside the city during World War II. Soviet troops seized the collection in 1945, but most of the works were returned in the mid-1950's. Although much of the city has been rebuilt since World War II, Dresden has a drab appearance in comparison with its former splendor. Melvin Croan

Dresden china, *DREHZ duhn,* is a type of porcelain that is produced in Meissen, Germany, near the city of Dresden. The Meissen factory became the first manufac-

Hard-paste porcelain by Johann Kändler; The Art Institute of Chicago

A Dresden china bowl was designed about 1737 by Johann Kändler as part of a tableware set called the *Swan Service.*

turer to produce true porcelain in Europe.

Augustus the Strong, Elector of Saxony and King of Poland, established the Meissen porcelain factory in 1710. The factory was directed by the German chemist Johann Böttger. In 1708, Böttger became the first European to make porcelain. At first, the factory produced hard red stoneware. In 1713, it began making the white porcelain for which it became famous.

The first great artistic period at the Meissen factory began in 1720, under the direction of Johann Höroldt, a German painter. Höroldt specialized in enameling Chinese landscapes and European scenes on porcelain (see **Enamel**). The European scenes featured featherlike trees and exotic floral designs. In 1733, the German sculptor Johann Kändler became factory director and designed beautiful Meissen porcelain ornamental figures and tableware. Kändler designed the famous *Swan Service* (1737-1741), a set of tableware in which the pieces were decorated with the raised figures of dolphins, swans, water plants, and mythical maidens. Kändler also introduced realistic porcelain flowers, which became one of the Meissen factory's most distinctive designs.

Meissen porcelain was first called Dresden china in the 1700's. The Meissen factory still produces porcelain today. Its trademark of two crossed swords remains one of the most famous in pottery.   William C. Gates, Jr.

See also **Porcelain; Böttger, Johann Friedrich.**

Dress. See Clothing.

Dressmaking. See Sewing.

Drew, Charles Richard (1904-1950), was an American physician known for his research on blood plasma and for setting up blood banks. Drew convinced physicians to use plasma, the liquid part of blood, for battlefield and other emergency transfusions. Previously, whole blood had been used for such transfusions. Plasma can be stored for long periods. But at the time that Drew conducted his research, whole blood could not be kept for more than a week. Also, unlike whole blood, plasma can be given to a person of any blood type. During the early part of World War II (1939-1945), Drew organized many blood bank programs. The plasma collected by blood banks saved millions of lives.

Drew was born in Washington, D.C. He graduated

AP/Wide World
Charles R. Drew

from McGill University Medical School in 1933 and joined the Howard University faculty in 1935. Drew did most of his research on plasma at Columbia University from 1938 to 1940. In 1940, Drew directed American efforts to send plasma to Great Britain. In 1941, he became the first director of a Red Cross program that collected plasma for the U.S. armed forces. Drew left the Red Cross that same year and became a professor of surgery at Howard University. He received the Spingarn Medal in 1944. That same year, Drew was appointed chief of staff at Freedmen's Hospital, which is associated with Howard. He became medical director of the hospital in 1946.   Aaron E. Klein

Dreyfus, *DRAY fuhs* or *DRY fuhs,* **Alfred** (1859-1935), was a Jewish French army officer who became the center of a bitter quarrel as a result of political injustice. He was arrested on Oct. 15, 1894, on suspicion of spying for Germany. In December, a military court found him guilty. It suspended him from the army and sentenced him to life imprisonment on Devils Island.

Throughout the trial, Dreyfus said he was innocent. In 1896, a member of the French general staff, Georges Picquart, found documents that convinced him of Dreyfus' innocence. But his superiors ordered him to drop the matter. Many noted people

Culver
Alfred Dreyfus

worked to get Dreyfus a new trial. Émile Zola wrote *J'accuse,* demanding justice (see **Zola, Émile**).

He received a second trial in 1899, but it was a mockery, because feeling against Jews was so bitter in the army. Many officials felt that the case was closed and that the army's honor was at stake. Testimony favorable to Dreyfus was barred, and the court again found him guilty. He was sentenced to 10 years' imprisonment, but President Émile Loubet pardoned Dreyfus after he had been confined for only a few days.

People throughout the world protested the trial. Finally, in 1906, the case was reviewed by the highest court in France, and Dreyfus was declared innocent.

In 1918, Dreyfus became a lieutenant colonel in the French army, and was enrolled in the Legion of Honor. At the outbreak of World War I, he commanded one of the forts defending Paris. He was born in Mulhouse, Alsace.   André Maurois

Drill, also called a *seeder,* is a tractor-drawn machine used to place seeds of small grains and grasses into soil. It plants seeds at the same depth in narrow rows spaced about 6 to 8 inches (15 to 20 centimeters) apart. The mechanism consists of a disk or hoe opener, a hopper, seed metering devices, and press wheels or short chains. The opener digs *furrows* (plowed rows) in the soil. The hopper is a long, narrow box that contains the seed to be planted. The seed metering devices are attached to the bottom of the hopper. They send measured amounts of seed through tubes into the furrows. The chains or press wheels then cover the seeds with soil.

There are two types of drills—*end-wheel* and *press-wheel.* An end-wheel drill is supported by two wheels, one at each side of the machine. The wheels drive the metering devices by means of gears and chains. Press-wheel drills are supported by wheels mounted behind each plowing piece. These wheels drive the metering devices, close the furrows, and press soil around the seed. Drills may be equipped with devices that plant seeds of grasses, alfalfa, and clover. Some drills can also distribute fertilizer.   Ronald T. Schuler

Drill is a tool used to bore holes into a variety of materials. These materials range from soft soil to hard rock, metal, plastics, and concrete. Drills are widely used to bore holes into wood or metal so screws or other fasteners can be inserted. Construction workers use drills to break up pavement and to dig foundations for buildings. Energy companies rely on drills to dig for oil and natural gas and to get rock samples. Dentists use small electric drills to remove tooth decay.

Some drills are small and hand operated. There are also handheld power drills. Drills called *drill presses* are mounted on tables or stand on the floor. Large drills must be mounted on masts that are supported by trucks or rigs.

The first drills were slender pieces of wood with points of sharp rock bound to them. They were invented

WORLD BOOK photo by Ralph Brunke

A handheld power drill is a useful tool for carpenters and for hobbyists who enjoy crafting objects from wood.

about 4000 B.C. The Italian artist and inventor Leonardo da Vinci designed the first mechanical drill about A.D. 1495. The first practical handheld power drill was patented in 1917. This article describes tools that drill metal, wood, and rock.

Metal drills turn a slender steel rod called a *bit.* Bits are removable and come in various sizes to make different-sized holes. One end of the bit fits into the drill. The other end of the bit has one or more cutting edges, which are called *lips.* When the drill turns the bit at a high speed, the lips cut into the metal to make a hole. Bits also have grooves, called *flutes.* As the bit rotates, flutes direct metal shavings out of the hole so the hole does not clog and cause the drill to jam. Flutes also allow cooling liquids to flow into the hole to prevent the bit from overheating.

Most metal drill bits are *twist bits.* Twist bits have two or more lips and two or more spiraling flutes. A special bit called a *spade bit* is used in many manufacturing processes to drill deep holes. A spade bit is a flat blade with one lip. The bit is clamped in a holder before it is fitted into the drill.

Wood drills usually use specially fluted twist bits called *auger bits.* An auger bit is easy to keep centered because it has a screwlike tip called a *feed screw.* Auger bits called *Jennings bits,* which have two spiraling flutes, are used in hand-operated drills. Handheld power drills take auger bits called *power bits,* which have one spiraling flute.

Rock drills are power drills that use a hammering action, a plowing action, or both. A *paving breaker,* also called a *jackhammer,* rapidly hammers a chisellike bit into such materials as concrete and blacktop. Jackhammers are often used to break up roads. They are also used to wreck buildings and to dig trenches (see **Pneumatic tool**).

Drills that plow without hammering are called *rotary* drills. Among rotary bits are *fishtails,* which have hardened carbon lips, and *diamond bits.* Diamond bits are studded with points of diamond to cut hard rock. They are often used in small, handheld drills to get samples of underground rock or ore.

Rotary drills called *augers* have spiraling, steel *screw* threads. Augers are often used to drill oil wells (see **Petroleum** [Drilling an oil well]).   M. O. M. Osman

Drilling. See Gas (Producing gas); **Machine tool** (Hole machining); **Petroleum.**

Drinking. See Alcoholism.

Drive-in. See Restaurant (Kinds of restaurants).

Driver, William (1803-1886), a sea captain, gave the name *Old Glory* to the United States flag. When he was 21 years old, Driver became licensed to command his first ship. As a farewell gift, his mother and some friends gave him a United States flag. Driver called the flag *Old Glory,* and flew it on his ship, the *Charles Doggett,* during his voyages around the world. In 1837, Driver settled in Nashville, Tenn. During the Civil War, he kept the flag carefully hidden inside a quilt so it would not be harmed. The Driver family donated the flag to the Smithsonian Institution in 1922. Driver was born in Salem, Mass.   Whitney Smith

Driver education. See Automobile (Driving safely).

Dromedary, *DRAHM uh DEHR ee,* also called *Arabian camel,* is a swift camel used mainly for transportation and food in dry parts of India, the Middle East, and Africa. It sometimes grows to be 7 feet (2 meters) tall. The dromedary has only one hump. It can live on small amounts of food and water and has great endurance for desert travel. The dromedary has a swinging pace and can travel at a rate of about 10 miles (16 kilometers) an hour. It can cover 100 miles (160 kilometers) in a day. It produces rich milk, and its hair is used for cloth. No true wild dromedaries exist. See also **Animal** (picture: Animals of the deserts); **Camel.**

Scientific classification. The dromedary belongs to the camel family, Camelidae. It is *Camelus dromedarius.*

Anne Innis Dagg

Drought, *drowt,* is a condition that results when the average rainfall for an area drops far below the normal amount for a long period of time. This condition is also called *drouth* (pronounced *drowth*). In areas that are not irrigated, the lack of rain causes farm crops to wither and die. Higher than normal temperatures usually accompany periods of drought. These high temperatures increase the stresses on plants and add to the crop damage. Forest and grass fires are more frequent and spread quickly due to the dry conditions. Much valuable timberland and rangeland has been burned during major droughts. Poor management of the soil can often lead to wind erosion. Often the dry and crumbled topsoil is blown away by hot, dry winds (see **Dust storm**). Streams, ponds, and wells often dry up during a drought, and animals suffer and may even die because of the lack of water. Water supplies for agricultural, industrial, and personal uses are greatly reduced during droughts. Water resource managers may impose water rationing in an attempt to deal with such shortages.

Long-range weather forecasters cannot predict with certainty just when a drought will occur. But people who study climate conditions have discovered that these drier-than-normal periods tend to alternate with wetter-than-normal periods in an irregular cycle. Droughts of the past show in the rings made by trees as they add wood each year. In wet periods, the year's layer of wood is thick. In dry periods, the ring is thin (see **Tree** [illustration: How a tree reveals its history]).

The Great Plains region of the United States suffered one of the worst droughts in its history from 1931 to 1938, and the effects were felt throughout the entire country. Few food crops could be grown, food became scarce, and prices went up. Hundreds of families in the Dust Bowl area had to be moved to farms in other locations with the help of the federal government (see **Dust Bowl**). From 1950 to 1954, the Southwest and the southern Great Plains suffered a severe drought. Hundreds of cattle ranchers were forced to ship their cattle to pasturelands in other regions of the country. To help ease this hardship, the federal government offered farmers emergency credit and seed grains at low prices. The worst drought since the 1930's struck the Midwest, northern Great Plains, and parts of the Southeast in 1988. It caused serious damage to grain crops.

Droughts have occurred in other areas of the United States and in other countries. In the early 1960's, a drought affected the Northeastern United States for several years, and from 1975 to 1977, a lack of winter snowfall resulted in severe drought conditions in the Western United States. Unusually dry conditions prevailed over western Europe from the fall of 1975 to the summer of 1976. Since the late 1960's, droughts have caused much suffering in Africa. The hardest-hit areas include Ethiopia and the Sahel, which lies south of the Sahara, Africa's great desert.   John A. Harrington, Jr.

Drowning is death caused by suffocation in water or other liquid. A person who cannot swim can keep from drowning by floating upon the surface of the water. Floating is accomplished by rolling over on the back and extending the body in a relaxed position. Failure to float is usually the result of fear, which causes the body to stiffen and sink. A person usually becomes unconscious less than two minutes after sinking. But death does not follow at once, for the heart continues to beat for several minutes. The belief that a person must come to the surface three times before finally sinking is false. The person may not rise at all, depending upon circumstances, especially upon the position of the arms while the person is struggling. If the arms are held above the head, the body sinks deeper into the water. If they are held down at the sides, the body will probably rise to the surface.

Methods of rescue. A drowning person should be rescued from a boat or with a life buoy whenever possible. This lessens the danger to the rescuer.

To rescue by swimming, approach the victim from the rear. Grasp the victim's hair or coat collar, and swim vigorously with the free hand and both legs. The side stroke should provide sufficient power to move two people through the water. If the victim cannot be approached from the rear and starts to sink, grasp one of the victim's hands and lie back in the water. Give a strong kick or two with the legs at the same time to keep from going under. A sharp pull with the right hand on that of the victim will turn the victim over on the back. Then you can swim with the victim and keep the person's head above water, using one of the following rescue methods: In the *cross-chest carry,* hold the victim against your upper hip in a back-floating position, while swimming on your side. This position close to the rescuer means greater security. It is an excellent carry for panic-stricken victims. In the *hair carry,* grasp the victim's hair at the back of the head, and stroke with your other arm. The hair carry is not as secure as the cross-chest carry, and should only be used to tow unconscious or semiconscious victims. It is a good position for towing victims long distances in smooth water.

Applying first aid. Breathing, or respiration, should be restored as soon as the victim has been rescued. The person administering artificial respiration must not give up easily. People who have gone under in extremely cold water have been saved after as many as eight hours. The preferred method of applying artificial respiration is mouth-to-mouth resuscitation. See **First aid** (Giving artificial respiration).

Drowning as a form of punishment. Drowning was a common form of punishment in most European countries from ancient times until the early 1600's. A condemned person sometimes received a choice of death by drowning or by hanging, or "by ditch or by gallows." The person usually chose drowning, since that was considered more honorable.   Carlotta M. Rinke

See also **Safety** (In water sports); **Swimming** (Water safety).

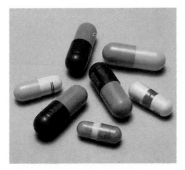

Capsules

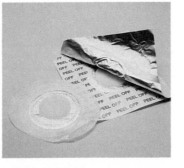

Transdermal patch

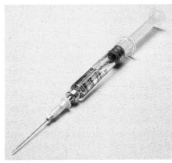

Injectable drug

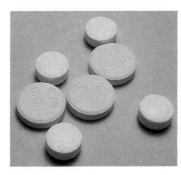

Tablets

Gel and cream

WORLD BOOK photos by Larry McCann

Liquid and inhalant

Modern drugs come in many forms and are administered in various ways. Most drugs are given orally. Drugs also may be applied to the skin, injected, or inhaled. Certain drugs may be obtained only with a doctor's prescription. Others may be purchased without a prescription.

Drug

Drug is one of the medical profession's most valuable tools. Doctors prescribe drugs to treat or prevent many diseases. Every year, penicillin and other germ-killing drugs save the lives of countless victims of meningitis, pneumonia, and other dangerous infectious diseases. Vaccines prevent such diseases as measles, polio, and smallpox. Analgesics lessen or eliminate pain. The use of these and many other kinds of drugs has helped millions of people live longer, healthier lives than would otherwise have been possible.

Most of our useful drugs were unknown before the 1900's. For example, the sulfa drugs and antibiotics, our best germ-fighting drugs, did not come into use until the late 1930's and early 1940's. Before that time, about 30 per cent of all pneumonia victims in the United States died of the disease. The new drugs quickly reduced the death rate from pneumonia in the United States to less than 5 per cent.

Polio vaccine was introduced in 1955. At that time, polio virus infected about 30,000 to 50,000 people every year in the United States. By 1960, use of the vaccine had reduced the number of new polio cases in the United

States to about 3,000 a year. In 1900, most Americans did not live past the age of 47. Today, Americans live an average of more than 70 years, in part because of the use of modern drugs.

But drugs can also cause sickness and death. Any drug, even a relatively safe one, may cause harm if it is used improperly. Aspirin, for example, is one of the safest and most useful drugs. Yet every year, aspirin kills children who mistake the pills for candy and eat too many of them. Any drug can kill if it is taken in a large enough dose. In addition, the widespread misuse of alcohol, cocaine, heroin, and other addictive drugs has become a serious problem.

We generally use the word *drugs* to mean only medicines and certain other chemical substances that people use, such as alcohol or marijuana. But *pharmacologists,* the scientists who study drugs, consider all chemicals that affect living things to be drugs. For example, they classify insecticides, weedkillers, and a wide variety of other substances as drugs. Even the chemicals in automobile exhaust and other substances that pollute the environment act like drugs because they affect living things.

This article deals chiefly with drugs that are used for medical purposes. Detailed information on the misuse of drugs can be found in the articles **Drug abuse** and **Drug addiction.**

Edward J. Cafruny, the contributor of this article, is Distinguished University Professor at the University of Medicine and Dentistry of New Jersey.

The many kinds of drugs people use can be classified in several ways. For example, they can be grouped according to their form, such as a capsule, gas, or liquid. Or they can be classified according to the way they are taken, such as by swallowing, inhaling, or injection. Drugs can also be grouped according to their chemical structure.

Pharmacologists generally classify drugs according to the major beneficial effect they have on the body. Classified in this way, many of the most widely used drugs belong to one of several dozen groups. Four especially important groups are (1) drugs that fight bacteria, (2) drugs that prevent infectious diseases, (3) drugs that affect the heart and blood vessels, and (4) drugs that affect the nervous system.

All drugs affect the body in more than one way. For example, some drugs taken to act on the nervous system also affect the heart. The action of these drugs on the heart is considered a *side effect.* The drugs discussed in this section, however, are classified according to their chief effect on the body.

Drugs that fight bacteria

Two main types of drugs kill or help the body kill bacteria: (1) antibiotics and (2) sulfonamides, or sulfa drugs. Doctors prescribe these drugs in treating meningitis, pneumonia, and many other infectious diseases. A large dose of penicillin or of certain other antibiotics kills disease-causing bacteria. A smaller dose of such an antibiotic keeps the bacteria from multiplying in the body and thus allows the body's natural defenses to destroy them. Other antibiotics and the sulfa drugs also prevent bacteria from multiplying in the body. In most cases, however, these drugs do not kill the bacteria. See **Antibiotic; Sulfa drug.**

Drugs that prevent infectious diseases

Two kinds of drugs prevent infectious diseases. They are (1) vaccines and (2) antiserums and globulins. Some of these drugs, such as polio vaccines, are especially valuable because there is no effective treatment for the disease they prevent.

Vaccines. There are several different kinds of vaccines. Each kind causes the body to produce substances, which are called *antibodies,* that fight a particular disease. The vaccine thus makes the body *immune* to the disease by providing resistance against attack by it. Vaccines have been developed against such infectious diseases as cholera, diphtheria, hepatitis, measles, and smallpox, as well as polio. In fact, vaccinations against smallpox have wiped out that disease. The last case of naturally occurring smallpox was reported in 1977. See **Immunization.**

Antiserums and globulins, like vaccines, prevent certain infectious diseases. But unlike vaccines, these drugs contain antibodies rather than substances that cause the body to produce antibodies. Therefore, the antiserums and globulins act more quickly than vaccines to prevent infection. Physicians prescribe these drugs after a person who has not been vaccinated is exposed to an infectious disease. Antiserums are used against such diseases as diphtheria and *tetanus* (lockjaw). Examples of diseases against which globulins protect include hepatitis, rabies, and tetanus. See **Serum; Globulin.**

Drugs that affect the heart and blood vessels

Drugs that affect the heart and blood vessels are known as *cardiovascular drugs.* Doctors prescribe them in treating diseases of the heart and blood vessels. Such diseases of the heart and blood vessels rank as the chief cause of death from disease in the United States, Canada, and many other countries. There are four major kinds of cardiovascular drugs: (1) antiarrhythmics, (2) cardiotonics, (3) vasodilators, and (4) antihypertensives.

Antiarrhythmics steady the heartbeat. People take these drugs to treat *tachycardia* and *fibrillation,* conditions in which the heart beats irregularly and at a rate much faster than normal.

Cardiotonics strengthen the heartbeat. These drugs cause the heart to beat more forcefully and thus increase circulation of the blood. Physicians prescribe them to treat conditions in which the heart pumps too weakly. The most widely used cardiotonic drugs are digoxin and digitoxin.

Vasodilators enlarge, or *dilate,* small blood vessels. These drugs are taken mostly to treat narrowing of the coronary arteries, the vessels that supply blood to the heart muscle. Drugs used to enlarge these arteries are called *coronary vasodilators.* Doctors prescribe them for people with such severe narrowing of the coronary arteries that they suffer chest pains while walking or exercising in some other way. Such persons are said to have *angina pectoris.* The most widely used coronary vasodi-

Rules for using drugs

No drug is absolutely safe. Proper use is beneficial. Improper use is harmful.

1. **Do not take a drug prescribed for someone else.** Only a physician or dentist can determine which drug will help you. A drug that works for someone else may not work for you because of differences in age, weight, or other physical characteristics. In addition, you may not have the same disease or disorder as someone else, even though the symptoms appear to be the same.

2. **Do not save prescription drugs for later use.** Obtain a new prescription each time illness occurs. You may have an illness that seems the same as an earlier one but is actually different.

3. **Do not keep nonprescription drugs too long.** All drugs change chemically in time. Some become weaker than intended. Other drugs contain substances that evaporate, making the medicines stronger than intended. If a drug label does not tell how long a drug will remain safe and effective, ask your pharmacist.

4. **Follow all instructions on drug labels.** The label tells how much of a drug to take and how often. It also tells under what conditions you should not take the drug. It may be dangerous to use more of a drug than the amount prescribed or recommended, or to ignore any other label instructions.

5. **Report unpleasant or unexpected drug effects** to your physician or dentist. Any drug may produce an unusual, unexpected effect.

6. **Keep all drugs in a safe place** away from children and pets. An overdose of any drug can cause sickness or even death.

lators are isosorbide dinitrate and nitroglycerin. Other kinds of drugs used in treating angina include calcium blockers and beta-blockers.

Antihypertensives are used in the treatment of *hypertension* (high blood pressure). Vasodilators and many other kinds of drugs are antihypertensives. Vasodilators lower blood pressure by causing the muscles in the walls of small blood vessels to relax. The blood is then able to flow at a lower pressure. Other antihypertensives act differently. Often, two or more kinds are given daily to the same patient.

Drugs that affect the nervous system

Many of the most widely used drugs affect the brain and other parts of the nervous system. These drugs include alcohol; the caffeine in cocoa, coffee, and tea; cocaine; marijuana; narcotics, such as heroin and morphine; and sleeping pills. Altogether, five major kinds of drugs affect the nervous system: (1) analgesics, (2) anesthetics, (3) hallucinogens, (4) stimulants, and (5) antianxiety and hypnotic drugs.

Analgesics relieve pain without causing unconsciousness or diminishing the other senses, such as the sense of touch or taste. For example, an analgesic may relieve a person's headache, but it will not prevent that person from feeling heat or cold or from tasting food.

There are two main kinds of analgesics: (1) narcotics and (2) nonnarcotics. Both kinds relieve pain. But the narcotics also produce drowsiness, a dazed condition, and often a feeling of well-being. Aspirin is one of the most commonly used nonnarcotic analgesics. The most widely used narcotics are *opiates,* which are obtained from the opium poppy, and certain related *synthetic* (artificially produced) drugs. Opiates include codeine, heroin, and morphine.

When pain is severe, physicians often prescribe a narcotic. For example, morphine is used to relieve the pain of severe injury and of cancer. But excessive use of narcotics leads to drug addiction, a condition in which a person has become so dependent on the drug that illness results if use of the drug is stopped. For this reason, physicians prescribe narcotics only if other analgesics will not work. See **Narcotic.**

Anesthetics eliminate sensation. *General anesthetics* eliminate sensation throughout the body, thus causing unconsciousness. These drugs, which include enflurane, halothane, and thiopental, are given during many kinds of surgical operations. *Local anesthetics* deaden the senses only in the area of the body to which they are applied. Dentists often give such local anesthetics as lidocaine and bupivacaine. Doctors use local anesthetics for eye surgery and other operations that do not require the patient to be unconscious. See **Anesthesia.**

Hallucinogens cause a person to *hallucinate*—that is, to see, hear, or otherwise sense something that exists only in the mind. These drugs are also called *psychedelic* (mind-revealing) drugs. They give people a distorted view of themselves and their surroundings. Hallucinogenic drugs include LSD, marijuana, mescaline, and PCP. Physicians have experimented with hallucinogens in treating mental illness. See **Hallucinogenic drug.**

Stimulants overcome sleepiness and tiredness. These drugs *stimulate,* or increase the activity of, the nervous system. Stimulants include caffeine, cocaine, and synthetic drugs known as *amphetamines.* Common names for amphetamines include "speed," "uppers," and "wakeups." See **Amphetamine.** Stimulants create a sense of well-being in most users, in addition to increasing mental and physical activity. But many people become depressed and uneasy as the effects wear off. They may then take the drug again to feel better, and they thus become dependent on it. For this reason, doctors seldom prescribe stimulants for tiredness. See **Stimulant.**

Antianxiety and hypnotic drugs reduce tension and worry by altering the nervous system. They include tranquilizers, sedatives, and alcohol.

Tranquilizers calm a person without causing much drowsiness if taken in a small enough dose. Larger doses may make the user sleepy as well as calmer. Many people who have difficulty adjusting to the stresses of daily life take mild tranquilizers. However, even the use of mild tranquilizers over a long period of time may make the user dependent on these drugs. Psychiatrists prescribe *antipsychotic drugs* and *antidepressant drugs* for people who have severe mental disorders that cannot be treated effectively with mild tranquilizers. These drugs may reduce a patient's extreme fears and worries. See **Tranquilizer.**

Sedatives, like tranquilizers, have a calming effect. But sedatives have greater ability than tranquilizers to make a person sleepy. As a result, physicians generally prescribe sedatives for patients who suffer from *insomnia* (the inability to sleep naturally). The most widely used sedatives are a group of synthetic drugs called *barbiturates.* These drugs include pentobarbital and secobarbital. Barbiturates are sometimes called "barbs," "downers," or "goofballs." There are also nonbarbiturate sedatives, such as chloral hydrate and paraldehyde. People who regularly use a sedative may become dependent on the drug and may have to increase the dose for the drug to be effective. See **Sedative; Barbiturate.**

Alcohol is the common name for ethyl alcohol, the drug found in alcoholic drinks. It relaxes most people and makes them drowsy. The use of alcohol, like the use of most other drugs that depress the nervous system, may make a person dependent on it. See **Alcoholism.**

Other kinds of drugs

People also use many other kinds of drugs besides those discussed above. These drugs include (1) diuretics, (2) hormones, (3) vitamins, (4) antitumor drugs, and (5) immunosuppressive drugs.

Diuretics increase the formation of urine. In certain diseases, the kidneys do not produce enough urine. As a result, fluid, salts, and wastes build up in the body. Diuretics correct this condition by causing the kidneys to produce more urine. Diuretics are also used to treat hypertension. See **Diuretic.**

Hormones are chemicals made by the body's glands. The hormones control many body functions, such as growth and reproduction. Certain animal hormones are similar to those produced by people, and scientists have created synthetic hormones. Natural and synthetic hormones are used as drugs in several ways.

Physicians prescribe hormones for patients whose glands produce insufficient amounts. For example, some people who have the disease diabetes mellitus do not produce enough of the hormone insulin. They must receive insulin injections. Doctors also prescribe hormones to treat diseases that do not result from a hormone deficiency. The hormones ACTH and cortisol, for example, are used in treating rheumatoid arthritis.

Hormones are also used as *oral contraceptives,* or *birth control pills,* which prevent pregnancy. These drugs work by interfering with the normal reproductive processes in a woman's body. See **Hormone; Birth control** (Methods of birth control).

Vitamins are essential to good health. Such diseases as rickets or scurvy develop if a person has certain vitamin deficiencies. The best way to obtain vitamins is to eat a well-balanced diet. But if necessary, a physician may prescribe vitamin pills or injections. See **Vitamin.**

Antitumor drugs destroy cancer cells. Although many such drugs have been developed, they all injure normal cells as well as cancer cells. But some antitumor drugs have been used to lengthen the life of patients with incurable cancer. Scientists hope to develop drugs that will destroy only cancer cells.

Immunosuppressive drugs. If foreign proteins somehow get into the bloodstream, they act as *antigens,* causing white blood cells to make antibodies against them (see **Immunity**). This process also occurs when an organ from one person is transplanted into another person. The antibodies formed begin to destroy the transplanted organ. Immunosuppressive drugs interfere with the body's formation of antibodies.

One use of immunosuppressive drugs is to prevent the destruction and rejection of transplanted organs. Azathioprine and cyclosporine are examples of immunosuppressive drugs.

How drugs work

Different drugs are *administered* (given) in different ways. But once in the body, almost all drugs work the same way—by altering the speed of cell activities.

Entrance into the body. Most drugs are administered orally. But drugs may also be given in several other ways. For example, they may be injected, inhaled, or applied to the skin. The method of administration depends on the form and purpose of a drug. An anesthetic gas, for example, must be inhaled to produce unconsciousness. Ointments are applied directly to the area being treated.

Each method of administration has advantages and disadvantages. For example, the easiest and safest way to take a drug is by swallowing it. But some drugs cannot be taken orally because stomach juices destroy them. Injected drugs act quickly in the body. But injection is somewhat painful, and it presents greater risk of infection than do other methods of administration.

Researchers are constantly developing new methods of administration. A device called a *transdermal patch* contains a layer of medication and is attached to the skin like a bandage. The patch slowly and continuously releases the drug, which seeps through the skin to the bloodstream. The coronary vasodilator nitroglycerin may be administered in this way. Another device, the *implantable pump,* consist of a small, metal disk with a chamber that can be filled with a drug. The pump is inserted in the body surgically and delivers the medication continuously. It may be refilled by injection.

Action in the body. Most drugs that are swallowed, inhaled, or injected enter the blood stream and travel throughout the body. They pass from the blood into the cells of the tissues where the drug action occurs. Only a few kinds of drugs—such as eye drops, local anesthetics, and nasal sprays—act before entering the bloodstream. When these drugs eventually enter the blood, the amount is usually too small to produce additional effects on the cells.

Almost all drugs create their effects by altering cell activities. To explain how drugs act on cells, pharmacologists developed the *receptor theory.* According to this theory, chemical reactions in every living cell control the cell's activities. Each controlling reaction causes a particular cell activity to begin, to speed up, or to slow

WORLD BOOK diagram

How the receptor theory explains drug action

According to the receptor theory, drugs produce their effects by attaching to *receptor molecules* in body cells. Normally, *activator molecules* produced in the body attach to a receptor molecule, *near right.* This chemical reaction causes a particular cell activity to speed up or slow down. Some drugs attach to a part of the receptor and thus keep the activator from forming a complete attachment, *center.* As a result, the particular cell activity is blocked. Other drugs are so similar to the activator that they form complete attachments themselves, *far right.* In such cases, the cell activity increases.

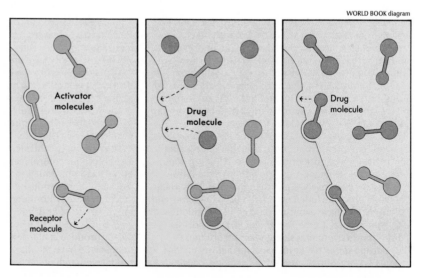

down. A drug acts on a cell by altering one or more of these chemical reactions. It does so by attaching to *receptor molecules* in each cell that are normally involved in the controlling chemical reaction.

The receptor theory not only explains how drugs work, but it also points up what drugs can and cannot do. Because they react with receptors that control cell activities, drugs can only alter the speed of those activities. They cannot create new cell activities.

In most cases, the chemical reaction between a drug and the body is not a one-way process. Drugs alter cell activity, but normal body processes also change most drugs. These processes transform a drug into one or more new substances, most of which are weaker than the original drug. This changing of drugs is called *biotransformation* or *drug metabolism*. It is one way in which the body protects itself against drugs. Most biotransformation occurs in the liver. A diseased liver takes longer than a healthy liver to change a drug into a weaker substance. As a result, physicians generally reduce drug dosage for a patient with liver disease. Otherwise, the drug would last longer in the body and thus exert too great an effect.

Effect on the body. All drugs can affect the body in both helpful and harmful ways. For example, a particular drug may produce a stronger heartbeat, relief from pain, or some other desired effect. But that drug, like all drugs, can also cause undesired effects—especially if the dose is too large.

Most drugs produce changes throughout the body because the drugs circulate through the bloodstream. As a result, most drugs used to affect one part of the body also affect other parts. For example, physicians sometimes prescribe morphine to relieve pain. Morphine alters the activities of cells in the brain and spinal cord and thus reduces the sensation of pain. But morphine also alters the function of cells in the body that are not involved in sensing pain. It may decrease the rate of breathing, cause vomiting, produce constipation, and create other undesired effects.

In general, a drug's effects are strengthened as the dose is increased and weakened as the dose is decreased. But all people do not react the same to a change in the dose of a drug. Doubling the dose, for example, may triple the strength of the drug effects in one person and not increase the effects in someone else.

The section *Kinds of drugs* describes the chief desired effects of various drugs. Effects other than those desired are called *adverse reactions*. Drugs produce three main kinds of adverse reactions: (1) side reactions, (2) hypersensitivity reactions, and (3) toxic reactions. The repeated use of alcohol, narcotics, and certain other drugs may create a condition called *drug dependence*.

Side reactions, or side effects, occur with all drugs. Physicians can anticipate these reactions and tell a patient what to expect. For example, many of morphine's harmful effects are side reactions and should therefore be expected. Most drugs cause weak side reactions that do not prevent use of the drug.

Hypersensitivity reactions, also called *allergic reactions,* occur only in persons allergic to a particular drug. Some of these reactions are minor but others are severe. Any drug may cause an allergic reaction in people highly sensitive to that drug. Some people cannot take such common drugs as aspirin or penicillin because they are allergic to them.

Toxic reactions result from drug poisoning. Such reactions damage cells and may kill a person. All drugs can have a mild toxic effect, and a large enough overdose of any drug will produce a severe toxic reaction.

Drug dependence. People who repeatedly take large amounts of such drugs as alcohol, amphetamines, barbiturates, or narcotics may become dependent on the drugs. These people have an intense psychological or physical need for a drug's effects. *Tolerance,* or resistance to a drug's effects, usually develops along with drug dependence. As drug use continues, tolerance increases. The drug user must thus take larger and larger doses to obtain the desired effects. The development of physical or psychological dependence, or both, is commonly called *drug addiction.* In most cases, a severe withdrawal illness occurs if a person stops taking the drug. See **Drug addiction; Drug abuse.**

Elimination from the body. The body eliminates drugs with other waste materials. Most drugs travel from the cells through the bloodstream to the kidneys and are eliminated in the urine. The body also eliminates drugs in sweat, tears, and solid wastes. Some anesthetics are eliminated almost entirely in exhaled breath.

How drugs are produced and sold

The production and sale of drugs used as medicines is a big business in many countries. The world's leading producers include France, Germany, Great Britain, Japan, Switzerland, and the United States.

This section deals chiefly with the production and sale of drugs in the United States. The U.S. drug, or *pharmaceutical,* industry includes over 1,000 drug companies and employs about 200,000 workers. New Jersey, New York, and Pennsylvania rank as the leading drug-producing states. Americans spend about $40 billion a year for drugs.

Sources of drugs

The pharmaceutical industry produces mostly synthetic drugs. Chemists working in the laboratories of

drug companies create these drugs from chemical elements. Other drugs produced by the pharmaceutical industry are obtained from plants, molds, animals, minerals, and genes and bacteria.

Chemical laboratories. Chemists have created many of our most valuable medicines. Most of these drugs do not occur naturally. Synthetic drugs duplicate or improve upon those obtained from plants, molds, bacteria, animals, or minerals. Pharmaceutical companies can produce many of these drugs at less cost and in greater quantity synthetically than by using the natural source. For example, the hormone cortisol, used to treat arthritis and many other ailments, can be obtained from the adrenal glands of cows and sheep. But drug companies can produce it cheaper synthetically. In addition, the

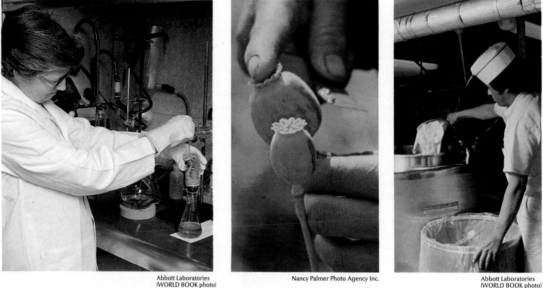

Abbott Laboratories
(WORLD BOOK photo)

Nancy Palmer Photo Agency Inc.

Abbott Laboratories
(WORLD BOOK photo)

Some sources of drugs. Most drugs are synthetic compounds created in drug company laboratories, *left.* Other drugs come from plants, animals, minerals, and bacteria. For example, opium poppies, *center,* supply opium, used to make such narcotics as codeine and morphine. Sodium chloride, or salt, and other substances are used in preparing *intravenous solutions, right,* which are injected into the veins of patients who cannot eat or drink.

synthetic form of cortisol causes fewer adverse reactions than the natural form of the hormone.

Plants and molds. Drug companies make several important medicines from plants and molds. These medicines include antibiotics, cardiotonics, and certain analgesics. For example, the antibiotic penicillin comes from a mold. The cardiotonic digitalis, a drug used to stimulate the heart, is obtained from the leaves of the purple foxglove, a flower. The pain reliever morphine is taken from opium, a drug that comes from the juice of the opium poppy. Plant drugs that pharmaceutical companies do not produce include such illegal drugs as marijuana and mescaline.

Animals. A number of important drugs—including several of the hormones used to treat arthritis, hormone deficiencies, and various other ailments—are obtained from the cells and tissues of animals. For example, millions of diabetes victims use insulin obtained from the pancreas of cattle and hogs. Physicians prescribe the hormone thyroxine, obtained from the thyroid gland of cattle and hogs, for patients whose thyroid gland produces too little of the hormone.

Minerals. Pharmaceutical companies produce several common drugs from minerals. For example, the mineral iodine is used in making tincture of iodine, a liquid that helps prevent infection when it is applied to cuts. The mineral silver nitrate is manufactured in powder form and rubbed onto wounds to stop bleeding and help prevent infection. Physicians also use silver nitrate in mild solution to treat certain eye and skin infections.

Genes and bacteria. Biologists and chemists have developed methods of genetic engineering by which human genes are inserted into bacterial cells. The genetically altered bacterial cell, called *recombinant DNA,*

manufactures a chemical substance identical to one that is made by human cells. The substance is then isolated and purified so it can be administered to patients whose bodies cannot make enough of it. Examples of drugs produced in this way include erythropoietin, a hormone that stimulates production of red blood cells; growth hormone, which regulates growth during childhood; and insulin, a hormone that controls the disease diabetes. See **Genetic engineering.**

Research and development

Pharmaceutical firms are continually developing new drugs. Although company chemists discover some new drugs by accident, the creation of most new products begins with an idea. This idea may be for a new kind of drug or for one that works better than existing drugs. A pharmaceutical company must then obtain such a drug, test it, and develop it into a safe, easy-to-use form. The entire process takes about 10 years for most drugs and costs many millions of dollars.

Creating a new drug is the task of a company's research chemists. They may make a new chemical compound or obtain the drug from a natural source. This work may take many months or even years. For example, researchers for one United States drug company spent two years testing soil from all parts of the world to find new antibiotics. The tests involved over 100,000 soil samples. The project resulted in the development of the antibiotic Terramycin, used to treat such diseases as bronchitis, pneumonia, and whooping cough.

In the process of creating a new drug, researchers perform tests with animals to see if the substance is safe and effective. They first give the substance to small animals, such as rats, mice, and guinea pigs. If the substance passes these tests, it is given to larger animals, such as dogs and monkeys. Researchers may test hundreds of substances before finding one that appears safe and effective. They then try to find out how this drug works, in what forms it can be given, how the animal body eliminates the drug, and what side effects it may have. The drug company then sends this and other information about the drug to the U.S. Food and Drug Administration (FDA)—a U.S. government agency—and asks for permission to conduct tests on people.

Testing with people. After receiving FDA approval, a drug company performs two series of *clinical tests* with the new drug. The company first tests the drug for safety in healthy human volunteers. If the results of these tests are satisfactory, the company checks the drug further in patients who have the disorder the drug is designed to correct.

Most clinical tests are supervised by a *clinical investigator,* a physician employed by the drug firm's research department. Physicians on the staffs of university hospitals cooperate with the clinical investigator by arranging for volunteers to take part in the second series of tests. The number of patients who receive the drug and the length of the tests depend on the disorder being treated and the kind of drug being tested. Most tests involve hundreds of patients and last from several months to a year. Some tests, however, involve thousands of patients and last several years.

Careful testing is one of a pharmaceutical company's most important responsibilities. Drug companies and the FDA constantly guard against the possibility of a harmful drug being sold to the public. But even the most careful testing cannot always reveal the possibility that a drug might produce an unexpected harmful effect. A tragic example of such an unexpected effect occurred in Europe during the early 1960's. Thousands of pregnant women who took a new sedative, thalidomide, gave birth to babies with no arms or legs or with some other deformities. The chances of such severe effects

occurring unexpectedly are, however, very small.

The drug company's clinical investigator and other scientists evaluate the results of the clinical tests. They also compare the new drug with those already in use. Other physicians and scientists continue to study the effects of the drug in animals. If the company decides it has developed a safe, effective drug, it will submit a *new drug application* to the FDA requesting approval to sell the drug. The section *The new drug application* describes this step in drug production.

Developing the finished product. Before selling a new drug, a company must develop it into a safe, easy-to-use form. Researchers determine what ingredients to add to the drug to make it into a capsule, liquid, pill, or other usable form. These ingredients, called *excipients,* must not interfere with the drug's action. Researchers also determine how fast the drug will break down chemically and lose its effectiveness. The company can include this information on the label if the breakdown occurs quickly. After all these steps, the company is ready to plan mass production of the drug.

Mass production

During research and development, a company produces only small quantities of a drug. The firm must determine whether the process used to produce small amounts will work for large-scale production. The company usually conducts production tests in an experimental *pilot plant* before beginning mass production. These production tests may indicate that small-scale methods must be changed. Sometimes these tests indicate that a new plant must be built to produce the drug.

A company has to plan its mass-production schedule carefully. If the firm produces too much of a drug, some of it might break down chemically and become worthless before it is sold. The company must also make certain that all batches of the drug have been made correctly. Samples of each batch are inspected. If such spot-checking reveals an error, the entire batch is either processed again or destroyed.

Distribution and sale

A new drug may be distributed and sold in one of two ways, depending on whether it is a prescription drug or a nonprescription drug. *Prescription drugs* may be sold only by a pharmacist and only if prescribed by a physician or dentist. *Nonprescription drugs* need not be sold by pharmacists and do not require a prescription. The FDA determines whether a drug may be sold as a prescription or nonprescription drug.

Prescription drugs include antibiotics, barbiturates, and certain tranquilizers. Because these drugs require a prescription, pharmaceutical companies direct their sales efforts for these drugs at physicians and dentists. The companies place advertisements in professional journals, mail out literature, and set up advertising displays at medical and dental meetings. Most drug firms also employ *medical service representatives* who call on doctors to tell them about the firm's products.

Nonprescription drugs, such as aspirin and some cough medicines, are considered safe enough to be sold *over the counter*—that is, without a prescription from a physician or dentist. A drugstore, grocery store, department store, or any other establishment may sell

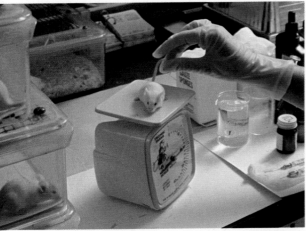

Abbott Laboratories (WORLD BOOK photo)

Tests with animals help researchers determine if a new drug is safe and effective. As part of the tests, each animal is weighed, *above,* to see if the drug's effects differ among animals of different sizes.

such drugs. As a result, pharmaceutical firms advertise nonprescription drugs widely to the public.

Drug names

All drugs produced by the U.S. pharmaceutical industry are given at least two names: (1) a chemical name and (2) a United States Adopted Name (USAN). In addition, a drug may have one or more trade names, or trademarks. For example, a certain diuretic has the chemical name 6-chloro-3, 4-dihydro-7-sulfamyl-2H1,2,4-benzothiadiazine, 1,1-dioxide. Its USAN is hydrochlorothiazide. The drug also has more than 20 trade names, including Esidrex, HydroDiuril, and Oretic.

The chemical name of a drug describes its chemical structure. It is the only name that identifies a drug exactly. But because most drugs have long, difficult chemical names—such as the above example—these names are not commonly used.

The United States Adopted Name, commonly referred to as the *generic* name, is usually an abbreviated chemical name. It provides a hint about a drug's chemical structure, as the name *hydrochlorothiazide* does in the example. But the USAN does not describe a drug fully. The USAN is shorter than the chemical name, and it is easier to use. The USAN Council, which is made up of pharmacists and scientists in other fields, selects all USAN's.

The trade name is given to a drug by the company that sells it. A number of firms may sell a particular drug. Each company may give the drug a different trade name, or it may market the drug under the drug's generic name. A drug may have 10, 20, or more trade names. State laws vary concerning prescriptions written for trade-named drugs. In some states, if a doctor prescribes a drug by its trade name, a pharmacist must fill the prescription with the trademarked drug. But in other states, a pharmacist may substitute a lower-priced trademarked or generic equivalent, as long as the doctor has not specifically prohibited such substitution. In still other states, a pharmacist may substitute an equivalent only if the doctor has indicated that such substitution is permissible. If a doctor prescribes a drug by its generic name, a pharmacist may fill the prescription with a suitable drug sold by any company.

Drug regulation

Almost all countries have laws regulating the manufacture, sale, and use of drugs. In the United States,

How a drug is mass-produced

Pharmaceutical companies manufacture drugs in a variety of forms, including capsules, liquids, and tablets. The pictures below show some of the steps in the mass production of tablets.

Drug powder poured into stamping machine

Machine stamps drug into tablet form

Tablets receive protective coating

Tablets bottled for distribution

every new drug sold must be approved by the FDA. In addition, the FDA inspects factories that manufacture drugs, and it checks the quality of drug samples taken from stores.

The United States Drug Enforcement Administration works to end the illegal use of narcotics and other drugs of abuse (see **Drug Enforcement Administration**). In addition, many states have laws concerning the manufacture, sale, and use of drugs. In Canada, the manufacture and sale of drugs is regulated by the Health Protection Branch of the federal Department of National Health and Welfare.

U.S. drug laws. The Federal Food, Drug, and Cosmetic Act of 1938 outlaws the sale of impure and falsely labeled drugs. It also requires manufacturers to prove to the FDA that a new drug is safe before they may sell it. In addition, the law requires that drug labels list active ingredients, directions for use, and warnings of possible harmful effects. Under the Drug Amendments Act of 1962, drug companies must prove that a new product is effective as well as safe. In 1975, the FDA issued regulations to ensure that all trade-named and generic equivalents of the same drug have identical actions in the body. In 1978, the FDA issued rules requiring that the labels of all prescription drugs and most nonprescription drugs carry an expiration date to show how long the drug will remain fully effective. The FDA controls the advertising of prescription drugs. The Federal Trade Commission (FTC) controls the advertising of nonprescription drugs.

The Comprehensive Drug Abuse Prevention and Control Act of 1970 strengthened federal regulation of the manufacture, sale, possession, and use of narcotics and other drugs of abuse. The act also called for increased federal assistance in the treatment of drug-dependent persons.

The Orphan Drug Act of 1983 encourages drug manufacturers in the United States to work with new drugs that can be used in the treatment of rare diseases. Such drugs are often referred to as *orphan drugs* because

pharmaceutical firms cannot afford to develop them. Research and marketing costs would exceed income from sales of the drugs. The Orphan Drug Act includes regulations that help reduce the expenses of developing and marketing orphan drugs. In addition, the act provides federal grants to pay for some of the costs of research and development.

The Federal Anti-Tampering Act of 1983 prohibits tampering with containers or labels for foods, drugs, or cosmetics. The purpose of the act is to prevent the unintentional use of incorrectly labeled or contaminated products.

The new drug application. In seeking FDA approval to sell a new drug, a drug company must submit a *new drug application*. The application must contain detailed information about the drug, including four important items: (1) records of tests that prove the drug is both safe and effective, (2) an account of the drug's composition, (3) a description of the methods used to manufacture the drug, and (4) the information to be included on the drug label. In addition, the company must provide the FDA with samples of the drug and each of its ingredients.

FDA scientists study each new drug application and conduct tests, if necessary, with the samples from the drug company. If they approve a drug, these scientists decide whether it will be sold as a prescription or nonprescription drug.

Drug standards. In the United States, standards of drug composition are established by *The United States Pharmacopeia-The National Formulary* (USP-NF). Federal law recognizes this publication as the official authority on drug standards. The USP-NF is revised continuously by a committee of the United States Pharmacopeial Convention. Each convention is attended by representatives from schools of medicine and pharmacy; from various federal agencies; and from associations of physicians, dentists, and pharmacists. Other professionals who are qualified to help determine drug standards also attend this convention.

History

Prehistoric peoples probably used drugs long before the first civilizations arose. It is likely they discovered that their aches and pains disappeared after they ate certain plants. They may have also noticed that animals ate certain plants only when ill and then recovered. Prehistoric people probably then ate the same plants when they felt sick.

Drugs in ancient times. The oldest known written record of drug use is a clay tablet from the ancient Sumerian civilization of the Middle East. This tablet, made in the 2000's B.C., lists about a dozen drug prescriptions. An Egyptian scroll from about 1550 B.C. names more than 800 prescriptions containing about 700 drugs. The ancient Chinese, Greeks, and Romans also used many drugs. In addition, the Romans opened the first drugstore and wrote the first prescriptions calling for definite amounts of drug ingredients.

Although ancient peoples used many drugs, most of the remedies were useless. Occasionally, people who had taken useless remedies recovered naturally. As a

Sumerian clay tablet; University Museums, University of Pennsylvania

The oldest written prescriptions ever found date from the 2000's B.C. They call mostly for various types of plant remedies.

result, they thought the drugs were responsible. However, ancient peoples did discover some effective drugs. The Greeks and Romans, for example, used opium to relieve pain. The Egyptians used castor oil as a laxative, and the Chinese ate liver to cure anemia.

Drugs in the Middle Ages. During the Middle Ages, which lasted from the A.D. 400's to the 1500's, interest in learning and science declined in Europe. As a result, Europeans produced little new information about drugs. But in the Middle East, Arab physicians added new discoveries to the knowledge of drugs they had acquired from the ancient Romans and Chinese. The Arabs later passed on their knowledge of drugs to Europeans.

Throughout the Middle Ages, the demand for drugs remained high, and pharmacies became increasingly common in Europe and the Arab world. But scientists had not yet learned how the human body functions, what causes infectious disease, or how drugs work. As a result, people continued to take many useless or harmful drugs, in addition to some effective ones.

Scientific advances. During the 1500's and 1600's, doctors and scientists made important advances in *pharmacology* (the study of drugs) and in other fields of science. These advances laid the foundation for later revolutionary progress in the development of drugs.

In the early 1500's, the Swiss physician Philippus Paracelsus pioneered in the use of minerals as drugs. He introduced many compounds of lead, mercury, and other minerals in the treatment of various diseases. But further progress in the development of drugs required advances in knowledge of the structure and functioning of the human body.

In 1543, the Flemish physician Andreas Vesalius, known as the founder of human anatomy, published the first complete description of the body's structure. His work destroyed many false beliefs about human anatomy. In the early 1600's, the English physician William Harvey discovered how blood—pumped by the heart—circulates through the body. Later in the 1600's, Anton van Leeuwenhoek, an amateur Dutch scientist, discovered bacteria. He used crude microscopes to study the

tiny organisms. But the role of germs as a cause of disease was not established until the 1800's.

The drug revolution began about 1800 and has continued to the present. During this period, scientists have discovered hundreds of drugs. They have also discovered the cause of many diseases, determined how drugs work, and learned much about how the body functions. In the process, the practice of medicine has been revolutionized, in large part by the use of drugs. Pharmacology has developed into a major science, and the manufacture of drugs has become a large industry.

In 1796, Edward Jenner, an English physician developed the first successful vaccination in an effort to prevent the deadly disease smallpox. He vaccinated a boy with pus from blisters on a woman infected with cowpox. The boy then caught cowpox, a minor disease related to smallpox. Jenner later injected smallpox matter into the boy. But the boy did not catch smallpox because his fight with cowpox had made his body *immune* (resistant) to smallpox. Jenner's discovery led to a search for vaccines against other diseases. This search gradually developed into the science of *immunology.*

Scientists learned how to *isolate* (separate) drugs from plants during the early 1800's. In 1806, morphine became the first of the plant drugs to be isolated. Within a few years, scientists had also isolated quinine.

In the 1840's, the use of anesthetics during surgery was introduced by two Americans working independently of each other—Crawford Long, a physician, and William T. G. Morton, a dentist. Later in the 1800's, the French scientist Louis Pasteur and the German physician Robert Koch established the *germ theory* of disease. Pasteur proved that germs cause infectious diseases and that killing the germs responsible stopped the spread of such diseases. Koch developed a method for determining which bacteria cause particular diseases.

The pace of the drug revolution quickened in the 1900's. In fact, most of the major drugs used today have been discovered since 1900. Important developments in hormone research followed the first isolation of a hormone in 1898. That year, an American pharmacologist, John J. Abel, isolated the hormone epinephrine, also called adrenalin. Scientists isolated several other hormones during the next 20 years. Then in the early 1920's, a research team led by Frederick Banting, a Canadian physician, discovered the hormone insulin. Since then, this drug has saved the lives of millions of diabetics.

In the early 1900's, Paul Ehrlich, a German scientist, developed a new method of treating infectious diseases. This method, called *chemotherapy,* involves the use of chemicals that attack disease-causing organisms. It is also used to destroy cancer cells. Ehrlich announced the discovery of the first chemotherapeutic drug, arsphenamine (Salvarsan), in 1910. His work led to the later discovery of the germ-fighting antibiotics and sulfa drugs.

The first antibiotic, penicillin, was discovered in 1928 by the British scientist Alexander Fleming. A German physician, Gerhard Domagk, discovered the first sulfa drug, Prontosil, in 1935. Scientists soon developed many other antibiotics and sulfa drugs. These "wonder drugs" proved to be remarkably effective against a variety of infectious diseases.

Many other important drugs have been discovered since 1900. Barbiturates, which reduce the activity of the

Drug milestones of the 1900's

1903 The first barbiturate, barbital, was introduced.

1910 The German scientist Paul Ehrlich introduced *chemotherapy,* a method of treating infectious disease by using chemicals to attack the disease-causing bacteria.

1922 A research team led by Frederick Banting, a Canadian physician, announced the discovery of the hormone insulin, used to treat diabetes.

1928 The British scientist Alexander Fleming discovered the first antibiotic, penicillin.

1930's Amphetamines were first used medically.

1935 Gerhard Domagk, a German physician, discovered the first sulfa drug, Prontosil.

1950's Scientists developed several important *synthetic* (artificially produced) tranquilizers, which came into widespread use.

1960 Birth control pills were introduced.

1970's and 1980's Drug researchers intensified their efforts to find drugs that will help cure cancer and many other diseases not yet conquered by medical science. Recombinant DNA methods were developed and used to produce interferons, hormones, and other drugs.

nervous system and the muscles, were introduced in 1903. Amphetamines, which stimulate the nervous system, were first used medically in the early 1930's. Scientists developed several important tranquilizers in the 1950's, and birth control pills appeared in 1960. During the late 1970's, scientists began using techniques of *recombinant DNA* to produce drugs, such as insulin and interferon. These techniques involve injecting human genes into bacterial cells, which produce some of the same chemicals in their own cells.

Growth of the drug industry. Until about 1800, there were few drug companies. Pharmacists themselves made almost all the drugs they sold. Then two revolutions, one in drugs and the other in industrial development, gave birth to the modern drug industry. The discovery of more and more drugs that required special training and equipment to produce made it increasingly difficult for a pharmacist to prepare drugs. At the same time, the Industrial Revolution in Europe led to the development of manufacturing methods that could be used to mass-produce drugs. As a result, many drug companies were established in Europe, and European firms dominated the world drug market for many years.

The beginning of the United States drug industry can be traced back to the Revolutionary War in America (1775-1783). The chief pharmacist of the American army, Andrew Craigie, set up a laboratory in Carlisle, Pa., to supply drugs to the military. After the war, Craigie opened his own laboratory and began a wholesale drug business. Soon other pharmacists set up drug companies. These companies grew as they adopted the mass-production techniques developed in Europe.

The American Civil War (1861-1865)—like the Revolutionary War—created a great demand for drugs and so furthered the growth of the U.S. pharmaceutical industry. But European companies continued to dominate the world drug market until World War I (1914-1918). Before the war, the United States imported most of its drugs from Germany. But such imports stopped when the United States joined the war against Germany in 1917. The American pharmaceutical industry then expanded rapidly to meet the country's drug needs. The United States soon began to export drugs and became one of the world's leading producers.

Over the years, the demand for drugs has increased rapidly as more and more drugs have been developed. The drug industry has grown with this demand and, through its discoveries, helped create it. Today, the United States leads all countries in drug production.

Drugs today benefit us tremendously. They also present us with some of our worst problems and greatest challenges. Drugs help prevent or control many diseases. They also relieve pain and tension and help the body function properly. But the misuse of alcohol, narcotics, and other drugs has led to addiction for millions of people. In addition, the widespread illegal use of drugs has become a major problem.

The challenges that drugs offer lie in the discovery of better medicines for treating cancer, cardiovascular diseases, and other crippling and deadly disorders. In the 1970's and 1980's, pharmaceutical researchers increased their efforts to find such drugs. Someday, scientists may develop drugs that lengthen life by slowing the aging process.   Edward J. Cafruny

Related articles in *World Book* include:

Drugs that fight bacteria

Antibiotic	Isoniazid	Sulfa drug
Cephalosporin	Penicillin	Tetracycline
Erythromycin	Streptomycin	

Drugs that affect the nervous system

Acetaminophen	Curare	Methadone
Alcohol	DMSO	Methamphet-
Amphetamine	Dramamine	amine
Analgesic	Ephedrine	Morphine
Aspirin	Ether	Narcotic
Barbiturate	Hallucinogenic	Nitrous oxide
Belladonna	drug	Opiate
Benzocaine	Hashish	Opium
Beta-blocker	Heroin	Procaine
Bromide	Ibuprofen	Quinine
Caffeine	Kola nut	Salicylic acid
Chloroform	Lidocaine	Scopolamine
Chlorpromazine	LSD	Sedative
Cinchona	Marijuana	Strychnine
Coca	Menthol	Thiopental
Cocaine	Mescaline	Tranquilizer
Codeine		

Other kinds of drugs

ACTH	Creosote	Iron
Anticoagulant	Cyclosporine	Laetrile
Antihistamine	Digitalis	Laxative
Antiseptic	Disulfiram	Liniment
Antitoxin	Diuretic	Magnesia
Arsenical	Emetic	Mercurochrome
Astringent	Epinephrine	Psyllium
BCG	Epsom salt	Salts
Calcium blocker	Eucalyptus	Serum
Camphor	Glauber's salt	Silver nitrate
Cascara sagrada	Hormone	Smelling salts
Castor oil	Insulin	Squill
Coagulant	Interferon	Steroid
Cod-liver oil	Iodine	Vitamin
Cortisone		

Other related articles

Anesthesia	Immunization
Antidote	Medicine
Birth control (Methods of birth	Mental illness (Drug therapy)
control)	Microencapsulation
Chelation therapy	Patent medicine
Chemotherapy	Pharmacology
Depressant	Pharmacopeia
DES	Pharmacy
Drug abuse	Placebo
Drug addiction	Pure food and drug laws
Drug Enforcement Administra-	Stimulant
tion	Tragacanth
Enzyme (Uses)	
Food and Drug Administration	

Outline

I. Kinds of drugs
- A. Drugs that fight bacteria
- B. Drugs that prevent infectious diseases
- C. Drugs that affect the heart and blood vessels
- D. Drugs that affect the nervous system
- E. Other kinds of drugs

II. How drugs work

A. Entrance into the body	C. Effect on the body
B. Action in the body	D. Elimination from the body

III. How drugs are produced and sold

A. Sources of drugs	D. Distribution and sale
B. Research and	E. Drug names
development	F. Drug regulation
C. Mass production	

IV. History

Drug abuse is commonly defined as the harmful, nonmedical use of a mind-altering drug. The continual misuse of one or more such drugs, also called *psychoactive drugs,* can lead to poor health and to personality and behavioral problems. Some experts use the term *drug abuse* to refer only to problems with illegal drugs, also called *street drugs.* Other experts include the harmful use of legal drugs, even ones prescribed by a doctor.

Cultural attitudes about a drug help determine whether its use is considered harmful. For example, both alcohol and marijuana can produce similar intoxication. However, most Americans consider the moderate use of alcohol as acceptable, but many regard any use of marijuana as dangerous. Such cultural attitudes are reflected in a number of drug laws. As a result, the sale of alcohol is legal in most parts of the United States, but the sale of marijuana is not.

Cultural attitudes also make it difficult to distinguish between the accepted use of certain drugs and the abuse of those drugs. Alcoholic beverages have been used by people in many societies for thousands of years. Yet, alcohol is one of the most widely abused drugs.

Commonly abused drugs. Many commonly abused drugs are illegal—that is, their possession and sale are forbidden by law. They include marijuana, cocaine, heroin, and such hallucinogenic drugs as LSD, PCP, and mescaline. Other abused drugs can be obtained legally only with a doctor's prescription. They include amphetamines, barbiturates and other sedatives, morphine, and tranquilizers. Still other abused drugs can be bought legally without a prescription in most nations. They include alcohol; nicotine, which is present in tobacco; and butyl nitrite and other inhalants, such as fumes from cleaning fluids, gasoline, and model airplane glue.

Why people abuse drugs. Many people continually use drugs because they want a pleasurable change in their state of mind. This pleasurable change may range from a mild "lift" to an intense psychoactive effect. Many people use such drugs as alcohol, marijuana, and cocaine to gain *euphoria* (a sense of well-being). This feeling is also called a "high." In larger doses, these drugs can alter a person's feelings and perceptions.

Many people experiment with drugs out of curiosity, for a thrill, to rebel, or because their friends use drugs. Others turn to drugs to escape depression or other personal problems, including difficulties with their schoolwork, job, or family. Regardless of why drug use began, many people continue the practice because they become dependent on a drug.

Effects of drug abuse. The regular use of certain drugs causes *dependence*—that is, the use of the drug becomes a hard-to-break habit. Drug dependence is partly due to *psychological dependence,* which involves a craving for the psychological experience a drug provides. It also is partly due to *physical dependence.* Physically dependent drug users develop *drug tolerance,* which means they need increasing doses of a drug to achieve the same effect. If a person develops drug tolerance and then stops using the drug, he or she will suffer from *drug withdrawal.* The body then needs the drug so badly that the user will seek more of the drug even though it is harmful. This condition is called *addiction.* Drug addiction ranks as one of the most serious health problems. For example, alcoholism or heroin addiction can destroy or seriously damage an individual's health and personal life. See **Drug addiction.**

The immediate effects of many abused drugs also involve extensive risks. Alcohol, marijuana, and tranquilizers decrease mental alertness and muscle coordination. Every year, thousands of traffic deaths and injuries are caused by people who drive under the influence of these drugs, especially alcohol. An overdose of alcohol, cocaine, sleeping pills, or heroin can cause coma or death. These drugs may paralyze respiration. An overdose of cocaine also can stop the heartbeat. Mixing drugs increases the risk of an overdose. Many illegal drugs are impure, and different batches have widely varying strengths. An overdose from a batch of great strength can kill the user.

Hallucinogenic drugs cause a person to have *hallucinations*—that is, to see or hear things that do not exist. PCP, a drug that causes users to feel apart from their surroundings, sometimes triggers violent reactions. In addition, users who inject drugs intravenously and share hypodermic needles or syringes are at risk of getting AIDS (Acquired Immune Deficiency Syndrome) and other diseases.

The cost of drug abuse in the United States is about $120 billion annually for alcohol, and about $60 billion annually for all other drugs. This total includes the expense of hospitalization, property damage, and time lost from work. An even greater cost occurs in the personal and family destruction caused by drug abuse.

Signs of drug abuse. Most drugs that are continually misused can influence a person's behavior. In some cases, this influence is obvious to other people. For example, excessive use of alcohol or sleeping pills causes poor muscle coordination, slurred speech, and sleepiness. People who use amphetamines and cocaine become restless and talkative. However, the effects of some drugs, such as tobacco and marijuana, may not be noticed by anyone other than the user.

Even parents and close friends may not be aware that a person is abusing drugs. Many drug abusers try to keep these activities secret. Long absences from home, school, or work, or a sharp drop in school or job performance, may indicate drug abuse. A sudden change in personality may also be a clue, but such a transformation often occurs without drugs.

Prevention of drug abuse. It is easier to prevent drug abuse than to stop the practice after it has started. Most people who abuse drugs begin doing so in their teens or early 20's. Parents of teen-agers should establish reasonable guidelines of behavior and discuss drug abuse openly with their children. Parents also should set an example for their children by not abusing drugs. If a young person develops a drug abuse problem, the parents should seek help from a physician, a professional counselor, or a community organization that provides such assistance.   David C. Lewis

Related articles in *World Book* include:

Adolescent (The use of drugs)	Hallucinogenic drug	Methamphetamine
Alcoholism	Hashish	Morphine
Amphetamine	Heroin	Narcotic
Barbiturate	LSD	Opium
Cocaine	Marijuana	Smoking
Drug Enforcement Administration	Mescaline	

See also *Drug abuse* in the Research Guide/Index, Volume 22, for a *Reading and Study Guide.*

Additional resources

Drug Abuse: Opposing Viewpoints. Ed. by Julie S. Bach. Greenhaven, 1988.
The Encyclopedia of Drug Abuse. Ed. by Robert O'Brien and Sidney Cohen. Facts on File, 1984.
Inciardi, James A. *The War on Drugs: Heroin, Cocaine, Crime, and Public Policy.* Mayfield Pub. Co., 1986.
Mind Drugs. Ed. by Margaret O. Hyde. 5th ed. Dodd, 1986.
Newman, Susan. *It Won't Happen to Me.* Perigee, 1987. Suitable for younger readers.
Woods, Geraldine. *Drug Use and Drug Abuse.* 2nd ed. Watts, 1986. For younger readers.

Drug addiction is the inability of a person to control the use of a drug. Such a person is called a *drug addict.* For addicts, drug use is more than a habit. The craving for the drug also involves *physical dependence.* That is, an addict's body depends on a drug so greatly that a painful withdrawal illness results if the drug is not used. In addition, addicts also develop a *tolerance* to the drug, and so doses that once satisfied the craving no longer do so. As a result, addicts need larger and larger doses to achieve the same effect.

For a discussion of some of the causes of drug addiction, see the *World Book* article on **Drug abuse.**

Addicting drugs. Three major groups of drugs can cause addiction: (1) *narcotics,* such as heroin and morphine; (2) *depressants,* including barbiturates, tranquilizers, and alcohol; and (3) *stimulants,* such as amphetamines, cocaine, and the nicotine in tobacco products.

Continued use or overuse of any of these types of drugs can cause addiction. Withdrawal from narcotics causes aching muscles, chills, runny nose and eyes, stomach cramps, and general body weakness. The initial symptoms resemble those of a bad cold. Withdrawal from depressants may cause insomnia and convulsions. It also may cause *delirium tremens,* a condition in which the victim becomes shaky and sees and hears things that are not present. Too swift a withdrawal from some depressants can cause death. Chronic high-dose users of stimulants may experience severe depression, fatigue, and long periods of sleep when they stop taking the drug. Cocaine withdrawal causes a condition called *cocaine hunger,* an intense craving for the drug. Overdoses of cocaine and *opiates* (narcotics made from opium) are major causes of medical emergencies and deaths.

The difference between addicting drugs and other habit-forming drugs is not clear in all cases. Some nonaddicting drugs—as well as the addicting drugs—cause a strong psychological craving that may make a drug habit as hard to break as physical dependence does. In addition, many nonaddicting drugs produce a tolerance in regular users. For such reasons, many experts use the term *drug dependence* rather than *addiction.*

Effects of drug addiction. Many addicts spend so much time under the influence of drugs or thinking about trying to get drugs that they neglect their health, work, family, and friends. They feel forced to keep taking the drug even though it endangers their lives. Addicts find it difficult to keep a job or to handle family responsibilities. They fail to eat well and to maintain personal cleanliness. As a result, many addicts suffer from malnutrition. Addicts who inject drugs may get such diseases as hepatitis, tetanus, or AIDS (acquired immune deficiency syndrome) from an unsterile needle.

For most addicts, the chief goal in life is obtaining more drugs. Narcotics cannot be obtained legally without a physician's prescription, but they may be bought illegally at very high prices. Some addicts turn to crime, such as robbery and prostitution, to support their habit. In most cases, addicts are not diagnosed until their lives are seriously damaged.

Treatment of drug addiction. An addict may be *detoxified* (withdrawn from using a drug) by slightly decreasing the daily dose over a period of weeks. Gradual withdrawal reduces the severity of withdrawal illness. But even after addicts have withdrawn completely, they feel irritable and restless for weeks or months. Some of the craving for the drug may remain for months or years. Many people who have withdrawn eventually return to drugs—and to readdiction. They do so partly because they have not solved the problems that first led them to drugs.

Some people who treat drug addiction believe that addicts can profit from treatment in groups composed of other addicts. These experts feel that by being confronted by other addicts, drug abusers can achieve a better understanding of themselves and their social responsibilities. These confrontations involve frank discussions of the problems of and motives for drug abuse. One group that uses such treatment, Alcoholics Anonymous (A.A.), has helped many people addicted to alcohol (see **Alcoholics Anonymous**). Other groups require members to live within a treatment community and adhere to strict rules of conduct while in the program.

Physicians use medications to treat some cases of addiction. For example, they may give heroin addicts a narcotic called *methadone*. Methadone develops physical dependence, but it satisfies the body's craving for heroin. Some methadone users can live almost normal lives (see **Methadone**). After detoxification, other medications, called *narcotic antagonists,* can be given to block the pleasant effects of heroin and prevent it from causing additional dependence. Physicians also use such drugs as clonidine or bromocriptine to detoxify opiate or cocaine addicts. A drug called *disulfiram* is used to treat alcoholism in detoxified alcoholics (see **Disulfiram**). No medication is known that will prevent cocaine relapse.

Control of drug addiction. Laws in the United States, Canada, and most other countries forbid the possession and sale of heroin. Other narcotics and addicting sedatives can be obtained legally only with a physician's prescription. Such laws, if they are fair and are rigorously enforced, probably limit addiction to certain drugs. They also probably decrease the total amount of drug addiction and drug abuse. But the strongest laws, which provide imprisonment and fines for individual users, have not eliminated drug addiction or drug abuse. Other solutions to the problem must also be sought. 	Mark S. Gold

See also **Drug abuse** and its list of *Related articles.*

Additional resources

Berger, Gilda. *Addiction: Its Causes, Problems, and Treatments.* Watts, 1982. Suitable for younger readers.
DuPont, Robert L. Jr. *Getting Tough on Gateway Drugs: A Guide for the Family.* Am. Psychiatric Pr., 1984. Suitable for younger readers.
Gold, Mark S. *The Facts About Drugs and Alcohol.* 3rd ed. Bantam, 1988.
Harris, Jonathan. *Drugged Athletes: The Crisis in American Sports.* Four Winds, 1987. Suitable for younger readers.
Mann, George A. *Recovery of Reality: Overcoming Chemical Dependency.* Harper, 1979.

Drug Enforcement Administration (DEA), an agency of the United States government, enforces federal laws and regulations dealing with narcotics and other dangerous drugs. The DEA is responsible for investigating illegal drug traffic and arresting suspected offenders. It also regulates the production and distribution of certain drugs.

The DEA investigates the smuggling of narcotics and dangerous drugs into the United States and the distribution of such drugs. It arrests suspected distributors, financiers, importers, and processors of illegal drugs. The agency cooperates with the Federal Bureau of Investigation and other federal agencies to prevent drug trafficking. It also works with state and local law enforcement organizations and with agencies of other nations to combat illegal drug traffic and abuse.

President Richard M. Nixon established the DEA in 1973 as part of the U.S. Department of Justice. The agency's functions had previously been performed by three Justice Department offices and the Bureau of Customs (now the U.S. Customs Service). The DEA has headquarters in Washington, D.C.

Critically reviewed by the Drug Enforcement Administration

Drug therapy. See Chemotherapy; Mental illness (Drug therapy).

Drugstore. See Drug; Pharmacy.

Druids, *DROO ihdz,* were the priestly, learned class among the Celts, a people of ancient Europe. The Druids were judges and lawmakers as well as priests. They led religious ceremonies, settled legal disputes, and served as leaders and advisers to their people.

Druidism, the religion of the Druids, involved the worship of many gods. The Druids regarded mistletoe and oak as sacred. They believed the soul was immortal and entered a new body after death. The Druids killed animals and possibly even human beings as sacrifices. They studied the flights of birds and the remains of sacrificed animals to foretell the future. The Romans, who conquered much of Europe between about 300 B.C. and about A.D. 100, tried to stop druidism. The religion finally died out after the Celts became Christians in the 400's and 500's.

During the 1600's, the descendants of the Celts became interested in their Druidic heritage. Today, several groups in Great Britain and Ireland practice what they believe to be ancient Druidism. They hold Druidic festivals at the beginning of spring, summer, autumn, and winter. A major celebration takes place at Stonehenge, a monument near Salisbury, England, that the Druids are said to have used. In Wales, festivals of music and poetry called *eisteddfods* (pronounced *ay STEHTH vahdz*) include Druidic rites. 	Christopher McIntosh

See also **Halloween** (The Celtic festival).

Drum is any member of about 200 species of fishes. Some drums are also called *croakers.* Drums get their name from the sound some of them make. These drums repeatedly tighten certain muscles on their swim bladder in the abdomen to produce vibrations that sound like drumming. Many kinds of drums live in warm, shallow ocean water near the shores of most continents. Some spend part of their early life in freshwater rivers or in bays where fresh and salt water are mixed. But only one species, the *freshwater drum,* spends its entire life in fresh water. The freshwater drum lives in large lakes

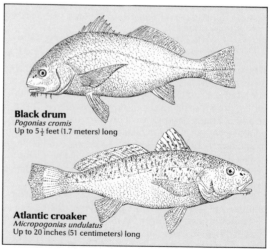

Black drum
Pogonias cromis
Up to 5 $\frac{1}{2}$ feet (1.7 meters) long

Atlantic croaker
Micropogonias undulatus
Up to 20 inches (51 centimeters) long

WORLD BOOK illustrations by Marion Pahl

Several kinds of drums are popular seafood. Commercial fishing crews catch black drum and Atlantic croakers off the Atlantic Coast of North America. These fish have firm, white flesh.

and rivers from Canada to Central America.

Drums range in size from species that weigh about 1 pound (0.45 kilogram) to those that weigh more than 100 pounds (45 kilograms). The *totuava,* which lives in the Gulf of California, is the heaviest. This rare fish weighs as much as 225 pounds (101 kilograms) and measures up to 6 feet (1.8 meters) long. Most drums have a scaly head; a blunt, rounded nose; and two upper fins separated by a notch.

Many drums, including the *red drum* and the *white croaker,* have teeth only in the rear of their mouth. These flat, grinding teeth enable the drums to eat clams, crabs, shrimp, and other shellfish that they find along the ocean floor. Other drums, including the *spotted seatrout* and the *weakfish,* have sharp front teeth that allow them to feed on such free-swimming animals as shrimp, squid, and small fish (see **Weakfish**).

Commercial fishing crews in the United States use nets to catch several kinds of drums, including the *Atlantic croaker,* the *black drum,* and the red drum. The drum's firm, white flesh makes it a popular seafood.

Two drums of the tropical Atlantic, the *jackknife-fish* and the *high-hat,* are favorites of aquarium owners. These small fish have an extremely high fin on their back, and interesting black-and-white markings.

Scientific classification. Drums make up the drum family, Sciaenidae.   William N. Eschmeyer

Drum is the oldest musical instrument. It is a member of the percussion family, which consists of instruments that are played by striking them with the hand, sticks, or other objects. Drums have also been used for various nonmusical purposes. For example, people of many cultures have used drums to communicate over long distances.

The *shell* (body) of a drum may be shaped like an open cylinder or a kettle. A thin covering called a *drumhead* is stretched tightly across the opening. Drumheads may be made of either calfskin or plastic. A cylinder-shaped drum generally has two drumheads. A kettle-shaped instrument has one.

A musician strikes the drumhead with sticks, with mallets, or with the hand to create vibrations that produce a sound. This sound *resonates* (increases) inside the shell of the drum.

The three most popular types of drums are the *snare drum,* the *bass drum,* and the *timpani.* Only the timpani can produce definite musical notes. The other types are used primarily as rhythm instruments.

The snare drum consists of a metal or wooden cylinder with a drumhead covering each opening. The drumhead used for playing is called the *batter head.* The opposite one is called the *snare head.* About 12 gut or wire strings called *snares* stretch across the snare head. A drummer strikes the batter head with two wooden

Some common types of drums

Drums are percussion instruments that provide rhythmic accompaniment in many kinds of music. A drum set consists of a number of drums of different sizes and types, along with cymbals. Most drum sets are used in popular music. Musicians usually play bongo drums in Latin-American music. Timpani are among the largest drums and are generally played in symphony orchestras.

© Pamella McReynolds

Bongo drums

© Pamella McReynolds

A drum set

Cameramann International, Ltd.

Timpani

sticks. The snares vibrate against the snare head, producing a full, crisp sound.

The bass drum resembles a large snare drum. The drumhead used for playing is called the *beating head,* and the opposite one is called the *resonating head.* At times, the drummer may play both heads at the same time. The drummer uses mallets to create a deep, booming sound. Various tone colors can be produced by using felt, wool, or wooden mallets.

The timpani are played in pairs or in groups of four. The drum is shaped like a kettle and is often called a *kettledrum.* It consists of a large copper or fiberglass shell with a single drumhead. A pedal mechanism enables the player to tune the drum to different pitches. Timpani produce a deep, resounding tone achieved by striking the drumhead with mallets. Different tone colors may be obtained by using a variety of mallets made of soft felt, hard felt, or wood.   John H. Beck

See also **Bongo drums; Conga drum; Tambourine; Tom-tom.**

Drumfish. See Drum.

Drumlin. See Glacier (How glaciers shape the land).

Drummond, William Henry (1854-1907), was a Canadian poet and physician. He was called the *poet of the habitants.* French-Canadian farmers once called themselves *habitants.* Drummond was interested in their way of life, and that of the *voyageurs* (trappers and boaters). Drummond turned their simple folk tales and legends into poems. He learned stories from farmers and backwoods people after he became a country doctor at the age of 30. His books of poetry include *The Habitant* (1897) and *The Voyageur* (1905). Drummond was born in County Leitrim, Ireland. He moved to Canada with his parents when he was 10 years old.   Rosemary Sullivan

Drunkenness. See Alcoholism.

Drupe, *droop,* is a fleshy fruit that has a single seed surrounded by a hard covering or *stone.* The pulp of a drupe is not divided into segments like the pulp of an orange. The whole drupe is usually covered with a thin skin. Drupes include the olive, plum, cherry, and peach. See also **Fruit** (illustration: Drupes).   Arthur W. Galston

Druses, *DROOZ ehz,* are an Arabic-speaking people of the Middle East. There are more than 500,000 Druses, who are also known as the *Druze* or *Druzes.* About half of them live in the Hauran districts of Syria. Most of the rest live in Lebanon and about 40,000 are in Israel. Some Druses have emigrated to the United States and Canada.

The Druses practice a secret religion related to Islam. Al-Hakim, a ruler of Egypt during the A.D. 1000's, founded the religion. He declared that he was God. When he died, Ismail al-Darazi, one of his followers, spread the religion to the people in the Syrian mountains. The name *Druse* probably comes from *Darazi.*

The Druses in Lebanon had little political representation. They played a key role in fighting that broke out against the government of Lebanon during the early 1980's.   Vernon Robert Dorjahn

Dry cell. See Battery (Kinds of batteries).

Dry cleaning is a process that removes dirt and stains from fabrics. Dry cleaning uses little or no water, but the process is not really "dry." It involves the use of liquids called *solvents.*

Dry-cleaning plants clean both clothing and household items such as draperies and bedspreads. Certain garments, including many of those made of wool or silk, must be dry cleaned to prevent shrinkage, fading, or other damage that might occur if the garment is washed in water. Some materials should not be dry cleaned. For example, dry cleaning may cause vinyl or artificial leather to crack or split. Most garments have care labels that tell how they should be cleaned.

How clothes are dry cleaned. Clothes are dry cleaned with others of the same color and type of fabric. Before cleaning, garments are sorted and may be *prespotted* to remove any stains that could become permanent during the dry-cleaning process.

The clothing is then put into a cleaning machine, which resembles a large home washing machine. It has a movable drum that is filled with liquid solvent instead of water. A special dry-cleaning detergent is usually added to the solvent to help remove soil. The drum rotates and the solvent circulates through the clothes. After the cleaning cycle, the solvent is drained from the machine and the drum spins rapidly to remove most of the solvent from the clothes. Finally, a machine called a *tumbler* blows warm air through the clothes to dry them completely. After cleaning, clothes are checked again in the spotting department to make sure all spots and stains are gone. The spotter uses a nozzle called a *steam gun* that can spray a jet of water vapor to wet the stain. Special stain-removing chemicals are used, depending on the nature of the stain and the type of fabric. Occasionally a stain cannot be removed without damage to the fabric or the dye.

From the spotting department, the garment goes to the presser or finisher. This worker uses presses, hand irons, and steaming equipment to remove wrinkles and restore the shape and texture of the garment.

Self-service, coin-operated dry-cleaning machines clean and dry clothes automatically. Some self-service stores also have pressing and spot-removing services. Self-service dry cleaning costs less than the professional process, but some garments require professional care.

The dry-cleaning industry is one of the largest service industries in the United States. It employs about 140,000 people in approximately 21,000 dry-cleaning plants. About 2,400 self-service laundries include coin-operated dry-cleaning equipment. In addition, many large hotels and department stores operate their own dry-cleaning departments.

Critically reviewed by the International Fabricare Institute

Dry dock is a dock in which a vessel can lie out of the water while repairs are being made below its water line (see Dock). The two chief kinds of dry docks are graving docks and floating docks.

Graving docks are used chiefly to repair large ships in shipyards. *Graving* was a term used in the days of wooden ships to mean cleaning a vessel's bottom and coating it with tar. A graving dock looks like a huge, concrete bathtub sunk into the ground. One end of the dock opens onto a harbor, river, or other waterway. When a ship enters the dock, shipyard workers place a huge floating or sliding *caisson,* or gate, against the open end. Pumps suck the water out and the vessel slowly sinks. Its *keel,* or bottom, comes to rest on wooden blocks placed on the floor of the dock. *Spars,* or long pieces of wood wedged between the ship and the sides of the dock, also help support the vessel.

© David R. Frazier

Dry docks at the Puget Sound Naval Shipyard in Bremerton, Wash., are used to repair various kinds of naval vessels.

When repairs are completed, workers flood the dock until the water reaches the same level as the water outside the gate. It is opened and the ship leaves.

Floating docks can be self-propelled or towed from place to place. They are important in war to repair ships in forward battle areas. A floating dock looks like a shoebox with the top and ends removed. Some types are built in U-shaped sections that can be assembled to make one large dock. The *hull,* or bottom, and *wing-walls,* or sides, of a floating dock contain compartments. Water enters these compartments, making the dock sink low enough to allow a ship to enter. Pumps then suck the water out and the dock rises, lifting the ship out of the water. Wooden blocks and spars similar to those used on graving docks help support the vessel. When repairs are completed, the compartments are flooded again until the dock sinks enough to allow the ship to float. Such docks can raise an average-sized ship in from one to two hours.   John F. Wing

Dry farming is a process of growing crops in semiarid regions without irrigation. Semiarid regions receive little rainfall during the crop-growing season. Therefore, farmers in these regions try to increase the amount of water that soaks into the soil during rainy or snowy periods. During the growing season, the crops absorb water stored in the soil.

Dry farming includes various practices that help increase soil moisture. Many farmers leave part of their cropland *fallow* (unplanted) each year. The fallow land stores moisture for the following year's crop. Instead of plowing the land, the farmer tills the soil about 3 inches (8 centimeters) deep. This technique, called *shallow cultivation,* kills weeds, which absorb moisture from the soil. It also exposes less soil to the air than plowing does and so reduces the amount of water that evaporates from the soil. Some farmers control weeds by applying chemical *herbicides,* rather than by tilling the soil.

Another dry-farming technique is *contour plowing,* which is practiced on sloping land. In contour plowing, the farmer plows across a slope, rather than up and down. The plowed soil forms furrows, which prevent rainwater from running down the slope. Thus, the water stays on the slope and filters into the ground.

After harvesting a crop, many farmers leave dead stalks and other plant wastes on the fields as a covering during the winter. The wastes create an uneven surface, to which snow sticks easily. These waste materials prevent some snow from being blown away by the wind. After the snow melts and soaks into the ground, the covering helps keep the moisture in the soil.

Only certain hardy crops, such as barley, sorghum, and wheat, can be grown by dry-farming methods. Even so, farmers must plant these crops as early as possible in the growing season so that the plants mature before the weather becomes too hot and dry.

Dry farming is practiced in semiarid regions of many countries, including Australia, Canada, China, Russia, and the United States. The largest dry-farming region in the United States lies in the Great Plains. Researchers have improved many dry-farming techniques and have developed new crop varieties that need little water. These improvements have increased food production in dry-farming regions.   Hayden Ferguson

Dry ice is solid carbon dioxide. The name *dry ice* refers to the fact that the substance changes from a solid to a gas without first becoming liquid. Because of this property, dry ice is widely used in industry to refrigerate food, medicine, and other materials that would be damaged by the melting of ordinary ice. Chemists use a mixture of dry ice and acetone or isopropyl alcohol to cool chemicals during certain reactions.

Dry ice is made in snowlike flakes or in blocks. Flakes are produced by cooling and compressing liquid or gaseous carbon dioxide. Blocks are formed by further compression of the flakes.

The chemical formula for dry ice is CO_2. Dry ice has a temperature of $-109.3°$ F. ($-78.5°$ C), which is much colder than the temperature of ordinary ice. For this reason, special care must be taken when handling dry ice to avoid frostbite.   Robert J. Ouellette

See also **Food, Frozen** (Dry-ice freezing); **Rainmaking** (Rainmaking methods).

Dry rot. See **Rot.**

Dry Tortugas, *tawr TOO guhz,* are a group of low coral islands, or *keys,* which lie about 60 miles (97 kilometers) west of Key West, Fla. The Spanish explorer Juan Ponce de León reached them in 1513, and called them the Tortugas (Spanish for turtles), because of the many turtles in the nearby waters. Spain ceded the Tortugas to the United States in 1819 along with Florida. Fort Jefferson was built on Garden Key in the Tortugas in 1846. The Tortugas became a federal bird reservation in 1908, and Fort Jefferson became a national monument in 1935.
Kathryn Abbey Hanna

Dry wall. See **Wallboard.**

Dryden, John (1631-1700), was the outstanding English writer of the *Restoration period* (about 1660 to 1700). He excelled as a poet, dramatist, and literary critic. Dryden believed that the individual is part of a society that has its roots in ancient Greece and Rome. He also believed that literature and the arts have value as civilizing forces. As a result, his writings deal with large social, political, and humanistic issues.

Dryden was born in Northamptonshire, and studied at Trinity College, Cambridge. He began writing after moving to London in the late 1650's. Dryden wrote only poetry at first, but later began writing plays to make a living. His finest play is *All for Love* (1677), an adaptation of Shakespeare's *Antony and Cleopatra.* Dryden simplified Shakespeare's story and concentrated on the tragic passions of the two famous lovers. *The Conquest of Granada* (1670, 1671), an imposing heroic drama, and *Marriage à la Mode* (1672), a light-hearted, sophisticated comedy, rank among the best of Dryden's plays.

Dryden's best poems sprang from his involvement with political controversies. In 1668, he was appointed poet laureate and in 1670 became the royal historiographer. He became involved in political disputes between King Charles II and Parliament. A Tory, he joined the king against the Whigs. Dryden's poem *Absalom and Achitophel* (1681) is a brilliant political satire based on Absalom's rebellion against King David, which is described in the Old Testament. *The Medal* (1682) is an even more biting attack on the Whigs. His most famous poem, *MacFlecknoe* (1682), is a satire written in mock-epic style against a literary foe, Thomas Shadwell.

Dryden also wrote to defend his religious faith. *Religio Laici* (1682) is a poem that defends the Church of England against its enemies. Dryden became a Roman Catholic about 1686, and wrote *The Hind and the Panther* (1687) in defense of Catholicism.

In 1688, King James II, a Catholic, lost his throne to William and Mary, who were Protestants. Dryden refused to swear allegiance to the new rulers, and he lost his government positions. He wrote a few plays and poems after 1688, but spent much of his time translating works to support himself. Dryden's most famous translations are the poems of Virgil (1697). "Alexander's Feast" (1697) is his best poem of the period.

Dryden also wrote much literary criticism. His best works include *An Essay of Dramatic Poesy* (1668), which expresses his admiration for Shakespeare; and his preface to a collection of fables published in 1700, in which he praised Chaucer.   Gary A. Stringer

See also **English literature** (Restoration literature).

Additional resources

McFadden, George. *Dryden: The Public Writer, 1660-1685.* Princeton, 1978.
Ward, Charles E. *The Life of John Dryden.* Univ. of North Carolina Press, 1961.

DT's. See Delirium tremens.
Dual Monarchy. See Austria-Hungary.
Duarte, *doo AHR tay,* **José Napoleón,** *hoh SAY nah poh lay OHN* (1926-1990), served as the elected president of El Salvador from 1984 to 1989. He had served as appointed president of a military junta from 1980 to 1982. During his presidency, Duarte could not end a civil war that had lasted 10 years and had resulted in the deaths of more than 60,000 people.

Duarte was born in San Salvador. In 1948, he graduated from the University of Notre Dame in Indiana. In 1960, Duarte helped organize the Christian Democratic Party in El Salvador. He served as mayor of San Salvador from 1964 to 1970. As mayor, he organized neighborhood groups to build or repair schools and health facilities.

©Sygma

José Duarte

Duarte ran for president in 1972. Early election returns showed him in the lead, but the ruling government altered the final results to show its own candidate as the winner. Duarte went into exile in Venezuela after some of his followers tried to overthrow the government and failed. He returned to El Salvador in 1979, after a military junta seized power. While serving as president, Duarte contracted cancer. He did not run for re-election in 1989.   Nathan A. Haverstock

See also **El Salvador** (Recent developments).

Du Barry, *doo BAR ee,* **Madame** (1746-1793), was the beautiful country girl who became the mistress of King Louis XV of France (see

Louis [XV]). She had little education. Instead, the beauty of this blue-eyed blonde and her pleasant manner were her greatest assets. She was not meddlesome, but jealous rivals and the king's ministers hated her so much that she had to use her influence upon the king in self-defense. By the time Louis XV died in 1774, she counted many friends at court.

She was born in Champagne, France. Her real name was Marie Jeanne Bécu. She first worked in a hat shop in Paris, but soon became the mistress of the Comte Jean du Barry. She met Louis in du Barry's gambling rooms. She married William du Barry, Jean's brother, to acquire the title Countess du Barry and thus gain enough social rank to be presented at court. This formality was required before she could become Louis XV's official mistress. In 1793, the French republicans accused her of aiding enemies of the French state. She was dragged to the guillotine just five weeks after Marie Antoinette's execution.   Richard M. Brace

Detail of portrait by Madame Vigée-Lebrun, private collection. Bulloz from Art Reference Bureau

Madame du Barry

Dubček, Alexander. See **Czechoslovakia** (The 1960's; Recent developments).
Du Bellay, *doo buh LAY,* **Joachim,** *zhaw a KEEM,* (1522-1560), was a French poet. With his friend Pierre de Ronsard, he founded a group of poets called the Pléiade. Du Bellay's essay *Defense and Glorification of the French Language* (1549) established the literary doctrines of the group.

Du Bellay was born in Anjou of a noble, but poor, family. He lived in Rome from 1553 to 1557, and he wrote the major parts of two brilliant volumes of verse, *Antiquities of Rome* and *Regrets* (both 1558), while there. In *Antiquities,* he praises the virtues of ancient Rome. In *Regrets,* written during a self-imposed exile from France, he deplores the corruption of modern Rome and speaks with both bitter disillusionment and longing of his native country.   Joel A. Hunt

See also **French literature** (The Pléiade).
Dubinsky, *doo BIHN skee,* **David** (1892-1982), an American labor leader, was president of the International Ladies' Garment Workers' Union from 1932 to 1966. He also helped found the Committee for Industrial Organization in 1935, which later became the Congress

of Industrial Organizations (CIO). He became a founding vice president of the American Federation of Labor Congress of Industrial Organizations (AFL-CIO) in 1955. He became noted for work in collective bargaining, labor's international affairs, and anti-racketeering. Born in Brest-Litovsk, Poland, Dubinsky was arrested for union activity there and was exiled to Siberia. He escaped and moved to the United States in 1911.   Jack Barbash

Dublin, *DUHB lihn* (pop. 502,749; met. area pop. 866,241), is the capital and largest city of the Republic of Ireland. It lies on the east coast of Ireland at the mouth of the River Liffey (see **Ireland** [map]). Dublin is the economic, political, and cultural center of Ireland. About a fourth of Ireland's people live in the Dublin area.

The city occupies a beautiful site, with Dublin Bay to the east and the Dublin Mountains to the south. Rolling plains extend west and north of Dublin. The River Liffey flows through the city.

Dublin has many wide streets and spacious squares that are lined with lovely houses and public buildings. Many of these buildings date from the 1700's. Large apartment and office buildings have been built during the 1900's. Residential areas are scattered throughout the city and spread into the suburbs.

Dublin's main shopping section lies along and near O'Connell and Grafton streets, which run north and south near the center of the city. O'Connell Street measures about 150 feet (46 meters) wide and is one of the widest streets in Europe. Statues of some famous Irish people stand down the center of this street.

A busy port and a manufacturing area are at the mouth of the River Liffey. Many office buildings and other important structures rise south of the river. This area includes Dublin Castle, St. Patrick's and Christ Church cathedrals, and the University of Dublin—also called Trinity College. Also in the area are the National Art Gallery, the National Library, the National Museum, and Leinster House—the meeting place of Ireland's parliament. Attractions north of the river include the Abbey Theatre and two historic buildings called Custom House and the Four Courts. Phoenix Park, which lies to the northwest, is one of the largest city parks in the world.

Economy. More than a fourth of Ireland's manufacturing industries are in Dublin. The city's products include chemicals, clothing, electrical equipment, electronics, furniture, machinery, metal products, printed materials, processed foods, textile products, tobacco, and a dark beer called *stout.* Construction, retail and wholesale trade, transportation and communications, and tourism and other service industries are also important. The city's port handles nearly half of Ireland's foreign trade. Ireland's main airport lies north of the city.

History. Vikings established Dublin in the mid-800's, though a small settlement had previously been on the site. The Viking town was named *Dublin,* from the Irish words *dubh,* meaning *black*; and *linn,* meaning *pool.* The name may refer to a pool of dark water in a branch of the River Liffey. The branch is now filled in by land. The Vikings built Christ Church Cathedral in the 1000's. Norman soldiers from England captured Dublin in 1170. The Normans erected St. Patrick's Cathedral and also built Dublin Castle. The castle was the center of British rule in Ireland for over 700 years.

Dublin expanded greatly during the 1700's. Although Ireland was controlled by England, an Irish parliament met in Dublin. Manufacturing and trade increased, and the city's cultural life flourished.

Dublin played an important part in most of the major events of Irish history. Fighting in the city during a rebellion against the British in 1916 caused much destruction in Dublin. Much property also was destroyed in the early 1920's, during Ireland's war of independence from Britain and a civil war that followed it.

Since the 1920's, the Dublin area has grown steadily. Some valuable old buildings have been destroyed to make room for new construction. Suburbs have expanded into the surrounding countryside. Today, city leaders face the problem of preserving as much as possible of what is valuable from the past while scheduling further growth for Dublin.   Desmond A. Gillmor

See also **Ireland** (pictures).

Dublin, *DUHB lihn,* **University of,** more generally known as Trinity College, Dublin, was founded in 1592 under a charter granted by Queen Elizabeth I. The financial support of this university came from funds and property given by James I. The university has faculties of arts, science, business, economic and social studies, engineering and systems sciences, and health sciences. It has about 8,400 undergraduate and postgraduate students.   Critically reviewed by the University of Dublin

Dubois, *DYOO BWAH,* **Eugène** (1858-1941), was a Dutch anatomist and physical anthropologist. While in Java in 1891-1892, he discovered the fossilized bones which he later named *Pithecanthropus erectus,* or *the apeman that walked erect* (see **Java man**). His discovery led to the theory of a single "missing link" in the chain of evolution joining apes and human beings. Later discoveries have led scientists to believe that Pithecanthropus is only one form among many in the human evolutionary process.   David B. Stout

Du Bois, *dyoo BWAH,* **Guy Pène,** *gee pehn* (1884-1958), was an American painter and art critic. Du Bois's early paintings were dark, loosely brushed but realistic impressions of modern city life. During the 1920's and 1930's, he produced his best-known paintings. These pictures realistically and often satirically portrayed styl-

© Richard Laird, FPG
Dublin stands at the mouth of the River Liffey. O'Connell Bridge, a major Dublin landmark, spans the river. The bridge is named for Daniel O'Connell, an Irish patriot.

ish women and stout, self-confident businessmen relaxing in art galleries, night clubs, restaurants, and theaters. Du Bois used sharp, bright colors and made his figures sleek, stiff, and sculptural.

Du Bois was born in New York City. For much of the period from 1913 to 1922, he edited a magazine called *Arts and Decoration*. Du Bois wrote many essays for a number of publications supporting American art and defending the values of realism and social observation in painting.   Sarah Burns

Du Bois, *doo BOYS,* **W. E. B.** (1868-1963), was one of the most important leaders of black protest in the United States. During the first half of the 1900's, he became the leading black opponent of racial discrimination. He also won fame as a historian and sociologist. Historians still use Du Bois's research on blacks in American society.

Du Bois was probably the first black American to express the idea of *Pan-Africanism.* Pan-Africanism is the belief that all people of African descent have common interests and should work together to conquer prejudice. In 1900, Du Bois predicted that humanity's chief problem of the new century would be "the color line."

William Edward Burghardt Du Bois was born in Great Barrington, Mass. He graduated from Fisk University in 1888. In 1895, he became the first black to receive a Ph.D. degree at Harvard University.

From 1897 to 1910, Du Bois taught history and economics at Atlanta University. He attended the First Pan-African Conference in London in 1900. He later organized Pan-African conferences in Europe and the United States. Du Bois received the Spingarn Medal in 1920. See **Spingarn Medal.**

Du Bois strongly opposed the noted black educator Booker T. Washington. Washington believed that blacks could advance themselves faster through hard work than by demands for equal rights (see **Washington, Booker T.**). But Du Bois declared that blacks must speak out constantly against discrimination. According to Du Bois, the best way to defeat prejudice was for college-educated blacks to lead the fight against it. Many of his ideas appear in a collection of essays called *The Souls of Black Folk* (1903). Du Bois' other works include *Black Reconstruction in America* (1935) and *The Autobiography of W. E. B. Du Bois* (1968).

Wide World
W. E. B. Du Bois

To fight racial discrimination, Du Bois founded the Niagara Movement in 1905 (see **Niagara Movement**). In 1909, he helped found the National Association for the Advancement of Colored People (NAACP). From 1910 to 1934, he was editor of the NAACP magazine *The Crisis.* Du Bois left the NAACP in 1934 and returned to the faculty at Atlanta University. From 1944 to 1948, he again worked for the NAACP. After 1948, Du Bois became increasingly dissatisfied with the slow progress of race relations in the United States. He came to regard Communism as a solution to the problems of blacks. In 1961, Du Bois joined the Communist Party and moved to Ghana.   Elliott Rudwick

See also **Black Americans** (The rise of new black leaders; picture).

Additional resources

DeMarco, Joseph P. *The Social Thought of W. E. B. DuBois.* Univ. Press of America, 1983.
Du Bois, W. E. B. *Writings.* Library of America, 1986.
Marable, Manning. *W. E. B. DuBois: Black Radical Democrat.* Twayne, 1986.
Rampersad, Arnold. *The Art and Imagination of W. E. B. Du Bois.* Harvard, 1976.

Du Bois, *dyoo BWAH,* **William Pène,** *pehn* (1916-   ), is an American writer and illustrator of books for children. He won the 1948 Newbery Medal for *The Twenty-One Balloons* (1947), the story of an old professor's amazing adventures while traveling in a hot-air balloon. Du Bois uses simple, lively language. His illustrations are clear, playful, and brightly colored.

Du Bois was born in Nutley, N.J. His father was Guy Pène du Bois, a noted painter and art critic. From age 8 to 14, du Bois lived in France. During that time, he acquired a love for France, the fantastic stories of French science-fiction writer Jules Verne, and especially the circus. These early interests influenced du Bois's books and pictures.   Sarah Burns

Dubos, *doo BAWS* or *doo BOH,* **René Jules,** *reh NAY zhool* (1901-1982), a French-American microbiologist, pioneered in the development of antibiotics, a type of drug. In 1939, Dubos developed tyrothricin, the first commercially produced antibiotic, from a substance made by soil bacteria. His work led other researchers to develop the antibiotics penicillin and streptomycin.

Dubos also investigated and wrote about human relationships to both the natural and social environment. He shared the 1969 Pulitzer Prize for general nonfiction for *So Human an Animal* (1968).

Dubos was born in Saint Brice, France, near Paris. In 1927, he earned a Ph.D. degree from Rutgers University and joined the Rockefeller Institute for Medical Research (now Rockefeller University). He became a United States citizen in 1938.   Isaac Asimov

Dubuffet, *dyoo byoo FEH,* **Jean,** *zhahn,* (1901-1985), was a French artist known for the primitive style of his works. Dubuffet's style draws its chief inspiration from crude wall drawings called *graffiti* and the art produced by children, insane people, and primitive cultures. His painting *Business Prospers,* which appears in the **Painting** article, is typical of his style.

Dubuffet was extremely interested in the materials used in painting. In many of his pictures, he used unusual combinations of substances such as sand, gravel, cement, glue, and tar to achieve especially rough textures. For example, he used plant leaves to create *The Gardener.* He produced other works by cutting up painted canvases and reassembling the pieces. Dubuffet often used simple or crude images to shock people who were used to beautiful pictures.

Dubuffet was born in Le Havre. He studied art as a young man but worked as a winemaker until he seriously devoted himself to painting in 1942. He influenced younger artists in the late 1940's and helped bring the return of recognizable subject matter to painting at a time when abstract art was popular.   Pamela A. Ivinski

Dubuque, *duh BYOOK,* Iowa (pop. 62,321; met. area pop. 93,745), is a port city on the west bank of the Mississippi River, opposite the Illinois-Wisconsin border. For location, see **Iowa** (political map). Dubuque was named for Julien Dubuque, who began to mine lead there in 1788. Lead mining and fur trading have been replaced by machinery manufacturing, meat packing, and tourism as the chief industries. Businesses in the city also produce plumbing supplies, furniture, fertilizers, and dairy products; and sell computer equipment and services, chiefly to medical facilities. Iowa's oldest brewery operates there. Clarke College, Loras College, the University of Dubuque and its theological seminary, and Wartburg Theological Seminary are in the city. Tourist attractions include greyhound races and paddle-wheel riverboat rides. Dubuque was first settled in 1833. A town government was organized in 1837. Iowa's first newspaper was published there in 1836. The city has a council-manager government.   Kenneth J. Amundson

Dubuque, *duh BYOOK,* **Julien** (1762-1810), a French-Canadian adventurer, was the first white person to settle in Iowa. He began mining lead ore in 1788 along the Mississippi River south of the present city of Dubuque. He had a Spanish title to his claim and named it "The Mine of Spain." He learned the language of his Indian neighbors and traded with them. He was born in Quebec province, Canada.   Thomas D. Clark

Ducat, *DUHK uht,* is a coin first issued by Roger II of Sicily, Duke of Apulia, in the mid-1100's. It was called a ducat because it was issued by authority of a duchy. Later the coin was used in all southern European countries, either in silver or in gold. The silver ones were worth between 75 cents and $1.10, and the gold ones, $1.46 to $2.32.   Burton H. Hobson

Duccio di Buoninsegna, *DOOT choh dee BWAW neen SAY nyah* (1250?-1319?), was the first great painter from Siena, Italy. He became noted for the graceful faces and the soft drapery of his figures. His painting grew out of the earlier Gothic and Byzantine styles, while anticipating the more humanistic art of the Renaissance. From 1308 to 1311, he painted *The Maestà,* the great altarpiece of the cathedral in Siena. It shows the Madonna enthroned, surrounded by angels and saints. Duccio also created miniature paintings for books. He was born in Siena. See also **Jesus Christ** (picture: Jesus restored a blind beggar's sight).   Vernon Hyde Minor

Duchamp, *doo SHAHN,* **Marcel** (1887-1968), was a French-born artist and a leader of the modern movement in art. Duchamp created works that challenged the traditional definition of art. His unconventional approach helped to develop an atmosphere of creative freedom for other artists and has continued to be influential.

Duchamp's best-known painting is *Nude Descending a Staircase, No. 2* (1912). The depiction of the human figure as a sequence of planes shows the influence of a style called *cubism* that was developed about 1910 in France. This painting first shocked Duchamp's older artistic colleagues in France in 1912. It caused an even greater sensation in 1913 when it was displayed at the New York Armory Show, the first large exhibition of modern art in the United States. The painting baffled and outraged many viewers, to whom it symbolized the unintelligibility of modern art.

Many of Duchamp's works were simply everyday objects that he gave titles and exhibited as art. He called these works *ready-mades.* Duchamp's most controversial ready-made was a common urinal that he titled *Fountain* and signed with the name "R. Mutt." By wittily designating ordinary objects as works of art, he hoped to make people examine their own standards of art.

The most important and complex work of Duchamp's career is the unfinished *The Bride Stripped Bare by Her Bachelors, Even,* sometimes known as the *Large Glass.* In this work of oil paint, wire, and lead foil enclosed in glass, Duchamp explored such themes as sexuality and the increasing mechanization of human life.

Duchamp was born in Blainville, France, near Rouen. In 1904, he went to Paris, where he met artists who later led modern art movements. Duchamp shared many ideas with artists known as *dadaists* and *surrealists,* but he was not identified exclusively with any group. He settled in the United States in 1942.   Pamela A. Ivinski

See also **Dadaism; Painting** (Dadaism; picture: *Chocolate Grinder, No. 1*); **Surrealism.**

Du Châtelet, Marquise. See **Voltaire** (Exile).
Duchess. See **Duke.**

Oil painting on canvas (1912); Philadelphia Museum of Art, Louise and Walter Arensberg Collection

Nude Descending a Staircase, No. 2, is Marcel Duchamp's most famous painting. It caused a sensation at the Armory Show of modern art in New York City in 1913. The painting shows motion by blending a series of movements into one picture.

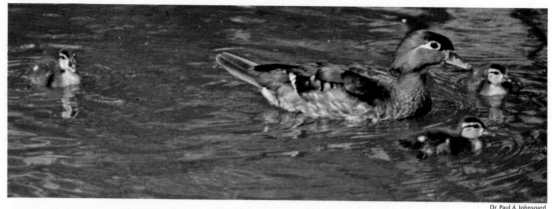

Dr. Paul A. Johnsgard

A wood duck and her ducklings stay close together so she can protect them from enemies. Most ducklings can swim on the day they are born, but they cannot fly for several weeks.

Duck is a bird with waterproof feathers and webbed feet. Ducks are related to geese and swans. But ducks have shorter necks and wings and flatter bills, and they quack or whistle rather than honk. Male ducks are called *drakes,* and females are called *ducks.*

Ducks live throughout the world in wetlands, including marshes and areas near rivers, ponds, lakes, and oceans. They live in arctic, temperate, and tropical regions for some or all of the year. Many kinds of ducks migrate long distances annually between their breeding grounds, where they rest and raise their young, and their wintering areas, where the water does not freeze. Some ducks migrate thousands of miles.

Most ducks are good to eat. Farmers raise the ducks that people buy to eat at home and in restaurants. Duck farming is a profitable business on Long Island, New York, and in the state of Washington, as well as in many parts of Europe, Australia, and New Zealand. Hunters also kill many kinds of wild ducks for food. But the sale of wild game is against the law in the United States.

The features of a duck

Ducks spend a lot of time in water, where their webbed feet serve as paddles for swimming and diving. They are graceful on water, but waddle clumsily when walking on land because their legs are set on the sides and toward the rear of the body. Most common wild ducks weigh from 2 to 4 pounds (0.9 to 1.8 kilograms), but some of the smaller species weigh less than 1 pound (0.45 kilogram).

The various kinds of ducks get their food in different ways, depending on their body features. Some ducks extend their long necks down through shallow water to pick food off the bottom. Others dive for food in deep water. Ducks that sift food have wide bills with edges

Facts in brief

Names: *Male,* drake; *female,* duck; *young,* duckling; *group,* flock.
Incubation period: 23 to 30 days, depending on species.
Number of eggs: 5 to 12, depending on species.
Length of life: 2 to 12 years (shoveler and mallard reported to 20 years).
Where found: All parts of the world except Antarctica.

that strain seeds, insects, and snails from the water. Some ducks have short bills that they use to pry barnacles from rocks or to grab clams. Others have long, narrow bills with sawlike edges for catching and holding fish.

Ducks protect themselves from cold water by waterproofing their feathers. They use their bills to rub the feathers with a waxy oil from a gland at the base of the tail. Under the oiled feathers is a layer of soft, fluffy feathers called *down.* Down helps insulate a duck's body because it traps air under the outside feathers.

Most drakes have bright-colored feathers. Their colors include green, blue, red, and chestnut. But drakes of some species are mostly black and white. Most females are brown and can hide by blending with the surroundings when incubating eggs or taking care of ducklings.

The life of a duck

Ducks seek mates during winter. The bright colors of the drakes attract females. A female usually leads her drake to the breeding grounds during the spring migration, often returning to the same wetland where she was hatched. The ability of ducks and other birds to return to the same places each year is called *homing behavior.* Once on the breeding grounds, each male defends a small territory from which he drives away other males or other pairs of his own species. The female builds a

Two types of duck bills

Diving ducks have long, narrow bills, *top,* with toothlike edges to hold fish. Dabbling ducks have short, broad bills for prying.

WORLD BOOK diagram by Margaret Estey

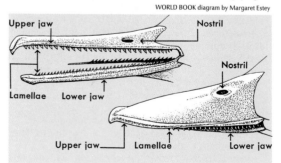

nest in a clump of grass or reeds, or in a hole in a tree.

Ducklings. The female duck lays from 5 to 12 eggs. After she starts to sit on the eggs to warm and protect them, the drake leaves to join other males. The ducklings hatch from three weeks to a month later.

Female redhead ducks of North America sometimes lay eggs in the nests of other species. They often depend on the other ducks to hatch the eggs and care for the young. Most ducklings look alike, and the new mother accepts them.

Ducklings can run, swim, and find food for themselves within 36 hours of hatching. A group of ducklings is called a *brood.* A mother duck keeps her brood together so she can protect it from predators. Animals that prey on ducklings include turtles, raccoons, hawks, and large fish. Sometimes the ducklings in one brood mix with another. As a result, some females end up with broods of 15 to 25 ducklings, while others have only 2 or 3. Ducklings grow quickly and have most of their feathers in about a month. They learn to fly in five to eight weeks.

Food. Ducks that do not dive for food are called *dabbling ducks.* They eat mostly wetland plants, including the seeds of aquatic weeds, grasses, sedges, and rushes. They also eat insects and other small animals that they find on or under the water. *Pochard ducks* dive to the bottom for roots, seeds, snails, insects, and small clams. In fresh water, pochards and dabbling ducks may eat many kinds of insects, including beetles, bugs, and dragonflies. In salt water, they feed on snails, barnacles, shrimp, and mussels, as well as on plants. *Wood ducks* eat acorns, small fruits, insects, and seeds.

Mergansers, a kind of sea duck, eat mostly fish, which they catch in either salt water or fresh water. *Eiders* and

Types of ducks Scientists classify ducks into eight separate groups called *tribes.* Members of six of the tribes are illustrated below. They are the dabbling duck, pochard, perching duck, sea duck, shelduck, and stiff-tailed duck. The other two tribes are called the steamer duck and the torrent duck.

Shelduck illustration by John F. Eggert; other illustrations by Athos Menaboni

Dabbling ducks (*Anatini*)

Mallard
Anas platyrhynchos
Found in Northern Hemisphere
(28 inches, or 71 centimeters)

Pochards (*Aythyini*)

Greater scaup
Aythya marila
Found in Northern Hemisphere
(20 inches, or 51 centimeters)

Perching ducks (*Cairinini*)

Mandarin duck
Aix galericulata
Found in eastern Asia and Japan
(20 inches, or 51 centimeters)

Sea ducks (*Mergini*)

Red-breasted merganser
Mergus serrator
Found in polar region, Northern Hemisphere
(23 inches, or 58 centimeters)

Shelducks (*Tadornini*)

Common shelduck
Tadorna tadorna
Found in Europe and Asia
(24 inches, or 61 centimeters)

Stiff-tailed ducks (*Oxyurini*)

Ruddy duck
Oxyura jamaicensis
Found in North and South America and West Indies
(17 inches, or 43 centimeters)

other sea ducks pull crabs, barnacles, and shrimp off rocks and weeds. They dig snails, cockles, mussels, and clams from the bottom, and also catch fish.

Habits. Once the female duck has nested, the drake usually leaves her and joins other drakes to *molt* (lose their old feathers). The drakes lose their bright colors and for several weeks have a brown color like that of the females. During this molt only, the drake also loses his flight feathers and cannot fly. He molts again in early fall and regains his male coloring. After her ducklings hatch, the female also molts, and replaces all her feathers.

After growing new feathers and after the young learn to fly, the ducks gather in flocks on large lakes, marshes, or shallow places in the ocean to migrate to their wintering grounds. They usually fly in long lines or "V" formations. Flocks use the same summer and winter areas year after year, even stopping to rest at the same spots along the way. Some ducks fly only a short distance. Others make long flights—from Alaska to Texas or Mexico, from Canada to Chesapeake Bay in Maryland and Virginia, or even to Central and South America.

Kinds of ducks

Scientists classify ducks into eight *tribes* (groups). Members of five of the eight tribes are found in North America. This section describes these five tribes. The scientific name of the tribe appears in parentheses after the common name.

Dabbling ducks (Anatini) include mallards, black ducks, pintails, baldpates, gadwalls, green-winged teals, blue-winged teals, cinnamon teals, and shovelers. These birds tip bottom-up in shallow water, stretching their necks to feed on the bottom. They take off from water in quick jumps. All dabbling ducks except gadwalls have shiny colored patches on their wings. Gadwalls have white wing patches.

Nearly all domestic ducks are dabbling ducks that developed from wild mallards. White Pekin ducks, which weigh about 8 pounds (3.6 kilograms), are the most commonly raised ducks in the United States.

Pochards (Aythyini) include canvasbacks, redheads, ringnecks, and greater and lesser scaups. They swim underwater with their wings closed and their legs sticking out to the sides. They have short wings and their legs

Walter Chandoha

White Pekins are the most common ducks raised commercially in the United States. They weigh about 8 pounds (3.6 kilograms).

are closer to the rear of the body than those of most other ducks. Pochards run along the surface of the water to get airborne.

Perching ducks (Cairinini) include wood ducks, mandarin ducks, and muscovy ducks. They are extremely colorful ducks of eastern North America and the tropical regions of Africa, Asia, and Central and South America. They often perch in trees.

Sea ducks (Mergini) include mergansers, eiders, scoters, old squaws, harlequins, buffleheads, and goldeneyes. Mergansers have long, narrow bills with sawlike edges to hold fish. Old squaws dive deeper—up to 180 feet (55 meters)—than any other water bird. Eiders produce down that is valuable as insulation in bedding and winter clothing. The Labrador duck, the only extinct duck of North America, was a sea duck.

WORLD BOOK illustration by Athos Menaboni

Most kinds of domestic ducks in the United States developed from wild mallards. Common species besides the White Pekin include, *left to right,* the Indian Runner, the Rouen, the Khaki Campbell, and the Buff. Duck farms supply domestic ducks to restaurants, stores, and homes.

Stiff-tailed ducks (Oxyurini). The ruddy duck is the only species of stiff-tailed duck found in the United States. Although ruddy ducks are among the smallest ducks, they lay eggs about twice as large as chicken eggs. Another stiff-tailed duck, the masked duck, is found in Mexico and Central and South America.

Protection of ducks

The Migratory Bird Treaty, signed by the United States and Canada in 1916, protects ducks and other waterfowl. The treaty requires both countries to manage migratory birds in ways that assure their future as a natural resource.

Today, various conservation agencies protect ducks. Laws regulate the number of ducks that hunters may kill. Refuge areas preserve important habitats. Nest boxes help wood ducks in places where trees with holes are scarce. Refuge managers raise and lower water levels in ways that produce good food plants and nesting cover for ducks. However, the destruction of their wetland habitats remains a major threat to ducks. Duck hunters buy special stamps to raise money to protect wetlands before the lands are drained for other purposes. In 1988, the United States and Canada adopted a plan to protect and improve wetlands in an effort to increase duck populations.

Scientific classification. Ducks are in the class Aves and in the order Anseriformes. They belong to the family Anatidae.

Eric G. Bolen

Related articles in *World Book* include:

Canvasback	Hunting	Pintail	Teal
Eider duck	Mallard	Shoveler	Wigeon
Gadwall	Merganser	Swan	Wood duck
Goose			

Duck hawk. See Falcon (The peregrine falcon).
Duckbill. See Platypus.
Ducking stool was a form of punishment usually given to "witches and nagging women" in England and the American Colonies from the 1600's to the early 1800's. The ducking stool was a chair fastened to the end of a long plank extended from the bank of a pond or stream. The victim of the punishment was tied securely to the chair and *ducked* (plunged) into the water several times.   Marion F. Lansing

See also **Colonial life in America** (picture: Public disgrace).
Duckweed is a tiny perennial water plant. It is the smallest flowering plant known. It floats on pools and ponds. It has no stems or true leaves. The plant consists of a *frond* (flat green structure) with a single hairlike root underneath. The flowers and fruits are so small they can barely be seen by the naked eye. Duckweed is sometimes grown for food for ducks and large goldfish. It has a healthful, laxative effect on some aquarium fish.

Scientific classification. The duckweed belongs to the duckweed family, Lemnaceae. It is a member of the genus *Lemna*. One species is *L. minor.*   Earl L. Core

Ducted propeller is a propeller that turns within a cylinderlike device called a *duct.* Ducted propellers are used primarily on air cushion vehicles. Putting a propeller inside a duct makes the propeller more efficient. The duct captures air normally thrown to the side by the propeller. This action increases the air pressure behind the propeller blades and increases the propeller's driving force. The increased thrust provided by a ducted propeller permits manufacturers to reduce the size of the propeller. Ducted propellers also operate more quietly than do propellers without ducts.   John D. Bogus

See also **Air cushion vehicle.**

Ductility, *duhk TIHL uh tee,* is the ability of certain solids to undergo permanent changes in shape without breaking. For example, a piece of copper can be drawn to make a thin wire. But the shape of a brick cannot be permanently changed except by breaking it.

Ductility is a valuable property of many metals, including aluminum, gold, iron, nickel, and silver. These metals can be drawn into wire, hammered into various shapes, or rolled into sheets. The term *malleability* is often used in place of ductility to describe the property of metals that allows them to be hammered into thin sheets. Metals are not the only ductile substances and not all metals are ductile. For example, modeling clay is a ductile nonmetallic substance and impure tungsten is a nonductile metal.   Johannes Weertman

See also **Malleability.**

Dude ranch is a Western-style ranch that receives paying guests. These guests are usually city dwellers who get little physical activity and contact with nature. Three brothers, Howard, Alden, and Willis Eaton, are believed to have established the West's first dude ranch near Sheridan, Wyo., in 1904.

Some dude ranches are regular cattle or sheep ranches that entertain a few guests as a sideline. But other ranches are devoted entirely to the business of entertaining *dudes* (guests). Most of the dude ranches are in the "cow country" of Montana, Wyoming, Arizona,

Bell Aerospace Textron

Ducted propellers power these high-speed amphibious landing craft used by the United States Navy to carry troops and equipment. Putting a propeller in a cylinderlike device called a *duct* makes the propeller more efficient and provides quieter operation than a propeller without a duct.

California, Nevada, Colorado, New Mexico, and Oregon. Guests go on horseback rides along mountain trails, hunt, fish, and in some cases help with the livestock.

Critically reviewed by the Dude Ranchers' Association

Dudley, Robert. See Leicester, Earl of.

Dudley, Thomas (1576-1653), was a colonial governor of Massachusetts. Born in Northampton, England, he became steward to the powerful Earl of Lincoln, whose estates he managed. He sailed with John Winthrop on the *Arbella* in 1630 as deputy governor of the colony. He became governor four times. A Puritan of the stern and harsh type, he often differed with the tolerant and kind Winthrop. He was a founder of First Church at Charlestown, Mass., and of Newtowne (now Cambridge, Mass.). He was an early promoter and overseer of Harvard College.   Bradford Smith

Due process of law is a basic principle in the American legal system that requires fairness in the government's dealing with persons. The term *due process of law* appears in the 5th and 14th amendments to the Constitution of the United States. These amendments forbid federal, state, and local governments from depriving a person of "life, liberty, or property, without due process of law." The Supreme Court of the United States has never clearly defined these words, and has applied them to a number of widely different situations.

The idea of due process of law dates from England's Magna Carta of 1215. One article in this document promises that no one shall be deprived of life, liberty, or property, except "by the lawful judgment of his peers or by the law of the land." Some early English *writs* (written legal orders) were designed to bring the government under a rule of law. For example, a writ of *habeas corpus* requires that the government show just cause before it can hold a person in custody. See **Magna Carta; Habeas corpus.**

Through law and custom, various safeguards have been developed in the United States to assure that persons accused of wrongdoing will be treated fairly. These safeguards are sometimes called *procedural due process.* Procedural due process includes the following requirements: (1) The law must be administered fairly. (2) People must be informed of the charges against them and must be given the opportunity for a fair hearing. (3) The person bringing the charges must not be allowed to judge the case. (4) Criminal laws must be clearly worded so that they give adequate warning of the action prohibited. Procedural due process concepts apply to civil and criminal cases.

Courts have also used the "due process" clauses of the 5th and 14th amendments to limit the content of laws, even though there was no procedural unfairness. For example, they have declared unconstitutional some laws restricting personal freedoms and business, on the ground that the laws violate due process of law. This practice involves the *substance* of public policy and is called *substantive due process.*   Sherman L. Cohn

See also **Civil rights; Constitution of the United States** (Amendments 5 and 14).

Duel is a form of combat between two armed persons. It is conducted according to set rules or a code, and it is normally fought in the presence of witnesses. From early times through the 1800's, men of high rank settled personal quarrels with weapons. They generally used swords or pistols. Duels resulted from disputes over property, charges of cowardice, insults to family or personal honor, and cheating at cards or dice.

The duel probably originated in the custom of Germanic *judicial combat,* a method of administering justice. In judicial combat, the accused person challenged the accuser to a trial with weapons. The gods were supposed to give victory to the innocent person. Queen Elizabeth I of England was the first to abolish the duel as a form of justice. Later, all civilized countries abandoned the practice. But some private duels are still fought.

Some duels were more deadly than others. About 1800, French honor was satisfied by wounds, but the American dueling code at that time demanded death. The phrase *to give satisfaction* could mean either that blood must be drawn, or that one of the contestants must die. At other times it meant only that the challenged party had faced his enemy's fire.

The man challenged had his choice of weapons. The sword became the main dueling weapon in England and France. Duelists generally used pistols in America. Each duelist chose a friend who was called his *second,* and a surgeon usually attended. To avoid the police, the meeting usually took place in a forest clearing at daybreak. When duelists used pistols, they usually faced each other at an agreed-upon distance and fired on a visible signal or a command.

Dueling was common in the United States up to the mid-1800's. Many famous Americans fought duels. Aaron Burr fatally wounded Alexander Hamilton on July 11, 1804, in a pistol duel. Burr blamed Hamilton for his defeat in an election for governor of New York (see **Hamilton, Alexander**). General Andrew Jackson killed Charles Dickinson on May 30, 1806, in a pistol duel. Jackson challenged Dickinson because Dickinson denounced him in the press. The quarrel started in a dispute over a horse race. Commodore James Barron killed Commodore Stephen Decatur on Mar. 22, 1820, in a pistol duel. Barron claimed Decatur was persecuting him. Henry Clay fought John Randolph on Apr. 8, 1826, in a pistol duel, but neither was hurt. Clay challenged Randolph because Randolph had made insulting remarks about him in the United States Senate (see **Randolph** [John Randolph of Roanoke]).

Tennessee outlawed dueling in 1801, and the District of Columbia banned it in 1839. Several other states did so soon after that. Since then, one who kills an opponent in a duel can be tried for murder or manslaughter. Some German students still duel secretly with swords as a sport. They try only to inflict cheek wounds in duels with fellow members of the fencing fraternities in the German universities.   Hugh M. Cole

Duff, Sir Lyman Poore (1865-1955), served on the Supreme Court of Canada from 1906 to 1944. During the last 11 years, he was chief justice. Canada became independent from Great Britain in 1931, and many of Duff's rulings strengthened the nation's central government. He upheld many federal laws challenged by provincial governments in Canada.

During World War II, Duff investigated charges that the government sent poorly equipped and untrained troops to help defend Hong Kong. Over 200 Canadians died and more than 2,000 were captured when Japan took Hong Kong in 1941. Duff's report supported the government's conduct but drew criticism in Canada.

Duff was born in Meaford, Ont. He received his law degree from the University of Toronto in 1889. King George V knighted him in 1934.   J. L. Granatstein

Dufferin and Ava, Marquess of (1826-1902), was a successful British diplomat who served as governor general of Canada from 1872 to 1878. As governor general, he helped convince the province of British Columbia to end its threat to withdraw from Canada during a delay in extending railroad service to the province. He also encouraged the province of Prince Edward Island to become part of Canada. Dufferin later served as British ambassador to Egypt, France, Italy, Russia, and Turkey. He was *viceroy* (ruler) of India from 1884 to 1888.

Dufferin was born in Florence, Italy. His given and family name was Frederick Temple Blackwood. He received his title in 1888.   Jacques Monet

Dufy, *dyoo FEE,* **Raoul,** *ra OOL* (1877-1953), was a French artist best known for his lively, decorative paintings. Dufy used bright colors and a simple style to portray a happy, carefree world. His subjects included landscapes, festivals, horse races, and figures. Dufy also illustrated books and made woodcuts. He also designed fabrics, tapestries, and theater costumes and sets.

Dufy was born in Le Havre. In 1900, he settled in Paris,

Water color (1932); the Baltimore Museum of Art, Saidie A. May Collection

Dufy's *Le Haras du Pin* shows the bright colors, sketchy details, and cheerful subject matter that typified his work.

where he painted briefly in the impressionist style. Dufy first attracted attention when he exhibited brightly colored pictures with the fauves (see **Fauves**). He then came under the influence of cubism but found that style too severe. By 1920, Dufy had developed his own personal style.   Willard E. Misfeldt

Du Gard, Roger Martin. See **Martin du Gard, Roger.**

Dugong, *DOO gahng,* is a plant-eating mammal that lives in the shallow, warm coastal waters of the Red Sea and the Indian Ocean, as far south as Australia. The dugong has a blunt, rounded snout with a bristly upper lip. Its whalelike body has a notched tail. The dugong uses its flippers to swim and to push sea grass near its mouth. Most dugongs are brownish or grayish. The male has two long upper tusks, and the ends of the upper jaw bend downward. The female gives birth to one

WORLD BOOK illustration by Donald C. Meighan

The dugong is a rare sea mammal.

calf at a time. Dugongs may grow about 10 feet (3 meters) long and weigh up to 650 pounds (295 kilograms).

Since the early 1900's, the dugong population has sharply declined. Laws protect the species in many areas. But many people still hunt the dugong for its hide, meat, and oil.

Scientific classification. The dugong is in the family Dugongidae and belongs to the order Sirenia. It is *Dugong dugon.*

Michael A. Bigg

See also **Manatee; Sea cow; Sirenia.**

Dugout. See **Boating** (Early boats); **Ship** (picture: Prehistoric and ancient Egyptian ships).

Duisburg, *DYOOS boork* (pop. 518,260), is a trading and manufacturing city in the Ruhr region of Germany (see **Germany** [political map]). It is the largest inland port of Western Europe. The city is built on the point where the Ruhr River flows into the Rhine and is connected with north German ports by the Rhine-Herne Canal. It is a gateway to the factories and mineral deposits of the Ruhr region. The city produces almost half of Germany's iron and steel. Duisburg's other products include chemicals, silks and woolens, soap, and tobacco.

Peter H. Merkl

Dukakis, *doo KAHK ihs,* **Michael Stanley** (1933-   ), was the Democratic presidential nominee in 1988. He lost the election to his Republican opponent, Vice President George Bush. Dukakis was serving his third term as governor of Massachusetts while he campaigned for the presidency. Before becoming governor, he had been elected to the Massachusetts House of Representatives four times.

Early life. Dukakis, the son of Greek immigrant parents, was born on Nov. 3, 1933, in Brookline, Mass. He graduated from Swarthmore College. From 1955 to 1957, he served in the U.S. Army in Korea. Dukakis earned a law degree from Harvard Law School in 1960.

In 1963, Dukakis married Katharine (Kitty) Dickson (1936-   ). They have three children—John (1958-   ), Mrs. Dukakis' son from a previous marriage; Andrea (1965-   ); and Kara (1968-   ).

Political career. In 1962, Dukakis was elected to the Massachusetts House of Representatives. He won reelection in 1964, 1966, and 1968. In 1970, he was nominated for lieutenant governor of Massachusetts, but the ticket was defeated.

Dukakis was elected governor of Massachusetts in 1974, defeating incumbent Francis W. Sargent. Under Dukakis, an estimated $500 million deficit in the state budget was eliminated. But many Massachusetts Democrats were dissatisfied that Dukakis had increased taxes and had cut spending on social programs. He lost the 1978 gubernatorial primary election to Edward J. King, who went on to victory in the general election.

Dukakis faced King again in the 1982 gubernatorial primary. He defeated King and then won the general election against Republican John W. Sears. Dukakis was reelected in 1986. During these terms as governor, Dukakis established a reputation as an effective manager and problem solver. He offered incentives to businesses that participated with the state government on such social programs as job training for welfare recipients. He also increased state tax revenues through stricter, more aggressive collection of taxes.

The 1988 Democratic National Convention nominated Dukakis for President and Senator Lloyd Bentsen of Texas for Vice President. Dukakis and Bentsen were defeated by Bush and his running mate, Senator Dan Quayle of Indiana. For the electoral vote, see **Electoral College** (table).

Dukakis was criticized for his handling of state finances in the late 1980's, at a time when Massachu-

Dukakis Headquarters
Michael Dukakis

setts was encountering severe financial difficulties. A decline in tax revenues and a sluggish state economy had led to large budget deficits. In 1989, Dukakis announced that he would not seek reelection as governor in 1990.

Robert L. Turner

See also **Democratic Party; Bentsen, Lloyd M., Jr.**

Dukas, *dyoo KAH,* **Paul Abraham** (1865-1935), was a French composer, music teacher, critic, and editor. He became best known for *The Sorcerer's Apprentice* (1897), written in a lively symphonic form called a *scherzo.* Dukas was a master of orchestration. He has been praised for the clarity of his music and for his ability to produce a variety of tone colors from different combinations of instruments.

Dukas was born in Paris. He taught at the National Conservatory of Music in Paris for several years. He also served as a music critic and prepared for publication and performance works by such composers as Ludwig van Beethoven, François Couperin, Jean-Philippe Rameau, and Domenico Scarlatti. Dukas composed only a few works in addition to *The Sorcerer's Apprentice.* They include the overture *Polyeucte* (1891), *Symphony in C* (1897), the opera *Ariadne and Bluebeard* (1907), and the ballet *The Peri* (1912). Vincent McDermott

Duke is a European title. It comes from the Latin word *dux* (leader), and is the title next highest to *prince.* In England, there are few dukes outside the royal family, where the sons have the title of Royal Duke. The wife of a duke is a *duchess,* the oldest son is a *lord* with the rank of *marquess,* and younger sons and daughters are called *lords* and *ladies.*

In early days, a duke was a leader in battle, and sometimes a ruler as well. The first English duke was the

Black Prince, oldest son of Edward III, who was made Duke of Cornwall in 1337. *Archduke* was a title used by members of the royal family of Habsburg from 1453 until the end of World War I. Marion F. Lansing

Duke, James Buchanan (1856-1925), an American businessman and philanthropist, organized the American Tobacco Company (now American Brands, Inc.) in 1890. He set up the Duke Endowment in 1924. He also gave funds to schools, hospitals, orphanages, and the Methodist Church. He was born near Durham, N.C. See also **Duke Endowment; Duke University.** J. R. Craf

Duke Endowment is a trust fund established in 1924 by James B. Duke, an American businessman. Its purpose is "to make provision in some measure for the needs of mankind along physical, mental, and spiritual lines." The original gift was about $40 million. Income of the endowment is distributed to specifically named beneficiaries in North and South Carolina. They include Duke University, Davidson College, Furman University, and Johnson C. Smith University; nonprofit hospitals and child care institutions; and rural United Methodist churches and retired United Methodist ministers. The endowment's main offices are at 200 S. Tryon Street, Charlotte, NC 28202. For assets, see **Foundations** (table).

Critically reviewed by the Duke Endowment

Duke University is a private coeducational school in Durham, N.C. It offers undergraduate programs in arts and sciences and engineering. It also has a graduate school and schools of business administration, divinity, forestry, law, and medicine. Courses lead to bachelor's, master's, and doctor's degrees.

The university library contains more than 6 million books and manuscripts. Duke Hospital is a noted teaching and training institution. The 7,200-acre (2,910-hectare) Duke Forest serves as a laboratory for the School of Forestry. The marine laboratory near Beaufort, N.C., is used for training and research in marine biology and oceanography.

The school originated in 1838 as an academy. It became Union Institute in 1839, and in 1859 it was renamed Trinity College. The school is named for the family of James B. Duke, a tobacco millionaire. His endowment in 1924 helped the college become a leading university. For the enrollment of Duke University, see **Universities and colleges** (table).

Critically reviewed by Duke University

Dukenfield, William Claude. See Fields, W. C.
Dukhobors. See Doukhobors.
Dulcimer, *DUHL suh muhr,* is a stringed musical instrument that produces soft, sweet sound. It is used chiefly to play folk songs.

There are two types of dulcimers. The *hammered dulcimer* has two or more strings of various lengths, which the player strikes with curved wooden hammers. The strings are stretched across a flat, trapezoid-shaped box. The *plucked dulcimer,* also called the *mountain dulcimer* or *Appalachian dulcimer,* is shaped like an hourglass or a teardrop. It has three or four strings. The player plucks or strums the strings with one hand and controls the pitch by pressing them down with the other. Dulcimers are traditionally held on the player's lap. They also may be hung from a strap around the neck or laid on a table.

The hammered dulcimer was invented in Arabia or

Persia about 5,000 years ago. The plucked dulcimer developed in the United States during the 1800's from dulcimers brought by European immigrants. Dulcimers gained widespread new popularity during the American folk music movement of the 1960's.   Melvin Berger

Dulles, *DUHL uhs,* **John Foster** (1888-1959), an American lawyer and diplomat, enjoyed a long and distinguished career in helping formulate the foreign policies of the United States. He won international acclaim in 1951 as the chief author of the Japanese peace treaty. He also negotiated the Australian, New Zealand, Philippine, and Japanese security treaties in 1950 and 1951. In 1953, Dulles became the 52nd secretary of state of the United States, serving in the Cabinet of President Dwight D. Eisenhower. He held this post until 1959, when he resigned because of poor health.

Dulles was born in Washington, D.C. He graduated from Princeton University, and received a law degree from George Washington University. His books include *War, Peace, and Change* (1939) and *War or Peace* (1950). Dulles helped in the formation of the United Nations. He later was a United States UN delegate. Dulles served as a United States senator from New York in 1949.

F. Jay Taylor

Duluth, *duh LOOTH* (pop. 92,811), is a city in northeastern Minnesota. It lies on the western shore of Lake Superior and St. Louis Bay. For location, see **Minnesota** (political map). Duluth and Superior, Wis.—which lies across the bay—are part of a metropolitan area with a population of 266,650. Duluth is built on a steep slope that rises about 800 feet (240 meters) above the shore of Lake Superior.

Duluth is a transportation center for products of the upper Midwest. The Duluth-Superior harbor is a major Great Lakes port. It is connected to the Atlantic Ocean by way of the St. Lawrence Seaway. It is the busiest freshwater port in North America. More than 110 docks are located along the 47 miles (76 kilometers) of harbor frontage. Port facilities include iron ore docks, coal docks, and grain elevators. An unusual feature of the port is a picturesque lift bridge that passes over the Duluth ship canal. The ship canal was constructed in 1871 by cutting through a sand bar called Minnesota Point. It was built to provide access to the Minnesota portion of St. Louis Bay.

Iron ore and coal are the chief products shipped from Duluth to other parts of the United States. Grain is the main international export. Important industries in Duluth include machine shops; paper mills; and printing, publishing, and meat-packing operations. Duluth is a major medical center. Duluth International Airport, freight railroads, and interstate and regional highways serve the city. Duluth is the seat of St. Louis County. It has a mayor-council form of government.

Duluth and its surrounding area make up an attractive vacation center. Skyline Parkway along the heights of the city offers scenic views of Duluth, Superior, and Lake Superior. The city has favorable conditions for summer and winter sports. The average temperature in July is 65° F. (18° C), and the average temperature in January is 6° F. (−14° C). The city's steep slope is the setting for the Spirit Mountain ski area. St. Louis Bay and the open lake are used for sailing. Duluth is close to good hunting and fishing areas. The city is the gateway to the scenic North Shore of Lake Superior.

Duluth has a symphony orchestra, community theater, and professional ballet company. The Depot—a restored railroad terminal—houses several community museums, the St. Louis County Historical Society, and the Lake Superior Museum of Transportation. The city is the home of the Duluth campus of the University of Minnesota and the College of St. Scholastica.

Duluth was named in honor of Daniel Greysolon, Sieur Duluth (or Du Lhut), a French explorer and trader who visited the site about 1679. In the 1700's, British traders replaced the French traders in the area. In 1817, John Jacob Astor's American Fur Company started a trading post at Fond du Lac, in what is now western Duluth. More people began to come to the area in the 1850's. Duluth was incorporated as a city in 1870. The population fell in the mid-1870's, and Duluth lost its status as a city. By about 1880, Duluth began to grow swiftly, as lumbering and sawmill activities increased. It was incorporated as a city again in 1887. Another period of growth began in the 1890's, when iron ore shipping developed.   Gordon L. Levine

Duma, *DOO muh,* was the name given to various legislative assemblies in Russia during the time when the czars ruled the country. *Duma* is a Russian word that can be translated as *a place for thinking.*

The most famous Duma was the lower house of an assembly that Czar Nicholas II established as a result of the Russian Revolution of 1905. He had no use for elected assemblies, but feared that there would be more revolts if he did not give the people a chance to participate in the government. The complicated laws on the election of the Duma gave voting rights to most men, but to no women. The voters were divided into four classes. Each class elected a certain number of members to electoral colleges, which chose members of the Duma. This voting structure was intended to give more weight to conservative voters who supported the

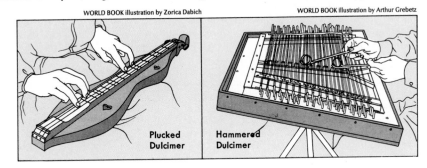

Types of dulcimers

The *plucked dulcimer* has three or four strings and is played with the fingers. The *hammered dulcimer* has two or more strings of various lengths, which are stretched across a trapezoid-shaped box. The player strikes the strings with curved wooden hammers.

WORLD BOOK illustration by Zorica Dabich   WORLD BOOK illustration by Arthur Grebetz

Plucked Dulcimer

Hammered Dulcimer

czar. In addition, laws passed by the Duma were to take effect only if approved by the czar and an upper house that he controlled.

The first Duma opened in 1906. But its members opposed the government so strongly that Nicholas dissolved it after 40 meetings and called for new elections. The second Duma, which opened in 1907, was no more cooperative. Nicholas dismissed it after a few months.

The electoral laws were changed in June 1907 to give still more weight to conservative voters. As a result, the third Duma was elected later in 1907. It cooperated with the czar's government, approving laws on important matters such as farm reform and education. This Duma completed its five-year term. A fourth Duma, similarly conservative, then was elected in 1912.

After World War I began in 1914, the fourth Duma became increasingly critical of Nicholas' leadership. In February 1917, when riots broke out in the Russian capital, Duma leaders formed a committee that pressed Nicholas to pass his power to a provisional government led by Duma members. Nicholas did this and gave up his throne. But the Duma no longer had much popular support and never met again.   Robert H. McNeal

See also **Nicholas II** (of Russia).

Dumas, *doo MAH,* **Alexandre,** *a lehk SAHN druh,* **père** (1802-1870), was a French novelist and playwright. His son was the French author Alexandre Dumas *fils* (son). *Père* means *father* in French. Dumas chose unusual real characters for his novels and plays. He often used their memoirs for historical detail and changed their lives into exciting tales of adventure.

Dumas is best known for his famous romantic novels *The Three Musketeers* (1844) and *The Count of Monte Cristo* (1844-1845). Dumas continued the story of *The Three Musketeers* in *Twenty Years After* (1845) and *The Viscount of Bragelonne* (1848-1850).

Although Dumas is best known for his novels, his plays are more important in the history of French literature. Dumas created two types of plays, the historical drama and the contemporary drama set in his own time. Dumas's historical plays include *Henry III and His Court* (1829) and *The Tower of Nesle* (1832). His first contemporary drama was *Antony* (1831). All three are melodramatic stories of passion and murder. These plays were among the earliest and most successful plays of the French romantic movement (see **Romanticism**). *Kean* (1836), one of Dumas's best-known plays, is about the English Shakespearean actor Edmund Kean, who lived during the early 1800's. It treats the nature of dramatic genius and the actor's alienation from society.

Dumas had many collaborators. The one who helped him the most was August Maquet. He wrote many novels with Dumas, including *The Three Musketeers,* though scholars disagree about how much Maquet contributed to them. Dumas also wrote histories, travelogues, and memoirs.

Dumas tried to shape his works to changing literary tastes. But during France's Second Empire (1852-1870), the quality of his work and his popularity fell. He was born in Villers-Cotterêts.   Thomas H. Goetz

Dumas, *doo MAH,* **Alexandre,** *a lehk SAHN druh,* **fils** (1824-1895), was a French writer. His father was the French author Alexandre Dumas *père* (father). *Fils* is the French word for *son.*

Dumas was born in Paris, the illegitimate son of Dumas *père.* The shame of illegitimacy caused the younger Dumas much suffering. It helps to explain his concern with the victims of society and his emphasis on stable family life in his works.

Dumas wrote both novels and plays, but his fame rests chiefly on his plays. His first play, *The Lady of the Camellias* (often called *Camille*), was a great success when performed in 1852. The tragic love story is set in the fashionable Parisian society of Dumas's time. The author based the play on his novel of the same name, which was published in 1848. Giuseppe Verdi used the story for his opera *La Traviata.*

Dumas came to believe that plays should teach social and moral lessons. He defended the family in *The Wife of Claude* (1873), *Denise* (1885), and *Francillon* (1887). Although he attacked wickedness, he also asked forgiveness for those who repent—as in *The Ideas of Madame Aubray* (1867). His plays, therefore, have a preaching tone, unpopular with many readers today. But the plays are well-constructed and often witty, and give a good picture of French upper-class society of his time.

Thomas H. Goetz

See also **Dumas, Alexandre,** *père.*

Du Maurier, *doo MAWR ee ay,* is the name of a family of English writers, artists, and actors.

George Louis Palmella Busson du Maurier (1834-1896) is known chiefly for his novels *Peter Ibbetson* (1892) and *Trilby* (1894). *Peter Ibbetson* is a tale of two lovers who could meet only in their dreams. *Trilby* is a story about artists in Paris. Trilby, the heroine, is an artist's model under the influence of Svengali, a hypnotist. Through hypnotism, she becomes a great singer. But she loses her power when Svengali dies.

George Du Maurier was born in Paris. He became an accomplished artist in black-and-white. He illustrated his own stories and those of many notable authors.

Sir Gerald du Maurier (1873-1934), the son of George du Maurier, was born in London. Gerald was an actor-manager who specialized in playing gentleman criminals in plays such as *Raffles* and *Bulldog Drummond.* He starred in the popular dramatic adaptation of *Trilby* and also played Shakespearean roles.

Daphne du Maurier (1907-1989), the second daughter of Gerald du Maurier, wrote several popular romantic novels tinged with adventure or mystery. *Rebecca* (1938) is a suspense novel about a young wife's experiences in a strange mansion that is dominated by the spirit of her husband's first wife.

Daphne du Maurier wrote two sea stories, *Jamaica Inn* (1936) and *Frenchman's Creek* (1941). Her other novels include *My Cousin Rachel* (1952), *The Glassblowers* (1963), and *The House on the Strand* (1969). She also wrote *Myself When Young* (1977), an autobiography. She was born in London and was married to Lieutenant General Sir Frederick Browning.   Harold Orel

Dumbarton Oaks, *duhm BAHR tuhn,* was the name of an international conference held in August-October 1944 at Dumbarton Oaks, an estate in Washington, D.C. The name was also given to the proposals agreed upon at the conference. Thirty-nine delegates from the United States, Great Britain, and the Soviet Union met to discuss plans for the creation of an international organization to be called the *United Nations.* After six weeks of talks, the Soviet delegates, as agreed in advance, left, and delegates from Nationalist China replaced them.

The conference gave more attention to establishing ways to deal with "the maintenance of international peace and security" than it did to setting up agencies to handle economic and social problems. The delegates agreed that provision must be made for the peaceful settlement of international disputes and for the power to enforce decisions. Their main achievement was the planning of a Security Council as the chief agency for settling conflicts and enforcing UN resolutions dealing with matters of war and peace among member states. Most provisions of the Dumbarton Oaks Proposals were put into the UN charter.   Robert J. Pranger

See also **San Francisco Conference; United Nations** (The Dumbarton Oaks Conference).

Dumont, Gabriel (1838-1906), served as military leader of the North West Rebellion, a revolt against the Canadian government in 1885. He helped Louis Riel lead the *métis* (persons of mixed white and Indian ancestry) in a fight for land rights. Riel was the métis' political head.

Dumont was born in Assiniboia, in what is now southern Manitoba. In the early 1870's, he moved to Saskatchewan. In 1873, Dumont became leader of a métis settlement in Saint Laurent, near Duck Lake. The métis surveyed their property by the traditional French system. Settlers laid out lots in strips so that most bordered a river or a

Public Archives of Canada
Gabriel Dumont

lake. But the Canadian government surveyed land in square lots and rejected the métis surveys. This dispute became the chief cause of the 1885 revolt.

In March 1885, Riel and Dumont formed a temporary government for the métis in Saskatchewan. Dumont's forces defeated mounted police at Duck Lake. Fighting between the métis and Canadian forces ended in May 1885, after Dumont's defeat at nearby Batoche. Dumont escaped. Several years later, the Canadian government granted him amnesty.   P. B. Waite

See also **North West Rebellion; Riel, Louis.**

Dún Laoghaire, *duhn LAIR uh* (pop. 54,715), is a town on the east coast of Ireland. It lies 7 miles (11 kilometers) southeast of Dublin (see **Ireland** [map]). *Dún Laoghaire* means *the fort of Laoghaire* in Gaelic. Laoghaire was an Irish king in the A.D. 400's. Dún Laoghaire is a residential area for people who work in Dublin. It is also a regional shopping center and has some light industries. In addition, it is a center of fishing, yachting, and other tourist activities. Ferries sail from Dún Laoghaire to Great Britain. The town has some Victorian architecture, but most of its buildings are modern.

Originally called Dunleary, the town was renamed Kingstown in 1821. Its development dates from the construction of its large harbor, begun in 1817. In 1834, a railway connected the town to Dublin. The town was named Dún Laoghaire in 1920. In 1930, it joined other nearby towns to form a borough.   Desmond A. Gillmor

Dunant, *doo NAHN,* **Jean Henri,** *zhahn ahn REE* (1828-1910), a Swiss banker, was the founder of the International Red Cross. As a young businessman, he accidentally saw the battle of Solferino in 1859. He was shocked at the lack of care given the wounded. His book, *Recollections of Solferino* (1862), influenced the rulers of Europe tremendously, and in 1863 the Permanent International Committee was organized in Geneva. In 1864, delegates of 16 countries agreed to the Geneva Convention for the treatment of wounded and prisoners (see **Geneva Conventions**). Dunant went bankrupt and for 15 years his whereabouts was unknown. He was found in 1890, living in an almshouse, and in 1901 shared the first Nobel Peace Prize. He was born in Geneva. See also **Red Cross** (History).   Alan Keith-Lucas

Dunbar, Paul Laurence (1872-1906), was one of the most popular American poets of the 1890's and early 1900's. He was perhaps the first black American to become nationally popular as a writer of both poetry and fiction. From 1896 to 1905, Dunbar published 12 books, more than any black American before 1950.

Dunbar wrote poetry in standard English about traditional poetic subjects and about the heroes of black Americans. In some of these poems, he experimented with metrical forms and rhyme schemes. He also wrote comic and sentimental poetry in dialect about black and white Americans. Editors of Dunbar's time preferred his dialect poetry and stories about former black slaves who seemed carefree, comic, and loyal to their former masters. Dunbar satisfied the demands of the editors but expressed fear that he would be remembered only as a writer of "a jingle in a broken tongue."

Some modern readers criticize Dunbar for not condemning racial stereotypes and discrimination against black Americans. In his poetry, Dunbar usually limited his racial concerns to themes praising blacks rather than attacking whites. He pointed out racial injustices bitterly or satirically in his essays and in such works as *The Strength of Gideon and Other Stories* (1900) and *The Sport of the Gods* (1902), a novel. Dunbar was born in Dayton, Ohio, the son of former slaves.

Bettmann Archive
Paul Dunbar

Darwin T. Turner

Duncan I, *DUHNG kuhn* (? -1040), succeeded his grandfather, Malcolm II, as king of Scotland in 1034. William Shakespeare's play *Macbeth* portrays the events in his life in a distorted manner (see **Macbeth**). Unsuccessful efforts to expand his kingdom marked Duncan's reign. He also failed to rule all Scotland. Macbeth of Moray, who had a claim to the throne by right of his wife, killed Duncan in a battle near Elgin.   Robert S. Hoyt

Duncan, *DUHNG kuhn,* **Isadora** (1877-1927), an American dancer, greatly influenced dancing in the 1900's. She rebelled against the rigid, formal training of classical ballet and created an individual form of expression. Influenced by the art of Greece, she often danced barefoot in a loose, flowing tunic. Duncan's dancing was

The Dance Collection, New York Public Library

Isadora Duncan was strongly influenced by classical Greek culture. She usually danced barefoot in a flowing tunic.

inspired mainly by literature and classical music. She based her first dances on poetry. Duncan also used images and forms taken from painting and sculpture. She found further inspiration in nature, and she used dance to mirror natural forms such as waves.

Isadora Duncan was born in San Francisco. She gained great success in Europe, where she first performed in 1899. She lived abroad during most of her career and established schools of dance for children in France, Germany, and Russia. Duncan's ideas inspired later generations to seek their own forms of dance expression.   Selma Landen Odom

See also **Dancing** (Modern dance).

Duncan, Robert (1919-1988), was an American poet. He was associated with a group of writers who worked during the 1950's at Black Mountain College, an experimental school in Black Mountain, N.C. These poets, including Robert Creeley and Charles Olson, are sometimes called the *Black Mountain poets.* Duncan was also a major figure in the *San Francisco Renaissance,* a cultural and artistic movement that occurred in the 1950's.

Duncan wrote hymns, lyrics, sonnets, and other forms of verse. He also wrote a verse play. Some of his works combine prose and poetry.

Duncan's most important early collections of poems include *The Opening of the Field* (1960) and *Roots and Branches* (1964). In these and several other works, he used religious and symbolic material, as well as references to Greek, Roman, and other ancient mythologies. In his later works, Duncan increasingly dealt with political and social issues. For example, in the collection *Bending the Bow* (1968), he attacked American participation in the Vietnam War. Many of Duncan's later poems were collected in *Ground Work: Before the War* (1984). Duncan was born in Oakland, Calif.   Clark Griffith

Dundee (pop. 177,674) is a major industrial center of Scotland and one of its largest cities. Dundee lies in east-central Scotland on the Firth of Tay—an arm of the North Sea. For location, see **Scotland** (political map).

Landmarks of Dundee include a huge civic building called Caird Hall, an old castle called Dudhope Castle, and the University of Dundee. Two bridges cross the firth, connecting Dundee with the other bank.

Dundee's many industries include shipping, and the manufacture of candy, marmalade, and gunny sacks and other items made from jute. Other products include cash registers, computers, tires, and watches.

Dundee has been an important trading center since the Middle Ages. It grew rapidly during the 1800's, and what was then the world's largest jute industry was established there. During the 1900's, the importance of Dundee's jute products industry and some other traditional industries declined. But a number of new industries have been established in the city.   H. R. Jones

Dune is a mound or ridge of loose sand that has been deposited by the wind. Dunes are common in all sandy regions. They are found along seacoasts, near rivers and lakes, and in deserts. Dunes may be long and narrow or shaped like a crescent. Some have three or more ridges that extend from a high central peak. In some areas, large dunes reach heights of 1,000 feet (300 meters).

Most dunes are found in large groups known as *dune fields.* Extremely large areas of dunes in the Sahara and other large deserts are called *sand seas.* Many dunes migrate across the land as the wind removes sand grains on one side of the dune and deposits them on the other side. Migrating dunes can block highways, bury houses, and destroy agricultural land.

Notable dune areas in the United States include Cape Cod in Massachusetts, Indiana Dunes State Park in Indiana, and Great Sand Dunes National Monument in Colorado. Others are White Sands National Monument in New Mexico and Death Valley National Monument and the Imperial Valley, both in California.   Wayne Lambert

See also **Desert; Sahara** (picture); **National Park System** (picture: Death Valley National Monument).

Dung beetle. See Scarab.

Dunham, *DUHN am,* **Katherine** (1912-   ), an American dancer and *choreographer* (dance creator), became noted for her interpretations of the dances of blacks of the West Indies and the United States. She

New York Public Library

Katherine Dunham became known for her choreography of black dances from throughout the world. Dunham and her company danced on Broadway in *A Tropical Revue* (1943), *above.*

made extensive studies of dances of Jamaica. In the late 1930's and early 1940's, Dunham served as a dancer and choreographer in motion pictures and stage musicals. She organized her own dance company, touring the United States and Europe with ballets which were based on African and Caribbean ceremonial and folk dances. Dunham operated her own school of dance.

Dunham was born in Chicago. She studied anthropology at the University of Chicago both as an undergraduate and a graduate student. Dunham described her experiences in Jamaica in *Journey to Accompong* (1946). Her autobiography, *A Touch of Innocence,* was published in 1959.   Selma Landen Odom

Duniway, Abigail Jane Scott (1834-1915), was a leader of the campaign for women's voting rights in the Pacific Northwest. Her efforts helped achieve *suffrage* (voting rights) for women in three states—Idaho in 1896, Washington in 1910, and Oregon in 1912.

Abigail Jane Scott was born in Tazewell County, Illinois. Her family moved to Oregon when she was 17 years old. In 1853, she married Benjamin C. Duniway, a farmer. He was injured nine years later and became an invalid. For several years, Mrs. Duniway supported her husband and their six children by operating a women's hat shop in Albany, Ore. During this time, she became increasingly aware of the unequal treatment of men and women by the law.

Oregon Historical Society
Abigail Duniway

In 1871, Mrs. Duniway moved her family to Portland, Ore. For the next 16 years, she published *The New Northwest,* a weekly newspaper that demanded equal rights for women. In 1873, Mrs. Duniway helped found the Oregon State Woman Suffrage Association. She continued to work for women's rights for most of her life.   Jesse L. Gilmore

Dunkerque, *DUHN kuhrk* (pop. 73,120; met. area pop. 200,000), is a French seaport and industrial center and the site of a dramatic Allied evacuation during World War II. Dunkerque—which is also spelled *Dunkirk* and *Dunquerque*—lies in northern France, where the English Channel meets the North Sea. For location, see **France** (political map).

Dunkerque has an excellent harbor and is one of the busiest ports in France. It is also a major center for petroleum refining and steel processing. Other industries include food processing, shipbuilding, and ship repair.

Dunkerque was founded by Saint Eloi in the A.D. 600's. By the 1500's, it had become a leading French port. In late May of 1940—during World War II—Germany won control of Belgium from the Allies. On May 26, thousands of British and French troops, and some Belgian troops, began retreating from Belgium to Dunkerque. Germany attacked the city and it was badly damaged. But from late May until June 4, more than 800 vessels evacuated about 338,000 Allied troops from Dunkerque to England. The vessels included cruisers,

Wide World
The escape from Dunkerque in 1940 became one of the most famous events of World War II. Allied ships and other vessels carried nearly 350,000 retreating troops to safety in England.

destroyers, gunboats, minesweepers, fishing boats, motorboats, and yachts. The evacuation ranks as one of the best-planned military movements in history. It has been called the Miracle of Dunkerque.   Mark Kesselman

See also **World War II** (The invasion of the Low Countries).

Dunkers. See Brethren, Church of the.

Dunlap, William (1766-1839), has been called the father of American drama. He was the first professional playwright in America, the first to produce his own plays, and the first to champion the cause of the native dramatist. He was also the first to adapt plays from the French and German, and his *History of the American Theatre* (1832) is the earliest account of the American stage. Of the 56 plays attributed to him, 27 are originals and 29 translations or adaptations. Dunlap's best-known original plays include *André* (1798), *Leicester* (1806), and *A Trip to Niagara* (1828).

Dunlap also wrote biographies and a valuable source book, *History of the Rise and Progress of the Arts of Design in the United States* (1834). He was also a successful painter. Dunlap was born in Perth Amboy, N.J.

Frederick C. Wilkins

Dunlop, John Boyd (1840-1921), a Scottish veterinarian, developed the *pneumatic* (air-filled) *tire.* He made the first ones to replace solid rubber tires on his son's tricycle so it would ride more comfortably. Dunlop's tire was tested and patented in Great Britain in 1888 and in the United States in 1890. He sold his tire patent and company in 1896.   Smith Hempstone Oliver

Dunne, *duhn,* **Finley Peter** (1867-1936), was an American humorist and journalist. He created the character of Mr. Dooley, an Irish Roman Catholic owner of a tavern in Chicago. Dooley expressed Dunne's social and political views in over 700 newspaper sketches from 1893 to 1919. In a comic Irish dialect, Dooley criticized American foreign policy, social fads, politicians, overly enthusiastic reformers, and the follies he saw in labor and management. As a neighborhood philosopher and independent businessman, Dooley became a spokesman for conservative older Americans.

Dunne was born in Chicago and had a personal background similar to that of Mr. Dooley. Dunne spent much of his adult life working as a newspaper and magazine editor.   Sarah Blacher Cohen

Dunning, John Ray (1907-1975), an American physicist, did research work that was important in developing the atomic bomb. Dunning produced high-energy particles for changing atoms of one kind into atoms of another kind, by using a cyclotron (see **Cyclotron**). With the cooperation of Alfred O. Nier, who separated small quantities of U-235 and U-238 from uranium, Dunning, E. T. Booth, and A. V. Grosse proved that slowly moving neutrons can cause U-235—but not U-238—to *fission,* or split (see **Uranium** [Radioactivity and fissionability]). Dunning also found that the neutron had magnetic properties.

Dunning pioneered in research on the discharge of neutrons from uranium fission. During World War II, he directed research in isotope separation which was put into large scale use at Oak Ridge, Tenn.

Dunning was born in Shelby, Nebr., and was graduated from Nebraska Wesleyan University. He received his Ph.D. degree at Columbia University. Dunning began teaching physics at Columbia in 1935. He was Dean of the School of Engineering and Applied Science at Columbia from 1950 until 1969.   Ralph E. Lapp

Duns Scotus, *duhnz SKOH tuhs,* **John** (1265 or 1266-1308), was one of the greatest theologians and philosophers of the Middle Ages. His ideas on God, knowledge, salvation, and the nature of being influenced many thinkers of the late Middle Ages.

According to tradition, Duns Scotus was born in Duns, Scotland, and entered the Franciscan religious order as a youth. His most important work was the *Opus Oxoniense* (*Oxford Work*). The book grew out of lectures Duns Scotus presented at Oxford University on *The Four Books of Sentences*, an influential medieval theological book by Peter Lombard. Duns Scotus also produced commentaries on Aristotle's ideas on logic and wrote *Quaestiones quodlibetales* (*Various Disputations*), which examines a variety of controversial philosophical and theological questions.

Duns Scotus also became known for his defense of the doctrine of the Immaculate Conception. According to this doctrine, the Virgin Mary was conceived free of original sin. His defense contributed to its recognition, centuries later, as an official doctrine of the Roman Catholic Church.   William J. Courtenay

See also **Scholasticism** (History).

Dunsany, Lord (1878-1957), wrote more than 50 books, including collections of stories, a novel, and an autobiography. He is remembered today for his tales, and for such plays as *The Gods of the Mountain* (1911) and *A Night at an Inn* (1916).

Dunsany's best work is in his short pieces and all his writings tend toward the form of the ironic fable. His writings often deal in the supernatural, and he invented his own mythology—"heavens and earths, and kings and peoples and customs, just as I need them." Nevertheless, his works show the influence of Oriental, Biblical, and classical literature.

Lord Dunsany was born Edward John Moreton Drax Plunkett in London of Irish parents. He was also a noted sportsman and soldier.   Martin Meisel

Dunstan, *DUHN stuhn,* **Saint** (909?-988), was an English religious reformer, statesman, and archbishop of Canterbury. He acted as an adviser to a number of kings of Wessex—a kingdom in southern England—including Kings Edmund, Edred, and Edgar. Dunstan also helped revive English monasteries by rebuilding them and by strengthening discipline among their residents. Many monasteries had been destroyed by the Danes, who had invaded England during the 800's. Dunstan also worked to unify England by helping make peace with Danes who lived in northern England.

Dunstan was born near Glastonbury. About 943, King Edmund made him abbot of a monastery at Glastonbury. In 956, Dunstan was banished from Wessex by King Edwig, whose conduct Dunstan had criticized. But Dunstan returned to Wessex after Edgar gained power there. Edgar made Dunstan bishop of London in 958 and archbishop of Canterbury in 959. Dunstan's feast day is May 19.   William J. Courtenay

Duodecimal numerals, *DOO uh DEHS uh muhl,* form a numeration system based on 12. The Romans, to whom the number 12 was sacred, used the duodecimal system in dividing the foot and pound into twelfths and the year into months. The words *inch* and *ounce* come from a Latin word meaning *twelfth.* The system used by merchants in counting by the dozen and by the gross (12 dozen or 144) is called a duodecimal system. The word *dozen* comes from a Latin word meaning *twelve.* Some writers argue that a duodecimal system could be used more easily than the decimal system, because 12 has more factors than 10.   John M. Smith

See also **Numeration systems.**

Duodenum. See **Stomach.**

Duplex. See **Housing** (Kinds of housing).

Duplicate bridge. See **Bridge** (Duplicate bridge).

Duplicator is a machine that makes copies of typed, printed, or handwritten matter or of illustrations. Printing and the use of carbon paper may be considered forms of duplicating. But the term *duplicator* usually refers to office equipment that makes copies of letters, forms, and similar items quickly and inexpensively. Duplicators may also be called *duplicating machines.*

There are several kinds of duplicators. They differ in size, price, quality of reproduction, and the number of copies they can produce. Three of the most common duplicating machines are the spirit duplicator, the stencil duplicator, and the offset duplicator. All of these machines require the preparation of a *master,* a special form from which copies are made.

Machines called *photocopiers* do not need a master to make copies. They duplicate originals—or even copies of originals—that appear on ordinary paper (see **Photocopying**).

Spirit duplicators are simple, inexpensive machines that make from 30 to 300 copies of an original. Many schools and small firms use them.

The material to be copied is typed on a paper master that is backed by another sheet of paper. The second sheet contains a waxy, dye-impregnated substance. The master is placed facedown on a drum on the duplicator. Blank sheets of paper are moistened in an alcohol-based solution and pressed against the master. The solution dissolves a portion of the dye in the image and transfers it to the copy paper in the form of the original typing.

This duplicator got its name from the alcohol in the solution.

Stencil duplicators are small, simple machines that can make from 10 to 5,000 copies. The most widely used stencil duplicator is a machine called a *mimeograph*. A strong, plastic-coated sheet is used as a master. A typewriter usually is used to cut through the coating, creating a path through which ink can flow. The master is placed in the machine on an ink-filled cylinder covered with an ink pad or belt. A roller presses a piece of paper against the master. The pressure squeezes ink from the pad, through the cuttings on the master, onto the paper. A digital stencil duplicator, which automated the duplicating process, was introduced in 1989.

Offset duplicators use the principle of offset printing (see **Offset**). A grease-base image is put on a paper or metal master by typing, printing, writing, or drawing. After the master has been made, it is placed on a drum in the duplicator. The master is inked on one cylinder and the image is transferred to a blanket cylinder. Then, the image is duplicated on a sheet of paper forced between the blanket cylinder and an impression cylinder. Businesses, schools, and churches use offset duplicators to make thousands of copies inexpensively.

Eileen Feretic

See also **Edison, Thomas A.** (picture: Mimeograph machine).

Du Pont, Éleuthère Irénée, *eh luh TYAYR ee ray NAY* (1771-1834), founded a gunpowder company in 1802 that was the forerunner of the present-day Du Pont Company. Throughout the 1800's, the firm was known as the premier gunpowder and explosives manufacturer in the United States.

Du Pont was born in Paris. His father was Pierre Samuel du Pont de Nemours, a well-known French economist. In 1799, Irénée emigrated to the United States. While on a hunting trip, he recognized the need for low-cost, quality gunpowder in his adopted country. Du Pont erected his gunpowder works near Wilmington, Del. The firm's sales increased steadily between 1804 and 1811. The sharp rise in demand accompanying the War of 1812 helped guarantee the company's success.   John A. Heitmann

Du Pont Company, officially E. I. du Pont de Nemours & Company, is one of the world's largest manufacturers and marketers of chemicals and chemical products. The company is also a supplier of energy resources. It has about 125 plants in the United States, and affiliates in Canada and other countries. These plants make industrial films and paints, plastics, X-ray film, electronic products, health-care products, pesticides, and a wide variety of basic chemicals. Other Du Pont products include such synthetic textile fibers as nylon, polyester, and acrylic. The company's headquarters are in Wilmington, Del.

Du Pont's energy subsidiary, Conoco Incorporated, explores for and produces crude oil and natural gas. Conoco's refineries manufacture a wide variety of petroleum products.

Éleuthère Irénée du Pont, a student of the famous French chemist Antoine Lavoisier, founded the company in 1802. At first the company made only gunpowder, but in 1880 it began producing high explosives. In 1890, Du Pont started producing a smokeless explosive based on nitrocellulose. It then became interested in the many useful applications of cellulose (see **Cellulose**). The company began manufacturing lacquers, adhesives, finishes, and plastics. Since the early 1900's, Du Pont has rapidly enlarged its list of products and product lines. Today, the company manufactures about 40,000 different products.

During World War II (1939-1945), Du Pont designed, built, and operated a $350-million center at Hanford, near Richland, Wash., for the manufacture of plutonium (see **Plutonium**). In 1950, Du Pont agreed to design, build, and operate the Savannah River plant in South Carolina for the Atomic Energy Commission. Other developments since the war include Orlon acrylic fiber, Dacron polyester fiber, Kevlar aramid fiber, and Teflon fluorocarbon resin.   Critically reviewed by the Du Pont Company

See also **Du Pont, Éleuthère Irénée; Manufacturing** (table).

Du Pont de Nemours, *doo PAHNT duh nuh MUR,* **Pierre Samuel** (1739-1817), was a French economist and statesman. His son, Éleuthère Irénée du Pont, founded what is now the Du Pont Company.

Du Pont was born in Paris. He first studied medicine but then turned to economics. He became famous as a member of a group of economists known as the *physiocrats,* who believed that governments should interfere less in economic life. The physiocrats also began the first organized study of how economies work. Du Pont wrote extensively on physiocratic doctrines, and he had a major impact on French economic policies at the time.

Du Pont got caught in political conflicts during the French Revolution (1789-1799). He fled with his family to the United States in 1799.   Barry W. Poulson

Duralumin, *du RAL yuh muhn,* is a term for any one of a group of aluminum-copper alloys. A typical duralumin alloy is made up of about 95 per cent aluminum, 4 per cent copper, 0.5 per cent magnesium, and 0.5 per cent manganese. Some duralumin alloys also include a small amount of silicon or iron. Duralumin has strength and lightness and is used in making aircraft parts and heavy-duty equipment. The term is obsolete in the United States but is used in other countries.

I. Melvin Bernstein

Durant, *duh RANT,* **Will** (1885-1981), was an American historian, philosopher, and educator. He first won recognition in 1926 for his *The Story of Philosophy.* He began his major historical series, *The Story of Civilization,* in 1935. Volumes in this series consist of *Our Oriental Heritage, The Life of Greece, Caesar and Christ, The Age of Faith, The Renaissance, The Reformation, The Age of Reason Begins, The Age of Louis XIV, The Age of Voltaire, Rousseau and Revolution,* and *The Age of Napoleon.* His wife, Ariel, was coauthor of the last five volumes. Durant described the artistic, intellectual, and spiritual developments of each period. William James Durant was born in North Adams, Mass.   Edwin H. Cady

Durant, *duh RANT,* **William Crapo** (1861-1947), an American manufacturer, became known as the "godfather" of the automobile industry. He outlined the principles of mass production, low costs, wide distribution, and increased profits. He organized General Motors Company in 1908 and lost control of it in 1910. He regained control in 1916, and the company was incorporated as General Motors Corporation. Durant was forced to resign from the corporation in 1920. He organized the Chevrolet Motor Company in 1911, but lost control of the company in 1920. He organized Durant Motors, Inc., in 1921, but it went bankrupt. Durant was born in Boston.   R. E. Westmeyer

Durante, *duh RAN tee,* **Jimmy** (1893-1980), was an American entertainer. Born James Francis Durante in New York City, he began his career playing the piano. His comic singing and clowning won him fame in vaudeville, the theater, nightclubs, movies, radio, and television. Durante made his large nose the object of many jokes and became known as the *Schnozzle.* In 1951, he received a Peabody Award for television entertainment. The entertainer's biography, *Schnozzola: The Story of Jimmy Durante,* was written by Gene Fowler.   Gerald Bordman

A. D. Cushman & Assoc.

Jimmy Durante

Duranty, *du RAN tee,* **Walter** (1884-1957), was a *New York Times* correspondent from 1913 to 1941. He also wrote novels, history, and books about his newspaper experiences. Duranty covered the French army in World War I, and was the *Times* Moscow correspondent from 1921 to 1934. A series of articles on the Soviet Union earned him a Pulitzer Prize in 1932. He was born in Liverpool, England.   John Eldridge Drewry

Durban, *DUR buhn* (pop. 677,760; met. area pop. 960,792), is the chief eastern seaport in South Africa. It is the largest city of Natal Province (see **Natal**). For location, see **South Africa** (political map).

Durban is a trading and industrial center and the most important resort city of South Africa. Durban is the most English of South Africa's cities in both language and culture. South Asians outnumber whites, however. Most Africans in Durban are Zulus. Durban was founded in 1834.   Bruce Fetter

Dürer, *DYUR uhr,* **Albrecht** (1471-1528), was the most famous painter and printmaker in the history of German art. He also became famous as a scholar and author. Dürer was the first writer to describe the concept of artistic genius and the first to publish scientific literature in German.

Dürer's published works include books on geometry and perspective, civil defense, and the measurements of the human body. In his studies on artistic theory, Dürer tried to explain idealized beauty as well as ugliness, and differences in human personality and appearance.

Dürer was born in Nuremberg. Between the ages of 13 and 40, he painted and drew a remarkable series of revealing self-portraits. He also wrote a travel diary and many letters, and completed a history of his family begun by his father. These self-portraits and writings have enabled historians to learn more about Dürer as a person than about any other northern European artist of his time.

Dürer's most famous oil paintings include *Self-Portrait* (1500); an altarpiece for the Church of the Germans in Venice, called *The Feast of the Rose Garlands* (1506); and

Four Apostles (1526), which was painted for the Nuremberg city hall. One of his most popular pictures is a brush drawing called *Praying Hands* (1508), which was a study for part of an altarpiece for a church in Frankfurt (am Main).

The Prado, Madrid

Albrecht Dürer (self-portrait)

Dürer was the first major artist to paint realistic water colors from nature. The best known of his nature studies include several landscapes done in the Austrian Alps and Italian Alps and scenes from the area around Nuremberg.

As a printmaker, Dürer created many woodcuts, most dealing with religious subjects. Some of his engravings portray traditional Christian subject matter. Other engravings picture Greek and Roman myths and allegories. In these prints, Dürer introduced idealized nude figures into German art. Dürer was also one of the first printmakers to experiment with etching.

Jane Campbell Hutchison

For examples of Dürer's work, see **Painting** (What do painters paint?); **Bookplate; Engraving; Four Horsemen of the Apocalypse; Horse** (Horses in history).

Durham, *DUR uhm* (pop. 86,700), is a fortress town in northern England. It stands on a hill that is almost completely surrounded by the River Wear. Durham Cathedral, which was begun in 1093, is a fine example of Norman architecture. Many tourists visit Durham to see the cathedral, as well as a Norman castle that houses the University of Durham.   M. Trevor Wild

Durham, *DUR uhm,* N.C. (pop. 100,538), is a tobacco-manufacturing and textile center in the northeastern part of the state. With Raleigh, it forms a metropolitan area of 561,222 people. For location, see **North Carolina** (political map). Cigarettes, smoking tobacco, machinery, and cotton goods are manufactured in Durham. Durham is the home of Duke University and North Carolina Central University.

Durham was settled in the 1850's. In 1865, General Joseph E. Johnston surrendered his Confederate army to Union General William T. Sherman at the Bennett Place, just west of the city. Durham has a council-manager form of government. It is the seat of Durham County.   Richard Jones

Durham, *DUR uhm,* **Earl of** (1792-1840), was a British political leader and governor general of Britain's Canadian colonies. A government report that he wrote about Canada in 1839 has long been considered an important document in Canadian history. But a number of scholars have shown that the report had little effect on Britain's policies toward its Canadian colonies.

Durham served as governor general of Canada for about four months. He went there in 1838 to investigate the causes of rebellions in the colonies of Upper Canada and Lower Canada (see **Rebellion of 1837-1838**). Durham resigned when the British Parliament disagreed with his mild punishment of the rebels.

After returning to Britain, Durham wrote his *Report on the Affairs of British North America.* The report

Paumgartner Altarpiece; Pinakothek, Munich, Germany (SCALA/Art Resource)

Dürer's *The Nativity* shows the influence of Italian Renaissance painting in its use of perspective and proportion. The picture is the central panel of an altarpiece completed in 1503.

urged the government to unify Upper and Lower Canada and to give the Canadian colonies self-government in local affairs. These proposals were later adopted. But they originally had been suggested by other people, and Durham's report was largely disregarded by the British Parliament.

Durham was born in London. His full name was John George Lambton. He was elected to Parliament in 1813. Durham became a Cabinet member in 1830 and helped write the Reform Bill of 1832. The reform bill gave most men of the middle class the right to vote. Durham served as a diplomat in Russia in 1832 and from 1835 to 1837. Lambton became Earl of Durham in 1833.

J. M. Bumsted

Durkheim, *DURK hym,* **Émile,** *ay MEEL* (1858-1917), was a French sociologist. His theories and writings helped establish the foundations of modern sociology. Durkheim disagreed with most social theorists of the late 1800's because they thought that individual psychology was the basis of sociology. Durkheim regarded sociology as the study of the society that surrounds and influences the individual. Durkheim explained his theories in his book *The Rules of Sociological Method* (1895).

In *The Division of Labor* (1893), Durkheim developed the theory that societies are bound together by two sources of unity. He called these sources *mechanical solidarity* and *organic solidarity.* Mechanical solidarity refers to similarities that many people in the society share, such as values and religious beliefs. Organic solidarity results from the division of labor into specialized jobs. Durkheim believed that the division of labor makes

people depend on one another and thus helps create unity in a society.

Durkheim studied thousands of cases of suicide to demonstrate his theory that a person commits suicide because of the influence of society. He explained this theory in *Suicide* (1897).

Durkheim was born in Épinal, France. He studied at the École Normale Supérieure in Paris and taught sociology at the University of Bordeaux and at the Sorbonne in Paris.   Neil J. Smelser

See also **Mythology** (Mythology and society).

Durocher, *duh ROH shehr,* **Leo** (1906-   ), became one of the most colorful figures in baseball. Durocher was known for his fiery temper, both as a player and, later, as a manager. He managed three National League pennant winners, the Brooklyn Dodgers in 1941 and the New York Giants in 1951 and 1954. The 1954 Giants swept four straight games from the Cleveland Indians in the World Series.

Leo Ernest Durocher was born in West Springfield, Mass. From 1928 to the early 1940's, he played in the majors as a shortstop with the New York Yankees, Cincinnati Reds, St. Louis Cardinals, and Dodgers. He managed the Dodgers from 1939 to 1946 and for part of the 1948 season. He managed the Giants from 1948 to 1955, the Chicago Cubs from 1966 to 1972, and the Houston Astros in 1972 and 1973.   Herman Weiskopf

Durrell, *DOOR uhl,* **Gerald** (1925-   ), is an English naturalist and author. He is best known for his work in wildlife preservation and his books on animals. Durrell describes his experiences with animals in light-hearted stories. Many are popular with young readers.

Durrell was born in Jamshedpur, India, of British parents. He was educated in Europe by private tutors. In 1947, Durrell began a career of leading zoological expeditions. He traveled to Cameroon, Madagascar, Mexico, Australia, and other places to collect animals for zoos in Europe and North America. Durrell began writing to help finance his expeditions. His first book was *The Overloaded Ark* (1953).

In the mid-1950's, Durrell decided to create his own zoo. He opened his zoo in Jersey, England, in 1959, and dedicated it to breeding endangered species. This zoo is known as the Jersey Zoological Park, and it is now operated by the Jersey Wildlife Preservation Trust. Durrell has written more than 30 books, including *A Zoo in My Luggage* (1960) and *The Stationary Ark* (1976). He also wrote *The Amateur Naturalist* (1983) with his wife, Lee.

Deborah A. Behler

Durrell, *DOOR uhl,* **Lawrence** (1912-   ), is an English novelist, travel writer, and poet. He is best known for his series of four novels called *The Alexandria Quartet.* The *Quartet* consists of *Justine* (1957), *Balthazar* (1958), *Mountolive* (1959), and *Clea* (1960). The novels are noted for their ornate language, unusual characters, and vivid descriptions of the Mediterranean Sea and the city of Alexandria, Egypt, during the late 1930's. Durrell describes a series of love affairs as viewed by the leading characters with different perspectives on what makes up the truth of their experience. Durrell champions all forms of love in the *Quartet,* but sees its expressions as leading to tragedy and despair.

Durrell was born in Darjeeling, India. He has lived most of his life in the eastern Mediterranean. His first novel, *The Black Book* (1938), reveals the influence of his close friend, the American novelist Henry Miller. Durrell describes life on the islands in and near Greece in *Prospero's Cell* (1945), *Reflections on a Marine Venus* (1953), *Bitter Lemons* (1957), and *The Greek Islands* (1978). He narrates a tour through the island of Sicily in *Sicilian Carousel* (1977). Durrell's poetry appears in *Collected Poems, 1931-1974* (1980).   Michael Seidel

Dürrenmatt, *DOO ruhn maht,* **Friedrich,** *FREE drihsh* (1921-   ), is a Swiss dramatist and novelist. Many of his plays are tragicomedies notable for their odd and arresting effects. His work shows a fascination with strange and paradoxical situations and characters. Dürrenmatt presents the world of his time in a state of decay and corruption. But some of his characters speak for his conviction that courage and goodness are possible. In his best-known play, *The Visit* (1956), the main character eventually atones for his own guilt, though he is surrounded by moral decay. Dürrenmatt also wrote *Romulus the Great* (1949), *The Marriage of Mr. Mississippi* (1952), *The Physicists* (1962), and *Play Strindberg* (1969). Dürrenmatt's fiction includes *Traps* (1956) and *The Pledge* (1958). Dürrenmatt was born near Bern.
Siegfried Mews

Duryea brothers, *DUR yay* or *DUR ee ay,* were two automobile pioneers. Charles E. Duryea (1861-1938) and J. Frank Duryea (1869-1967) built the first successful gasoline-powered car in America. Their one-cylinder model made a trial run in 1893 in Springfield, Mass. A second model they built won the $2,000 first prize in the Chicago *Times-Herald* race on Thanksgiving Day in 1895. This was the nation's first gasoline-automobile race. The brothers formed the Duryea Motor Wagon Company in Springfield in 1895, and produced 13 cars in 1896.

In 1898, Frank Duryea joined the Stevens Arms Company. There, he designed the four- and six-cylinder Stevens-Duryea automobiles. Charles was born in Canton, Ill., and Frank in Washburn, Ill.   William L. Bailey

Du Sable, *du SAH bul,* **Jean Baptiste Point** (1745-1818), a black American pioneer, was the first known settler to build a house and open a trading post in what became Chicago. His name is also spelled Sable, De Sable, and De Saible.

Du Sable was probably born in Haiti. He came to the Chicago area during the 1770's. He made friends with the Indians, and married a Potawatomi Indian. He had a farm near Peoria in 1773. Du Sable built a log cabin on the north bank of the Chicago River about 1779. He operated his trading post in part of the cabin, and became rich trading with the Indians.
Edgar Allan Toppin

Detail of an aquatint by an unknown artist. Courtesy of Chicago Historical Society

Jean du Sable

See also **Chicago** (History).

Duse, *DOO zay,* **Eleonora,** *eh leh aw NAW rah* (1859-1924), an Italian actress, has been called "the greatest actress of her time." Duse seemed to live her parts instead of act them. Critics praised her natural and sincere act-

ing. Although shy, Duse felt at home on the stage.

Gabriele D'Annunzio wrote some of his best plays for her, including *La Gioconda* and *Francesca da Rimini* (see **D'Annunzio, Gabriele**). He fell in love with her and wrote a book, *The Flame of Life* (1900), based on their love story. She went into retirement for almost 20 years because of this book. She was one of the first major actresses to act in Henrik Ibsen's plays *Hedda Gabler* and *The Lady from the Sea.* She also acted in *Camille* and *Cavalleria Rusticana.*

Duse was born on a train while her actor parents were traveling in Italy. At 14, she played Juliet in *Romeo and Juliet.* She made several successful tours in the United States and other countries.   Richard Moody

Dushanbe, *doo SHAHN buh* (pop. 539,000), is the capital and largest city of the Tadzhik Soviet Socialist Republic in the Soviet Union. It lies in a cotton-growing valley at the foot of the Gissar Range of the Tian Shan mountains. For location, see **Union of Soviet Socialist Republics** (political map). Dushanbe is the scientific, cultural, and educational center of the republic. Much of the republic's industry is centered in the city. Dushanbe's products include silk, textiles, processed foods, and machinery. Hydroelectric stations that are located nearby supply power to the city and also to metals and chemical plants in the vicinity.

Dushanbe was established in 1926 by the merger of three small villages. In 1929, the government changed the city's name to Stalinabad in honor of the Soviet dictator Joseph Stalin. During the "destalinization" campaign of 1961, the name was changed back to Dushanbe.
Leslie Dienes

Düsseldorf, *DOOS uhl dawrf* (pop. 561,686), is a commercial and industrial city in Germany. It lies on the Rhine River (see **Germany** [political map]).

Düsseldorf has many beautiful buildings, parks, and gardens, and fashionable shops. Landmarks include St. Lambertus Church, a Gothic structure built in the 1200's; and the town hall, which dates from the 1500's. Düsseldorf is the home of a well-known art academy and a medical school. The city has a large harbor that is a base for important shipping and tourist cruise industries. Other industry includes banking, commerce, and the manufacture of chemicals, iron, and steel.

Düsseldorf was chartered as a city in 1288, though settlements existed on the city's present site as early as the 700's. Allied bombing raids during World War II (1939-1945) badly damaged many sections of the city. But the damaged areas were soon rebuilt.   Peter H. Merkl

Dust is made up of small particles of all kinds of solid matter. A speck of true dust is smaller than $\frac{1}{1,000}$ of a millimeter ($\frac{4}{100,000}$ of an inch). Coarser dust may be as large as $\frac{5}{1,000}$ of a millimeter ($\frac{2}{10,000}$ of an inch).

The greatest part of all ordinary dust in the atmosphere consists of mineral matter picked up by the wind. It comes from such places as bare soil, crumbling rock ledges, mud flats, and plowed fields.

Volcanic dust is a special kind of dust that comes from volcanoes. Explosions of volcanoes change solid lava into powder and spray liquid lava into the air, forming tiny drops and shreds of glass. Volcanoes have spread large amounts of their dust over the earth.

Dust deposits. True dust is repeatedly picked up by the wind or washed into streams. Coarser dust settles rapidly. Two kinds of dust deposits cover hills and valleys. One is volcanic dust. The other is ordinary mineral dust blown from the bare mud flats that once lay in front of the great ice sheets covering North America and Europe. The rich soil called *loess,* found in Europe, Asia, and North America, is made of such dust (see **Loess**).

Importance to human beings. Condensing water vapor settles on dust particles and forms water droplets. When these droplets unite with others, rain or snow may form (see **Rain**). Dust also may keep many of the sun's rays from reaching the earth.

Large amounts of mineral dust are always in the air of some quarries, mines, and factories. This dust may collect in workers' lungs and cause a disease called *silicosis* (see **Silicosis**). Dust also can serve as a carrier for disease bacteria. The spore stages of some disease bacteria can be thought of as dust particles themselves. The same is true of certain mold spores and the pollens which produce hay fever, asthma, and other allergies.

Ernest E. Wahlstrom

See also **Dust Bowl; Dust storm; Air** (Particles in the air); **Air cleaner.**

Dust Bowl refers to a series of destructive wind and dust storms that struck the United States during the 1930's. These storms ranked among the worst environmental disasters in world history. Most of the damage occurred from 1935 to 1938 in the southern Great Plains, and so this area also became known as the Dust Bowl. Altogether, the storms damaged about 50 million acres (20 million hectares) of land, mainly in Colorado, Kansas, New Mexico, Oklahoma, and Texas. An additional 50 million acres were endangered before conservation measures began to take effect.

The soil of the Dust Bowl had become dry and loose by the early 1930's. This occurred partly because much

AP/Wide World

Dust storms of the 1930's, such as the one above, blew the powdery topsoil away in great clouds. The droughts that contributed to the dust storms damaged crops in most of the Southwest and Great Plains, causing great hardship.

The Dust Bowl, an area of the Great Plains, was formed by severe dust storms of the 1930's. Dust storms swept across other parts of the Great Plains during the 1950's, 1960's, and 1970's.

of the area's natural grassland was converted to wheatland during the early 1900's. But the wheat, as it was grown then, did not adequately protect the ground against winds. In addition, the remaining grasslands were destroyed through the grazing of too much livestock. Furthermore, a drought that lasted seven years began in 1931. Thus, the soil was easily eroded and blown when strong winds whipped through the region.

Dust storms had struck the Great Plains before, but they were never as large and destructive as those of the 1930's. One of the first major storms struck in May 1934. It carried about 350 million short tons (318 million metric tons) of dirt all the way to the East Coast. About 40 big storms swept through the Dust Bowl in 1935, with dust often reducing visibility to less than a mile (1.6 kilometers).

Most of the storms came in the spring. At that time, the snow had melted, the winds were unusually strong, and the new crops were not big enough to hold the soil. Many people and animals caught in the open during the storms had their lungs badly damaged or became lost. Dirt had to be shoveled out of houses and away from barn doors. Cars and farm machines were ruined. The region's agricultural economy was wrecked as farmers could find little to harvest. One of the most dramatic results was the mass departure of thousands of bankrupt and discouraged farm families, many of whom went to California to seek a better life. *The Grapes of Wrath* (1939) by John Steinbeck describes the unhappy plight many of these migrants faced.

The federal government sent aid to the Dust Bowl. The Soil Conservation Service, which was set up in 1935, taught farmers ways to slow erosion and protect the soil. In addition, more than 18,500 miles (29,800 kilometers) of trees were planted in small belts to break the force of the winds. As the crisis passed, however, many farmers abandoned the protective farming methods. During droughts in the 1950's and the 1970's, dust storms again damaged the region.   Donald Worster

Additional resources

Ganzel, Bill. *Dust Bowl Descent.* Univ. of Nebraska Press, 1984. A photographic comparison of the Great Plains in the 1930's and 1970's.
Hurt, R. Douglas. *The Dust Bowl: An Agricultural and Social History.* Nelson-Hall, 1981.
Low, Ann M. *Dust Bowl Diary.* Univ. of Nebraska Press, 1984. Life in North Dakota during the 1930's.
Worster, Donald E. *Dust Bowl: The Southern Plains in the 1930's.* Oxford, 1979.

Dust devil is a whirling column of air. It is caused by the rising of an overheated layer of air near the ground. Dust devils occur most frequently in deserts, where the sun heats the air near the dry ground to a high temperature. The motion of the air as it rises can often be seen because it may carry sand and dust 1,000 feet (300 meters) or more above the earth.   Margaret A. LeMone

Dust explosion occurs when a cloud of burnable dust is ignited, causing an intense release of energy. Such explosions can damage property and kill people.

Explosive dust clouds can be produced by certain industrial operations. Common dusts that explode include those of cereal grains, coal, cocoa, cotton, pigment, sugar, and wood. Even metal dusts can explode.

A dust explosion begins with the ignition of a small group of dust particles in a concentrated dust cloud. These particles ignite nearby particles which, in turn, ignite others. The heat spreads until a fireball engulfs the entire cloud. The burning cloud produces large amounts of energy and expanding gas. If the exploding cloud is in a confined space, such as a silo or other building, pressure builds rapidly, and the explosion can cause great damage.

In the past, explosions of coal dust and grain dust caused more property damage and loss of life than did any other kinds of dust explosions. Today, the coal-mining industry and other industries control dust clouds to reduce explosions.   Norman J. Alvares

Dust storm is a strong, turbulent wind that carries fine particles of clay, silt, and other earthy material for long distances. The particles are swept up and remain suspended in the air during a dust storm. Most of the particles measure less than $\frac{1}{500}$ inch ($\frac{1}{16}$ millimeter) in diameter. Dust storms occur where the ground has little or no protective vegetation because of low rainfall, grazing, or poor farming practices. Dust storms play an important role in soil erosion.

A dust storm may cover hundreds of miles and rise to a height of more than 10,000 feet (305 meters). It carries as much as 4,000 short tons of dust particles per cubic mile of air (875 metric tons per cubic kilometer). Winds of at least 25 miles per hour (40 kilometers per hour) are associated with dust storms.

In the United States, a dust storm is reported when blowing dust reduces visibility below $\frac{5}{8}$ mile (1 kilome-

ter). During the 1930's, parts of Colorado, Kansas, New Mexico, Oklahoma, and Texas were hit by dust storms that resulted from soil erosion. Today, dust storms occur in parts of northern Africa, Asia, and Europe.
          Richard A. Dirks

See also **Dust Bowl; Shelter belt.**

Dutch. See Netherlands.

Dutch Antilles. See Netherlands Antilles.

Dutch East India Company was a powerful trading company that helped establish Dutch rule in what is now Indonesia. In 1602, the Dutch government granted the company a monopoly on trade between Asia and the Netherlands. The company also received broad governmental and military powers, including the right to rule territories and to wage war in Asia.

By 1700, the company had gained control of the cinnamon, clove, and nutmeg trade in the East Indies. It had trading posts in many Asian countries and ruled parts of what are now South Africa and Sri Lanka and most of present-day Indonesia.

In the 1700's, the demand for textiles from India, tea from China, and coffee from Arabia and Java exceeded that for spices. The Dutch East India Company had strong competition from the English East India Company and other traders. The Dutch company lost money and was disbanded in 1799.   John E. Wills, Jr.

See also **East India Company; Indonesia** (History); **Netherlands** (History); **South Africa** (History).

Dutch East Indies. See Indonesia (History).

Dutch elm disease is a severe disease of the elm tree. It is caused by a fungus carried by the native elm bark beetle and the smaller European bark beetle. It can

WORLD BOOK illustration
by Oxford Illustrators Limited

The European bark beetle is one of the two kinds of beetles that spread Dutch elm fungus disease from tree to tree.

cause the death of a large elm in four to eight weeks.

Dutch elm disease usually begins with a wilting of the younger leaves in the upper part of the tree. Later, lower branches become infected. By midsummer, many of the leaves turn yellow and then brown, and they curl and drop off. Some of the leaves remain attached to twigs. When diseased branches are cut, long brown streaks can be seen beneath the bark.

The best way to control Dutch elm disease is to plant disease-resistant elms. But few varieties of elms are immune to all strains of the fungus. The use of insecticides that control the beetles helps limit the spread of the disease. Spraying the trees with fungicides is not very effective. Many cities and towns have ordinances that require the removal of diseased trees.

Dutch elm disease is so called because the Dutch first

observed it in the Netherlands in 1919. It became known in the United States in 1930 and was limited to an area close to New York City. The disease now afflicts elm trees throughout the nation. Jerry T. Walker

Dutch Guiana. See Suriname.

Dutch language. See Netherlands (People).

Dutch oven is a covered metal cooking pot. Modern Dutch ovens are usually made of aluminum. American pioneers used a cast-iron Dutch oven with a rimmed lid. The pot was set on hot coals, and coals were also placed on the lid. Brick ovens in fireplaces and chimneys are sometimes called Dutch ovens.

Dutch pins. See Bowling (History).

Dutch Reformed Church. See Reformed Church in America.

Dutch West India Company was formed by Dutch merchants and chartered by the government of the Netherlands in 1621. The company was given trading and colonizing privileges for a period of 24 years in North America, the West Indies, and Africa. The colony of New Netherland included parts of what are now the states of New York, New Jersey, Delaware, and Connecticut. The colony was founded by the Dutch West India Company and had headquarters in New Amsterdam (now New York City). See also **New Netherland; Patroon system.** J. Salwyn Schapiro

Dutch West Indies. See Netherlands Antilles.

Dutchman's-breeches, also called *white heart,* is a small, delicate plant with flattened, heart-shaped flowers. This perennial grows from Nova Scotia to Georgia and west to Nebraska. It is also found in Washington and Oregon. The plant has lacy, fernlike leaves. The stems of the plant are brittle and contain a watery sap. The stem grows from an underground tuber (see **Tuber**).

Dutchman's-breeches gets its name from the shape of its flowers. Each leafless flower stalk has four to ten nodding fragrant flowers that look like baggy trousers hanging upside down. The flowers are waxy white or pinkish-white with yellow tips.

WORLD BOOK illustration by Robert Hynes

Dutchman's-breeches

Scientific classification. Dutchman's-breeches is a member of the fumitory family, Fumariaceae. It is *Dicentra cucullaria.*

Robert W. Hoshaw

Duty, in economics. See **Customs; Tariff.**

Duvalier, *doo vahl YAY,* **François,** *frahn SWA* (1907-1971), was the president of Haiti from 1957 until his death in 1971. Duvalier ruled as a dictator and allowed no one to oppose him. He was elected to a seven-year term as president in 1957. In 1961, before his term ended, he declared himself reelected. He was elected president for life in 1964 by the National Assembly, whose members he had selected.

Duvalier was a physician and an authority on voodoo, a kind of religion practiced by most Haitians. He used the Haitian peasants' fear of voodoo to maintain his power (see **Voodoo**). Many peasants believed he had magical powers. Duvalier also controlled the armed forces and a feared secret police force that the people call the *Tontons Macoutes* (bogeymen).

Duvalier was born in Port-au-Prince, Haiti. He graduated from the National University of Haiti medical school in 1934. He was secretary of labor and public health in 1949 and 1950, and adviser to a public health commission from 1952 to 1954. After François Duvalier died, his son—Jean-Claude Duvalier—became president. Jean-Claude also ruled as a dictator. Rebels overthrew his government in 1986, and he fled from Haiti. See **Haiti** (History). Thomas G. Mathews

Duvoisin, *dyoo vwah ZAN,* **Roger Antoine** (1904-1980), was a children's artist and illustrator. He won the 1948 Caldecott Medal for his illustrations for *White Snow, Bright Snow,* written by Alvin Tresselt. Duvoisin wrote and illustrated several popular children's books, including the *Petunia* and *Veronica* series. He also illustrated the *Happy Lion* series written by his wife, Louise Fatio. Duvoisin was born in Geneva, Switzerland, and moved to the United States in 1927. He became a U.S. citizen in 1938. He wrote and illustrated his first children's book, *A Little Boy Was Drawing,* for his son in 1932. Jill P. May

Dvina River, *dvee NAH,* is the name of two rivers in the Soviet Union. One, called the Western Dvina or Daugava, rises west of Moscow and flows into the Gulf of Riga at Riga, Latvia. This river is 633 miles (1,019 kilometers) long.

Another river, the Northern Dvina, is an important waterway in the northwestern part of the Soviet Union. The Northern Dvina, formed by the Sukhona and Vychegda rivers, is 455 miles (732 kilometers) long. It flows into the White Sea at the port of Archangel. Steamboats travel on the Northern Dvina. It is connected to the Neva and Volga rivers by the Northern Dvina Canal. For the location of both of the rivers, see **Union of Soviet Socialist Republics** (terrain map). Theodore Shabad

Dvořák, *DVAWR zhahk,* **Antonín,** *AN TAW nyeen* (1841-1904), was a Czech composer. He and Bedřich Smetana are considered the founders of the Czech national school of music. Dvořák composed in a variety of musical forms, including songs, *chamber music* (compositions played by small groups), choral works, operas, symphonies, and dances. He is best known for his symphony *From the New World* (1893). This work was his ninth and last symphony. However, it is also known as his fifth symphony because Dvořák started numbering his symphonies only after 1880. This symphony is a good example of the non-Germanic romanticism of the late 1800's.

The folk music of the Czechs and other Slavic peoples was the main source of Dvořák's music. Dvořák's songs have passages of powerful dramatic expression and skillful use of melody. His best-known songs include *Moravian Duos* (1876), *Gypsy Melodies* (1880), and *Biblical Songs* (1894). His most famous chamber work is the piano trio *Dumky* (1891). The music in his chamber works, as well as in such orchestral works as the *Carnival* overture (1892), is lyrical and powerful. Dvořák's major choral works include the famous *Stabat Mater* (1876), composed after the death of two of his children; and the oratorio *St. Ludmila* (1886). *Rusalka (The Water-*

Nymph, 1900) is the best of his several operas.

Dvořák was born in Nelahozeves, a small village near Prague. At the age of 16, he went to Prague to study music. The Czech National Theater was founded in 1862, and Dvořák became a viola player in its orchestra. Dvořák began composing at about the same time. He was his own greatest critic, and, in 1873, he burned the scores of most of the works he had composed.

A performance of the cantata *Hymnus* in 1873 marked the first public performance of a Dvořák work. The work received great acclaim. Dvořák soon applied for a *stipend* (grant) offered to musicians by the government. He submitted the score of a symphony to support his application. The judges, including Johannes Brahms, were so impressed by the power of Dvořák's music that they granted him a three-year stipend. This occasion also began a lifelong friendship with Brahms, who used his influence to help get Dvořák's compositions published.

In 1878, Dvořák composed the first set of his well-known *Slavonic Dances.* A performance of it in 1879 in London made Dvořák known in England. Beginning in 1884, Dvořák visited England many times to conduct performances of his orchestral and his choral works.

In 1891, Dvořák became professor of musical composition at the Prague Conservatory. His growing fame and the success of his works in the United States brought him an offer to serve as director of the National Conservatory of Music in New York City. Dvořák held this position from 1892 to 1895. At the same time, he conducted, and he visited Czech and other Slavic settlements in the Midwest.

Dvořák composed *From the New World* while living in the United States. Its popular second movement uses the theme of the black American spiritual, "Goin' Home."

Steven E. Gilbert

Dwarf is an unusually small adult human being, animal, or plant. Human dwarfs who have normal body proportions are also called *midgets.* Other human dwarfs have abnormal proportions. There are several kinds of dwarf animals, including dwarf cattle and toy dogs. Dwarf plants include ornamental fruit trees and several varieties of flowers, such as marigolds and dahlias.

Dwarfism occurs both in individual organisms and in entire groups of organisms. Such groups include African Pygmies, Shetland ponies, and dwarf trees. Dwarfism may result from an inherited defect or from problems that affect a developing baby during pregnancy. A wide variety of diseases, very poor nutrition, or severe emotional deprivation also can interfere with growth.

This article discusses human dwarfism, which occurs as the result of an underdeveloped skeleton. The growth of the bony skeleton depends on the formation of tissue called *cartilage* (see **Cartilage; Bone** [Development of bones]). Dwarfism results when the cartilage cells do not grow and divide properly. Such improper development may occur because of defective cartilage cells or interference with the growth of otherwise normal cartilage cells. Defective cartilage cells cause *chondrodystrophic dwarfism,* in which the defect is restricted to the cartilage cells, or *chromosome-related dwarfism,* in which there is a more widespread cellular disorder. Interference with the growth of normal cartilage cells results in either *hormonal dwarfism* or *nonhormonal dwarfism.*

Chondrodystrophic dwarfism occurs when only certain cartilage cells are defective. The term *chondrodystrophic* means *badly developed cartilage.* Most chondrodystrophic dwarfs have abnormal body proportions. The defective cells occur only in the spine or only in the arms and legs. Consequently, either the *torso* (chest and abdomen) or the limbs grow unusually short.

Chromosome-related dwarfism results when all the cells of the body are defective. Such defects involve a disturbance in the number of *chromosomes* per cell. The chromosomes are the cell structures that contain *genes.* Genes provide the cell with information on how to grow and divide. Each body cell normally has 46 chromosomes. If a cell has an extra chromosome or is missing a part of a chromosome or a whole chromosome, growth may be affected. One such disorder that results in dwarfism is *Turner's syndrome.*

Hormonal dwarfism may occur when a hormone deficiency interferes with the growth of normal cartilage cells. Hormones are chemical substances secreted by various glands. These substances circulate through the blood and influence cells to act in certain ways.

There are three major hormones or hormonelike substances needed for growth: (1) *growth-hormone-releasing hormone* (GHRH) from the *hypothalamus,* a hor-

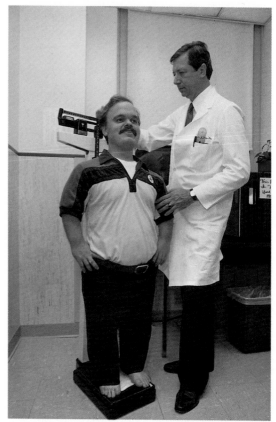

Margaret Thomas, The Washington Post

Dwarfism occurs when the bones' cartilage cells do not grow properly. As a result, such body parts as the arms, legs, and torso may be underdeveloped. This photo shows a dwarf and his physician, who is of normal height.

mone-producing center in the brain; (2) *growth hormone* (GH) from the pituitary gland; and (3) *somatomedin C,* produced by the liver and probably other tissues, including bone and cartilage. GHRH stimulates the pituitary gland to release GH. GH probably stimulates growth in some cells, but more importantly, it stimulates release of somatomedin C. Somatomedin C can accelerate growth in many types of cells. Extreme emotional neglect or abuse produces a reversible form of dwarfism probably by interfering with one or more of these hormones through effects on the nervous system. Other hormones, including *insulin* from the pancreas and *thyroxine* from the thyroid gland, also influence growth.

An individual with a deficiency of any of the major growth-promoting hormones is usually normally proportioned but much shorter than other members of his or her family. Such individuals appear much younger than their actual age and grow at a slower rate than normal. They reach their final height and may become sexually mature in their mid-20's.

Physicians use GH to stimulate growth in some types of patients with subnormal growth. In the past, GH was extracted from human pituitary glands. Today, it is made in the laboratory by genetic engineering methods.

Nonhormonal dwarfism occurs if disease or severely impaired nourishment blunts the growth of cartilage cells. For example, diseases of the bowel or kidneys may interfere with growth. Many nonhormonal and hormonal interferences with growth can be corrected, with rapid "catch-up" growth taking place after treatment. A child who appears to be growing too slowly should be examined by a physician to determine whether the child's growth is normal.   Jesse Roth

See also **Bonsai; Pygmies; Shetland pony; Toy dog.**

Dwarf star. See Star (The size of stars; diagram).

Dwight, John (1635?-1703), was an important early English potter. He developed and manufactured high-quality stoneware at his factory in Fulham, now a London suburb. His stoneware led to the establishment of England as a world center for ceramics production.

Dwight was probably born in Oxfordshire. He settled in Fulham between 1671 and 1673. Dwight took out his first patent for stoneware in 1671. The patent was renewed in 1684 for a hard red stoneware that was a great improvement over earlier English ceramics. Dwight improved his stoneware to the point that he was able to use it to make sculptures. These sculptures included small figures of mythological characters and full-sized portrait heads. The heads marked the peak of English ceramic art in the late 1600's.   John W. Keefe

Dyaks, *DY aks,* are a group of people most of whom live in Sarawak, eastern Malaysia. The name is also spelled *Dayaks* (pronounced *DY aks*). There are two groups of Dyaks—the *Ibans,* also called *Sea Dyaks,* and the *Land Dyaks.* The approximately 350,000 Ibans make up about 31 per cent of Sarawak's population. They live along the seacoast and rivers. The 96,000 Land Dyaks compose about 9 per cent of the population. They live inland and call themselves by the name of their village or locality.

Most Dyaks wear traditional clothing—sarongs for women and brightly colored *loincloths* (cloth wrapped around the hips) for men. However, many Dyaks have adopted Western dress.

Most Dyaks live in bamboo houses called *long houses,* which are built on poles. The floors are from 6 to 15 feet (1.8 to 4.5 meters) above the ground. Long houses measure from 30 to 1,000 feet (9 to 300 meters) long. As many as 50 families may live in one long house, each in a separate room. See **Indonesia** (picture: A Dyak long house).

Most Dyaks are farmers or plantation workers, and their major crop is rice. Some teach school or hold civil service or factory jobs. Others are skilled boat makers or weavers. Most Dyaks follow traditional religions. Some are Christians or Muslims.   Donn V. Hart

M. P. L. Fogden, Bruce Coleman, Ltd.

Dyaks are a Southeast Asian people who mainly live in eastern Malaysia. The group shown above are Ibans, or Sea Dyaks, who live along rivers. Many earn their living by making boats.

Dye is a chemical compound used to produce long-lasting colors in materials. The textile industry uses dyes to color fibers, yarns, and fabrics. Manufacturers also dye food, fur, ink, leather, paper, plastics, and wood. This article discusses textile dyeing.

Until the 1850's, all dyes were made from natural sources, such as various parts of plants or of certain animals. During the late 1800's and early 1900's, chemists developed synthetic dyes. These dyes hold their color better and cost less to produce than natural dyes. Today, industry uses synthetic dyes almost entirely.

How dyes work

A dye must be dissolved before it can work. When textiles are placed into a *dyebath* (dye solution), the fibers absorb the molecules of the dye. These molecules give the fibers the desired color.

Dyed textiles vary in their ability to hold color. However, all textiles can be made *colorfast* to at least some extent. A colorfast fabric does not change color under normal use. For example, a fabric is *lightfast* if it does not fade in sunlight. It is also *washfast* if it keeps its color after being laundered. Such substances as chlorine bleach and perspiration may also affect the colors of fabrics. Many dyes resist color changes from such substances.

To improve the colorfastness of some fabrics, dyers add substances called *mordants* to dyebaths. Mordants combine with the dye molecules and fix them firmly in the fibers. The chief mordants include tannic acid and soluble compounds of such metals as aluminum, chromium, copper, iron, and tin.

Kinds of dyes

Synthetic dyes. The chief kinds of synthetic dyes include (1) acid dyes, (2) azoic or developed dyes, (3) basic dyes, (4) direct dyes, (5) disperse dyes, (6) premetalized dyes, (7) reactive dyes, (8) sulfur dyes, and (9) vat dyes. Pigments are sometimes used to color textiles. But pigments do not dissolve, and so they are not true dyes. Manufacturers use adhesives to fix pigments to fibers.

Acid dyes are dissolved in acid solutions. These dyes give bright colors to nylon, silk, and wool.

Azoic or developed dyes involve a reaction of two colorless chemicals to produce a deeply colored dye in the fiber. This chemical reaction increases brightness and wash-fastness in fabrics made of acrylic, cotton, nylon, and rayon.

Basic dyes are dissolved in alkaline solutions. They provide many brilliant colors and are used on acrylic, wool, and other fibers.

Direct dyes color fibers without the help of a mordant, though salt is used to help achieve deep shades. Dyers use these dyes on such fibers as cotton and rayon.

Disperse dyes dissolve only slightly in water. Dyeing at high temperatures helps dissolve the insoluble dye particles, allowing them to be absorbed into the fibers. Disperse dyes color acetate, acrylic, nylon, and polyester.

Premetalized dyes contain such metals as copper and chromium, which improve colorfastness. Such dyes are widely used on acrylic, nylon, and wool.

Reactive dyes form a strong chemical bond with certain fibers, including cotton, nylon, rayon, and wool. These dyes produce bright, washfast colors.

Sulfur dyes and *vat dyes* are insoluble in water and are dissolved in an alkaline solution. Fibers colored with such dyes also receive an oxygen treatment to help fix the dyes. Vat dyes rank among the most colorfast dyes. Dyers use sulfur dyes and vat dyes chiefly on cotton and rayon.

Natural dyes. Most natural dyes came from such parts of plants as the bark, berries, flowers, leaves, and roots. The madder plant, which grows in Asia and Europe, supplied bright red dyes for many fabrics, including linen and silk. People in many lands obtained *saffron,* a yellow dye, from the crocus plant. They used saffron on such textiles as silk and wool. Natural *indigo,* a dark blue dye, comes from the indigo plant, which grows chiefly in India. Dyers used it on cotton, wool, and other fibers, and it is still used on denim fabrics. *Logwood* is another natural dye that is still used. It comes from a tree that grows in Central America, Mexico, and the West Indies. Logwood supplies black and brown dyes for such materials as cotton, fur, and silk. *Henna,* an orange-brown dye made from a shrub of North Africa and the Middle East, was used to color leather. Henna is sometimes used to dye human hair.

Leading animal dyes included *carmine* and *Tyrian purple.* Carmine, a bright red dye, was made from the dried bodies of an insect of Mexico and Central America. Tyrian purple was a rare, expensive dye that came

from certain shellfish of the Aegean and Mediterranean seas.

Dyeing textile materials

Textiles are dyed at various stages. If textile fibers are dyed before being spun into yarn, the process is called *stock dyeing.* In *yarn dyeing,* or *skein dyeing,* the fibers are dyed after they are made into yarn. Most stock and yarn dyeing takes place in large vats. In *piece dyeing,* manufacturers apply the dyes after the yarn is made into cloth. Piece dyeing is used for most solid-color fabrics. Some dyeing machines pull the cloth through the dyebath. Others have squeeze rolls that force dye into the cloth. Some machines can continuously dye about 100 yards (91 meters) of fabric per minute.

Manufacturers print designs on some fabrics. A machine applies different colors to various areas by means of screens or engraved rolls. These areas form a pattern. See **Silk-screen printing; Textile.**

History

People have dyed fabrics and other materials for more than 5,000 years. Dyers have also used mordants for several thousand years.

In 1856, an English chemist named William H. Perkin discovered the first synthetic dye accidentally. This dye, called *mauve,* is pale purple. Perkin produced mauve when he tried to make quinine from a coal tar product called aniline.

Before World War I (1914-1918), Germany made most of the world's dyes. During the war, the Germans cut off their supply of dyes. As a result, the dye industry in the United States grew rapidly. Since the 1940's, chemists have invented many synthetic textile fibers—and have developed thousands of synthetic dyes to combine with them. United States industries use about 8,000 different synthetic dyes.   Howard L. Needles

Related articles in *World Book* include:

Aniline	Indigo	Madder	Saffron
Batik	Lake (dye)	Mauve	Stain
Catechu	Leather (Final	Mordant	Tie dyeing
Coal tar	processing)	Phoenicia	Turmeric
Color	Logwood	(Trade)	
Henna			

Dyer, Mary (? -1660), a colonist from England, became a martyr to the Quaker faith. With her husband, William, she arrived in Massachusetts about 1635. Because of religious intolerance, they later moved to Rhode Island. In 1650 she returned to England, and joined the Society of Friends, or Quakers. Seven years later, she came back to America. She was arrested repeatedly for "bearing witness to her faith." Finally, in Boston, she was charged with sedition, convicted, and hanged.   Ian C. C. Graham

Dylan, *DIHL uhn,* **Bob** (1941-   ), an American composer, singer, and musician, was the most influential folk-song writer of the early 1960's. His early songs often protested what many people considered the wrongs of society. These songs include "Blowin' in the Wind" (1962) and "The Times They Are A-Changin' " (1963). One of his biggest hits was "Like a Rolling Stone" (1965).

Dylan was born in Duluth, Minn. His given and family name was Robert Allen Zimmerman. In 1961, he moved to New York City to meet his idol, folk singer Woody

Guthrie. During the early part of his career, Dylan accompanied himself on acoustical guitar and harmonica. By the mid-1960's, he was performing with a rock band that used electric guitars.

Dylan has shifted musical directions several times. In the late 1960's and early 1970's, he moved toward country music. In the late 1970's, he wrote music with a Christian message.

Sam Emerson, Sygma
Bob Dylan

He continued to influence songwriters in the 1980's, making music that mixed spiritual and nonreligious themes.   Don McLeese

Dynamics, *dy NAM ihks,* in physics, is the study of objects that change their speed or the direction of their motion because of forces acting upon them. Sir Isaac Newton expressed the relationship of these forces and changes in motion in his second law of motion. This law states that the force applied to an object is equal to the mass of that object multiplied by its acceleration in the direction of the force (see **Force** [Measuring force]; **Motion** [Newton's laws of motion]). See also **Mechanics; Statics.**   James D. Chalupnik

Dynamics, Group. See Group dynamics.

Dynamite is one of the most important industrial explosives. It is used to blast out damsites, canal beds, mines, quarries, and the foundations for large buildings. It also has been used for demolition in warfare.

The principal explosive in dynamite is an oily liquid called *nitroglycerin.* It is mixed with other materials—some explosive and some nonexplosive—and packed in cylinders made of waxed paper or plastics. These cylinders, called *cartridges,* range from $\frac{7}{8}$ to 8 inches (22 to 200 millimeters) in diameter and from 4 to 30 inches (10 to 76 centimeters) in length.

To use dynamite, workers insert an explosive device called a *detonating cap* or *blasting cap* into one end of the cartridge. They place the cartridge in a hole bored into the material to be blasted. Earth is packed around and behind the cartridge. After moving to safety, the workers set off the detonating cap—and the explosion—by means of a fuse or an electric current.

Kinds of dynamite. There are four chief varieties of dynamite: (1) *straight dynamite,* (2) *ammonia dynamite,* (3) *straight gelatin,* and (4) *ammonia gelatin.*

Straight dynamite contains nitroglycerin and an absorbent, chemically reactive mixture, such as wood pulp and sodium nitrate. It is the oldest type and has been replaced by ammonia dynamite for most uses.

Ammonia dynamite is stronger, safer, and cheaper than straight dynamite. It contains ammonium nitrate and produces fewer toxic fumes and cooler gases than other dynamites do. It is called a *permissible explosive,* which means that it can be used safely in mines where extreme heat could ignite dust or gas in the air.

Straight gelatin is made from a stiff gel called *blasting gelatin.* Blasting gelatin consists of nitroglycerin mixed with a small amount of an explosive called *guncotton* (see **Guncotton**). Sodium nitrate and other ingredients

© David R. Frazier
Dynamite has many industrial uses. This silver miner is placing cartridges of the explosive in holes drilled in the mine.

are added to make straight gelatin. Straight gelatin has been replaced by ammonia gelatin for most uses.

Ammonia gelatin is made by adding ammonium nitrate and other ingredients to blasting gelatin. Ammonia gelatin is waterproof. It is used for underwater blasting.

History. Dynamite was invented in 1867 by Alfred Nobel, a Swedish chemist and the founder of the Nobel Prizes. Nobel discovered that *kieselguhr,* a type of chalky earth, absorbed a great deal of nitroglycerin. He found that kieselguhr soaked with nitroglycerin could serve as an explosive that was much less dangerous to handle than pure nitroglycerin. It also was much more powerful than the gunpowder explosives then used for blasting. From his discovery, Nobel developed straight dynamite and blasting gelatin.

In the early 1900's, ammonia dynamite and ammonia gelatin were developed. During the mid-1900's, many blasting operators began to use a mixture of ammonium nitrate and fuel oil, called ANFO, instead of dynamite. They also used *slurry explosives.* Slurry explosives are slushy mixtures of chemicals called *nitrocarbonitrates.* ANFO and slurry explosives are cheaper to use than dynamite but need dynamite or other explosives to detonate them.   James E. Kennedy

See also **Explosive; Fuse; Nitroglycerin; Nobel, Alfred B.; TNT.**

Dynamo. See Electric generator.

Dynamotor, *DY nuh мон tuhr,* is an electric machine that can be used as both a motor and a generator. It can change a direct current (DC) from high to lower voltage, or from low to higher voltage. Transformers can handle only alternating current (AC). The dynamotor might be called a direct-current transformer. Its armature has two windings, and each winding can be used as either a motor winding or a generator winding. Dynamotors are seldom used today. Most have been replaced by electronic *DC to DC converters.* These devices convert the input DC to AC, raise or lower the AC voltage using some form of transformer, and then convert the AC voltage to output DC voltage.   Donald W. Novotny

Dyne, *dyn,* is a unit of force. A dyne is defined as the force that acting upon 1 gram of matter will give it an acceleration of 1 centimeter per second for every second the force acts (1 centimeter per second per second). The dyne is part of the centimeter-gram-second (CGS) system, an early version of the metric system of measurement. In the present metric system, called the International System of Units (SI), the *newton* is used instead of the dyne to measure force (see **Newton**). The dyne corresponds to the *poundal* in the customary, or English, system of measurement.   Leland F. Webb

Dysentery, DIHS uhn TEHR ee, is a disease involving inflammation of the lining of the large intestine. The inflammation, which is caused by microscopic organisms, produces abdominal pain and diarrhea. The bowel movements may contain mucus and blood. Some cases of dysentery include fever or vomiting.

Diarrhea causes people with dysentery to lose fluids and salts necessary to their bodies. The disease can be fatal if the body becomes dehydrated.

Dysentery strikes people of all ages throughout the world, but some forms of the disease occur more frequently in tropical countries. It can be particularly dangerous to infants, the elderly, and people in weak physical condition.

Causes and symptoms. Dysentery is caused by several types of microorganisms, including *salmonella* bacteria, *shigella* bacteria, and one-celled organisms called *amebas.* Shigella and amebas cause most dysentery. Shigella produce *shigellosis,* also called *bacillary dysentery.* Shigellosis begins suddenly and involves high fever and severe diarrhea. If untreated, the disease may disappear in a few weeks. However, some cases result in fatal dehydration.

Amebas cause *amebic dysentery,* which begins gradually and rarely produces high fever. It can cause diarrhea for years, however, and may produce *ulcers* (open sores) in the large intestine. Later, the infection may spread to the liver. Amebic dysentery seldom is fatal.

Spread. The organisms that cause dysentery are transmitted through the *feces* (solid body wastes) of infected individuals. Some people, known as *carriers,* spread the disease but have no symptoms of it.

The bacteria and amebas enter the body through the mouth, in most cases in food or water. Flies and unwashed hands can transfer feces to food. Fruits and vegetables must be thoroughly washed if they have been treated with fertilizer containing human feces.

Epidemics of dysentery have occurred where people live in overcrowded conditions and have poor sanitation. In the past, the disease was common in hospitals, prisons, and army camps. During some wars, more soldiers died from dysentery than in battle. Improved sanitation during the 1900's has greatly reduced the number of cases of dysentery. However, epidemics of the disease still occur in developing countries.

Diagnosis and treatment. Physicians diagnose dysentery after finding shigella or amebas in samples of the patient's feces or intestinal tissues. Treatment includes replacing fluids and body salts that the patient has lost. Physicians also use certain antibiotics to speed recovery from dysentery.   James L. Franklin

Dyslexia, dihs LEHK see uh, is a term that refers to many reading disabilities. Originally, the term referred only to those disabilities thought to be the result of a disorder in the central nervous system. However, many

people began to use the term to describe a broad range of reading problems, and even spelling and writing problems. Thus, *dyslexia* came to mean simply *poor reading* to many people. Many educators no longer use the term because of the confusion over its meaning.

Some specialists still use the term dyslexia in its original sense. Research indicates that dyslexia may be caused by abnormal development of the baby's brain during the mother's pregnancy period. The abnormalities interfere with the brain's ability to understand written material. For example, dyslexics reverse words and letters, so that they read *was* for *saw* or *d* for *p* or *b*. Many such persons also have difficulty remembering the sequence of letters in a word and in distinguishing right from left.

Before a child is diagnosed as dyslexic, other more specific possible causes of the reading problem should be ruled out. These possibilities include limited intelligence; poor eyesight or hearing; immaturity in emotional, intellectual, or physical development; inappropriate teaching; or unstable home conditions.

Special tests are used to detect dyslexia, but some educators question their value. In fact, many learning experts doubt that dyslexia actually exists. They argue that a diagnosis of dyslexia lumps together various problems that cause poor reading. These specialists maintain that the problems should be specifically identified for each poor reader. In this way, a person can be given the most appropriate treatment or training.   Roger Farr

Additional resources

Hornsby, Bevé. *Overcoming Dyslexia.* Dunitz, 1984.
Huston, Anne M. *Common Sense About Dyslexia.* Madison Books, 1987.
Savage, John F. *Dyslexia: Understanding Reading Problems.* Messner, 1985. For younger readers.

Dyspepsia, dihs PEHP see uh, is a term which is loosely used to refer to a disorder in digestion. Dyspepsia involves such symptoms as pain in the upper abdomen, heartburn, belching, fullness and heaviness in the stomach region, and spitting up food or sour-tasting liquid. Dyspepsia may be caused by ulcers of the stomach or duodenum, hyperacidity, cancer of the stomach, gallstones, infection of the gall bladder, colitis, constipation, adhesions, chronic appendicitis, and worry and nervousness. It can be treated only by treating the disorder which is causing it. In many cases, proper diet is part of the treatment.   Andrew G. Plaut

See also **Indigestion.**

Dysprosium, dihs PROH see uhm (chemical symbol, Dy), is one of the rare-earth metals. Its atomic number is 66, and its atomic weight is 162.50. Its density is 8.559 grams per cubic centimeter at 25° C (see **Density**). It has a melting point of 1412° C and a boiling point of 2567° C. The name comes from the Greek word *dysprositos,* meaning *hard to get.* French scientist Paul Émile Lecoq de Boisbaudran discovered dysprosium in 1886. It is found associated with erbium, holmium, and other rare earths in the minerals gadolinite, euxenite, xenotime, and others. Dysprosium is best separated from the other rare earths by solvent extraction or ion-exchange processes (see **Ion**). When cooled to low temperatures, it is strongly attracted by a magnet.   Larry C. Thompson

See also **Rare earth.**

Dystrophy, Muscular. See Muscular dystrophy.